Critical Thinking, Reading, and Writing

A Brief Guide to Argument

Critical Thinking, Reading, and Writing

A Brief Guide to Argument

SYLVAN BARNET
Professor of English, Late of Tufts University

HUGO BEDAU
Professor of Philosophy, Late of Tufts University

JOHN O'HARA
*Professor of Critical Thinking,
Reading, and Writing, Stockton University*

bedford/st.martin's
Macmillan Learning

Boston | New York

For Bedford/St. Martin's

Vice President, Editorial, Macmillan Learning Humanities: Leasa Burton
Senior Program Manager: John E. Sullivan III
Executive Marketing Manager: Joy Fisher Williams
Director of Content Development, Humanities: Jane Knetzger
Senior Developmental Editor: Leah Rang
Assistant Editor: Cari Goldfine
Editorial Assistant: Alex Markle
Senior Content Project Manager: Peter Jacoby
Senior Workflow Project Supervisor: Joe Ford
Senior Workflow Project Manager: Paul Rohloff
Production Supervisor: Robin Besofsky
Media Product Manager: Rand Thomas
Media Editor: Julia Domenicucci
Editorial Services: Lumina Datamatics, Inc.
Composition: Lumina Datamatics, Inc.
Text Permissions Manager: Kalina Ingham
Senior Text Researcher: Elaine Kosta, Lumina Datamatics, Inc.
Photo Permissions Editor: Angela Boehler
Photo Researcher: Brittani Morgan Grimes, Lumina Datamatics, Inc.
Director of Design, Content Management: Diana Blume
Text Design: Lumina Datamatics, Inc.
Design Motif Opener Pattern: Irtsya/Shutterstock
Cover Design: William Boardman
Cover Image: Torben Giehler, German, born in 1973, *BOOGIE WOOGIE*, 1999, Acrylic on canvas, 205.7 × 195.6 cm (81 × 77 in.), Museum of Fine Arts, Boston, The Living New England Artist Purchase Fund, created by The Stephen and Sybil Stone Foundation 1999.499. Photo ©2020 Museum of Fine Arts, Boston.
Printing and Binding: LSC Communications

ISBN 978-1-319-19451-2

Acknowledgments
Text acknowledgments and copyrights appear at the back of the book on pages 467–69, which constitute an extension of the copyright page. Art acknowledgments and copyrights appear on the same page as the art selections they cover.

Preface

He who knows only his own side of the cause knows little. — JOHN STUART MILL

Critical Thinking, Reading, and Writing: A Brief Guide to Argument is a book about reading other people's arguments and writing your own arguments — and it is also a collection of dozens of selections, ranging from Plato to the present, with a strong emphasis on critical thinking, reading, and writing about current issues.

Since the first edition, the quotation above has reflected the view of argument that underlies this book: In writing an essay, an author engages in a serious effort to discover his or her own ideas and, having found them, to contribute to a multisided conversation. The writer is not setting out to trounce an opponent. That is partly why we avoid expressions such as "marshaling evidence," "attacking an opponent," and "defending a thesis." Edmund Burke once wrote, "Our antagonist is our helper," and we agree that views and perspectives contrary to our own can help us sharpen our own thinking and writing. True, on television and social media we see pundits on the right and left who have made up their minds and who are indifferent or hostile to others' analysis and opinions. But in an academic community, and indeed in our daily lives, we learn by listening to others and by questioning our own ideas.

Two other foundational assumptions of this book are that arguments occur in a variety of forms, including but not limited to words on a page, and that arguments are shaped by the contexts in which they are made. In this edition, we reaffirm these beliefs with an expanded focus on visual rhetoric and information literacy, with heightened sensitivity to the interplay between argument and persuasion. We also recognize that academic and cultural discourses may make different arguments — asking different kinds of questions, making different kinds of claims, and using different kinds of evidence to support their views. Part Three, which focuses on approaches to argument, examines how philosophers, psychologists, literary critics, and debaters formulate arguments according to their unique purposes.

Just as arguments are instruments of inquiry and learning as well as expression, *Critical Thinking, Reading, and Writing* aims to help students learn to think, read, and write in more effective ways. As *critical thinkers and readers*, students in courses that use this book should develop their abilities to

- ask good questions about the reasoning processes that shape arguments;
- understand why information is selected and how it is presented persuasively by producers of arguments;
- account for variation and discrepancy in diverse perspectives on issues;
- understand how various contexts inform the production and reception of ideas;
- analyze and evaluate the strength of the evidence, reasoning, and assumptions undergirding arguments; and
- reflect upon, interrogate, and judge the (stated and unstated) consequences of arguments.

As *critical writers*, students develop their abilities to

- summarize an argument accurately, identifying the thesis, support, and conclusion;
- analyze an argument by reasoning logically and convincingly about it;
- produce a clear and purposeful argument of their own appropriate to a situation or discourse;
- communicate effectively for a specific audience (using appropriate language, tone, style, depth, and detail);
- explore sources of information and incorporate them selectively and skillfully, with proper documentation; and
- synthesize all information, ideas, terms, and concepts in an orderly and coherent way.

We think about and draft a response to something we have read, and in the very act of drafting, we may find — if we think critically about the words we are putting down on paper — that we are changing (perhaps slightly, perhaps radically) our own position. In short, one reason we write is so that we can improve our ideas. And even if we do not drastically change our views, we and our readers at least come to a better understanding of why we hold the views we do.

Enduring Features

ANALYZING AND CRAFTING ARGUMENTS

Part One, Critical Thinking and Reading (Chapters 1–4), and Part Two, Critical Writing (Chapters 5–7), together offer a short course in methods of thinking about and writing arguments. By "thinking," we mean *critical* thinking — serious analytic thought, including analysis of one's own perspectives, assumptions, and predispositions as one encounters (and produces) arguments; by "writing," we mean *critical* writing — the use of effective, respectable techniques for reasoned, convincing analysis, not merely gut feelings and persuasive gimmicks. (We are reminded of the notorious note scribbled in the margin of a politician's speech: "Argument weak; shout here").

We offer lots of advice about how to set forth an argument, but we do not offer instruction in dissembling, deceiving, or practicing one-upmanship; rather, we discuss responsible ways of arguing persuasively. We know that before one can write a persuasive argument, one must learn about an issue and clarify one's own ideas — a process that includes thinking critically about others' positions (even when they are agreeable) and being critical about one's own positions before setting them forth responsibly. Therefore, we devote Chapter 1 to critical thinking; Chapters 2, 3, and 4 to critical reading (including reading images in Chapter 4); and Chapters 5, 6, and 7 to critical writing.

Parts One and Two, then, offer a preliminary (but we hope substantial) discussion of such topics as

- identifying assumptions;
- getting ideas by means of invention strategies;
- finding, evaluating, and citing printed and electronic sources;
- interpreting visual sources;
- evaluating kinds of evidence; and
- organizing material as well as an introduction to some ways of thinking.

Parts One and Two together contain thirty selections (eight are student essays) for analysis and discussion.

INQUIRY AND INVENTION

In the first chapter, we emphasize how the process of critical thinking is a generative process. We focus on identifying the purpose, fairness, and consequences of arguments to various stakeholders and on analyzing ideas and concepts by asking questions — and then asking still further questions — to inspire fair-minded learning.

Our instruction throughout the book is accompanied by essays and images that embody and challenge concepts in critical thinking and argument. Each essay is accompanied by a list of Topics for Critical Thinking and Writing, which is not surprising given the emphasis we place on evaluating arguments, asking questions, and investigating further so as to generate new ideas. Among the chief questions writers should ask, we suggest, are "What is X?" and "What is the value of X?" By asking such questions — for instance (to look only at these two types of questions), "Is the fetus a person?" or "Is Arthur Miller a better playwright than Tennessee Williams?" — a writer probably will find pathways for discovering new sources, new questions, and new ideas, at least after a few moments of head scratching. Developing an argument by identifying issues is nothing new. Indeed, it goes back to an ancient method of argument used by classical rhetoricians, who identified a stasis (an issue) and then asked questions about it: Did *X* do such and such? If so, was the action bad? If bad, how bad? (Finding an issue or stasis — a position where one stands — by asking questions is discussed in Chapter 6.)

STYLES OF ARGUMENTATION

In keeping with our emphasis on writing as well as reading, we raise issues not only of what can roughly be called the "content" of the essays, but also of what can (equally roughly) be called the "style" — that is, the *ways* in which the arguments are set forth. Content and style, of course, cannot finally be kept apart. As Cardinal Newman said, "Thought and meaning are inseparable from each other. . . . *Style is thinking out into language.*" In our Topics for Critical Thinking and Writing, we sometimes ask the student

- to evaluate the effectiveness of an essay's opening paragraph,
- to explain a shift in tone from one paragraph to the next, or
- to characterize the persona of the author as revealed in the whole essay.

In short, this book is not designed as an introduction to some powerful ideas (although in fact it is that, too); rather, it is designed as an aid to thinking about and *writing* well-reasoned, effective arguments on important political, social, scientific, ethical, legal, and religious issues.

The selections reprinted in this book also illustrate different styles of argument that arise, at least in part, from the different disciplinary backgrounds of the various authors. Essays by journalists, lawyers, social scientists, policy analysts, philosophers, critics, activists, and other writers — including first-year undergraduates — will be found in these pages. These authors develop and present their views in arguments that have distinctive features reflecting their special training and concerns. The differences in argumentative styles found in these essays foreshadow the differences students will encounter in the readings assigned in many of their other courses.

In Part Three, Further Views on Argument (Chapters 8–12), we acknowledge and detail some of the different approaches to argument and emphasize their potential usefulness to a particular writing situation — or as a means of framing an argument course or unit.

- Chapter 8, A Philosopher's View: The Toulmin Model, is a summary of the philosopher Stephen Toulmin's method for analyzing arguments, covering claims, grounds, warrants, backing, modal qualifiers, and rebuttals. This summary will assist those who wish to apply Toulmin's methods to the readings in this book.

- Chapter 9, A Logician's View: Deduction, Induction, and Fallacies, offers a more rigorous analysis of these topics than is usually found in composition courses and reexamines from a logician's point of view material introduced in Chapter 3.

- Chapter 10, A Psychologist's View: Rogerian Argument, with an essay by psychotherapist Carl R. Rogers, complements the discussion of audience, organization, and tone in Chapter 6.

- Chapter 11, A Literary Critic's View: Arguing about Literature, should help students see the things literary critics argue about and *how* they argue. Students can apply what they learn not only to the literary readings that appear in the chapter (poems by Robert Frost and Richard Blanco and a story by Kate Chopin) but also to the literary texts that appear in Chapter 14.

- Chapter 12, A Debater's View: Individual Oral Presentations and Debate, introduces students to standard presentation strategies and debate format.

What's New in the Tenth Edition

This tenth edition brings significant changes. The authors of the first eight editions established a firm foundation for the book: Hugo Bedau, professor of philosophy, brought analytical rigor to the instruction in argumentation, and Sylvan Barnet, professor of English, contributed expertise in writing instruction. They have since turned the project over to John O'Hara, professor of critical thinking, to contribute a third dimension, augmenting and enriching the material on critical thinking throughout, especially in the early chapters. Other changes have been made to ensure practical instruction and current topics.

Fresh and Timely New Readings and Casebooks. More than a third of the total featured essays are new, as are topics such as identity politics, fake news, student loan forgiveness, the sentience of animals, and video games as sports. Existing topics such as free speech have been carefully considered and updated to reflect our contemporary discourse and perspectives.

Inspired by feedback from instructors teaching argument, this edition now features a casebook on an issue relevant to students' lives now as well as a collection of perspectives from philosophy, literature, and politics.

- Chapter 13, A College Education: What Is Its Purpose? presents multiple perspectives on a topic relevant to students' lives now: Should students focus their studies in STEM fields in the hopes of securing a more stable future and contributing to the economy, or should college be a place where students learn empathy, citizenship, and critical thinking — attributes often instilled by the humanities?

- Chapter 14, What Is the Ideal Society? provides a philosophical and theoretical context for several of the contemporary arguments in the book, but this chapter is also useful by itself as a means of thinking and writing about a concept that has been written about for centuries. The voices here range from Thomas More, Thomas Jefferson, and Martin Luther King Jr. to literary figures W. H. Auden, Walt Whitman, and Ursula K. Le Guin.

A Sharper Focus on Fostering Critical Thinking and Information Literacy. Early chapters in Part One on critical reading and writing are updated to include an explanation of confirmation bias, a survey-analyze-evaluate process for working through an issue, an understanding of obstacles to critical thinking, and strategies for approaching an issue (or an assignment). Chapter 7, Using Sources, has been extensively updated to help students interrogate their sources for reliability, relevance, and accuracy. Given that today's digital natives seek and find information online, new sections on finding reliable sources provide instruction and visual examples of sponsored content, fake news sites, and scholarly databases so that students can evaluate and use research effectively.

More Visual Guidance. In response to reviewer feedback, we have revised and updated some of the instruction to design new Visual Guides and create additional entry points to critical thinking. Colorful graphics and flowcharts aid students in designing their own paths through common argument tasks such as writing a critical summary and organizing an analysis.

In addition to the student essays that are marked to show the writers' strategies, this edition features annotated essays that make argument moves visible. Several selections by professional writers provide support for understanding argument during the reading process and highlight writers' rhetorical moves and persuasive strategies.

Writing Prompts That Support Major Course Assignments. Each chapter on critical thinking, reading, and writing now features a capstone writing prompt that allows students to practice argument in common assignment genres: examining assumptions and exploring an issue, critical summary, rhetorical analysis, visual analysis, argument analysis, argument, research paper, and literary criticism.

Acknowledgments

The authors would like to thank those who have strengthened this book by their comments and advice on the tenth edition: Christine F. Brown, Penn State Brandywine; Michael D. Bryant, Moorpark College; Deanna L. Gabrielson, Morehead State University; Erin Galope, Eastfield Community College; Carolyn Mason, Virginia State University; Annette Moore, Mitchell Community College; Jeffrey Nishimura, Los Angeles City College; Jessica L. Parker, Metropolitan State University of Denver; Elizabeth Simmons, Collin College; Eric D. Sullivan, Metropolitan Community College–Longview; Meghan Tutolo, University of Pittsburgh at Greensburg; and Renee Vas, Riverside City College.

We are also deeply indebted to the people at Bedford/St. Martin's, especially to our thoughtful and supportive editor, Leah Rang, whose input, review, and feedback helped shape both the written chapters and the reading selections in this edition. Maura Shea, John Sullivan, and Adam Whitehurst, our editors for preceding editions, have also left a lasting impression on the book; without their work on the first several editions, there probably would not be a tenth. Others at Bedford/St. Martin's to whom we are deeply indebted include Edwin Hill, Leasa Burton, Joy Fisher Williams, Peter Jacoby, Cari Goldfine, and Theresa Carcaldi, all of whom have offered countless valuable (and invaluable) suggestions. Special thanks go to Lexi DeConti and Alex Markle who were there for every step of this edition to provide insight and commentary, particularly so in the selection and layout of visual elements new to this edition. We would also like to thank Hilary Newman, Kalina Ingham, Arthur Johnson, Elaine Kosta, Angela Boehler, and Brittani Morgan Grimes, who adeptly managed art research and text permissions. Intelligent, informed, firm yet courteous, persuasive, and persistent — all these folks know how to think and argue.

Bedford/St. Martin's Puts You First

From day one, our goal has been simple: to provide inspiring resources that are grounded in best practices for teaching reading and writing. For more than thirty-five years, Bedford/St. Martin's has partnered with the field, listening to teachers, scholars, and students about the support writers need. We are committed to helping every writing instructor make the most of our resources.

How can we help *you*?

- Our editors can align our resources to your outcomes through correlation and transition guides for your syllabus. Just ask us.
- Our sales representatives specialize in helping you find the right materials to support your course goals.
- Our *Bits* blog on the Bedford/St. Martin's English Community (**community .macmillan.com**) publishes fresh teaching ideas weekly. You'll also find easily downloadable professional resources and links to author webinars on our community site.

Contact your Bedford/St. Martin's sales representative or visit **macmillanlearning.com** to learn more.

PRINT AND DIGITAL OPTIONS FOR *CRITICAL THINKING, READING, AND WRITING*

Choose the format that works best for your course and ask about our packaging options that offer savings for students.

Print

- *Paperback edition.* To order the paperback edition, use ISBN 978-1-319-19451-2.
- *Loose-leaf edition.* This format does not have a traditional binding; its pages are loose and hole punched to provide flexibility and a lower price to students. It can be packaged with our digital space for additional savings. To order the loose-leaf packaged with Achieve, use ISBN 978-1-319-33629-5.

Digital

- *Innovative digital learning space.* Bedford/St. Martin's suite of digital tools makes it easy to get everyone on the same page by putting student writers at the center. For details, visit **macmillanlearning.com/college/us/englishdigital**.

- *Popular e-book formats.* For details about our e-book partners, visit **macmillanlearning.com/ebooks**.

- *Inclusive Access.* Enable every student to receive their course materials through your LMS on the first day of class. Macmillan Learning's Inclusive Access program is the easiest, most affordable way to ensure that all students have access to quality educational resources. Find out more at **macmillanlearning.com/inclusiveaccess**.

YOUR COURSE, YOUR WAY

No two writing programs or classrooms are exactly alike. Our Curriculum Solutions team works with you to design custom options that provide the resources your students need. (Options below require enrollment minimums.)

- *ForeWords for English.* Customize any print resource to fit the focus of your course or program by choosing from a range of prepared topics, such as Sentence Guides for Academic Writers.

- *Macmillan Author Program (MAP).* Add excerpts or package acclaimed works from Macmillan's trade imprints to connect students with prominent authors and public conversations. A list of popular examples or academic themes is available upon request.

- *Bedford Select.* Build your own print handbook or anthology from a database of more than 900 selections, and add your own materials to create your ideal text. Package with any Bedford/St. Martin's text for additional savings. Visit **macmillanlearning.com/bedfordselect**.

INSTRUCTOR RESOURCES

You have a lot to do in your course. We want to make it easy for you to find the support you need — and to get it quickly.

Resources for Teaching Critical Thinking, Reading, and Writing is available as a PDF that can be downloaded from **macmillanlearning.com**. The instructor's manual includes sample syllabi, notes for every selection and chapter, and additional topics for classroom discussion and student writing assignments.

How *Critical Thinking, Reading, and Writing* Supports WPA Outcomes for First-Year Composition

The following chart provides information on how *Critical Thinking, Reading, and Writing* helps students build proficiency and achieve the learning outcomes set by the Council of Writing Program Administrators that writing programs across the country use to assess their students' work.

Rhetorical Knowledge	
Learn and use key rhetorical concepts through analyzing and composing a variety of texts	**Part One, Critical Thinking and Reading**, moves students from analyzing and evaluating an issue to analyzing specific written and visual arguments. • **Chapter 3, Critical Reading: Getting Deeper into Arguments**, gives students a vocabulary for key concepts of Aristotelian rhetoric — *ethos, logos, pathos* — and distinguishes between rational strategies (e.g., induction, deduction) and nonrational appeals (e.g., satire, irony, emotional appeals). • **Chapter 4, Visual Rhetoric: Thinking about Images as Arguments**, shows students how these strategies can be applied to visual arguments such as photographs, political cartoons, advertisements, and graphs. **Part Two, Critical Writing**, guides students from analysis to composing their own arguments. • **Chapter 5, Writing an Analysis of an Argument**, guides students through examining thesis, purpose, methods, persona, and the intended audience. An argument and a student's analysis, annotated to highlight the students' rhetorical strategies (pp. 188–90) explicate the process of assessing and evaluating an argument. • **Chapter 6, Developing an Argument of Your Own**, asks students to imagine and compose for their own audience (Imagining an Audience, pp. 216–18). **Select student essays are direct responses** to the professional selections and therefore model analysis and evaluation of a text.

Gain experience reading and composing in several genres to understand how genre conventions shape and are shaped by readers' and writers' practices and purposes	*Critical Thinking, Reading, and Writing* boasts fifty-four readings (including ten student essays) from a variety of sources, genres, and times. Selections for analysis and discussion include source-based arguments from professionals in different disciplines — journalists, lawyers, social scientists, policy analysts, philosophers, critics, activists, literary figures, and students. **Part Three, Further Views on Argument**, covers five different approaches to argument, providing students with multiple perspectives on how to both examine and craft arguments in different argument genres: Chapter 8, A Philosopher's View: The Toulmin Model; Chapter 9, A Logician's View: Deduction, Induction, and Fallacies; Chapter 10, A Psychologist's View: Rogerian Argument; Chapter 11, A Literary Critic's View: Arguing about Literature; and Chapter 12, A Debater's View: Individual Oral Presentations and Debate. The **Topics for Critical Thinking and Writing** that follow every reading in the text point to stylistic choices, heightening students' awareness of writing conventions. In Chapter 7, Using Sources, helpful tables detail the genre conventions of scholarly, popular, and trade sources (p. 258), as well as types of fake news (p. 267).
Develop facility in responding to a variety of situations and contexts calling for purposeful shifts in voice, tone, level of formality, design, medium, and/or structure	Each chapter on critical thinking, reading, and writing features a capstone writing prompt that allows students to practice argument in common assignment genres: examining assumptions and exploring an issue, critical summary, rhetorical analysis, visual analysis, argument analysis, argument, research paper, and literary criticism. Thinking Critically activities help scaffold composing in different genres. See, for example, Thinking Critically: Identifying Ethos (p. 78) and Thinking Critically: Examining Language to Analyze an Author's Argument (p. 186).
Understand and use a variety of technologies to address a range of audiences	The authors of *Critical Thinking, Reading, and Writing* assume students will be composing in different media; therefore, instruction throughout emphasizes the affordances and constraints of composing in analog and digital when taking notes, evaluating and citing sources, presenting, and more.

Match the capacities of different environments (e.g., print and electronic) to varying rhetorical situations	In additional to coverage noted above that helps students understand the rhetorical situation, specific guidance on composing in different environments includes using images in writing (Chapter 4) and delivering oral and electronic presentations (Chapter 12).
Critical Thinking, Reading, and Composing	
Use composing and reading for inquiry, learning, critical thinking, and communicating in various rhetorical contexts	**Chapter 1, Critical Thinking**, emphasizes how the process of critical thinking is a generative process through acts of inquiry, reading, and writing. See Generating Ideas: Writing as a Way of Thinking (pp. 12–17). **Chapter 6, Developing an Argument of Your Own**, includes further guidance on inquiry and invention as part of the composing process. See Getting Ideas: Argument as an Instrument of Inquiry (p. 206), Revision as Invention (p. 210), and Asking Questions with Stasis Theory (pp. 210–13).
Read a diverse range of texts, attending especially to relationships between assertion and evidence, to patterns of organization, to the interplay between verbal and nonverbal elements, and to how these features function for different audiences and situations	**The fifty-four selections are sourced from diverse authors, disciplines, and genres.** The casebooks (Chapters 13 and 14) highlight the different patterns of organization and rhetorical strategies used by different authors writing on the same topic. **Topics for Critical Thinking and Writing** that follow every reading prompt students to analyze the organization of arguments, the reliability of sources and their responsible use, and the effectiveness of arguments for the audience and situation. Several sections highlight the importance of strong organization to deliver sound logic, reasoning, and support for claims. See, for example: • Types of Reasoning (pp. 80–85) • Evidence: Experimentation, Examples, Authoritative Testimony, and Numerical Data (pp. 92–102) • Drafting and Revising Argument (pp. 220–34) **Part Three, Further Views on Argument**, covers how five different argument approaches — Toulmin, formal logic, Rogerian, literary criticism, and debate — organize and use claims and support according to their different purposes.

Locate and evaluate (for credibility, sufficiency, accuracy, timeliness, bias, and so on) primary and secondary research materials, including journal articles and essays, books, scholarly and professionally established and maintained databases or archives, and informal electronic networks and internet sources	**Chapter 7, Using Sources**, is a comprehensive resource for finding and evaluating primary and secondary sources. • Finding Sources (pp. 248–55) advises students on finding sources online, in databases, and in libraries. • Performing Your Own Primary Research (pp. 271–75) guides students in interviewing peers and local authorities as well as conducting surveys and observations. • Evaluating Sources (pp. 255–71) helps students analyze the credibility, accuracy, and timeliness of sources. In this edition, Chapter 7 has been heavily updated to correlate with the Framework for Information Literacy for Higher Education from the Association of College and Research Libraries. Notable new entries that serve students' current research challenges include • Entering a Discourse (pp. 243–45) • Why Finding Reliable Internet Sources Is So Challenging (pp. 262–64) • A Word on "Fake News" (pp. 264–66)
Use strategies — such as interpretation, synthesis, response, critique, and design/redesign — to compose texts that integrate the writer's ideas with those from appropriate sources	**Synthesizing Sources** (p. 275) emphasizes the importance of synthesis as a way of thinking. **Chapter 7, Using Sources**, covers best practices for paraphrasing and summarizing and avoiding plagiarism. Two sample student papers — one following MLA guidelines (pp. 302–8) and one following APA (pp. 309–13) — model outcomes for the research and writing process.
Processes	
Develop a writing project through multiple drafts	**Chapter 6, Developing an Argument of Your Own,** guides students through the writing process: generating ideas, developing and supporting a convincing thesis, imagining an audience, using transitions, maintaining a consistent tone and persona, and peer review. A sample student essay shows one student's process from rough notes to a final draft (pp. 236–40).
Develop flexible strategies for reading, drafting, reviewing, collaborating, revising, rewriting, rereading, and editing	**Chapter 2, Critical Reading: Getting Started,** covers active reading strategies such as previewing, underlining, highlighting, annotating, and rereading. A sample essay and a Thinking Critically: Previewing activity give students practice.

Use composing processes and tools as a means to discover and reconsider ideas	**Chapter 1, Critical Thinking**, and **Chapter 6, Developing an Argument of Your Own**, offer ample means of using composing to discover ideas and interrogate assumptions. Notable sections include • Survey, Analyze, and Evaluate the Issue (pp. 6–7) • Prompting Yourself: Classical Topics and Invention (pp. 16–17) • Three Brainstorming Strategies: Freewriting, Listing, and Diagramming (pp. 206–10)
Experience the collaborative and social aspects of writing processes	A new section on understanding and entering discourse (pp. 243–45) emphasizes the social aspect of writing. **Exercises** throughout the text offer opportunities for practicing and apply critical thinking and argument concepts in small groups.
Learn to give and to act on productive feedback to works in progress	**Chapter 6, Developing an Argument of Your Own**, covers the importance of peer review (pp. 234–36) and includes a Checklist for Peer Review of a Draft of an Argument that walks students through questions to ask when reviewing peers' work and providing feedback.
Adapt composing processes for a variety of technologies and modalities	**Reading, Writing, and Researching Tip** boxes highlight strategies for adapting writing to specific contexts, such as slide presentations. Instruction throughout *Critical Thinking, Reading, and Writing* emphasizes the affordances and constraints of composing in analog and digital when taking notes, evaluating and citing sources, presenting, and more.
Reflect on the development of composing practices and how those practices influence their work	**Checklists** in every chapter invite students to reflect on their reading and writing processes, and **Thinking Critically** boxes throughout the text prompt students to apply the concepts they've learned via interactive exercises.
Knowledge of Conventions	
Develop knowledge of linguistic structures, including grammar, punctuation, and spelling, through practice in composing and revising	**Part Two, Critical Writing**, shows students how to recognize the characteristics of writing and teaches how those qualities contribute to effective (or ineffective) writing (see first outcome for more information). **Chapter 6, Developing an Argument of Your Own**, discusses how to establish an appropriate tone and persona; eliminate *we, one,* and *I* in argumentative writing; and avoid sexist language. Thinking Critically: Eliminating *We, One,* and *I* (p. 233) gives students a chance to put these concepts into practice, and a Checklist for Establishing Tone and Persona (p. 234) allows students to self-review and revise.

Understand why genre conventions for structure, paragraphing, tone, and mechanics vary	**Chapter 5, Writing an Analysis of an Argument**, helps students examine how an author's methods differ in relation to their purpose and audience. **Part Three, Further Views on Argument**, delves into expectations for different kinds of arguments.
Gain experience negotiating variations in genre conventions	**Assignments** at the end of every critical thinking, reading, and writing chapter prompt students to write common argument genres such as a critical summary, rhetorical analysis, or analysis of an argument. Additional prompts include multimodal composing.
Learn common formats and/ or design features for different kinds of texts	**Previewing** (pp. 33–36) introduces students to design and genre features such as headings, subheadings, and abstracts to aid in basic comprehension and source evaluation. **Chapter 4, Visual Rhetoric: Thinking about Images as Arguments**, includes dozens of examples of visual arguments in different genres and highlights their design features. **MLA and APA style formatting conventions** are covered in detail in Chapter 7, Using Sources. Sample student papers in each style provide models.
Explore the concepts of intellectual property (such as fair use and copyright) that motivate documentation conventions	**Chapter 2, Critical Reading: Getting Started**, teaches best practices for recognizing and avoiding plagiarism and offers guidance on ethical paraphrase and summary. See, for example, Patchwriting and Plagiarism (pp. 49–50), **Chapter 7, Using Sources**, includes robust coverage of MLA and APA documentation styles, which discuss formatting conventions and include annotated sample student papers. • Compiling an Annotated Bibliography (pp. 278–79) shows students how to properly document and summarize their sources. • Quoting from Sources (pp. 279–83) shows students how to responsibly quote and integrate sources into their writing. • Checklists for evaluating print sources, websites, and fake news, avoiding plagiarism, and general strategies for source-based papers reinforce these concepts.
Practice applying citation conventions systematically in their own work	**MLA and APA style**, conveniently identified by blue- and green-edged pages, offer guidance on citation conventions, including dozens of models for in-text citations and reference lists.

Contents

PART THREE   FURTHER VIEWS ON ARGUMENT   315

8   A PHILOSOPHER'S VIEW: THE TOULMIN MODEL   317

Critical Thinking, Reading, and Writing

A Brief Guide to Argument

PART ONE

Critical Thinking and Reading

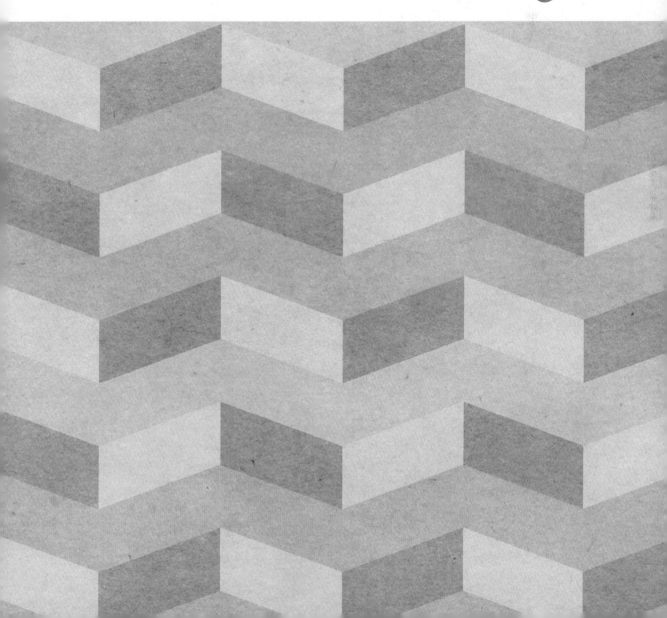

1

Critical Thinking

What is the hardest task in the world? To think.　　　　　　　— RALPH WALDO EMERSON

In all affairs it's a healthy thing now and then to hang a question mark on the things you have long taken for granted.　　　　　　　— BERTRAND RUSSELL

Although Emerson said the hardest task in the world is simply "to think," he was using the word *think* in the sense of *critical thinking*. By itself, *thinking* can mean almost any sort of cognitive activity, from idle daydreaming ("I'd like to go camping") to simple reasoning ("but if I go this week, I won't be able to study for my chemistry exam"). Thinking by itself may include forms of deliberation and decision-making that occur so automatically they hardly register in our consciousness ("What if I do go camping? I won't be likely to pass the exam. Then what? I better stay home and study").

When we add the adjective *critical* to the noun *thinking*, we begin to examine this thinking process consciously. When we do so, we see that even our simplest decisions involve a fairly elaborate series of calculations. Just in choosing to study and not to go camping, for instance, we weighed the relative importance of each activity (both are important in different ways); considered our goals, obligations, and commitments (to ourselves, our parents, peers, and professors); posed questions and predicted outcomes (using experience and observation as evidence); and resolved to take the most prudent course of action (i.e., made a decision).

Many people associate being critical with fault-finding and nit-picking. The word *critic* might conjure an image of a sneering art or food critic eager to gripe about everything that's wrong with a particular work of art or menu item. People's low estimation of the stereotypical critic comes to light humorously in Samuel Beckett's play *Waiting for Godot*, when the two vagabond heroes, Vladimir and Estragon, engage in a name-calling contest to see who can hurl the worst insult at the other. Estragon wins hands-down when he fires the ultimate invective:

V: Moron!

E: Vermin!

V: Abortion!

E: Morpion!

V: Sewer-rat!

E: Curate!

V: Cretin!

E: (*with finality*) Crritic!

V: Oh! (*He wilts, vanquished, and turns away*)

However, being a good *critical* thinker isn't the same as being a "critic" in the derogatory sense. Quite the reverse: Because critical thinkers approach difficult questions and seek intelligent answers, they must be open-minded and self-aware, and they must analyze *their own* thinking as rigorously as they analyze others'. They must be alert to *their own* limitations and biases, the quality of evidence *they themselves* offer, the logic *they* use, and the conclusions *they* draw. In college, we may not aspire to become critics, but we all should aspire to become better critical thinkers.

Becoming more aware of our thought processes is a first step in practicing critical thinking. The word *critical* comes from the Greek word *krinein*, meaning "to separate, to choose"; above all, it implies *conscious* inquiry. It suggests that by breaking apart, or examining, our reasoning we can understand better the basis of our judgments and decisions — ultimately, so that we can make better ones.

Thinking through an Issue

When thinking about an issue, no matter how simple or controversial, we want to do it in a way that's fair to all parties and not just a snap judgment. Critical thinking means questioning not only the beliefs and assumptions of others, but also *one's own* beliefs and assumptions. When developing an argument, you ought to be identifying important problems, exploring relevant issues, and evaluating available evidence fairly — not merely collecting information to support a preestablished conclusion.

ANALYZING AND EVALUATING FROM MULTIPLE PERSPECTIVES

Let's think critically about an issue related to religious freedom, equality, and the law — one that we hope brings some humor to the activity but also inspires careful thinking and debate. In 2005, in response to pressure from some religious groups, the Kansas Board of Education gave preliminary approval for teaching alternatives to evolution in public school science classes. New policies would require science teachers to present "intelligent design" — the idea that the universe was created by an intentional, conscious force such as God — as an equally plausible explanation for natural selection and human development.

In a quixotic challenge to the legislation, twenty-four-year-old physics graduate Bobby Henderson wrote an open letter to the Kansas school board that quickly became popular on the internet and then was published in the *New York Times*. Henderson appealed for recognition of another theory that he said was equally valid: that an all-powerful deity called the

Flying Spaghetti Monster created the world. While clearly writing satirically on behalf of science, Henderson nevertheless kept a straight face and argued that if creationism were to be taught as a theory in science classes, then "Pastafarianism" must also be taught as another legitimate possibility. "I think we can all look forward to the time," he wrote, "when these three theories are given equal time in our science classes. . . . One third time for Intelligent Design; one third time for Flying Spaghetti Monsterism (Pastafarianism); and one third time for logical conjecture based on overwhelming observable evidence."

Under the establishment clause of the First Amendment, members of the Church of the Flying Spaghetti Monster were permitted to install a monument on the lawn of a Crossville, Tennessee, courthouse in 2008.

Since that time, the Church of the Flying Spaghetti Monster has become a creative venue where secularists and atheists construct elaborate mythologies, religious texts, and rituals, most of which involve cartoonish pirates and various noodle-and-sauce images. ("R'amen," they say at the end of their prayers.) However, although tongue in cheek, many followers have also used the organization seriously as a means to champion the First Amendment's establishment clause, which prohibits government institutions from *establishing*, or preferring, any one religion over another. Pastafarians have challenged policies and laws in various states that appear to discriminate among religions or to provide exceptions or exemptions based on religion. In Tennessee, Virginia, and Wisconsin, church members have successfully petitioned for permission to display statues or signs of the Flying Spaghetti Monster in places where other religious icons are permitted, such as on state government properties. One petition in Oklahoma argued that because the state allows a marble and granite Ten Commandments monument on the state courthouse lawn, then a statue of the Flying Spaghetti Monster must also be permitted; this effort ultimately forced the state to remove the Ten Commandments monument in 2015. Since then, individuals in California, Georgia, Florida, Texas, and Utah have asserted their right to wear religious head coverings in their driver's license photos — a religious exemption afforded to Muslims in those states — and have had their pictures taken with colanders on their heads.

Let's stop for a moment. Take stock of your initial reactions to the Church of the Flying Spaghetti Monster. Some responses might be quite uncritical, quite unthinking: "That's outrageous!" or "What a funny idea!" Others might be the type of snap judgment we discussed earlier: "These people are making fun of real religions!" or "They're just causing trouble." Think about it: If your hometown approved placing a Christmas tree on the town square during the holiday season and the Church of the Flying Spaghetti Monster argued that it, too, should be allowed to set up its holiday symbol — perhaps a statue — as a matter of religious equality, should it be afforded equal space? Why, or why not?

Be careful to exercise critical thinking here. Can one simply say, "No, that belief is ridiculous," in response to a religious claim? What if members of a different religious group were asking for equal space? Should a menorah (a Jewish holiday symbol) be allowed? A mural celebrating Kwanzaa? A Native American symbol? Can some religious expressions be included in public spaces and not others? If so, why? If not, why not?

In thinking critically about a topic, we must try to see it from all sides before reaching a conclusion. Critical thinking requires us to understand our own position and also see the other side. One mainstay of critical thinking is a *willingness to identify and consider objections to our own beliefs*. We conduct an argument with ourselves, advancing and then questioning different opinions. If someone were proposing a Spaghetti Monster holiday display, we should ask

- **Who** is *for* and *against* the proposition?
- **Why** are they *for* or *against* it?
- **What** can be said *for* and *against* the proposition?

When thinking critically, it's important to ask key questions about various positions. It is also important to weigh competing interests and predict the outcomes of any decision or action we take. Remember that to be fair, we must adopt a skeptical attitude not only toward views opposed to our own but also toward our own views and our own common sense — that is, toward ideas that seem to us obviously right. If we assume that we have a monopoly on the truth and dismiss those who disagree with us as misguided fools or if we assume that opponents are acting out of self-interest (or a desire to harass the community) and we don't analyze their views, we're being critical, but we aren't engaging in critical thinking.

SURVEY, ANALYZE, AND EVALUATE THE ISSUE

Seeing an issue such as the Church of the Flying Spaghetti Monster from multiple perspectives will require you to gather information — to find out what people are saying and thinking. You'll likely want to gather perspectives and opinions from religious leaders, community members, and legal experts and analyze them alongside one another (after all, you wouldn't want the town to be sued for discrimination). You'll want to examine points on which people agree and disagree. Try to familiarize yourself with current debates — perhaps about religious equality, free speech, or the separation of church and state — and consider the responsibility of public institutions to accommodate different viewpoints and various constituencies. Ask yourself: What are the bigger issues at stake? Finally, you'll want to evaluate the evidence used by all sides to support their claims. Remember that the Church of the Flying Spaghetti Monster didn't gain so much traction by being easy to dismiss. You'll certainly have to think beyond a knee-jerk value judgment like, "No, a Spaghetti Monster statue would be ugly."

To summarize our process, consider doing the following to enhance your ability to consider multiple perspectives:

1. **Survey different viewpoints**, considering as many as possible and paying attention to who stands to gain and lose in any debate.
2. **Analyze the conflicts**, identifying and separating out the problems or points of debate and trying to see the bigger issues at stake.
3. **Evaluate the ideas**, judging the merit of various claims and arguments and measuring the weight of the evidence.

If you survey, analyze, and evaluate comprehensively, you'll have better and more informed ideas; you'll generate a wide variety of ideas, each triggered by your own responses and the ideas your research brings to light. In short — and this point is key — *argument is an instrument of learning, decision-making, and persuasion.* You will be able to find your position by thinking through the issue and developing your argument. As you do so, you should be as thorough as possible and sensitive to the ideas and rights of many different people. After all, you may have to present your argument to the town council or community. If you simply decided that a Spaghetti Monster statue was insulting to other religions and ignored the law in your argument, you could be setting up your town for a lawsuit.

Use the Visual Guide: Evaluating a Proposal below to pursue some lines of questioning for evaluating a proposed regulation, policy, or procedure. Apply this line of thinking to the Flying Spaghetti Monster issue.

What do you think? If you were on your hometown's city council and a petition came through from the Church of the Flying Spaghetti Monster to permit a Spaghetti Monster display alongside the traditional Christmas tree and menorah on the town square, how would you answer the questions presented in the Visual Guide? How would you vote? Why? How would you explain your vote to opponents of the Spaghetti Monster display?

Visual Guide: Evaluating a Proposal

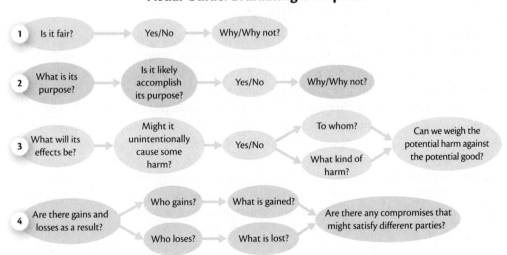

OBSTACLES TO CRITICAL THINKING

Because critical thinking requires engaging seriously with potentially difficult topics, topics about which you may already have strong opinions, and topics that elicit powerful emotional responses, it's important to recognize the ways in which your thinking may be compromised or clouded. The following attitudes might impede or otherwise negatively affect critical thinking in real life:

1. The topic is too controversial. I do not want to take a position on it.
2. The topic hits "too close to home" (i.e., "I have had direct experience with this").
3. The topic disgusts/angers/bores me.
4. Everyone I know thinks roughly the same thing I do about this topic.
5. Others may judge me if I verbalize what I think.
6. My opinion on this topic is X because it benefits me, my family, or my kind the most.
7. My parents raised me to think X about this topic.
8. One of my favorite celebrities believes X about this topic, so I should agree.
9. I know what I think, but my solutions are probably unrealistic. You can't change the system.
10. The answer is just common sense. Anyone who thinks differently lacks common sense.

Think about how each attitude might be detrimental to engagement with the question of approving a Flying Spaghetti Monster statue or might work as an impediment to drawing sound conclusions and making decisions on any issue.

ANTICIPATING COUNTERARGUMENTS

As we have shown, we generate ideas not only by supporting our initial thoughts, but also imagining opposing responses to them — sometimes called *counterpoints* or *counterpositions,* which help us clarify our thoughts. When we draw conclusions, we may also find **counterarguments** to our own position (other positions and points collected logically together toward a different conclusion). Sometimes, we avoid counterarguments — or avoid taking them seriously — because we do not want to face them or we simply cannot see things from another perspective. But we should try to take counterarguments seriously because they ultimately strengthen our thinking. When we write, they demonstrate that we have taken the time to consider other perspectives. We mention counterarguments here because they're an important component in argument, as you've already seen in our illustrations; we also spend more time discussing them in the Rebuttals section in Chapter 8.

> **WRITING TIP**
> Early in the process of conceiving your ideas on a topic, stop to ask yourself, "What might someone reasonably offer as an *objection* to my view?"

Critical Thinking at Work: From a Cluster to a Short Essay

Clustering is a type of brainstorming and a way of generating ideas, so it is a good tool for the process of thinking through an issue. Here's an example showing a student developing ideas about an issue related to the Church of the Flying Spaghetti Monster. The student, Alexa Cabrera, was assigned to write approximately 500 words about a specific legal challenge made by a member of the Church of the Flying Spaghetti Monster. She selected the case of Stephen Cavanaugh, a prisoner who had made a complaint against the Nebraska State Penitentiary after being denied the right to practice Pastafarianism while incarcerated there. Because the Department of Corrections had denied him those privileges, Cavanaugh filed suit citing civil rights violations and asked for his rights to be accommodated.

Alexa began thinking through her argument with a cluster, offering an initial idea and then building on it. Notice the role of counterpoints in the beginning of her cluster. Notice, too, that her cluster is not as elaborate as our earlier one. Her cluster was a *first* step, not a road map of the final essay. Finally, notice that Alexa's cluster contains ideas that did *not* make it into the final essay and that her essay — the product of several revised drafts — introduces points she had *not* thought of while clustering. In other words, the thinking process does not end when you begin the writing stage. Instead, writing an argument is a *continuous* process of thinking and learning as well as a method of persuasion.

Counterpoints	Supporting Points	Opposing Points	Counterpoints
Some people think prison should be punitive.	Religion is important to prisoners and to their rehabilitation. Isn't that the point of prison?	Prisoners are being punished. Why should religious beliefs be accommodated at all?	What legal rights are prisoners entitled to? (Do research.)

Cavanaugh requires special treatments for only one person, himself, just to be provocative and exert power.

But that's not the point. It's equity: Whatever is being done for one group must be done for all.

Cruel and unusual punishment protections? (Do research.)

First Amendment

Initial Idea

Prisoners should be allowed to practice any religion.

Is that true for *all*?

All religions' essential observances should be accommodated.

"Pastafarianism" is not a "real" religion.

Who decides what is a "real" religion?

Some accommodations can't be made (pilgrimages, certain objects) but reasonable ones can be.

You can't just let people make up their own religions and the accommodations they want.

What is the legal definition of a real religion? (Do research.)

Alexa Cabrera

Professor Regina Dacus

English 112

8 October 2016

Stirred and Strained: Pastafarians Should Be Allowed
to Practice in Prison

Stephen Cavanaugh is a member of the Church of the Flying Spaghetti Monster (FSM), a mostly web-based religious group notable for its members' demands that they be treated under the First Amendment like any other religion. The group strives to show that if Christians can place Nativity scenes on public grounds or if Muslims can wear head coverings in state driver's license photographs, then by god (or by pasta, as the case may be), they can too. Cavanaugh is in the Nebraska State Penitentiary, where inmates are permitted under the Religious Land Use and Institutionalized Persons Act (RLUIPA) to exercise religious freedoms guaranteed by the First Amendment. He wants the same rights and privileges given to incarcerated Christians, Muslims, Jews, and Buddhists — namely, to be able to wear religious clothing, to eat specially prepared meals, and to be given resources, space, and time to conduct worship with his fellow "believers." For Cavanaugh, this means being able to dress up as a pirate, eat pasta on selected holidays, order satirical holy books, and lead a weekly "prayer" group. Many people consider these requests absurd, but Cavanaugh should be permitted under the First Amendment and the RLUIPA to practice his faith.

Some arguments against Cavanaugh are easier to dismiss than others. One of these simply casts aside the spiritual needs and concerns of prisoners: They are being punished, after all, so why should they receive any religious accommodations? This position is both immoral and unconstitutional. Religion is an important sustaining force for prisoners who might otherwise struggle to find meaning and purpose in life, and it is protected by the First Amendment *because* it helps prisoners find purpose and become rehabilitated — the fundamental goal of correctional facilities (even for those serving life without parole). Another argument sees religion as important as long as it conforms to Judeo-Christian belief structures, which has for a long time been the only spiritual path available in American prisons. But today, in our diverse society, the RLUIPA *requires* prisons to provide religious accommodations for all faiths equally unless an undue administrative, financial, or security burden can be proven. Obviously, many religious observances cannot be accommodated. Prisons cannot permit inmates to carry crosses and staves, construct temples and sweat lodges, or make required religious pilgrimages. However, as long as *some* reasonable religious accommodations can be and are made for some groups—such as Catholics being offered fish on Fridays or Jewish and Muslim prisoners receiving kosher and halal meals—then all religious groups must be similarly accommodated.

The more challenging question about the Church of the Flying Spaghetti Monster is whether it is a religion at all, whether it deserves equal treatment among more established religions. When Cavanaugh was first denied his request, the prison claimed that FSM was not a religion but a "parody" of religion. The Nebraska State Penitentiary suggested it could not grant privileges to anyone who presents his whimsical desires as part of a religious philosophy. In dealing with a humorous and politically motivated "religion" without a strong tradition and whose founder may write a new gospel at any time, should the prison have to keep up with the possibility of constantly changing prisoner demands? Can anyone just make up a religion and then expect to be accommodated?

For better or worse, the answer is yes—as long as the accommodations represent valid forms of observance, are reasonable, and do not pose a substantial burden to the institution. Many religions have councils that at times alter the tenets of their faith. The state does not have the authority to determine what is or is not a "real" religion or religious practice. It does have an obligation under the RLUIPA to accommodate not just some but all forms of faith for incarcerated persons. As long as individuals sincerely hold certain beliefs, and as long as the accommodations requested meet the standards of reasonability and equity, state prisons, like all other government agencies and institutions, cannot discriminate. Some might argue that Cavanaugh's

---

Writer cites law's requirements.

Last sentence sustains the thesis and anticipates that readers may agree on this point but still not consider the FSM a religion.

Paragraph 3: Raises a possible counterposition and gives it due respect.

Responds to opposing position; writer is still discussing reasonable and fair treatment of inmates, not "anything goes."

Writer reminds readers that the state cannot determine a "real" or "unreal" religion, just as it cannot judge the depth, rigor, or literalness of an inmate's belief.

Rebuts the counterargument. → faith is not sincere — that he does not *really* believe that the Earth was literally created by a ball of pasta with meatball-shaped eyes. But this is not the point. The government cannot apply a religious test to

Writer makes a shrewd rhetorical move, appealing to the democratic value of fairness. → measure the degree of one's sincerity or faith. Like others in the Flying Spaghetti Monster movement — secularists, atheists, and professed believers — Cavanaugh should not be treated as an exploiter of religious freedom. In fact, in a pluralistic society with laws to ensure religious freedom and equality, his challenge helps protect all faiths.

Topics for Critical Thinking and Writing

1. A paper begins with its title, not with its first paragraph. A good title makes readers curious and may let them know where the essay will take them. Does this title have that effect on you? Why, or why not? What other title would you suggest?

2. Are you convinced from this essay that it would be unfair to deny Cavanaugh and other Pastafarian inmates their demands? Why, or why not?

3. How would you define a "real" religion? Can it be any belief deeply and sincerely felt, or does it require something more? Explain your answer.

Generating Ideas: Writing as a Way of Thinking

"To learn to write," Robert Frost said, "is to learn to have ideas." But how does one "learn to have ideas"?

Sometimes, we discover ideas while talking with others. A friend shares an opinion about some issue, and we — who have never really thought much about the matter — find ourselves saying that we see their point but have a different opinion. We are, in a sense, offering a counterpoint, saying, "Well, yes, I see your point, but I'm not of that opinion. I see it differently — not as *X*, but as *Y*." For example, imagine someone is arguing against the US border wall proposal put forth by US President Donald Trump. Another person could say:

> *Yes*, I see your point that a wall will be expensive, *but* the fact is we do already have substantial border fences, and we spend a lot of money on enforcement. The wall proposal only strengthens what we already do and may even amount to long-term savings.

A third person might respond, "*Yes*, I see your point about money, *but* the wall will be destructive to the environment, which outweighs the financial savings." A fourth might add, "*Yes, and* a wall is also a symbol of division." Often, we get ideas when we add to others' observations. Maybe we find ourselves agreeing with someone and would like to extend the observation to include another position, too. We are essentially saying, "*Yes*, *X*, sure, and also *Y*, too."

Here's another example of how that might play out:

> *Yes*, a "soda tax" on high-sugar beverages would discourage unhealthy behaviors and generate much-needed revenue for the city, *and* come to think of it, it may encourage drink companies to lower the sugar content of their products.

Mere chance — a response a friend's comment — seems to have produced an idea. However, learning to have ideas is not usually a matter of chance. Or if chance *is* involved, well, as Louis Pasteur put it, "Chance favors the prepared mind." Lurking in the mind are bits of information, opinions that may arise in an unexpected circumstance — when talking, when listening to a lecture or a classroom discussion, or especially when reading.

Consider Archimedes, the ancient Greek mathematician who discovered a method to determine the volume of an irregularly shaped object. Here's how the story goes: A king gave a goldsmith a specific weight of gold and asked him to make a crown in the shape of laurel leaves. When the job was finished, the king weighed the crown and found that it matched the weight of the gold he had provided. Nevertheless, he suspected that the goldsmith might have substituted some silver for some of the gold. How could the king find out (without melting or otherwise damaging the crown) if the crown was pure gold?

For Archimedes, meditating on this problem produced no ideas at first, but when he entered a bathtub he noticed that the water level rose as he immersed his body. He suddenly realized that he could determine the purity of the crown by measuring the amount of water it displaced. Since silver is less dense than gold, it takes a greater volume of silver to equal a given weight of gold. In his excitement at his idea to measure equal weights and relative volumes by immersing the crown in water, Archimedes is said to have leaped out of the tub and run naked through the street, shouting "*Eureka!*" (Greek for "I have found [it]!").

Why do we tell this story? Partly because we like it, but chiefly because the word *eureka* captures that moment of unexpectedly finding an idea. Finding an idea can sometimes feel like reaching under the couch to retrieve a dog toy and finding a ten-dollar bill instead: "Hey, look what I found! *Eureka!*" But we rarely luck into ideas in this way. Actually, the word *eureka* comes from the same Greek word that has given us the word **heuristic** (pronounced hyoo-RIS-tik), which refers to a *method* or *process* of discovering ideas.

Sculpture in Manchester, England, depicting Archimedes's bathtub "Eureka" moment.

When you're asked to think about something you've read in this book, if your first response is that you have no ideas, please do not just take a bath like Archimedes did. A better method is to immerse yourself not in water but in the issues at hand. You can do this by listening to what's being said in the world around you — both in and out of the classroom, as well as in the world of magazines, newspapers, books, and other media — and thinking about your responses to what you hear.

One of the most basic methods to discover ideas is the one we mention above — "Yes, *but* I see it differently" or "Yes, *and also.*" This process can help you respond to a work and begin to develop ideas.

CONFRONTING UNFAMILIAR ISSUES

Generating ideas can be a challenge when you, as a student, are asked to read about and respond to new or unfamiliar issues. Sometimes, students wonder why they have to engage in particular topics and generate ideas about them. "I want to be a speech pathologist," one might say, "so why do I need to read essays and formulate ideas about capital punishment?"

One answer is that a college curriculum should spur students to think about pressing issues facing our society, so learning about capital punishment is important to all students. But this isn't the only answer. One could never study "all" the important social problems we face (and many of them change very rapidly). Instead, colleges seek to equip students with tools, methods, and habits of mind that enable them to confront arguments about *any* potential issue or problem. The primary goal of a college education (and of this book) is to help students develop an *intellectual apparatus* — a tool kit that can be applied to any subject matter, any issue.

The techniques presented in this book offer a practical framework for approaching issues, thinking about them carefully, asking good questions, identifying problems, and offering reasonable solutions — not necessarily because we want you to form opinions about the specific issues we have selected (although we hope you do), but because we want you to practice critical thinking, reading, and writing in ways that transfer to other aspects of your education as well as to your personal, professional, and civic life.

The Nigerian novelist Chinua Achebe said, "The writer must march up front." Rather than thinking that you must "agree or disagree" with the authors whose positions you'll read about in this book, imagine that you'll be practicing how to discover your own unique point of view by finding pathways into debates, negotiating different positions, and generating new ideas. So when you confront a new or unfamiliar issue in this book (or elsewhere), consider the strategies discussed in this chapter as practical methods — *heuristics* — for generating new ideas from the information at hand. That is what critical thinking (and writing) is all about.

USING CLUSTERING TO DISCOVER IDEAS

As you can see from the student cluster on the Pastafarian issue, we're big fans of clustering as a practical method for generating ideas and thinking through your argument. If you think with pencil and paper in hand and let your mind make associations by clustering, you'll find (perhaps to your surprise) that you have plenty of interesting ideas and that some can lead to satisfying conclusions. Doubtless you'll also have some ideas that represent gut reactions or poorly thought-out conclusions, but that's okay. When clustering, allow your thoughts to take shape without restriction; you can look over your ideas again and organize them later.

To start clustering, take a sheet of paper and jot down what you think is the most basic issue or the fundamental conflict. This will help shape the questions you ask and frame your initial idea. Write down your initial idea — your opinion on the issue or debate at hand — and then develop supporting ideas, explore counterpositions (and rebuttals), and jot down where you need to do some research, eventually leading you to a tighter argument. Review the cluster in this chapter on page 9 to help you work through an issue.

> **WRITING TIP**
> If you decide to generate ideas for your essay by clustering, don't worry that some ideas may be off the cuff or even nonsense. Just get ideas down on paper. You can evaluate them later.

APPROACHING AN ISSUE (OR AN ASSIGNMENT)

Anyone who has played baseball can tell you that one of the most challenging things to do is hit the ball. So, coaches often instruct their players to develop an *approach* to hitting. The hitter's approach begins in the dugout. First, you watch the pitcher. You make observations. What kind of pitches are being thrown? Are they largely inside pitches or outside pitches, high or low, fast or slow? Answering these questions can help determine what you do as you get ready to bat. You must also ask: What is the game situation? Are you attempting to hit long into the outfield or just get the ball in play, perhaps to advance your runners already on the bases? Once you step into the batter's box, where should you set your feet — farther away from the plate or close to it? In short, you are asking questions: *What am I facing? What is my goal?* and, quite literally, *Where do I stand?*

Not everyone plays baseball, but this metaphor is intended to get you thinking about how to prepare for an argument by asking some key questions:

- What should you look for in an issue or problem?
- What kinds of challenges will opponents likely throw at you?
- How will you position yourself?
- What do you want to achieve?

A critical thinker's approach, like a baseball batter's, is the preparation for the argument. It involves assessing issues, identifying key problems, and discovering your ideas.

In real life, and in this book, you may be given an assignment to think critically or make an argument. A professor (or a textbook author) assigning a prompt is much like a coach instructing you on your approach, and examining the assignment prompt carefully is like reading the pitcher. Ask: What is being thrown at you? How should you strategize to meet the challenges?

Perhaps the assignment prompts you to consider a certain aspect of an issue, compare two arguments, or take a side in a debate. Here is an example of an assignment that calls for a specific approach:

> At the time a county clerk in Kentucky named Kim Davis was refusing to sign marriage licenses for same-sex couples, some of her supporters compared her to civil

rights activists like Rosa Parks, who intentionally broke segregation laws in order to challenge them. Are Kim Davis's actions justifiable in the same way Rosa Parks's were? Are the two figures equivalent crusaders for justice?

A prompt like this doesn't tell you *what* to think, but *what to ask* and *how to argue*. It tells you to *compare, analyze,* and *evaluate*. In your comparison of Davis and Parks, you must judge whether or not their actions were morally or politically equivalent and then argue yes or no. You are being prompted to consider the motivations, purposes, and justifications for each figure's actions.

Many assignments call for these elements of comparison, analysis, and evaluation. They ask the questions and tell you how to argue. But by figuring out what to ask and how to argue yourself, you can develop arguments without prompts provided by your professors. When facing issues in your life, work, or society, you will sometimes have to prompt *yourself* to figure out what to think (and what to argue).

PROMPTING YOURSELF: CLASSICAL TOPICS AND INVENTION

One way of generating new ideas by prompting yourself is to consider what the ancient rhetoricians called **topics** — from the Greek *topoi,* meaning "places." (We see this word as a root in our word *topography,* a description of place.) Today, we often use the word *topic* to describe something very specific, as when a professor or committee leader says, "Today our topic for discussion is the proposed bike lane on our campus drive." But for the ancients, such as Aristotle in Greece and Cicero in Rome, the *topoi* (or topics) were more conceptual and were seen as the basic elements of arguments, debates, and conversations. Among the classical topics were *definition, comparison, relationship,* and *testimony.* When formulated as questions, they prompted thoughtful people to invent (from the Latin *invenire,* "to come upon, to find") ideas.

If you're at a loss for ideas when confronted with an issue — and an assignment to write about it — you might discover ideas by turning to the relevant classical topics, framing them as questions, and jotting down your responses. We'll use our campus bike lane as an example issue.

Definition: What are the elements in the debate?

What is a road? What is a bike lane? What is a college campus? How might these definitions help you think through the issues? If, for example, you define a *road* as a way people travel (especially students), a *bike lane* as a pathway for a certain means of safe transportation, and a *campus* as a place where students must be able to live and learn safely, then you may be able to discover a reasonable starting point for an argument: *Because many students use bikes and they need to get to class safely, a bike lane on campus is a reasonable accommodation.* Simply defining the basic elements within an issue may guide your thinking on a question.

Comparison: What are the elements like or unlike?

Comparing students to nonstudents, cars to bikes, or campuses to other public spaces may also help you discover your position. You may find that students have a special need for bikes that nonstudents do not have. Or you may find that bikes, compared to cars, are cheaper and more environmentally friendly. Maybe campus roads are not the same as some other public roads; they may be more like roads in parks, cutting through spaces of leisure, quietude, and study. Making comparisons like these can help you evaluate the various reasons bicycle lanes may be called for on campus. You may also compare other cases: Have other colleges built bike lanes? If so, to what effect?

Relationship: What are the causes and effects in play?

Think of relationships as "*if . . . then*" propositions. If we decided to build bike lanes, then we would likely increase safety and access on campus and help the environment. However, if we build bike lanes, then we would also spend a great deal of money, which may affect other budget priorities, some of which may also increase other kinds of access and safety. The point: Teasing out the relationships of actions to their consequences can help produce ideas. (You may also explore the consequences of nonactions: If we did not build bike lanes, then we would not be keeping up with institutions that are building them, making our school less attractive to new students.)

Testimony: What are the major opinions and forms of evidence?

All ideas need to be justified in consideration of opinions and evidence. What do drivers think? What do students think? What do experts and respected leaders say? What laws or rules are applicable? What evidence has been (or can be) gathered to testify to the need for bike lanes (or the lack of such a need)? Have there been accidents? Are students or drivers complaining about the risks? Gathering testimony — assessing data, trends, currents, opinions, and attitudes — can help inspire ideas.

The classical *topoi* are not solutions to any problems at hand, but a means of discovering solutions. They provide a set of categories that can work as guidelines to formulating an opinion or argument. In other words, they offer a way to organize the *process* of invention, of thinking through an issue to determine what you think and what position you want to take.

An Essay for Generating Ideas

Consider the following brief essay about the Food and Drug Administration's approval, in 2015, of a genetically engineered salmon. Although GMO (genetically modified organism) foods and medicines are common in the United States, this salmon will soon be the first genetically modified animal approved for food consumption in the United States. After you read the essay, refer to Thinking Critically: Generating Ideas with Topics (p. 19), which asks you to begin jotting down ideas on a sheet of paper along the lines of the classical topics. As an example of how to respond to the questions, we've included columns related to the Stephen Cavanaugh case. As you attempt to formulate ideas related to the essay about genetically engineered salmon, answer the questions related to the classical topics. There's no need to limit yourself to one answer per item as we did.

NINA FEDOROFF

Nina Fedoroff (b. 1942) is a molecular biologist and winner, in 2007, of the National Medal of Science. She served as science and technology advisor to the US secretary of state from 2007 to 2010 and is an emeritus Evan Pugh professor at Penn State University. The following essay originally appeared in the *New York Times* in December 2015.

The Genetically Engineered Salmon Is a Boon for Consumers and Sustainability

This is great news for consumers and the environment. Wild salmon populations have long been in deep trouble because of overfishing, and open-water cage farming of salmon pollutes coastal waters, propagates fish diseases, and sacrifices a lot of wild-caught fish to be consumed as salmon feed.

The fish is virtually identical to wild salmon, but it is a more sustainable food source, growing faster to maturity.

But just imagine, you'll soon be able to eat salmon guilt-free. AquaBounty has spent more than 20 years developing and testing this faster-growing salmon that will require less feed to bring it to a marketable size. It can be farmed economically in closed, on-land facilities that recirculate water and don't dump waste into the sea. Since the fish live in clean, managed water, they don't get diseases that are spread among caged fish in the sea. And the growing facilities could be closer to markets, cutting shipping costs.

All of these elements take pressure off wild salmon and make salmon farming more sustainable.

Much of the concern about AquaBounty's 5 salmon centers around several bits of added DNA, taken from another fish, that let the salmon grow continuously, not just seasonally. That does not make them "unnatural" or dangerous, it just makes them grow to market size on less feed.

We've been tinkering with our plants and animals to serve our food needs for somewhere between 10 and 20 thousand years. We created corn, for example. The seed-bearing structure of the original "wild" version, called teosinte, looked very different from the modern-day ear, packed with hundreds of soft, starch-and-protein-filled kernels. And it's people who developed the tomatoes we eat today. Mother Nature's are tiny: A pioneering breeder described them in an 1893 grower's guide as "small, hollow, tough, watery" fruits.

But there's money (and fame) in being anti-G.M.O. The organic food marketers want to sell their food, which is over-priced because organic farming is inefficient — not because the food's better — so they tell scare stories about the dangers of G.M.O.s.

There is also no reason to fear that these genetically engineered salmon will escape and destroy wild populations. Only sterile females will be grown for food. And since the fish will be grown in contained facilities on land, escapees can't survive either.

AquaBounty's salmon is salmon, plain and simple. I, for one, can't wait to taste it.

THINKING CRITICALLY *Generating Ideas with Topics*

Use the classical topics (pp. 16–17) to think through an issue. Provide the relevant information for a topic of your choice or for the topic of genetically engineered salmon explored in Fedoroff's essay. We have provided the issue of Steven Cavanaugh and the Church of the Flying Spaghetti Monster as an example.

TOPICS	QUESTIONS	EXAMPLE TOPIC: *PASTAFARIANISM*	YOUR TOPIC
Definition *Categories* *Descriptions* *Definitions* *Explanations*	What is it?	Define terms: *creationism* *religious freedom* *civil rights*	
Comparison *Similarities* *Differences* *Analogies* *Applications*	What is it like or unlike?	Civil disobedience Other struggles for religious rights	
Relationships *Antecedents* *Precedents* *Consequences* *Outcomes*	What are some causes and effects? (*If . . . , then*)	If Pastafarianism is permitted to continue, then . . . If prisoners cannot worship freely, then . . .	
Testimony *Statistics* *Maxims* *Laws* *Authorities/ Quotations*	What forms of evidence and opinion exist?	What have courts said in the past? What do supporters and/ or detractors say? What laws exist to protect members of religions?	

THINKING CRITICALLY ABOUT THE ISSUE

What follows is an inner dialogue that you might engage in as you think critically about the question of genetically engineered salmon.

> The purpose of genetically engineered salmon is to protect against the ecological effects of overfishing—that seems to be a good thing.
>
> Another purpose is to protect consumers by ensuring that the price of salmon, one of the most commonly eaten fish, will not become so high that few people could afford it.
>
> But other issues are apparent. Should we turn to altering the genes of animals to protect the environment or consumer prices? Are there other solutions, like eating less salmon or regulating overfishing?
>
> Who gains and who loses, and what do they stand to gain or lose, by Federal Drug Administration (FDA) approval of genetically modified salmon?
>
> The author says no one should worry about "several bits of DNA added," but come to think of it, is this modification unethical or dangerous in any way? Is it okay to create a new type of animal by altering genes?
>
> The author attacks anti-GMO activists, saying they're just after money (and fame — why fame?). Isn't money (and fame?) also the goal of AquaBounty and other GMO food producers?

Part of the job is **analytic**, recognizing the elements or complexities of the whole, and part is **evaluative**, judging the adequacy of all the ideas, one by one. Both tasks require critical thinking in the form of analyzing and evaluating, and those processes themselves require a self-conscious and disciplined *approach*.

So far, we have jotted down a few thoughts and then immediately given some second thoughts contrary to the first. Be aware that your own counterpositions might not come to mind right away. They might not occur until you reread your notes or try to explain the issue to a friend, until you do some preliminary reading on the subject, or even until you begin drafting an essay aimed at supporting or undermining the FDA rules. Most likely, some good ideas won't occur until a second or third or fourth draft — or even until after you have published or turned in your work.

Here are some further thoughts on the issue of genetically modified salmon to show how different perspectives and questions lead to different approaches.

> According to one article, the FDA is not requiring companies to label the salmon as genetically engineered. Should this information at least be made available to consumers? Maybe their religious, ethical, or personal preferences would be not to eat modified fish species. If the fish were properly labeled and people knew of any risks associated with eating it, consumers could avoid it if they wished.
>
> ▪ *Possible perspectives*: Social (consumer interest)

- *Questions*: How should consumers expect to be protected by the government in an era of new scientific developments such as GMOs and in relation to their right to know what goes into their food? How should the government respond to new scientific advances such as GMOs?
- *Approach*: Might I argue that the new regulations are okay, but strict labeling should be required?

It's actually pretty amazing that scientists have helped solve the problem of the dwindling salmon population from overfishing by making a genetic modification that allows fish to grow large and fast and sustainably. Like any new thing, people who are uncomfortable with technological change will resist the new processes but will soon become accustomed to them once their fears are allayed. I'll bet at one time, people were hesitant to accept the light bulb as an advancement. Like all new advances, once it is accepted, it will be a boost to consumers, the environment, and business.

- *Possible perspectives*: Scientific (technological change)
- *Questions*: What other technologies were resisted in the past and are now commonplace, and what lessons can we learn from them? Which technologies are now keystones for our economy? How has science contributed to solving food crises and environmental crises?
- *Approach*: Might I argue that people should be more open to technological innovation as a way to solve environmental, social, and economic issues related to the food supply?

Doubtless there is much that we haven't asked or thought about, but we hope you'll agree that the issue deserves careful thought. Some of these questions require you to do **research** on the topic. Some raise issues of fact, and relevant evidence probably is available. To reach a conclusion in which you have confidence, you'll likely have to do some research to find out what the facts — the objective data — are. Merely explaining your position without giving the evidence will not be convincing.

Even without doing any research, however, you might want to look over the pros and cons, perhaps adding some new thoughts or modifying or even rejecting (for reasons that you can specify) some of those already given. If you do think further about this issue (and we hope that you will), notice an interesting point about *your own* thinking: It probably isn't *linear* (moving in a straight line from *A* to *B* to *C*) but *recursive*, moving from *A* to *C* and back to *B* or starting over at *C* and then back to *A* and *B*. By zigging and zagging almost despite yourself, you'll reach a conclusion that may finally seem correct. In retrospect, it might seem obvious; *now* you can chart a nice line from *A* to *B* to *C* — but that probably wasn't at all evident at the start.

A CHECKLIST FOR CRITICAL THINKING

- ☐ Does my thinking show open-mindedness and intellectual curiosity?
- ☐ Am I approaching my subject from a particular perspective?
- ☐ Can I examine the assumptions that come with my approach?
- ☐ Am I willing to entertain different ideas, both those that I encounter while reading and those that come to mind while writing?
- ☐ Am I willing to exert myself — for instance, to do research — to acquire information, identify different viewpoints, and evaluate evidence?

A Short Essay Calling for Critical Thinking

When reading an essay, we expect the writer to have thought carefully about the topic. We don't want to read every false start, every fuzzy thought, and every ill-organized paragraph that the writer knocked off. Yes, writers make false starts, put down fuzzy thoughts, and write ill-organized paragraphs, but then they revise and revise yet again, ultimately producing a readable essay that seems effortlessly written. Still — and this is our main point — writers of argumentative essays need to show readers that they have made some effort; they need to show *how* they got to their views. It isn't enough for the writer to say, "I believe *X*"; rather, he or she must in effect say, "I believe *X* because I see things from this perspective. Others believe *Y* or *Z*, and although from their perspective, their answers might sound reasonable, my inquiry shows another way to think or act about the issue. There may be value in *Y* or *Z* (or maybe not), and on the surface they may be plausible (or maybe they are not plausible), but their beliefs do not take into account what I am arguing, that *X* is a better alternative because. . . ." Obviously you don't need to follow that exact pattern (although you could); the point is that writers often need to make their critical thinking explicit to convince their readers of the argument they make.

Notice in the following short essay — on employers using biometric devices to monitor employees' performance — that the author, Lynn Stuart Parramore, positions herself against new workplace technologies in a compelling way. As you read, think critically about how she presents her position and how she encourages readers to sympathize with her views. Ask questions about what she includes and excludes, whether she presents other perspectives amply or fairly, and what additional positions might be valid on these recent developments in the rapidly growing field of biometrics in business.

LYNN STUART PARRAMORE

Lynn Stuart Parramore is a senior research analyst at the Institute for New Economic Thinking and a senior editor of *AlterNet*, as well as a frequent contributor to *Reuters*, *HuffPost*, and other outlets. Reprinted here is an essay published by *Al Jazeera America* on September 18, 2015.

Provocative title leaves readers with a sense of Parramore's argument.

→ *Fitbits for Bosses*

The writer throws in an ominous proposition, the "behavior-monitoring device," that could become routine.

→ Imagine you've just arrived at your job with the Anywhere Bank call center. You switch on your computer and adjust the height of your chair. Then, you slide on the headset, positioning the mic in front of your lips. All that's left to do is to activate your behavior-monitoring device — the gadget hanging from your neck that tracks your tone of voice, your heart rate, and your physical movements throughout the day, sending real-time reports to your supervisor.

A scene from a dystopian movie? Nope. It's already happening in America. Welcome to the brave new world of workplace biosurveillance.

It's obvious that wearable tracking technology has gone mainstream: Just look at the explosion of smart watches and activity monitors that allow people to count steps and check their calorie intake. But this technology has simultaneously been creeping into workplaces: The military uses sensors that scan for injuries, monitor heart rate, and check hydration. More and more, professional athletes are strapping on devices that track every conceivable dimension of performance. Smart ice skates that measure a skater's jump. Clothes that measure an athlete's breathing and collect muscle data. At this year's tryouts in Indianapolis, some NFL hopefuls wore the "Adidas miCoach," a device that sends data on speed and acceleration straight to trainers' iPads. Over the objection of many athletes, coaches and team owners are keen to track off-the-field activity, too, such as sleep patterns and diet. With million-dollar players at stake, big money seems poised to trump privacy.

Now employers from industries that don't even require much physical labor are getting in on the game.

Finance is adopting sophisticated analytics to ensure business performance from high-dollar employees. Cambridge neuroscientist and former Goldman Sachs trader John Coates works with companies to figure out how monitoring biological signals can lead to trading success; his research focuses on measuring hormones that increase confidence and other desirable states as well as those that produce negative, stressful states. In a report for Bloomberg, Coates explained that he is working with "three or four hedge funds" to apply an "early-warning system" that would alert supervisors when traders are getting into the hormonal danger zone. He calls this process "human optimization."

People who do the most basic, underpaid work in our society are increasingly subject to physical monitoring, too — and it extends far beyond the ubiquitous urine test. Bank of America has started using smart badges that monitor the voice and behavior patterns of call-center workers, partnering with the creepily named Humanyze, a company specializing in "people analytics." Humanyze is the brainchild of the MIT Media Lab, the fancy research institute at the Massachusetts Institute of Technology dedicated to the "betterment of humanity," which, incidentally, receives a quarter of its funding from taxpayers. Humanyze concocted a computer dashboard complete with graphs and pie charts that can display the location of employees (Were you hanging out in the lounge today?) and their "social context" (Do you spend a lot of time alone?).

Humanyze founder Ben Waber points out that companies already spend enormous resources collecting analytics on their customers. Why not their employees?

A growing number of workers are being monitored by GPS, often installed on their smartphones. In the U.S. the Supreme Court ruled that law enforcement officials need a warrant to use GPS devices to track a suspect. But employers don't worry over such formalities in keeping tabs on employees, especially those who are mobile, such as truck drivers. A *Washington Post* report on GPS surveillance noted a 2012 study by the research firm Aberdeen Group, which showed that 62 percent of "field

Science-fiction language and references to a dystopian "brave new world" assist sense of foreboding.

Presents as "obvious" the fact that biosurveillance technology has gone mainstream, "creeping" into the workplace. "So what?" Parramore is about to tell us.

Single sentence turns the focus from two specialized fields to everyday jobs.

Extends the dystopian theme and sci-fi language: Phrases like "alert supervisors" and "human optimization" hint at deeper control by managers.

Parramore enhances her argument through strong language and ironic, sardonic tone: "creepily named," "concocted."

Parramore quotes Humanyze's founder but presents his statement as anything but appealing.

Supports claims with examples from a research study and a case study.

employees" — those who regularly perform duties away from the office — are tracked this way. In May, a California woman filed a lawsuit against her former employer, Intermex Wire Transfer, for forcing her to install a tracking app on her phone, which she was required to keep on 24/7. She described feeling like a prisoner wearing an ankle bracelet. After removing the app, the woman was fired.

Sensitive to Big Brother accusations, the biosurveillance industry is trying to keep testing and tool evaluations under the radar. Proponents of the technology point to its potential to improve health conditions in the workplace and enhance public safety. Wouldn't it be better, they argue, if nuclear power plant operators, airline pilots, and oil rig operatives had their physical state closely monitored on the job?

Young Americans nurtured in a digital world where their behavior is relentlessly 10 collected and monitored by advertisers may shrug at an employer's demands for a biosurveillance badge. In a world of insecure employment, what choice do they have, anyway? Despite the revelations of alarming National Security Agency spying and increased government and corporate surveillance since 9/11, the young haven't had much experience yet with what's at stake for them personally. What could possibly go wrong?

A lot: Surveillance has a way of dehumanizing workers. It prevents us from experimenting and exercising our creativity on the job because it tends to uphold the status quo and hold back change. Surveillance makes everyone seem suspicious, creating perceptions and expectations of dishonesty. It makes us feel manipulated. Some researchers have found that increased monitoring actually decreases productivity.

Philosopher and social theorist Michel Foucault observed that the relationship between the watcher and the watched is mostly about power. The power of the observer is enhanced, while the person observed feels more powerless. When an employer or manager interprets our personal data, she gets to make categorical judgments about us and determine how to predict our behavior.

What if she uses the information to discriminate? Coerce? Selectively apply the rules? The data she uses to make her judgments may not even be telling the truth: Researchers have warned that big data can produce big errors. People looking at numbers tend to use them to confirm their own biases, cherry-picking the information that supports their beliefs and ditching the rest. And since algorithms are constructed by human beings, they are not immune to human biases, either. A consumer might be labeled "unlikely to pay a credit card bill" because of an ethnic name, thus promulgating a harmful stereotype.

As Americans, we like to tell ourselves that we value freedom and undue interference from authority. But when we are subjected to surveillance, we feel disempowered and disrespected. We may be more inclined to accept the government getting involved because of fears about terrorism — but when it comes to surveillance on the job, our tendency to object may be chilled by weakened worker protections and increased employment insecurity.

Instead of producing an efficient and productive workplace, biosurveillance may 15 instead deliver troops of distracted, apathetic employees who feel loss of control and decreased job satisfaction. Instead of feeling like part of a team, surveilled workers may develop an us-versus-them mentality and look for opportunities to thwart the monitoring schemes of Big Boss.

Perhaps what we really need is biosurveillance from the bottom up — members of Congress and CEOs could don devices that could, say, detect when they are lying or how their hormones are behaving. Colorful PowerPoints could display the results of data collection on public billboards for the masses to pore over. In the name of safety and efficiency, maybe we ought to ensure that those whose behavior can do society the most harm do not escape the panopticon.

> Concludes by suggesting that those in power most need to be watched "in the name of safety and efficiency" — ostensibly the terms used to justify the practice as applied to workers.

Topics for Critical Thinking and Writing

1. Do you think biometric measurement by employers is ever justified, or do the privacy and security of one's own body always trump the concerns of employers? Why, or why not?

2. If your teachers or parents could monitor the time you spent, and how you felt, while doing homework and studying, what benefits and drawbacks might result? What types of personal monitoring of children are already in place (or possible) in schools and homes, and are these methods different from biometric surveillance?

3. Do you think Lynn Stuart Parramore fairly portrays the founder of Humanyze and others who see potential in the possibilities for biometric monitoring? Why, or why not? In what other ways might biometric measurements help employees and employers?

4. List some examples of Parramore's use of language, word choice, and phrasing that would influence readers to be suspicious of biometric monitoring. How does this language make the essay more or less effective or convincing?

5. In what way does Parramore's recommendation in the final paragraph support or contradict her argument about individuals' basic rights to privacy?

Examining Assumptions

In Chapter 3, we will discuss **assumptions** in some detail. Here we introduce the topic by emphasizing the importance of *identifying* and *examining* assumptions — those you'll encounter in the writings of others and those you'll rely on in your own essays.

With this in mind, let's again consider some of the assumptions suggested in this chapter's earlier readings. The student who wrote about Stephen Cavanaugh's case pointed out that Nebraska prison officials simply did not see the Church of the Flying Spaghetti Monster as a real religion. Their assumption was that some religions can be more or less "real" than others or can make more sense than others. Assumptions may be *explicit* or *implicit*, stated or unstated. In this case, the prison officials were forthright about their assumptions in their stated claim about the church, perhaps believing their point was obvious to anyone who thought seriously about the idea of a Flying Spaghetti Monster. It didn't occur to them to consider that even major and mainstream religions honor stories, claims, and rituals that seem absurd to others.

An implicit assumption is one that is not stated but, rather, is taken for granted. It works like an underlying belief that structures an argument. In Lynn Stuart Parramore's essay on workplace biometric devices, the unstated assumption is that these sorts of technological monitors in the workplace represent a kind of evil "big brother" intent on subduing and exploiting employees with newer and newer forms of invasion of privacy. Parramore's assumption, while not stated directly, is evident in her choice of language, as we've pointed out above with terms such as *dystopian* and *brave new world*.

Another way to discern her assumption is by looking at the scenarios and selections of examples she chooses. For example, in imagining a company that would seek to know how much time an employee spends in the lounge area or alone, Parramore sees only obsessive monitoring of employees for the purposes of regulating their time. But what if these technologies could enable a company to discover that productivity or worker satisfaction increases in proportion to the amount of time employees spend collaborating in the lounge? Maybe workplace conditions would improve instead of deteriorating (a bigger lounge, more comfortable chairs), and maybe more efforts would be made for team-building and improving interpersonal employee relations. From a position that is skeptical about how employers might use such technologies, biometric surveillance of employees appears to be a dramatic overreach on the part of industries that use them. Biometric devices are seen as an intrusion and perhaps a violation of workers' privacy rights. However, from a business or an organizational strategy perspective, these technologies could be seen as ways to improve workplace heath and productivity.

Assumptions can be powerful sources of ideas and opinions. Understanding our own and others' assumptions is a major part of critical thinking. Assumptions about race, class, disability, sex, and gender are among the most powerful sources of social inequality. The following essay by Helen Benedict was published in 2015, two years after the US Department of Defense lifted the ban on women in combat roles in the armed forces and shortly after Defense Secretary Ashton Carter further lifted exclusions pertaining to women by granting them access to serve in all capacities in combat, including in elite special forces units. One assumption we may make about these developments is that the changed regulations resulted in an equal-access military. However, as Benedict argues, women in the military continue to face obstacles to equality, many of which themselves are based on social assumptions about gender.

A CHECKLIST FOR EXAMINING ASSUMPTIONS

☐ Have I identified any of the assumptions presupposed in the writer's argument?

☐ Are these assumptions explicit or implicit?

☐ Are these assumptions important to the author's argument, or are they only incidental?

☐ Does the author give any evidence of being aware of the hidden assumptions in her or his argument?

(continues on next page)

HELEN BENEDICT

Helen Benedict (b. 1952) is a professor at Columbia University's Graduate School of Journalism. She is best known for her journalism on social injustice and the Iraq War as well as her seven novels, most recently *Wolf Season*, which received *Publishers Weekly's* Best Contemporary War Novel award in 2018.

The Military Has a Man Problem

Army Specialist Laura Naylor, a Wisconsin native, spent a year in Baghdad with the 32nd Military Police Company in 2003 and 2004. During that time, she — like all of the more than quarter-million women deployed to Iraq and Afghanistan — was officially banned from ground combat. That technicality didn't slow down Naylor when an IED[1] hit her convoy and it began to take fire from a nearby building. "We had to search this house nearby, thinking they were the ones doing the shooting, and I was the lead person the whole way. I had a flashlight in one hand, a pistol in the other, and I'd kick the door open with my foot, look both ways, give the all clear, go to the next room, do the same thing," she recounted to me a few years later. "We were interchangeable with the infantry."

A friend in her unit, Specialist Caryle Garcia, was wounded when a roadside bomb

went off beside her Humvee. Garcia was her team's gunner, her body exposed from the chest up above the Humvee's roof. Their close friend, 20-year-old Specialist Michelle Witmer, became the first National Guardswoman ever killed in action after being shot during another ambush. Witmer's death was a grim marker in a steady march that has seen one woman after another achieve milestones in military service since the September 11, 2001, attacks that would have been unimaginable just a generation ago. During the Vietnam War, female soldiers were not even allowed to carry guns.

In early 2013, outgoing Defense Secretary Leon Panetta, with the backing of the Joint Chiefs of Staff, finally lifted the ban on women serving in ground combat, belatedly admitting they had already been doing so. "Women have shown great courage and sacrifice on and off the battlefield," he said, "and proven their ability to serve in an expanding number of roles." President Barack Obama heralded the

---

[1]**IED** improvised explosive device; an unconventional bomb. [Editors' note]

move, which remains politically controversial on Capitol Hill, saying, "Valor knows no gender." Since Panetta's decree, the debate has centered on whether, now that women can serve in previously all-male combat units, they have the ability to actually do it. The Marine Corps, Army and Special Forces have all been busily, and publicly, putting women to the test, running them through training courses and assessments, and announcing gravely how many have passed or failed.

Yet to many female soldiers and the men who have witnessed their competence in battle over the past 13-plus years, this debate seems like closing the barn door after the horse has bolted — ignoring that the distinction between "rear echelon" and "front line" in these wars is obsolete. Of the roughly 300,000 American women who have deployed to the Afghanistan and Iraq wars since 2001, at least 800 have been wounded, and, as of last count, at least 144 have been killed. Two women have earned Silver Stars, the military's third-highest award.

For generations now, the debate over women in combat has put the onus on women to prove they can handle the infantry and other traditionally all-male units. Yet today's wars have made it clear that the military's problem lies not with its women, their ability or their courage. The military's problem, instead, is with some of its men — and a deeply ingrained macho culture that denigrates, insults and abuses women.

In eight years of covering women at war, I have noticed a pattern in attitudes toward women in the military: The men who have served with women are more than satisfied with their work, while the men who are most resistant to serving alongside women have never done it.

"Oh, it's too rough for women," such men tend to say. Others complain, "Women would ruin our camaraderie" or "We'd be competing for women instead of looking out for ourselves." As retired Gen. Gordon R. Sullivan, a former Army chief of staff, wrote, lifting the combat ban against women would be "confusing" and "detrimental to units."

These attitudes reveal deeply patriarchal, condescending and creaky stereotypes about women, as if they are capable of being nothing more than soft, sexy objects of romance — or sexual prey.

Some of the very same types of prejudiced objections were once raised against black and gay men entering the military, even though they had demonstrated their military prowess long before they were openly welcomed into the ranks. As former chairman of the Joint Chiefs Gen. John Shalikashvili wrote in 2007, many within the military were originally concerned that "letting people who were openly gay serve would lower morale, harm recruitment and undermine unit cohesion."

And yet, even after President Harry 10 Truman forced the racial integration of the military in 1948 and even after the fall of "don't ask, don't tell" in 2011, the military is still standing. And nobody questions any longer whether black or gay people can serve as well as straight white men.

Canada, Denmark and Norway have allowed women to serve in combat since the 1980s. Canadian commanders found no "negative effect on operational performance or team cohesion," according to one report; neither did military leaders in Norway. Israel, which added women to combat units years ago, has found that they "exhibit superior skills" in discipline, shooting and weapons use.

Today's debate about women would be less antediluvian if, instead of questioning whether women can do the job they've already been doing for years, it focused on why so many men in all-male companies still don't want to work with women. To what sort of all-male camaraderie are they clinging, and why?

In some ways, it may seem hard to blame the men who feel this way. Military training inculcates these attitudes deep into their souls. Drill instructors dress down recruits by taunting them with suggestions that their girlfriends and wives are being unfaithful. Military cadences and songs can be astonishingly misogynist. One example from the Naval Academy: "*Who can take a chainsaw / Cut the bitch in two / F--- the bottom half / And give the upper half to you. . . .*"

Long after racist language was banned from training, drill instructors regularly insult male recruits by calling them "ladies," "pussies," "girls" and worse. As an Iraq veteran wrote about his time in Marine boot camp in 2008, "The Drill Instructor's nightly homiletic speeches, full of an unabashed hatred of women, were part of the second phase of boot camp: the process of rebuilding recruits into Marines."

In other words, stoking men's hatred and 15 suspicion of women is a way of firing up those men to kill.

One of the most common objections put forth by men who don't want to work with women is that they would be so concerned with protecting the women in their units that it would risk the mission. That is, they would be too chivalrous to be good soldiers.

But as more data on the military's rampant sexual harassment and abuse come out, this chivalry argument becomes harder to believe. Given that half the women deployed to Iraq and Afghanistan reported being sexually harassed, and one in four reported being sexually assaulted, according to a Department of Veterans Affairs study, evidence of this gallantry is, to say the least, scant. Former Army Sgt. Rebekah Havrilla, who says she was raped while serving in Afghanistan, testified before the Senate Armed Services Committee: "I had no faith in my chain of command as my first sergeant previously had sexual harassment accusations against him and the unit climate was extremely sexist and hostile in nature towards women."

If the military wants to get serious about inviting female soldiers to play ever-larger roles in war, it will have to find ways to change the attitude of so many of its own soldiers, sailors, airmen and Marines.

Stories from recent years about the depths of the military's misogyny are legendary. In 2013, the head of the Air Force's sexual assault prevention office at the Pentagon, Jeffrey Krusinski, was himself arrested and charged with sexual battery by police in Arlington, Virginia, after allegedly accosting a woman in a parking lot. (He was later acquitted by a jury.) An Army sergeant at Fort Hood who worked as a sexual abuse educator was investigated for running a prostitution ring. The married Army general in charge of Fort Jackson, who oversaw training for many Army recruits, was suspended after allegedly physically attacking his girlfriend.

If these are examples of the people in 20 charge of ensuring respectful treatment of women, is it any surprise that new recruits see women as less than equals? Not long after Krusinski's arrest, West Point's rugby team was disbanded after lewd emails about fellow female cadets surfaced that the school said suggested "a culture of disrespect towards women."

Until the military recognizes women as equal human beings, how can it recognize them as equal soldiers? As Colleen Bushnell, who was sexually assaulted while in the Air Force and now is an advocate for survivors, has said, "This is a predator problem, not a female problem."

Military culture may well be the last bastion of male protectionism in modern society, so it is no surprise that its arguments against admitting women fully are the same as those used whenever women first enter a previously all-male field — whether that is firefighting, policing, politics, sports or voting. Indeed, many of the objections macho military types make to women today mirror those their grandfathers and great-grandfathers made when women were trying to enter public life.

Yet there's precious little evidence that all-male cultures produce anything better than co-ed cultures, just as there is no evidence at all that the presence of women as voters, golfers, politicians, police officers, firefighters — or presidents — ruins anything other than male privilege.

War has changed. It is simply unfeasible to keep women off the front lines. "We're getting blown up right alongside the guys," as one female soldier who served in Iraq told me. "We're in combat! So there's no reason to keep us segregated anymore."

Admitting that the military's problem 25 with female soldiers is actually a man's problem, however, will necessitate stronger military and political leadership than we have yet seen. It will require a wholesale shift in how the military builds respect among its troops. And it means teaching the men who don't want to work with women that they must either respect their female comrades or leave. As Australia's Army chief, David Morrison, put it to his troops in 2013, "Female soldiers and officers have proven themselves worthy of the best traditions of the Australian army. . . . If that does not suit you, then get out. . . . There is no place for you amongst this band of brothers and sisters."

American military leaders, take note.

Topics for Critical Thinking and Writing

1. What purpose do the first two paragraphs of Helen Benedict's essay serve in her overall argument?

2. Identify Benedict's thesis. In your own words, what is she arguing?

3. In the past, what assumptions about women were the basis for excluding them from military combat service? How does Benedict see those assumptions still at work, despite formal recognition that women are capable of combat roles in the service?

4. What examples does Benedict use to make comparisons? How do her comparisons help advance her argument about the "man problem" in the military?

5. What changes or actions may be taken to reduce or eliminate the "man problem" in the military? If you were to make an argument about what can be done to solve the problem, what specific areas of military life could be addressed, and what new procedures might be instituted?

6. Construct an argument to defend your position on this question: Because women are now permitted to serve in all military combat positions, should all women, like all men, have to register for Selective Service and be subject to the military draft, if one were needed?

ASSIGNMENTS FOR CRITICAL THINKING

1. Choose one of the following topics and write down all the pro and con arguments you can think of in, say, ten minutes. Then, at least an hour or two later, return to your notes and see whether you can add to them. Finally, write a balanced dialogue between two imagined speakers who hold opposing views on the issue. You'll doubtless have to revise your dialogue several times, and in revising your drafts, you'll likely come up with further ideas. Present *both* sides as strongly as possible. (You may want to give the two speakers distinct characters, or personas.) After you have completed the exercise, write an exploratory essay in which you first identify the issue, then work through different perspectives, positions, ideas, and solutions related to your issue.

    If none of the suggested topics that follow interests you, ask your instructor about the possibility of choosing a topic of your own. Suggested topics:

    a. Colleges with large athletic programs should pay student athletes a salary or stipend.
    b. Bicyclists and motorcyclists should be required by law to wear helmets.
    c. High school teachers should have the right to carry concealed firearms in schools.
    d. Smoking should be prohibited on all college campuses, including in all buildings *and* outdoors.
    e. Honors students should have the privilege of registering for classes earlier than other students.
    f. Students should have the right to drop out of school at any age.
    g. Comfort animals — such as dogs, cats, ferrets, and snakes — that have been recommended to patients by doctors or therapists to ease anxiety should be allowed in college classrooms.

2. In April 2012, Williams College in Williamstown, Massachusetts, hosted a lecture and film screening of work by Jiz Lee, described in campus advertisements as a "genderqueer porn star." After inviting the adult entertainer to campus, the college came under fire by some students and members of the public (especially after the story was reported by national media). Opponents questioned the appropriateness and academic value of the event, which was brought to campus by the Mike Dively Committee, an endowment established to help "develop understanding of human sexuality and sexual orientation and their impact on culture." Proponents argued that (1) pornography is a subject that deserves critical analysis and commentary, (2) the Dively series is intended to create conversations about sexuality and sexual orientation in society and culture, and (3) treating any potential subject in an academic setting under the circumstances of the program is appropriate. What are your views? Should adult film stars ever be invited to college campuses? Should pornography constitute a subject of analysis on campus? Why, or why not?

    Now, imagine you're a student member of your campus programming board. Some faculty members from the Gender and Sexuality Program come to your committee seeking funds to invite a female former adult film star to campus to lecture on "The Reality of Pornography." Faculty and student sponsors have assured your committee that the visit by the actress in question is part of an effort to educate students and the public about the adult film industry and its impact on women. Graphic images and short film clips will be shown. Use the thinking strategies in this chapter to pose as many questions as you can about the potential benefits and risks of approving this invitation. How would you vote, and why? (If you can find a peer who has an opposing view, construct a debate on the issue.)

3. In 1984, the US Congress passed the National Minimum Drinking Age Act, mandating that all states implement and enforce raising the minimum drinking age from eighteen to twenty-one years. Through this legislation, the United States became one of a handful of developed countries to have such a high drinking age. In 2009, John McCardell, president emeritus of Middlebury College in Vermont, wrote a declaration signed by 136 college presidents supporting returning the drinking age to eighteen. McCardell's organization, Choose Responsibly, says that people age eighteen to twenty should be treated as the adults they are — for example, in terms of voting, serving on juries and in the military, or buying legal weapons. The organization encourages educational programs and awareness efforts that would introduce alcohol-related issues to young college students and demystify and discourage problem drinking. Lowering the drinking age is opposed by the organization Mothers Against Drunk Drivers, whose members argue that raising it to twenty-one has curbed traffic accidents and fatalities caused by drunk driving. How would you approach this question of returning the drinking age to eighteen? What perspectives should matter most? Apply the critical thinking questions from the section Survey, Analyze, and Evaluate the Issue (pp. 6–7) and decide: Should the drinking age be lowered to eighteen? Argue why or why not, trying to anticipate and address the counterarguments likely to be made against your position.

2

Critical Reading: Getting Started

Some books are to be tasted, others to be swallowed, and some few to be chewed and digested.
— FRANCIS BACON

Read parts of a newspaper quickly or an encyclopedia entry, or a fast-food thriller, but do not insult yourself or a book which has been created with its author's painstakingly acquired skill and effort, by seeing how fast you can dispose of it.
— SUSAN HILL

Active Reading

In the passages that we quote above, two good points are made. The first is that some types of reading do not need to be fully read at all — a taste of what they offer is enough. Some types of reading can be taken in completely and quickly, swallowed whole like a fast-food meal. But some types of reading call for much closer attention. Classical works of literature, for example, may require thoughtful consideration of their language, their meanings, and their relevancy to the present. Similarly, many arguments (usually essays, editorials, articles) require thoughtful deliberation, especially about the ideas they express.

But how do you know the difference between a book (or an essay) that may be read quickly and one that deserves to be read slowly? How can you judge the value of a piece of writing *before* deciding to read it carefully? And if you *do* decide a text is worth reading slowly and carefully, how do you prepare to think critically about it?

PREVIEWING

Even before reading a single word of a text, you may evaluate it to some degree. **Previewing** is a strategy for reading that allows you to use prior knowledge — such as the expectations of your teacher or your understanding of how certain kinds of texts generally work — to help guide your reading. Skilled readers rarely read a text "cold"; instead, they think about it in terms of what they already know. They first examine the text, **skimming** to identify and evaluate the following:

- the author
- the place of publication

- the **genre**, or type of writing
- the table of contents
- headnotes or an abstract (if available)
- the title and subtitle
- section headings
- other information that stands out at a glance (such as images, graphs, and tables)

By previewing and skimming effectively, you can quickly ascertain quite a bit of information about an article or essay. You can detect the author's claims and methods, see the evidence he or she uses (experience, statistics, quotations, etc.), examine the tone and difficulty level, and determine whether the piece of writing offers useful ideas for you. These strategies work well if you're researching a topic and need to review many essays — you can read efficiently to find those that are most important or relevant to you or those that offer different perspectives. Of course, if you do find an essay to be compelling during previewing and skimming, you can begin "chewing and digesting," as Francis Bacon put it — reading more closely and carefully (or else putting it aside for later when you can give it more time).

> **READING TIP**
> Instead of imagining previewing and slower, more careful reading as two separate stages, think of previewing as an activity that helps you decide — at any time — whether or not you should begin engaging in more careful reading.

One of the first things you can do to begin previewing a piece of writing is to identify the **author** — not just by name but also in terms of any other information you may know or can find out. You might already know, for example, that a work by Martin Luther King Jr. will probably deal with civil rights. You know that it will be serious and eloquent. You know that King's words will likely be related to the social conditions of the 1950s and 1960s and that he will be speaking in a somewhat different language than you are accustomed to. In contrast, if Stephen King is the author, you would change your expectations, probably anticipating the essay to be about fear, the craft of writing, or King's experiences as a horror novelist. You may also know that this King writes for a broad audience, so his essay won't be terribly difficult to understand. But even if you don't know the author, you can often discern something about him or her by looking at biographical information provided in the text or by doing a quick internet search. You can use this information to predict the subject of an essay and its style, as well as its author's possible assumptions and biases.

The **place of publication** may also reveal something about the essay in terms of its subject, style, and approach. For instance, the *National Review* is a conservative journal. If you notice that an essay on affirmative action was published in the *National Review*, you can tentatively assume that the essay will not endorse affirmative action. In contrast, knowing that *Ms.* magazine is a liberal publication, you can guess that an essay on affirmative action published there will probably be an endorsement. You often can learn a good deal about a magazine or journal simply by flipping through it and noticing the kinds of articles in it. The advertisements also tell you what kind of audience the magazine or journal likely has. If you don't know anything about a publication, you can quickly research it on the internet to find out more.

The **title** of an essay, too, may give an idea of what to expect. Of course, a title may announce only the subject and not the author's thesis or point of view ("On Gun Control"; "Should Drugs Be Legal?"). A title may also be opaque or mysterious ("The Chokehold"). Fairly often, though, a title will indicate the thesis (as in "Give Children the Vote" or "We Need Campaign Finance Reform Now"). If you can tell more or less what to expect from a title, you can probably take in some of the major points even on a quick reading. Glancing at subtitles, and any section headings and subheadings, too, can help you map the progression of an argument without fully reading the entire text.

THESIS   Sometimes, you can find the **thesis** (the main point or major claim) of an essay by looking at the first paragraph. Other times, especially if the paragraphs are short, you can locate the thesis within the first several paragraphs. Depending on what you discover while skimming, you can speed up or slow down your reading as needed while you locate the thesis and get a sense of how the argument for it is structured. As we noted, if the essay has sections, pay attention to headings and subheadings to see how the thesis is supported by other minor claims.

CONTEXT   When engaging with a text, you also consider the role of **context** — the situational conditions in which a piece was written. Context — literally, "with the text" — can refer to the time period, geographical location, cultural climate, political environment, or any other setting that helps you orient a piece of writing to the conditions surrounding it. Recognizing the context can reveal a lot about how an author treats a subject. For example, an essay about gun control written before the mass shootings of the past ten years might have a less urgent approach and advocate more lenient measures than one written today. An article about transgender identity or police brutality might convey different assumptions about those topics depending on whether it was written before or after the increased recognition of transgender rights or before or after the protests of the Black Lives Matter movement. Social conditions, in short, affect how writers and readers think.

Anything you read exists in at least two broad contexts: the context of its *production* (where and when it was written or published) and the context of its *consumption* (where and when it is encountered and read). One thing all good critical readers do when considering the validity of claims and arguments is to take *both* types of context into account. This means asking questions not only about the approaches, assumptions, and beliefs about certain subjects that were in place when an essay was written, but also about how current events and new trends in thinking that occurred after the original publication date may generate different issues and challenges related to the subject of the essay. The state of affairs in the time and place in which that argument is made *and received* matters to the questions you might ask, the evidence you might consider, and the responses you might produce.

Consider these words, spoken by Abraham Lincoln in his famous debates with Stephen Douglas, when the two campaigned against each other for a US Senate seat in 1858. Douglas had accused Lincoln of holding the then-unpopular view that the black race and white race were equal. Lincoln defended himself against these charges:

> I will say then that I am not, nor ever have been, in favor of bringing about in any way the social and political equality of the white and black races [Applause], that

I am not nor ever have been in favor of making voters or jurors of negroes, nor of qualifying them to hold office, nor to intermarry with white people; and I will say in addition to this that there is a physical difference between the white and black races which I believe will forever forbid the two races living together on terms of social and political equality. And inasmuch as they cannot so live, while they do remain together there must be the position of superior and inferior, and I as much as any other man am in favor of having the superior position assigned to the white race.

Lincoln's ideas about race in this speech may surprise you. If you saw this quotation somewhere, it might make you think that Abraham Lincoln held racist views despite his reputation as "The Great Emancipator." However, it is crucial to put his words in context to develop a fuller, more mature understanding of them. Historians, for example, read these words in light of common and even "scientific" beliefs about race in the 1850s, informed by the situation at hand (a campaign speech, in which he might feel free to overstate or appeal to popular beliefs), and with knowledge of Lincoln's uncompromising efforts later to abolish slavery. How does consideration of these historical contexts help you understand Lincoln's words? How does consideration of the context in which you read it shape your understanding, given your expectations and your prior knowledge about Lincoln?

THE "FIRST AND LAST" RULE   You may apply the "first and last" rule when skimming essays. This rule assumes that somewhere early and late in the writing you can locate the author's key points. Opening paragraphs are good places to seek out the author's central thesis, and final paragraphs are good places to seek out conclusive statements such as "Finally, then, *it is time that we . . .*" or "Given this evidence, *it is clear that . . .*" Final paragraphs are particularly important because they often summarize the argument and restate the thesis.

> **WRITING TIP**
> You can arrange elements in a sentence according to the "first and last" rule to control what points you want to emphasize most.

The first and last rule works because authors often place main points of emphasis at the beginnings and endings of essays, but they also do the same within individual paragraphs. Authors do not usually bury key ideas in the middle of long essays, and neither do they surround the key ideas of paragraphs with bulky text. Further, authors try not to hide their most important points in the middle of long sentences. Often, the main point of a sentence can be found by looking at the elements stated first and last. (Of course, there are always exceptions to the rule.) Consider the following sentences, each of which contains the same basic information arranged in different ways:

Here, the time period and the new smoking prohibitions get the most emphasis:

> Over the past fifteen years, the rate of smoking among New York City residents declined by more than 35% because of new health trends and new tobacco restrictions.

Here, the place and the percentage are most emphasized:

> In New York City, new tobacco restrictions and new health trends helped lower the smoking rate over fifteen years by more than 35%.

A SHORT ESSAY FOR PREVIEWING PRACTICE

Before skimming the following essay, apply the previewing techniques discussed on pages 33–36 and complete the Thinking Critically: Previewing activity below.

THINKING CRITICALLY *Previewing*

The following activity lists typical types of questions readers use while previewing. Provide the missing information for Sanjay Gupta and his essay "Why I Changed My Mind on Weed" (p. 38) or another essay of your choosing.

PREVIEWING STRATEGIES	TYPES OF QUESTIONS	ANSWERS
Author	Who is the author? What expertise and credibility does the author have? How difficult is the writing likely to be?	
Title	What does the title reveal about the essay's content? Does it give any clues about how the argument will take shape? Do headings or subheadings reveal any further information?	
Place of Publication	How does the place of publication help you understand the argument? What type of audiences will it be likely to target?	
Context	By placing the article in the context of its time — given trends in the conversations about or popular understandings of the subject — what can you expect about the author's position?	
Skimming	As you skim over the first several paragraphs, where do you first realize what the argument of the essay is? What major forms of evidence support the argument?	

SANJAY GUPTA

Dr. Sanjay Gupta (b. 1969) is a neurosurgeon and multiple Emmy Award–winning television personality. As a leading public health expert, he is most well known as CNN's chief medical correspondent. In 2011, *Forbes* magazine named him one of the ten most influential celebrities in the United States. The essay below originally appeared on CNN.com in August 2013.

Why I Changed My Mind on Weed

Over the last year, I have been working on a new documentary called "Weed." The title "Weed" may sound cavalier, but the content is not.

I traveled around the world to interview medical leaders, experts, growers and patients. I spoke candidly to them, asking tough questions. What I found was stunning.

Long before I began this project, I had steadily reviewed the scientific literature on medical marijuana from the United States and thought it was fairly unimpressive. Reading these papers five years ago, it was hard to make a case for medicinal marijuana. I even wrote about this in a *Time* magazine article, back in 2009, titled "Why I Would Vote No on Pot."

Well, I am here to apologize.

I apologize because I didn't look hard 5 enough, until now. I didn't look far enough. I didn't review papers from smaller labs in other countries doing some remarkable research, and I was too dismissive of the loud chorus of legitimate patients whose symptoms improved on cannabis.

Instead, I lumped them with the high-visibility malingerers, just looking to get high. I mistakenly believed the Drug Enforcement Agency listed marijuana as a Schedule 1 substance because of sound scientific proof. Surely, they must have quality reasoning as to why marijuana is in the category of the most dangerous drugs that have "no accepted medicinal use and a high potential for abuse."

They didn't have the science to support that claim, and I now know that when it comes to marijuana neither of those things are true. It doesn't have a high potential for abuse, and there are very legitimate medical applications. In fact, sometimes marijuana is the only thing that works. Take the case of Charlotte Figi, whom I met in Colorado. She started having seizures soon after birth. By age 3, she was having 300 a week, despite being on 7 different medications. Medical marijuana has calmed her brain, limiting her seizures to 2 or 3 per month.

I have seen more patients like Charlotte first hand, spent time with them and come to the realization that it is irresponsible not to provide the best care we can as a medical community, care that could involve marijuana.

We have been terribly and systematically misled for nearly 70 years in the United States, and I apologize for my own role in that.

I hope this article and upcoming docu- 10 mentary will help set the record straight.

On August 14, 1970, the Assistant Secretary of Health, Dr. Roger O. Egeberg, wrote a letter recommending the plant, marijuana, be classified as a Schedule 1 substance, and it has remained that way for nearly 45 years. My research started with a careful reading of that decades-old letter. What I found was unsettling. Egeberg had carefully chosen his words:

"Since there is still a considerable void in our knowledge of the plant and effects of the active drug contained in it, our recommendation is that marijuana be retained within Schedule 1 at least until the completion of certain studies now under way to resolve the issue."

Not because of sound science, but because of its absence, marijuana was classified as a Schedule 1 substance. Again, the year was 1970. Egeberg mentions studies that are under way, but many were never completed. As my investigation continued, however, I realized Egeberg did in fact have important research already available to him, some of it from more than 25 years earlier.

HIGH RISK OF ABUSE

In 1944, New York mayor Fiorello LaGuardia commissioned research to be performed by the New York Academy of Science. Among their conclusions: they found marijuana did not lead to significant addiction in the medical sense of the word. They also did not find any evidence marijuana led to morphine, heroin or cocaine addiction.

We now know that while estimates vary, 15 marijuana leads to dependence in around 9 to 10% of its adult users. By comparison, cocaine, a Schedule 2 substance "with less abuse potential than Schedule 1 drugs," hooks 20% of those who use it. Around 25% of heroin users become addicted.

The worst is tobacco, where the number is closer to 30% of smokers, many of whom go on to die because of their addiction.

There is clear evidence that in some people marijuana use can lead to withdrawal symptoms, including insomnia, anxiety and nausea. Even considering this, it is hard to make a case that it has a high potential for abuse. The physical symptoms of marijuana addiction are nothing like those of the other drugs I've mentioned. I have seen the withdrawal from alcohol, and it can be life threatening.

I do want to mention a concern that I think about as a father. Young, developing brains are likely more susceptible to harm from marijuana than adult brains. Some recent studies suggest that regular use in teenage years leads to a permanent decrease in IQ. Other research hints at a possible heightened risk of developing psychosis.

Much in the same way I wouldn't let my own children drink alcohol, I wouldn't permit marijuana until they are adults. If they are adamant about trying marijuana, I will urge them to wait until they're in their mid-20s, when their brains are fully developed.

MEDICAL BENEFIT

While investigating, I realized something 20 else quite important. Medical marijuana is not new, and the medical community has been writing about it for a long time. There were in fact hundreds of journal articles, mostly documenting the benefits. Most of those papers, however, were written between the years 1840 and 1930. The papers described the use of medical marijuana to treat "neuralgia, convulsive disorders, emaciation," among other things.

A search through the U.S. National Library of Medicine this past year pulled up nearly 20,000 more recent papers. But the majority were research into the harm of marijuana, such as "Bad trip due to anticholinergic effect of cannabis," or "Cannabis induced pancreatitis" and "Marijuana use and risk of lung cancer."

In my quick running of the numbers, I calculated about 6% of the current U.S. marijuana studies investigate the benefits of medical marijuana. The rest are designed to investigate harm. That imbalance paints a highly distorted picture.

THE CHALLENGES OF MARIJUANA RESEARCH

To do studies on marijuana in the United States today, you need two important things.

First of all, you need marijuana. And marijuana is illegal. You see the problem. Scientists can get research marijuana from a special farm in Mississippi, which is astonishingly located in the middle of the Ole Miss campus, but it is challenging. When I visited this year, there was no marijuana being grown.

The second thing you need is approval, and the scientists I interviewed kept reminding me how tedious that can be. While a cancer study may first be evaluated by the National Cancer Institute, or a pain study may go through the National Institute for Neurological Disorders, there is one more approval required for marijuana: NIDA, the National Institute on Drug Abuse. It is an organization that has a core mission of studying drug abuse, as opposed to benefit.

Stuck in the middle are the legitimate patients who depend on marijuana as a medicine, oftentimes as their only good option.

Keep in mind that up until 1943, marijuana was part of the United States drug pharmacopeia. One of the conditions for which it was prescribed was neuropathic pain. It is a miserable pain that's tough to treat. My own patients have described it as "lancinating, burning and a barrage of pins and needles." While marijuana has long been documented to be effective for this awful pain, the most common medications prescribed today come from the poppy plant, including morphine, oxycodone and dilaudid.

Here is the problem. Most of these medications don't work very well for this kind of pain, and tolerance is a real problem.

Most frightening to me is that someone dies in the United States every 19 minutes from a prescription drug overdose, mostly accidental. Every 19 minutes. It is a horrifying statistic. As much as I searched, I could not find a documented case of death from marijuana overdose.

It is perhaps no surprise then that 76% of 30 physicians recently surveyed said they would approve the use of marijuana to help ease a woman's pain from breast cancer.

When marijuana became a Schedule 1 substance, there was a request to fill a "void in our knowledge." In the United States, that has been challenging because of the infrastructure surrounding the study of an illegal substance, with a drug abuse organization at the heart of the approval process. And yet, despite the hurdles, we have made considerable progress that continues today.

Looking forward, I am especially intrigued by studies like those in Spain and Israel looking at the anti-cancer effects of marijuana and its components. I'm intrigued by the neuroprotective study by Lev Meschoulam in Israel, and research in Israel and the United States on whether the drug might help alleviate symptoms of PTSD. I promise to do my part to help, genuinely and honestly, fill the remaining void in our knowledge.

Citizens in 20 states and the District of Columbia have now voted to approve marijuana for medical applications, and more states will be making that choice soon. As for Dr. Roger Egeberg, who wrote that letter in 1970, he passed away 16 years ago.

I wonder what he would think if he were alive today.

Exercise: The "First and Last" Rule

When writing, you can emphasize main points by using the first and last rule (see p. 36). Try it yourself by considering the following list of observations from Gupta's essay. Rearrange the statements any way you wish to write a single paragraph, using the first and last rule to emphasize the elements that you find most important. (You do not have to include all the details; you might want to add in some others, and feel free to rephrase them.) Next, compare your sentences to your classmates'. How do they compare in terms of emphasis?

- Gupta is one of the most respected voices in public health.
- Gupta argues for the legalization of medical marijuana.
- Gupta's letter was written for CNN News.
- Gupta rejects his previous position on medical marijuana and apologizes for his oversight.
- The article was important because it represented a shift in approach by a leading doctor.

READING WITH A CAREFUL EYE: UNDERLINING, HIGHLIGHTING, ANNOTATING

Once you have a general idea of the work — not only an idea of its topic and thesis but also a sense of the way in which the thesis is argued — you can go back and start reading it carefully.

As you read, **underline** or **highlight** key passages and make **annotations** in the margins. Because you're reading actively, or interacting with the text, you won't simply let your eye rove across the page.

- Highlight the chief points so that later when reviewing the essay you can easily locate the main passages.
- Don't overdo it. If you find yourself highlighting most of a page, you're probably not distinguishing the key points clearly enough.
- Make your marginal annotations brief and selective. They may consist of hints or clues, comments like "doesn't follow," "good," "compare with Jones," "check this," and "really?"
- Highlight key definitions. In the margin you might write "good," "in contrast," or "?" if you think the definition is correct, incorrect, or unclear.
- Use tools to highlight or annotate when using software to read a digital essay. Also consider copying and pasting passages that you would normally highlight into a new document file. Clearly identify these passages as direct quotations to avoid plagiarism, and type your annotations next to them using the review functions.

In all these ways, you interact with the text and lay the groundwork for eventually writing your own essay on what you have read.

What you annotate will depend largely on your **purpose**. If you're reading an essay to see how the writer organizes an argument, you'll annotate one sort of thing. If you're reading to challenge the thesis, you'll annotate other things. Here is a passage from an essay by Charles R. Lawrence titled "On Racist Speech," with a student's rather skeptical, even aggressive, annotations. But notice that the student apparently made at least one of the annotations — "Definition of 'fighting words'" — chiefly to remind herself to locate where the definition of an important term appears in the essay. The essay is presented in full on page 69.

<table>
<tr>
<td>Example of such a policy?</td>
<td>University officials who have formulated <u>policies</u> to respond to incidents of racial harassment have been characterized in the press as "thought police," but such policies generally do nothing more than</td>
</tr>
<tr>
<td>?</td>
<td>impose (sanctions) against intentional face-to-face insults. When <u>racist</u></td>
</tr>
<tr>
<td>Example?</td>
<td>speech takes the form of <u>face-to-face insults</u>, catcalls, or other assaul-</td>
</tr>
<tr>
<td>What about sexist speech?</td>
<td>tive speech aimed at an individual or small group of persons, it falls directly within the "<u>fighting words</u>" exception to First Amendment</td>
</tr>
<tr>
<td>Definition of "fighting words"</td>
<td>protection. The Supreme Court has held that <u>words "which 'by their very utterance inflict</u> injury or tend to incite an immediate breach of the peace'" are not protected by the First Amendment.</td>
</tr>
</table>

<table>
<tr>
<td>Really? Probably depends on the individual.</td>
<td>If the purpose of the First Amendment is to foster the greatest amount of speech, racial insults disserve that purpose. Assaultive racist speech functions as a preemptive strike. The <u>invective is</u> experienced as a blow, not as a <u>proffered idea</u>, and once the blow is struck, it is unlikely that a dialogue will follow. Racial insults are par-</td>
</tr>
<tr>
<td>Why must speech always seek "to discover truth"?</td>
<td>ticularly undeserving of First Amendment protection because the perpetrator's <u>intention is not to discover truth</u> or initiate dialogue</td>
</tr>
<tr>
<td>How does he know?</td>
<td>but to injure the victim. <u>In most situations</u>, members of minority groups realize that they are likely to lose if they respond to epithets by fighting and are forced to remain silent and submissive.</td>
</tr>
</table>

READING: FAST AND SLOW

Earlier, we recommended skimming as a quick previewing strategy to help you determine the author's purpose, general argument, and major forms of supporting evidence. Then we suggested a way to go a bit deeper, annotating as you read. However, once you determine that a particular text is worth digging into even further, you should alter your strategy so that you can engage with the argument in an even more analytical way. If critical thinking involves "taking apart" a specimen to help you understand it, then doing so with a text is akin to taking apart any complex system to understand better how it works (as with an automobile engine, for example). If you can see how all the parts of an argument work in relation to one another, you can see why they are convincing — or may *sound* convincing even when you disagree with them. But since your task is not just to understand arguments but also to evaluate, judge, and offer possible alternatives to them, you should be alert to areas where improvements can be made, where new questions may be asked, and where new parts can be added to support or challenge the conclusions. To do all this, you must *read more slowly*.

Reading slowly is sometimes called **close reading**, a technique that traces a text's details and patterns. Close reading means, for starters, paying attention to the *language* of an essay. By doing this, you can see how words and their meanings lend support to an argument — but perhaps also reveal assumptions on the part of an author. For example, an author who calls his city's crime problem a "monster" might argue for harsher law enforcement than another who refers to crime as a "sickness," who might argue for investigating the root causes of crime.

To develop new perspectives and solutions related to the issues presented in this book, you must interrogate the readings and test whether or not they hold up to your intellectual scrutiny. The issues raised in this book — and the arguments made about them — require more comment than President Calvin Coolidge supposedly provided when his wife, who hadn't been able to attend church one Sunday, asked him what the preacher talked about in his sermon. "Sin," Coolidge said. His wife persisted: "What did the preacher say about it?" Coolidge's response: "He was against it."

But, again, when we say that most of the arguments in this book require close reading, we don't mean that they are obscure or overly difficult; we mean, rather, that you have to approach them thoughtfully and deliberately, always examining their alternatives.

Some arguments appear convincing simply because all the parts work so well together. Such arguments may appear airtight and indisputable not because they offer the only reasonable or viable position, but just because they are so well constructed, because they appeal to common assumptions or rely on widely shared concepts. To close read effectively, you must employ **analysis**, another word from the Greek: *analusis*, "to loosen; to undo." We like this as a metaphor for close reading analysis because it suggests looking for the ways an argument has been put together and how it might be taken apart again.

When close reading, we often discover areas where an argument can be improved upon or challenged. The following patterns of thought may help you discover those spaces:

- The language in the article is characterized by . . .
- Although the argument is convincing, its assumptions are that . . .
- Although the argument is convincing, it fails to consider *X* alternative perspective . . .
- Although the argument does a good job offering . . . , it could be further improved by offering more of . . .
- The argument, rather than being convincing, instead proves or shows . . .
- Although the author looks at evidence showing . . . , he doesn't attend fully to other evidence showing . . .
- An audience might agree with this argument if they also believed . . .
- An audience might oppose this argument if they believed . . .
- The author's perspective is shaped by the values and interests of . . .
- An opponent's perspective might be shaped by the values and interests of . . .

As these sentence beginnings demonstrate, it takes close reading and analytical skill to decide whether to agree or disagree with an argument, or to draw a different conclusion, or to conceive of a new argument. You must practice disassembling arguments piece by piece, considering words, sentences, and paragraphs thoughtfully, one by one. Above all, go slow! In this vein, recall an episode from Lewis Carroll's *Through the Looking-Glass*:

> "Can you do Addition?" the White Queen asked. "What's one and one and one and one and one and one and one and one and one and one?"
>
> "I don't know," said Alice. "I lost count."
>
> "She can't do Addition," the Red Queen said.

Alice with the Red Queen and the White Queen.

It's easy enough to add one and one and one and so on, and of course Alice can do addition — but not at the pace that the White Queen sets. Similarly, you may find it difficult to perform thorough and thoughtful analysis if you read too quickly. Fortunately, you can set your own pace in reading the essays in this book. Skimming won't work, but slow and close reading — and thinking carefully about what you're reading — will.

When you first pick up an essay, you may indeed want to skim it, but if it is compelling enough, you will have to settle down to read it slowly, and perhaps you will read it more than one time. The effort could be worthwhile.

DEFINING TERMS AND CONCEPTS

Writers often attempt to provide a provisional definition of important terms and concepts to advance their arguments. They ask readers, in a way, to accept a definition for the purposes of the argument at hand. Readers may do so, but if they want to argue a different position, they must do so according to the definition offered by the author, or else they must offer their own definition.

Before going further, allow us to define the difference between a **term** and a **concept**. A rule of thumb is that a *term* is more concrete and fixed than a *concept*. You may be able to find an authoritative source (like a federal law or an official policy) to help define a word as a *term*. An author may write, for example, "According to the legal definition, the term 'exploitation' means *A*, *B*, and *C*" (a technical definition). It may be difficult to contend with an author who offers a definition of a term in a strict way such as this. Unless you can find a different standard, you may have to start out on the same basic ground: an agreed-upon definition.

A *concept* is more open-ended and may have a generally agreed-upon definition but rarely a strict or unchanging one. Writers may say, "For the purposes of this argument, let's define 'exploitation' as a moral concept that involves *A*, *B*, and *C*" (a broad definition). Concepts can be abstract but can also function powerfully in argumentation; love, justice, morality, psyche, health, freedom, bravery, masculinity — these are all concepts. You may look up such words in the dictionary, but it won't offer a strict definition and won't say much about how to apply the concept. Arguments that rely predominantly on concepts may be more easily added to or challenged, because concepts are so much more open-ended than terms.

To illustrate how terms and concepts work, suppose you're reading an argument about whether a certain set of images is pornography or art. For the present purpose, let's use a famous example from 1992, when American photographer Sally Mann published *Immediate Family*, a controversial book featuring numerous images of her three children (then ages twelve, ten, and seven) in various states of nakedness during their childhood on a rural Virginia farm. Mann is considered a great photographer and artist ("America's Best Photographer," according to *Time* magazine in 2001), and *Immediate Family* is very well regarded in the art community ("one of the great photograph books of our time," according to the *New Republic*). But some critics couldn't separate the images of Mann's own naked children from the label "child pornography."

WRITING TIP
When defining a term conceptually, you may cite an authoritative person, such as an expert in a field ("Stephen Hawking defines time as . . ."), or you might cite a respected leader or important text ("Mahatma Gandhi defines love as . . ."; "The bible says . . ."). Alternatively, you can combine several views and insert your own provisional definition.

If you wished to argue against this position, you might begin by asking, "What is *child pornography*? What is *art*?" If someone were to define child pornography to include *any* images of nude children, that definition would include photographs taken for any reason — medical, sociological, anthropological, scientific — and would include even the innocent photographs taken by proud parents of their children swimming, bathing, and so on. It would also apply to some of the world's great art. Most people do not seriously think the mere image of the naked body, child or adult, is pornography. If you wanted to argue that Mann's photographs are not child pornography, you could draw upon the legal term itself and apply it to the images. You could also offer your own conceptual definition of art and apply that to the images.

Sometimes whether a word is used as a term or a concept has major implications for certain groups and interests. In recent years, for example, the dairy industry has lobbied the Food and Drug Administration to force producers of soy- and almond-based drinks to stop using the word *milk* to describe them. The dairy industry claims that "milk" is a term with a technical definition: a high-fat, high-protein liquid secreted by female animals to nourish their young. It argues that calling soy- and almond-based products "milk" runs the risk of deceiving consumers by suggesting that these drinks are nutritionally equivalent to "real" milk. Obviously, for marketing purposes the producers of the drinks prefer avoiding the term "almond water" or "soy drink." They argue that the word "milk" is more conceptual, commonly used to describe different liquids, such as milk of magnesia, rose milk, and coconut milk. The two sides are fundamentally disagreeing about the definition of the word.

In 2018, the FDA signaled that a legal definition of milk might be on the horizon. It does make us wonder if we will be soon eating "legume paste" instead of peanut butter (given that peanuts are not technically "nuts" and mashed peanuts are not technically butter).

Summarizing and Paraphrasing

After previewing, skimming, and a first reading (maybe even a second one), perhaps the next best step, particularly with a fairly difficult essay, is to reread it (again). Simultaneously, take notes on a sheet of paper, summarizing each paragraph in a sentence or two, and then write an overall summary of the whole argument. Writing a **summary** will help you understand the contents and see the strengths and weaknesses of the piece. It will also help you prepare for writing by providing a snapshot of the argument in your notes.

Don't confuse a summary with a paraphrase. A **paraphrase** is a word-by-word or phrase-by-phrase rewording of a text, a sort of translation of the author's language into your own. A paraphrase is therefore as long as the original or even longer; a summary is much shorter. An entire essay, even a whole book, may be summarized in a page, in a paragraph, even in a sentence. Obviously, a summary will leave out most details, but it will accurately state the essential thesis or claim of the original.

Why would anyone summarize, and why would anyone paraphrase? Because, as we've already said, these two activities — in different ways — help you comprehend an author's ideas and offer ways to introduce those ideas into your arguments in a way that readers can follow. Summaries and paraphrases can help you

- **validate** the basis of your ideas by providing an instance in which someone else wrote about the same topic
- **support** your argument by showing readers where someone else "got it right" (corroborating your ideas) or "got it wrong" (countering your ideas, but giving you a chance to refute that position in favor of your own)
- **clarify** in short order the complex ideas contained in another author's work
- **lend authority** to your voice by showing readers that you have considered the topic carefully by consulting other sources
- **build new ideas** from existing ideas on the topic, enabling you to insert your voice into an ongoing debate made evident by the summary or paraphrase

When you *summarize*, you're standing back, saying briefly what the whole adds up to; you're seeing the forest, as the saying goes, not the individual trees. When you *paraphrase*, you're inching through the forest, scrutinizing each tree — finding a synonym for almost every word in the original in an effort to ensure that you know exactly what the original is saying. (Keep in mind that when you incorporate a summary or a paraphrase into your own essay, you should acknowledge the source and state that you are summarizing or paraphrasing.)

Let's examine the distinction between summary and paraphrase in connection with the first two paragraphs of Paul Goodman's essay "A Proposal to Abolish Grading," excerpted from his book *Compulsory Miseducation and the Community of Scholars* (1966):

> Let half a dozen of the prestigious universities — Chicago, Stanford, the Ivy League — abolish grading, and use testing only and entirely for pedagogic purposes as teachers see fit.

Anyone who knows the frantic temper of the present schools will understand the transvaluation of values that would be effected by this modest innovation. For most of the students, the competitive grade has come to be the essence. The naïve teacher points to the beauty of the subject and the ingenuity of the research; the shrewd student asks if he is responsible for that on the final exam.

A *summary* of these two paragraphs might read like this:

> If some top universities used tests only to help students learn and not for grades, students would stop worrying about whether they got an A, B, or C and might begin to share the teacher's interest in the beauty of the subject.

Notice that the summary doesn't convey Goodman's style or voice (e.g., the wry tone in his pointed contrast between "the naïve teacher" and "the shrewd student"). That is not the purpose of summary.

Now for a *paraphrase*. Suppose you're not sure what Goodman is getting at, maybe because you're uncertain about the meanings of some words (e.g., *pedagogic* and *transvaluation*), or you just want to make sure you understand the point.

> Suppose some of the top universities — such as Chicago, Stanford, Harvard, Yale, and others in the Ivy League — stopped using grades and instead used tests only to help students learn.
>
> Everyone who is aware of the rat race in schools today will understand the enormous shift in values about learning that would come about by this small change. At present, idealistic instructors talk about how beautiful their subjects are, but smart students know that grades are what count. They only want to know if that subject will be on the exam.

In short, you may decide to paraphrase an important text if you want the reader to see the passage itself but you know that the full passage will be puzzling. In this situation, you offer help, *paraphrasing* before making your own point about the author's claim.

A second good reason to offer a paraphrase is if there is substantial disagreement about what the text says. The Second Amendment to the US Constitution is a good example of this sort of text:

> A well regulated Militia being necessary to the security of a free State, the right of the people to keep and bear Arms shall not be infringed.

Exactly what, one might ask, is a "Militia"? What does it mean for a militia to be "well regulated"? And does "the

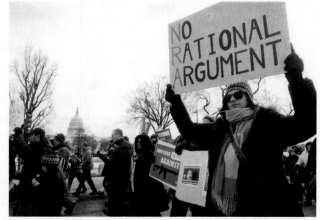

Gun control supporters marching in Washington, DC.

people" mean each individual or the citizenry as a unified group? After all, elsewhere in the document, where the Constitution speaks of individuals, it speaks of a "man" or a "person," not "the people." To speak of "the people" is to use a term (some argue) that sounds like a reference to a unified group — perhaps the citizens of each of the thirteen states — rather than a reference to individuals. However, if Congress did mean a unified group rather than individuals, why didn't it say, "Congress shall not prohibit the states from organizing militias"?

In fact, thousands of pages have been written about that sentence, and if you're going to write about it, you certainly have to let readers know exactly how you interpret each word. In short, you almost surely will paraphrase the sentence, going word by word, giving readers your own sense of what each word or phrase means. Here is one possible paraphrase:

> Because an independent society needs the protection of an armed force if it is to remain free, the government may not limit the right of the individuals (who may someday form the militia needed to keep the society free) to possess weapons.

In this interpretation, the Constitution grants individuals the right to possess weapons, and that is that.

Other students of the Constitution, however, offer very different paraphrases, usually along these lines:

> Because each state that is now part of the United States may need to protect its freedom (from the new national government), the national government may not infringe on the right of each state to form its own disciplined militia.

This paraphrase says that the federal government may not prevent each state from having a militia; it says nothing about every individual person having a right to possess weapons.

The first paraphrase might be offered by the National Rifle Association or any other group that interprets the Constitution as guaranteeing individuals the right to own guns. The second paraphrase might be offered by groups that seek to limit the ownership of guns.

Why paraphrase? Here are two reasons you might paraphrase a passage:

1. To help yourself understand it. In this case, the paraphrase does not appear in your essay.

2. To help your reader understand a passage that is especially important but

---

A CHECKLIST FOR A PARAPHRASE

☐ Do I have a good reason for offering a paraphrase rather than a summary?

☐ Is the paraphrase entirely in my own words — a word-by-word "translation" — rather than a patchwork of the source's words and my own, with some of my own rearrangement of phrases and clauses?

☐ Do I not only cite the source but also explicitly say that the entire passage is a paraphrase?

that is not immediately clear. In this case, you paraphrase to let the reader know exactly what the passage means. This paraphrase does appear in your essay.

Patchwriting and Plagiarism

We have indicated that only rarely will you have reason to paraphrase in your essays. In your notes, you might sometimes copy word for word (quote), paraphrase, or summarize, but if you produce a medley of borrowed words and original words in your essays, you are **patchwriting**, and it can be dangerous: If you submit such a medley, you risk the charge of **plagiarism** *even if you have rearranged the phrases and clauses, and even if you have cited your source.*

Here's an example. First, we give the source: a paragraph from Helen Benedict's essay on the "man problem" in the military reprinted in full beginning on page 27:

> For generations now, the debate over women in combat has put the onus on women to prove they can handle the infantry and other traditionally all-male units. Yet today's wars have made it clear that the military's problem lies not with its women, their ability or their courage. The military's problem, instead, is with some of its men — and a deeply ingrained macho culture that denigrates, insults and abuses women.

Here is a student's patchwriting version:

> Over the past two generations, debates about women's roles in the military have focused on whether or not they can handle the infantry duty. Yet everyday they do. Helen Benedict points out that women are not the problem in the military — the men are, especially those who hold ideas ingrained in a macho culture that is insulting and abusive to women.

As you can see, the student writer has used patchwriting because she followed the source almost phrase by phrase, making small verbal changes here and there, such as substituting new words and key phrases, while at other points using the same vocabulary slightly rearranged. That is, the sequence of ideas and their arrangement, as well as most of the language, are entirely or almost entirely derived from the source, even if some of the words are different. Thus, even if the student cites the source, it is plagiarism.

What the student should have done is either (1) *quote the passage exactly,* setting it off to indicate that it's a quotation and indicating the source, or (2) *summarize it briefly* and credit the source — maybe in a version such as this:

> Helen Benedict points out that arguments used in the past to keep women out of military combat roles were unfounded. Women have proved themselves time and time again since the ban on women in combat roles was lifted. However, Benedict argues, even though women now have the opportunity to serve, they are by no means "equal" in the military. Benedict details the sexist

culture in the military—what she calls the military's "man problem"—a problem that subjects women to a deeply hostile environment.

The above example frankly summarizes a source and attributes it to the author, Benedict. The reader knows these ideas are Benedict's, not the writer's. This allows the writer to build on her source's ideas to establish—and distinguish—her own argument.

Citing a source is not enough to protect you from the charge of plagiarism. Citing a source tells the reader that some fact or idea—or some groups of words enclosed within quotation marks or set off by indentation—comes from the named source; it does *not* tell the reader that almost everything in the paragraph is, in effect, someone else's writing with a few words changed, a few words added, and a few phrases moved.

The best way to avoid introducing patchwriting into your final essay is to make certain that when taking notes you indicate, *in the notes themselves*, what sort of notes they are. For example:

- When quoting word for word, put the passage within quotation marks and cite the page number(s) of the source.

- When paraphrasing—perhaps to ensure that you understand the writer's idea or because your readers won't understand the source's highly technical language unless you put it into simpler language—use some sign, perhaps (*par*), to remind yourself later that this passage is a paraphrase and thus is not really *your* writing.

- When summarizing, use a different key, such as (*sum*), and cite the page(s) or online location of the source.

If you have taken notes properly, with indications of the sort we've mentioned, when writing your paper you can say things like the following:

- *X*'s first reason is simple. *X* says, ". . ." (here you quote *X*'s words, putting them within quotation marks).

- *X*'s point can be summarized thus: . . . (here you cite the page).

- *X*, writing for lawyers, uses some technical language, but we can paraphrase her conclusion in this way: . . . (here you give the citation).

For additional information about plagiarism, see the section A Note on Plagiarizing on pages 276–78 in Chapter 7.

Strategies for Summarizing

As with paraphrases, summaries can help you establish your understanding of an essay or article. Summarizing each paragraph or each group of closely related paragraphs will enable you to follow the threads of the argument and will ultimately provide a useful map of the essay. Then, when rereading the essay, you may want to underline passages that you now realize are the author's key ideas — for instance, definitions, generalizations, and summaries. You may also want to jot notes in the margins, questioning the logic, expressing your uncertainty, or calling attention to other writers who see the matter differently.

How long should your summaries be? They can be as short as a single sentence or as long as an entire paragraph. Here's a one-sentence summary of Martin Luther King Jr.'s famous essay "Letter from Birmingham Jail," which King wrote after his arrest for marching against racial segregation and injustice in Birmingham, Alabama.

> In his letter, King argues that the time is ripe for nonviolent protest throughout the segregated South, dismissing claims by local clergymen who opposed him and arguing that unjust laws need to be challenged by black people who have been patient and silent for too long.

WRITING TIP
Your essay is *likely to include brief summaries* of points of view with which you agree or disagree, but it will *rarely include a paraphrase* unless the original is obscure and you feel compelled to present a passage at length in words that are clearer than those of the original. If you do paraphrase, explicitly identify the material as a paraphrase. Never submit patchwriting.

King's essay, however, is quite long. Obviously, our one-sentence summary cannot convey substantial portions of King's eloquent arguments, sacrificing almost all the nuance of his rationale, but it serves as an efficient summation and allows the writer to move on to his or her own analysis promptly.

A longer summary might try to capture more nuance, especially if, for the purposes of your essay, you need to capture more. How much you summarize depends largely on the *purpose* of your summary (see again our list of reasons to summarize on p. 46). Here is a longer summary of King's letter:

> In his letter, King argues that the time is ripe for nonviolent protest in the segregated South despite the criticism he and his fellow civil rights activists received from various authorities, especially the eight local clergymen who wrote a public statement against him. King addresses their criticism point by point, first claiming his essential right to be in Birmingham with his famous statement, "injustice anywhere is a threat to justice everywhere," and then saying that those who see the timing of his group's nonviolent direct action as inconvenient must recognize at least two things: one, that his "legitimate and unavoidable impatience" resulted from undelivered promises by authorities in the past; and two, that African Americans had long been told over and over again to wait for change with no change forthcoming. "This 'wait' has almost always meant 'never,'" King writes. For those who criticized his leadership, which encouraged people to break laws prohibiting their march, King says that breaking *unjust* laws may actually be construed as a *just* act. For those who called him an extremist, he revels in the definition ("was not Jesus an extremist in love?" he asks) and reminds them of the more extremist groups who call for violence in the face of blatant discrimination and brutality (and who will surely rise, King suggests, if no redress is forthcoming for the peaceful southern protestors he leads). Finally, King rails against "silence," saying that to hold one's tongue in the face of segregation is tantamount to supporting it — a blow to "white moderates" who believe in change but do nothing to help bring it about.

This summary, obviously much longer than the first, raises numerous points from King's argument and preserves through quotation some of King's original tone and substance. It sacrifices much, of course, but seeks to provide a thorough account of a long and complex document containing many primary and secondary claims.

If your instructor asks for a summary of an essay, most often he or she won't want you to include your own thoughts about the content. Of course, you'll be using your own words, but try to "put yourself in the original author's shoes" and provide a summary that reflects the approach taken by the source. It should *not* contain ideas that the original piece doesn't express. If you use exact words and phrases drawn from the source, enclose them in quotation marks.

Summaries may be written for exercises in reading comprehension, but the point of summarizing when writing an essay is to assist your own argument. A faithful summary — one without your own ideas interjected — can be effective when using a source as an example or showing another writer's concordance with your argument. Consider the following paragraph written by a student who wanted to use Henry David Thoreau's 1849 essay, "Resistance to Civil Government," to make a point in her paper on sweatshops and other poor labor conditions in the supply chains of our everyday products. Thoreau famously argued that many northerners who objected to slavery in the United States did not always realize how economically tied up in slavery they were. He argued that true opposition to slavery meant withdrawing fully from all economic activity related to it. The student was arguing that if a person today purchases goods manufactured in sweatshops or under other inadequate labor conditions, he or she is in a sense just as responsible for the abuses of labor as the companies who operate them. Thoreau provided a convenient precedent. Notice how the student offers a summary (underlined) along the way and how it assists her argument.

> Americans today are so disconnected from the source and origins of the products they buy that it is entirely possible for them one day to march against global warming and the next to collect a dividend in their 401k from companies that are the worst offenders. It is possible to weep over a news report on child labor in China and then post an emotional plea for justice on Facebook using a mobile device made by Chinese child laborers. In 1849, Henry David Thoreau wrote in "Resistance to Civil Government" how ironic it was to see his fellow citizens in Boston opposed to slavery in the South, yet who read the daily news and commodity prices and "fall asleep over them both," not recognizing their own investments in, or patronage of, the very thing that offends their consciences. To Thoreau, such "gross inconsistency" makes even well-intentioned people "agents of injustice." Similarly, today we do not see the connections between our consumer habits and the various kinds of oppression that underlie our purchases — forms of oppression we would never support directly and outright.

The embedded short summary addresses only one point of Thoreau's original essay, but it shows how summaries may serve in an integrative way — as analogy, example, or illustration — to support an argument even without adding the writer's own commentary or analysis.

CRITICAL SUMMARY

When writing a longer summary that you intend to integrate into your argument, you may interject your own ideas; the appropriate term for this writing is **critical summary**. It signifies that you're offering more than a thorough and accurate account of an original source, because you're adding your evaluation of it as well. Think of it as weaving together your neutral summary with your own argument so that the summary meshes seamlessly with your overall writing goal. Along the way, during the summary, you may appraise the original author's ideas, commenting on them as you go — even while being faithful to the original.

How can you faithfully account for an author's argument while commenting on its merits or shortcomings? One way is to offer examples from the original. In addition, you might assess the quality of those examples or present others that the author didn't consider. Remember, being critical doesn't necessarily mean refuting the author. Your summary can refute, support, or be more balanced, simply recognizing where the original author succeeds and fails.

> **WRITING TIP**
>
> When writing a critical summary, you can problematize by examining areas not considered by the author. Ask: What has the author missed? What evidence or examples have been misinterpreted?

A STRATEGY FOR WRITING A CRITICAL SUMMARY   Follow these five steps when writing a critical summary:

1. **Introduce** the summary. You don't have to provide all these elements, but consider offering the *author's name* and *expertise*, the *title* of the source, the *place* of publication, the *year* of publication, or any other relevant information. You may also start to explain the author's main point that you are summarizing:

> Pioneering feminist Betty Friedan, in her landmark book *The Feminine Mystique* (1963), argued that . . .

Don't overdo it. Select the most important details carefully and work toward concision. Remember that this is a summary, so "get in and get out." That is, move quickly back to your analysis.

2. **Explain** the major point the source makes. Here you have a chance to tell your readers what the original author is saying, so be faithful to the original but also highlight the point you're summarizing:

> Pioneering feminist Betty Friedan, in her landmark book *The Feminine Mystique* (1963), argued that women of the early 1960s were falling victim to a media-created image of ideal femininity that pressured them to prioritize homemaking, beauty, and maternity above almost all other concerns.

Here you can control the readers' understanding through simple adjectives such as *pioneering* and *landmark*. (Compare how "*stalwart* feminist Betty Friedan, in her *provocative* book" might dispose the reader to interpret your material differently.)

3. **Exemplify** by offering one or more representative examples or evidence on which the original author draws. Feel free to quote if needed, although it is not required in a summary.

> Friedan examines post–World War II trends that included the lowering of the marriage age, the rise of the mass media, and what she calls "the problem that has no name" — that of feminine unfulfillment, or what we might today call "depression."

Feel free to use a short quotation or utilize signature terms, phrases, or concepts from the source.

4. **Problematize** by placing your assessment, analysis, or question into the summary.

> Although the word *depression* never comes up in Friedan's work, one could assume that terms like *malaise, suffering,* and *housewives' fatigue* signal an emerging understanding of the relationship between stereotypical media representations of social identity and mental health.

If you're working toward a balanced critique or rebuttal, here is a good place to insert your ideas or those of someone with a slightly different view. Consider utility phrases that help tie these elements of critical summary together. More adjectives and strong verbs can help indicate your critique and judgment. For example:

> In her *careful* analysis of contemporary horror films, Simpson looks at movies like *X, Y,* and *Z,* showing how *inadequately* women are represented as *weak, vulnerable* victims in need of rescue, mostly by men. Nevertheless, while her analysis is *convincing,* her examples *ignore* films such as *A, B,* and *C,* and this glaring omission shows . . .

5. **Extend** by tying the summary to your argument, helping transition out of the critical summary and back into your own analysis. Imagine your final task as saying (without saying) something like, *And this summary is important to my overall thesis because it shows . . .*

> Friedan's work should raise questions about how women are portrayed in the media today and about what mental health consequences are attributable to the ubiquitous and consistent messages given to women about their bodies, occupations, and social roles.

It is possible to use this method — **Introduce, Explain, Exemplify, Problematize,** and **Extend** — in many ways, but essentially it is a way of providing a critical summary, any element of which can be enhanced or built upon as needed. When you're writing your own critical summary, refer to the Visual Guide (p. 55) for reference.

Visual Guide: Writing a Critical Summary

1 INTRODUCE

Who is the *author*? What is his or her expertise or significance?

What type of *source* is it? When was it published?

2 EXPLAIN

What (and how) is the author arguing? What is the author trying to achieve?

3 EXEMPLIFY

What evidence does the author use to support the argument, thesis, and/or perspective in this essay?

What examples or descriptions of the author's evidence can you include in your summary?

4 PROBLEMATIZE

What are your concerns about the author's interpretation, approach, methodology, or conclusions?

Do you notice any assumptions and predispositions that might have affected the author's interpretations?

What perspectives were left out? What further evidence (or contrary evidence) was overlooked?

5 EXTEND

What the author has done well? Not so well? What more could have been done, if anything?

What might further research reveal?

What other perspectives might have informed or improved the analysis?

What new directions could be opened in light of the author's analysis or your own critical summary?

If your source's ideas were implemented or acted upon, what might be the consequences or implications?

A SHORT ESSAY FOR SUMMARIZING PRACTICE

The following piece by Susan Jacoby is annotated to provide a "rough summary" in the margins, more or less paragraph by paragraph, the kind you might make if you are outlining an essay or argument.

SUSAN JACOBY

Susan Jacoby (b. 1946), a journalist since the age of seventeen, is well known for her feminist writings. "A First Amendment Junkie" (our title) appeared in the Hers column in the *New York Times* in 1978. Notice that her argument zigs and zags, not because Jacoby is careless but because in building a strong case to support her point of view, she must consider some widely held views that she does *not* accept; she must set these forth and then give her reasons for rejecting them.

A First Amendment Junkie

Paragraph 1: Although feminists usually support the First Amendment, when it comes to pornography many feminists take the position of opposing the Equal Rights Amendment, abortion, and other causes of the women's movement.

It is no news that many women are defecting from the ranks of civil libertarians on the issue of obscenity. The conviction of Larry Flynt, publisher of *Hustler* magazine — before his metamorphosis into a born-again Christian — was greeted with unabashed feminist approval. Harry Reems, the unknown actor who was convicted by a Memphis jury for conspiring to distribute the movie *Deep Throat*, has carried on his legal battles with almost no support from women who ordinarily regard themselves as supporters of the First Amendment. Feminist writers and scholars have even discussed the possibility of making common cause against pornography with adversaries of the women's movement — including opponents of the Equal Rights Amendment and "right-to-life" forces.

Paragraph 2: Larry Flynt produces garbage, but Jacoby thinks his conviction represents an unconstitutional limitation of freedom of speech.

All of this is deeply disturbing to a woman writer who believes, as I always have and still do, in an absolute interpretation of the First Amendment. Nothing in Larry Flynt's garbage convinces me that the late Justice Hugo L. Black was wrong in his opinion that "the Federal Government is without any power whatsoever under the Constitution to put any type of burden on free speech and expression of ideas of any kind (as distinguished from conduct)." Many women I like and respect tell me I am wrong; I cannot remember having become involved in so many heated discussions of a public issue since the end of the Vietnam War. A feminist writer described my views as those of a "First Amendment junkie."

Paragraphs 3, 4: Feminists who want to censor pornography argue that it poses a greater threat to women than similar repulsive speech poses to other groups. They can make this case, but it is absurd to say that pornography is a "greater threat" to women than "neo-Nazi . . . extermination camps."

Many feminist arguments for controls on pornography carry the implicit conviction that porn books, magazines, and movies pose a greater threat to women than similarly repulsive exercises of free speech pose to other offended groups. This conviction has, of course, been shared by everyone — regardless of race, creed, or sex — who has ever argued in favor of abridging the First Amendment. It is the argument used by some Jews who have withdrawn their support from the American Civil Liberties Union because it has defended the right of American Nazis to march through a community inhabited by survivors of Hitler's concentration camps.

If feminists want to argue that the protection of the Constitution should not be extended to *any* particularly odious or threatening form of speech, they have a reasonable argument (although I don't agree with it). But it is ridiculous to suggest that the porn shops on 42nd Street are more disgusting to women than a march of neo-Nazis is to survivors of the extermination camps.

The arguments over pornography also blur the vital distinction between expression of ideas and conduct. When I say I believe unreservedly in the First Amendment, someone always comes back at me with the issue of "kiddie porn." But kiddie porn is not a First Amendment issue. It is an issue of the abuse of power — the power adults have over children — and not of obscenity. Parents and promoters have no more right to use their children to make porn movies than they do to send them to work in coal mines. The responsible adults should be prosecuted, just as adults who use children for back-breaking farm labor should be prosecuted.

Paragraph 5: Trust in the First Amendment is not refuted by kiddie porn; kiddie porn is an issue of child abuse.

Susan Brownmiller, in *Against Our Will: Men, Women, and Rape*, has described pornography as "the undiluted essence of antifemale propaganda." I think this is a fair description of some types of pornography, especially of the brutish subspecies that equates sex with death and portrays women primarily as objects of violence.

The equation of sex and violence, personified by some glossy rock record album covers as well as by *Hustler*, has fed the illusion that censorship of pornography can be conducted on a more rational basis than other types of censorship. Are all pictures of naked women obscene? Clearly not, says a friend. A Renoir nude is art, she says, and *Hustler* is trash. "Any reasonable person" knows that.

Paragraphs 6, 7, 8: Some feminists think censorship of pornography can be more "rational" than other kinds of censorship, but a picture of a nude woman strikes some women as base and others as "lovely." There is no unanimity.

But what about something between art and trash — something, say, along the lines of *Playboy* or *Penthouse* magazines? I asked five women for their reactions to one picture in *Penthouse* and got responses that ranged from "lovely" and "sensuous" to "revolting" and "demeaning." Feminists, like everyone else, seldom have rational reasons for their preferences in erotica. Like members of juries, they tend to disagree when confronted with something that falls short of 100 percent vulgarity.

In any case, feminists will not be the arbiters of good taste if it becomes easier to harass, prosecute, and convict people on obscenity charges. Most of the people who want to censor girlie magazines are equally opposed to open discussion of issues that are of vital concern to women: rape, abortion, menstruation, contraception, lesbianism — in fact, the entire range of sexual experience from a woman's viewpoint.

Paragraphs 9, 10: If feminists censor girlie magazines, they are unwittingly helping opponents of the women's movement censor discussions of rape, abortion, and so on.

Feminist writers and editors and filmmakers have limited financial resources: Confronted by a determined prosecutor, Hugh Hefner[1] will fare better than Susan Brownmiller. Would the Memphis jurors who convicted Harry Reems for his role in *Deep Throat* be inclined to take a more positive view of paintings of the female genitalia done by sensitive feminist artists? *Ms.* magazine has printed color reproductions of some of those art works; *Ms.* is already banned from a number of high school libraries because someone considers it threatening and/or obscene.

---

[1] **Hugh Hefner** Founder and longtime publisher of *Playboy* magazine.

Paragraphs 11, 12:
Like other would-be
censors, feminists want
to use the power of the
state to achieve what
they have not achieved
in "the marketplace
of ideas." They lack
faith in "democratic
persuasion."

Paragraphs 13, 14: This
attempt at censorship
reveals a "desire to shift
responsibility from indi-
viduals to institutions."
The responsibility is
properly the parents'.

Paragraph 15: We can't
have too much of the
First Amendment.

Feminists who want to censor what they regard as harmful pornography have essentially the same motivation as other would-be censors: They want to use the power of the state to accomplish what they have been unable to achieve in the marketplace of ideas and images. The impulse to censor places no faith in the possibilities of democratic persuasion.

It isn't easy to persuade certain men that they have better uses for $1.95 each month than to spend it on a copy of *Hustler*. Well, then, give the men no choice in the matter.

I believe there is also a connection between the impulse toward censorship on the part of people who used to consider themselves civil libertarians and a more general desire to shift responsibility from individuals to institutions. When I saw the movie *Looking for Mr. Goodbar*, I was stunned by its series of visual images equating sex and violence, coupled with what seems to me the mindless message (a distortion of the fine Judith Rossner novel) that casual sex equals death. When I came out of the movie, I was even more shocked to see parents standing in line with children between the ages of ten and fourteen.

I simply don't know why a parent would take a child to see such a movie, any more than I understand why people feel they can't turn off a television set their child is watching. Whenever I say that, my friends tell me I don't know how it is because I don't have children. True, but I do have parents. When I was a child, they did turn off the TV. They didn't expect the Federal Communications Commission to do their job for them.

I am a First Amendment junkie. You can't OD on the First Amendment, because 15 free speech is its own best antidote.

SUMMARIZING JACOBY   If we want to present a *brief summary* in the form of one coherent paragraph — perhaps as part of an essay arguing for or against — we might write something like the one shown in the paragraph below. (Of course, we would introduce it with a lead-in along these lines: "Susan Jacoby, writing in the *New York Times*, offers a forceful argument against censorship of pornography. Jacoby's view, briefly, is . . .")

> When it comes to censorship of pornography, some feminists take a position shared by opponents of the feminist movement. They argue that pornography poses a greater threat to women than other forms of offensive speech offer to other groups, but this interpretation is simply a mistake. Pointing to kiddie porn is also a mistake, for kiddie porn is an issue involving not the First Amendment but child abuse. Feminists who support censorship of pornography will inadvertently aid those who wish to censor discussions of abortion and rape or censor art that is published in magazines such as *Ms.* The solution is not for individuals to turn to institutions (i.e., for the government to limit the First Amendment) but for individuals to accept the responsibility for teaching young people not to equate sex with violence.

In contrast, a *critical summary* of Jacoby — an evaluative summary in which we introduce our own ideas and examples — might look like this:

Susan Jacoby, writing for the *New York Times* in 1978, offers a forceful argument against censorship of pornography, but one that does not have foresight of the internet age and the new availability of extreme and exploitative forms of pornography. While she dismisses claims by feminists that pornography should be censored because it constitutes violence against women, what would Jacoby think of such things as "revenge porn" and "voyeuristic porn" today or the array of elaborate sadistic fantasies readily available to anyone with access to a search engine? Jacoby says that censoring pornography is a step toward censoring art, and she proudly wears the tag "First Amendment junkie," ostensibly to protect what she finds artistic (such as images of female genitalia in *Ms.* magazine). However, her argument does not help us account for these new forms of exploitation and violence disguised as art or "free speech." Perhaps she would see revenge porn and voyeur porn in the same the way she sees kiddie porn — not so much as an issue of free speech but as an issue of other crimes. Perhaps she would hold her position that we can avoid pornography by just "turning off the TV," but the new internet pornography is intrusive, entering our lives and the lives of our children whether we like it or not. Education is part of the solution, Jacoby would agree, but we could also consider . . .

[Margin annotations:]

Introduces author, source, and year and characterizes the argument as "forceful"

Problematizes Jacoby's claims by introducing present-day contexts

Explains Jacoby's argument

Problematizes Jacoby's claim by pointing out its omissions in the current context

Extends Jacoby's argument to a new issue related to today's media environment

This example not only summarizes and applies the other techniques presented in this chapter (e.g., accounting for context and questioning definitions of terms and concepts) but also weaves them together with a central argument that offers a new response and a practicable solution.

A CHECKLIST FOR A SUMMARY

- ❏ Have I adequately previewed the work?
- ❏ Can I state the thesis?
- ❏ If I have written a summary, is it accurate?
- ❏ Does my summary mention all the chief points?
- ❏ If there are inconsistencies, are they in the summary or the original selection?
- ❏ Will my summary be clear and helpful?
- ❏ Have I considered the audience for whom the author is writing?

Essays for Analysis

GWEN WILDE

This essay was written for a composition course at Tufts University.

Why the Pledge of Allegiance Should Be Revised (Student Essay)

All Americans are familiar with the Pledge of Allegiance, even if they cannot always recite it perfectly, but probably relatively few know that the *original* Pledge did *not* include the words "under God." The original Pledge of Allegiance, published in the September 8, 1892, issue of the *Youth's Companion,* ran thus:

> I pledge allegiance to my flag, and to the Republic for which it stands: one Nation indivisible, with Liberty and justice for all. (Djupe 329)

In 1923, at the first National Flag Conference in Washington, DC, it was argued that immigrants might be confused by the words "my Flag," and it was proposed that the words be changed to "the Flag of the United States." The following year it was changed again, to "the Flag of the United States of America," and this wording became the official — or, rather, unofficial — wording, unofficial because no wording had ever been nationally adopted (Djupe 329).

In 1942, the United States Congress included the Pledge in the United States Flag Code (4 USC 4, 2006), thus for the first time officially sanctioning the Pledge. In 1954, President Dwight D. Eisenhower approved adding the words "under God." Thus, since 1954 the Pledge reads:

> I pledge allegiance to the flag of the United States of America, and to the Republic for which it stands: one nation under God, indivisible, with Liberty and Justice for all. (Djupe 329)

In my view, the addition of the words "under God" is inappropriate, and they are needlessly divisive — an odd addition indeed to a nation that is said to be "indivisible."

Very simply put, the Pledge in its latest 5 form requires all Americans to say something that some Americans do not believe. I say "requires" because although the courts have ruled that students may not be compelled to recite the Pledge, in effect peer pressure does compel all but the bravest to join in the recitation. When President Eisenhower authorized the change, he said, "In this way we are reaffirming the transcendence of religious faith in America's heritage and future; in this way we shall constantly strengthen those spiritual weapons which forever will be our country's most powerful resource in peace and war" (Sterner).

Exactly what did Eisenhower mean when he spoke of "the transcendence of religious faith in America's heritage" and when he spoke of "spiritual weapons"? I am not sure what "the transcendence of religious faith in America's heritage" means. Of course, many Americans have been and are deeply religious — no one doubts it — but the phrase certainly goes far beyond saying that many Americans have been devout. In any case, many Americans have *not* been devout, and many Americans have *not* believed in "spiritual weapons," but they have nevertheless been patriotic Americans. Some of them have fought and died to keep America free.

In short, the words "under God" cannot be uttered in good faith by many Americans. True, something like 70 or even 80% of Americans say they are affiliated with some form of Christianity, and approximately another 3% say they are Jewish. I don't have the figures for persons of other faiths, but in any case we can surely all agree that although a majority of Americans say they have a religious affiliation, nevertheless several million Americans do *not* believe in God.

If one remains silent while others are reciting the Pledge, or even if one remains silent only while others are speaking the words "under God," one is open to the charge that one is unpatriotic, is "unwilling to recite the Pledge of Allegiance." In the Pledge, patriotism is connected with religious belief, and it is this connection that makes it divisive and (to be blunt) un-American. Admittedly, the belief is not very specific: one is not required to say that one believes in the divinity of Jesus, or in the power of Jehovah, but the fact remains, one is required to express belief in a divine power, and if one doesn't express this belief one is — according to the Pledge — somehow not fully an American, maybe even un-American.

Please notice that I am not arguing that the Pledge is unconstitutional. I understand that the First Amendment to the Constitution says that "Congress shall make no law respecting an establishment of religion, or prohibiting the free exercise thereof." I am not arguing that the words "under God" in the Pledge add up to the "establishment of religion," but they certainly do assert a religious doctrine. Like the words "In God We Trust," found on all American money, the words

"under God" express an idea that many Americans do not hold, and there is no reason why these Americans — loyal people who may be called upon to defend the country with their lives — should be required to say that America is a nation "under God."

It has been argued, even by members of 10 the Supreme Court, that the words "under God" are not to be taken terribly seriously, not to be taken to say what they seem to say. For instance, Chief Justice Rehnquist wrote:

> To give the parent of such a child a sort of "heckler's veto" over a patriotic ceremony willingly participated in by other students, simply because the Pledge of Allegiance contains the descriptive phrase "under God," is an unwarranted extension of the establishment clause, an extension which would have the unfortunate effect of prohibiting a commendable patriotic observance. (qtd. in Stephens et al. 104)

Chief Justice Rehnquist here calls "under God" a "descriptive phrase," but descriptive of *what*? If a phrase is a "descriptive phrase," it describes something, real or imagined. For many Americans, this phrase does *not* describe a reality. These Americans may perhaps be mistaken — if so, they may learn of their error at Judgment Day — but the fact is, millions of intelligent Americans do not believe in God.

Notice, too, that Chief Justice Rehnquist goes on to say that reciting the Pledge is "a commendable patriotic observance." Exactly. That is my point. It is a *patriotic* observance, and it should not be connected with religion. When we announce that we respect the flag — that we are loyal Americans — we should not also have to announce that we hold a particular religious belief, in this case a belief in monotheism, a belief that there is a God and that God rules.

One other argument defending the words "under God" is often heard: The words "In God We Trust" appear on our money. It is claimed that these words on American money are analogous to the words "under God" in the Pledge. But the situation really is very different. When we hand some coins over, or some paper money, we are concentrating on the business transaction, and we are not making any affirmation about God or our country. But when we recite the Pledge — even if we remain silent at the point when we are supposed to say "under God" — we are very conscious that we are supposed to make this affirmation, an affirmation that many Americans cannot in good faith make, even though they certainly can unthinkingly hand over (or accept) money with the words "In God We Trust."

Because I believe that *reciting* the Pledge is to be taken seriously, with a full awareness of the words that is quite different from when we hand over some money, I cannot understand the recent comment of Supreme Court Justice Souter, who in a case said that the phrase "under God" is "so tepid, so diluted, so far from compulsory prayer, that it should, in effect, be beneath the constitutional radar" (qtd. in "Guide"). I don't follow his reasoning that the phrase should be "beneath the constitutional radar," but in any case I am willing to put aside the issue of constitutionality. I am willing to grant that this phrase does not in any significant sense signify the "establishment of religion" (prohibited by the First Amendment) in the United States. I insist, nevertheless, that the phrase is neither "tepid" nor "diluted." It means what it says — it *must* and *should* mean what it says, to everyone who utters it — and, since millions of loyal Americans cannot say it, it should not be included in a statement in which Americans affirm their loyalty to our great country.

In short, the Pledge, which ought to unite 15 all of us, is divisive; it includes a phrase that many patriotic Americans cannot bring themselves to utter. Yes, they can remain silent when others recite these two words, but, again, why should they have to remain silent? The Pledge of Allegiance should be something that *everyone* can say, say out loud, and say with pride. We hear much talk of returning to the ideas of the Founding Fathers. The Founding Fathers did not create the Pledge of Allegiance, but we do know that they never mentioned God in the Constitution. Indeed, the only reference to religion, in the so-called establishment clause of the First Amendment, says, again, that "Congress shall make no law respecting an establishment of religion, or prohibiting the free exercise thereof." Those who wish to exercise religion are indeed free to do so, but the place to do so is not in a pledge that is required of all schoolchildren and of all new citizens.

WORKS CITED

Djupe, Paul A. "Pledge of Allegiance." *Encyclopedia of American Religion and Politics*. Edited by Paul A. Djupe and Laura R. Olson, Facts on File, 2003.

"Guide to Covering 'Under God' Pledge Decision." *ReligionLink*, 17 Sept. 2005, religionlink.com/database/guide-to-covering-under-god/.

Stephens, Otis H., et al., editors. *American Constitutional Law*. 6th ed., vol. 1, Cengage Learning, 2014.

Sterner, Doug. "The Pledge of Allegiance." *Home of Heroes*, homeofheroes.com/hallofheroes/1st_floor/flag/1bfc_pledge_print.html. Accessed 13 Apr. 2016.

Topics for Critical Thinking and Writing

1. Summarize the essay in a paragraph.

2. What words are defined in this essay? Are they defined more as terms or as concepts? Explain *how* the author, Gwen Wilde, defines one word or phrase.

3. Does Wilde give enough weight to the fact that no one is compelled to recite the Pledge of Allegiance? Explain your answer.

4. What arguments does Wilde offer in support of her position?

5. Does Wilde show an adequate awareness of counterarguments? Identify one place where she raises and refutes a counterargument.

6. What is Wilde's strongest argument? Are any of her arguments notably weak? If so, how could they be strengthened?

7. What assumptions — tacit or explicit — does Wilde make? Do you agree or disagree with them? Explain your response.

8. What do you take the words "under God" to mean? Do they mean "under God's special protection"? Or "acting in accordance with God's rules"? Or "accountable to God"? Or something else? Explain.

9. Chief Justice Rehnquist wrote that the words "under God" are a "descriptive phrase." What do you think he meant by this?

10. What is the purpose of the Pledge of Allegiance? Does the phrase "under God" promote or defeat that purpose? Explain your answer.

11. What do you think about substituting "with religious freedom" for "under God"? Set forth your response, supported by reasons, in about 250 words.

12. Wilde makes a distinction between the reference to God on US money and the reference to God in the Pledge of Allegiance. Do you agree with her that the two cases are not analogous? Explain.

13. What readers might *not* agree with Wilde's arguments? What values do they hold? How might you try to persuade an audience who disagrees with Wilde to consider her proposal?

14. Putting aside your own views on the issue, what grade would you give this essay as a work of argumentative writing? Support your evaluation with reasons.

15. Consider how you would summarize a photograph such as this one by following the steps of introducing, explaining, exemplifying, problematizing, and extending it (see pp. 53–55).

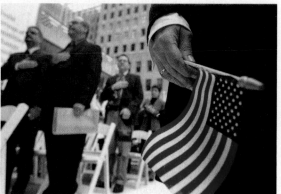

Spencer Platt/Getty Images News/Getty Images

ZACHARY SHEMTOB AND DAVID LAT

Zachary Shemtob, formerly editor in chief of the *Georgetown Law Review*, is a clerk in the US District Court for the Southern District of New York. David Lat is a former federal prosecutor. Their essay originally appeared in the *New York Times* in 2011.

Executions Should Be Televised

Earlier this month, Georgia conducted its third execution this year. This would have passed relatively unnoticed if not for a controversy surrounding its videotaping. Lawyers for the condemned inmate, Andrew Grant DeYoung, had persuaded a judge to allow the recording of his last moments as part of an effort to obtain evidence on whether lethal injection caused unnecessary suffering.

Though he argued for videotaping, one of Mr. DeYoung's defense lawyers, Brian Kammer, spoke out against releasing the footage to the public. "It's a horrible thing that Andrew DeYoung had to go through," Mr. Kammer said, "and it's not for the public to see that."

We respectfully disagree. Executions in the United States ought to be made public.

Right now, executions are generally open only to the press and a few select witnesses. For the rest of us, the vague contours are provided in the morning paper. Yet a functioning democracy demands maximum accountability and transparency. As long as executions remain behind closed doors, those are impossible. The people should have the right to see what is being done in their name and with their tax dollars.

This is particularly relevant given the current debate on whether specific methods of lethal injection constitute cruel and unusual punishment and therefore violate the Constitution.

There is a dramatic difference between reading or hearing of such an event and observing it through image and sound. (This is obvious to those who saw the footage of Saddam Hussein's hanging in 2006 or the death of Neda Agha-Soltan during the protests in Iran in 2009.) We are not calling for opening executions completely to the public — conducting them before a live crowd — but rather for broadcasting them live or recording them for future release, on the web or TV.

When another Georgia inmate, Roy Blankenship, was executed in June, the prisoner jerked his head, grimaced, gasped, and lurched, according to a medical expert's affidavit. The *Atlanta Journal-Constitution* reported that Mr. DeYoung, executed in the same manner, "showed no violent signs in death." Voters should not have to rely on media accounts to understand what takes place when a man is put to death.

Cameras record legislative sessions and presidential debates, and courtrooms are allowing greater television access. When he was an Illinois state senator, President Obama successfully pressed for the videotaping of homicide interrogations and confessions. The most serious penalty of all surely demands equal if not greater scrutiny.

Opponents of our proposal offer many objections. State lawyers argued that making Mr. DeYoung's execution public raised safety concerns. While rioting and pickpocketing occasionally marred executions in the public square in the eighteenth and nineteenth centuries, modern security and technology obviate this concern. Little would change in the death chamber; the faces of witnesses and executioners could be edited out, for privacy reasons, before a video was released.

Of greater concern is the possibility that [10] broadcasting executions could have a numbing effect. Douglas A. Berman, a law professor, fears that people might come to equate human executions with putting pets to sleep. Yet this seems overstated. While public indifference might result over time, the initial broadcasts would undoubtedly get attention and stir debate.

Still others say that broadcasting an execution would offer an unbalanced picture — making the condemned seem helpless and sympathetic, while keeping the victims of the crime out of the picture. But this is beside the point: the defendant is being executed precisely because a jury found that his crimes were so heinous that he deserved to die.

Ultimately the main opposition to our idea seems to flow from an unthinking disgust — a sense that public executions are archaic, noxious, even barbarous. Albert Camus related in his essay "Reflections on the Guillotine" that

viewing executions turned him against capital punishment. The legal scholar John D. Bessler suggests that public executions might have the same effect on the public today; Sister Helen Prejean, the death penalty abolitionist, has urged just such a strategy.

That is not our view. We leave open the possibility that making executions public could strengthen support for them; undecided viewers might find them less disturbing than anticipated.

Like many of our fellow citizens, we are deeply conflicted about the death penalty and how it has been administered. Our focus is on accountability and openness. As Justice John Paul Stevens wrote in *Baze v. Rees*, a 2008 case involving a challenge to lethal injection, capital punishment is too often "the product of habit and inattention rather than an acceptable deliberative process that weighs the costs and risks of administering that penalty against its identifiable benefits."

A democracy demands a citizenry as informed [15] as possible about the costs and benefits of society's ultimate punishment.

Topics for Critical Thinking and Writing

1. In paragraphs 9–13, Zachary Shemtob and David Lat discuss objections to their position. Are you satisfied with their responses to the objections, or do you think they do not satisfactorily dispose of one or more of the objections? Explain.

2. In paragraph 4, the authors say that "[t]he people should have the right to see what is being done in their name and with their tax dollars." But in terms of *rights*, should the person being executed have a right to die in privacy? Articulate a position that weighs the public's right to see what is being done with its tax dollars against death row prisoners' rights to privacy.

3. In the concluding paragraph, the authors imply that their proposal, if enacted, will help inform citizens "about the costs and benefits of society's ultimate punishment." Do you agree? Why, or why not? What reasons do the authors offer to support their proposal?

4. In your view, what is the strongest argument the authors give on behalf of their proposal? What is the weakest? Explain why you made these choices.

A Casebook for Critical Reading: Should Some Kinds of Speech Be Censored?

In addition to the essays by Jacoby, Wilde, and Shemtob and Lat, we present two additional essays on the topic of free speech and censorship. We suggest you read each one through to get its gist and then read it a second time, writing down after each paragraph a sentence or two summarizing the paragraph. Consider the essays individually and also in relation to one another, keeping in mind the First Amendment to the Constitution, which reads, in its entirety, as follows:

> Congress shall make no law respecting an establishment of religion, or prohibiting the free exercise thereof; or abridging the freedom of speech, or of the press; or the right of the people peaceably to assemble, and to petition the government for a redress of grievances.

SUZANNE NOSSEL

Suzanne Nossel, a graduate of Harvard Law School, is a leading voice on issues related to freedom of expression. She has held executive roles in Amnesty International USA and Human Rights Watch and is currently the chief executive officer of PEN America, a leading human rights advocacy group. Nossel's writing has appeared in several prominent newspapers and in scholarly journals such as *Foreign Affairs, Dissent,* and *Democracy.* She is a feature columnist for *Foreign Policy* magazine, where this essay first appeared in October 2017.

The Pro–Free Speech Way to Fight Fake News

After the gunfire ended, false claims that the Las Vegas carnage was the work of Islamic State terrorists or left-leaning Donald Trump opponents flooded Facebook pages, YouTube searches, and news feeds. Again, we saw how so-called "fake news" can fuel chaos and stoke hatred. Like most fraudulent news, those deceptive articles are protected speech under the First Amendment and international free expression safeguards. Unless they cross specific legal red lines — such as those barring defamation or libel — fake news stories are not illegal, and our government does not have the power to prohibit or censor them.

But the fact that fake news is free speech does not nullify the danger it poses for open discourse, freedom of opinion, or democratic governance. The rise of fraudulent news and the related erosion of public trust in mainstream journalism pose a looming crisis for free expression. Usually, free expression advocacy centers on the defense of contested speech from efforts at suppression, but it also demands steps to fortify the open and reasoned debate that underpins the value of free speech in our society and our lives. The championing of free speech must not privilege any immutable notion of the truth to the exclusion of others. But this doesn't mean that free speech proponents should be indifferent to the quest for truth, or to attempts to deliberately undermine the public's ability to distinguish fact from falsehood.

Both the First Amendment and international law define free speech to include the right to receive and impart information. The power of free speech is inextricably tied to the opportunity to be heard and believed, and to persuade. Fake news undermines precisely these sources of power. If public discourse becomes so flooded with disinformation that listeners can no longer distinguish signal from noise, they will tune out. Autocrats know this well and thus tightly control the flow of information. They purvey falsehoods to mislead, confuse, and — ultimately — to instill a sense of the futility of speech that saps the will to cry foul, protest, or resist. On social media, the problem is not one of control, but of chaos. The ferocious pace with which false information can spread can make defending the truth or correcting the record seem like mission impossible, or an invitation to opponents to double down in spreading deceit.

The problem of fraudulent news right now is compounded by social and political divisions that undercut the traditional ways in which truth ordinarily prevails. Investigations, exposés, and studies fall short in a situation where a significant portion of the population distrusts a wide array of sources they perceive as politically or ideologically hostile — including sources that traditionally commanded broad if not universal respect.

The debate over solutions to fraudulent news has centered on what the government, news outlets, social media platforms, and civil society actors like fact-checking groups can do. Each has an important role to play, but they also must respect sharp limits to their interventions. Of course, no president should routinely denigrate legitimate news that he dislikes — as Donald Trump continually does. But Trump's misuse of his authority merely reminds us that it's for good reasons that the Constitution forbids the government from adjudicating which news is true and which is false. Google and Facebook, as private platforms, should monitor their sites to make sure that dangerous conspiracy theories don't go viral — but if they over-police what appears on their pages, they'll create new impairments for edgy speech. Certainly, news outlets should strive to uphold professional and ethical standards, but they alone can't convince cynical readers to trust them. Similarly, those who believe fake news tend to distrust the fact-checking outlets that try to tell them the stories are bogus.

Ultimately, the power of fake news is in the minds of the beholders — namely, news consumers. We need a news consumers' equivalent of the venerable Consumers Union that, starting in the 1930s, mobilized millions behind taking an informed approach to purchases, or the more recent drive to empower individuals to take charge of their health by reading labels, counting steps, and getting tested for risk factors.

When there were only a few dishwashers to choose from, buyers didn't need *Consumer Reports* to sort through their features and flaws. But when the appliance shopper began to face information overload, trusted arbiters were established to help them sort out the good from the bad. In decades past, news consumption centered on newspapers, magazines, and network shows that had undergone layers of editing and fact-checking. Most consumers saw little necessity to educate themselves about the political leanings of media owners, modes of attribution for quotes, journalistic sourcing protocols, the meaning of datelines, or other indicators of veracity.

Now, with the proliferation of overtly partisan media, lower barriers to entry into public discourse, and information flooding across the web and cable news, consumers need new tools to sort through choices and make informed decisions about where to invest their attention and trust. The fight against fake news will hinge not on inculcating trust in specific sources of authority but on instilling skepticism, curiosity, and a sense of agency among consumers, who are the best bulwark against the merchants of deceit.

A news consumers' movement should include several prongs, building on PEN America's newly released "News Consumers Bill of Rights and Responsibilities" from its new report, "Faking News: Fraudulent News and the Fight for Truth." The movement should furnish credible information to help consumers weigh the reliability of varied news sources. It should include an advocacy arm to prod newsrooms, internet platforms, and social media giants into being transparent about their decisions as to what news is elevated and how it is marked. This movement should advance news literacy curricula in schools and equip the next generation to navigate the information ocean they were born into. It should conduct outreach to diverse constituencies and strive continually to avoid ideological bias. It should develop an investigative research arm to expose, name, and shame the purveyors of fraudulent news and their financial backers. And it might provide periodic ranking of, and reporting on, newsrooms and other outlets to hold them accountable to their audiences. The movement should also mobilize the public to become good news consumers by encouraging them to apply a critical eye to news sources, favor those that are trustworthy, validate reports before sharing them on social media, and report errors when they see them.

Recognizing fraudulent news as a threat to 10 free expression cannot be grounds to justify a cure — in the form of new government or corporate restrictions on speech — that may end up being worse than the disease. Unscrupulous profiteers and political opportunists may never cease in their efforts to infect the global information flow of information to serve their purposes. The best prescription against the epidemic of fake news is to inoculate consumers by building up their ability to defend themselves.

Topics for Critical Thinking and Writing

1. What problem does Suzanne Nossel identify for free speech advocates in paragraph 2? Why do you think she believes that free speech advocates should defend fake news despite its potential to spread falsehoods?

2. In paragraph 3, Nossel writes, "The power of free speech is inextricably tied to the opportunity to be heard and believed, and to persuade." In 250 words or so, explain how critical thinking provides both the means to support fake news and fight against it.

3. Examine Nossel's argument in paragraph 6. Do you agree or disagree with the idea of an organization that would label information sources – a sort of *Consumer Reports* for fake news? Do you think it would work? Why or why not?

4. What news sources do you rely upon, and why do you see them as credible and trustworthy? Trace your news sources and evaluate each of them. What criteria do they have to meet for you to trust them?

5. Do you believe that social media platforms like Facebook and Twitter are good for free speech in an open society or bad for it? Explain your answer in about 350 words, using specific examples to support your ideas.

CHARLES R. LAWRENCE III

Charles R. Lawrence III (b. 1943), author of numerous articles in law journals and coauthor of *We Won't Go Back: Making the Case for Affirmative Action* (1997), teaches law at the William S. Richardson School of Law at the University of Hawai'i at Manoa. This essay originally appeared in the *Chronicle of Higher Education* (October 25, 1989), a publication read chiefly by faculty and administrators at colleges and universities. An amplified version of the essay appeared in the *Duke Law Journal* (February 1990).

On Racist Speech

I have spent the better part of my life as a dissenter. As a high school student, I was threatened with suspension for my refusal to participate in a civil defense drill, and I have been a conspicuous consumer of my First Amendment liberties ever since. There are very strong reasons for protecting even racist speech. Perhaps the most important of these is that such protection reinforces our society's commitment to tolerance as a value, and that by protecting bad speech from government regulation, we will be forced to combat it as a community.

But I also have a deeply felt apprehension about the resurgence of racial violence and the corresponding rise in the incidence of verbal and symbolic assault and harassment to which blacks and other traditionally subjugated and excluded groups are subjected. I am troubled by the way the debate has been framed in response to the recent surge of racist incidents on college and university campuses and in response to some universities' attempts to regulate harassing speech. The problem has been framed as one in which the liberty of free speech is in conflict with the elimination of racism. I believe this has placed the bigot on the moral high ground and fanned the rising flames of racism.

Above all, I am troubled that we have not listened to the real victims, that we have shown so little understanding of their injury, and that we have abandoned those whose race, gender, or sexual preference continues to make them second-class citizens. It seems to me a very sad irony that the first instinct of civil libertarians has been to challenge even the smallest, most narrowly framed efforts by universities to provide black and other minority students with the protection the Constitution guarantees them.

The landmark case of *Brown v. Board of Education* is not a case that we normally think of as a case about speech. But *Brown* can be broadly read as articulating the principle of equal citizenship. *Brown* held that segregated schools were inherently unequal because of the *message* that segregation conveyed — that black children were an untouchable caste, unfit to go to school with white children. If we understand the necessity of eliminating the system of signs and symbols that signal the inferiority of blacks, then we should hesitate before proclaiming that all racist speech that stops short of physical violence must be defended.

University officials who have formu- 5 lated policies to respond to incidents of racial harassment have been characterized in the press as "thought police," but such policies generally do nothing more than impose sanctions against intentional face-to-face insults. When racist speech takes the form of face-to-face insults, catcalls, or other assaultive speech aimed at an individual or small group of persons, it falls directly within the "fighting words" exception to First Amendment protection. The Supreme Court has held that words which "by their very utterance inflict injury or tend to incite an immediate breach of the peace" are not protected by the First Amendment.

If the purpose of the First Amendment is to foster the greatest amount of speech, racial insults disserve that purpose. Assaultive racist speech functions as a preemptive strike. The invective is experienced as a blow, not as a proffered idea, and once the blow is struck, it is unlikely that a dialogue will follow. Racial insults are particularly undeserving of First Amendment protection because the perpetrator's intention is not to discover truth or initiate dialogue but to injure the victim. In most situations, members of minority groups realize that they are likely to lose if they respond to epithets by fighting and are forced to remain silent and submissive.

Courts have held that offensive speech may not be regulated in public forums such as streets where the listener may avoid the speech by moving on, but the regulation of otherwise protected speech has been permitted when the speech invades the privacy of the unwilling listener's home or when the unwilling listener cannot avoid the speech. Racist posters, fliers, and graffiti in dormitories, bathrooms, and other common living spaces would seem to clearly fall within the reasoning of these cases. Minority students should not be required to remain in their rooms in order to avoid racial assault. Minimally, they should find a safe haven in their dorms and in all other common rooms that are a part of their daily routine.

I would also argue that the university's responsibility for ensuring that these students receive an equal educational opportunity provides a compelling justification for regulations that ensure them safe passage in all common areas. A minority student should not have to risk becoming the target of racially assaulting speech every time he or she chooses to walk across campus. Regulating vilifying speech that cannot be anticipated or avoided would not preclude announced speeches and rallies — situations that would give minority-group members and their allies the chance to organize counterdemonstrations or avoid the speech altogether.

The most commonly advanced argument against the regulation of racist speech proceeds something like this: We recognize that minority groups suffer pain and injury as the result of racist speech, but we must allow this hate mongering for the benefit of society as a whole. Freedom of speech is the lifeblood of our democratic system. It is especially important for minorities because often it is their only vehicle for rallying support for the redress of their grievances. It will be impossible to formulate a prohibition so precise that it will prevent the racist speech you want to suppress without catching in the same net all kinds of speech that it would be unconscionable for a democratic society to suppress.

Whenever we make such arguments, we 10 are striking a balance on the one hand between our concern for the continued free flow of ideas and the democratic process dependent on that flow, and, on the other, our desire to further the cause of equality. There can be no meaningful discussion of how we should reconcile our commitment to equality and our commitment to free speech until it is acknowledged that there is real harm inflicted by racist speech and that this harm is far from trivial.

To engage in a debate about the First Amendment and racist speech without a full understanding of the nature and extent of that harm is to risk making the First Amendment an instrument of domination rather than a vehicle of liberation. We have not all known the experience of victimization by racist, misogynist, and homophobic speech, nor do we equally share the burden of the societal harm it inflicts. We are often quick to say that we have heard the cry of the victims when we have not.

The *Brown* case is again instructive because it speaks directly to the psychic injury inflicted by racist speech by noting that the symbolic message of segregation affected "the hearts and minds" of Negro children "in a way unlikely ever to be undone." Racial epithets and harassment often cause deep emotional scarring and feelings of anxiety and fear that pervade every aspect of a victim's life.

Brown also recognized that black children did not have an equal opportunity to learn and participate in the school community if they bore the additional burden of being subjected to the humiliation and psychic assault contained in the message of segregation. University students bear an analogous burden when they are forced to live and work in an environment where at any moment they may be subjected to denigrating verbal harassment and assault. The same injury was addressed by the Supreme Court when it held that sexual harassment that creates a hostile or abusive work environment violates the ban on sex discrimination in employment of Title VII of the Civil Rights Act of 1964.

Carefully drafted university regulations would bar the use of words as assault weapons and leave unregulated even the most heinous of ideas when those ideas are presented at times and places and in manners that provide an opportunity for reasoned rebuttal or escape from immediate injury. The history of the development of the right to free speech has been one of carefully evaluating the importance of free expression and its effects on other important societal interests. We have drawn the line between protected and unprotected speech before without dire results. (Courts have, for example, exempted from the protection of the First Amendment obscene speech and speech that disseminates official secrets, that defames or libels another person, or that is used to form a conspiracy or monopoly.)

Blacks and other people of color are [15] skeptical about the argument that even the most injurious speech must remain unregulated because, in an unregulated marketplace of ideas, the best ones will rise to the top and gain acceptance. Our experience tells us quite the opposite. We have seen too many good liberal politicians shy away from the issues that might brand them as being too closely allied with us.

Whenever we decide that racist speech must be tolerated because of the importance of maintaining societal tolerance for all unpopular speech, we are asking blacks and other subordinated groups to bear the burden for the good of all. We must be careful that the ease with which we strike the balance against the regulation of racist speech is in no way influenced by the fact that the cost will be borne by others. We must be certain that those who will pay that price are fairly represented in our deliberations and that they are heard.

At the core of the argument that we should resist all government regulation of speech is the ideal that the best cure for bad speech is good, that ideas that affirm equality and the worth of all individuals will ultimately prevail. This is an empty ideal unless those of us who would fight racism are vigilant and unequivocal in that fight. We must look for ways to offer assistance and support to students whose speech and political participation are chilled in a climate of racial harassment.

Civil rights lawyers might consider suing on behalf of blacks whose right to an equal education is denied by a university's failure to ensure a nondiscriminatory educational climate or conditions of employment. We must embark upon the development of a First Amendment jurisprudence grounded in the reality of our history and our contemporary experience. We must think hard about how best to launch legal attacks against the most indefensible forms of hate speech. Good lawyers can create exceptions and narrow interpretations that limit the harm of hate speech without opening the floodgates of censorship.

Everyone concerned with these issues must find ways to engage actively in actions that resist and counter the racist ideas that we would have the First Amendment protect. If we fail in this, the victims of hate speech must rightly assume that we are on the oppressors' side.

Topics for Critical Thinking and Writing

1. Summarize Charles Lawrence's essay in a paragraph. (You may find it useful first to summarize each paragraph in a sentence and then to revise these summary sentences into a paragraph.)

2. In one sentence, state Lawrence's thesis (his main point).

3. Why do you suppose Lawrence included his first paragraph? What does it contribute to his argument?

4. In paragraph 8, Lawrence speaks of "racially assaulting speech" and of "vilifying speech." It's easy to think of words that fit these descriptions, but what about other words? Is *Uncle Tom*, used by an African American about another African American who is eager to please whites, an example of "racially assaulting speech"? Or consider the word *gay*. Surely this word is acceptable because it's widely used by homosexuals, but what about *queer* (used by some homosexuals but sometimes derogatory when used by heterosexuals)? What might make these words seem "assaulting" or "vilifying"?

5. Find out if your college or university has a code — perhaps online — governing hate speech. If it does, summarize and evaluate it in no more than 500 words, capturing its key provisions and requirements. If your college has no such code, make a case for why such a policy should be developed and made available to students and faculty.

ASSIGNMENTS FOR CRITICAL READING

Definition in Three Parts

1. Construct a definition (three to five sentences) of *cyberbullying*. If you use sources, cite them.

2. Find a technical definition of cyberbullying as defined by a law, rule, or code, and compare it to your definition in exercise 1 above. What limits and restrictions are included? (Be sure to cite your source.)

3. Given the admittedly scanty information that we have on the Evans case, do you think a suspension was reasonable in light of the definitions of cyberbullying above? If you think it was reasonable, explain why. If you think it was unreasonable, explain why. Indicate also whether you think a different punishment might have been appropriate. Your essay should be about 250 to 300 words in length.

Letter to the Editor

Your college newspaper has published a letter that links a hateful attribute to a group and that clearly displays hatred for the entire group. (For instance, the letter charges that interracial marriages should be made illegal because "African Americans carry a criminal gene" or that "Jews should not be elected to office because their loyalty is to Israel, not the United States" or that "Muslims should not be allowed to enter the country because they are intent on destroying America.") The letter generates many letters of response; some, supporting the editor's decision to publish the letter, make these points:

- The writer of the offending letter is a student in the college, and she has a right to express her views.
- The point of view expressed is probably held only by a few persons, but conceivably it expresses a view held by a significant number of students.
- Editors should not act as censors.
- The First Amendment guarantees freedom of speech.
- Freedom of expression is healthy — that is, society gains.

In contrast, among the letters opposing the editor's decision to publish, some make points along these lines:

- Not every view of every nutty student can be printed; editors must make responsible choices.
- The First Amendment, which prohibits the government from controlling the press, has nothing to do with a college newspaper.
- Letters of this sort do not foster healthy discussion; they merely heat things up.

Write a 250- to 500-word letter to the editor expressing your view of the decision to publish the first letter. (If you wish, you can assume that the letter addressed one of the topics we specify in the second sentence of this exercise. In any case, address the general issue of the editor's decision, not just the specific issue of the charge or charges made in the first letter.)

Critical Summary

Write a critical summary of an essay you have read in this book. In a critical summary, you are relating the argument, but along the way adding your opinion and perspective, commenting on the quality of evidence, pointing out where the argument succeeds and fails, and asking further questions.

Use the moves in the following list to guide your summary, and refer to the Visual Guide: Writing a Critical Summary on page 55. You can combine some of these moves into one sentence, reorder information, provide quotations, and begin problematizing at any point by inserting your position through careful use of words and phrases, adding an evaluative sentence of your own, or providing commentary on a quote or paraphrase from the essay.

- **Introduce:** Provide the author and title and contextualize the information.
- **Explain:** Identify and describe the thesis and argument.
- **Exemplify:** Provide some of the author's original evidence.
- **Problematize:** Pose critical questions or provide an evaluation of the argument.
- **Extend:** Ask further questions or apply, test, or consider the argument in ways that support your evaluation of it.

For more on writing a critical summary, see the following sections in Chapter 2: Summarizing and Paraphrasing (pp. 46–49), Patchwriting and Plagiarism (pp. 49–50), and A Checklist for a Summary (p. 59).

3

Critical Reading: Getting Deeper into Arguments

Not everything that is faced can be changed, but nothing can be changed until it is faced.
— JAMES BALDWIN

Persuasion, Argument, and Rhetorical Appeals

When we think seriously about an argument, not only do we encounter ideas that may be unfamiliar, but also we are forced to examine our own cherished opinions — and perhaps for the first time really see the strengths and weaknesses of what we believe. As the philosopher John Stuart Mill put it, "He who knows only his own side of the case knows little."

It is useful to distinguish between **persuasion** and **argument**. Persuasion has the broader meaning. To **persuade** is to convince someone else to accept or adopt your position. To be persuasive does not necessarily mean your argument is sound. Persuasion can be accomplished

- by giving reasons (i.e., by argument, by logic);
- by appealing to the emotions; or
- by bullying, lying to, or threatening someone.

Argument, we mean to say, represents only one form of persuasion, but a special one: one that elevates the cognitive or intellectual capacity for reason. Rhetoricians often use the Greek word *logos*, which means "word" or "reason," to denote this aspect of persuasive writing. An appeal to reason may by conducted by using such things as

- physical evidence, data, and facts;
- the testimony of experts, authorities, or respected persons;
- common sense; or
- probability.

Visual Guide: Evaluating Persuasive Appeals

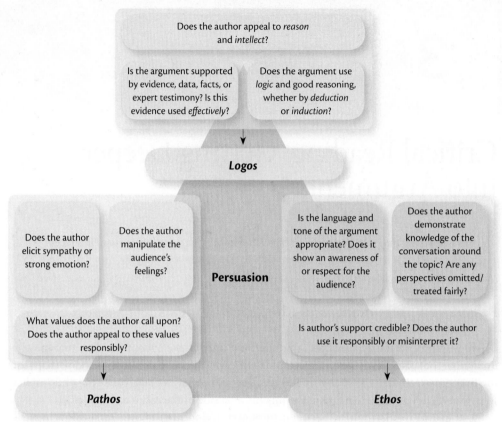

Does the author appeal to *reason* and *intellect*?

Is the argument supported by evidence, data, facts, or expert testimony? Is this evidence used *effectively*?

Does the argument use *logic* and good reasoning, whether by *deduction* or *induction*?

Logos

Does the author elicit sympathy or strong emotion?

Does the author manipulate the audience's feelings?

Is the language and tone of the argument appropriate? Does it show an awareness of or respect for the audience?

Does the author demonstrate knowledge of the conversation around the topic? Are any perspectives omitted/treated fairly?

Persuasion

What values does the author call upon? Does the author appeal to these values responsibly?

Is author's support credible? Does the author use it responsibly or misinterpret it?

Pathos

Ethos

Put it this way: The goal of *argument* is to convince by demonstrating the truth (or probable truth) of an assertion, whereas the goal of *persuasion* is simply to convince by any means whatsoever. **Logos**, the root word of *logic*, means appealing to the intellect to make rational claims and reasoned judgments.

An appeal to the emotions is known as ***pathos***, which is Greek for "feeling," and elicits the sym*path*ies (note the root word here) in one form or another. Appeals to the sympathies may call upon any number of emotions, such as anger, fear, pity, or envy, or they may call upon passionate feelings about honor, duty, family, or patriotism. In critical thinking, we may be tempted to privilege the mind (*logos*) over the heart (*pathos*), but we must note that emotions inform decision-making in important ways, too, and most arguments use *logos* and *pathos*, reason and passion, in different degrees. Most of this book is about argument in the sense of presenting reasonable support of claims, but reason is not the whole story.

If an argument is to be effective, it must be presented persuasively, and writers may convincingly call upon readers' feelings to make a sound argument. Consider two broad arguments that were made in 2018 about the Department of Homeland Security's policy of separating families of illegal immigrants at the US–Mexico border. Many conservatives argued by appealing to reason: The law requires all illegal immigrants to be detained and

Images of children held in detention centers, such as this one from 2014, appealed to the emotions of Americans in 2018. What aspects of this photograph make it particularly convincing as an appeal to emotions and values?

John Moore/Getty Images News/Getty Images

processed, and children need special accommodations and, therefore, separate detention centers. However, many liberals argued by appealing primarily to emotions, using heart-rending images and stories of incarcerated children separated from their parents to inspire public outcry. In response, just over a month after it started, President Donald Trump signed an executive order stopping the practice of separating families at the border.

In short, emotion won the day over reason — yet in no way can we say that feelings led us astray. Emotions can, in fact, guide us toward wise choices because emotions are often closely connected to values, ideals, morals, ethics, and principles. Feelings can impassion us to make rash decisions, sure, but they can also inspire bold ones. And reason, a powerful tool of the intellect, can just as soon lead us toward the dark rather than the light. As the poet Emily Dickinson wrote, "Much madness is divinest sense / To a discerning eye / Much sense the starkest madness." To conduct our lives strictly according to pure reason *or* pure feeling would lead, we think, to an intolerable existence in either case. We rely upon both of these faculties, and we need both kinds of appeals.

Because of this, most arguments do not divide easily along the lines of *logos* and *pathos*. Nor do arguments always imply two opposing speakers and positions. Of course, arguments *may* put reason and passion in opposition and present clearly opposing positions, but it is not a *requirement* that arguments do so, nor that they contain any special degree of *logos* or *pathos*. For example, the Declaration of Independence is an argument, one that sets forth the colonists' reasons for declaring their independence (*logos*) but also includes powerful language that condemns tyranny and appeals to "Life, Liberty, and the Pursuit of Happiness," words that evoke strong emotion (*pathos*). Even everyday arguments utilize both kinds of appeals. If you were explaining to your parents why you are changing your major, you might supply reasons and justifications for your decision (perhaps by comparing statistics about overall costs, future income potential, and job prospects), thus constructing a *rational* argument based on *logos*, but you may also be appealing to your family's passionate beliefs about happiness, using emotional persuasion to convince them you are making the right choice.

> **WRITING TIP**
> An argument doesn't require two opposing positions. Even when writing only for oneself, trying to clarify one's thinking by setting forth reasons and justifications for an idea, the result is an argument.

In addition to *logos* and *pathos*, the Greek philosopher Aristotle (384–322 BCE) defined a third type of rhetorical appeal. **Ethos**, the Greek word for "character," involves the careful presentation of self, what Aristotle called "the speaker's personal character when the speech is so spoken as to make us think him credible" (*Rhetoric* 1.2.1356a.4-15). Aristotle emphasized the importance of impressing upon the audience that the speaker is a person of authority, good sense, and moral integrity. When writers convey their *ethos*, their trustworthiness or good character, they may

- establish authority and credibility (e.g., by demonstrating or stating expertise, credentials, or experience),

- use language appropriate to the setting (e.g., by avoiding vulgar language, slang, and colloquialism),

- demonstrate familiarity with their audience (e.g., by achieving the right tone and level of complexity),

- show fair-mindedness (e.g., by offering other points of view in goodwill and by recognizing that contrary points of view may have some merit), or

- show attention to detail (e.g., by citing relevant statistics and careful interpretation of evidence).

THINKING CRITICALLY *Identifying Ethos*

For each method listed, locate a sentence in one of the readings in this book. Provide a quotation that shows the author establishing *ethos*.

METHOD	EXAMPLES	YOUR TURN
Use personal experience or credentials to establish authority.	"As a student who works and attends school full-time, I can speak firsthand about . . ."	
Acknowledge weaknesses, exceptions, and complexities.	"Although I have shown that *X* is important, investigation into *Y* is also necessary to truly understand . . ." "Understandably, my solution may be seen as too simple or reductive, but it may work as a starting point for . . ."	
Mention the qualifications of any sources as a way to boost your own credibility.	"According to *X*, author and noted professor of *Y* at *Z* University, . . ."	

In short, writers who are concerned with *ethos* — and all writers should be — employ devices that persuade readers that they are reliable, intelligent persons in whom their readers can have confidence.

Reason, Rationalization, and Confirmation Bias

We know that if we set our minds to a problem, we can often find reasons (not always necessarily sound ones) for almost anything we want to justify. In an entertaining example from Benjamin Franklin's *Autobiography*, Franklin tells of being hungry and wrestling with his vegetarianism on a voyage from Boston while watching his fellow passengers hauling in cod from the sea:

> Hitherto I had stuck to my resolution of not eating animal food, and on this occasion, I considered with my master Tryon the taking of every fish as a kind of unprovoked murder, since none of them had or ever could do us any injury that might justify the slaughter. All this seemed very reasonable.

However, once the fish was fried,

> it smelt admirably well. I balanced some time between principle and inclination, till I recollected that when the fish were opened I saw smaller fish taken out of their stomachs. Then thought I, if you eat one another, I don't see why we mayn't eat you. So I dined upon cod very heartily and continued to eat with other people, returning only now and then occasionally to a vegetable diet. So convenient a thing it is to be a *reasonable creature*, since it enables one to find or make a reason for everything one has a mind to do.

Franklin is being playful in commenting on how rationalizations work, but he touches on a truth: If necessary, we can find reasons to justify whatever we want. That is, instead of reasoning, we may *rationalize* (a self-serving but dishonest form of reasoning), like the fox in Aesop's fables who, finding the grapes he desired were out of reach, consoled himself with the thought that they were probably sour.

Another aspect of rationalization is **confirmation bias**. Confirmation bias is a type of cognitive bias that describes the tendency to seek out, find, and employ evidence that reinforces our inclinations or preexisting beliefs. In this process, only *confirmatory* ideas, information, and data are accounted for and taken seriously while disconfirming data are ignored or treated with skepticism. In other words, whether consciously or unconsciously, we ignore the full picture, disregard other perspectives without first listening to them, and search only for support for our position, no matter how credible or representative it is. Cognitive bias occurs most when deeply ingrained beliefs or views impede our ability to interpret information fairly. It also occurs when students write papers and research only tidbits of sources — easy quotes or factoids — that support their thesis, rather than fully reading the source material to get the full picture of what the source's argument is. (Be careful of this in your own writing; cherry-picking evidence from sources often leads to misinterpretation, which will damage your own *ethos*.)

Perhaps we can never be certain that we aren't rationalizing or falling victim to confirmation bias, except when being playful like Franklin. But we can think critically about how our own reasoning process can be affected by our own self-interest, beliefs, and worldviews. The more we can be alert to the ways these shape our thinking, the more fairly we can reason.

Types of Reasoning

Reason may not be the only way of finding the truth, but it is a way on which we often rely when making arguments, whether we are making them to ourselves or others. Traditionally, arguments are often said to be **inductive** or **deductive**; that is, to proceed along two different pathways toward their conclusions. (We spend some time discussing logical reasoning here, but a more in depth discussion can also be found in Chapter 9, A Logician's View: Deduction, Induction, and Fallacies.)

INDUCTION

Inductive reasoning, or *induction,* is essentially a process of thinking in which patterns of evidence and examples accumulate until the thinker draws a reasonable conclusion from what has been observed. One might say, for example: "In my experience, the subway always arrives promptly at 6:00 a.m., so I infer from this evidence that it will also run promptly today at 6:00 a.m." Induction uses information about observed cases to reach a conclusion about unobserved cases.

> **WRITING TIP**
> By far the most common way to test the adequacy of an inductive argument is to consider one or more **counterexamples**. If the counterexamples are numerous, genuine, and reliable, the generalization can be challenged.

The word *induction* comes from the Latin *in ducere,* "to lead into" or "to lead up to." In inductive reasoning, we draw from the specific to make generalizations about reality. We discern patterns and expand toward an explanation or a theory. If, on a fishing trip, a green-eyed horsefly bites you (specific incident), you may reasonably conclude that other flies like it in the area will also bite you (generalization). Although it seems obvious, you used induction to infer a conclusion. Your inferences might be even broader: You may be tempted to generalize that these green-eyed horseflies are native to the area and that other fishing streams in the area are likely to have them. Induction has taken your reasoning from a specific example to a general theory of reality.

DEDUCTION

In Latin, the term *deduction* means "lead down from," the opposite of induction's tendency "to lead up to." *Deductive reasoning* is the mental process of moving down from one given, true statement through another true statement to produce a reasonable conclusion. That is to say, the generalizations come first, and the specific conclusion is, because of them, therefore proven true.

One of the best ways to think through an argument, especially a deductive argument, is to use a syllogism, so in the next section we examine more closely how syllogisms work.

PREMISES AND SYLLOGISMS

In classical argument, a **syllogism** — Latin for "a reckoning together" — is often used to show the truth or factuality of a conclusion. A syllogism shows two or more propositions called **premises** that are given, or assumed to be true. The word *premise* comes from a Latin word meaning "to set in front." A deductive argument is said to be **valid** if its internal logic is so strong that it makes it impossible for the premises to be true and the conclusion nevertheless to be false. A classical syllogism therefore joins the premises with a third statement presented as a logical conclusion. Thus, premises are set down before the argument begins.

The classic example of a syllogism is this:

Premise: All human beings are mortal.

Premise: Socrates is a human being.

Conclusion: Socrates is mortal.

The purpose of a syllogism is simply to present reasons that establish the truth of a conclusion. Truth can be demonstrated if the argument satisfies both of two independent criteria:

1. All of the premises *must be true*.

2. The syllogism *must be valid*.

If each premise is *true* and the syllogism is *valid*, then the argument is said to be **sound**.

SOUND ARGUMENTS: TRUE AND VALID   But how do we tell in any given case if an argument is sound? We can perform two different tests, one for the *truth* of each of the premises and another for the overall *validity* of the conclusions drawn from the premises.

The basic test for the **truth** of a premise is to determine whether what it asserts corresponds with reality; if it does, then it is true, and if it doesn't, then it is false. The truth of a premise depends on its content — what it asserts — and the evidence provided for it.

The basic test for **validity** is different. A valid argument is one in which the conclusion *necessarily follows* from the premises, so that if all the premises are true, then the conclusion must be true, too. Consider this syllogism:

Extracting oil from the Arctic Wildlife Refuge would adversely affect the local ecology.

Adversely affecting the local ecology is undesirable unless there is no better alternative fuel source.

Alex Segre/Shutterstock.com

The great fictional detective Sherlock Holmes was credited with having unusual powers of deduction. Holmes could see the logical consequences of many and apparently disconnected premises.

Therefore, extracting oil from the Arctic Wildlife Refuge is undesirable unless there is no better alternative fuel source.

Here, if we grant the premises to be true and the conclusion necessarily follows from the premises, then the argument is valid.

VALID BUT NOT SOUND   Part of being a good critical thinker is the ability to analyze the premises and determine the validity and soundness of an argument. The problem is that arguments can have many premises, or premises that are quite complex, making it difficult to ascertain their truth. Suppose that one or more of a syllogism's premises are false but the syllogism itself is valid. What does that indicate about the truth of the conclusion? Consider this example:

All Americans prefer vanilla ice cream to other flavors.

Jimmy Fallon is an American.

Therefore, Jimmy Fallon prefers vanilla ice cream to other flavors.

The first (or major) premise in this syllogism is false. Yet the argument passes our formal test for validity: If one grants both premises, then one must accept the conclusion. So we can say that the conclusion *follows from* its premises, even though the premises *do not prove* the conclusion. This is not as paradoxical as it may sound. For all we know, the argument's conclusion may in fact be true; Jimmy Fallon may indeed prefer vanilla ice cream, and the odds are that he does because consumption statistics show that a majority of Americans prefer vanilla. Nevertheless, if the conclusion in this syllogism is true, it's not because this argument proved it.

TRUE BUT NOT VALID   Some arguments may have true premises yet nevertheless have false conclusions. This occurs when the premises are not related to one another, or when conclusions do not *necessarily* follow from the premises. Consider this syllogism:

X minority group is disadvantaged in schools.

John Doe is a member of *X* minority group.

Therefore, John Doe is disadvantaged in school.

Here, let's grant that the premises are true. Let's also grant that the conclusion may well be true: John Doe could indeed be disadvantaged. But it's also possible that the conclusion is false. Suppose you were to argue that minority groups aren't the only ones who are disadvantaged. Consider, for example, how a learning disability may affect a student's success. In short, the truth of the two premises is no guarantee that the conclusion is also true.

Chemists may use litmus paper to determine instantly whether the liquid in a test tube is an acid or a base; unfortunately, we cannot subject most arguments to a litmus test like this to determine their reasonability. Logicians beginning with Aristotle have developed techniques to test any given argument, no matter how complex or subtle, for centuries; we cannot hope to express the results of their labor in a few pages. Apart from advising you to consult Chapter 9, A Logician's View: Deduction, Induction, and Fallacies, all we can do here is reiterate the core questions you must always ask when evaluating any argument:

- Is it vulnerable to criticism on the grounds that one (or more) of its premises is false?
- Does one of the premises not necessarily relate to another premise?
- Even if all the premises were true, would the conclusion still not necessarily follow?

ENTHYMEMES   Much reasoning that occurs in writing happens in a form of a special form called an **enthymeme**, an incomplete or abbreviated syllogism in which a conclusion is drawn without stating one or more of the premises. To use the classical example, we might say

Socrates is mortal because he is human.

Here, the unstated premise is that all humans are mortal; the premise is missing but remains operative.

We can reason better about what we read and write by thinking about the things that "go without saying." The rhetoric of advertisers and politicians, for example, can sometimes be dismantled by thinking about how enthymemes work to hide the implicit premises. Consider the following claim:

You will improve your complexion by using Clear-Away.

The premises and conclusion here might be presented as a syllogism:

Unstated premise: All people who use Clear-Away improve their complexion.

Premise: You use Clear-Away.

Conclusion: You will improve your complexion.

Or consider this example:

Jim Hartman doesn't know accurate statistics on crime in his state; therefore, he is unqualified to be governor.

This might be stated as this syllogism:

> People who do not know accurate statistics about crime in their states are unqualified to be governor.
>
> Jim Hartman doesn't know accurate statistics.
>
> Jim Hartman is unqualified to be governor.

Occasionally, it is not the premises that are unstated in an enthymeme, but the conclusions that are left out. Consider this example:

> Lucky Charms breakfast cereal is fortified with vitamins!

The premises and conclusion might be stated this way:

> All food fortified with vitamins is healthy.
>
> Lucky Charms cereal is a food fortified with vitamins.
>
> Lucky Charms cereal is healthy.

Just these few examples should indicate that our alertness to the unstated premises or conclusions of an enthymeme can be valuable.

A WORD ON WEAK AND INVALID ARGUMENTS   Inductive and deductive arguments can both be critically examined and challenged by searching for weaknesses in their premises or weaknesses in the inferences that lead to their conclusions. Below, for example, you will see an inductive argument presented as a syllogism. (Inductive arguments are not typically presented as such; when they are, they are called "statistical" or "nondeductive" syllogisms.) Working inductively, however, we can present two premises based on observations and draw a generalization:

> Every fish we have taken from the harbor has a fungus.
>
> Every fish we observed with the fungus has died.
>
> All the fish in the harbor are dying of a fungus.

Now, examine the probability of this conclusion. It may well be true that all the fish in the harbor are dying, yet this is still not a *valid* conclusion. It is not valid because the conclusion does not *necessarily follow* from the premises. In fact, inductive arguments are not referred to as valid or invalid at all, or sound or unsound, but as *strong* or *weak* depending on the probability of the conclusion. The example above has *weak induction* because we do not have information about *how many or what types of fish were sampled* or further *what other factors might have contributed to the deaths of the sampled fish.*

When we reason inductively, weaknesses frequently lie in the size and the quality of the **sample**. If we're offering an argument concerning the political leanings of sorority and fraternity members at our campus, we cannot interview *every* member, so instead we select a sample. But we must ask if the sample is a fair one: Is it representative of the larger group? We may interview five members of Alpha Tau Omega and find that all five are Republicans, yet we cannot conclude

> **WRITING TIP**
> An argument that uses samples ought to tell the reader how the samples were chosen. If it doesn't provide this information, the reader should treat the argument with suspicion.

that all members of fraternities at our school are Republicans. To get a more *representative sample*, we would measure opinions from across the various sororities and fraternities.

A larger sample doesn't necessarily mean a *representative* one, however. A poll of the political leanings of college students would tell us very little if it included only students at small private colleges. We could not use that data to extrapolate about *all* college students. Ask yourself: Why not?

Inductive arguments are susceptible to challenges because they tend to generalize, or "lead up" from observations to a conclusion. They are always contingent upon new observations and new data and are susceptible to overgeneralization (which occurs when we extend the application or relevancy of the observed cases too far). Deductive arguments, on the other hand, which "lead down" from their premises toward a conclusion, often posit facts or principles as their premises. Therefore, because deduction can (although it does not always) produce incontrovertible truths, deductive arguments tend to be more reliable than inductive arguments, which can be very strong but never attain 100 percent certainty. When they are sound, deductive arguments based on incontrovertibly true premises provide an *absolutely* necessary conclusion.

Some Procedures in Argument

DEFINITIONS

In our current discussion, we are primarily analyzing the logic of arguments — the *logos* — and prioritizing the procedures of thinking and argument that emphasize reason. Another important element to this kind of thought is *definition*. Earlier, in the section Defining Terms and Concepts in Chapter 2 (pp. 44–45), we discussed how definitions of key terms and concepts underpin arguments. As to whether or not a local stream is "polluted," for example, you may use a strict (terminological) or loose (conceptual) definition of the word *pollution* to argue either way. You might define the word *pollution* as a term set forth by your state's environmental protection agency, which perhaps requires that water contains a minimum threshold of toxins, or you might describe *pollution* according to your own concept of having a lot of garbage lying alongside of it. Either definition may help you argue for a state cleanup effort. When we define key words, we're answering the question "What is it?" and setting out our definition for the purposes of the argument at hand. In answering this question as precisely as we can, we can then find, clarify, and develop ideas accordingly.

Trying to decide the best way to define key terms and concepts is often difficult — and sometimes controversial. Consider one of the most contentious debates in our society: abortion rights. Many arguments about abortion depend on a definition of "life." Traditionally, human life has been seen as beginning at birth. Nowadays, most people see "life" as something that begins at least at viability (the capacity of a fetus to live independently of the uterine environment). But modern science has made it possible to see the beginning of "life" in different ways. Some who want abortion to be prohibited by law define life as beginning with *brain birth*, the point at which "integrated brain functioning begins to emerge." Still others see life beginning as early as fertilization. Whatever the merits of these definitions, the debate itself is convincing evidence of just how important it can be to define your important terms and concepts when making arguments.

STIPULATION   When you are writing, you may define your terms and concepts by **stipulating** definitions. The word *stipulate* comes from the Latin verb *stipulari*, meaning "to bargain" or "to secure a guarantee." When you stipulate, you ask the reader to agree with a certain definition for the sake of the argument at hand (although, of course, a reader may not want to make that bargain). For example, you may write one of the following:

- If we can agree the definition of *X* is *Y*, then . . .
- If we can agree the strict definition of *X* does not include *Y*, then . . .

Establishing your definition then allows the reader to consider and evaluate your argument according to your definition.

In contracts, you can often find stipulated definitions made very explicitly because, in a legal context, key terms need to be precisely defined and agreed upon by all parties to avoid disputes. For example, consider this language from a portion of a California home insurance policy covering damage caused by an earthquake:

> For the purposes of this policy . . . the term Earthquake shall mean seismic activity, including earth movement, landslide, mudslide, sinkhole, subsidence, volcanic eruption, or Tsunami, as defined herein. . . . The term Tsunami shall mean a wave or series of waves caused by underwater earthquakes and/or seismic activity, including, but not limited to, volcanic eruptions, landslides, earth movement, mudslide, sinkhole, or subsidence. In no event shall this Company be liable for any loss caused directly or indirectly by fire, explosion or other excluded perils as defined herein.

Parties mutually agree to certain definitions by signing the contract itself. Other forms of writing also require comprehensive definitions. For instance, if you were a legislator writing a law to limit "internet gambling" in your state, you must have a very precise definition of what that means. (The actual legal definition of internet gambling in the US legal code is more than 1,000 words!)

You do not have to be writing a contract or a law to make stipulative definitions. In your arguments, you may stipulate a definition in the following cases:

- when you are seeking to secure a shared understanding of the meaning of a term or concept
- when no fixed or standard definition is available

If you are call something *undemocratic*, you must define what you mean by *democratic*. If you call a painting or a poem a *masterpiece*, you may want to try to define that word, perhaps by offering criteria art must meet to be called a masterpiece. What is your definition of what it means for a nation to *advance*? What definition of *cruel and unusual punishment* will you use in your argument about solitary confinement? How are you defining *food insecurity* in your call to end hunger on campus? Not everyone may accept your stipulative definitions, and there will likely be defensible alternatives. However, when you stipulate a definition, your audience knows what *you* mean by the term.

Consider the opening paragraph of a 1975 essay by Richard B. Brandt titled "The Morality and Rationality of Suicide." Notice that the author does two things:

- He first stipulates a definition.
- Then, aware that the definition may strike some readers as too broad and therefore unreasonable or odd, he offers a reason on behalf of his definition.

"Suicide" is conveniently defined, for our purposes, as doing something which results in one's death, either from the intention of ending one's life or the intention to bring about some other state of affairs (such as relief from pain) which one thinks it certain or highly probable can be achieved only by means of death or will produce death. It may seem odd to classify an act of heroic self-sacrifice on the part of a soldier as suicide. It is simpler, however, not to try to define "suicide" so that an act of suicide is always irrational or immoral in some way; if we adopt a neutral definition like the above we can still proceed to ask when an act of suicide in that sense is rational, morally justifiable, and so on, so that all evaluations anyone might wish to make can still be made. (61)

Sometimes, a definition that at first seems extremely odd can be made acceptable by offering strong reasons in its support. Sometimes, in fact, an odd definition marks a great intellectual leap forward. For instance, in 1990 the US Supreme Court recognized that *speech* includes symbolic nonverbal expressions such as protesting against a war by wearing armbands or by flying the American flag upside down. Such actions — although they are nonverbal — are considered speech because they express ideas or emotions. More controversially, in 2010 the Supreme Court ruled in *Citizens United vs. Federal Election Commission* that corporate spending in the form of campaign contributions constitutes speech and cannot be limited under the First Amendment. This decision spurred unprecedented spending on elections by corporations and today remains a divisive definition of speech.

Our object with these examples is to make one overall point clear: An argument will be most fruitful if the participants first share an understanding of the concepts they are talking about.

SYNONYM   One way to define a term or concept is through **synonym**. For example, *pornography* can be defined, at least roughly, as "obscenity" (something indecent). But definition by synonym is usually only a start; you then have to define or explain the synonym, too, because, in fact, *pornography* and *obscenity* are not exact synonyms. Imagine writing, "This company's strategy is essentially a *con game*" or "Spanking children is *child abuse*." In each case, synonyms were provided to help define the terms of the argument, but now the synonyms need to be explained.

EXAMPLE   Another way to define a word is to point to an example (sometimes called an **ostensive definition**, from the Latin *ostendere*, "to show"). This method can be very helpful, ensuring that both writer and reader are talking about the same thing — and adding not only clarity but vivid detail. If you are reviewing a movie and you want to define "tween movies," you could point to specific examples of the kinds of films you mean. You could say that "tween movies" are those films marketed to a certain age demographic — young people between eight and sixteen years old — but the definition may be made concrete and visible by quickly surveying such films: "Tween movies include films that feature plots developed around preteen or teenage characters, such as *The Sandlot* (1993) and *High School Musical* (2006)." Or imagine you are attempting to define American folk heroes as those characters, whether based on real people or wholly invented, whose stories have been exaggerated and transformed in various genres, such as *Johnny Appleseed*, *John Henry*, and *Casey Jones*.

Definitions by example also have their limitations, so choosing the right examples, ones that have all the central or typical characteristics and that will best avoid misinterpretation, is important to using this method of definition effectively. A few decades ago, many people pointed to James Joyce's *Ulysses* and D. H. Lawrence's *Lady Chatterley's Lover* as examples of obscene novels. Today these books are regarded as literary masterpieces. It's possible that they can be obscene and also be literary masterpieces. (Joyce's wife is reported to have said of her husband, "He may have been a great writer, but . . . he had a very dirty mind.")

ESTABLISHING SUFFICIENT AND NECESSARY CONDITIONS   A final way to define a term or concept is by establishing its *sufficient and necessary conditions*. For writers, this just means controlling definitions by offering certain preconditions. For example, if you say a "sport" is defined as any activity meeting *sufficient* conditions of competition and

"*It all depends on how you define 'chop.'*"

Tom Cheney, The New Yorker Collection/The Cartoon Bank

physical endurance, you can also argue that video gaming, which meets those criteria, may be called a sport. (See Matthew Walther's essay, "Sorry Nerds: Video Games Are Not a Sport," on p. 194 on this very subject.) If you were to argue vaping should not be subject to the same rules on your campus as smoking, you could define "smoking" as an activity requiring the *necessary* conditions of combustion and smoke, neither of which is a feature of a vaporizer.

One common way in formal logic to distinguish between sufficient and necessary conditions is to imagine them phrased as conditional propositions. Sufficient conditions are usually presented as "if, then" propositions, whereas necessary conditions are usually presented as "*if and only if*, then . . ." propositions. Suppose we want to define the word *circle* and are conscious of the need to keep circles distinct from other geometric figures such as rectangles and spheres. We might express our definition by citing sufficient and necessary conditions as follows: "Anything is a circle *if and only if* it is a closed plane figure and all points on the circumference are equidistant from the center." Using the connective "if and only if" between the definition and the term being defined helps make the definition neither too exclusive (too narrow) nor too inclusive (too broad). Of course, for most ordinary purposes we don't require such a formally precise definition.

Exercise: Definitions

Read the selections below and (a) identify the term or concept being defined; (b) explain which type of definition it is (stipulation, synonym, example); and (c) use details from the examples to support your answer.

> Marriage is primarily an economic arrangement, an insurance pact. It differs from the ordinary life insurance agreement only in that it is more binding, more exacting. Its returns are insignificantly small compared with the investments. In taking out an insurance policy one pays for it in dollars and cents, always at liberty to discontinue payments. If, however, woman's premium is a husband, she pays for it with her name, her privacy, her self-respect, her very life, "until death doth part."
>
> — Emma Goldman, *Marriage and Love* (1911)

> Pentagon spending is reaching into areas of American life previously neglected: entertainment, popular consumer brands, sports. Rick and Donna's home is full of this incursion. As they putter around the kitchen, getting ready for the day ahead, they move from the wall cabinets (purchased at DoD contractor Lowe's Home Center) to the refrigerator (from defense contractor Maytag), choosing their breakfast from a cavalcade of products made by Pentagon contractors. These companies that, quite literally, feed the Pentagon's war machine, are the same firms that fill the shelves of America's kitchens. . . . No part of the hours of the day will be lacking in products produced by Pentagon contractors . . . 3M Post-It notes, Microsoft Windows software, Lexmark printers, Canon Photocopiers, AT&T telephones, Maxwell House coffee from Altria.
>
> — Nicholas Turse, *The Complex* (2008)

A slander is a spoken defamation, whether that act of speech is public and one-time or recorded and redistributed. Slander also includes defamation by gesture, which could include making a gesture that suggests professional incompetence or mental illness. Slander carries the additional burden for a plaintiff of having to prove that they suffered actual loss due to the false statement.

— Mitch Ratcliffe, *How to Prevent Against Online Libel and Defamation* (2009)

When considering a subject as abstract and intangible as peace, it is important to define the term itself. In the context of this discussion, peace may be defined as it is in Webster's dictionary as a community's "freedom from civil disturbance, or a state of security or order provided for by law or custom."

— Kincaid Fitzgerald, *Peace in the Global Neighborhood* [student paper at Leiden University] (2018)

ASSUMPTIONS

Even the longest and most complex chains of reasoning or proof, and even most carefully constructed definitions, are fastened to assumptions — one or more *unexamined beliefs*. These taken-for-granted, hidden, or neglected beliefs affect how writers and readers make inferences and draw conclusions. If you attend a birthday party, you might *assume* that cake will be served. If the ceiling is wet, you may *assume* that the roof is leaking.

However, false assumptions can be dangerous. If you assume that a person of a certain race, class, or gender will behave in predictable ways, you may be stereotyping that individual and making guesses about that person's actions without evidence. If you assume that traffic will stop at a red light and you proceed through an intersection without looking, you could end up in a car crash. Suppose a business executive assumes that sales are down because of poor marketing and not the quality of her company's product; she could end up ignoring the real problem and wasting time and money on a new advertising campaign instead of improving the product.

Assumptions are sometimes deeply embedded in our value systems and therefore hard to recognize. Consider this case: When education researchers questioned race and class disparities on the SAT exam in the early 2000s, they found it odd that minorities and other economically disadvantaged students performed worse than their white, middle-class counterparts on the *easier* verbal and math questions, *not* the more difficult ones. That is, some basic vocabulary words like *horse* and *canoe* were likely to be misidentified by minority and lower-income students than more challenging words like *anathema* and *intractable*. (Colloquially, *horse* could be a verb, as in "play around," or it could refer to heroin. *Canoe*, meanwhile, describes what happens to a cigar when one side burns faster than another.) Researchers found that the problem was the assumptions made by the test designers, not the student test-takers. The more "difficult" words typically learned in school or in textbooks were understood more uniformly among all students. The test designers had assumed that persons of all socioeconomic groups hear language the same way and therefore that their proficiency could be measured using the same linguistic standards. By challenging the assumptions of the exam, researchers were able to challenge the disparities in exam results. As a result, college admissions boards began to regard the SAT as a weaker indicator of academic potential for some groups, while test designers began to address other deeply embedded assumptions in the exam.

Sometimes assumptions may be stated explicitly, especially when writers feel confident that readers share their values. Benjamin Franklin, for example, argued against paying salaries to the holders of executive offices in the federal government on the grounds that men are moved by ambition (love of power) and by avarice (love of money) and that powerful positions conferring wealth incite men to do their worst. These assumptions he stated, although he felt no need to argue them at length because he also guessed that his readers shared them.

"Let me guess. You want French and you want ranch?"

Assumptions may also be unstated. Writers, painstakingly arguing specific points, may choose to keep one or more of their argument's assumptions tacit, or unspoken. Or they may be completely unaware of an underlying assumption they hold. For example, Franklin didn't even bother to state two other assumptions:

- Persons of wealth who accept an unpaying job (after all, only persons of wealth could afford to hold unpaid government jobs) will have at heart the interests of all classes of people, not only the interests of their own class.
- Those wealthy government servants will be male.

Probably Franklin didn't state these assumptions because he thought they were perfectly obvious. But if you think critically about the first assumption listed above, you may find reasons to doubt that people who attain wealth will no longer be motivated by self-interest. The second assumption runs even more deeply: Although women could not vote in Franklin's time, there were no legal restrictions on women running for office, yet the assumption Franklin shared with his audience was that politics was a male domain. Both of these assumptions have now shifted to a great extent: We now assume that paying legislators ensures that the government does not consist only of people whose incomes may give them an inadequate view of the needs of others, and our society now assumes that people who are not (or who do not identify as) male can also hold government positions. After the midterm elections of 2018, more than 100 women occupied seats in the US House of Representatives for the first time in history.

Good critical thinking involves sharpening your ability to identify assumptions, especially those that seem so self-evident, or commonsensical, that they hardly need to be stated. When you are evaluating arguments or writing your own, you should question the basic ideas upon which a writer's claims rest and ask yourself if there are other, contradictory, or opposed ideas that could be considered. If there are, you can explore the alternative forms of understanding — alternative assumptions — to test or to critique an argument and perhaps offer a different analysis or a different possibility for action. When you are hunting for assumptions (your own and others'), try the following:

- **Identify** the ideas, claims, or values that are presented as obvious, natural, or given (so much so that they are sometimes not even stated).

- **Examine** those ideas to test for their commonality, universality, and necessity. Are other ways of thinking possible?

- **Determine** whether or not contradictory ideas, claims, or values provide a fruitful new way of interpreting or understanding the information at hand.

Exercise: Assumptions

Read the following sentences and identify the assumptions that are embedded in them. State the assumptions and then challenge the claims of each sentence.

- Jamaican Blue Mountain coffee is expensive; therefore, it must be high-quality coffee.
- All students were given a syllabus detailing the policies and procedures for this course, so they all know the absence policy.
- If you do not vote, you have no right to complain about politicians.
- Someday Joseph will ask Jill to marry him.
- It's hard to believe the president is wasting time golfing when there is an economic crisis at hand.
- After decades of increasing divorce rates in the United States, the divorce rate has dropped by 18 percent in the past ten years; clearly, staying married is more popular now than it was in the past.
- Although my downtown apartment is close to my workplace, crime has been on the rise in the city, so I am moving to the suburbs where I am safer.

EVIDENCE: EXPERIMENTATION, EXAMPLES, AUTHORITATIVE TESTIMONY, AND NUMERICAL DATA

In a courtroom, evidence bearing on the guilt of the accused is introduced by the prosecution, and evidence to the contrary is introduced by the defense. Not all evidence is admissible (e.g., hearsay is not, even if it's true), and the law of evidence is a highly developed subject in jurisprudence. In daily life, the sources of evidence are less disciplined. Daily experience, a memorable observation, or an unusual event — any or all of these may serve as evidence for (or against) some belief, theory, hypothesis, or explanation a person develops.

In making arguments, people in different disciplines use different kinds of evidence to support their claims. For example:

- In literary studies, texts (works of literature, letters, journals, notes, and other kinds of writing) are the chief forms of evidence.

- In the social sciences, field research (interviews, observations, surveys, data) usually provides the evidence.

- In the hard sciences, reports of experiments are the usual evidence; if an assertion cannot be tested — if one cannot show it to be false — it is an *opinion*, not a scientific hypothesis.

When you are offering evidence to support your arguments, you are drawing on the specific information that makes your claims visible, concrete, *evident*. For example, in arguing that the entertainment industry needs to address the problem of sexual harassment among powerful male celebrities, you could point to the many men who have been accused of these behaviors. Each instance constitutes **evidence** for the problem. If you are arguing that bump stocks (devices that allow semiautomatic guns to operate like automatic ones) should be banned, you will point to specific cases in which bump stocks were used to commit crimes in order to show the need for regulation. Evidence can take many forms. Here, we discuss three broad categories of evidence.

EXPERIMENTATION   Often, the forms of evidence that scientists use, whether in the natural and mathematical sciences or in the social sciences, is the result of **experimentation**. Experiments are deliberately contrived situations, often complex in their methodology or the technologies they use, that are designed to yield particular observations. What the ordinary person does with unaided eye and ear, the scientist does much more carefully and thoroughly, often in controlled situations and with the help of laboratory instruments. For example, a natural scientist studying the biological effects of a certain chemical might expose specially bred rodents to carefully monitored doses of the chemical and then measure the effects. A health scientist might design a study in which people who exercise regularly are compared to people who do not in order to argue the beneficial effects of consistent exercise on heart health. A psychologist might introduce a certain type of therapy to a group of people and then compare the results to other treatment methods.

It's no surprise that society attaches much more weight to the findings of scientists than to the corroborative (much less the contrary) experiences of ordinary people. No one today would seriously argue that the sun really does go around the earth just because it looks that way, nor would we argue that the introduction of carcinogens to the human body through smoking does not increase the risk for cancers. Yet because some kinds of scientific validation (such as repeatability) produce unarguable fact, we sometimes assume that all forms of experimentation are equal in their ability to point to truth. However, we should also be skeptical, since experiment designs can also be flawed — by bad design, bad samples, measurement error, or a host of other problems. Moreover, the results of experimentation can also be used to make different kinds of arguments. Consider that the same scientific data are used by people who argue that humans are the primary cause of climate change as well as by people who deny that humans play a significant role in climate change.

EXAMPLES   Unlike the hard sciences, the variety, extent, and reliability of the evidence obtained in the humanities — and in daily life — are quite different from those obtained in the laboratory. In all forms of writing, examples constitute the primary evidence. We follow here with an explanation of examples and a description of several common forms of examples.

Nearly all arguments use examples. Suppose we argue that a candidate is untrustworthy and shouldn't be elected to public office. We may point to episodes in his career — his misuse of funds in 2008 and the false charges he made against an opponent in 2016 — as examples of his untrustworthiness. Or if we're arguing that President Harry Truman ordered the atom bomb dropped to save American (and, for that matter, Japanese) lives that otherwise would have been lost in a hard-fought invasion of Japan, we could point to the fierce resistance of the Japanese defenders in battles on the islands of Saipan, Iwo Jima, and Okinawa, where Japanese soldiers fought to the death rather than surrender. These examples indicate that the Japanese defenders of the main islands would have fought to their deaths without surrendering, even though they knew defeat was certain.

An *example* is a type of *sample*. These two words come from the same Old French word, *essample*, from the Latin *exemplum*, which means "something taken out" — that is, a selection from the group, something held up as indicative. A Yiddish proverb shrewdly says, "'For example' is no proof," but the evidence of well-chosen examples can go a long way toward helping a writer convince an audience.

In arguments, three sorts of examples are especially common:

- real events
- invented instances (artificial or hypothetical cases)
- analogies

We will treat each of these briefly.

Real Events   In referring to Truman's decision to drop the atom bomb, we touched upon examples drawn from real events — the various named battles — to demonstrate our claim that it was ultimately the best option. Yet an example drawn from reality may not be as clear-cut as we would like. We used the Japanese army's behavior on Saipan and on Iwo Jima as evidence for our claim that the Japanese later would have fought to the death in an American invasion of Japan. This, we argued, would therefore have inflicted terrible losses on the Japanese and on the Americans. Our examples could be countered by evidence that in June and July 1945 certain Japanese diplomats sent out secret peace feelers to Switzerland and offered to surrender if the Emperor Hirohito could retain power so that in August 1945, when Truman authorized dropping the bomb, the situation was very different. If we were to argue that Truman should *not* have dropped the bomb, we could cite those peace feelers specifically, indicating a Japanese willingness to end the war without such destruction.

But most arguments using real events require further support. Some may argue that we are not currently under threat of a nuclear war, and they may offer examples of various agreements made among nuclear-armed nations as evidence. But such an argument needs more support because of the weight of counterexamples. As much as nations have sought to reduce the nuclear threat, arguing that the threat does not exist ignores many examples showing that nuclear war remains a possibility: The continuation of some nuclear programs, the development of new nuclear weapons systems, and documented attempts by terrorists to acquire nuclear material on the black market — all these real events provide counterexamples that could challenge the claim that nuclear war is no longer a possibility.

In short, *real* events are often so entangled in historical circumstances that they might not be adequate or fully relevant evidence in the case being argued. When using real events as examples (a perfectly valid strategy), the writer must

- demonstrate that they are representative,
- anticipate counterexamples, and
- argue against counterexamples, showing that one's own examples can be considered outside of other contexts.

Thus, in our earlier argument against Truman's use of the atomic bomb, we might raise the facts of the fierceness of Japanese resistance in specific earlier battles but then argue that they are not relevant because our examples show that the Japanese were seeking peace. Similarly, if others were arguing that Truman did the right thing, they could mention the peace feelers, but argue that it would not have desirable to permit the emperor to retain power.

Invented Instances　An **invented instance** is an **artificial** or **hypothetical** example. Take this case: A writer poses a dilemma in his argument that "Stand Your Ground" laws are morally indefensible. (These laws allow individuals the right to protect themselves against threats of bodily harm, to the point of using lethal force in self-defense.) In his discussion, he raises the most famous of these cases, involving the death of unarmed Florida teenager Trayvon Martin, who was killed in 2012 by a self-appointed neighborhood watchman named George Zimmerman, who mistook the African American youth as a threat. He writes: "If Trayvon Martin had been of age and legally armed, in fact, he would have had the right to kill Zimmerman when Zimmerman approached him in a hostile way." By imagining this scenario, the writer asks readers to apply the principles of justice underlying the law to the reverse scenario: What happens when neither party is clear about which of them is standing his ground? Even though the example isn't "real" — although it alters the details of a real event — it sets forth the problem in a clear way.

Offering an invented instance is something like a drawing of the parts of an atom in a physics textbook. It is admittedly false, but by virtue of its simplification it sets forth the relevant details very clearly. Thus, in a discussion of legal rights and moral obligation, the philosopher Charles Frankel says:

> It would be nonsense to say, for example, that a nonswimmer has a moral duty to swim to the help of a drowning man.

If Frankel were talking about a real event and a real person, he could get bogged down in details about the actual person and the circumstances of the event, losing his power to put the moral dilemma forward in its clearest terms.

When an example is invented, it is almost certain to support the writer's point — after all, the writer is making it up, so it is bound to be the ideal example. That said, invented instances have drawbacks. First and foremost, they cannot serve as the highest quality of evidence. A purely hypothetical example can illustrate a point, but it cannot substitute for actual events. Sometimes, hypothetical examples are so fanciful that they fail to convince the reader. Here is — what else? — an example of what we mean: The philosopher Judith Jarvis Thomson, in the course of an argument entitled "A Defense of Abortion," asks you to imagine waking up one day and finding that against your will a celebrated violinist has been hooked up to your body for life support. She then asks: Do you have the right to unplug the violinist? Whatever you answer, you have to agree that such a scenario is not exactly the same as asking whether or not a woman has a right to an abortion.

But we add one point: Even a highly fanciful invented case can have the valuable effect of forcing us to see where we stand. A person may say that she is, in all circumstances, against torture — but what would she say if a writer proposed a scenario in which the location of a ticking bomb were known only by one person and extracting that information through torture could save hundreds or thousands of lives? Artificial cases of this sort can help us examine our beliefs; nevertheless, they often create exceptional scenarios that may not be generalized convincingly to support an argument.

Analogies   The third sort of example, **analogy**, is a kind of comparison. Here's an example:

> Before the Roman Empire declined as a world power, it exhibited a decline in morals and in physical stamina; our society today shows a decline in both morals (consider the high divorce rate and the crime rate) and physical culture (consider obesity in children). America, like Rome, will decline as a world power.

Strictly speaking, an analogy is an extended comparison in which different things are shown to be similar in several ways. Thus, if one wants to argue that a head of state should have extraordinary power during wartime, one can offer an analogy that, during wartime, the state is like a ship in a storm: The crew is needed to lend its help, but the major decisions are best left to the captain. Notice that an analogy like this compares things that are relatively *un*like, similar to metaphor and simile. Simply comparing the plight of one state to another is not an analogy; it's merely an inductive inference from one case of the same sort to another such case.

Let's consider another analogy. We have already glanced at Judith Thomson's hypothetical case in which the reader wakes up to find herself hooked up to a violinist in need of life support. Thomson uses this situation as an analogy in an argument about abortion. The reader stands for the mother; the violinist, for the unwanted fetus. You may want

"Do you mind if I use yet another sports analogy?"

to think about whether this analogy holds up: Is a pregnant woman really like a person hooked up to such a machine? Is an embryo or fetus really equivalent to a celebrated violin player?

The problem with argument by analogy is this: Because different things are similar in some ways does not mean they are similar in all ways. Thomson's argument is basically developed on the premise that being the reader hooked up to a violinist is like being the pregnant mother hooked up to a fetus. But those two things are obviously quite different. Similarly, a state is not a ship in a storm. The government is not a business. As Bishop Butler is said to have remarked in the early eighteenth century, "Everything is what it is, and not another thing."

Analogies can be convincing, however, when they simplify complex issues. "Don't change horses in midstream" isn't a statement about riding horses across a river but, rather, about changing a course of action in critical times. Still, in the end, analogies don't necessarily prove anything. What may be true about riding horses across a stream may not be true about, say, choosing a new leader in troubled times. What is true for one need not be true for the other.

Analogies can be helpful in developing our thoughts and in helping listeners or readers understand a point we're trying to make. It is sometimes argued, for instance, that newspaper and television reporters and their confidential sources should share the right to confidential privilege, like the doctor–patient, attorney–client, or priest–confessor relationship. The analogy is worth thinking about: Do the similarities run deep enough, or are there fundamental differences in the types of confidentiality we should expect between journalists and their sources and between people and their doctors, lawyers, or priests?

AUTHORITATIVE TESTIMONY   Another form of evidence is **testimony**, the citation or quotation of authorities. In daily life, we rely heavily on authorities of all sorts: We get a doctor's opinion about our health, we read a book because an intelligent friend recommends it, we see a movie because a critic gave it a good review, and we pay at least a little attention to the weather forecaster.

In setting forth an argument, one often tries to show that one's view is supported by notable figures — perhaps Jefferson, Lincoln, Martin Luther King Jr., or scientists who won a Nobel Prize — but authorities do not have to be figures of such a high stature. You may recall that when talking about medical marijuana legalization in Chapter 2, we presented an open letter by Sanjay Gupta. To make certain that you were impressed by his ideas, we described him as CNN's chief medical correspondent and a leading public health expert. In our Chapter 2 discussion of Sally Mann, we qualified our description of her controversial photographs by noting that *Time* magazine called her "America's Best Photographer" and the *New Republic* called her book "one of the great photograph books of our time." But heed some words of caution:

- Be sure that the authority, however notable, is *an authority on the topic in question*. (A well-known biologist might be an authority on vitamins but not on the justice of war.)

- Be sure that the authority is *unbiased*. (A chemist employed by the tobacco industry isn't likely to admit that smoking may be harmful, and a producer of violent video games isn't likely to admit that playing those games stimulates violence.)

- Beware of *nameless* authorities: "a thousand doctors," "leading educators," "researchers at a major medical school." (If possible, offer at least one specific name.)

- Be careful when using authorities who indeed were great authorities in their day but *who now may be out of date.* (Examples include Adam Smith on economics, Julius Caesar on the art of war, Louis Pasteur on medicine.)

- Cite authorities *whose opinions your readers will value.* (William F. Buckley Jr.'s conservative/libertarian opinions mean a good deal to readers of the magazine that he founded, the *National Review*, but probably not to most liberal thinkers. Gloria Steinem's liberal/feminist opinions carry weight with readers of the magazines that she cofounded, *New York* and *Ms.* magazine, but probably not with most conservative thinkers.)

THINKING CRITICALLY *Authoritative Testimony*

Locate one authority on each issue and use the table to examine whether or not that person is an adequate authority. In the last box, explain why this is a reliable testimony.

ISSUE	EXPERT NAME AND QUALIFICATIONS	TIME PERIOD	PLACE OF PUBLICATION	YOUR EXPLANATION
Recreational marijuana				
Spanking children				
How to manage test anxiety				
Restoring voting rights to felons				
The quality of the latest Academy Award–winning Best Picture				

One other point: *You* may be an authority. You probably aren't nationally known, but on some topics you might have the authority of personal experience. You may have been injured on a motorcycle while riding without wearing a helmet, or you may have escaped injury because you wore a helmet. You may have dropped out of school and then returned. You may have tutored a student whose native language isn't English, you may be such a student who has received tutoring, or you may have attended a school with a bilingual education program. In short, your personal testimony on topics relating to these issues may be invaluable, and a reader will probably consider it seriously.

NUMERICAL DATA   The last sort of evidence we discuss here is data based on math or collections of numbers, also referred to as **quantitative** or **statistical** evidence. Sometimes quantitative evidence offers firm answers. Suppose the awarding of honors at graduation from college is determined based on a student's cumulative grade-point average (GPA). The undisputed assumption is that the nearer a student's GPA is to a perfect record (4.0), the more deserving he or she is of highest honors. Consequently, a student with a GPA of 3.9 at the end of her senior year is a stronger candidate for honors than another student with a GPA of 3.6. When faculty members determine the academic merits of graduating seniors, they know that these quantitative, statistical differences in student GPAs will be the basic (if not the only) kind of evidence under discussion.

Here, numbers prove to be reliable evidence, used to justify the argument that one student deserves honors more than another. However, in many cases, numbers do not simply speak for themselves. Numerical information can be presented in many forms. Graphs, tables, and pie charts are familiar ways of presenting quantitative data in an eye-catching manner, but how the numbers are organized, interpreted, and presented can make a difference in how well they support an argument's claims. (See the section Visuals as Aids to Clarity: Maps, Graphs, and Pie Charts on pp. 159–63 in Chapter 4 for more on graphs.)

Let's look how some different kinds of numbers are commonly used as evidence.

Presenting Numbers   In an argument, you may need to evaluate whether it is more persuasive to present numbers in percentages or real numbers. For example, arguing that the murder rate increased by 30 percent in one city sounds more compelling than saying there were thirteen murders this year compared to ten last year (only three more, but a technical increase of 30 percent). Should an argument examining the federal budget say that it (1) underwent a *twofold increase* over the decade, (2) increased by *100 percent*, (3) *doubled*, or (4) was *one-half of its current amount ten years ago*? As you can see, these are equivalent ways of saying the same thing, but by making a choice among them, a writer can play up or play down the increase to support different arguments in more or less dramatic ways.

Other kinds of choices may be made in interpreting numbers: Suppose in a given city in 2017, 1 percent of the victims in fatal automobile accidents were bicyclists. In the same city in 2018, the percentage of bicyclists killed in automobile accidents was 2 percent. Was the increase 1 percent (not an alarming figure), or was it 100 percent (a staggering figure)? The answer is both, depending on whether we're comparing (1) bicycle deaths in automobile accidents *with all deaths in automobile accidents* (that's an increase of 1 percent) or (2) bicycle deaths in automobile accidents *only with other bicycle deaths in automobile accidents* (an increase of 100 percent). An honest statement would say that bicycle deaths due to automobile accidents doubled in 2018, increasing from 1 to 2 percent. But here's another point: Although every such death is lamentable, if there was only one such death in 2017 and two in 2018, the increase from one death to two — an increase of 100 percent! — hardly suggests a growing problem that needs attention. No one would be surprised to learn that in the following years there were no deaths at all, or only one or two.

Consider how different calculations can impact the meaning of numerical data. Here are some statistics that pop up in conversations about wealth distribution in the United States. In 2017, the Census Bureau calculated that the **median** household income in the United States was $61,372, meaning that half of households earned less than this amount and half earned above it. However, the **average** — technically, the **mean** — household income in the same year was $86,220, or $24,848 (or 40 percent) higher. Which number more accurately represents the typical household income? Both are "correct," but both are calculated with different measures (median and mean). If a politician wanted to argue that the United States has a strong middle class, he might use the average (mean) income as evidence, a number calculated by dividing the total income of all households by the total number of households. If another politician wished to make a rebuttal, she could point out that the average income paints a rosy picture because the wealthiest households skew the average higher. The median income (representing the number above and below which two halves of all households fall) should be the measure we use, the rebutting politician could argue, because it helps reduce the effect of the limitless ceiling of higher incomes and the finite floor of lower incomes at zero.

Our point: This just shows how different methods of calculating — or how writers may use the results of those different methods — can produce different understandings of an issue.

Unreliable Statistical Evidence   Because we know that 90 percent is greater than 75 percent, we're usually ready to grant that any claim supported by 90 percent of cases is more likely to be true than an alternative claim supported in only 75 percent of cases. The greater the difference, the greater our confidence. Yet statistics often get a bad name because it's so easy to misuse them (unintentionally or not) and so difficult to be sure that they were gathered correctly in the first place. (One old saying goes, "There are lies, damned lies, and statistics.") Every branch of social science and natural science needs statistical information, and countless decisions in public and private life are based on quantitative data in statistical form. It's therefore important to be sensitive to the sources and reliability of the statistics and to develop a healthy skepticism when you confront statistics whose parentage is not fully explained. Always ask: Who gathered the statistics? For what purpose?

Consider this example of statistics, from the self-described "culture jammer" Kalle Lasn, the founder of AdBusters, a group that commonly criticizes aspects of consumer society:

Advertisements are the most prevalent and toxic of the mental pollutants.

From the moment your radio alarm sounds in the morning to the wee hours of late-night TV, microjolts of commercial pollution flood into your brain at the rate of about three thousand marketing messages per day. (Kalle Lasn, *Culture Jam* [1999], 18–19)

Lasn's book includes endnotes as documentation, so, being curious about the statistics, we turned to the appropriate page and found this information concerning the source of his data:

> "three thousand marketing messages per day." Mark Landler, Walecia Konrad, Zachary Schiller, and Lois Therrien, "What Happened to Advertising?" *BusinessWeek*, September 23, 1991, page 66. Leslie Savan in *The Sponsored Life* (Temple University Press, 1994), page 1, estimated that "16,000 ads flicker across an individual's consciousness daily." I did an informal survey in March 1995 and found the number to be closer to 1,500 (this included all marketing messages, corporate images, logos, ads, brand names, on TV, radio, billboards, buildings, signs, clothing, appliances, in cyberspace, etc., over a typical twenty-four hour period in my life). (219)

Well, this endnote is odd. In the earlier passage, the author asserted that about "three thousand marketing messages per day" flood into a person's brain. In the documentation, he cites a source for that statistic from *BusinessWeek* — although we haven't the faintest idea how the authors of the *BusinessWeek* article came up with that figure. Oddly, he goes on to offer a very different figure (16,000 ads) and then, to our confusion, offers yet a third figure (1,500) based on his own "informal survey."

Probably the one thing we can safely say about all three figures is that none of them means very much. Even if the compilers of the statistics explained exactly how they counted — let's say that among countless other criteria they assumed that the average person reads one magazine per day and that the average magazine contains 124 advertisements — it would be hard to take them seriously. After all, in leafing through a magazine, some people may read many ads and some may read none. Some people may read some ads carefully — but perhaps just to enjoy their absurdity. Our point: Although Lasn said, without implying any uncertainty, that "about three thousand marketing messages per day" reach an individual, it's evident from the endnote that even he is confused about the figure he gives.

WRITING TIP
When writing, consider presenting your numerical data in ways that have the most impact. A quarter, 25%, and 1 out of 4 are all the same but may resonate differently with your audience. But be ethical; don't try to manipulate your reader.

We'd like to make a final point about the unreliability of some statistical information — data that looks impressive but that is, in fact, insubstantial. Consider Marilyn Jager Adams's book *Beginning to Read: Thinking and Learning about Print* (1994), in which she pointed out that poor families read to their preschool children only 25 hours per year over a five-year period, whereas in the same period middle-income families read to their preschool children 1,000 to 1,700 hours. The figures were much quoted in newspapers and by children's advocacy groups. Adams could not, of course, interview every family in these two groups; she had to rely on samples. What were her samples? For poor families, she selected twenty-four children in twenty families, all in Southern California. (Ask yourself: Can families from only one geographic area provide an adequate sample for a topic such as this?) And how many families constituted Adams's sample of middle-class families? Exactly one — her own. We leave it to you to judge the validity of her findings.

Sometimes the definition of what is being counted can affect the statistical results. Sociologist Joel Best notes in his book *Stat Spotting* an interesting case: When research several years ago showed that "one-fifth [20 percent] of college students practice self-injury," the dramatic statistic attracted journalists and news media who published all kinds of worrying articles. But a closer look at the study revealed not only that the survey was limited to two Ivy League universities (a sampling problem), but also that it *defined* self-injury in a very broad way, to include minor acts that most psychologists would consider to be within the range of normal behavior — such as pinching, scratching, or hitting oneself. In actuality, as another analysis showed, only 1.6 percent of college students reported injuring themselves to the point of needing medical treatment — quite a lot fewer than 20 percent.

We are not suggesting that everyone who uses statistics is trying to deceive (or is unconsciously being deceived by them). We suggest only that statistics are open to widely different interpretations and that often those columns of numbers, which appear to be so precise with their decimal points and their complex formulas, may actually be imprecise and possibly worthless if they're based on insufficient samples, erroneous methodologies, or biased interpretation.

A CHECKLIST FOR EVALUATING STATISTICAL EVIDENCE

Regard statistical evidence (like all other evidence) cautiously and don't accept it until you have thought about these questions:

☐ Was the evidence compiled by a disinterested (impartial) source? The source's name doesn't always reveal its particular angle (e.g., People for the American Way), but sometimes it lets you know what to expect (e.g., National Rifle Association, American Civil Liberties Union).

☐ Is it based on an adequate sample?

☐ What is the definition of the thing being counted or measured?

☐ Is the statistical evidence recent enough to be relevant?

☐ How many of the factors likely to be relevant were identified and measured?

☐ Are the figures open to a different and equally plausible interpretation?

☐ If a percentage is cited, is it the average (or *mean*), or is it the median?

Nonrational Appeals

In talking about induction and deduction, definitions, and types of evidence, we've been talking about means of rational persuasion, things normally falling under the purview of *logos*. However, as mentioned earlier, there are also other means of persuasion. Force is an example. If Stacey kicks Janée, and threatens to destroy Janée's means of livelihood, and threatens Janée's life, Stacey may persuade Janée to cooperate or agree with her. Writers, of course, cannot use such kinds of force on their readers (nor would they want to, we hope). But they do have at their disposal forms of persuasion that are more associated with *pathos*. These types of appeals do not rely on rational logic or inference (*logos*), but predominantly on the feeling — the emotions — of readers.

SATIRE, IRONY, SARCASM

One form of irrational but sometimes highly effective persuasion is **satire** — that is, witty ridicule. A cartoonist may persuade viewers that a politician's views are unsound by caricaturing (thus ridiculing) her appearance or by presenting a grotesquely distorted (funny, but unfair) picture of the issue she supports.

Satiric artists often use caricature; satiric writers, also seeking to persuade by means of ridicule, often use **verbal irony**. This sort of irony contrasts what is said and what is meant. For instance, words of praise may actually imply blame (when Shakespeare's Cassius says,

How does this mural by street artist Banksy use visual irony?

"Brutus is an honorable man," he wants those who hear him to think that Brutus is dishonorable). Occasionally, words of modesty may actually imply superiority ("Of course, I'm too dumb to understand this problem"). Such language, when heavy-handed, is **sarcasm** ("You're a great guy," someone who is actually criticizing you says). If it's witty and clever, we call it irony rather than sarcasm.

Although ridicule isn't a form of reasoning, passages of ridicule, especially verbal irony, sometimes appear in argument essays. These passages, like reasons or like appeals to the emotions, are efforts to persuade the reader to accept the writer's point of view. The key to using humor in an argument is, on the one hand, to avoid wisecracking like a smart aleck and, on the other hand, to avoid mere clownishness. In other words, if you get too silly, acerbic, or outright insulting, you may damage your *ethos* and alienate your audience.

EMOTIONAL APPEALS

It is sometimes said that good argumentative writing appeals only to reason, never to emotion, and that any emotional appeal is illegitimate and irrelevant. "Tears are not arguments," the Brazilian writer Machado de Assis said. Logic textbooks may even stigmatize with Latin labels the various sorts of emotional appeal — for instance, *argumentum ad populam* (appeal to the prejudices of the mob, as in "Come on, we all know that schools don't teach anything anymore") and *argumentum ad misericordiam* (appeal to pity, as in "No one ought to blame this poor kid for stabbing a classmate because his mother was often institutionalized").

LEARNING FROM SHAKESPEARE   True, appeals to emotion may distract from the facts of the case; they may blind the audience by, in effect, throwing dust in its eyes or by provoking tears. A classic example occurs in Shakespeare's *Julius Caesar*, when Marc Antony addresses the Roman populace after Brutus, Cassius, and Casca have conspired to assassinate Caesar. The real issue is whether Caesar was becoming tyrannical (as the assassins claim). Antony turns from the evidence and stirs the crowd against the assassins by appealing to its emotions. Shakespeare drew from an ancient Roman biographical writing, Plutarch's *Lives of the Noble Grecians and Romans*. Plutarch says this about Antony:

> [P]erceiving that his words moved the common people to compassion, . . . [he] framed his eloquence to make their hearts yearn [i.e., grieve] the more, and, taking Caesar's gown all bloody in his hand, he laid it open to the sight of them all, showing what a number of cuts and holes it had upon it. Therewithal the people fell presently into such a rage and mutiny that there was no more order kept.

Here's how Shakespeare reinterpreted the event in his play:

> Friends, Romans, countrymen, lend me your ears;
> I come to bury Caesar, not to praise him.

After briefly offering insubstantial evidence that Caesar gave no signs of behaving tyrannically (e.g., "When that the poor have cried, Caesar hath wept"), Antony begins to play directly on his hearers' emotions. Descending from the platform so that he may be in closer contact with his audience (like a modern politician, he wants to work the crowd), he calls attention to Caesar's bloody toga:

> If you have tears, prepare to shed them now.
> You all do know this mantle; I remember
> The first time ever Caesar put it on:
> 'Twas on a summer's evening, in his tent,
> That day he overcame the Nervii.
> Look, in this place ran Cassius' dagger through;
> See what a rent the envious Casca made;
> Through this, the well-belovèd Brutus stabbed . . .

In these few lines, Antony accomplishes the following:

- He prepares the audience by suggesting to them how they should respond ("If you have tears, prepare to shed them now").
- He flatters them by implying that they, like Antony, were intimates of Caesar (he credits them with being familiar with Caesar's garment).
- He then evokes a personal memory of a specific time ("a summer's evening") — the day that Caesar won a battle against the Nervii, a particularly fierce tribe in what is now France. (In fact, Antony was not at the battle and did not join Caesar until three years later.)

Antony doesn't mind being free with the facts; his point here is not to set the record straight but to stir people against the assassins. He goes on, daringly but successfully, to identify one particular slit in the garment with Cassius's dagger, another with Casca's, and a third with Brutus's. Antony cannot know which dagger made which slit, but his rhetorical trick works.

Notice, too, that Antony arranges the three assassins in climactic order, since Brutus (Antony claims) was especially beloved by Caesar:

> Judge, O you gods, how dearly Caesar loved him!
> This was the most unkindest cut of all;
> For when the noble Caesar saw him stab,
> Ingratitude, more strong than traitor's arms,
> Quite vanquished him. Then burst his mighty heart.

Nice. According to Antony, the noble-minded Caesar — Antony's words have erased all thought of the tyrannical Caesar — died not from wounds inflicted by daggers but from the heartbreaking perception of Brutus's ingratitude. Doubtless there wasn't a dry eye in the crowd. Let's all hope that if we are ever put on trial, we'll have a lawyer as skilled in evoking sympathy as Antony.

ARE EMOTIONAL APPEALS FALLACIOUS?   Antony's oration was obviously successful in the play and apparently was successful in real life, but it is the sort of speech that prompts logicians to write disapprovingly of attempts to stir feeling in an audience. (As mentioned earlier, the evocation of emotion in an audience is **pathos**, from the Greek word for "emotion" or "suffering.") There is nothing inherently wrong in stimulating an audience's emotions when attempting to establish a claim, but when an emotional appeal confuses the issue being argued or shifts attention away from the facts, we can reasonably speak of the emotional appeal as a fallacy.

No fallacy is involved, however, when an emotional appeal heightens the facts, bringing them home to the audience rather than masking them. In talking about legislation that would govern police actions, for example, it's legitimate to show a photograph of the battered, bloodied face of an alleged victim of police brutality. True, such a photograph cannot tell the whole truth; it cannot tell if the subject threatened the officer with a gun or repeatedly resisted an order to surrender. But it can demonstrate that the victim was severely beaten and (like a comparable description in words) evoke emotions that may properly affect the audience's decision about the permissible use of police violence. Similarly, an animal rights activist who argues that calves are cruelly confined might reasonably talk about the inhumanely small size of their pens, in which they cannot turn around or even lie down. Others may argue that calves don't care about turning around or have no right to turn around, but the evocative verbal description of their pens, which makes an emotional appeal, cannot be called fallacious or irrelevant.

THINKING CRITICALLY *Nonrational Appeals*

Identify the emotion summoned by the following nonrational appeals and explain how the claim may be countered by logic or reason.

NONRATIONAL APPEAL	EMOTION	LOGICAL COUNTER
Football players and other athletes should not be allowed to kneel for the National Anthem to protest police violence because it disrespects the American flag and all those people who died defending it.		
Nowadays, it seems anything goes on television, and even primetime shows feature foul language, sex, and violence. Don't they realize children are watching?		
The Powerball jackpot this week is more than $500 million. Even if you don't normally play the lottery, it's time to buy a ticket!		

In appealing to emotions, then, keep in mind these strategies:

- Do not falsify (especially by oversimplifying) the issue.
- Do not distract attention from the facts of the case.
- Do think ethically about how emotional appeals may affect the audience.

You should focus on the facts and offer reasons (essentially, statements linked with "because"), but you may also legitimately bring the facts home to your readers by seeking to provoke appropriate emotions. Your words will be fallacious only if you stimulate emotions that aren't connected with the facts of the case.

Does All Writing Contain Arguments?

Our answer to the question in the heading is no — however, *most* writing probably *does* contain an argument of sorts. The writer wants to persuade the reader to see things the way the writer sees them — at least until the end of the essay. After all, even a recipe for a cherry pie in a food magazine — a piece of writing that's primarily expository (how to do it) rather than argumentative (how a reasonable person ought to think about this topic) — probably starts out with a hint of an argument, such as "*Because* [a sign that a *reason* will be offered] this pie can be made quickly and with ingredients (canned cherries) that are always available, give it a try. It will surely become one of your favorites." Clearly, such a statement cannot stand as a formal argument — a discussion that addresses counterarguments, relies chiefly on logic and little if any emotional appeal, and draws a conclusion that seems irrefutable.

Still, the statement is technically an argument on behalf of making a pie with canned cherries. In this case, we can identify a claim (the pie will become a favorite) and two *reasons* in support of the claim:

- It can be made quickly.
- The chief ingredient — because it is canned — can always be at hand.

There are two underlying *assumptions*:

- Readers don't have a great deal of time to waste in the kitchen.
- Canned cherries are just as tasty as fresh cherries — and even if they aren't, no one who eats the pie will know the difference.

When we read a lead-in to a recipe, then, we won't find a formal argument, but we'll probably see a few words that seek to persuade us to keep reading. And most writing does contain such material — sentences that engage our interest and give us a reason to keep reading. If the recipe is difficult and time consuming, the lead-in may say this:

> Although this recipe for a cherry pie, using fresh cherries that you will have to pit, is a bit more time consuming than the usual recipes that call for canned cherries, once you have tasted it you will never go back to canned cherries.

Again, although the logic is scarcely compelling, the persuasive element is evident. The assumption is that readers have a discriminating palate; once they've tasted a pie made with fresh cherries, they'll never again enjoy the canned stuff. The writer isn't making a formal argument with abundant evidence and detailed refutation of counterarguments, but we know where he stands and how he wishes us to respond.

In short, almost all writers are trying to persuade readers to see things *their* way. As you read the essays in this chapter, keep in mind the questions in the checklist for analyzing an argument. They can help you take apart an argument and discover where strengths and weakness lie and perhaps find new points to make (and things to say) in important discussions and debates.

A CHECKLIST FOR ANALYZING AN ARGUMENT

Thesis and Claims

☐ Is the author's claim or thesis clear?

☐ Are any parts of the argument based on *logos*, *pathos*, or *ethos*?

☐ Are any premises false or questionable?

☐ Is the logic — deductive or inductive — valid?

☐ Are important terms and concepts defined satisfactorily?

☐ Does the writer make assumptions that are problematic for his or her argument?

Support and Evidence

☐ Does the writer use evidence to support his or her claims?

☐ Are the examples — imagined, invented, or hypothetical — relevant and convincing?

☐ Are the statistics (if any) relevant, accurate, and complete?

☐ Are other interpretations of evidence possible?

☐ Can authorities who offer evidence be considered impartial?

Fairness

☐ Are alternative viewpoints and counterexamples adequately considered?

☐ Is there any evidence of dishonesty or of a discreditable attempt to manipulate the reader?

☐ Is the writer's tone and use of language appropriate to the subject and the audience?

An Example: An Argument and a Look at the Writer's Strategies

The following essay, "The Reign of Recycling" by John Tierney, concerns the efficacy of recycling—whether or not it is helping the environment in significant ways or if it has gone beyond its originally good intentions to become an unsustainable or even counterproductive measure. We follow Tierney's essay with some comments about the ways in which he constructs his argument.

JOHN TIERNEY

John Tierney (b. 1953) is an award-winning journalist for the *New York Times* who publishes frequently on issues related to science, environmentalism, and politics. He has also published extensively in magazines such as the *Atlantic, Rolling Stone, Newsweek, Discover,* and *Esquire.* Known for his skepticism toward climate science and big government, Tierney is regarded as a conservative critic. This essay appeared in the *New York Times* in 2015.

The Reign of Recycling

If you live in the United States, you probably do some form of recycling. It's likely that you separate paper from plastic and glass and metal. You rinse the bottles and cans, and you might put food scraps in a container destined for a composting facility. As you sort everything into the right bins, you probably assume that recycling is helping your community and protecting the environment. But is it? Are you in fact wasting your time?

In 1996, I wrote a long article[1] for *The New York Times Magazine* arguing that the recycling process as we carried it out was wasteful. I presented plenty of evidence that recycling was costly and ineffectual, but its defenders said that it was unfair to rush to judgment. Noting that the modern recycling movement had really just begun just a few years earlier, they predicted it would flourish as the industry matured and the public learned how to recycle properly.

So, what's happened since then? While it's true that the recycling message has reached more people than ever, when it comes to the bottom line, both economically and environmentally, not much has changed at all.

Despite decades of exhortations and mandates, it's still typically more expensive for municipalities to recycle household waste than to send it to a landfill. Prices for recyclable materials have plummeted because of lower oil prices and reduced demand for them overseas. The slump has forced some recycling companies to shut plants and cancel plans for new technologies. The mood is so gloomy that one industry

Reign in the title suggests that recycling is a powerful, perhaps even tyrannical, trend.

Tierney presents a common assumption—recycling is helping—but questions it.

Establishes *ethos*: he has long been familiar with (and right about) the central issues and questions.

Tierney's thesis:
Premise: Recycling was costly and ineffectual in 1996.
Premise: Not much has changed since 1996.
Conclusion: Recycling remains costly and ineffectual.

Tierney gestures toward evidence, but he does not present concrete examples.

---

[1]John Tierney, "Recycling Is Garbage," *New York Times,* June 30, 1996, nyti.ms/2kqksIS. [All citations in this selection are the editors'; they appeared as hyperlinks in the original publication.]

veteran tried to cheer up her colleagues this summer with an article in a trade journal titled, "Recycling Is Not Dead!"[2]

While politicians set higher and higher goals, the national rate of recycling has stagnated in recent years. Yes, it's popular in affluent neighborhoods like Park Slope in Brooklyn and in cities like San Francisco, but residents of the Bronx and Houston don't have the same fervor for sorting garbage in their spare time.

The future for recycling looks even worse. As cities move beyond recycling paper and metals, and into glass, food scraps and assorted plastics, the costs rise sharply while the environmental benefits decline and sometimes vanish. "If you believe recycling is good for the planet and that we need to do more of it, then there's a crisis to confront," says David P. Steiner, the chief executive officer of Waste Management, the largest recycler of household trash in the United States. "Trying to turn garbage into gold costs a lot more than expected. We need to ask ourselves: What is the goal here?"

Recycling has been relentlessly promoted as a goal in and of itself: an unalloyed public good and private virtue that is indoctrinated in students from kindergarten through college. As a result, otherwise well-informed and educated people have no idea of the relative costs and benefits.

They probably don't know, for instance, that to reduce carbon emissions, you'll accomplish a lot more by sorting paper and aluminum cans than by worrying about yogurt containers and half-eaten slices of pizza. Most people also assume that recycling plastic bottles must be doing lots for the planet. They've been encouraged by the Environmental Protection Agency, which assures the public that recycling plastic results in less carbon being released into the atmosphere.

But how much difference does it make? Here's some perspective: To offset the greenhouse impact of one passenger's round-trip flight between New York and London, you'd have to recycle roughly 40,000 plastic bottles, assuming you fly coach. If you sit in business- or first-class, where each passenger takes up more space, it could be more like 100,000.

Even those statistics might be misleading. New York and other cities instruct people to rinse the bottles before putting them in the recycling bin, but the E.P.A.'s life-cycle calculation doesn't take that water into account. That single omission can make a big difference, according to Chris Goodall, the author of "How to Live a Low-Carbon Life." Mr. Goodall calculates that if you wash plastic in water that was heated by coal-derived electricity, then the net effect of your recycling could be *more* carbon in the atmosphere.

To many public officials, recycling is a question of morality, not cost-benefit analysis. Mayor Bill de Blasio of New York declared that by 2030 the city would no longer send any garbage to landfills. "This is the way of the future if we're going to save our earth," he explained[3] while announcing that New York would join San Francisco,

---

[2]Patty Moore, "Recycling Is Not Dead," *Resource Recycling*, July 1, 2015, resource-recycling.com/node/6130.

[3] Jill Jorgensen, "Bill de Blasio Calls for the End of Garbage by 2030," *Observer*, April 22, 2015, observer.com/2015/04 /bill-de-blasio-calls-for-the-end-of-garbage-by-2030/.

Margin notes:

Notice Tierney quotes an expert authority for corroborating evidence. Why would a Waste Management executive agree with Tierney?

Tierney suggests the EPA itself may not be trustworthy. Note that the EPA is commonly a target of pro-business conservatives.

Proposes that people who think they are doing good for the environment are actually doing worse. How ironic!

Begins to address "zero waste" proposals, implicitly criticizing New York's decision to pursue such a goal.

Seattle and other cities in moving toward a "zero waste" policy, which would require an unprecedented level of recycling.

The national rate of recycling rose during the 1990s to 25 percent, meeting the goal set by an E.P.A. official, J. Winston Porter. He advised state officials that no more than about 35 percent of the nation's trash was worth recycling, but some ignored him and set goals of 50 percent and higher. Most of those goals were never met and the national rate has been stuck around 34 percent in recent years.

"It makes sense to recycle commercial cardboard and some paper, as well as selected metals and plastics," he says. "But other materials rarely make sense, including food waste and other compostables. The zero-waste goal makes no sense at all — it's very expensive with almost no real environmental benefit."

> Tierney cites another authority, J. Winston Porter, but he may be shifting the issue; Porter actually says some forms of recycling are good.

One of the original goals of the recycling movement was to avert a supposed crisis because there was no room left in the nation's landfills. But that media-inspired fear was never realistic in a country with so much open space. In reporting the 1996 article I found that all the trash generated by Americans for the next 1,000 years[4] would fit on one-tenth of 1 percent of the land available for grazing. And that tiny amount of land wouldn't be lost forever, because landfills are typically covered with grass and converted to parkland, like the Freshkills Park being created on Staten Island. The United States Open tennis tournament is played on the site of an old landfill — and one that never had the linings and other environmental safeguards required today.

> Tierney undermines assumptions that landfills are bad.

Though most cities shun landfills, they have been welcomed in rural communities 15 that reap large economic benefits (and have plenty of greenery to buffer residents from the sights and smells). Consequently, the great landfill shortage has not arrived, and neither have the shortages of raw materials that were supposed to make recycling profitable.

With the economic rationale gone, advocates for recycling have switched to environmental arguments. Researchers have calculated that there are indeed such benefits to recycling, but not in the way that many people imagine.

> Counterarguments are raised, but Tierney uses them to defend landfills.

Most of these benefits do not come from reducing the need for landfills and incinerators. A modern well-lined landfill in a rural area can have relatively little environmental impact. Decomposing garbage releases methane, a potent greenhouse gas, but landfill operators have started capturing it and using it to generate electricity. Modern incinerators, while politically unpopular in the United States, release so few pollutants that they've been widely accepted in the eco-conscious countries of Northern Europe and Japan for generating clean energy.

Moreover, recycling operations have their own environmental costs, like extra trucks on the road and pollution from recycling operations. Composting facilities around the country have inspired complaints about nauseating odors, swarming rats, and defecating sea gulls. After New York City started sending food waste to be composted in Delaware, the unhappy neighbors of the composting plant successfully campaigned to shut it down last year.

> Pathos: In arguing against composting facilities, Tierney turns stomachs.

---

[4] A. Clark Wiseman. *U.S. Wastepaper Recycling Policies: Issues and Ethics* (1990; *Google Books*), books.google.com /books/about/U_S_Wastepaper_Recycling_Policies.html?id=m9YsAQAAMAAJ.

The environmental benefits of recycling come chiefly from reducing the need to manufacture new products — less mining, drilling and logging. But that's not so appealing to the workers in those industries and to the communities that have accepted the environmental trade-offs that come with those jobs.

Tierney establishes common ground.

Nearly everyone, though, approves of one potential benefit of recycling: reduced 20 emissions of greenhouse gases. Its advocates often cite an estimate by the E.P.A. that recycling municipal solid waste in the United States saves the equivalent of 186 million metric tons of carbon dioxide, comparable to removing the emissions of 39 million cars.

According to the E.P.A.'s estimates, virtually all the greenhouse benefits — more than 90 percent — come from just a few materials: paper, cardboard and metals like the aluminum in soda cans. That's because recycling one ton of metal or paper saves about three tons of carbon dioxide, a much bigger payoff than the other materials analyzed by the E.P.A. Recycling one ton of plastic saves only slightly more than one ton of carbon dioxide. A ton of food saves a little less than a ton. For glass, you have to recycle three tons in order to get about one ton of greenhouse benefits. Worst of all is yard waste: it takes 20 tons of it to save a single ton of carbon dioxide.

Tierney mixes a fraction and a percentage to present his numerical data. But America still has a huge carbon footprint. Is Tierney downplaying the impact of recycling here?

Once you exclude paper products and metals, the total annual savings in the United States from recycling everything else in municipal trash — plastics, glass, food, yard trimmings, textiles, rubber, leather — is only two-tenths of 1 percent of America's carbon footprint.

As a business, recycling is on the wrong side of two long-term global economic trends. For centuries, the real cost of labor has been increasing while the real cost of raw materials has been declining. That's why we can afford to buy so much more stuff than our ancestors could. As a labor-intensive activity, recycling is an increasingly expensive way to produce materials that are less and less valuable.

Recyclers have tried to improve the economics by automating the sorting process, but they've been frustrated by politicians eager to increase recycling rates by adding new materials of little value. The more types of trash that are recycled, the more difficult it becomes to sort the valuable from the worthless.

In New York City, the net cost of recycling a ton of trash is now $300 more than 25 it would cost to bury the trash instead. That adds up to millions of extra dollars per year — about half the budget of the parks department — that New Yorkers are spending for the privilege of recycling. That money could buy far more valuable benefits, including more significant reductions in greenhouse emissions.

So what is a socially conscious, sensible person to do?

Tierney claims his source is "the most thorough" study without defining his criteria. The source title indicates that it is a study of Japan. Does this use of evidence effectively support Tierney's claim?

It would be much simpler and more effective to impose the equivalent of a carbon tax on garbage, as Thomas C. Kinnaman has proposed after conducting what is probably the most thorough comparison of the social costs[5] of recycling, landfilling and incineration. Dr. Kinnaman, an economist at Bucknell University, considered everything from environmental damage to the pleasure that some people take in recycling (the "warm glow" that makes them willing to pay extra to do it).

---

[5] Thomas C. Kinnaman et al., "The Socially Optimal Recycling Rate: Evidence from Japan," *Journal of Environmental Economics and Management*, vol. 68, no. 1 (2014): 54–70, digitalcommons.bucknell.edu/fac_journ/774/.

He concludes that the social good would be optimized by subsidizing the recycling of some metals, and by imposing a $15 tax on each ton of trash that goes to the landfill. That tax would offset the environmental costs, chiefly the greenhouse impact, and allow each municipality to make a guilt-free choice based on local economics and its citizens' wishes. The result, Dr. Kinnaman predicts, would be a lot less recycling than there is today.

Then why do so many public officials keep vowing to do more of it? Special-interest politics is one reason — pressure from green groups — but it's also because recycling intuitively appeals to many voters: It makes people feel virtuous, especially affluent people who feel guilty about their enormous environmental footprint. It is less an ethical activity than a religious ritual, like the ones performed by Catholics to obtain indulgences for their sins.

Religious rituals don't need any practical justification for the believers who perform them voluntarily. But many recyclers want more than just the freedom to practice their religion. They want to make these rituals mandatory for everyone else, too, ◄——
with stiff fines for sinners who don't sort properly. Seattle has become so aggressive that the city is being sued by residents who maintain that the inspectors rooting through their trash are violating their constitutional right to privacy.

> **Definition by synonym: recycling is a religion.**

It would take legions of garbage police to enforce a zero-waste society, but true believers insist that's the future. When Mayor de Blasio promised to eliminate garbage in New York, he said it was "ludicrous" and "outdated" to keep sending garbage to landfills. Recycling, he declared, was the only way for New York to become "a truly sustainable city."

But cities have been burying garbage for thousands of years, and it's still the easiest and cheapest solution for trash. The recycling movement is floundering, and its survival depends on continual subsidies, sermons and policing. How can you build a sustainable city with a strategy that can't even sustain itself?

> **Tierney ends by proposing a solution: the status quo.**

Topics for Critical Thinking and Writing

1. What kinds of claims make John Tierney's essay persuasive? How might he be more convincing?

2. What assumptions are at work in Tierney's essay? For example, what are some of the assumptions about environmentalism that he challenges?

3. In paragraph 29, Tierney defines environmentally conscious behaviors as a "religious ritual." What kind of definition is this? How do you know? (For a refresher, see pp. 44–45.)

4. What does Tierney identify as the main problem, and what solution is he proposing? Provide a summary of his solution, tracing his line of reasoning.

5. Find at least three places where Tierney offers examples to support his claims. What kind of examples are they? Do they stand up to scrutiny?

6. Does Tierney rely more on *logos*, *pathos*, or *ethos*? How and where? In your opinion, should he have relied on one (or more) of these appeals more heavily than he did? Explain your answer.

KWAME ANTHONY APPIAH

Kwame Anthony Appiah (b. 1954) established his reputation as a philosopher at Cornell, Yale, Harvard, Princeton, and New York University. He is a noted cultural theorist, African historian, and novelist decorated with awards and recognitions for more than a dozen books, most recently *As If: Idealization and Ideals* (2017) and *The Lies that Bind: Rethinking Identity* (2018).

Go Ahead, Speak for Yourself

"As a white man," Joe begins, prefacing an insight, revelation, objection or confirmation he's eager to share — but let's stop him right there. Aside from the fact that he's white, and a man, what's his point? What does it signify when people use this now ubiquitous formula ("As a such-and-such, I . . .") to affix an identity to an observation?

Typically, it's an assertion of authority: As a member of this or that social group, I have experiences that lend my remarks special weight. The experiences, being representative of that group, might even qualify me to represent that group. Occasionally, the formula is an avowal of humility. It can be both at once. ("As a working-class woman, I'm struggling to understand Virginia Woolf's blithe assumptions of privilege.") The incantation seems indispensable. But it can also be — to use another much-loved formula — problematic.

The "as a" concept is an inherent feature of identities. For a group label like "white men" to qualify as a social identity, there must be times when the people to whom it applies act as members of that group, and are treated as members of that group. We make lives *as* men and women, *as* blacks and whites, *as* teachers and musicians. Yet the very word "identity" points toward the trouble: It comes from the Latin *idem*, meaning "the same." Because

members of a given identity group have experiences that depend on a host of other social factors, they're *not* the same.

Being a black lesbian, for instance, isn't a matter of simply combining African-American, female and homosexual ways of being in the world; identities interact in complex ways. That's why Kimberle Crenshaw, a feminist legal theorist and civil-rights activist, introduced the notion of intersectionality, which stresses the complexity with which different forms of subordination relate to one another. Racism can make white men shrink from black men and abuse black women. Homophobia can lead men in South Africa to rape gay women but murder gay men. Sexism in the United States in the 1950s kept middle-class white women at home and sent working-class black women to work for them.

Let's go back to Joe, with his NPR mug and 5 his man bun. (Or are you picturing a "Make America Great Again" tank top and a high-and-tight?) Having an identity doesn't, by itself, authorize you to speak on behalf of everyone of that identity. So it can't really be that he's speaking for all white men. But he can at least speak to what it's like to live as a white man, right?

Not if we take the point about intersectionality. If Joe had grown up in Northern Ireland as a gay white Catholic man, his experiences might be rather different from those of his gay white *Protestant* male friends there — let alone those of his childhood pen pal, a straight, Cincinnati-raised reform Jew. While identity affects your experiences, there's no guarantee that what you've learned from them is going to be the same as what other people of the same identity have learned.

We've been here before. In the academy during the identity-conscious 1980s, many humanists thought that we'd reached peak "as a." Some worried that the locution had devolved into mere prepositional posturing. The literary theorist Barbara Johnson wrote, "If I tried to 'speak as a lesbian,' wouldn't I be processing my understanding of myself through media-induced images of what a lesbian is or through my own idealizations of what a lesbian *should* be?" In the effort to be "real," she saw something fake. Another prominent theorist, Gayatri Chakravorty Spivak, thought that the "as a" move was "a distancing from oneself," whereby the speaker became a self-appointed representative of an abstraction, some generalized perspective, and suppressed the actual multiplicity of her identities. "One is not just one thing," she observed.

It's because we're not just one thing that, in everyday conversation, "as a" can be useful as a way to spotlight some specific feature of who we are. Comedians do a lot of this sort of identity-cuing. In W. Kamau Bell's recent Netflix special, "Private School Negro," the "as a" cue, explicit or implicit, singles out various of his identities over the course of an hour. Sometimes he's speaking as a parent, who has to go camping because his kids enjoy camping. Sometimes he's speaking as an African-American, who, for ancestral reasons, doesn't see the appeal of camping ("sleeping outdoors *on purpose*?"). Sometimes — as in a story about having been asked his weight before boarding a small aircraft — he's speaking as

"a man, a heterosexual, cisgender *Dad* man." (Hence: "I have no idea how much I weigh.")

The switch in identities can be the whole point of the joke. Here's Chris Rock, talking about his life in an affluent New Jersey suburb: "As a black man, I'm against the cops, but as a man with property, well, I need the cops. If someone steals something, I can't call the Crips!" Drawing attention to certain identities you have is often a natural way of drawing attention to the contours of your beliefs, values or concerns.

But *caveat auditor*: Let the listener beware. 10 Representing an identity is usually volunteer work, but sometimes the representative is conjured into being. Years ago, a slightly dotty countess I knew in the Hampstead area of London used to point out a leather-jacketed man on a park bench and inform her companions, with a knowing look, "He's the *head gay*." She was convinced that gays had the equivalent of a pontiff or prime minister who could speak on behalf of all his people.

Because people's experiences vary so much, the "as a" move is always in peril of presumption. When I was a student at the University of Cambridge in the 1970s, gay men were *très chic*: You couldn't have a serious party without some of us scattered around like throw pillows. Do my experiences entitle me to speak for a queer farmworker who is coming of age in Emmett, Idaho? Nobody appointed me head gay.

If someone is advocating policies for gay men to adopt, or for others to adopt toward gay men, what matters, surely, isn't whether the person is gay but whether the policies are sensible. As a gay man, you could oppose same-sex marriage (it's just submitting to our culture's heteronormativity, and anyway monogamy is a patriarchal invention) or advocate same-sex marriage (it's an affirmation of equal dignity and a way to sustain gay couples). Because members of an identity group won't be identical, your "as a" doesn't settle anything. The same holds for religious, vocational and national identities.

And, of course, for racial identities. In the 1990s the black novelist Trey Ellis wrote a screenplay, "The Inkwell," which drew on his childhood in the milieu of the black bourgeoisie. A white studio head (for whom race presumably eclipsed class) gave it to Matty Rich, a young black director who'd grown up in a New York City housing project. Mr. Rich apparently worried that the script wasn't "black enough" and proposed turning the protagonist's father, a schoolteacher, into a garbage man. Suffice to say, it didn't end well. Are we really going to settle these perennial debates over authenticity with a flurry of "as a" arrowheads?

Somehow, we can't stop trying. Ever since Donald Trump eked out his surprising electoral victory, political analysts have been looking for people to speak for the supposedly disgruntled white working-class voters who, switching from their former Democratic allegiances, gave Mr. Trump the edge.

But about a third of working-class whites voted for Hillary Clinton. Nobody explaining why white working-class voters went for Mr. Trump would be speaking for the millions of white working-class voters who didn't. One person could say that she spoke *as* a white working-class woman in explaining why she voted for Mrs. Clinton just as truthfully as her sister could make the claim in explaining her support for Mr. Trump — each teeing us up to think about how her class and race might figure into the story. No harm in that. Neither one, however, could accurately claim to speak *for* the white working class. Neither has an exclusive on being representative.

So we might do well to ease up on "as a" — on the urge to underwrite our observations with our identities. "For me," Professor Spivak once tartly remarked, "the question 'Who should speak' is less crucial than 'Who will listen?'"

But tell that to Joe, as he takes a sip of kombucha — or is it Pabst Blue Ribbon? All right, Joe, let's hear what you've got to say. The speaking-as-a convention isn't going anywhere; in truth, it often serves a purpose. But here's another phrase you might try on for size: "Speaking for myself . . ."

Topics for Critical Thinking and Writing

1. In paragraph 2, Kwame Anthony Appiah says that speaking through the lens of an identity group is usually "an assertion of authority." How is this so? In your opinion, are there experiences that are unique to one's identity that allow them to speak with more or less authority on certain topics? If so, identify the topics and give an example.

2. How does Appiah define the term *intersectionality* in this essay? Is it adequately defined? Paraphrase the definition of *intersectionality* in this essay and then look up the term in a reputable resource and provide another definition. Does the new definition clarify or contradict Appiah's definition? How so?

3. Where does Appiah use humor or sarcasm in this essay? Explain how his humor serves to support the argument. Is it the most effective choice for the argument? Why or why not?

4. Appiah writes at length about how speaking "as a" certain identity is inadequate for establishing authority and therefore not legitimate. Explain how Appiah's concerns are really concerns about inductive reasoning and sampling. (See Types of Reasoning, pp. 80–85.)

5. Does Appiah's essay appeal more to *logos, ethos,* or *pathos*? How do you know? Was this an effective choice for his audience?

6. Examine your own identity categories and write about whether you feel you have the authority to speak "as" one of those categories. Why do you think you do? Are there identity categories in which you fit that you would not feel authoritative in speaking for the larger group? Why not?

NAUSICAA RENNER

Nausicaa Renner is digital editor of the *Columbia Journalism Review* and senior editor of *n+1*, a digital and print magazine on literature, culture, and politics. Renner's writerly interests include current events, psychoanalysis, and social media. Her essays have appeared numerously in these publications and others, including the *New York Times Magazine, Bookforum,* the *Nation,* and *National Review.*

How Do You Explain the "Obvious"?

There's nothing more persuasive than the obvious. To appeal to it is to ask people to be bigger, better, more noble — to take a sweeping look at the facts, admit what is plain and do the right thing. Tell me with a fixed gaze and an air of confidence that something is obvious. I will be tempted to believe you, if only to join in the clarity and sense of purpose that comes with accepting what is staring me in the face.

In July 2018, after President Trump's meeting with Vladimir Putin in Helsinki, David Remnick, the editor of *The New Yorker,* called on congressional Republicans to recognize the obvious. Trump, he wrote, had spent his trip working "to humiliate the leaders of Western Europe and declare them 'foes'; to fracture longstanding military, economic and political alliances; and to absolve Russia of its attempts to undermine the 2016 election. He did so clearly, repeatedly and with conviction." *Use your heads,* Remnick seemed to say, inviting G.O.P. leadership out of the darkness and into the light,

asking which of them would "stand up not to applaud the Great Leader but to find the capacity to say what is obvious and what is true." *New York* magazine went further, using the blunt instrument of obviousness to impugn the Republican Party: "G.O.P. Senators: Trump's Obvious Russia Lie Is Good Enough for Us," read one headline, soon after the president claimed that he had, during a news conference with Putin, accidentally said "would" when he meant "wouldn't." ("It should have been obvious," he said, defending himself. "I thought it would be obvious.")

The obvious is a common tool in political arguments; there is something about calling on voters' "common sense" that makes the opposition look like sophists and weasels, waffling and equivocating. The obvious cuts through nonsense. It asks why we have hundreds of pages of tax law instead of one; it insists on straightforward fixes for immigration policy. And part of the appeal of universal health care is simply that it's universal: no compromises, no complex incentive systems, no loopholes, less a policy than a statement of rights. In a recent *Vox* article, Tim Higginbotham and Chris Middleman wrote that Medicare-for-all plans present a "resolute vision, one in which our common well-being and dignity take obvious precedence over the profits of a few." The stance is sure of itself; it has the certitude to weigh health care against profit and reach a decisive answer, while others remain lost in a mental fog.

But we also appeal to the obvious as a last-ditch effort when, after decades of conflict, we're further than ever from clarity. After the 2012 shooting at Sandy Hook Elementary School, President Obama gave an emotional speech at a vigil for the 20 children and six adults who were killed, asking the nation to look at itself: "Are we really prepared to say that we're powerless in the face of such carnage, that the politics are too hard?" A few years later, in a speech calling for bipartisan agreement on gun laws, he noted that after Sandy Hook, 90 percent of Americans supported a "common-sense compromise" bill. But Republicans had voted that bill down. The speech had a ring of desperation and defeat: If we can't agree on something this obvious, the president seemed to ask, what can we agree on?

In Edgar Allan Poe's "The Purloined Letter," the detective Auguste Dupin is able to find a stolen letter in the apartment of an unscrupulous government minister — a letter no one else could find, because everyone else assumed it would be treated as if it were valuable and hidden. Instead, the letter was hiding in plain sight, not carefully preserved but crumpled and torn like trash. It escapes detection "by dint of being extremely obvious." We prefer our politicians to be like Dupin: able to rise above the mire of small details and see the whole.

This is harder than it sounds. The letter either pops out or it doesn't. The obvious can be like a Magic Eye poster, one of those novelties whose hidden 3-D image only leaps out at you when you look at it just right: You can't really help someone else see it. It has been a signature move of the Trump administration to disrupt the obvious, beginning with a debate over the size of the crowd at the moment the president was sworn in. The mind is great at coming up with viable alternatives to ideas it doesn't want to accept, and those unwilling to accept invocations of the obvious, like Remnick's, find themselves safely tangled in a web of possibilities. With Trump, "rather than acknowledge the obvious, the supporters spin theories of 'Art of the Deal,'" wrote Jim Schutze in a column in the *Dallas Observer*, "imputing all kinds of cleverness and guile, saying he pretends to be an idiot as part of a wily strategy." At its least extreme, this entails a belief that there is some cunning in Trump's most transparent lies and clumsiest public statements; at its most extreme, it puts him at the center of an elaborate plot to destroy the "deep state." What is "obvious" is taken as false because it's *too* obvious.

This is because the obvious is, essentially, a shortcut: It appeals to a set of values we'd formed some consensus around, a set of ideas we once agreed no serious person would question. To call something "obvious" or "common sense" is to call it settled and refuse to relitigate it or revisit all the work that went into determining it was so inarguable in the first place. In a recent book, "At War with the Obvious," the psychoanalyst Donald Moss writes that "the obvious is adaptive. It mutates under pressure, like cells." If you need evidence of this, he writes, consider the status of gay, queer and trans people over the past few decades. In the 1990s, the American mainstream found it obvious that gay people should have no right to marry; today, it's regarded by many as broadly obvious that they should. An idea that was once marginal enough to require laborious defense gradually became so self-evident that it was hardly worth explaining; like the crumpled letter, its presence was taken for granted.

The difficulty is that, later, when such propositions are threatened, people may find themselves shocked, out of practice, struggling to defend their values with the passion or eloquence that first brought them into existence. Last month, for instance, Michael Anton, a former national-security official in the Trump administration, published a *Washington Post* op-ed arguing that, contrary to the understanding of most readers, birthright citizenship was based in a misreading of the law and should be ended by executive order. The fury that met this suggestion was sputtering: For anyone not already immersed in constitutional law, being horrified by Anton's claims meant arguing in favor of something that had long been so obvious that it was easy to forget what made it obvious in the first place. Justin Fox, a columnist for *Bloomberg Opinion*, allowed that a majority of the world's nations didn't offer birthright citizenship. But the claim that the authors of the 14th Amendment intended anything else, he wrote, "is, to anyone who takes the time to read a few pages of congressional debate, obviously false."

America is built on an appeal to the obvious. The Declaration of Independence holds its truths to be "self-evident" — axiomatic, irreducible, not needing justification because they justify themselves. (It was not obvious to the authors that those truths applied to all Americans, though this seems obvious to most of us now.)

What Americans have confronted lately 10 is a state of affairs in which many of our most basic paradigms are no longer obvious to everyone. Appeals to obviousness seem to wilt as soon as they appear. "Are we prepared to say that such violence visited on our children, year after year after year, is somehow the price of our freedom?" asked Obama in his Sandy Hook speech. This was a rhetorical question; the obvious answer is supposed to be "no." But what if some Americans answer with "yes"?

Politicians and the press still invoke obviousness in the hope of summoning some conviction we all still share, some bedrock of group belief we can agree on. To see them fail, repeatedly, is unsettling; it makes our deepest values seem impotent. It had seemed obvious to some that a modern presidential administration would not defend white nationalists or that the United States government would seek to avoid taking babies from their parents' arms — or that a man who bragged about harassing women wouldn't be elected in the first place. In the summer of 2017, NPR celebrated the Fourth of July by tweeting, line by line, the text of the Declaration of Independence; its account was immediately attacked by angry Americans accusing the organization of spreading seditious anti-Trump propaganda. The nation's founding values have come to seem, somehow, unfamiliar and contentious; we can't recognize the Declaration of Independence when we see it. Let the obvious sit too long and it becomes like an animal in a zoo: pointed at, but never exercised, and idly wandered past by people who have forgotten how powerful it is in action.

Topics for Critical Thinking and Writing

1. In her first paragraph, Nausicaa Renner refers to an "appeal" to the obvious. What kind of appeal is this? Is it more of an appeal to reason (*logos*) or an appeal to emotion (*pathos*)? Or is it something else? Explain your answer.

2. Does Renner use an inductive or deductive means in describing the "obvious"? (See Types of Reasoning, pp. 80–85.) Explain.

3. What other strategies does Renner use to define the "obvious"?

4. What does Renner's central argument compel readers to *do*, if anything? Does she recommend any specific course of action? If so, how do you think it could benefit you?

5. Make a short list of things — three or four ideas, customs, or beliefs — that seemed obvious at one time in history but are no longer taken as obvious. What do you think will be the major changes in the obvious over the next generation?

ANNA LISA RAYA

Daughter of a second-generation Mexican American father and a Puerto Rican mother, Anna Lisa Raya grew up in Los Angeles. In 1994, while she was an undergraduate at Columbia University in New York, she wrote and published this essay on identity.

It's Hard Enough Being Me (Student Essay)

When I entered college, I *discovered* I was Latina. Until then, I had never questioned who I was or where I was from: My father is a second-generation Mexican American, born and raised in Los Angeles, and my mother was born in Puerto Rico and raised in Compton, California. My home is El Sereno, a predominantly Mexican neighborhood in L.A. Every close friend I have back home is Mexican. So I was always just Mexican. Though sometimes I was just Puerto Rican — like when we would visit Mamo (my grandma) or hang out with my Aunt Titi.

Upon arriving in New York as a first-year student, 3,000 miles from home, I not only experienced extreme culture shock, but for the first time I had to define myself according to the broad term "Latina." Although culture shock and identity crisis are common for the newly minted collegian who goes away to school, my experience as a newly minted Latina was, and still is, even more complicating. In El Sereno, I felt like I was part of a majority, whereas at the College I am a minority.

I've discovered that many Latinos like myself have undergone similar experiences. We face discrimination for being a minority in this country while also facing criticism for being "whitewashed" or "sellouts" in the countries of our heritage. But as an ethnic group in college, we are forced to define ourselves according to some vague, generalized Latino experience. This requires us to know our history, our language, our music, and our religion. I can't even be a content "Puerto Mexican" because I have to be a politically-and-socially-aware-Latina-with-a-chip-on-my-shoulder-because-of-how-repressed-I-am-in-this-country.

I am none of the above. I am the quintessential imperfect Latina. I can't dance salsa to save my life, I learned about Montezuma and the Aztecs in sixth grade, and I haven't prayed to the *Virgen de Guadalupe* in years.

Apparently I don't even look Latina. I [5] can't count how many times people have just assumed that I'm white or asked me if I'm Asian. True, my friends back home call me *güera* ("whitey") because I have green eyes and pale skin, but that was as bad as it got. I never thought I would wish my skin were a darker shade or my hair a curlier texture, but since I've been in college, I have — many times.

Another thing: My Spanish is terrible. Every time I call home, I berate my mama for not teaching me Spanish when I was a child. In fact, not knowing how to speak the language of my home countries is the biggest problem that I have encountered, as have many Latinos. In Mexico there is a term, *pocha*, which is used by native Mexicans to ridicule Mexican Americans. It expresses a deep-rooted antagonism and dislike for those of us who were raised on the other side of the border. Our failed attempts to speak pure, Mexican Spanish are largely responsible for the dislike. Other Latin American natives have this same attitude. No matter how well a Latino speaks Spanish, it can never be good enough.

Yet Latinos can't even speak Spanish in the U.S. without running the risk of being called "spic" or "wetback." That is precisely why my mother refused to teach me Spanish when I was a child. The fact that she spoke Spanish was constantly used against her: It prevented her from getting good jobs, and it would have placed me in bilingual education — a construct of the Los Angeles public school system that has proved to be more of a hindrance to intellectual development than a help.

To be fully Latina in college, however, I *must* know Spanish. I must satisfy the equation: Latina [equals] Spanish-speaking.

So I'm stuck in this black hole of an identity crisis, and college isn't making my life any easier, as I thought it would. In high school, I was being prepared for an adulthood in which I would be an individual, in which I wouldn't have to wear a Catholic school uniform anymore. But though I led an anonymous adolescence, I knew who I was. I knew I was different from white, black, or Asian people. I knew there was a language other than English that I could call my own if I only knew how to speak it better. I knew there were historical reasons why I was in this country, distinct reasons that make my existence here easier or more difficult than other people's existence. Ultimately, I was content.

Now I feel pushed into a corner, always [10] defining, defending, and proving myself to classmates, professors, or employers. Trying to understand who and why I am, while understanding Plato or Homer, is a lot to ask of myself.

A month ago, I heard three Nuyorican (Puerto Ricans born and raised in New York) writers discuss how New York City has influenced their writing. One problem I have faced as a young writer is finding a voice that is true to my community. I was surprised and reassured to discover that as Latinos, these writers had faced similar pressures and conflicts as myself; some weren't even taught Spanish in childhood. I will never forget the advice that one of them gave me that evening: She said that I need to be true to myself. "Because people will always complain about what you are doing — you're a 'gringa' or a 'spic' no matter what," she explained. "So you might as well do things for yourself and not for them."

I don't know why it has taken 20 years to hear this advice, but I'm going to give it a try. *Soy yo* and no one else. *Punto.*[1]

---

[1] **Soy yo . . . Punto.** I'm me . . . Period (Spanish). [Editors' note]

Topics for Critical Thinking and Writing

1. When Anna Lisa Raya says she *"discovered"* she was Latina (para. 1), to what kind of event is she referring? Was she coerced or persuaded to declare herself as Latina, or did it come about in some other way? Explain.

2. Is Raya glad or sorry she didn't learn Spanish as a child? What evidence in her essay indicates one way or the other?

3. What is an "identity crisis" (para. 9)? Does everyone go through such a crisis upon entering college? Did you? Or is this an experience that only racial minorities in predominantly white American colleges undergo? Explain your responses.

RONALD TAKAKI

Ronald Takaki (1939–2009), the grandson of agricultural laborers who emigrated from Japan, was a professor of ethnic studies at the University of California–Berkeley. He edited *From Different Shores: Perspectives on Race and Ethnicity in America* (1987) and wrote (among other works) *Strangers from a Different Shore: A History of Asian-Americans* (1989). The essay reprinted here appeared originally in the *New York Times* on June 16, 1990.

The Harmful Myth of Asian Superiority

Asian Americans have increasingly come to be viewed as a "model minority." But are they as successful as claimed? And for whom are they supposed to be a model?

Asian Americans have been described in the media as "excessively, even provocatively" successful in gaining admission to universities. Asian American shopkeepers have been congratulated, as well as criticized, for their ubiquity and entrepreneurial effectiveness.

If Asian Americans can make it, many politicians and pundits ask, why can't African Americans? Such comparisons pit minorities against each other and generate African American resentment toward Asian Americans. The victims are blamed for their plight, rather than racism and an economy that has made many young African American workers superfluous.

The celebration of Asian Americans has obscured reality. For example, figures on the high earnings of Asian Americans relative to Caucasians are misleading. Most Asian Americans live in California, Hawaii, and New York — states with higher incomes and higher costs of living than the national average.

Even Japanese Americans, often touted for 5 their upward mobility, have not reached equality. While Japanese American men in California earned an average income comparable to Caucasian men in 1980, they did so only by acquiring more education and working more hours.

Comparing family incomes is even more deceptive. Some Asian American groups do have higher family incomes than Caucasians. But they have more workers per family.

The "model minority" image homogenizes Asian Americans and hides their differences. For example, while thousands of Vietnamese American young people attend universities, others are on the streets. They live in motels and hang out in pool halls in places like East Los Angeles; some join gangs.

Twenty-five percent of the people in New York City's Chinatown lived below the poverty level in 1980, compared with 17 percent of the city's population. Some 60 percent of the workers in the Chinatowns of Los Angeles and San Francisco are crowded into low-paying jobs in garment factories and restaurants.

"Most immigrants coming into Chinatown with a language barrier cannot go outside this confined area into the mainstream of American industry," a Chinese immigrant said. "Before, I was a painter in Hong Kong, but I can't do it here. I got no license, no education. I want a living; so it's dishwasher, janitor, or cook."

Hmong and Mien refugees from Laos have 10 unemployment rates that reach as high as 80 percent. A 1987 California study showed that three out of ten Southeast Asian refugee families had been on welfare for four to ten years.

Although college-educated Asian Americans are entering the professions and earning good salaries, many hit the "glass ceiling" — the barrier through which high management positions can be seen but not reached. In 1988, only 8 percent of Asian Americans were "officials" and "managers," compared with 12 percent for all groups.

Finally, the triumph of Korean immigrants has been exaggerated. In 1988, Koreans in the New York metropolitan area earned only 68 percent of the median income of non-Asians. More than three-quarters of Korean greengrocers, those so-called paragons of bootstrap entrepreneurialism, came to America with a college education. Engineers, teachers, or administrators while in Korea, they became shopkeepers after their arrival. For many of them, the greengrocery represents dashed dreams, a step downward in status.

For all their hard work and long hours, most Korean shopkeepers do not actually earn very much: $17,000 to $35,000 a year, usually representing the income from the labor of an entire family.

But most Korean immigrants do not become shopkeepers. Instead, many find themselves trapped as clerks in grocery stores, service workers in restaurants, seamstresses in garment factories, and janitors in hotels.

Most Asian Americans know their "suc- 15 cess" is largely a myth. They also see how the celebration of Asian Americans as a "model minority" perpetuates their inequality and exacerbates relations between them and African Americans.

Topics for Critical Thinking and Writing

1. What is the thesis of Ronald Takaki's essay? What evidence does he offer for its truth? Do you find his argument convincing? Explain your answers to these questions.

2. Takaki several times uses statistics to make a point. What effect do the statistics have on the reader? Do some of the statistics seem more convincing than others? Explain your responses.

3. Consider the title of Takaki's essay. To what group(s) is the myth of Asian superiority harmful?

4. Suppose you believed that Asian Americans are economically more successful in America today, relative to white Americans, than African Americans are. Does Takaki agree or disagree with you? Why, or why not? What evidence, if any, does he cite to support or reject the belief?

5. Takaki attacks the "myth" of Asian American success and thus rejects the idea that Asian Americans are a "model minority" (recall the opening and closing paragraphs). Do you think a model is possible to describe any minority group? Why, or why not?

JAMES Q. WILSON

James Q. Wilson (1931–2012) was Collins Professor of Management and Public Policy at the University of California–Los Angeles. Among his books are *Thinking about Crime* (1975), *Bureaucracy* (1989), *The Moral Sense* (1993), and *Moral Judgment* (1997). This essay appeared originally in the *New York Times Magazine* on March 20, 1994.

Just Take Away Their Guns

The president wants still tougher gun control legislation and thinks it will work. The public supports more gun control laws but suspects they won't work. The public is right.

Legal restraints on the lawful purchase of guns will have little effect on the illegal use of guns. There are some 200 million guns in private ownership, about one-third of them handguns. Only about 2 percent of the latter are employed to commit crimes. It would take a Draconian,[1] and politically impossible, confiscation of legally purchased guns to make much of a difference in the number used by criminals. Moreover, only about one-sixth of the handguns used by serious criminals are purchased from a gun shop or pawnshop. Most of these handguns are stolen, borrowed, or obtained through private purchases that wouldn't be affected by gun laws.

What is worse, any successful effort to shrink the stock of legally purchased guns (or of ammunition) would reduce the capacity of law-abiding people to defend themselves. Gun control advocates scoff at the importance of self-defense, but they are wrong to do so. Based on a household survey, Gary Kleck, a criminologist at Florida State University, has estimated that every year, guns are used — that is, displayed or fired — for defensive purposes more than a million times, not counting their

use by the police. If his estimate is correct, this means that the number of people who defend themselves with a gun exceeds the number of arrests for violent crimes and burglaries.

Our goal should not be the disarming of law-abiding citizens. It should be to reduce the number of people who carry guns unlawfully, especially in places — on streets, in taverns — where the mere presence of a gun can increase the hazards we all face. The most effective way to reduce illegal gun-carrying is to encourage the police to take guns away from people who carry them without a permit. This means encouraging the police to make street frisks.

The Fourth Amendment to the Consti- 5 tution bans "unreasonable searches and seizures." In 1968 the Supreme Court decided (*Terry v. Ohio*) that a frisk — patting down a person's outer clothing — is proper if the officer has a "reasonable suspicion" that the person is armed and dangerous. If a pat-down reveals an object that might be a gun, the officer can enter the suspect's pocket to remove it. If the gun is being carried illegally, the suspect can be arrested.

The reasonable-suspicion test is much less stringent than the probable-cause standard the police must meet in order to make an arrest. A reasonable suspicion, however, is more than just a hunch; it must be supported by specific facts. The courts have held, not always consistently, that these facts include

---

[1] **Draconian** Harsh or severe, often excessively so. [Editors' note]

someone acting in a way that leads an experienced officer to conclude criminal activity may be afoot; someone fleeing at the approach of an officer; a person who fits a drug courier profile; a motorist stopped for a traffic violation who has a suspicious bulge in his pocket; a suspect identified by a reliable informant as carrying a gun. The Supreme Court has also upheld frisking people on probation or parole.

Some police departments frisk a lot of people, but usually the police frisk rather few, at least for the purpose of detecting illegal guns. In 1992 the police arrested about 240,000 people for illegally possessing or carrying a weapon. This is only about one-fourth as many as were arrested for public drunkenness. The average police officer will make *no* weapons arrests and confiscate *no* guns during any given year. Mark Moore, a professor of public policy at Harvard University, found that most weapons arrests were made because a citizen complained, not because the police were out looking for guns.

It is easy to see why. Many cities suffer from a shortage of officers, and even those with ample law-enforcement personnel worry about having their cases thrown out for constitutional reasons or being accused of police harassment. But the risk of violating the Constitution or engaging in actual, as opposed to perceived, harassment can be substantially reduced.

Each patrol officer can be given a list of people on probation or parole who live on that officer's beat and be rewarded for making frequent stops to insure that they are not carrying guns. Officers can be trained to recognize the kinds of actions that the Court will accept as providing the "reasonable suspicion" necessary for a stop and frisk. Membership in a gang known for assaults and drug dealing could be made the basis, by statute or Court precedent, for gun frisks.

The available evidence supports the claim 10 that self-defense is a legitimate form of deterrence. People who report to the National Crime Survey that they defended themselves with a weapon were less likely to lose property in a robbery or be injured in an assault than those who did not defend themselves. Statistics have shown that would-be burglars are threatened by gun-wielding victims about as many times a year as they are arrested (and much more often than they are sent to prison) and that the chances of a burglar being shot are about the same as his chances of going to jail. Criminals know these facts even if gun control advocates do not and so are less likely to burgle occupied homes in America than occupied ones in Europe, where the residents rarely have guns.

Some gun control advocates may concede these points but rejoin that the cost of self-defense is self-injury: Handgun owners are more likely to shoot themselves or their loved ones than a criminal. Not quite. Most gun accidents involve rifles and shotguns, not handguns. Moreover, the rate of fatal gun accidents has been declining while the level of gun ownership has been rising. There are fatal gun accidents just as there are fatal car accidents, but in fewer than 2 percent of the gun fatalities was the victim someone mistaken for an intruder.

Those who urge us to forbid or severely restrict the sale of guns ignore these facts. Worse, they adopt a position that is politically absurd. In effect, they say, "Your government, having failed to protect your person and your property from criminal assault, now intends to deprive you of the opportunity to protect yourself."

Opponents of gun control make a different mistake. The National Rifle Association and its allies tell us that "guns don't kill, people kill" and urge the Government to punish more severely people who use guns to commit crimes. Locking up criminals does protect society from future crimes, and the prospect of being locked up may deter criminals. But our experience with meting out tougher sentences is mixed. The tougher the prospective sentence the less likely it is to be imposed, or at least to be imposed swiftly. If the Legislature adds on time for crimes committed with a gun, prosecutors often bargain away the add-ons; even when they do not, the judges in many states are reluctant to impose add-ons.

Worse, the presence of a gun can contribute to the magnitude of the crime even on the part of those who worry about serving a long prison sentence. Many criminals carry guns not to rob stores but to protect themselves from other armed criminals. Gang violence has become more threatening to bystanders as gang members have begun to arm themselves. People may commit crimes, but guns make some crimes worse. Guns often convert spontaneous outbursts of anger into fatal encounters. When some people carry them on the streets, others will want to carry them to protect themselves, and an urban arms race will be under way.

And modern science can be enlisted to 15 help. Metal detectors at airports have reduced the number of airplane bombings and sky-jackings to nearly zero. But these detectors only work at very close range. What is needed is a device that will enable the police to detect the presence of a large lump of metal in someone's pocket from a distance of ten or fifteen feet. Receiving such a signal could supply the officer with reasonable grounds for a pat-down. Underemployed nuclear physicists and electronics engineers in the post-cold-war era surely have the talents for designing a better gun detector.

Even if we do all these things, there will still be complaints. Innocent people will be stopped. Young black and Hispanic men will probably be stopped more often than older white Anglo males or women of any race. But if we are serious about reducing drive-by shootings, fatal gang wars and lethal quarrels in public places, we must get illegal guns off the street. We cannot do this by multiplying the forms one fills out at gun shops or by pretending that guns are not a problem until a criminal uses one.

Topics for Critical Thinking and Writing

1. If you had to single out one sentence in James Wilson's essay that best states his thesis, what sentence would that be? Why do you think it states, better than any other sentence, the essay's thesis?

2. In paragraph 3, Wilson reviews research by a criminologist purporting to show that guns are important for self-defense in American households. Evaluate the evidence: Does the research as reported show that displaying or firing guns in self-defense actually prevented crimes? Or wounded aggressors? Suppose you were also told that in households where guns may be used defensively, thousands of innocent people are injured and hundreds are killed — for instance, children who find a loaded gun and play with it. Would you regard these injuries and deaths as a fair trade-off? Explain. What does the research presented by Wilson really show?

3. In a brief statement, explain the difference between the "reasonable suspicion" test (para. 5) and the "probable cause standard" (para. 6) that the courts use in deciding whether a street frisk is lawful. (You may want to organize your essay into two paragraphs, one on each topic, or perhaps into three if you include a brief introductory paragraph.)

4. Wilson reports in paragraph 7 that the police arrest four times as many drunks on the streets as they do people carrying unlicensed firearms. Does this strike you as absurd, reasonable, or mysterious? Does Wilson explain it to your satisfaction? Why, or why not?

5. In paragraph 12, Wilson says that people who want to severely restrict the ownership of guns are in effect saying, " 'Your government, having failed to protect your person and your property from criminal assault, now intends to deprive you of the opportunity to protect yourself.' " What reply might an advocate of severe restrictions make? (Even if you strongly believe Wilson's summary is accurate, put yourself in the shoes of an advocate of gun control and come up with the best reply that you can.)

6. In his final paragraph, Wilson grants that his proposal entails a difficulty: "Innocent people will be stopped. Young black and Hispanic men will probably be stopped more often than older white Anglo males or women of any race." Assuming that his predictions are accurate, is his proposal therefore fatally flawed and worth no further thought, or (taking the other extreme view) will innocent people who fall into certain classifications just have to put up with frisking for the public good? Explain your response.

BERNIE SANDERS

Bernie Sanders (b. 1941), former mayor of Burlington, Vermont, was elected to the US Congress in 1990, becoming the first independent to win a seat since 1950. In 2006, he won election as US senator from Vermont and, in 2016, made an unsuccessful but widely popular bid to earn the nomination of the Democratic Party for the US presidency. A self-avowed "democratic socialist," Sanders has advocated throughout his life for civil rights and workers' rights.

We Must Make Public Colleges and Universities Tuition Free

Our nation needs the best-educated workforce in the world to succeed in the ever more competitive global economy. Sadly, we are moving further and further away from that goal. As recently as 1995, the United States led the world in college graduation rates, but today we have fallen to 11th place. We are now behind such countries as Japan, South Korea, Canada, England, Ireland, Australia, and Switzerland. Eleventh place is not the place for a great nation like the United States.

Why is this so important? Because fifty years ago, if you had a high school degree, odds were that you could get a decent job and make it into the middle class. But that is no longer the case. While not all middle-class jobs in today's economy require post-secondary education, an increasing number do. By 2020, two-thirds of all jobs in the United States will require some education beyond high school.

And these jobs tend to pay better, too. Nationally, a worker with an associate's degree will earn about $360,000 more over their career than a worker with a high school diploma. And a worker with a bachelor's degree will earn almost $1 million more.

If it makes sense to get a college degree, why aren't more high school students enrolling in and graduating from college? The main reason is because the ever-rising cost of higher education puts college out of reach for many families, or requires students to take on a mountain of debt.

It's time to change that dynamic. It's time to 5 make public colleges and universities tuition-free for the working families of our country. It is time for every child to understand that if they study hard and take their school work seriously they will be able to get a higher education, regardless of their family's income. It's time to reduce the outrageous burden of student debt that is weighing down the lives of millions of college graduates.

Today, our system of higher education is in a state of crisis. As tuition and fees steadily rise and as states cut funding for colleges and universities year after year, American families are finding it increasingly difficult to afford college. Every year, hundreds of thousands of bright young people can't get a higher education because it is simply too expensive. Equally disgraceful, millions of college graduates have had to take on life-long debt for the "crime" of getting the education they need.

Some 44 million Americans already owe more than $1.3 trillion in student loans, and the vast majority of current college students will graduate deeply in debt. For most graduates, this debt will take many years to repay, which not only impacts their career choices, but also their ability to get married, have kids, or buy a home.

In the richest country in the history of the world, everyone who has the desire and the ability should be able to get a college education regardless of their background and ability to pay. That's why I introduced the *College for All Act,* to make public colleges and universities in America tuition-free for families

earning $125,000 per year or less — which covers 86 percent of our population.

This is not a radical idea. Many other nations around the world invest in an educated workforce that isn't burdened with enormous student debt. In Germany, Finland, Denmark, Iceland, Norway, and Sweden public colleges and universities are free. In Germany, public colleges are free not only for Germans, but also for international students.

It wasn't that long ago that our own gov- 10 ernment understood the value of investing in higher education. In 1944, Congress passed the GI Bill, which provided a free college education to millions of World War II veterans. This was one of the most successful pieces of legislation in modern history, laying the groundwork for the extraordinary post-war economic boom and an unprecedented expansion of the middle class.

But it was not just the federal government that acted. In 1965, average tuition at a four-year state public university was just $256, and many excellent colleges — such as the City University of New York — did not charge any tuition at all. The University of California system, considered by many to be the crown jewel of public higher education in this country, did not charge tuition until the 1980s.

The good news is that governors, state legislators, and local officials around the country now understand the crisis and are acting. This year, the City College of San Francisco began offering tuition-free college, and its enrollment for residents is up by 51 percent compared to last year. In New York, tens of thousands will go to the city's public colleges and universities this year without paying tuition. Similar programs have popped up in Tennessee, Oregon, Detroit and Chicago.

We are making progress on this issue, but we still have a long way to go. Making America great is not spending tens of billions more on weapons systems or providing trillions in tax breaks for the very rich. Rather, it is having a well-educated population that can compete in the global economy, and making it possible that every American, regardless of income, has the opportunity to get the education they need to thrive.

Topics for Critical Thinking and Writing

1. Examine the first paragraph of Bernie Sanders's essay and describe Sanders's approach to his argument. How does he use rhetorical appeals? Assumptions? Definition?

2. Use the structure of the syllogism (see Premises and Syllogisms, pp. 81–85) to list a series of premises in Sanders's argument that lead to the conclusion, "Therefore, we must make US colleges and universities tuition free." (Keep in mind that you can list as many premises as you want.) Do you think the argument is *valid*? If you had to work to undermine it, where would you point in the premises to show areas that are challengeable?

3. How does Sanders's argument use emotional appeals (*pathos*)?

4. Do you think Sanders provides a thoughtful consideration of opposing viewpoints? What negative consequences can you think of that might result from passing the College for All Act?

5. Examine Sanders's use of numbers. How does he use numerical data to support his argument? Do you find his presentation of numbers effective or misleading? How might he have presented them differently?

ASSIGNMENTS FOR CRITICAL READING

1. Choose one of the essays in this book and write a rhetorical analysis. In other words, investigate *how* the author makes his or her argument in order to convince the intended audience. Here are some questions to consider as you plan your analysis:

   - What is the writer's claim or thesis?

   - Who is the writer's audience?

   - What is the writer's purpose? What outcome does the writer want to see?

   - In what ways is the argument based on *logos*, *pathos*, or *ethos*? What is the balance of these appeals?

   - What types of support (evidence) is offered on behalf of the claim?

   - What emotions are evoked by the argument and how?

   - How does the writer establish credibility?

   - Are the writer's strategies effective in convincing the intended audience? If not, what should the writer have done differently?

   Use A Checklist for Analyzing an Argument on page 108 to further guide your analysis.

2. Write your own definition for any term or concept you can imagine needing a definition — or *redefinition* — and develop it into a paragraph or full essay using one (or more) of the definition types discussed in this chapter: stipulation, synonym, example, or establishing sufficient and necessary conditions. Here are some ideas to help you. You may also supply your own term or concept or apply this exercise to a current argument you are writing.

hipster culture	American-made car	capital punishment
apocalyptic anxiety	wasting time	alcoholism
the 1960s	being a good neighbor	stereotypes (or stereotypes of *X*)

4

Visual Rhetoric: Thinking about Images as Arguments

"What is the use of a book," thought Alice, "without pictures or conversations?"

— LEWIS CARROLL

All photographs are accurate. None of them is the truth.

— RICHARD AVEDON

Uses of Visual Images

Most visual materials that accompany written arguments serve one of several functions. One of the most common is to appeal to the reader's emotions (e.g., a photograph of a sad-eyed calf in a narrow pen assists an argument against eating veal by inspiring sympathy for the animal). Pictures can also serve as visual evidence, offering proof that something occurred or appeared in a certain way at a certain moment (e.g., a security photograph shows the face of a bank robber to a jury). Pictures can help clarify numerical data (e.g., a graph shows five decades of law school enrollment by males and females). They can also add humor or satire to an essay (a photograph of an executive wearing a blindfold made of dollar bills supports an argument that companies are blinded by their profit motives). In this chapter, we concentrate on thinking critically about visual images. This means reading images in the same way we read print (or electronic) texts: by looking closely at them and discerning not only *what* they show but also *how* and *why* they show what they do and how they convey a particular message or argument.

When we discussed the appeal to emotion, **pathos**, in Chapter 3 (see Persuasion, Argument, and Rhetorical Appeals, pages 75–79), we explained how certain words and ideas can muster the emotions of an audience. Images can do the same without words or with minimal, carefully selected, and thoughtfully displayed words. In a very immediate way, they can make us laugh, cry, or gasp. Furthermore, when used as evidence, some images, graphs, and visuals have an additional advantage over words: They carry a high level of what communications scholars call *indexical value*, meaning that they seem to point to what is true and indisputable.

In courtrooms today, trial lawyers and prosecutors help stir the audience's emotions when they

- hold up a murder weapon for jurors to see,
- introduce victims of crime as witnesses, or
- exhibit images of a bloody corpse or a crime scene.

Whether presented sincerely or gratuitously, visuals can have a significantly persuasive effect. Visuals may be rationally connected to an argument: A gruesome image of a diseased lung in an anti-smoking ad makes a reasonable claim, as does a photograph of crime scene that establishes the veracity of the locations of evidence. But the immediate impact of a photograph is more often on the viewer's heart (*pathos*) rather than mind (*logos*). Speaking of those appeals, we can also say that images can help establish *ethos*: Think about how lawyers might present to the jury images of defendants portrayed in wholesome contexts — receiving an award, hugging a family member — in order to bolster their character or credibility (even if their defendants are actually lacking these qualities).

Like any kind of evidence, images make statements and support arguments. When the US Congress debated whether to allow drilling in the Arctic National Wildlife Refuge (ANWR), opponents and supporters both used images to support their verbal arguments:

- *Opponents* of drilling showed beautiful pictures of polar bears frolicking, wildflowers in bloom, and caribou on the move, arguing that such a landscape would be despoiled.
- *Proponents* of drilling showed bleak pictures of what they called "barren land" and "a frozen wasteland," pointing to a useless and barely habitable environment.

Both sides knew very well that images are powerfully persuasive, and they didn't hesitate to use them as supplements to words.

These two photographs, both of the Arctic National Wildlife Refuge, show different uses of images to argue about the value and use of land.

We invite you to reflect upon the appropriateness of using such images in arguments. Was either side manipulating the "reality" of the ANWR? Both images were *real*, after all. Each side selected a particular *kind* of image for a specific **purpose** — to support its position on drilling in the ANWR. Neither side was being dishonest, and both were showing true pictures, but both were also appealing to emotions.

Exercise: Responding to Images

In a paragraph, discuss how these images of the ANWR offer reasonable support (*logos*) and emotional support (*pathos*) for an argument. Go further: Examine the source of the photographs and also discuss how *ethos* is established.

TYPES OF EMOTIONAL APPEALS

After reading Chapter 3, you understand much about how arguments appeal to reason through induction and deduction, by definitions and examples, by drawing conclusions, and so forth. You also learned something about *persuasion*, which is a broad term that can include appeals to various kinds of emotions — for example, an **appeal to pity**, such as the image of a sad-eyed calf mentioned at the beginning of this chapter. You might be moved emotionally by such an image and say, "Well, I am never eating meat again because doing so implies the inhumane treatment of helpless animals," and regard the image as both *reasonable* and *emotionally powerful*. Or you might say, "Although it's emotionally powerful, this image doesn't describe the condition of every calf. Some are treated humanely, slaughtered humanely, and eaten ethically." In your argument, you might include an alternative image of a pasture-raised calf on an organic, locally owned farm (although you too would be appealing to emotions).

The point is that images can be persuasive even if they don't make good or complete arguments. The gangster Al Capone famously said, "You can get a lot more done with a kind word and a gun than with a kind word alone." A threat of violence — do this *or else* — is actually a *kind* of an argument, just one that appeals exclusively to the emotions — specifically, to fear.

Although they do not threaten violence, advertisers commonly use the **appeal to fear** as a persuasive technique. The appeal to fear is a threat of sorts. Showing a scary burglary, a visceral car crash, embarrassing age spots, or a nasty cockroach infestation can successfully convince consumers to buy a product — a home security system, a new car insurance policy, an age-defying skin cream, a pesticide. Such images generate fear and anxiety at the same time they offer the solution for it.

However, appeals to fear — like all the appeals we will discuss — are not confined to the world of advertising. Appeals to fear often drive political arguments, especially during a campaign season. Even arguments about art and culture can utilize fear to support an argument. In 1985, the Parents Music Resource Center (PMRC), founded by Tipper Gore (then wife of politician Al Gore), argued that some popular music was undermining society

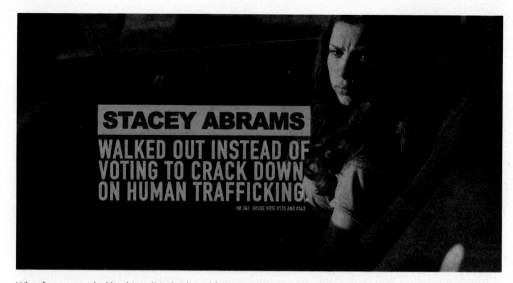

What fears are evoked by this political video ad from Georgia, distributed during the 2018 midterm elections?

by promoting occult beliefs, precocious sexuality, and drug and alcohol use. After a US Senate hearing was convened, the PMRC successfully lobbied the recording industry to require "Parental Advisory" warnings on all music deemed inappropriate for children.

There are different kinds of fear to which writers can appeal. Appeals to fear are at work in a recently named phenomenon called FOMO, or Fear of Missing Out, which occurs when someone adopts the latest trends, attends events, or otherwise engages in some activity because they worry about not being part of it. FOMO occurs too when we are hurried to take advantage of a scarce or limited-time opportunity.

Violence and fear can also support arguments made to end acts of terror and cruelty. Images played a crucial role in the antislavery movement in the nineteenth century. The collection shown on page 135 offers three different types of visuals and three depictions of the slave experience. The first is a diagram showing how human cargo was packed into a slave ship; it was distributed with Thomas Clarkson's *Essay on the Slavery and Commerce of the Human Species* (1804), one of the first antislavery treatises. Following is Civil War surgeon Frederick W. Mercer's photograph (April 2, 1863) of Gordon, a "badly lacerated" runaway slave. Images such as the slave ship and the runaway slave worked against slave owners' claims that slavery was a humane institution — claims that also were supported by illustrations, such as the woodcut *Attention Paid to a Poor Sick Negro* from Josiah Priest's *In Defence of Slavery* (1843). Examine each picture closely and consider whether you think they make appeals to reason or emotion.

Appeal to self-interest is another persuasive tactic that speakers and writers can use. Consider these remarks, which use the word *interest* in the sense of "self-interest":

Diagram "Description of a Slave Ship," distributed with Thomas Clarkson's *Essay on the Slavery and Commerce of the Human Species* (1804).

Frederick W. Mercer's photograph (April 2, 1863) of Gordon, a "badly lacerated" runaway slave.

Attention Paid to a Poor Sick Negro, a woodcut from Josiah Priest's *In Defense of Slavery* (1843).

Would you persuade, speak of Interest, not Reason. — BENJAMIN FRANKLIN

There are two levers for moving men — interest and fear. — NAPOLEON BONAPARTE

Appeals to self-interest may be quite persuasive because they speak directly to what benefits *you* the most, not necessarily what benefits others in the community, society, or world. Such appeals are also common in advertising. "You can save bundles by shopping at Maxi-Mart," a commercial might claim, without making reference to third-world sweatshop labor conditions in the supply chain, the negative impact of global commerce, or other troublesome aspects of what you see only as a great savings for yourself. Maxi-Mart would never say, "Maxi-Mart offers low prices by buying products made cheaply on the other side of the world and shipping them to the United States on inefficient fuel-guzzling cargo ships."

You may be familiar with other types of advertising that speak to the senses more than reason. These kinds of appeals don't necessarily make *good* arguments for the products in question, but they can be highly persuasive — sometimes affecting us subconsciously — because they speak so much to our individual feelings and interests. Of course, as with all appeals, those made to self-interest can be seen in all kinds of arguments, but the appeals of advertisements are often so blunt and obvious that they help us highlight their effects. Thinking critically about appeals in advertisements can be helpful then in developing our ability to analyze other basic kinds of appeals in words and other kinds of images.

Here is a list of some other emotional appeals commonly used in advertising:

- sexual appeals (e.g., a bikini-clad model standing near a product)
- bandwagon appeals (e.g., crowds of people rushing to a sale)
- humor appeals (e.g., a cartoon animal drinking *X* brand of beverage)
- celebrity appeals (e.g., a famous person driving *X* brand of car)
- testimonial appeals (e.g., a doctor giving *X* brand of vitamins to her kids)
- identity appeals (e.g., a "good family" going to *X* restaurant)
- prejudice appeals (e.g., a "loser" drinking *X* brand of beer)
- lifestyle appeals (e.g., a jar of *X* brand of mustard on a silver platter)
- stereotype appeals (e.g., a Latinx person enjoying *X* brand of salsa)
- patriotic appeals (e.g., *X* brand of mattress alongside an American flag)

Exercise: Emotional Appeals in Visual Arguments

Select two of the appeals listed above and think of another real-life instance outside advertising in which the type of appeal occurs, either in words or images. For example, images of former pro football quarterback Colin Kaepernick have been used to appeal to the patriotism of audiences in arguments about the appropriateness of his dissent: kneeling on the football field during the national anthem to protest police violence against African Americans.

Seeing versus Looking: Reading Advertisements

Advertising is one of the most common forms of visual persuasion we encounter in everyday life. The influence of advertising in our culture is pervasive and subtle. Part of its power comes from our habit of internalizing the intended messages of words and images without thinking deeply about them. Once we begin decoding the ways in which advertisements are constructed — once we view them critically — we can understand how (or if) they work as arguments. We may then make better decisions about whether to buy particular products and what factors convinced us or failed to convince us. Further, by sharpening our critical skills, we can approach images in all their forms with a more careful and skeptical approach.

To read any image critically, it helps to consider some basic rules from the field of **semiotics,** the study of signs and symbols. Fundamental to semiotic analysis is the idea that visual signs have shared meanings in a culture. If you approach a sink and see a red faucet and a blue faucet, you can be pretty sure which one will produce hot water and which one will produce cold water. Thus, one of the first strategies we can use in reading advertisements critically is **deconstructing** them, taking them apart to see what makes them work.

For starters, it's helpful to remember that advertisements are enormously expensive to produce and disseminate, so nothing is left to chance. Teams of people typically scrutinize every part of an advertisement to ensure it communicates the intended message — although this doesn't imply that viewers must accept those messages. Taking apart an advertisement (or any image) means examining each visual element carefully in order to understand its purpose, its strategy, and effect.

Consider this 2007 advertisement for Nike shoes featuring basketball star LeBron James. Already, you should see the celebrity appeal — an implicit claim that Nike shoes

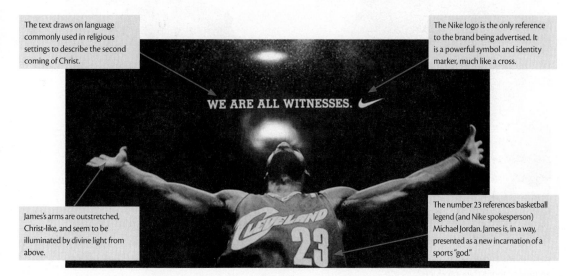

A Nike advertisement featuring basketball star Lebron James, annotated to show a deconstruction of the image.

help make James a star player. The ad creates an association between the shoes and the sports champion. But look closer, paying attention to how the elements work together to make meaning.

Let's also consider this advertisement in the context of James's famous 2014 return to the Cleveland Cavaliers, his hometown team, after leaving the team abruptly to play four seasons with the Miami Heat. James's own second coming resonated with themes of forgiveness, redemption, and salvation among Cleveland sports fans. In 2018, James signed with the Los Angeles Lakers in free agency. In one of his first public statements about his decision, James said, "I believe the Lakers is a historical franchise, we all know that, but it's a championship franchise and that's what we're trying to get back to. And I'm happy to be part of the culture and be a part of us getting back to that point." Considering these comments, we wonder if this same image of James in a Lakers jersey would have the same resonance.

In the ad on p. 137, all these associations work together to elevate James, Jordan, and Nike to exalted status. Of course, our description here is tongue in cheek. We're not gullible enough to believe this literally, and the ad's producers don't expect us to be; but they do hope that such an impression will be powerful enough to make us think of Nike the next time we shop for athletic shoes. If sports gods wear Nike, why shouldn't we?

This kind of analysis is possible when we recognize a difference between *seeing* and *looking*. **Seeing** is a physiological process involving light, the eye, and the brain. **Looking**, however, is a social process involving the mind. It suggests apprehending an image in terms

How do the DKNY and Bulova advertisements use the symbolic, connotative meanings of the apple to make an argument about their products?

of symbolic, metaphorical, and other social and cultural meanings. To do this, we must think beyond the *literal* meaning of an image or image element and consider its *figurative* meanings. If you look up *apple* in the dictionary, you'll find its literal, **denotative** meaning — a round fruit with thin red or green skin and a crisp flesh. But an apple also communicates figurative, **connotative** meanings. Connotative meanings are the cultural or emotional associations that an image suggests.

The connotative meaning of an apple in Western culture dates back to the biblical story of the Garden of Eden, where Eve, tempted by a serpent, eats the fruit from the forbidden tree of knowledge and brings about the end of paradise on earth. Throughout Western culture, apples have come to represent knowledge and the pursuit of knowledge. Think of the ubiquitous Apple logo gracing so many mobile phones, tablets, and laptops: With its prominent bite, it symbolizes the way technology opens up new worlds of knowing. Sometimes, apples represent forbidden knowledge, temptation, or seduction — and biting into one suggests giving in to desires for new understandings and experiences. The story of Snow White offers just one example of an apple used as a symbol of temptation.

When you are looking — and not just seeing in the simplest sense — you are attempting to discern the ways in which symbolic meanings are used to communicate a message. Take, for example, the following advertisement for Play-Doh, one of the most enduring and popular toys of the past century. First developed in 1930s, Play-Doh has sold billions of canisters around the world. Today, Play-Doh competes with a wide array of technological toys for children, such as smartphones and video game systems.

The ad for Play-Doh featured here makes an argument with just a single line of text: "No In-App Purchases." These words are set below the image of a shopping cart with a plus sign made of Play-Doh, which has come to be an almost universally recognized symbol for an electronic shopping cart online. Both the words and the icon are textured and look a little rough at the edges, suggesting that they are also made of Play-Doh. In a blue open space suggesting three-dimensionality, the advertisement seems to make a case for the role of real-life,

An advertisement for the timeless toy, Play-Doh, that takes on its digital competitors.

non-digital play in the development of children. It presents Play-Doh as a traditional, value-based proposition without manipulative sales tactics, something trustworthy and honest. The way children play has changed dramatically since the 1930s, but by fashioning the electronic icon and text out of a nearly century-old product, the ad implies that just because a toy — or anything else — is new and high-tech, that does not make it inherently better than old-fashioned things. After all, the product being advertised has stood the test of time; how long will an app on a smartphone or tablet last until it is replaced with a newer version requiring a new update?

Levels of Images

One helpful way of deriving the meanings of images by *looking* at them is to use *seeing* first as a way to define what is plainly or literally present in them. You can begin by *seeing* — identifying the elements that are indisputably "there" in an image (the denotative level). In a sense, you are merely taking an inventory of what is visible and evident. Then you move on to *looking* — interpreting the meanings suggested by the elements that are present (the connotative level). Arguably, when we *see*, we pay attention only to the denotative level — that is, we observe just the explicit elements of the image. We aren't concerned with the meaning of the image's elements yet, just with the fact that they're present.

When we *look*, we move to the connotative level — that is, we speculate on the elements' deeper meanings: what they suggest figuratively, symbolically, or metaphorically in our cultural system. We may also consider the relationship of different elements to one another.

Seeing	Looking
Denotation	Connotation
Literal	Figurative
What is present	What it means
Understanding/Textual	Interpreting/Subtextual/Contextual

Further questions we can ask have to do with the contexts in which they are created, disseminated, and received. Within each of those, other questions arise.

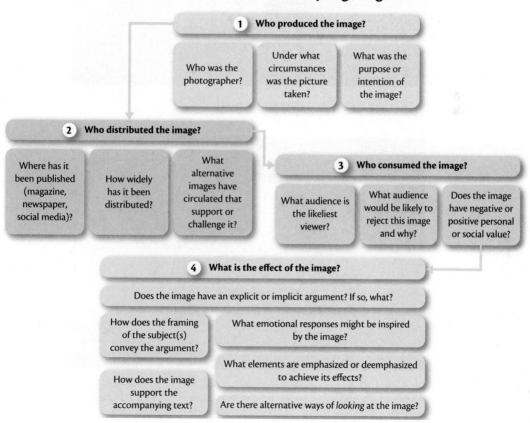

Visual Guide: Analyzing Images

1 Who produced the image?

- Who was the photographer?
- Under what circumstances was the picture taken?
- What was the purpose or intention of the image?

2 Who distributed the image?

- Where has it been published (magazine, newspaper, social media)?
- How widely has it been distributed?
- What alternative images have circulated that support or challenge it?

3 Who consumed the image?

- What audience is the likeliest viewer?
- What audience would be likely to reject this image and why?
- Does the image have negative or positive personal or social value?

4 What is the effect of the image?

- Does the image have an explicit or implicit argument? If so, what?
- How does the framing of the subject(s) convey the argument?
- What emotional responses might be inspired by the image?
- What elements are emphasized or deemphasized to achieve its effects?
- How does the image support the accompanying text?
- Are there alternative ways of *looking* at the image?

Exercise: Seeing versus Looking

Examine the images below and do the following:

1. *See* the image. Thoroughly describe the image. Write down as many elements as possible that you see: colors, shapes, text, people, objects, lighting, framing, perspective, and so forth.

2. *Look* at the image. Take the elements you have observed and relate what they suggest by considering their figurative meanings, their meanings in relation to one another, and their meanings in the context of the images' production and consumption.

Ferdinando Scianna/Magnum Photos

Cattle grazing in a California pasture near a wind farm in 1996.

Moms Demand Action, a national public safety advocacy group against gun violence, published this advertisement in 2013. The text reads, "One child is holding something that's been banned in America to protect them. Guess which one."

Documenting Reality: Reading Photographs

As we learned with the uses of images relating to the Arctic National Wildlife Refuge (see p. 132), photographs can serve as evidence but have a peculiar relationship to the truth. We must never forget that images are constructed, selected, and used for specific purposes.

When advertisers use images, we know they're trying to convince consumers to purchase a product or service. But when images serve as documentary evidence, we often assume that they're showing the "truth" of the matter at hand. When we see an image in the newspaper or a magazine, we may assume that it captures a particular event or moment in time *as it really happened*. Our level of skepticism may be lower than when we are looking at images designed to persuade us.

But these kind of images — historical images, images of events, news photographs, and the like — are not free from the potential for manipulation or for (conscious or unconscious) bias. Consider how liberal and conservative media sources portray the nation's president in images: One source may show him proud and smiling in bright light with the American flag behind him, whereas another might show him scowling in a darkened image suggestive of evil intent. Both are "real" images, but the framing, tinting, setting, and background can inspire significantly different responses in viewers.

As we saw with the image of LeBron James, certain postures, facial expressions, and settings can contribute to a photograph's interpretation. Martin Luther King Jr.'s great speech of August 28, 1963, "I Have a Dream," still reads very well on the page, but part of its immense appeal derives from its setting: King spoke to some 200,000 people in Washington, DC, as he stood on the steps of the Lincoln Memorial. That setting, rich with associations of slavery and freedom, strongly assists King's argument. In fact, images of King delivering his speech are nearly inseparable from the very argument he was making. The visual aspects — the setting (the Lincoln Memorial with the Washington Monument and the Capitol in the distance) and King's gestures — are part of the speech's persuasive rhetoric.

Derrick Alridge, a historian, examined dozens of accounts of Martin Luther King Jr. in history books, and he found that images of King present him overwhelmingly as a messianic figure — standing before crowds, leading them, addressing them in postures reminiscent of a prophet. Although King is an admirable figure, Alridge asserts, history books err by presenting him as more than human. Doing so ignores his personal struggles and failures and makes a myth out of the real man. This myth suggests he was the epicenter of the civil rights movement, an effort that was actually conducted in different ways via different strategies on the part of many other figures whom King eclipsed. We may even get the idea that the entire civil rights movement began and ended with

Martin Luther King Jr. delivering his "I Have a Dream" speech on August 28, 1963, from the steps of the Lincoln Memorial.

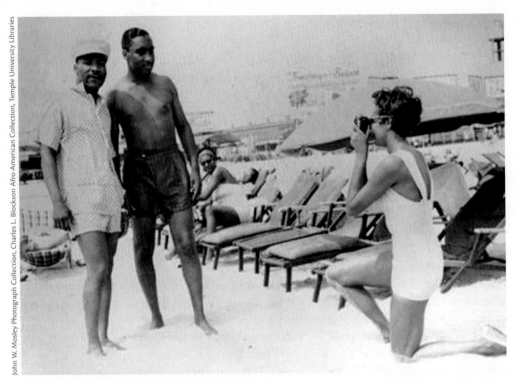

Martin Luther King Jr. on "Chicken Bone Beach" in Atlantic City.

King alone. When history books present King as a holy prophet, Alridge argues, it becomes easier to focus on his gospel of love, equality, and justice and not on the specific policies and politics he advocated — his avowed socialist stances, for instance. In short, while photographs of King seek to help us remember, they may actually portray him in a way that causes us to forget other things — for example, that his approval rating among whites at the time of his death was lower than 30 percent and among blacks lower than 50 percent.

A WORD ON "ALTERNATIVE FACTS"

All this discussion of "seeing and looking" is intended to underscore how much photographs that seem to provide a clear window into reality are not absolute guarantors of truth. How images are selected, created, and circulated has much to do with their meaning and value. Furthermore, in the digital age, it's remarkably easy to alter photographs. Because of this, we have become more suspicious of photographs as direct evidence of reality. We retain our skepticism when we encounter images of celebrities on the internet who have been obviously "Photoshopped." However, we sometimes do not anticipate the degree to which all kinds of published images may be altered for persuasive purposes. When those purposes are the result of political or ideological bias, we are particularly vulnerable to misinformation because of our assumptions about the reality or truth-value of images.

One memorable moment brings to light how disputes over the truth of images matter. During the inauguration of President Donald Trump, some media outlets were accused by the president of deliberately downplaying the crowd size by comparing images of that day to images of larger crowds at the 2009 Obama inaugural. "[W]e caught them [the media] in a real beauty," the president said. Probably referring to a tweet by the *New York Times* showing side-by-side images of the two inaugurals, White House Press Secretary Sean Spicer said that the photographs "were intentionally framed . . . to minimize the enormous support that had gathered on the National Mall."

Spicer's claim may or may not have been true, but he insisted that "this was the largest audience ever to witness an inauguration, period." He referred to what his colleague Kellyanne Conway now famously called "alternative facts": his calculations of the crowd size, the ridership levels on the DC Metro system, and images of the inauguration ceremony produced by the National Park Service, which had been cropped in such a way as to depict a larger crowd size.

We think this story gets us to the heart of what is meant by alternative facts. To be blunt, the phrase simply

A *New York Times* tweet comparing the crowd sizes at the Obama and Trump inaugurals in 2009 and 2017 drew the ire of the White House, which accused the media of bias.

AP Photo/Patrick Semansky

Empty spaces were cropped out of this image produced by the National Park Service at the White House's request for more flattering images of the crowd size at the 2017 inauguration. These images were subsequently released to media outlets.

means alternative *beliefs* or alternative *forms of evidence* that people present as facts. Although two contradictory facts can't be true, two depictions of the same event may be presented, and therefore seen and interpreted, as factual. To counteract our own tendency to think that "seeing is believing," we can be more critical about images by approaching them through three broad frameworks: accommodation, resistance, and negotiation.

Accommodating, Resisting, and Negotiating the Meaning of Images

Most images are produced, selected, and published so as to have a specific effect on readers and viewers. This dominant meaning of an image supposes that the audience will react in a predictable way or take away a specific message, usually based on the widespread **cultural codes** that operate within a society. Images of elegant women in designer dresses, rugged men driving pickup trucks, stodgy teachers, cutthroat CEOs, hipster computer programmers, and so on speak to generally accepted notions of what certain types of people are like. An image of a suburban couple in an automobile advertisement washing their new car subconsciously confirms and perpetuates a certain ideal of middle-class suburban life (a heterosexual couple, a well-trimmed lawn, a neatly painted house and picket fence — and a brand-new midsize sedan). An image of a teary-eyed young woman accepting a diamond ring from a handsome man will likely touch the viewer in a particular way, in part because of our society's cultural codes about the rituals of romantic love and marriage, gender roles, and the diamond ring as a sign of love and commitment.

These examples demonstrate that images can be constructed according to dominant connotations of gender, class, and racial, sexual, and political identity. When analyzing an image, ask yourself what cultural codes it endorses, what ideals it establishes as natural, and what social norms or modes of everyday life it idealizes or assumes.

As image consumers, we often **accommodate** (i.e., passively accept) those messages and cultural codes promoted by media images. For example, in the hypothetical advertisement featuring a marriage proposal — a man kneeling, a woman crying sentimentally — you might not decide to buy a diamond, but you might accept the messages that diamond rings are the appropriate objects to represent love and commitment. Further, you might accept the cultural codes about the rituals of romantic love, marriage, and gender roles, sharing the assumption that men should propose to women and that women are more emotional than men.

When you *accommodate* cultural codes without understanding them critically, you allow the media that perpetuate these codes to interpret the world for you. That is, you accept their interpretations without questioning the social and cultural values implicit in their assumptions, many of which may actually run counter to your own or others' social and cultural values. When analyzing an image, ask yourself what cultural codes it endorses, what ideals it establishes as natural, and what social norms it assumes or idealizes.

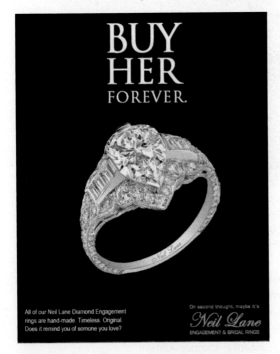

What cultural codes does this ad accommodate?

If you **resist** the cultural codes of an image, you actively criticize its message and meaning. Suppose you (1) question how the ad presents gender roles and marriage, (2) claim that it idealizes heterosexual marriage, and (3) point out that it confirms and extends traditional gender roles in which men are active and bold and women are passive and emotional. Moreover, you (4) argue that the diamond ring represents a misguided commodification of love because diamonds are kept deliberately scarce by large companies and, as such, are overvalued and overpriced; meanwhile, you say, the ad prompts young couples to spend precious money at a time when their joint assets might be better saved, and because many diamonds come from third-world countries under essentially slave labor conditions, the diamond is more a symbol of oppression than of love. If your analysis follows such paths, you *resist* the dominant message of the image in question. Sometimes, this is called an *oppositional reading*.

Negotiation, or a *negotiated reading*, the most useful mode of reading and viewing, involves a middle path — a process of revision that seeks to recognize and change the conditions that give rise to certain negative aspects of cultural codes. Negotiation implies a practical intervention into common viewing processes that help construct and maintain social conditions and relations. A negotiated reading enables you to emphasize the ways in which individuals, social groups, and others relate to images and their dominant meanings and how different personal and cultural perspectives can challenge those meanings. This intervention can be important when inequalities or stereotypes are perpetuated by cultural codes. Without intervention, there can be no revision, no positive social or cultural change. You *negotiate* cultural codes when:

- you understand the underlying messages of images and accept the general cultural implications of these codes, *but*

- you acknowledge that in some circumstances the general codes do not apply.

Memes often use humor to present oppositional ideas. However, in doing so, they sometimes reaffirm other cultural codes and assumptions.

The Saturday Evening Post

LEGO...the most creative adventure you can give to a child

Colorful, durable, snap-together tiles that can build almost anything.
Snap...and build. Snap again...and build again. New fun every day!

Lego is Imagination. Expression. Experiment. Creating. It's the most
doing-making-building-thinking way to play that's ever been devised. Put
magical Lego into the hands of a five-year-old and the will make you a
camel. A little boy will turn his Lego into an airplane on Monday... snap
apart and it's a train on Tuesday, a skyscraper on Wednesday. A twelve-
year-old might even build a whole city! There's great adventure in each box
of these smooth, shiny, plastic tiles. For Christmas stockings $1.95, $2.95,
$4.95 sets. Lots more pieces in the $7.95, $10.95, $16.95 sets. Enough
Lego to build a town in the big $25.00 set. Supplemental kits with choice
of all Lego parts including extra trees, gas pumps, etc., available at 50¢.

A product of Sineapher Bros., Inc., Denver 17, Colo. In Canada Elio Samsonite of Canada, Ltd., Stratford, Ont. Prices slightly higher.

LEGO System by Samsonite®

Exercise: Accommodating, Resisting, and Negotiating Images

Examine the image shown here of an advertisement for Lego building blocks or choose your own ad, PSA, or other image. Provide brief examples of how a viewer could accommodate, resist, or negotiate the images in the add.

Are Some Images Not Fit to Be Shown?: Politics and Pictures

Images of suffering — either human or animal — can be immensely persuasive. In the nineteenth century, for instance, the antislavery movement made extremely effective use of images in its campaign. We reproduced two antislavery images earlier in this chapter, as well as a counterimage that sought to assure viewers that slavery was a beneficent system (p. 135). But are there some images not fit to print?

Until recently, many newspapers did not print pictures of lynched African Americans, hanged and burned and maimed. The reasons for not printing such images probably differed between South and North: Southern papers may have considered the images to be discreditable to whites, and northern papers may have deemed the images too revolting. Even today, when it's commonplace for newspapers and television news to show pictures of dead victims of war, famine, or traffic accidents, one rarely sees bodies that are horribly maimed. (For traffic accidents, the body is usually covered, and we see only the smashed car.) The US government refused to release photographs showing the bodies of American soldiers killed in the war in Iraq, and it was most reluctant to show pictures of dead Iraqi soldiers and civilians. Only after many Iraqis refused to believe that former Iraqi president Saddam Hussein's two sons had been killed did the US government reluctantly release pictures showing the two men's blood-spattered faces — and some American newspapers and television programs refused to use the images.

There have been notable exceptions to this practice, such as Huynh Cong (Nick) Ut's 1972 photograph of children fleeing a napalm attack in Vietnam (p. 149), which was widely reproduced in the United States and won the photographer a Pulitzer Prize in 1973. It's impossible to measure the influence of this particular photograph, but many people believe that it played a substantial role in increasing public pressure to end the Vietnam War. Another widely reproduced picture of horrifying violence is Eddie Adams's 1968 picture (p. 150) of a South Vietnamese chief of police allied with the United States firing a pistol into the head of a Viet Cong prisoner.

Huynh Cong (Nick) Ut, *The Terror of War: Children on Route 1 near Trang Bang*, 1972.

The issue remains: Are some images unacceptable? For instance, although capital punishment — by methods including lethal injection, hanging, shooting, and electrocution — is legal in parts of the United States, every state prohibits the publication of pictures showing the execution.

AN ARGUMENT ON PUBLISHING IMAGES

A twenty-first-century example concerning the appropriateness of showing certain images arose early in 2006. In September 2005, a Danish newspaper, accused of being afraid to show political cartoons that were hostile to Muslim terrorists, responded by publishing twelve cartoons. One cartoon showed the prophet Muhammad wearing a turban that looked like a bomb. The images at first didn't arouse much attention, but when they were reprinted in Norway in January 2006, they attracted worldwide attention and outraged Muslims, most of whom regard any depiction of Muhammad as blasphemous. Some Muslims in various Islamic nations burned Danish embassies and engaged in other acts of violence. Most non-Muslims agreed that the images were in bad taste, and, apparently in deference to Islamic sensibilities (but possibly also out of fear of reprisals), very few Western newspapers reprinted the cartoons when they covered the news events. Most newspapers (including the *New York Times*) merely described the images. The editors of these papers believed that readers should be told the news, but that because the drawings were so offensive to some persons, they should be described rather than reprinted. A controversy then arose: Do readers of a newspaper deserve to *see* the evidence for themselves, or can a newspaper adequately fulfill its mission by offering only a verbal description? These questions arose again after the 2007 bombing of

Eddie Adams, *Execution of Viet Cong Prisoner, Saigon*, 1968.

the French satirical newspaper *Charlie Hebdo* and then after another mass shooting at the same newspaper in 2015 that claimed the lives of twelve editors and staff members.

Persons who argued that the images should be reproduced in the media generally made these points:

- Newspapers should yield neither to the delicate sensibilities of some readers nor to threats of violence.

- Jews for the most part do not believe that God should be depicted (the prohibition against "graven images" appears in Exodus 20.3), but they raise no objections to such Christian images as the ceiling of the Sistine Chapel. Further, when Andres Serrano (a Christian) in 1989 exhibited a photograph of a small plastic crucifix submerged in urine, it outraged a wider public (several US senators condemned it because the artist had received federal funds), but virtually all newspapers showed the image, and many even printed its title, *Piss Christ*. The subject was judged to be newsworthy, and the fact that some viewers would regard the image as blasphemous was not considered highly relevant.

- Our society values freedom of speech, and newspapers should not be intimidated. When certain pictures are a matter of news, readers should be able to see them.

In contrast, opposing voices made these points:

- Newspapers must recognize deep-seated religious beliefs. They should indeed report the news, but there is no reason to *show* images that some people regard as blasphemous. The images can be adequately *described* in words.

- The Jewish response to Christian images of God, and even the tolerant Christians' response to Serrano's image of the crucifix immersed in urine, are irrelevant to the issue of whether a Western newspaper should represent images of the prophet Muhammad. Virtually all Muslims regard depictions of Muhammad as blasphemous, and that's what counts.

- Despite all the Western talk about freedom of the press, the press does *not* reproduce all images that become matters of news. For instance, news items about the sale of child pornography do not include images of the pornographic photos.

Exercises: Thinking about Images

1. In June 2006, two American soldiers were captured in Iraq. Later their bodies were found, dismembered and beheaded. Should newspapers have shown photographs of the mutilated bodies? Why, or why not? (In July 2006, insurgents in Iraq posted images on the internet showing a soldier's severed head beside his body.)

2. Hugh Hewitt, an Evangelical Christian, offered a comparison to the cartoon of Muhammad wearing a bomb-like turban. Suppose, he asked, an abortion clinic were bombed by someone claiming to be an Evangelical Christian. Would newspapers publish "a cartoon of Christ's crown of thorns transformed into sticks of TNT"? Do you think they would? If you were the editor of a newspaper, would you? Why, or why not?

3. A week after the 2015 attack on *Charlie Hebdo*, and in response to media hesitancy to republish the offending images of Muhammad, the Index on Censorship and several other journalistic organizations called for all newspapers to publish them simultaneously and globally on January 8, 2015. "This unspeakable act of violence has challenged and assailed the entire press," said Lucie Morillon of Reporters Without Borders. "Journalism as a whole is in mourning. In the name of all those who have fallen in the defense of these fundamental values, we must continue *Charlie Hebdo*'s fight for the right to freedom of information." Evaluate this position.

4. Examine the image shown here by photojournalist Paul Fusco of the November 22, 2003, funeral for Sgt. Scott C. Rose, who was killed in Iraq. In an argumentative essay of about 500 words, argue your view on this photograph. Is such a photograph so intimately personal that it should not be made public? What possible uses of this photograph can you imagine?

© Paul Fusco/Magnum Photos

Writing about Political Cartoons

Most editorial pages print political cartoons as well as editorials. Like the writers of editorials, cartoonists seek to persuade, but they rarely use words to *argue* a point. True, they may use a few words in speech balloons or in captions, but generally the drawing does most of the work. Because their aim usually is to convince the viewer that some person's action or proposal is ridiculous, cartoonists almost always **caricature** their subjects: They exaggerate the subject's distinctive features to the point at which the subject becomes grotesque and ridiculous — absurd, laughable, contemptible.

We agree that it's unfair to suggest that because, say, a politician who proposes a new law dresses in outdated clothes and has a distinctive jawline, his proposal is ridiculous, but that's the way cartoonists work. Further, cartoonists are concerned with producing a striking image, not with exploring an issue, so they almost always oversimplify, implying that there really is no other sane view.

In the course of saying that (1) the figures in a cartoon are ridiculous and *therefore* their ideas are contemptible and (2) there is only one side to the issue, cartoonists often use **symbolism**. Here's a list of common symbols:

- symbolic figures (e.g., the US government as Uncle Sam)
- animals (e.g., the Democratic Party as donkey and the Republican Party as elephant)
- buildings (e.g., the White House as representing the nation's president)
- things (e.g., a bag with a dollar sign on it as representing a bribe)

For anyone brought up in American culture, these symbols (like the human figures they represent) are obvious, and cartoonists assume that viewers will instantly recognize the symbols and figures, will get the joke, and will see the absurdity of whatever issue the cartoonist is seeking to demolish.

In writing about the argument presented in a cartoon, normally you will discuss the ways in which the cartoon makes its point. Caricature usually implies, "This is ridiculous, as you can plainly see by the absurdity of the figures depicted" or "What *X*'s proposal adds up to, despite its apparent complexity, is nothing more than . . ." As we have said, this sort of persuasion, chiefly by ridicule, probably is unfair: Almost always the issue is more complicated than the cartoonist indicates. But cartoons work largely by ridicule and the omission of counterarguments, and we shouldn't reject the possibility that the cartoonist has indeed highlighted the absurdity of the issue.

In analyzing the cartoon and determining the cartoonist's attitude, consider the following elements:

- the relative size of the figures in the image
- the quality of the lines (e.g., thin and spidery, thick and seemingly aggressive)

- the amount of empty space in comparison with the amount of heavily inked space (a drawing with lots of inky areas conveys a more oppressive tone than a drawing that's largely open)
- the degree to which text is important, as well as its content and tone (e.g., witty, heavy-handed)

Your essay will likely include an *evaluation* of the cartoon. Indeed, the *thesis* underlying your analytic/argumentative essay may be that the cartoon is effective (persuasive) for such-and-such reasons but unfair for such-and-such other reasons.

The cartoon by Pulitzer Prize–winning cartoonist Walt Handelsman responds to recent breaches of political decorum. It depicts a group of Washington, DC, tourists being driven past what the guide calls "The Museum of Modern American Political Discourse," a building in the shape of a giant toilet. The toilet as a symbol of the level of political discussion dominates the cartoon, effectively driving home the point that Americans are watching our leaders sink to new lows as they debate the future of our nation. By drawing the toilet on a scale similar to that of familiar monuments in Washington, Handelsman may be pointing out that today's politicians, rather than being remembered for great achievements like those of George Washington or Abraham Lincoln, will instead be remembered for their rudeness and aggression. If you were accommodating the meaning of this cartoon, you might agree with Handelsman, but if you were resisting its message, you could point out that it blames politicians solely for the state of political discourse and portrays the "people" as separate from it (or subject to it); however, as we must recognize, political discourse is also in bad shape among the people themselves, too.

Walt Handelsman/Chicago Tribune/TNS

THINKING CRITICALLY *Analysis of a Political Cartoon*

Find a recent political cartoon to analyze, pulled from a print or online news publication. For each Type of Analysis section in the chart below, provide your own answer based on the cartoon.

TYPE OF ANALYSIS	QUESTIONS TO ASK	YOUR ANSWER
Context	Who is the artist? Where and when was the cartoon published? What situations, issues, or political conditions does it respond to?	
Description	What do you see in the cartoon? What elements does it include?	
Analysis	Looking more closely at the images and considering their meanings, how does the cartoon make its point? Is it effective? How could you accommodate, resist, or negotiate the meanings of this image?	

A CHECKLIST FOR ANALYZING POLITICAL CARTOONS

☐ Is there a lead-in?

☐ Is there a brief but accurate description of the drawing?

☐ Is the source of the cartoon cited (perhaps with a comment by the cartoonist)?

☐ Is there a brief report of the event or issue that the cartoon is targeting, as well as an explanation of all the symbols?

☐ Is there a statement of the cartoonist's claim (thesis)?

☐ Is there an analysis of the evidence, if any, that the image offers in support of the claim?

☐ Is there an analysis of the ways in which the drawing's content and style help convey the message?

☐ Is there adequate evaluation of the drawing's effectiveness?

☐ Is there adequate evaluation of the effectiveness of the text (caption or speech balloons) and of the fairness of the cartoon?

Ryan Kwon

Professor Carter

English 101

17 September 2018

The American Pipe Dream?

Visual arguments are powerful tools used by photographers, advertisers, and artists to persuade an audience. Two powerful examples of visual arguments about a shared subject, the so-called American Dream, occur in two different types of images, yet they both point to important questions about the attainability of the dream in two different contexts. The first is Margaret Bourke-White's 1937 photograph of flood victims, and the second is Mike Keefe's 2012 political cartoon from InToon.com. Both images, although seventy-five years apart, aim to persuade the audience that the ideology of the American Dream is unattainable in reality. While Bourke-White does so through the use of appeals to irony, juxtaposition, and color contrast, Keefe does so through heavy symbolism and carefully selected text. By comparing these two images, we can see how the American dream is—and always was—elusive.

> *Thesis:* Two visual arguments from different contexts reveal the irony of the American Dream.

Bourke-White's photo of flood victims waiting in a bread line in 1937 (Fig. 1) is not a staged photo like an advertisement, but on closer inspection, it utilizes visual framing to undermine the ideology of the American Dream through appeals to irony, juxtaposition, and color contrast. The billboard is loaded with emotive, powerful phrases like, "World's Highest Standard of Living" and "There's no way like the American Way." The family in the billboard image is nicely dressed, smiling, and driving a shiny, new car. This billboard presents the good life that the American Dream is known to give its citizens.

> Makes use of an "inventory" of elements in the photograph—billboard, words, clothing, smiles, car, dog, empty baskets.

However, the juxtaposition of this billboard with the line of flood victims beneath it creates an appeal to irony. The American good life is

Margaret Bourke-White/Time & Life Pictures/Getty Images

Fig. 1. Margaret Bourke-White, *Kentucky Flood* (1937).

Kwon recognizes visual metaphor: Being stuck in line is a symbol for social immobility.	physically above the heads of the people in line, as if it were nothing more than a dream. The family on the billboard is "free" in the sense that they are on the open road. Even the dog appears to be smiling. Meanwhile, the flood victims, stuck in line, are not moving at all. Unlike the family, they do not appear to be enjoying the privileges of ownership: their baskets are (literally and figuratively) empty. The billboard creates the illusion that all American citizens can live the good life simply by being a citizen, but the realities of the flood victims in this photograph say otherwise.
Placing the photograph in historical context helps interpret meaning. More on how the form and visual details of the photograph add meaning.	The audience must also take into account that in 1937, racism and segregation of blacks from whites was heavily prominent. Since the billboard pictures a white family, it excludes minorities from the American Dream. Therefore, this photograph demonstrates specifically that minorities are unable to attain the American Dream. The color contrast in this photo further emphasizes the division between light and dark, black people and white people. The billboard is bright, white, and promising, in a

Fig. 2. Mike Keefe, "The American Pipe Dream with Attached Mirage . . ." (2012).

dreamlike world above the heads the real individuals who are shadowed and dark, demonstrating that the American Dream is nothing more than an unattainable dream for some.

Keefe's more recent political cartoon (Fig. 2) also demolishes the attainability of the American Dream, but adds a more modern perspective through the use of symbolism and carefully selected text. The description of the cartoon reads, "The American Pipe Dream with Attached Mirage . . ." Since political cartoons are meant to be read in a matter of seconds by the audience, it is important for the cartoonist to get his or her message across quickly. Keefe manages to do so by setting the tone with this description. A white family, like the one in Bourke-White's photo, is drawn struggling to climb up a desert mountain, demonstrated by their wide eyes, their open mouths, and the beads of sweat surrounding the man's head. They are struggling because they are weighed down by four objects: a prison ball named "Underemployment"; a treasure chest of "Credit Card Debt"; a big bag of "Student Loans"; and a wide-eyed infant. The prison ball weighs the man

Again, author shows how visual details can be interpreted as metaphors.

down because without steady income from a secure job, he cannot support his family. Credit card debt is represented as a treasure chest because a credit card can buy lots of material items, but one must pay off the bill. Leaving the bill unpaid means all of the so-called treasures are taken away. The woman is literally carrying baggage, and that baggage is the amount of student loans that add into the credit card debt. Finally, having a child without a job and with heavy debt is an extra expense. With all of these items weighing the family down, it is no surprise they are struggling to achieve the American Dream, represented by the floating mirage of a suburban home.

The American Dream is floating above the struggling family in Keefe's image, much like the billboard in Bourke-White's photo. This time, however, it is a white family who is struggling to achieve the American Dream, the same kind of family who, ironically, were once the face of it. Thus, Keefe's cartoon manages to express the modern unattainability of the American Dream for all to its audience in a matter of moments, in a way that is just as effective as Bourke-White's photograph.

Clearly, visuals are powerful tools that can persuade an audience to take a stance on a certain political ideology, such as the American Dream. Both Bourke-White and Keefe make their stances about the unattainability of the American Dream clear, and even build off of each other to make the message stronger, despite their works being created in two different contexts. While textual arguments are certainly accredited more for their persuasion, visual arguments play a powerful role with the ability to persuade an audience.

> Author uses evidence from the image to establish the American Dream as something unreachable—always an ideal, but not a reality for all.

Works Cited

Bourke-White, Margaret. *Kentucky Flood. Life*, Time Inc., 1937, images.google.com/hosted/life/bdb4f71a5f11cf96.html.

Keefe, Mike. "American Pipe Dream." *InToon.com,* The Association of American Editorial Cartoonists, 13 Apr. 2012, editorialcartoonists .com/cartoon/display.cfm/110032/. Accessed 20 Sep. 2018.

Visuals as Aids to Clarity: Maps, Graphs, and Pie Charts

Often, writers use visual aids that are not images but still present information or data graphically in order to support a point. Maps were part of the argument in the debate over drilling in the Arctic National Wildlife Refuge we discussed at the beginning of this chapter.

- Advocates of drilling argued that it would take place only in a tiny area. Their drawn map showed the entire state of Alaska, with a smaller inset showing a much smaller part of the state that was the refuge. The map points out the drilling area with an arrow, implying it is too insignificant of an area to matter because it is too miniscule to show.

- Opponents utilized a close-up image to show the extent of industrial sprawl and roads that would have to be constructed across the refuge for drilling to take place. The map uses many icons to show how intrusive the drilling would be to this green natural area. The inset Alaska map is much smaller, deemphasizing the size of the refuge relative to the state.

By changing the scale and orienting viewers to the information in different ways, maps of the same area support different arguments.

Graphs, tables, and pie charts usually present quantitative data in visual form, helping writers clarify dry, statistical assertions. For instance, a line graph may illustrate how many immigrants came to the United States in each decade of the twentieth century.

A bar graph (with bars running either horizontally or vertically) offers similar information. In the Coming to America graph on page 160, we can see at a glance that, say, the second bar on the lower left is almost double the height of the first, indicating that the number of immigrants almost doubled between 1850 and 1860.

A pie chart is a circle divided into wedges so that we can see, literally, how a whole comprises its parts. We can see, for instance, in the From Near and Far chart

Maps showing the refuge in different ways for different purposes: advocates of drilling used the map on the top to emphasize size, and opponents used the map on the bottom to emphasize industrial transformation.

on page 160, an entire pie representing the regions of foreign-born US immigrants: 32 percent were born in Central America and Mexico, 40 percent in Asia, 9 percent in Europe, and so on.

COMING TO AMERICA . . .

Both the percentage and number of foreign-born people in the United States dropped
during much of the twentieth century, but after 1970, the tide was turning again.

. . . FROM NEAR AND FAR

Central America, Mexico, and Asia contribute
most to the foreign-born population.

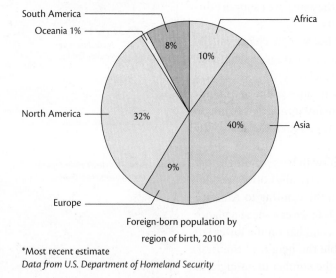

Foreign-born population by
region of birth, 2010

*Most recent estimate
Data from U.S. Department of Homeland Security

A WORD ON MISLEADING OR MANIPULATIVE VISUAL DATA

Because maps, charts, tables, and graphs offer empirical data to support arguments, they
communicate a high degree of reliability and tend to be convincing. "Numbers don't
lie," it is sometimes said, and to some extent this is true. It's difficult to spin a fact like
1 + 1 = 2. However, as author Charles Seife notes in his book *Proofiness*, numbers are

cold facts, but the measurements that numbers actually chart aren't always so clear or free from bias and manipulation. Consider two examples of advertising claims that Seife cites — one for a L'Oréal mascara offering "twelve times more impact" and another for a new and improved Vaseline product that "delivers 70% more moisture in every drop." Such measurements *sound* good but remain relatively meaningless. (How was eyelash "impact" measured? What is a percentage value of moisture?)

Another way data can be relatively meaningless is when it addresses only part of the question at stake. In 2013, a Mayo Clinic study found that drinking coffee regularly lowered participants' risk of the liver disease known as primary sclerosing cholangitis (PSC). But PSC is already listed as a "rare disease" by the Centers for Disease Control and Prevention, affecting fewer than 1 in 2,000 people. So even if drinking coffee lowered the risk of PSC by 25 percent, a person's chances would improve only slightly from 0.0005 percent chance to 0.0004 percent chance — hardly a change at all, and hardly a rationale for drinking more coffee. Yet statistical information showing a 25 percent reduction in PSC sounds significant, even more so when provided under a headline proclaiming "Drinking coffee helps prevent liver disease."

A CHECKLIST FOR CHARTS AND GRAPHS

☐ Is the source authoritative?

☐ Is the source cited?

☐ Will the chart or graph be intelligible to the intended audience?

☐ Is the caption, if any, clear and helpful?

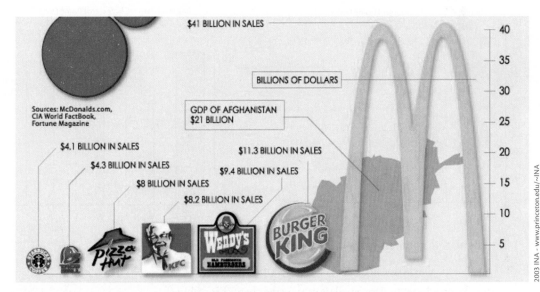

Sources: McDonalds.com, CIA World FactBook, Fortune Magazine

$41 BILLION IN SALES

BILLIONS OF DOLLARS

GDP OF AFGHANISTAN $21 BILLION

$4.1 BILLION IN SALES
$4.3 BILLION IN SALES
$8 BILLION IN SALES
$8.2 BILLION IN SALES
$11.3 BILLION IN SALES
$9.4 BILLION IN SALES

2003 INA – www.princeton.edu/~INA

In this graph, McDonald's $41 billion in sales are shown to be about 3.5 times higher than the revenues of its next closest competitor, Burger King (at $11.3 billion), but the McDonald's logo graphic is about 13 times larger than Burger King's.

Consider other uses of numbers that Seife shows in his book to constitute "proofiness" (his title and word to describe the misuse of numbers as evidence):

- In his 2006 State of the Union Address, George W. Bush declared No Child Left Behind (NCLB) a success: "[B]ecause we acted," he said, "students are performing better in reading and math." (True, fourth to eighth graders showed improved scores, but other grade levels declined. In addition, fourth- to eighth-grade reading and math scores had been improving at an unchanged rate both before and after the NCLB legislation.)

- In 2000, the *New York Times* reported "Researchers Link Bad Debt to Bad Health" (the "dark side of the economic boom"). The researchers claimed that debt causes more illness, but in doing so they committed the correlation-causation fallacy: Just because two phenomena are correlated does not mean they are causally related. (Example: More people wear shorts in the summer and more people eat ice cream in the summer than during other seasons, but wearing shorts does not *cause* higher ice cream consumption.)

Finally, consider the following graph showing that eating Quaker Oats decreases cholesterol levels after just four weeks of daily servings. The bar graph suggests that cholesterol levels will plummet. But a careful look at the graph reveals that the vertical axis doesn't begin at zero. In this case, a relatively small change has been (mis)represented as much bigger than it actually is.

A more accurate representation of cholesterol levels after four weeks of eating Quaker Oats, using a graph that starts at zero, would look more like the second graph — showing essentially unchanged levels.

Be alert to common ways in which graphs can be misleading:

- Vertical axis doesn't start at zero or skips numbers.
- Scale is given in very small units to make changes look big.
- Pie charts don't accurately divide on scale with percentages shown.
- Oversized graphics don't match the numbers they represent.

Exercise: Misleading Visuals

Examine these two graphs and describe how the way data from the Bureau of Labor Statistics is visualized presents two different stories about the declining unemployment rate in the United States.

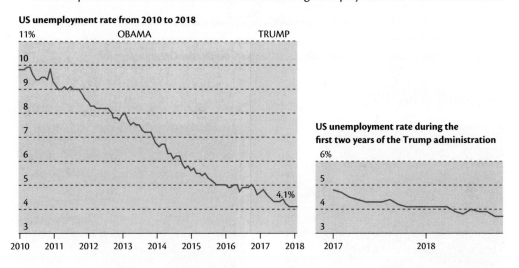

Using Visuals in Your Own Paper

Every paper uses some degree of visual persuasion, merely in its appearance. Consider these elements of a paper's "look": title page; margins (ample, but not so wide that they indicate the writer's inability to produce a paper of the assigned length); double-spaced text for the reader's convenience; headings and subheadings that indicate the progression of the argument; para-graphing; and so on. But you may also want to use visuals such as pictures, graphs, tables, or pie charts to provide examples, help readers digest statistical data more quickly, or simply liven up your essay or presentation. Keep a few guidelines in mind as you work with visuals, "writing" them into your own argument with as much care as you would read them in others' arguments:

- Consider your audience's needs and attitudes and select the type of visuals — graphs, drawings, photographs — likely to be most persuasive to that audience.
- Consider the effect of color, composition, and placement within your document. Because images are most effective when they appear near the text that they supplement, do not group all images at the end of the paper.

Remember especially that images are almost never self-supporting or self-explanatory. They may be evidence for your argument (e.g., Ut's photograph of napalm victims is *very* compelling evidence of suffering), but they aren't arguments themselves.

- Be sure to explain each visual that you use, integrating it into the verbal text that provides the logic and principal support behind your thesis.
- Be sure to cite the source of any visual that you paste into your argument.

Additional Images for Analysis

DOROTHEA LANGE

In 1936, photographer Dorothea Lange (1895–1965) took a series of a migrant mother and her children. Widely reprinted in the nation's newspapers, these photographs helped dramatize for the American public the poverty of displaced workers during the Great Depression.

Migrant Mother

Art Resource, NY

Library of Congress, Prints & Photographs Division, Reproduction number LC-DIG-fsa-8b29516.

Topics for Critical Thinking and Writing

1. Dorothea Lange drew increasingly near to her subject as she took a series of pictures. Make a list of details gained and lost by framing the mother and children more closely. The final shot in the series (right) became the most famous and most widely reprinted. Do you find it more effective than the other? Why, or why not?

2. Notice the expression on the mother's face, the position of her body, and the way she interacts with her children. What sorts of relationships are implied? Why is it significant that she doesn't look at her children or at the camera? How do the photographs' effects change according to how much you can see of the children's faces?

3. These photographs constitute a sort of persuasive "speech." Of what, exactly, might the photographer be trying to persuade her viewers? Write a brief essay (about 250 words) explaining Lange's purpose for her photographs and how she achieves that purpose. What assumptions does she make about her original audience? What sorts of evidence does she use to reach them?

UNITED STATES GOVERNMENT

During World War II, the US government produced a series of recruitment posters bearing the legend "This is the enemy." These posters depicted racially stereotyped images of both German and Japanese soldiers, typically engaged in acts of savage violence or clandestine surveillance.

World War II Recruitment Poster

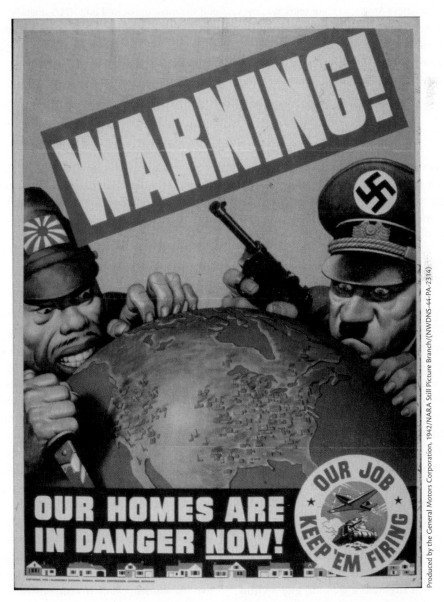

Produced by the General Motors Corporation, 1942/NARA Still Picture Branch/(NWDNS-44-PA-2314)

1. It has been claimed that one role of propaganda is to dehumanize the enemy so that (1) soldiers will feel less remorse about killing opposing soldiers and (2) civilians will continue to support the war effort. What specific features of this poster contribute to this propaganda function?

2. Some would claim that such a racially provocative image of a Japanese person should never have been used because of the potential harm to all Asians, including patriotic Asian Americans. (Did you know that the 442nd Regimental Combat Team, consisting solely of Japanese American volunteers, was by war's end the most decorated unit in US military history for its size and length of service?) Others believe that the ordinary rules do not apply in times of national crisis and that, as an old saying has it, "All's fair in love and war." In an essay of about 500 words, argue for one or the other of these propositions. Refer to this poster as one piece of your evidence.

NORA EPHRON

Nora Ephron (1941–2012) attended Wellesley College and then worked as a reporter for the *New York Post* and as a columnist and senior editor for *Esquire*. Ephron wrote screenplays and directed films, including *Sleepless in Seattle* (1993) and *You've Got Mail* (1998), and continued to write essays on a wide variety of topics. "The Boston Photographs" is from her collection *Scribble, Scribble: Notes on the Media* (1978).

The Boston Photographs

"I made all kinds of pictures because I thought it would be a good rescue shot over the ladder . . . never dreamed it would be anything else. . . . I kept having to move around because of the light set. The sky was bright and they were in deep shadow. I was making pictures with a motor drive and he, the fire fighter, was reaching up and, I don't know, everything started falling. I followed the girl down taking pictures. . . . I made three or four frames. I realized what was going on and I completely turned around, because I didn't want to see her hit."

You probably saw the photographs. In most newspapers, there were three of them. The first showed some people on a fire escape — a fireman, a woman, and a child.

The fireman had a nice strong jaw and looked very brave. The woman was holding the child. Smoke was pouring from the building behind them. A rescue ladder was approaching, just a few feet away, and the fireman had one arm around the woman and one arm reaching out toward the ladder. The second picture showed the fire escape slipping off the building. The child had fallen on the escape and seemed about to slide off the edge. The woman was grasping desperately at the legs of the fireman, who had managed to grab the ladder. The third picture showed the woman and child in midair, falling to the ground. Their arms and legs were outstretched, horribly distended. A potted plant was falling too. The caption said that the woman, Diana Bryant, nineteen, died in the fall. The child landed on the woman's body and lived.

The pictures were taken by Stanley Forman, thirty, of the *Boston Herald American.* He used a motor-driven Nikon F set at 1/250, f5.6-S. Because of the motor, the camera can click off three frames a second. More than four hundred newspapers in the United States alone carried the photographs: The tear sheets from overseas are still coming in. The *New York Times* ran them on the first page of its second section; a paper in south Georgia gave them nineteen columns; the *Chicago Tribune,* the *Washington Post,* and the *Washington Star* filled almost half their front pages, the *Star* under a somewhat redundant headline that read: SENSATIONAL PHOTOS OF RESCUE ATTEMPT THAT FAILED.

The photographs are indeed sensational. They are pictures of death in action, of that split second when luck runs out, and it is impossible to look at them without feeling their extraordinary impact and remembering, in an almost subconscious way, the morbid fantasy of falling, falling off a building, falling to one's death. Beyond that, the pictures are classics, old-fashioned but perfect examples of photojournalism at its most spectacular. They're throwbacks, really, fire pictures, 1930s tabloid shots; at the same time they're technically superb and thoroughly modern — the sequence could not have been taken at all until the development of the motor-driven camera some sixteen years ago.

Most newspaper editors anticipate some 5 reader reaction to photographs like Forman's; even so, the response around the country was enormous, and almost all of it was negative. I have read hundreds of the letters that were printed in letters-to-the-editor sections, and they repeat the same points. "Invading the privacy of death." "Cheap sensationalism." "I thought I was reading the *National Enquirer.*" "Assigning the agony of a human being in terror of imminent death to the status of a side-show act." "A tawdry way to sell newspapers." The *Seattle Times* received sixty letters and calls; its managing editor even got a couple of them at home. A reader wrote the *Philadelphia Inquirer:* "*Jaws* and *Towering Inferno* are playing downtown; don't take business away from people who pay good money to advertise in your own paper." Another reader wrote the *Chicago Sun-Times:* "I shall try to hide my disappointment that Miss Bryant wasn't wearing a skirt when she fell to her death. You could have had some award-winning photographs of her underpants as her skirt billowed over her head, you voyeurs." Several newspaper editors wrote columns defending the pictures: Thomas Keevil of the *Costa Mesa* (California) *Daily Pilot* printed a ballot for readers to vote on whether they would have printed the pictures; Marshall L. Stone of Maine's *Bangor Daily News,* which refused to print the famous assassination picture of the Vietcong prisoner in Saigon, claimed that the Boston pictures showed the dangers of fire escapes and raised questions about slumlords. (The burning building was a five-story brick apartment house on Marlborough Street in the Back Bay section of Boston.)

For the last five years, the *Washington Post* has employed various journalists as ombudsmen, whose job is to monitor the paper on behalf of the public. The *Post's* current ombudsman is Charles Seib, former managing editor of the *Washington Star;* the day the Boston photographs appeared, the paper received over seventy calls in protest. As Seib later wrote in a column about the pictures, it was "the largest reaction to a published item that I have experienced in eight months as the *Post's* ombudsman. . . .

"In the *Post*'s newsroom, on the other hand, I found no doubts, no second thoughts . . . the question was not whether they should be printed but how they should be displayed. When I talked to editors . . . they used words like 'interesting' and 'riveting' and 'gripping' to describe them. The pictures told of something about life in the ghetto, they said (although the neighborhood where the tragedy occurred is not a ghetto, I am told). They dramatized the need to check on the safety of fire escapes. They dramatically conveyed something that had happened, and that is the business we're in. They were news. . . .

"Was publication of that [third] picture a bow to the same taste for the morbidly sensational that makes gold mines of disaster movies? Most papers will not print the picture of a dead body except in the most unusual circumstances. Does the fact that the final picture was taken a millisecond before the young woman died make a difference? Most papers will not print a picture of a bare female breast. Is that a more inappropriate subject for display than the picture of a human being's last agonized instant of life?" Seib offered no answers to the questions he raised, but he went on to say that although as an editor he would probably have run the pictures, as a reader he was revolted by them.

In conclusion, Seib wrote: "Any editor who decided to print those pictures without giving at least a moment's thought to what purpose they served and what their effect was likely to be on the reader should ask another question: Have I become so preoccupied with manufacturing a product according to professional traditions and standards that I have forgotten about the consumer, the reader?"

It should be clear that the phone calls 10 and letters and Seib's own reaction were

Stanley Forman

Stanley Forman

CHAPTER 4 | VISUAL RHETORIC: THINKING ABOUT IMAGES AS ARGUMENTS occasioned by one factor alone: the death of the woman. Obviously, had she survived the fall, no one would have protested; the pictures would have had a completely different impact. Equally obviously, had the child died as well — or instead — Seib would undoubtedly have received ten times the phone calls he did. In each case, the pictures would have been exactly the same — only the captions, and thus the responses, would have been different.

But the questions Seib raises are worth discussing — though not exactly for the reasons he mentions. For it may be that the real lesson of the Boston photographs is not the danger that editors will be forgetful of reader reaction, but that they will continue to censor pictures of death precisely because of that reaction. The protests Seib fielded were really a variation on an old theme — and we saw plenty of it during the Nixon-Agnew years — the "Why doesn't the press print the good news?" argument. In this case, of course, the objections were all dressed up and cleverly disguised as righteous indignation about the privacy of death. This is a form of puritanism that is often justifiable; just as often it is merely puritanical.

Seib takes it for granted that the widespread though fairly recent newspaper policy against printing pictures of dead bodies is a sound one; I don't know that it makes any sense at all. I recognize that printing pictures of corpses raises all sorts of problems about taste and titillation and sensationalism; the fact is, however, that people die. Death happens to be one of life's main events. And it is irresponsible — and more than that, inaccurate — for newspapers to fail to show it, or to show it only when an astonishing set of photos comes in over the Associated Press wire. Most papers covering fatal automobile accidents will print pictures

Stanley Forman

Stanley Forman

of mangled cars. But the significance of fatal automobile accidents is not that a great deal of steel is twisted but that people die. Why not show it? That's what accidents are about. Throughout the Vietnam War, editors were reluctant to print atrocity pictures. Why *not* print them? That's what that was about. Murder victims are almost never photographed; they are granted their privacy. But their relatives are relentlessly pictured on their way in and out of hospitals and morgues and funerals.

I'm not advocating that newspapers print these things in order to teach their readers a lesson. The *Post* editors justified their printing of the Boston pictures with several arguments in that direction; every one of them is irrelevant. The pictures don't show anything about slum life; the incident could have happened anywhere, and it did. It is extremely unlikely that anyone who saw them rushed out and had his fire escape strengthened. And the pictures were not news — at least they were not national news. It is not news in Washington, or New York, or Los Angeles that a woman was killed in a Boston fire. The only newsworthy thing about the pictures is that they were taken. They deserve to be printed because they are great pictures, breathtaking pictures of something that happened. That they disturb readers is exactly as it should be: that's why photojournalism is often more powerful than written journalism.

Topics for Critical Thinking and Writing

1. In paragraph 5, Nora Ephron refers to "the famous assassination picture of the Vietcong prisoner in Saigon" (see p. 150). The photo shows the face of a prisoner who is about to be shot in the head at close range. Jot down the reasons you would or would not approve of printing this photo in a newspaper. Think, too, about this: If the photo on page 150 weren't about a war — if it didn't include the soldiers and the burning village in the rear but instead showed children fleeing from an abusive parent or an abusive sibling — would you approve of printing it in a newspaper?

2. In paragraph 9, Ephron quotes a newspaperman as saying that before printing Forman's pictures of the woman and the child falling from the fire escape, editors should have asked themselves "what purpose they served and what their effect was likely to be on the reader." If you were an editor, what would your answers be? By the way, the pictures were *not* taken in a poor neighborhood, and they did *not* expose slum conditions.

3. In fifty words or so, write a precise description of what you see in the third of the Boston photographs. Do you think readers of your description would be "revolted" by the picture (para. 8), as were many viewers, the *Washington Post*'s ombudsman among them? Why, or why not?

4. Ephron thinks it would be good for newspapers to publish more photographs of death and dying (paras. 11–13). In an essay of approximately 500 words, state her reasons and your evaluation of them. In the context of the internet age, when gruesome and grisly photographs and videos showing death are widely available, do you think Ephron's ideas still hold up? Why, or why not?

ASSIGNMENTS IN VISUAL RHETORIC

1. Choose a visual text and analyze its argument. Then evaluate whether the argument is effective or not. Support your analysis and evaluation with strong evidence and detail from the visual. (Advertisements, public service announcements, and political cartoons work particularly well for this assignment, although photographs and other visuals can also be rich resources.)

   - Identify the author(s) of the image. Who was the photographer/artist/designer? Who produced or sponsored the image?

   - Identify the intended audience for the image. Consumers? Art lovers? Newspaper reader of a particular political leaning? A particular demographic (age, gender, race, nationality, etc.)? Explain how you know that is the intended audience (context of publication, producer of the image, etc.).

   - Identify and describe the central argument of the image. If you cannot identify the argument, explain why you cannot really describe what the argument is.

   - Does the image appeal primarily to reason (*logos*), perhaps even using statistics, charts, graphs, tables, or illustrations? Does it appeal to feelings (*pathos*), evoking emotional responses or deeply held values? Or does it appeal to credibility and character (*ethos*), suggesting good sense, trustworthiness, or prudence? Use details from the image to explain how you know.

   - Are there any assumptions you can identify in the argument, either assumptions held by the creator or by the audience?

   - Are there any visual symbols present that contribute to the argument?

   - What single aspect of the image immediately captures your attention? Why exactly does it stand out? Its size? Position on the page? Beauty? Grotesqueness? Humor? How does the visceral impact of this element contribute to the visual's overall argument?

   - What is the relation of any text to the image? Does the visual part do most of the work, or does it serve to attract us and lead us on to read the text?

   - What elements at first go unnoticed or seem to be superfluous to the image? Are they important? If so, how? If not, why are they present?

2. Watch the commercials that air during a television show or examine the print advertisements in a popular magazine. Identify as many examples as possible of the types of appeals mentioned in Types of Emotional Appeals on pages 133–36. Select two good examples and explain what you think is the intended (or unintended) effect of the appeals. Is there a rational basis for the appeals you selected? Or are the appeals irrational even if they are effective? Or are they a little of both? Are the advertisements' appeals effective for the intended audience? Explain.

3. Imagine that you work for a business and are asked to advertise one of the products above in a campaign that will be placed in a publication such as *Time* or *Newsweek*. Design the advertisement according to your purpose and in consideration of your audience. In addition, write a 250- to 500-word analysis of your advertisement, identifying your target audience (college students? young couples about to buy their first home? retired persons? environmental activists?) and your message and explaining the strategy you employ to persuade this audience and sell your product.

4. Gather some of the graphic materials used to promote and reflect your college or university — including a screen shot of its website, the college catalog, and the brochures and other materials sent to prospective students — and choose one of the following options:

   ▪ What is the dominant image that your college or university administration seems to be promoting? Are there different, even competing, images of your school at work? How accurate is the story that these materials tell about your campus? Write an essay (approximately 500 words) in which you explain to prospective students the ways in which the promotional materials capture, or fail to capture, the true spirit of your campus.

   ▪ Compare the website of your institution to one or two from very different institutions — perhaps a community college, a large state university, or an elite private college. How do you account for the similarities and differences among the images shown on the two different sites?

PART TWO

Critical Writing

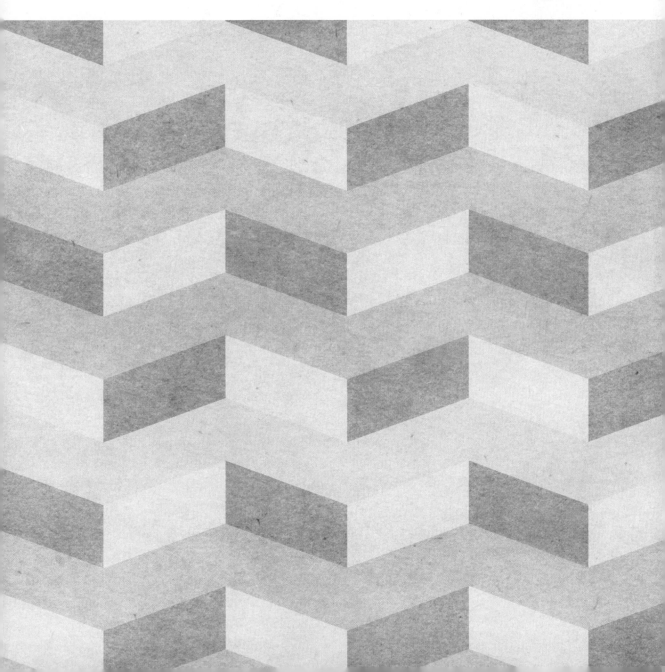

5

Writing an Analysis of an Argument

To expect truth to come from thinking signifies that we mistake the need to think with the urge to know. Thinking can and must be employed in the attempt to know, but in the exercise of this function it is never itself; it is but the handmaiden of an altogether different enterprise.

— HANNAH ARENDT

I don't wait for moods. You accomplish nothing if you do that. Your mind must know it has got to get down to work.

— PEARL S. BUCK

Fear not those who argue but those who dodge.

— MARIE VON EBNER-ESCHENBACH

Analyzing an Argument

Most of your writing in other courses will require you to write an analysis of someone else's writing. In a political science course, you may have to analyze, say, an essay first published in *Foreign Affairs*, perhaps reprinted in your textbook, that argues against raising tariffs on foreign goods. A course in sociology may require you to analyze a report on the correlation between fatal accidents and drunk drivers under the age of twenty-one. In much of your college writing, you will be asked to set forth reasoned responses to your reading as preparation for making arguments of your own.

EXAMINING THE AUTHOR'S THESIS

Obviously, you must understand an essay before you can analyze it thoughtfully. You must read it several times — not just skim it — and (the hard part) you must think critically about it. You'll find that your thinking is stimulated if you take notes and if you ask yourself questions about the material. Are there any websites or organizations dedicated to the material you are analyzing? If there are, visit some to see what others are saying about the material you are reviewing. Notes will help you keep track of the writer's thoughts and also of your own responses to the writer's thesis. The writer probably *does* have a **thesis** — a main claim or point — and if so, you must try to locate it. Perhaps the thesis is explicitly stated in the title, in a sentence or two near the beginning of the essay, or in a concluding paragraph, or perhaps it is not directly stated and you will have to infer it from the essay as a whole.

Notice that we said the writer *probably* has a thesis, stated or unstated. Much of what you read will indeed be primarily an **argument**: a writer explicitly or implicitly trying to support some thesis and to convince readers to agree with it. But some of what you read will be relatively neutral, with the argument just faintly discernible — or even with no argument at all. A work may, for instance, chiefly be a report: Here is the data, or here is what *X, Y,* and *Z* said; make of it what you will. A report might simply state how various ethnic groups voted in an election, for example. In a report of this sort, of course, the writer hopes to persuade readers that the facts are correct, but no thesis is advanced — at least not consciously; the writer is not evidently arguing a point and trying to change readers' minds. Such a document differs greatly from an essay by a political analyst who presents those same findings to persuade a candidate to sacrifice the votes of one ethnic bloc to get more votes from other blocs.

If you are looking for evidence that what you are reading is an argument, look for the presence of two elements:

- Transitions implying the drawing of a conclusion (such as *therefore, because, for the reason that,* and *consequently*) and

- Verbs implying proof (such as *confirms, verifies, accounts for, implies, proves, disproves, is (in)consistent with, refutes,* and *it follows that*).

Keep your eye out for such terms and examine their role whenever they appear. If the essay does not seem to be advancing a clear thesis, think of one it might support or some conventional belief it might undermine. That could be the implicit thesis. (See also Thinking Critically: Examining Language to Analyze an Author's Argument on p. 186.)

EXAMINING THE AUTHOR'S PURPOSE

While reading an argument, try to form a clear idea of the author's **purpose**. A first question is this: Judging from the essay or the book, is the purpose to persuade, or is it to report? An analysis of a persuasive argument requires more investment in the analysis of language and rhetoric, whereas an analysis of a pure report (a work apparently without a thesis or argumentative angle) calls for dealing chiefly with the accuracy of the report. (The analysis must also consider whether the report really has an argument built into it, consciously or unconsciously.)

Purpose can mean many things because people write for many reasons. We write notes and emails sometimes with a purpose to persuade:

Dear Professor, please forgive my absence from class this morning. I hit a deer on the way to class. Thankfully, only my car got damaged. I do hope I can make up the exam.

Such an email seems simple enough, but this note is a pretty carefully constructed argument. It establishes *ethos* (in a polite and formal tone) and appeals to *pathos* (by pointing to a sympathetic circumstance). It reasons, without really stating it, that the unforeseeable nature of the event is a good excuse to allow a make-up exam. If necessary, it could feasibly be underwritten by evidence (such as an accident report or an image of the damaged car).

In formal writing, purposes may vary. Sometimes, writers are trying to change an opinion, arguing that a certain perspective or interpretation of events is the correct one. A historian may assemble evidence from the past to argue that something occurred a certain way or that one event bore a relationship to some other events. A literary scholar might examine a novel and argue that some constellation of details amounts to something significant. In the sciences, the interpretation of data could be an effort to persuade. In opinion columns, blogs, and newspapers, people routinely write editorials sharing their perspectives and interpretations of the world. Whether the purpose is to change minds, challenge common assumptions, criticize institutionalized ideas, or argue that people should take some specific action, all arguments have a purpose.

When you are analyzing arguments, you will have a specific purpose. Perhaps you want simply to inform, attempting to convey someone else's argument as accurately as you can as if it were a report. Or perhaps you want to affirm (or challenge) the argument, making another argument (or counterargument) or your own. You might also satirize the argument, the writer, or the kind of thinking it represents. Whenever you analyze an argument, you are paying special attention to the author, context, language, medium — everything about the setting of an argument — and how those details and choices help the author achieve his or her purpose.

EXAMINING THE AUTHOR'S METHODS

If the essay advances a thesis to achieve a clear purpose, you will want to analyze the strategies or **methods** of argument that allegedly support the thesis.

- Is the argument aimed at a particular audience? Do the author's chosen methods work for that particular audience?

- Does the writer quote authorities? What publications does the writer draw from? Are these authorities competent in this field? Does the writer consider equally competent authorities who take a different view?

- Does the writer use statistics? If so, who compiled them, and are they appropriate to the point being argued? Can they be interpreted differently?

- Does the writer build the argument by using examples or analogies? Are they satisfactory?

- Does the writer include images (photos, graphs, charts, screenshots)? Are the image sources reliable? Do they support the writer's argument well, perhaps by an appeal to *logos* or *pathos*?

- Are the writer's assumptions acceptable?

- Does the writer consider all relevant factors? Has he or she omitted some points that you think should be discussed? For instance, should the author recognize certain opposing positions and perhaps concede something to them?

- Does the writer seek to persuade by means of humor or ridicule? If so, is the humor or ridicule fair? Is it supported also by rational argument?

EXAMINING THE AUTHOR'S PERSONA

You will probably also want to analyze something a bit more elusive than the author's explicit arguments: the author's self-presentation. Does the author seek to persuade readers partly by presenting himself or herself as conscientious, friendly, self-effacing, authoritative, or in some other light? Most writers, while they present evidence, also present themselves (or, more precisely, they present the image of themselves that they wish us to behold). In persuasive writing, this **persona** — this presentation of self, which can often be discerned from *language*, *voice*, and *tone* of the author — may be no less important than the presentation of evidence. In some cases, the persona may not much matter, but the point is that you should look at the author's self-presentation to consider if it's significant.

In establishing a persona, writers adopt various rhetorical strategies, ranging from the level of vocabulary they use, to their specific word choices, to the way they approach or organize their argument. The author of an essay may be polite, for example, and show fair-mindedness and open-mindedness, treating the opposition with great courtesy and expressing interest in hearing other views. Such a tactic is itself a persuasive device. Another author may use a technical vocabulary and rely on a range of hard evidence such as statistics. This reliance on a scientific tone and seemingly objective truths is itself a way of seeking to persuade — a rational way, to be sure, but a mode of persuasion nonetheless.

Consider these further examples:

- A writer who speaks of an opponent's "gimmicks" instead of "strategy" probably is trying to downgrade the opponent and also to convey the self-image of a street-wise person.

- A writer who uses legalistic language and cites numerous court cases is seeking to reveal her fluency in the law and her research capabilities to convince readers she is authoritative.

- A writer who seems professorial or pedantic, referencing a lot of classical figures and citing intellectual sources, is hoping to present himself as a person of deep knowledge and wisdom.

- A writer who draws a lot of examples from daily life in their ordinary neighborhood is wanting to be seen as a regular, commonsense person.

On a larger scale, then, consider not only the language, voice, and tone of the author, but also the *kind* of evidence that is used and the *ways* in which it is organized and presented. One writer may first bombard the reader with facts and then spend relatively little time drawing conclusions. Another may rely chiefly on generalizations, waiting until the end of the essay to bring the thesis home with a few details. Another may begin with a few facts and spend most of the space reflecting on these. All such devices deserve comment in your analysis.

The writer's persona may color the thesis and help it develop in a distinctive way. If we accept the thesis, it is no doubt partly because the writer has won our goodwill by persuading us of his or her good character or *ethos*. Good writers present themselves not as know-it-alls, wise guys, or bullies, but as decent people whom the reader presumably would like to invite to dinner.

In short, the author's self-presentation usually matters. A full analysis of an argument must recognize its effect, whether positive or negative.

EXAMINING THE AUTHOR'S AUDIENCE

Another key element in understanding an argument lies in thinking about the intended audience—how the author perceives the audience and what strategies the author uses to connect to it. We have already said something about the creation of the author's persona. An author with a loyal following is, almost by definition, someone who in earlier writings has presented an engaging persona, a persona with a trustworthy *ethos*. A trusted author can sometimes cut corners and can perhaps adopt a colloquial tone that would be unacceptable in the writing of an unknown author. The acclaimed mythologian Joseph Campbell once said, "You can always tell an author who is still working under the authorities by the number of footnotes he provides in his text."

Authors who want to convince their audiences need to think about how they present information and how they present themselves. Consider how you prefer people to talk to you. What sorts of language do you find engaging? Much, of course, depends on the circumstances, notably the topic, the audience, and the place. A joke may be useful in an argument about whether the government should regulate junk food, but almost surely a joke will be inappropriate — will backfire, will alienate the audience — in an argument about abortion. The *way* an author addresses the reader (through an invented persona) can have a significant impact on the reader's perception of the author, which is to say perception of the author's *views* and *argument*. A slip in tone or an error of fact, however small, may be enough for the audience to dismiss the author's argument. When you write your own arguments, understanding audience means thinking about all the possible audiences who may come into contact with your writing or your message and thinking about the consequences of what you write and where it is published.

Consider the impact of President Donald Trump's frequent use of Twitter to share his opinions and ideas. In that venue, he commonly castigates his political opponents (and sometimes his friends) and rails against policies and people he disagrees with. For many people, including some Republicans, not only does he generalize and oversimplify — after all, he is limited to a special number of characters — but his curious uses of capitalization and common misspellings are seen to detract from his *ethos*. For others, who may argue that Twitter is only one limited channel of communication where misspellings and solecisms are common, Trump's *ethos* is not damaged. Regardless of whether you think Trump strengthens or weakens his *ethos* through his tweets, they are on public record and will doubtlessly be analyzed long into the future; as the ancient Roman poet Horace said, *"Nescit vox missa reverti"* ("The word once spoken can never be recalled"), or, in plain proverbial English, "Think twice before you speak."

A tweet from Donald Trump claiming that Barack Obama ordered surveillance in Trump Tower during the 2016 US presidential campaign.

Our point is that we must consider the author's persona in conjunction with the publication type or venue in which an argument occurs in order to fully analyze the argument — whether it is occurring in a tweet, an editorial, a magazine article, a review, or a scholarly essay — because each publication context has a specific intended audience to whom the author is appealing.

Consider your own social media usage. Have you ever seen something posted by a friend or influencer on Facebook, Instagram, or Twitter and then swiftly taken down again? Have you ever received a text message or email not intended for you? Just as you must consider the purposes of the authors in those cases, when you are reading more formal essays it is equally important to think about who wrote them (author and author's persona) and for whom they were intended (audience). These factors can help you better discern the perspective and intentions of the author, which can significantly inform the ways evidence was gathered, interpreted, and represented.

A CHECKLIST FOR ANALYZING AN AUTHOR'S INTENDED AUDIENCE

- ❏ Where did the piece appear? Who published it? Why, in your view, might someone have found it worth publishing?

- ❏ In what technological format does this piece appear? Print journal? Online magazine? Blog? What does the technological format say about the piece, the author, or the audience?

- ❏ Is the writing relatively informal — for instance, a tweet or a Facebook status update? Why is this medium good or bad for the message?

- ❏ Who is the intended audience? Are there other audiences who may also have an interest but whom the author has failed to consider?

- ❏ If *you* are the intended audience, what shared values do you have with the author?

- ❏ What strategies does the writer use to create a connection with the audience?

ORGANIZING YOUR ANALYSIS

In writing an analysis of an argument, it is usually a good idea at the start of your analysis — if not in the first paragraph, then in the second or third — to let the reader know the purpose (and thesis, if there is one) of the work you are analyzing and then to summarize the work briefly, noting its main points.

Throughout the essay, you will want to analyze the strategies or methods of argument that allegedly support the thesis. Thus, you will probably find it useful (and your readers will certainly find it helpful) to write out *your* thesis (your evaluation or judgment). You might say, for instance, that the essay is impressive but not conclusive, or is undermined by convincing contrary evidence, or relies too much on unsupported generalizations, or is wholly admirable. It all depends on what you conclude as you go through the process of analyzing the argument at hand.

And then, of course, comes the job of setting forth your analysis and the support for your thesis. There is no one way of going about this work, and the organization of your analysis may or may not follow the organization of the work you are analyzing. (The Visual Guide: Organizing Your Analysis graphic shows some options, but there are, of course, others that may better suit your argument.)

Especially in analyzing a work in which the author's persona, ideas, and methods are blended, you will want to spend some time commenting on the persona. Whether you discuss it near the beginning of your analysis or near the end will depend on how you want to construct your essay, and this decision will partly depend on the work you are analyzing. For example, if the author's persona is kept in the background and is thus relatively invisible, you may want to make that point fairly early to get it out of the way and then concentrate on more interesting matters. If, however, the persona is interesting — and perhaps seductive, whether because it seems so scrupulously objective or so engagingly subjective — you may want to hint at this quality early in your essay and then develop the point while you consider the arguments.

Visual Guide: Organizing Your Analysis

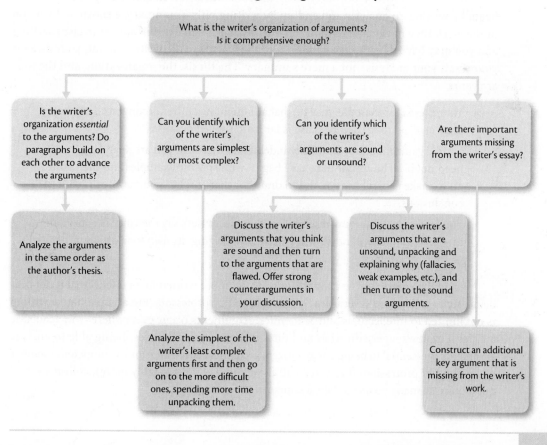

What is the writer's organization of arguments? Is it comprehensive enough?

Is the writer's organization *essential* to the arguments? Do paragraphs build on each other to advance the arguments?

Can you identify which of the writer's arguments are simplest or most complex?

Can you identify which of the writer's arguments are sound or unsound?

Are there important arguments missing from the writer's essay?

Analyze the arguments in the same order as the author's thesis.

Discuss the writer's arguments that you think are sound and then turn to the arguments that are flawed. Offer strong counterarguments in your discussion.

Discuss the writer's arguments that are unsound, unpacking and explaining why (fallacies, weak examples, etc.), and then turn to the sound arguments.

Analyze the simplest of the writer's least complex arguments first and then go on to the more difficult ones, spending more time unpacking them.

Construct an additional key argument that is missing from the writer's work.

A good conclusion for an analysis of an argument might offer a reassessment of the major points made by the author and a final statement about the validity or viability of the argument. You also have a chance in the conclusion to test the author's argument further, perhaps applying it to new or different situations that highlight its effectiveness or show where it falls short. If readers were to accept or reject the argument, what would be the implications? What other arguments would gain or lose currency by accepting or rejecting this one? Does the argument represent a new kind of potential or a new kind of threat — in a general sense, does it disrupt or attempt to disrupt current thinking, and, if so, is that a good or bad thing?

SUMMARY VERSUS ANALYSIS

In the last few pages, we have tried to persuade you that, in writing an analysis of a reading:

- Most of the nonliterary material that you will read is designed to argue, to report, or to do both. Read and reread thoughtfully, and take careful notes.

- Most of this material also presents the writer's personality, or voice, and this voice usually merits attention in an analysis.

There is yet another point, equally obvious but often neglected by students who begin by writing an analysis and end up by writing only a summary, a shortened version of the work they have read: Although your essay is an analysis of someone else's writing and you may have to include a summary of the work you are writing about, your essay is *your* essay, your analysis, not a mere summary. The thesis, the organization, and the tone are yours.

- Your thesis, for example, may be that although the author is convinced she has presented a strong case, her case is far from proved because . . .

- Your organization may be deeply indebted to the work you are analyzing, but it need not be. The author may have begun with specific examples and then gone on to make generalizations and to draw conclusions, but you may begin with the conclusions.

- Your tone, similarly, may resemble your subject's (let's say the voice is courteous academic), but it will nevertheless have its own ring, its own tone of, say, urgency, caution, or coolness.

Most of the essays that we have included thus far are written in an intellectual if not academic style, and indeed several are by students and by professors. But argumentative writing is not limited to intellectuals and academics. Arguments occur everywhere — in academic articles and newspaper editorials and on the backs of cereal boxes. Being able to analyze arguments is essential to being a wise citizen, a skeptical consumer, and a competent member of any field or profession. If it weren't all these things (and probably more), colleges would not require so many people to take a course in the subject.

An Argument, Its Elements, and a Student's Analysis of the Argument

In many types of media, we are exposed to the opinions and judgments of others, often capable writers, who argue their positions clearly, reasonably, and convincingly. We want to think carefully before we accept an argument, so we encourage skepticism but not entrenchment in your own position. You must be willing to hear and seriously consider different positions. Consider the following argument by columnist Nicholas Kristof, published in the *New York Times* in 2005. Analyze the essay and, after you do, examine our analysis of Kristof's argument, as well as the analysis provided by student Theresa Carcaldi, to see how it matches your own.

NICHOLAS D. KRISTOF

Nicholas D. Kristof (b. 1959), a two-time Pulitzer Prize winner, grew up on a farm in Oregon. After graduating from Harvard, he was awarded a Rhodes scholarship to Oxford, where he studied law. In 1984, he joined the *New York Times* as a correspondent, and since 2001 he has written as a columnist. The editorial that follows first appeared in the *New York Times* in 2005.

For Environmental Balance, Pick Up a Rifle

Here's a quick quiz: Which large American mammal kills the most humans each year?

It's not the bear, which kills about two people a year in North America. Nor is it the wolf, which in modern times hasn't killed anyone in this country. It's not the cougar, which kills one person every year or two.

Rather, it's the deer. Unchecked by predators, deer populations are exploding in a way that is profoundly unnatural and that is destroying the ecosystem in many parts of the country. In a wilderness, there might be ten deer per square mile; in parts of New Jersey, there are up to 200 per square mile.

One result is ticks and Lyme disease, but deer also kill people more directly. A study for the insurance industry estimated that deer kill about 150 people a year in car crashes nationwide and cause $1 billion in damage. Granted, deer aren't stalking us, and they come out worse in these collisions — but it's still true that in a typical year, an American is less likely to be killed by Osama bin Laden[1] than by Bambi.

If the symbol of the environment's being 5 out of whack in the 1960s was the Cuyahoga River in Cleveland catching fire, one such symbol today is deer congregating around what they think of as salad bars and what we think of as suburbs.

So what do we do? Let's bring back hunting.

Now, you've probably just spilled your coffee. These days, among the university-educated crowd in the cities, hunting is viewed as barbaric.

The upshot is that towns in New York and New Jersey are talking about using birth control to keep deer populations down. (Liberals presumably support free condoms, while conservatives back abstinence education.) Deer contraception hasn't been very successful, though.

Meanwhile, the same population bomb has spread to bears. A bear hunt has been scheduled for this week in New Jersey — prompting outrage from some animal rights groups (there's also talk of bear contraception: make love, not cubs).

As for deer, partly because hunting is per- 10 ceived as brutal and vaguely psychopathic, towns are taking out contracts on deer through discreet private companies. Greenwich, Connecticut, budgeted $47,000 this year to pay a company to shoot eighty deer from raised platforms over four nights — as well as $8,000 for deer birth control.

Look, this is ridiculous.

---

[1] The Al-Qaeda leader and mastermind of the 9/11 attack who was still at large at Kristof's writing. [Editors' note]

We have an environmental imbalance caused in part by the decline of hunting. Humans first wiped out certain predators—like wolves and cougars—but then expanded their own role as predators to sustain a rough ecological balance. These days, though, hunters are on the decline.

According to "Families Afield: An Initiative for the Future of Hunting," a report by an alliance of shooting organizations, for every hundred hunters who die or stop hunting, only sixty-nine hunters take their place.

I was raised on *Bambi*—but also, as an Oregon farm boy, on venison and elk meat. But deer are not pets, and dead deer are as natural as live deer. To wring one's hands over them, perhaps after polishing off a hamburger, is soggy sentimentality.

What's the alternative to hunting? Is it 15 preferable that deer die of disease and hunger? Or, as the editor of *Adirondack Explorer* magazine suggested, do we introduce wolves into the burbs?

To their credit, many environmentalists agree that hunting can be green. The New Jersey Audubon Society this year advocated deer hunting as an ecological necessity.

There's another reason to encourage hunting: it connects people with the outdoors and creates a broader constituency for wilderness preservation. At a time when America's wilderness is being gobbled away for logging, mining, or oil drilling, that's a huge boon.

Granted, hunting isn't advisable in suburban backyards, and I don't expect many soccer moms to install gun racks in their minivans. But it's an abdication of environmental responsibility to eliminate other predators and then refuse to assume the job ourselves. In that case, the collisions with humans will simply get worse.

In October, for example, Wayne Goldsberry was sitting in a home in northwestern Arkansas when he heard glass breaking in the next room. It was a home invasion—by a buck.

Mr. Goldsberry, who is six feet one inch 20 and weighs two hundred pounds, wrestled with the intruder for forty minutes. Blood spattered the walls before he managed to break the buck's neck.

So it's time to reestablish a balance in the natural world—by accepting the idea that hunting is as natural as bird-watching.

Topics for Critical Thinking and Writing

1. What is Nicholas Kristof's chief thesis? (State it in one sentence.)

2. Does Kristof make any assumptions—tacit or explicit—with which you agree or disagree? Why?

3. Is the slightly humorous tone of Kristof's essay inappropriate for a discussion of deliberately killing wild animals? Why, or why not?

4. What kind of evidence does Kristof offer to justify his claim that more hunting is needed? What interpretations of Kristof's evidence could be made if you were trying to challenge him?

5. Do you agree that "hunting is as natural as bird-watching" (para. 21)? In any case, do you think that an appeal to what is "natural" is a good argument for expanding the use of hunting? Why, or why not?

6. To whom is Kristof talking? How do you know?

THE ESSAY ANALYZED

By now you have read and begun to analyze Kristof's essay. Now let's examine his argument with an eye to identifying those elements we mentioned earlier in this chapter that deserve notice when examining *any* argument: the author's *thesis, purpose, methods, persona,* and *audience* (see Analyzing an Argument, pp. 175–83). It is important to point out that analysis does not always (or even usually) happen in a linear way.

When analyzing, we always consider the author, the publication type, and the context in which the argument was written. We knew that Kristof is a self-described progressive but is also known to take provocative positions somewhat out of step with typical liberal attitudes (for example, Kristof argued elsewhere in several *New York Times* editorials that sweatshops in foreign countries could be a good thing, a necessary stage on the way to progress). Thus, we could better interpret his argument about hunting deer: Although it involves guns and the killing of animals, it presents ethical and ecological reasons likely to be valued by liberals. We also knew that the essay appeared in a newspaper, the *New York Times*, where paragraphs are customarily very short, partly to allow for easy reading. Taking all this information together, we can assume that Kristof's intended audience was a commonsense, urban (or suburban) moderate who might hold typical liberal values about guns and hunting. This assumption allows us to read Kristof's tone — funny and acerbic but not cutting or insulting — as one suitable to the writer's purpose: to challenge a relatively sympathetic audience and at the same time gently ridicule their more "bleeding-heart" brethren.

Thesis   Kristof does not *announce* the thesis in its full form until paragraph 6 ("Let's bring back hunting"); instead he begins with evidence that builds up to the thesis. (It's worth noting that his paragraphs are very short, and if the essay were published in a book instead of a newspaper, Kristof's first two paragraphs probably would be combined, as would the third and fourth.)

Purpose   He wants to *persuade* readers to adopt his view. Kristof does not show that his essay is argumentative by using key terms that normally mark argumentative prose: *in conclusion, therefore,* or *because of this.* Almost the only traces of the language of argument are "Granted" (para. 18) and "So" (i.e., *therefore*) in his final paragraph. But the argument is clear — if unusual — and he wants readers to accept his argument as *true.* Possibly, part of his purpose is that he wants to make this argument specifically to a liberal audience unlikely to assume that hunting or guns could be a solution.

Methods   Kristof offers evidence identifying the problem of deer overpopulation, pointing out the annual number of deaths, and comparing that number — with a reference to a global terrorist — to the number of deaths from terrorism. He also points out other hazards such as Lyme disease and the economic impact of deer overpopulation. Kristof's methods of presenting evidence include providing **statistics** (paras. 3, 4, 10, and 13), giving **examples** (paras. 10, 19–20), and citing **authorities** (paras. 13 and 16).

Persona   Kristof presents himself as a confident, no-nonsense fellow, a newspaper columnist. A folksy tone ("Here's a quick quiz") and informal, humorous language establish a good relationship with readers. A well-known columnist, Kristof is a progressive who often takes nontypical views and presents a voice of "common sense." His readers probably know what to expect, and they read him with pleasure.

Audience   Kristof is known to be progressive, and he knows his audience is, too ("Now you've probably just spilled your coffee," he says when he proposes hunting as a solution). But he also mocks the "the university-educated crowd in the cities, [for whom] hunting is viewed as barbaric" (para. 7). So he is mocking liberal dogmas even though his audience is presumable of the same ilk. But he is not conservative (in fact, he spoofs them, too). Ordinarily, it is a bad idea to make fun of persons, whether they're you're intended audience or not; impartial readers rarely want to align themselves with someone who mocks others. In the essay we are looking at, however, Kristof gets away with this smart-guy tone because he not only has loyal readers but also has written the entire essay in a highly informal or playful manner.

Let's now turn to a student's written analysis of Kristof's essay and then to our own analysis of the student's analysis.

Theresa Carcaldi

Professor Markle

ENG 120

13 July 2018

For Sound Argument, Drop the Jokes:

How Kristof Falls Short in Convincing His Audience

In recent years, the action of hunting wild animals has become controversial. However, the *New York Times* columnist Nicholas D. Kristof attempts to argue for the necessity of hunting deer in America in his piece, "For Environmental Balance, Pick up a Rifle." Kristof certainly engages his audience in this newspaper column, especially progressive-minded readers who might believe any expansion of guns or hunting is abhorrent. He presents evidence that at first seems convincing; however, it is clear that the soundness of his argument falls short as a result of replacing his arguments with jokes, failing to provide adequate evidence, and including lines that are both incapable of relating to a majority of the population as well as disbelieving.

Before describing why Kristof's essay falls short of being sound, it is first important to concede the fact that Kristof's essay appeared in a newspaper column that is meant to be read in a quick manner, so the tone of his essay as well as its length and lack of evidence and full development of ideas is to be expected. His sarcastic, conversational tone is layered with occasional jokes and creates a friendly relationship with the audience that sets the stage for trust between author and reader. Therefore, some initial evidence sets out the problems of deer overpopulation in a way likely to be accepted, including dramatic statistics about human highway deaths caused by deer and the incident rates of Lyme disease spread by deer. By doing this, Kristof appeals to fear in the basic structure of his argument: the drastic rise in the deer population is wreaking havoc across America, and the solution to this problem is to hunt more deer.

No doubt, deer do cause serious problems. As Kristof says, deer "kill people more directly" each year than any other mammal (para. 4). However, the evidence is mostly unconvincing. By showing the deer threat to be more significant than the threat of terrorism, Kristof intends to highlight the

---

Carcaldi examines the paradox of the title—for a liberal goal, use a gun.

Note in Carcaldi's thesis her primary critique of Kristof's argument.

Analyzes how Kristof establishes *ethos*.

Points out Kristof's persuasive strategy.

Accounts for the fact that there is a problem, but takes issue with how that problem is overdramatized.

often irrationality of his audience's anxieties. However, his sample is too small: just because deaths caused by deer in a single year exceed that of terrorism in America, that does not mean that a major terrorist attack will not happen in the future.

Even with the threats deer do pose, the idea of hunting being the best solution is unconvincing. While Kristof states in paragraph 16 that the New Jersey Audubon Society "advocated deer hunting as an ecological necessity," this is only convincing if the audience is aware of what the New Jersey Audubon Society advocates for—which Kristof fails to explain. To add, Kristof proposes that the present alternative to deer hunting is to let the deer perish from natural causes like "disease and hunger" (para. 15). While this appeal to the audience's sensitivities about animal cruelty is good evidence for supporting deer hunting, Kristof does not fully explain why other solutions, such as deer birth control, are inadequate; instead, he just jokes about it, poking fun at the oversensitive "make love, not cubs" crowd. Rather than giving an argument, in other words, he makes a joke, then adds a further one that "Liberals presumably support free condoms, while conservatives back abstinence education" (para. 8). While this may make the audience laugh, it also suggests that people's political attitudes often prevent them from using common sense. This is an appeal to humor and to common sense, but is certainly not a fully stated reason for why deer contraception is not a solution. Kristof once states, "Deer contraception hasn't been very successful" (para. 8), yet does not explain why—he merely makes a statement without evidence, which does not contribute to a sound argument.

In addition, Kristof ends his essay with unbelievable statements. First, he claims hunting "connects people with the outdoors and creates a broader constituency for wilderness preservation" (para. 17). This statement contradicts his previous statement that "Humans first wiped out certain predators—like wolves and cougars" (para. 12). After stating the negative effects hunting has had on wildlife preservation, it is difficult to

Carcaldi reinterprets and challenges the evidence Kristof uses.

Suggests that the argument Kristof makes is presented as one (although not the only or best) solution.

Acknowledges other types of appeals Kristof makes.

claim that hunting nowadays would be any different. Finally, Kristof ends with "hunting is as natural as bird-watching" (para. 21). While hunting in the wild is certainly natural, it goes without saying that hunting with manmade weapons is far from being natural. Thus, with these two statements, not only does Kristof contradict himself, but he jeopardizes his audience's trust. While Kristof may use transitions of argumentation, such as "Granted" (para. 3), "Meanwhile" (para. 9), and "To their credit" (para. 16), his writing is primarily based on unsupported statements and jokes rather than sound reasoning. Ultimately, his essay is left labeled as an unsound argument.

> Carcaldi concludes by reiterating her own thesis and main points.

Clearly, Kristof has written an engaging article about a controversial topic and has written it well for the medium in which it was produced and for the audience he sought. However, this does not mean his argument is logical and sound. As a result of his lack of evidence, his often overconfident statements, and the logical fallacies ridden throughout the piece, his argument is left unsound, and his audience is left utterly unconvinced that the only solution to the deer issue across America is to hunt them.

AN ANALYSIS OF THE STUDENT'S ANALYSIS

Carcaldi's essay seems to us to be excellent, doubtless the product of a good deal of thoughtful revision. She does not cover every possible aspect of Kristof's essay — she concentrates on Kristof's reasoning and says very little about his style — but we think Carcaldi does a good job in a short space. What makes her essay effective?

- She has a strong title ("For Sound Argument, Drop the Jokes: How Kristof Falls Short in Convincing His Audience") that is of at least a little interest; it picks up Kristof's method of using humor, and it gives a hint of what is to come.

- She promptly identifies Kristof's subject and gives us a hint of where she will be going, telling us outright that it is "clear that the soundness of his essay falls short."

- She recognizes Kristof's audience at the start and analyzes his use of language and his assumptions with that knowledge in mind.

- She uses a few brief quotations to give us a feel for Kristof's essay and to let us hear the evidence for itself, but she does not pad her essay with long quotations.

- She considers all Kristof's main points.

- She organizes her essay reasonably, letting us hear Kristof's thesis, letting us know the degree to which she accepts it, and finally letting us know her specific reservations about Kristof's essay.

- She concludes without the formality of "in conclusion" but structures her analysis in such a way as to account for the charm or effectiveness of Kristof's essay but not agree with his solutions.

- Notice, finally, that she sticks closely to Kristof's essay. She does not go off on a tangent about the virtues of vegetarianism or the dreadful politics of the *New York Times*, the newspaper that published Kristof's essay. She was asked to analyze the essay, and she has done so.

A CHECKLIST FOR WRITING AN ANALYSIS OF AN ARGUMENT

☐ Have I accurately stated the writer's thesis (claim) and summarized his or her supporting reasons?

☐ Have I indicated early in the essay where I will be taking my reader (i.e., have I indicated my general response to the essay I am analyzing)?

☐ Have I called attention to the strengths, if any, and the weaknesses, if any, of the essay?

☐ Have I commented on the ways *logos* (logic, reasoning), *pathos* (emotion), and *ethos* (character of the writer) are presented in the essay?

☐ Have I explained any disagreements I might have about definitions of important terms and concepts?

☐ Have I examined the chief uses of evidence in the essay and offered supporting or refuting evidence or interpretation?

☐ Have I used occasional brief quotations to let my reader hear the author's tone and to ensure fairness and accuracy?

☐ Is my analysis effectively organized?

☐ Have I taken account of the author's audience(s)?

☐ Does my essay, perhaps in the concluding paragraphs, indicate my agreement or disagreement with the writer but also my view of the essay as a piece of argumentative writing?

☐ Is my tone appropriate?

JEFF JACOBY

Jeff Jacoby (b. 1959) is a columnist for the *Boston Globe*, where this essay was originally published on the op-ed page on February 20, 1997. As an opinion columnist, Jacoby is known for his conservative slant: In 1999, he won the Breindal Prize for opinion journalism from Rupert Murdoch's News Corporation, and in 2004, he won the Thomas Paine Award from the Institute for Justice, a libertarian law firm.

Bring Back Flogging

Boston's Puritan forefathers did not indulge miscreants lightly.

For selling arms and gunpowder to Indians in 1632, Richard Hopkins was sentenced to be "whipt, & branded with a hott iron on one of his cheekes." Joseph Gatchell, convicted of blasphemy in 1684, was ordered "to stand in pillory, have his head and hand put in & have his toung drawne forth out of his mouth, & peirct through with a hott iron." When Hannah Newell pleaded guilty to adultery in 1694, the court ordered "fifteen stripes Severally to be laid on upon her naked back at the Common Whipping post." Her consort, the aptly named Lambert Despair, fared worse: He was sentenced to twenty-five lashes "and that on the next Thursday Immediately after Lecture he stand upon the Pillory for . . . a full hower with Adultery in Capitall letters written upon his brest."

Corporal punishment for criminals did not vanish with the Puritans — Delaware didn't get around to repealing it until 1972 — but for all relevant purposes, it has been out of fashion for at least 150 years. The day is long past when the stocks had an honored place on the Boston Common, or when offenders were publicly flogged. Now we practice a more enlightened, more humane way of disciplining wrongdoers: We lock them up in cages.

Imprisonment has become our penalty of choice for almost every offense in the criminal code. Commit murder; go to prison. Sell cocaine; go to prison. Kite checks; go to prison. It is an all-purpose punishment, suitable — or so it would seem — for crimes violent and nonviolent, motivated by hate or by greed, plotted coldly or committed in a fit of passion. If anything, our preference for incarceration is deepening — behold the slew of mandatory minimum sentences for drug crimes and "three-strikes-you're-out" life terms for recidivists. Some 1.6 million Americans are behind bars today. That represents a 250 percent increase since 1980, and the number is climbing.

We cage criminals at a rate unsurpassed 5 in the free world, yet few of us believe that the criminal justice system is a success. Crime is out of control, despite the deluded happy talk by some politicians about how "safe" cities have become. For most wrongdoers, the odds of being arrested, prosecuted, convicted, and incarcerated are reassuringly long. Fifty-eight percent of all murders do *not* result in a prison term. Likewise 98 percent of all burglaries.

Many states have gone on prison-building sprees, yet the penal system is choked to bursting. To ease the pressure, nearly all convicted felons are released early — or not locked up at all. "About three of every four convicted criminals," says John DiIulio, a noted Princeton criminologist, "are on the streets without meaningful probation or parole supervision." And while everyone knows that amateur thugs should be deterred before they become career criminals, it is almost unheard of for judges to send first- or second-time offenders to prison.

Meanwhile, the price of keeping criminals in cages is appalling — a common estimate is $30,000 per inmate per year. (To be sure, the cost to society of turning many inmates loose would be even higher.) For tens of thousands of convicts, prison is a graduate school of criminal studies: They emerge more ruthless and savvy than when they entered. And for many offenders, there is even a certain cachet to doing time — a stint in prison becomes a sign of manhood, a status symbol.

But there would be no cachet in chaining a criminal to an outdoor post and flogging him. If young punks were horsewhipped in public after their first conviction, fewer of them would harden into lifelong felons. A humiliating and painful paddling can be applied to the rear end of a crook for a lot less than $30,000 — and prove a lot more educational than ten years' worth of prison meals and lockdowns.

Are we quite certain the Puritans have nothing to teach us about dealing with criminals?

Of course, their crimes are not our crimes: 10 We do not arrest blasphemers or adulterers, and only gun control fanatics would criminalize the sale of weapons to Indians. (They would criminalize the sale of weapons to anybody.) Nor would the ordeal suffered by poor Joseph Gatchell — the tongue "peirct through" with a hot poker — be regarded today as anything less than torture.

But what is the objection to corporal punishment that doesn't maim or mutilate? Instead of a prison term, why not sentence at least some criminals — say, thieves and drunk drivers — to a public whipping?

"Too degrading," some will say. "Too brutal." But where is it written that being whipped is more degrading than being caged? Why is it more brutal to flog a wrongdoer than to throw him in prison — where the risk of being beaten, raped, or murdered is terrifyingly high?

The *Globe* reported in 1994 that more than two hundred thousand prison inmates are raped each year, usually to the indifference of the guards. "The horrors experienced by many young inmates, particularly those who . . . are convicted of nonviolent offenses," former Supreme Court Justice Harry Blackmun has written, "border on the unimaginable." Are those horrors preferable to the short, sharp shame of corporal punishment?

Perhaps the Puritans were more enlightened than we think, at least on the subject of punishment. Their sanctions were humiliating and painful, but quick and cheap. Maybe we should readopt a few.

Topics for Critical Thinking and Writing

1. When Jeff Jacoby says (para. 3) that today we are more "enlightened" than our Puritan forefathers because where they used flogging, "We lock them up in cages," is he being ironic? Explain.

2. Suppose you agree with Jacoby. Explain precisely (1) what you mean by *flogging* (does Jacoby explain what he means?) and (2) how much flogging is appropriate for different crimes such as housebreaking, rape, robbery, and murder.

3. In an essay of about 250 words, explain why you think that flogging would be more (or less) degrading and brutal than imprisonment.

4. At the end of his essay Jacoby draws to our attention the terrible risk of being raped in prison as an argument in favor of replacing imprisonment with flogging. Do you think this is sound reasoning? Why, or why not?

5. Jacoby draws the line (para. 11) at punishment that would "maim or mutilate." Why draw the line here? Some societies punish thieves by amputating a hand. Suppose we knew that this practice really did seriously reduce theft. Should we adopt it? How about adopting castration (surgical or chemical) for rapists? For child molesters? Explain your response.

MATTHEW WALTHER

Matthew Walther is a national correspondent at the *Week*, a widely circulated online and print magazine of news, opinion, and commentary published in both UK and US editions. Walther also contributes to the *Spectator of London*, the *Catholic Herald*, and the *National Review*. This piece was first published in May 2018.

Sorry, Nerds: Video Games Are Not a Sport

As a columnist you hate to get a reputation for having anything negative to say about a large group of people. Which is why I am often at great pains to admit that nerd culture has given the world lots of wonderful things and not just wizard erotica, minarchism, and all the anti-anti arguments about racism and misogyny you can find on Reddit. I just don't know what they are yet.

My biggest problem with nerd culture, though, is not that it exists but that it has territorial ambitions. Two decades ago, comic books were still a fringe phenomenon; now they are the only things directors are allowed to make films about, notwithstanding mumblecore and Oscar bait. Oh well. Movie tickets are too expensive anyway. But at sports I feel like it is necessary to draw a line in the sand and, unlike President Obama, to act when my opponents cross it.

In 2016 something called the National Association of Collegiate Esports was established

in order to regulate competitions between young adult gamers, taking over a role that had previously belonged to their mothers who needed the garbage taken out. Two years earlier, a private university in Illinois created the nation's first varsity gaming team and began awarding "athletic" scholarships to skilled players. Imagine being that kid's parents. "Oh, yes, Dylan just got accepted with an athletic scholarship." "That's wonderful. Cross country, right?" "No, *Wario's Woods*."

Video games are not a sport. On the loosest imaginable definition a sport involves not only skill and competition but physical exertion and at least the possibility of injury. Even darts and pool and ping pong are, in the broadest sense, sports. Sitting on a couch interacting with your television set is not a sport, otherwise watching CNN with your grandfather would be one. So would self-abuse.

It's actually not difficult to understand 5 why universities are getting into this business.

Even for those not lucky enough to make first string on U.C. Berkeley's traveling *Overwatch* team — which has an actual coach — there are plenty of opportunities on our nation's college campuses for people who want to pretend that there is no difference between *FIFA* and FIFA. At Western Michigan University in Kalamazoo, a mid-tier state school, it was recently announced that the administration is spending half a million dollars on "a new facility" for "multiplayer video games."

This is just a continuation of what these colleges have done for decades now when they advertised wave pools and cool dining facilities and hip-looking plate-glass dorms. Undergraduate education is actually a four-year-long debt-financed summer camp for lazy overgrown teenagers. It has nothing to do with the life of the mind, and even less to do with old-fashioned vocational training. One worthless piece of paper is as good as any other, which means that the directional state former polytechnics have to find some non-academic means of competing with each other for the loan dollars that will one day crush their underemployed 20-something graduates.

Which is not to say that no opportunities await the Doug Fluties of *Mario Kart*. As I write this, hundreds of millions of dollars are being made streaming video games on the internet by people with few or any other marketable skills. The amount of revenue generated by advertising and sponsorships from "esports" is soon expected to reach $1 billion annually.

Treating video games as sports is a civilizational rather than a semantic problem. Enjoyed in moderation, they are probably a harmless pastime like anything else. But increasingly the reality is not 10-year-olds leveling up their Pikachus on the school bus or even high-school kids unwinding with a little *Goldeneye* but adults — almost all of them men — in their 20s, 30s, and even 40s playing games for hours every day. Gaming is not only a compulsion, but something far more sinister — what one game designer has called "a simulation of being an expert." In a country without meaningful or well-paying opportunities for work young people disappear into their fantasies of competence in which they fly airplanes and score touchdowns and perform daring commando raids without having to go further than the refrigerator.

Video games are, in other words, another of those illusions we peddle to convince people that the world's problems do not exist. Sports, by comparison, are very much of this world. Compared with what's going on inside a PlayStation the most insignificant Saturday afternoon baseball game between two clubs with losing records is a thing of epochal significance, brimming with meaningful human drama.

Topics for Critical Thinking and Writing

1. In his first paragraph, does Matthew Walther define his key terms, *nerds* and *sports*? If so, where? If not, provide the definitions you think Walther assumes.

2. In paragraph 2, why do you think that Walther takes a dig at President Obama? How do you think this affects his relationship with the audience (*ethos*)?

3. Overall, how would you characterize Walther's tone and language? What about it makes it effective and persuasive — or not?

4. What kinds of evidence does Walther provide to support his position that video games are not a sport? Is the evidence adequate enough to be convincing?

5. What assumptions does Walther make about the motivations for people playing video games? Are his assumptions fair? Why, or why not?

6. How does Walther compare "real sports" to video games? Do you think he is right or wrong that video games do not offer the same types of "meaningful human drama" that sports do? Why?

JUSTIN CRONIN

Justin Cronin (b. 1962) is an award-winning writer of five best-selling novels and a winner of the Hemingway Foundation/PEN Award. Educated at Harvard and the Iowa Writer's Workshop, Cronin taught at La Salle University in Philadelphia, Pennsylvania, and at Rice University in Houston, Texas. The following selection was published in the *New York Times* in 2013.

Confessions of a Liberal Gun Owner

I am a New England liberal, born and bred. I have lived most of my life in the Northeast — Boston, New York, and Philadelphia — and my politics are devoutly Democratic. In three decades, I have voted for a Republican exactly once, holding my nose, in a mayoral election in which the Democratic candidate seemed mentally unbalanced.

I am also a Texas resident and a gun owner. I have half a dozen pistols in my safe, all semiautomatics, the largest capable of holding twenty rounds. I go to the range at least once a week, have applied for a concealed carry license, and am planning to take a tactical training course in the spring. I'm currently shopping for a shotgun, either a Remington 870 Express Tactical or a Mossberg 500 Flex with a pistol grip and adjustable stock.

Except for shotguns (firing one feels like being punched by a prizefighter), I enjoy shooting. At the range where I practice, most of the staff knows me by sight if not by name. I'm the guy in the metrosexual eyeglasses and Ralph Lauren polo, and I ask a lot of questions: What's the best way to maintain my

sight picture with both eyes open? How do I clear a stove-piped round?

There is pleasure to be had in exercising one's rights, learning something new in mid-life, and mastering the operation of a complex tool, which is one thing a gun is. But I won't deny the seductive psychological power that firearms possess. I grew up playing shooting games, pretending to be Starsky or Hutch or one of the patrolmen on *Adam-12*, the two most boring TV cops in history.

A prevailing theory holds that boys are simultaneously aware of their own physical powerlessness and society's mandate that they serve as protectors of the innocent. Pretending to shoot a bad guy assuages this anxiety, which never goes away completely. This explanation makes sense to me. Another word for it is catharsis, and you could say that, as a novelist, I've made my living from it.

There are a lot of reasons that a gun feels right in my hand, but I also own firearms to protect my family. I hope I never have to use one for this purpose, and I doubt I ever will. But I am my family's last line of defense. I have chosen to meet this responsibility, in part, by being armed. It wasn't a choice I made lightly. I am aware that, statistically speaking, a gun in the home represents a far greater danger to its inhabitants than to an intruder. But not every choice we make is data-driven. A lot comes from the gut.

Apart from the ones in policemen's holsters, I don't think I saw a working firearm until the year after college, when a friend's girlfriend, after four cosmopolitans, decided to show off the .38 revolver she kept in her purse. (Half the party guests dived for cover, including me.)

It wasn't until my mid-forties that my education in guns began, in the course of writing a novel in which pistols, shotguns, and rifles, but also heavy weaponry like the AR-15 and its military analogue, the M-16, were widely used. I suspected that much of the gunplay I'd witnessed in movies and television was completely wrong (it is) and hired an instructor for a daylong private lesson "to shoot everything in the store." The gentleman who met me at the range was someone whom I would have called "a gun nut." A former New Yorker, he had relocated to Texas because of its lax gun laws and claimed to keep a pistol within arm's reach even when he showered. He was perfect, in other words, for my purpose.

My relationship to firearms might have ended there, if not for a coincidence of weather. Everybody remembers Hurricane Katrina; fewer recall Hurricane Rita, an even more intense storm that headed straight for Houston less than a month later. My wife and I arranged to stay at a friend's house in Austin, packed up the kids and dog, and headed out of town — or tried to. As many as 3.7 million people had the same idea, making Rita one of the largest evacuations in history, with predictable results.

By two in the morning, after six hours on 10 the road, we had made it all of fifty miles. The scene was like a snapshot from the Apocalypse: crowds milling restlessly, gas stations and minimarts picked clean and heaped with trash, families sleeping by the side of the road. The situation had the hopped-up feel of barely bottled chaos. After Katrina, nobody had any illusions that help was on its way. It also occurred to me that there were probably a lot of guns out there — this was Texas, after all. Here I was with two tiny children, a couple of thousand dollars in cash, a late-model S.U.V. with half a tank of gas and not so much as a heavy book to throw. When my wife wouldn't let me get out of the car so the dog could do his business, that was it for me. We jumped the median, turned around, and were home in under an hour.

As it happened, Rita made a last-minute turn away from Houston. But what if it hadn't? I believe people are basically good, but not all of them and not all the time. Like most citizens of our modern, technological world, I am wholly reliant upon a fragile web of services to meet my most basic needs. What would happen if those services collapsed? Chaos, that's what.

It didn't happen overnight, but before too long my Northeastern liberal sensibilities, while intact on other issues, had shifted on the question of gun ownership. For my first pistol I selected a little Walther .380. I shot it enough to decide it was junk, upgraded to a full-size Springfield 9-millimeter, liked it but wanted something with a thumb safety, found a nice Smith & Wesson subcompact that fit the bill, but along the way got a little bit of a gun-crush on the Beretta M-9 — and so on.

Lots of people on both sides of the aisle own firearms, or don't, for reasons that supersede their broader political and cultural affiliations. Let me be clear: my personal armory notwithstanding, I think guns are woefully under-regulated. It's far too easy to buy a gun — I once bought one in a parking lot — and I loathe the National Rifle Association. Some of the Obama administration's proposals strike me as more symbolic than effective, with some 300 million firearms on the loose. But the White House's recommendations seem like a good starting point and nothing that would prevent me from protecting my family in a crisis. The AR-15 is a fascinating weapon, and, frankly, a gas to shoot. So is a tank, and I don't need to own a tank.

Alas, the days of à la carte politics like mine seem over, if they ever even existed. The bigger culprit is the far right and the lunatic pronouncements of those like Rush Limbaugh. But in the weeks since Newtown, I've watched my Facebook feed, which is dominated by my coastal friends, fill up with antigun dispatches that seemed divorced from reality. I agree it would be nice if the world had exactly zero guns in it. But I don't see that happening, and calling gun owners "a bunch of inbred rednecks" doesn't do much to advance rational discussion.

Thus, my secret life — though I guess it's 15 not such a secret anymore. My wife is afraid of my guns (though she also says she's glad I have them). My sixteen-year-old daughter is a different story. The week before her fall semester exams, we allowed her to skip school for a day, a tradition in our house. The rule is, she gets to do whatever she wants. This time, she asked to take a pistol lesson. She's an NPR listener like me, but she's also grown up in Texas, and the fact that one in five American women is a victim of sexual assault is not lost on her. In the windowless classroom off the range, the instructor ran her through the basics, demonstrating with a Glock 9-millimeter: how to hold it, load it, pull back the slide.

"You'll probably have trouble with that part," he said. "A lot of the women do."

"Oh really?" my daughter replied, and with a cagey smile proceeded to rack her weapon with such authority you could have heard it in the parking lot.

A proud-papa moment? I confess it was.

Topics for Critical Thinking and Writing

1. This essay could with equal accuracy be called "Confessions of a Texas Gun Owner." Why do you suppose Justin Cronin chose the title he did rather than our imagined title?

2. Why does Cronin devote so many sentences to autobiographical matters since, in fact, none of the autobiography actually involves using a gun to protect himself or his family against an intruder?

3. How would you characterize Cronin's persona as he presents it in this essay? Do you feel that his persona effectively connects with you as a reader? Why, or why not?

4. What *arguments* does Cronin offer on behalf of gun ownership? Do you think his thesis might have been strengthened if he had cited statistics or authorities, or do you think that such evidence probably would have been inappropriate in a highly personal essay? Explain your response.

5. In paragraph 12, Cronin writes, "It didn't happen overnight, but before too long my Northeastern liberal sensibilities . . . had shifted on the question of gun ownership." Why did his attitude shift?

6. In paragraph 13, Cronin says that he believes "guns are woefully under-regulated" and that he "loathe[s] the National Rifle Association," but he doesn't go into any detail about what

sorts of regulations he favors. Do you think his essay might have been more convincing if he had given us details along these lines? Explain.

7. Each of Cronin's last three paragraphs is very short. We have discussed how, in general, a short paragraph is usually an underdeveloped paragraph. Do you think these paragraphs are underdeveloped, or do you think Cronin knows exactly what he is doing? Explain.

CARL SAFINA

Carl Safina (b. 1955) is a marine biologist and author whose work on animal and ocean conservation has been recognized in McArthur, Pew, and Guggenheim Fellowships and whose books have earned him awards ranging from a National Academies literary award to John Burroughs, James Beard, and George Rabb medals. He holds the Endowed Chair for Nature and Humanity at Stony Brook University and is the founding director of the not-for-profit foundation The Safina Center. He has published widely in the *New York Times*, *Orion*, and *Audubon* magazines and was host of the ten-part PBS series *Saving the Ocean with Carl Safina* in 2013. The selection below is from his book *Beyond Words: What Animals Think and Feel* (2015).

Never Mind Theory

Experiments showed at first that wolves could not follow human hand pointing to find hidden food. Dogs often can. But the wolves had been tested with a fence separating them from the human who was pointing. Dog tests were of course barrier-free, and dogs usually had their most familiar human companions with them. When experimenters finally leveled the playing field, wolves did as well as dogs — with no training.

Experiments can be powerful for learning about behavior. But sometimes, experimental situations are so pinched and artificial — as with wolves behind fences — that they hide capabilities they're trying to investigate. Real-life behaviors and decisions can't always be stuffed into an experiment.

Any ecologist who watches free-living animals feels humbled by the depth and nuance of how they negotiate the world and how easily they slip the noose of human observation as they go about their business of working to keep themselves and their babies alive.

On the other hand, laboratory studies seem preoccupied with "testing" academically generated concepts such as "self-awareness" and — my pet peeve — "theory of mind." It's not that these *ideas* aren't helpful. They are. It's that animals don't care about academic classifications and testing setups. They have no interest in arguments over wafer-thin slices of categories, such as whether an otter smashing a clam with a stone is using a tool but a gull dropping a clam on a stone is not using a tool. They care about survival. Some academic researchers, meanwhile, chop concepts into so many pieces, you'd think behavior was shish kebab. So in this section I want to have a little fun with some muddles that behavioral scientists have created. We'll be blowing away some smoke and breaking some mirrors. And as for the kebab, the first skewer goes to "theory of mind."

"Theory of mind" — such an awkward phrase — is an idea. Exactly what the idea is depends on whom you ask. Naomi Angoff Chedd, who works with autistic children, tells me it is "knowing that another can have thoughts that differ from yours." I like that definition; it's helpful. Dolphin researcher Diana Reiss says it's the ability to feel that "I have an idea of what's on your mind." That's different. Still others assert — oddly, I think — that it's the ability "to read the minds of others." The "mind-reading" camp gets the most press, and its adherents get the most carried away with themselves. Italian neuroscientist and philosopher Vittorio Gallese writes of "our sophisticated mind-reading abilities."

I don't know about you (I guess that's my point), but I cannot read anyone's mind. Informed guessing based on experience and body language is just about all we can really do. If a sketchy-looking stranger crosses the street to come toward us, our first problem is that we *can't* know what they're thinking. If "theory of mind" is defined as understanding that another can hold thoughts different from yours, then fine, there's that. But claims about humans' "sophisticated mind-reading abilities" are nonsense. That's why we say, "How are you?"

"Theory of mind" was coined in 1978 by researchers who tested chimpanzees. With an impressive lack of human insight into what could be an appropriate context or meaningful to a chimp, they showed chimpanzees videotapes of human actors trying to access out-of-reach bananas, or trying to play music while the record player was unplugged, or shivering because a heater wasn't working, and so on. A chimpanzee was supposed to prove that it understood the human's problem by choosing a photo of the solution to the problem. It was supposed to choose, for instance, "a lit wick for the malfunctioning heater." No, the researchers *weren't* kidding. If the chimps didn't select the correct photo, the researchers declared that chimpanzees didn't understand the videotaped human actor's problem and, thus, had no "theory of mind." (Now, imagine you're a chimp, led into a room, shown a video of a man shivering next to a heater, and without anyone being able to explain the problem, the experiment, or the uses of fire, you're supposed to choose a lit wick. Imagine, for that matter, that you're Thomas Jefferson being shown a video of a man trying to play a phonograph that is unplugged. You'd have no idea what you were looking at.) In the decades since, and many studies later, scientists in the field have finally suggested that those results might have been affected by the test's setup. Science marches on. Well, hello.

So far, some scientists grant theory-of-mind ability — basically, understanding that another can have thoughts and motives that differ from yours — to apes and dolphins. A few allow elephants and crows. Occasional researchers have admitted dogs. But many continue to insist that theory of mind is "uniquely human." Even while I was writing this, science journalist Katherine Harmon wrote, "In most animal species, scientists have failed to see even a glimmer of evidence."

Not a glimmer? It's *blinding*. People who don't see the evidence aren't paying attention. Frans de Waal pays attention. The shenanigans of chimps who like to spray water on unsuspecting zoo visitors, he says, reflects, "a complex, and familiar, inner life."

Whether researchers do or don't think that chimpanzees, dogs, and other animals "have theory of mind" hardly matters. What matters: What do they have, and how do they have it? What do dogs do? And what motivates them? Rather than asking whether a dog or chimp follows a human gaze, let's ask how dogs and chimps direct one another's attention.

Humans are better at reading humans than we are at reading dogs. Dolphins are better at reading dolphins. Chimps at chimp reading. We judge the sketchy stranger's friendly or evil intent by their body language. But so do our dogs. Other animals are highly skilled body-language readers. The stakes can be life or death, and they can't ask questions. Our orphaned raccoon, Maddox (whom we bottle-raised but never caged; she lived free-range), could sometimes read my intent almost as fast as the thought occurred to me, though I couldn't understand what cue I was giving. She'd suddenly bristle and put her back up, for instance, if I'd just decided that it was time to stop playing in the kitchen and usher her outdoors. I used to joke that I had a mind-reading raccoon. (It must have been something in the way I looked at her, but, wow, was she sharp. And so were her teeth.)

Watching free-living animals negotiate the world on their terms shows you their rich mental abilities. And you can start by looking at who's scampering around your house, gazing up at you imploringly, awaiting your response.

In the morning I'm making coffee, and because it's chilly I raise the screens and lower the storm windows; the phone rings, and I answer it. Chula follows all my movements, looking me in the eyes for any clues that I might wish to interact — or perhaps move toward the jar of treats. She does not understand coffee, screens, or phones. A human from most of our history or a Native American from an intact tribe in 1880 or a hunter-gatherer today would also not understand anything I am doing. The difference between my crazy dog and Crazy Horse is that Crazy Horse could have learned everything I am doing (and perhaps vice versa). But, again, the point is not whether dogs are just like us. The point is that they are like themselves. The interesting question is: What are they like?

Our daughter, Alexandra, aged twenty, sees our other dog, Jude, appear at the screen door and indicate his desire to come in. Usually the doggies are both either in or out together, but Chula happens to be inside when Jude comes to the screen. Alex sees the whole thing and describes it like this: "Jude whined to be let in. Chula went to the screen and stared at Jude like, 'Ha,' as if teasing him like she does before they start playing; then she put her paw to the door, but just lightly, just like a person would open the door, and just opened the door and turned and went back to the bone she'd been chewing. She knew what she was doing. She had already turned around by the time Jude entered. She just got up to open the door, like, 'Okay, fine, come in.' The specific thing that was so interesting," Alex wants to emphasize, "was how she opened the door for him and then turned away and went back to what she'd been doing, just as I myself would have let Jude in."

We grab our jackets, and Chula and Jude get excited. They hope — it's safe to say — that we're taking them for a run. I open the door and say, "Car," and they run for the car's back hatch.

At the river, we let them out. They love this, of course. A swan sees them running along the shore. He steps gingerly into the water, paddling just out of easy reach. The dogs go into the water up to their bellies and bark at the swan a few times. The swan is actually stemming the current in place, not paddling away, not even drifting away. Either he doesn't want to move from this point along the shore, or he's taunting them, or he feels some conflict between challenging them and fleeing. But it's not nesting season, and the swans are not being territorial with one another. It seems he's taunting the dogs, but why would he? I don't know why he's holding right there — but he must know. Is this his idea of fun?

Chula weighs her option of swimming to the swan. You can see her trying to figure out what to do next. She wades deep enough to almost float but seems to understand that this won't work for her. The swan clearly understands that this won't work for Chula, because he is staring directly at her from just a few strokes away, but not moving one feather farther. In a minute the dogs realize that this is not going to get any more fun for them, and they splash to shore and gambol off.

The swan just showed that he understood that he needed to avoid the dogs *and* that he understood the limitations of their movement in water. He understands how to use the water to stay completely safe while holding himself so close that, were he on land, the dogs could cover the distance in two bounds, requiring perhaps half a second. The swan demonstrated theory of mind and mastery of medium.

Farther down the shore, Chula bounds into the water near where some mallard ducks are floating. They, too, paddle to deeper water but do not fly. A few hundred yards farther along the shore, the river enters Long Island Sound. The river's mouth is perhaps a hundred yards across. Out in mid-river, several hundred scaup — another kind of duck — are diving for mussels. They ignore the dogs. But when four humans appear on the far shore, all the ducks fly up in alarm, leaving the vicinity of the river and flying out into the Sound. As they pass over other sitting groups of scaup and long-tailed ducks, those ducks also take flight and head out over the Sound, in a wide-spreading panic.

Why would the ducks merely paddle away from their age-old enemy the wolf (in domesticated form) yet become panicked by the mere appearance of humans on a farther shore? Because the ducks understand a dog's limits and have learned that humans can kill at great distance — that's why. They know that causing harm can be on a human's mind, and they have some concept either of death or attack or great danger. And because for millions of years of evolution they had no experience of guns, their accurate judgment about what constitutes differing safe distances from dogs and humans is learned and recent. Do they "have" a theory of mind? The question gets less interesting as the richness of behaviors and perceptions become more apparent. What the birds do and why; that's what's so interesting.

When we get home, I towel off Chula, [20] whose fur is full of sand and damp with brackish water. She endures it but doesn't love it. Yet as soon as I unfurl the towel, Jude dives headlong into it, tail wagging widely as he snaps his jaws randomly while prancing like a terry-cloth ghost. Jude loves playing blindman's buff. The game is to grab and release his muzzle while he's blindly snapping. Take the towel off, he stops snapping and tries to get into the towel again. Chula has no interest in this game, or in Jude when he's being so silly.

Later, in the yard surrounding our house, the dogs chase each other in totally unnecessary play. They fake each other out when racing around the shed or cottage. Chula will try to double back to intercept Jude, but Jude will stop to see from which way Chula is coming. They know what is going on, and they seem to understand that the other is trying to fool them. That's "theory of mind," too. One is evaluating what the other is thinking, each showing clear understanding that the other might be faked into a false belief about which direction they'll be charging from. Because they're playing, there's both cleverness and humor in this. (Unless they're just two unconscious machines interacting without sensation or perception. Some people still insist that "we can't be sure." That's what I mean by denial.)

A dog who has never before seen a ball would not bring it to a person and lay it at their feet. But a dog experienced with balls comes to invite play. They envision the game, plan a way to start it, and execute the plan with a human partner who they understand is knowing. Theory of mind.

Any dog who goes into a play bow is inviting you, understanding that you might engage. (The play bow isn't strictly canine; Maddox the raccoon frequently invited play this way.) Dogs and others don't play-bow to trees, chairs, or other inanimate objects. Our puppy Emi play-bowed to the first ball she ever saw when I rolled it her way. She assumed anything moving so purposefully along the floor had to be alive — but she did that only once. In moments she realized that this was a wonderful new thing but that it was inanimate, not capable of an aware response or voluntary play. It therefore needed no further invitation, nor consideration, nor restraint in being chewed, flung, and pounced on.

Chula once barked at a life-sized concrete dog, but only once — a sniff told her that its shape had lied. A dog — or an elephant, say — often validates the authenticity of things by scent. A dog that loves chasing rabbits will give one perfunctory sniff to a porcelain rabbit. It obviously recognizes rabbits on sight but is too clever to be fooled by a fake. To a dog, if it looks like a duck and quacks like a duck, it's not a duck unless it *smells* like a duck.

These little stories reveal dogs' shrewd 25 ability to discern what has a mind — and what doesn't. Theory thereof. You can't bring swimming swans and flocks of diving ducks into a lab. Sometimes, rather than "testing" animals in contraptions and contrived setups where they can't be who they are, we might simply define the concept we're interested in, then watch the animals in free-living situations appropriate to their lives. Do they show an understanding that others hold different thoughts and agendas and can even be fooled? Yes. It's happening all around us, twenty-four/seven, blindingly obvious. But you have to have your eyes open. Lab psychologists and philosophers of behavior often don't seem to know about how perceptions function in the real world. I wish they'd go outside, watch, and have some fun.

Topics for Critical Thinking and Writing

1. Does the reader have to infer Carl Safina's thesis, or does he state it directly? What, in your opinion, is the closest thing to a thesis statement Safina offers?

2. What assumptions does Safina propose are among the shortcomings of scientific research into animal intelligence?

3. What is Safina's persona in this essay? Is his presentation of himself effective? How do you think it contributes to his argument overall?

4. What is Safina's fundamental dispute with the ways researchers have tested animals with the theory of mind? How does he establish his form of evidence as a vital alternative to scientific understandings?

5. Define the terms *anthropomorphism* and *anthropocentrism*. Think of an example of each, and argue whether or not either concept helps or hurts Safina's argument.

6. Safina's language and voice might appeal to a specific audience. What do you think are some potential characteristics of Safina's likeliest readers? Who do you think might disagree with him, and what do you think would be their primary criticism? Are those criticisms valid?

7. Write down your own thoughts on the intelligence of your own or a friend's pet. Closely examine your own assumptions about what the pet is thinking — or what the pet is thinking about you — and then share your thoughts with classmates. Do their experiences with their own pets support or undermine your assumptions? Could any of these experiences be used to support or refute Safina? How so?

ASSIGNMENT FOR WRITING AN ANALYSIS OF AN ARGUMENT

Choose a selection not yet discussed in class or an essay assigned by your instructor. In an essay of 500 words, analyze and evaluate the essay. In writing an analysis of a reading, do the following:

- Read and reread thoughtfully the essay you are analyzing. Composing and keeping notes in the margins or in new documents will help you think about what you are reading.

- Be sure to examine the author's thesis, purpose, methods, persona, intended audience, and tone.

- Examine closely the *organization* of an argument. Is the thesis explicitly or implicitly stated, at the very beginning or somewhere later in the essay? What is the author's strongest piece of evidence? Is it presented right off the bat and then supported by further evidence, or does the essay build up to the key evidence? Is the organization effective?

- Remember that although your essay is an analysis of someone else's writing and you may have to include a summary of the work you are writing about, your essay is *your* essay, your analysis, not a mere summary; the thesis, the organization, and the tone are yours.

6

Developing an Argument of Your Own

The difficult part in an argument is not to defend one's opinion but to know what it is.
— ANDRÉ MAUROIS

No greater misfortune could happen to anyone than that of developing a dislike for argument.
— PLATO

Planning an Argument

First, hear the wisdom of Mark Twain: "When the Lord finished the world, He pronounced it good. That is what I said about my first work, too. But Time, I tell you, Time takes the confidence out of these incautious early opinions."

All of us, teachers and students, have our moments of confidence, when we feel certain that our thoughts and judgments are settled. However, for the most part we know too that new information and new experiences can always change our early opinions on matters. To execute a well-informed, well-reasoned argument takes time and effort, and most of all a willingness to revise: to revise our thinking as we learn, and our writing as we produce it. Clear, thoughtful, seemingly effortless prose is not common on the first try. Good writing requires rethinking and revision. In a live conversation we can always claim ignorance and cover ourselves with such expressions as "Well, I don't know, but I sort of think . . . ," and we can always revise our words instantly ("Oh, well, I didn't mean it that way"). However, once we have had the chance to learn about and reason through an issue, and are committed to writing down our thoughts — and once we have handed in the final version of our writing — we are helpless. We are (putting it strongly) naked to our enemies.

Producing the strongest arguments requires good planning — but that can be difficult when you do not yet know what to think about something. Thus, planning your argument starts with developing it.

GETTING IDEAS: ARGUMENT AS AN INSTRUMENT OF INQUIRY

In Chapter 1, we quoted Robert Frost, "To learn to write is to learn to have ideas," and we offered strategies about generating ideas, a process traditionally called **invention**. A moment ago we said that we often improve our ideas when explaining them to someone else. Partly, of course, we're responding to questions or objections raised by our companion in the conversation. But in writing we must respond to other writers and also to ourselves: Almost as soon as we think we know what we have to say, we may find that it won't do. If we're lucky, we may find a better idea surfacing. One of the best ways of getting ideas is to talk things over.

When it comes to writing, the process of "talking things over" usually begins with a dialogue between yourself and a text that you're reading: Your notes, your summary, and your annotations are a kind of dialogue between you and the author. You can also have a dialogue with classmates and friends about your topic to try out and develop ideas. You may be arguing, but not chiefly to persuade; rather, you're using argument to find the truth — testing ideas, playing the devil's advocate, speaking hypothetically. Through reading, taking notes, and talking, you may find that you have developed some clear ideas that can be put into writing. So you take up a sheet of blank paper, but then a paralyzing thought suddenly strikes: "I have ideas but just can't put them into words." The blank white page (or screen) stares back at you.

All writers, even professional ones, are familiar with this experience. Good writers know that waiting for inspiration is usually not the best strategy. You may be waiting a long time. The best thing to do is begin. Recall some of what we said in Chapter 1: *Writing is a way of thinking.* It's a way of *getting and developing ideas. Argument* is an instrument of inquiry as well as persuasion. It is an important *method* of *critical thinking.* It helps us clarify what we think. One reason we have trouble writing is our fear of putting ourselves on record, but another reason is our fear that we have no ideas worth putting down. However, by writing notes — or even free associations — and by writing a draft, no matter how weak, we can begin to think our way toward good ideas.

When you are planning an argument, talking with others can help, but sometimes there isn't time to chat live. Take advantage of the tools at your disposal. Use the internet, including your email, social media, search engines, blogs, and wikis, to involve yourself in the conversation. Posting on social media or writing a blog entry in a public space about your topic can foster conversations about the topic and help you discover what others think — and your own opinions. Using the internet to uncover and refine a topic is common practice, especially early in the brainstorming process.

THREE BRAINSTORMING STRATEGIES: FREEWRITING, LISTING, AND DIAGRAMMING

If you are facing an issue, debate, or topic and don't know what to write, it is likely because you don't yet know what you think. If, after talking about the topic with yourself (via your reading notes) and others (via any means), you are still unclear on what you think, try one of three strategies: freewriting, listing, or diagramming.

FREEWRITING   Write for five or six minutes, nonstop, without censoring what you produce. You may use what you write to improve your thinking. You may even dim your computer screen so you won't be tempted to look up and fiddle too soon with what you've just written. Once you have spent the time writing out your ideas, you can use what you've written to look further into the subject at hand.

Freewriting should be totally free. As a topic, let's imagine the writer below is thinking about how children's toys are constructed for different genders. The student is reflecting on the release of the Nerf Rebelle, a type of toy gun made specifically for girls. A good freewrite might look like this:

> FREEWRITING: Nerf released a new toy made for girls, the Nerf Rebelle gun. It was an attempt the company made to offer toys for girls that have been traditionally made for boys. This seems good — showing an effort toward equality between the sexes. Or is Nerf just trying to broaden its market and sell more toys (after all, boys are only half the population)? Or is it both? That could be my central question. But it is not like the gun is gender-neutral. It is pink and purple and has feminine-looking designs on it. And with its "elle" ending the gun sounds small, cute, and girly. Does this toy represent true equality between the sexes, or does it just offer more in the way of feminine stereotypes? It shoots foam arrows, unlike the boys' version of the gun, which shoots bullets. This suggests Cupid, maybe — a figure whose arrows inspire love. A stereotype that girls aren't saving the world with their weapons but seeking love and marriage. What kind of messages does this send to young girls? Is it the same message suggested by the gun? How does this work in other areas of life, like business and politics?

Notice that the writer here is jumping around, generating and exploring ideas while writing. Later she can return to the freewriting and begin organizing her ideas and observations. Notice that right in the middle of the freewriting she made a connection between the toy and Cupid, and by extension to the larger culture in which forms of contemporary femininity can be found. This connection seems significant, and it may help the student to broaden her argument from a critique of the company's motives early on, to a more evidence-based piece about assumptions underlying certain trends in consumer and media culture. The point is that freewriting in this case led to new paths of inquiry and may have inspired further research into different kinds of toys and media.

LISTING   Writing down keywords, just as you do when making a shopping list, is another way of generating ideas. When you make a shopping list, you write *ketchup*, and the act of writing it reminds you that you also need hamburger rolls — and *that* in turn reminds you that you also need tuna fish. Similarly, when preparing a list of ideas for a paper, just writing down one item will often generate another. Of course, when you look over the list, you'll probably drop some of these ideas — the dinner menu will change — but you'll be making progress. If you have a smartphone or tablet, use it to write down your thoughts. You can even email these notes to yourself so you can access them later, or you can store them digitally in the cloud.

Here's an example of a student listing questions and making associations that could help him focus on a specific argument within a larger debate. The subject here is whether prostitution should be legalized. Key terms are underlined.

> LIST: Prostitutes & Law
>   What types of prostitutes exist?
>   How has the law traditionally policed sex in history and in different places?
>   How many prostitutes are arrested every year?
>   Individual rights vs. public good?
>   Why shouldn't people be allowed to sell sex?
>   Could prostitution be taxed?
>   Who gains or suffers most from enforcement? From legalization?
>   If it were legal, could its negative effects be better controlled?
>   Aren't "escort services" really prostitution rings for people with more money?
>   Who goes into the "oldest business" and why?

Notice that the student doesn't really know the answers yet but is asking questions by free-associating and seeing what turns up as a productive line of analysis. The questions range from the definition of prostitution to its effects, and they might inspire the student to do some basic internet research or even deeper research. Once you make a list, see if you can observe patterns or similarities among the items you listed or if you invented a question worthy of its own thesis statement (e.g., "The enforcement of prostitution laws hurts *X* group unequally, and it uses a lot of public money that could better be used in other areas or toward regulating the trade rather than jailing people").

DIAGRAMMING   Sketching a visual representation of an essay is a kind of listing. Three methods of diagramming are especially common.

Clustering   As we discuss on page 9, you can make an effective cluster by writing, in the middle of a sheet of paper, a word or phrase summarizing your topic (e.g., *fracking*, the process of forcing high pressure into rock to extract natural resources; see diagram), circling it, and then writing down and circling a related word or idea (e.g., *energy independence*). You then circle these phrases and continue jotting down ideas, making connections, and indicating relationships. Here, the economic and environmental impacts of fracking seem to be the focus. Whether you realize it or not, an argument is taking shape.

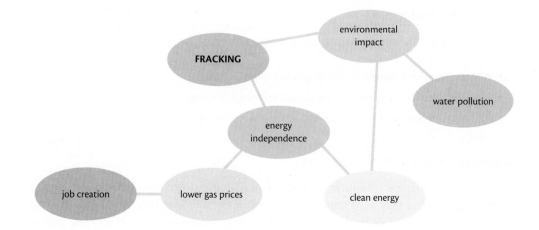

Branching   Some writers find it useful to draw a tree, moving from the central topic to the main branches (chief ideas) and then to the twigs (aspects of the chief ideas).

Comparing in columns   Draw a line down the middle of the page and then set up two columns showing oppositions. For instance, if you are concerned with the environmental and economic impacts of fracking, you might produce columns that look something like this:

Environmental	Economic
water pollution	employment
chemicals used	independence from unstable oil-producing countries
gas leaks	cheaper fuel
toxic waste	cheaper electricity

All these methods can, of course, be executed with pen and paper, but you may also be able to use them on your computer, depending on the capabilities of your software. You might also find templates from a good website helpful.

Exercise: Brainstorming

Consider these topics by using freewriting, listing, or diagramming:

- What is the biggest threat to national security today?
- Should your college require students to study a foreign language?
- Should monuments to Confederate leaders be removed from public spaces?

REVISION AS INVENTION

Whether you're using a computer or a pen, you may put down some words and almost immediately see that they need improvement, not simply a little polishing but a substantial overhaul. You write, "Race should be counted in college admissions for two reasons," and as soon as you write those words, a third reason comes to mind. Or perhaps one of those "two reasons" no longer seems very good. As E. M. Forster said, "How can I know what I think till I see what I say?" We have to see what we say — we have to get something down on the page — before we realize that we need to make it better.

Writing, then, is really **rewriting** — that is, **revising** — and a revision is a *re-vision*, a second look. The essay that you submit — whether as hard copy or as digital file — should be clear and may appear to be effortlessly composed, but in all likelihood the clarity and apparent ease are the result of a struggle with yourself during which you refined your first thoughts. You begin by putting down ideas, perhaps in random order, but sooner or later comes the job of looking at them critically, developing what's useful in them and removing what isn't. If you follow this procedure, you will be in the company of Picasso, who said that he "advanced by means of destruction." Any passages that you cut or destroy can be kept in another file in case you want to revisit those deletions later. Sometimes, you end up restoring them and developing what you discarded into a new essay with a new direction.

Whether you advance bit by bit (writing a sentence, revising it, writing the next, etc.) or whether you write an entire first draft and then revise it and revise it again and again is chiefly a matter of temperament. Probably most people combine both approaches, backing up occasionally but trying to get to the end fairly soon so that they can see rather quickly what they know, or think they know, and can then start the real work of thinking, of converting their initial ideas into something substantial.

ASKING QUESTIONS WITH STASIS THEORY

Generating ideas, we said when talking about **topics** and invention strategies in Chapter 1 (p. 16), is mostly a matter of asking (and then thinking about) questions. In this book, we include questions at the end of each argumentative essay not to torment you, but to help you think about the arguments — for instance, to turn your attention to especially important matters. If your instructor asks you to write an answer to one of these questions, you are lucky: Examining the question will stimulate your mind to work in a specific direction.

Another method of using your own questions is to use **stasis theory**, an invention process used by ancient rhetoricians like Aristotle and Cicero to work through a topic and find what facts and judgments "hold." (*Stasis* means something like "stability," so you can image the process as leading you to what is true about a topic or issue.) If your instructor doesn't assign a topic for an argumentative essay, you'll find that some ideas may be generated by applying the four key questions of stasis theory. These four questions, for the ancients, sought to establish the facts, the meaning, the importance, and the action needed in a given situation. We present an example of using stasis theory below.

First, consider these questions in general:

1. What is *X*? (*definition*)
2. What is the value or seriousness of *X*? (*quality*)
3. What are the causes (or the consequences) of *X*? (*fact*)
4. What should (or could or must) we do about *X*? (*policy*)

Let's spend a moment looking at each of these questions.

1. What is X? Suppose your topic was capital punishment; *defining* what that is could be its own argument, although you would certainly want to go beyond saying simply, "Capital punishment is the legally authorized killing of a person." That does not need to be argued. Similarly, we can hardly argue about which states utilize capital punishment and which do not, or about how many people have been sentenced to death in the United States in the past ten years — a glance at the appropriate reports will answer those questions. You might instead define the uses, limits, evolution, or means of capital punishment as administered in the United States. Which uses might constitute cruel and unusual punishment? How has the death penalty changed over time, and what does that say about a changing society? Is the death penalty discriminatory? Your definition does not necessarily have to argue that it should or should not be abolished, or that it should or should not be applied fairly. You might be doing enough just by establishing a clear definition of the topic and its problems. An argument about abortion, for example, might concentrate strictly on the definition of a "person" or of the "viability" of a fetus, or even the definition of "when life begins." Arguments of this sort may make a claim — and may take a stand — but they do not also have to argue for an action. You may establish a clear definition of the problem and leave it to others for possible responses.

2. What is the value or seriousness of X? Assessing the value of a topic or issue is thinking about its meaning and how it reflects or relates to a larger significance, whether personal, social, political, religious, and so on. Why should a general audience of American readers care about your examination of the death penalty? Why should your target audience — lawyers, Catholics, general voters, or whomever — care? What is the *seriousness* of discrimination in the criminal

- to set forth an assessment
- to convince readers that the assessment is reasonable

In writing an evaluation, you have to rely on criteria, and these will vary depending on your topic. What criteria serve best in making an evaluation? Probably some or all of the following:

- testimony of authorities
- inductive evidence
- appeals to logic ("it follows, therefore, that . . .")
- appeals to emotion

> **WRITING TIP**
> College courses often call for arguments about art and literature. In writing an evaluation, you have to rely on criteria particular to literature. For instance, in comparing the artistic merit of plays by Tennessee Williams and Arthur Miller, you may want to talk about the quality of the character-ization, the importance of the theme, and so on.

3. *What are the causes (or the consequences) of X?* When you ask about the causes and consequences of an issue, you are assessing the real or conjectured facts of the matter. Think about this in relation to the topic of capital punishment: You might look at what the actual or probable effects are (or would be) for various groups of people either personally affected or professionally interested in this aspect of our justice system.

Consider also this example concerning the academic performance of girls in single-sex schools. It is pretty much agreed (based on statistical evidence) that the graduates of these schools do better, as a group, than girls who graduate from coeducational schools. But why? What is the *cause*? Administrators of girls' schools usually attribute the success to the fact that their classrooms offer an atmosphere free from male intimidation: Girls allegedly gain confidence and become more expressive without the presence of boys. This may be the answer, but skeptics have attributed the graduates' success to two other causes:

- Most single-sex schools require parents to pay tuition, and it is a documented fact that the children of well-to-do parents do better, academically, than the children of poorer parents.
- Most single-sex schools are selective private schools whose students are chosen based upon academic promise — that is, students who have *already done well academically.*

The lesson? Be cautious in attributing a cause. There may be multiple causes and factors. The kinds of support that usually accompany claims of consequence and cause include the following:

- factual data, especially statistics
- analogies ("The Roman Empire declined because of *X* and *Y*"; "Our society exhibits *X* and *Y*; therefore . . .")
- inductive evidence

4. What should (or could or must) we do about X?   Whether you end up arguing that a problem exists to identify it, diagnose its larger importance, or demonstrate its unfortunate consequences, you may find yourself in a position to recommend a partial or full solution to the problem. What action should be taken, and by whom? Continuing our example, should the death penalty be abolished? Should parents change the ways they discipline their children? Should the law allow eighteen-year-olds to drink alcohol? Should eighteen-year-old women be required to register for Selective Service? Should steroid use by athletes be banned? These questions involve conduct and policy; how you answer them will reveal your values and principles.

(See the Visual Guide: Organizing Your Argument on p. 225 for an example of how an argument of policy might be structured.)

Support for claims of policy usually include the following:

- statistics

- testimony of authorities

- appeals to common sense and to the reader's moral sense

Again, an argument may be entirely based on one, two, three, or all of the four basic questions discussed in this section. Someone interested in analyzing the debate over censorship of fake news may construct the argument exclusively about what fake news *is* (a question of definition); about the *seriousness* of fake news in a democratic society (a question of quality); about how efforts to curb fake news limit free speech (a question of fact); or that some entity or institution, such as the US government or Facebook, should act to limit fake news (a question of policy). Of course, all of these questions could also be combined in a more comprehensive argument.

As you work through various questions and discover your argument, keep in mind that other elements of critical thinking and argument we have discussed up to this point are still relevant. You should still address different perspectives and possible objections to your ideas — counterarguments — and refute them if possible. Most of all, you should be careful to support your ideas with carefully selected evidence and examples.

THE THESIS OR MAIN POINT

Let's assume that you are writing an argumentative essay — perhaps an evaluation of an argument in this book — and you have what seems to be a pretty good draft or at least a collection of notes that are the result of hard thinking. You really do have ideas now, and you want to present them effectively. How will you organize your essay? No one formula works best for every essayist and for every essay, but it is usually advisable to formulate a basic **thesis** (a claim, a central point, a chief position) and to state it early. Every

> **WRITING TIP**
> If a question seems relevant or a piece of evidence inspires new questions and answers in your mind, it's a good idea to start writing — even just fragmentary sentences if necessary. You'll probably find that one idea leads to another and that new questions and issues begin to appear. Even if your ideas seem weak as you write them, don't be discouraged; you will have put something on paper, and returning to these words, perhaps in five minutes or even the next day, you'll probably find that some ideas aren't at all bad and may stimulate even better ones.

essay that is any good, even a book-length one, has a thesis (a main point), which can be stated briefly, usually in one sentence. Remember Calvin Coolidge's alleged remark to his wife on the preacher's sermon on sin: "He was against it." Don't confuse the **topic** (sin) with the thesis (sin is bad). The thesis is the argumentative theme, the author's primary claim or contention, the proposition that the rest of the essay will explain and defend. Of course, the thesis may sound commonplace, but the book or essay or sermon ought to develop it in an interesting and convincing way.

When you formulate a thesis and ask questions about it — such as who the readers are, what they believe, what they know, and what they need to know — you also begin to get ideas about how to organize the material (or, at least, you realize that you'll have to work out some sort of organization). The thesis may be clear and simple, but the reasons (the argument) may take many pages. The thesis is the point; the argument sets forth the evidence that supports the thesis.

RAISING THE STAKES OF YOUR THESIS   Imagine walking across campus and coming upon a person ready to perform on a tightrope suspended between two buildings. He is wearing a glittering leotard and is eyeing up his challenge very seriously. Here's the thing, though: His tightrope is only *one foot off the ground*. Would you stop and watch him walk across it? Maybe, maybe not. Most people are likely to take a look and move on. If you did spend a few minutes watching, you wouldn't be very worried about the performer falling. If he lost his balance momentarily, you wouldn't gasp in horror. And if he walked across the tightrope masterfully, you might be somewhat impressed but not enraptured.

Now imagine the rope being *a hundred feet off the ground*. You and many others would almost certainly stop and witness the feat. The audience would likely be captivated, nervous about the performer potentially falling, "oohing" if he momentarily lost his balance, and cheering if he crossed the rope successfully.

Consider the tightrope as your thesis statement, the performer as writer, and the act of crossing as the argument. What we call "low-stakes" thesis statements are comparable to low tightropes: A low-stakes thesis statement itself may be interesting, but not much about it is vital to any particular audience. Low-stakes thesis statements lack a sense of importance or

Kay Nietfeld/DPA/Getty Images

Edu Silva 2ev/Shutterstock.com

Considering thesis statements as tightropes strung at different heights can help you consider the stakes of your argument.

relevance. They may restate what is already widely known and accepted, or they may make a good point but not discuss any consequences. Some examples:

Good nutrition and exercise can lead to a healthy life.

Our education system focuses too much on standardized tests.

Children's beauty pageants are exploitative.

Students can write well-organized, clear, and direct papers on these topics, but if the thesis is "low stakes" like these, the performance would be similar to that of an expert walking across a tightrope that is only one foot off the ground. The argument may be well executed, but few in the audience will be inspired by it.

However, if you raise the stakes by "raising the tightrope," you can compel readers to *want* to read and keep reading. There are several ways to raise the tightrope. First, *think about what is socially, culturally, or politically important* about your thesis statement and argument. Some writing instructors tell students to ask themselves "So what?" about the thesis, but this can be a vague directive. Here are some better questions:

- Why is your thesis important?
- What is the impact of your thesis on a particular group or demographic?
- What are the consequences of what you claim?
- What could happen if your position were *not* recognized?
- How can your argument benefit readers or compel them to action (by doing something or adopting a new belief)?
- What will readers *gain* by accepting your argument as convincing?

In formulating your thesis, keep in mind the following points.

- *Different thesis statements may speak to different target audiences.* An argument about changes in estate tax laws may not thrill all audiences, but for a defined group — accountants, lawyers, or the elderly, for instance — it may be quite controversial and highly relevant.
- *Not all audiences are equal — or equally interested in your thesis or argument.* In this book, we generally select topics of broad importance. However, in a literature course, a film history course, or a political science course, you'll calibrate your thesis statements and arguments to an audience that is invested in those fields.

> ### A CHECKLIST FOR A THESIS STATEMENT
>
> ☐ Does the statement make an arguable assertion rather than (1) merely assert an unarguable fact, (2) merely announce a topic, or (3) declare an unarguable opinion or belief?
>
> ☐ Is the statement broad enough to cover the entire argument that I will be presenting, and is it narrow enough for me to cover the topic in the space allotted?
>
> ☐ Does the thesis have consequences beneficial to some audience or consequences that would be detrimental if it were not accepted? (In other words, are there stakes?)

THINKING CRITICALLY *"Walking the Tightrope"*

Examine the low-stakes thesis statements provided below and expand each one into a high-stakes thesis by including the importance of asserting it and by proposing a possible response. The first one has been done as an example.

LOW-STAKES THESIS	HIGH-STAKES THESIS
Good nutrition and exercise can lead to a healthy life.	One way to help solve the epidemic obesity problem in the United States is to remind consumers of a basic fact accepted by nearly all reputable health experts: Good nutrition and exercise can lead to a healthy life.
Every qualified American should vote.	
Spanking children is good/bad.	
Electric cars will reduce air pollution.	

In writing about the steep decline in bee populations, your argument might look quite different if you're speaking to ecologists as opposed to gardeners. (We will discuss audience more in the following section.)

- *Be wary of compare-and-contrast arguments.* One of the most basic approaches to writing is to compare and contrast, a maneuver that produces a low-tightrope thesis. It normally looks like this: "*X* and *Y* are similar in some ways and different in others." But if you think about it, *anything* can be compared and contrasted in this way, and doing so doesn't necessarily *tell* anything important. So, if you're writing a compare-and-contrast paper, make sure to include the reasons why it is important to compare and contrast these things. What benefit does the comparison yield? What significance does it have to some audience or some issue?

IMAGINING AN AUDIENCE

Raising the tightrope of your thesis will also require you to imagine the *audience* you're addressing. The questions that you ask yourself in generating thoughts on a topic will primarily relate to the topic, but additional questions that consider the audience are always relevant:

- Who are my readers?
- What do they believe?

- What common ground do we share?
- What do I want my readers to believe?
- What do they need to know?
- Why should they care?

Let's think about these questions. The literal answer to the first probably is "my teacher," but (unless you receive instructions to the contrary) you should not write specifically for your teacher. Instead, you should write for an audience that is, generally speaking, like your classmates. In short, your imagined audience is literate, intelligent, and moderately well informed, but its members don't know everything that you know, and they don't know your response to the problem being addressed. Your audience needs more information along those lines to make an intelligent decision about the issue.

For example, in writing about how children's toys shape the minds of young boys and girls differently, it may not be enough to simply say, "Toys are part of the gender socialization process." ("Sure they are," the audience might already agree.) However, if you raise the stakes based on who your intended audience is and the audience's level of intelligence, you have an opportunity to direct a more complex argument that results from this observation: You frame the questions, lay out the issues, identify the problems, and note the complications that arise because of your basic thesis. You could point out that toys have a significant impact on the interests, identities, skills, and capabilities that children develop and carry into adulthood. Because toys are so significant, is it important to ask questions about whether they perpetuate gender-based stereotypes? Do toys help perpetuate social inequalities between the sexes? Most children think toys are "just fun," but they may be teaching kids to conform unthinkingly to the social expectations of their sex, to accept designated sex-based social roles, and to cultivate talents differently based on sex. What we want you to see is that asking broader questions about the implications of your argument extends it further and gives it social importance to make it relevant to your audience.

> **WRITING TIP**
> If you wish to persuade, finding premises that you share with your audience can help establish common ground, a function of *ethos*.

What audiences should be concerned with your topic? Maybe you're addressing the general public who buys toys for children at least some of the time. Maybe you're addressing parents who are raising young children. Maybe you're addressing consumer advocates, encouraging them to pressure toy manufacturers and retailers to produce more gender-neutral offerings. The point is that your essay should contain (and sustain) an assessment of the impact of your high-stakes thesis, and it should set out a clear course of action for a particular audience.

That said, if you know your audience well, you can argue for different courses of action that are most likely to be persuasive. You may not be very convincing if you argue to parents in general that they should avoid all Disney-themed toys. Perhaps you should argue simply that parents should be conscious of the gender messages that toys convey, offer their kids diverse toys, and talk to their children while playing with them about alternatives to the stereotypical messages that the toys convey. However, if you're writing for a magazine called *Radical Parenting* and your essay is titled "Buying Toys the Gender-Neutral Way," your audience and its expectations — therefore, your thesis and argument — may look far different. The bottom line is not just to know your audience but to define it.

The essays in this book are from many different sources with many different audiences. An essay from the *New York Times* addresses educated general readers; an essay from *Ms.* magazine targets readers sympathetic to feminism. An essay from *Commonweal*, a Roman Catholic publication for nonspecialists, is likely to differ in point of view or tone from one in *Time*, even though both articles may advance approximately the same position. The *Commonweal* article may, for example, effectively cite church fathers and distinguished Roman Catholic writers as authorities, whereas the *Time* article would probably cite few or none of these figures because a non-Catholic audience might be unfamiliar with them or, even if familiar, might be unimpressed by their views.

The tone as well as the gist of the argument is in some degree shaped by the audience. For instance, popular journals, such as *National Review* and *Ms.* magazine, are more likely to use ridicule than are journals chiefly addressed to, say, an academic audience.

Instructors sometimes tell students to imagine their audience as their classmates. What they probably mean is that your argument should be addressed to people invested in the world of ideas, not just your literal classmates. Again, ask yourself the following questions:

- "What do my readers need to know?"
- "What do I want them to believe?"

Exercise: Imagining Your Audience

Consider one of the four topics below and write your responses to each question for your chosen topic.

Animal intelligence   Free college tuition   Screen time   Minimum wage

1. Who are my readers?
2. What do they believe?
3. What common ground do we share?
4. What do I want my readers to believe?
5. What do they need to know?
6. Why should they care?

ADDRESSING OPPOSITION AND ESTABLISHING COMMON GROUND

Presumably, your imagined audience does not share all your views. But why? By putting yourself into your readers' shoes — and your essay will almost surely summarize the views that you're going to speak against — and by thinking about what your audience knows or thinks it knows, you will also generate ideas. Ask yourself:

- Why does your audience not share your views? What views do they hold?
- How can these readers hold a position that to you seems unreasonable?

You may also spend time online reviewing websites dedicated to your topic to discover facts and assess common views and opinions.

Let's assume that you believe the minimum wage should be raised, but you know that some people hold a different view. Why do they hold it? Try to state their view *in a way that would be satisfactory to them.* Having done so, you may perceive that your conclusions and theirs differ because they're based on different premises — perhaps different ideas about how the economy works — or different definitions, concepts, or assumptions about fairness or employment. Examine the opposition's premises carefully and explain, first to yourself (and ultimately to your readers) why you see things differently.

Perhaps some facts are in dispute, such as whether or not an oil pipeline poses a serious threat to the local ecology. The thing to do, then, is to check the facts. If you search online on a reputable website or in a database and find that environmental harms have not been common in cases of other pipelines, yet you are still against one in your own area, you can't premise your argument on the harm the pipeline is likely to cause. You'll have to develop an argument that takes account of the facts and interprets them reasonably.

Among the relevant facts there surely are some that your audience or your opponent will not dispute. The same is true of the values relevant to the discussion; both sides very likely believe in some of the same values. These areas of shared agreement are crucial to effective persuasion in argument.

There are two good reasons for identifying and isolating the areas of agreement:

- There is no point in disputing facts or values on which you and your readers already agree.
- It usually helps establish goodwill between yourself and your opponent when you can point to shared beliefs, assumptions, facts, and values.

Recall that in composing college papers it's usually best to write for a general audience, an audience rather like your classmates but without the specific knowledge that they all share as students enrolled in one course. If the topic is raising the minimum wage, the audience presumably consists of supporters and nonsupporters, as well as people who hold no opinion at all (*yet*, perhaps, until they read your ideas). Thinking "What do readers need to know?" may prompt you to give statistics about the rising cost of living and the number of people who make just the minimum wage. Or if you're arguing against raising the minimum wage, it may prompt you to cite studies showing how doing so increases the cost of goods and

A protest for a higher minimum wage.

Cem Ozdel/Anadolu Agency/Getty Images

the rate of unemployment. If you are writing for a general audience, asking "What does the audience believe?" is important because many people will not be familiar with the basic facts about the minimum wage and the implications of raising it. You will likely be painting with broad strokes, arguing from the widest possible perspectives. But if the audience is specialized, such as a group of economists, a union group, or a sector of small business owners who fear that rate hikes will interfere with their business, an effective essay will have to address their special beliefs.

In addressing the beliefs of your likely opponents, you must try to establish some common ground. If you advocate for the minimum wage hike, you should recognize the possibility that this represents a threat to some proprietors of small businesses. But perhaps you can argue that increases in the minimum wage typically result in more spending at small businesses, which would be good for small business owners in the long run. This is how your thoughts in imagining an audience can prompt you to think of other kinds of evidence — perhaps testimony or statistics on this issue, for example.

A CHECKLIST FOR IMAGINING AN AUDIENCE

☐ Have I identified my readers as a general or more specific audience?

☐ Do I understand how much my readers need to be told based on what I believe they already know?

☐ Have I provided necessary background (including definitions of special terms) if the imagined readers probably are not especially familiar with the topic?

☐ Am I able to identify whether or not my readers are likely to be neutral, sympathetic, or hostile to my views?

    ☐ For neutral audience members, have I offered good reasons to persuade them?

    ☐ If they're sympathetic, have I done more than merely reaffirm their present beliefs? That is, have I perhaps enriched their views or encouraged them to act?

    ☐ If they're hostile, will they nevertheless feel respected and informed by my position? Have I taken account of their positions and recognized their strengths but also called attention to their limitations? Have I offered a position that might persuade them to modify their position?

Drafting and Revising an Argument

There is no one way to begin writing. As we have suggested earlier in this chapter, sometimes the best way to get started writing is just to start writing, building ideas, and seeing where your pen (or keyboard) takes you. But, alas, at a certain point, you will want to begin organizing your essay more deliberately, considering your purpose, audience, language, and the organization of your ideas.

THE TITLE

One of the first things you might do in planning an argument is invent a **title**, where you can announce the thesis or topic explicitly, or simply attract the attention of readers in a unique or imaginative way. If you examine the titles of essays in this book, you can see titles that announce their positions and topics both more and less explicitly than others:

"We Must Make Public Colleges and Universities Tuition-Free" (announces thesis)

"The Boston Photographs" (announces topic)

"A First Amendment Junkie" (invites readers' curiosity)

Be prepared to rethink your title *after* completing the last draft of your paper. A working title can help guide your inquiry, but do not hesitate to rethink your title after you have written your argument to ensure it accurately represents your position and analysis.

> **WRITING TIP**
> It's better to invent a simple, direct, informative title than a strained, puzzling, or overly cute one. You want to engage readers, not turn them off.

THE OPENING PARAGRAPHS

Opening paragraphs are difficult to write, so don't worry about writing an effective opening when you're drafting. Just get some words down on paper and keep going. But when you revise your first draft, you should begin to think seriously about the effect of your opening.

A good introduction arouses readers' interest and prepares them for the rest of the paper. How? One convenient method of writing an introduction is to offer a "hook" first — something to simultaneously attract the reader and set the stage for the essay. The following table lists some strategies for opening paragraphs.

Hook	Description	Example
Anecdote	A brief story or vignette	I was having lunch recently in the newly built food court, and I noticed the word *organic* on my package of carrots, and I began to wonder . . .
Statistic	A relevant (sobering, shocking, attention-grabbing) number	According to a 2017 Common Sense Media report, American children between the ages of 0 and 8 spend an average of 2.25 hours per day of "screen time" . . .

(Continued)

Hook	Description	Example
Noteworthy event	A recent news story, real-life account, or interesting illustration of the current situation	When the president said this year in his State of the Union address that more must be done for the nation's infrastructure, he touched on an issue that . . .
Analogy	A case similar in structure but different in detail from the point being established	When a leopard stalks its prey, it can spend a full day establishing a prime ambush position, then all at once dart at over 35 miles per hour and jump over 20 feet to close the deal. This is something like . . .
Quotation	Wise, poignant, or landmark words framing your discussion	In 1903, W. E. B. Du Bois said in *The Souls of Black Folk* that "the problem of the twentieth century is the problem of the color line." In the twenty-first century, . . .
Historical account	A brief account of the back-ground or evolution of the topic	The evolution of the monster movie extends from early films such as *Nosferatu* (1922) and *The Hunchback of Notre Dame* (1923) to today's renditions such as *The Babadook* (2014) and *Slenderman* (2018). In that evolution, we can see . . .

You may set your hook quickly, provide a more elaborate version, or even combine the strategies listed in the table. In addition to grabbing readers' attention, opening paragraphs also usually do at least one (and often all) of the following:

- prepare readers for the topic (naming the topic, giving some idea of its impor-tance, noting conventional beliefs about it, or relaying in brief what people are saying about it)
- provide readers with definitions of key terms and concepts (stipulating, quoting an authority, etc.)
- establish a context for your argument by linking your subject, topic, and views to relevant social issues, debates, and trends
- reveal the thesis
- provide readers a map of the argument (giving a sense of how the essay will be organized)

You may not wish to announce your thesis in the title, but if you don't announce it there, you should set it forth early in the argument, in the introductory paragraph or paragraphs. Although it is possible for the thesis to be blurted out in the first line, usually writers spend some time preparing the argument before providing the thesis. And although it is possible never to state the thesis directly but only imply it throughout the argument, thesis statements may also be bold and daring.

Another thing you can do in an introduction is spend some time outlining the general subject into which your topic fits. The subject is the general area in which your questions and research reside, whereas your specific topic might be narrower. For example, the subject of your paper may be workers' rights, or immigration, or national security, but your topic will usually be something that falls within that subject — the minimum wage, or the border wall, or WikiLeaks, for example. You may go to great lengths to frame your topic within a subject, or you may just mention it, but it usually helps to position your discussion in a larger framework.

After announcing the topic, giving the necessary background and context, and stating your position in as engaging a manner as possible, you will do well to give the reader an idea of *how* you will proceed — that is, how the essay will be organized. It is not a requirement that all writers must state exactly what they will be doing in each part of their essay — and in fact, it may not be an effective strategy for certain audiences and purposes. Nevertheless, at any point in your introduction, you may announce that there are, say, four common objections to your thesis and that you will take them up one by one. You could add that you will move from the weakest (or most widely held) to the strongest (or least familiar), after which you will advance your own view in greater detail. Or you might announce that three primary views of an issue exist, and you will spell them out before moving on.

Not every writer states plans like this outright. But if your analysis is methodical and perhaps complex, you can tell readers where you will be taking them and by what route. In effect, you are giving them a look at your own outline. How far you go to clue the reader in to your method of analysis is up to you, just as it is up to you to decide how much background, context, definition, and so on you include. Ultimately, these decisions will impact the length and style of your introduction and set the foundations for the rest of your argument.

It is important to note that all the elements of introductions we have laid out so far do not have to be included categorically or in a formulaic way. You might do more background work, you might provide a very detailed account of competing perspectives in order to position yourself within a debate, you might offer both an anecdote and a statistic, or you might combine some elements and leave out others. The following introduction has been annotated to show the writer's choices.

According to a 2017 Common Sense Media report, American children ◄——— Hooks reader with a dramatic statistic.
between the ages of 0 and 8 spend an average of 2.25 hours per day
involved in "screen time," a term used to denote the total time a child ◄——— Defines a key term.

| | spends in front of any visual electronic media, whether television, video game, or internet. If that is correct, then children are spending a whopping 34 days — a full month and then some — each year on "screens." The debate over how much screen time is appropriate for children, and what its ultimate effects are on children's development, has been lively in the fully connected digital world. But since the advent of the iPhone in 2007, the debate has heated up even more. One group of investors, JANA Partners, recently worried about the "toxic" effects of the current levels of screen time on children, and others have correlated increasing levels of anxiety and depression in children with high levels of internet usage. To understand the potential impact of screen time on children, and what may be done about it, it is important first to examine what kinds of screen time might be positive or negative. As I will show, some kinds of screen time act as positive influences in children's life, increasing children's creativity and in some instances sociability. While there may be negative impacts to some kinds of "screen time" or too much "screen time" (even with positive or educational media), if parents and educators understand more about how to select and control children's media usage, we can work toward a practical solution in a society where these kinds of technologies are not likely to disappear. |

Author inserts her own voice to express concern.

Contextualizes the debate about screen time.

Provides a "map" of how the analysis will proceed.

Concedes to possible counterpoints, but enters into the conversation with a relevant, impactful thesis.

ORGANIZING THE BODY OF THE ESSAY

We begin with a wise remark by a newspaper columnist, Robert Cromier: "The beautiful part of writing is that you don't have to get it right the first time — unlike, say, a brain surgeon."

In drafting an essay, you will, of course, begin with an organization that seems appropriate, but you may find, in rereading the draft, that some other organization is better. For a start, in the Visual Guide: Organizing Your Argument, we offer three types of organization that are common in argumentative essays. Please note, however, that we do not mean to suggest that essays should be formulaic. These general structures need to be considered alongside your argument's needs to present counterpoints at the appropriate times, to relate an anecdote in the middle of things, or to introduce shorter summaries of others' arguments. Occasionally, these items warrant new paragraphs. The best writers know how to manage structure and how to go down little rabbit holes to explore a point further (perhaps with an analogy, anecdote, or example) but without being *digressive*, departing too far from the main point.

Even if you were to adhere closely to the patterns, you have a lot of room for variation. But let's assume that in the introductory paragraphs you have sketched the topic (and have shown, or implied, that the reader doubtless is interested in it) and have fairly and courteously set forth the opposition's view, recognizing its merits ("I grant that," "admittedly," "it is true that") and indicating the degree to which you can share part of that view. You now want to set forth arguments explaining why you differ on some essentials.

Visual Guide: Organizing Your Argument

Argument of Policy	Inductive Argument	Deductive Argument
1. Explanation of the problem or issue	1. Introduction	1. Introduction/Thesis
2. Why the reader should care about the issue	2. Example 1	2. Point 1 supporting thesis
3. Statement of alternative (but less adequate) solutions	3. Counter	3. Point 2 supporting thesis
4. Arguments in favor of your proposed solution	4. Example 2	4. Point 3 supporting thesis
5. Arguments answering possible objections	5. Example 3	5. Counterarguments with rebuttals
6. Reaffirmation of the merit of the proposed solution	6. Thesis/Conclusion	6. Summary/Conclusion

In presenting your own position, you can begin with either your strongest or your weakest reasons. Each method of organization has advantages and disadvantages.

- If you begin with your strongest examples or reasons, your essay could impress your readers and then peter out, leaving them asking, "Is that all?"

- If you begin with your weakest material, you build to a climax, but readers may not still be with you because they may have felt that the beginning of the essay was frivolous or irrelevant.

The obvious solution is to ensure that even your weakest argument demonstrates strength. Yet because we are not always so fortunate to have equally strong reasons, you can always assure your readers explicitly how you are going to proceed. For example, you may go ahead and say that stronger points will soon follow and you offer this point first to show that you are aware of it and that, slight though it is, it deserves some attention. The body of the essay, then, is devoted to arguing a position in whatever ways you need to explain yourself best.

Doubtless you'll sometimes be uncertain, while drafting an essay, whether to present a given point before or after another point, or when you should explain why you are proceeding the way you are.

> **WRITING TIP**
> By acknowledging arguments other than your own — and possible objections to your points — you let readers know that you've done your homework and build their trust. You also have a chance to preempt critiques of your ideas, which helps you be more persuasive.

When you write, and certainly when you revise, try to put yourself into the reader's shoes: Which point do you think the reader needs to know first? Which point *leads to* which further point? Your argument should not be a mere list of points; rather, it should clearly integrate one point with another in order to develop an idea and transition smoothly from one idea to the next. However, in all likelihood you won't have a strong sense of the best organization until you have written a draft and have reread it.

CHECKING TRANSITIONS   Make sure, in revising, that the reader can move easily from the beginning of a paragraph to the end and from one paragraph to the next. Transitions help signal the connections between units of the argument. For example ("For example" is a transition, indicating that an illustration will follow), they may illustrate, establish a sequence, connect logically, amplify, compare, contrast, summarize, or concede (see Thinking Critically: Using Transitions in Argument). Transitions serve as guideposts that enable the reader to move easily through your essay.

When writers revise an early draft, they chiefly do these tasks:

- They **unify** the essay by eliminating irrelevancies.
- They **organize** the essay by keeping in mind the imagined audience.
- They **clarify** the essay by fleshing out thin paragraphs, by ensuring that the transitions are adequate, and by making certain that generalizations are adequately supported by concrete details and examples.

We are not talking here about polish or elegance; we are talking about fundamental matters. Be especially careful not to abuse the logical connectives (*thus, as a result,* and so on). If you write several sentences followed by *therefore* or a similar word or phrase, be sure that what you write after the *therefore* really *does follow* from what has gone before. Logical connectives are not mere transitional devices that link disconnected bits of prose. They are supposed to mark a real movement of thought, which is the essence of an argument.

THE ENDING

What about concluding paragraphs, in which you summarize the main points and reaffirm your position? A conclusion — the word comes from the Latin *claudere,* "to shut" — ought to provide a sense of closure, but it can be much more than a restatement of the writer's thesis.

THINKING CRITICALLY *Using Transitions in Argument*

Fill in examples of the types of transitions listed below, using topics of your choice. The first one has been done as an example.

TYPE OF TRANSITION	TYPE OF LANGUAGE USED	EXAMPLE OF TRANSITION
Illustrate	*for example, for instance, consider this case*	"Many television crime dramas contain scenes of graphic violence. For example, in an episode of *Law and Order . . .*"
Establish a sequence	*a more important objection, a stronger example, the best reason*	
Connect logically	*thus, as a result, therefore, so, it follows*	
Amplify	*further, in addition to, moreover*	
Compare	*similarly, in a like manner, just as, analogously*	
Contrast	*on the one hand . . . on the other hand, but, in contrast, however*	
Summarize	*in short, briefly*	
Concede	*admittedly, granted, to be sure*	

It can, for instance, make a quiet, emotional appeal by suggesting that the issue is important and that the ball is now in the reader's court.

If you can look back over your essay and add something that both enriches it and wraps it up, fine; but don't feel compelled to say, "Thus, in conclusion, I have argued X, Y, and Z, and I have refuted Jones." After all, *conclusion* can have two meanings: (1) ending, or finish, as the ending of a joke or a novel; or (2) judgment or decision reached after deliberation. Your essay should finish effectively (the first sense), but it need not announce a judgment (the second).

If the essay is fairly short, so that a reader can keep its general gist in mind, you may not need to restate your view. Just make sure that you have covered the ground and that your last sentence is a good one. Notice that the student essay presented later in this chapter (p. 239) doesn't end with a formal conclusion, although it ends conclusively, with a note of finality.

By "a note of finality" we do *not* mean a triumphant crowing. It's far better to end with the suggestion that you hope you have by now indicated why those who hold a different view may want to modify it and accept yours.

If you study the essays in this book or the editorials and op-ed pieces in a newspaper, you will notice that writers often provide a sense of closure by using one of the following devices:

- a return to something stated in the introduction
- a glance at the wider implications of the issue (i.e., what would happen if your solution were implemented or not)
- a hint toward unasked or answered questions that the audience might consider in light of the writer's argument (i.e., predict new questions or issues, and let them ring out at the end as guides to further thinking)
- a suggestion that the reader can take some specific action or do some further research (i.e., the ball is now in the reader's court)
- an anecdote that illustrates the thesis in an engaging way (i.e., a brief account, real or imagined, that brings your ideas into a visible form)
- a brief summary (i.e., a recap. But note that this sort of ending may seem unnecessary and tedious if the paper is short and the summary merely repeats what the writer has already said.)

USES OF AN OUTLINE

Outlines may seem rigid to many writers, especially to those who compose online, where we're accustomed to cutting, copying, moving, and deleting as we draft. You're probably familiar with the structure known as a **formal outline**. Major points are indicated by I, II, III; points within major points are indicated by A, B, C; divisions within A, B, C are indicated by 1, 2, 3; and so on. Thus:

    I. Arguments for opening all Olympic sports to professionals

        A. Fairness

            1. Some Olympic sports are already open to professionals.

            2. Some athletes who really are not professionals are classified as professionals.

        B. Quality (achievements would be higher)

However, an outline—whether you write it before drafting or use it to evaluate the organization of something you've already written—is meant to be a guide rather than a straitjacket.

THE OUTLINE AS A PRELIMINARY GUIDE   Some writers sketch an outline as soon as they think they know what they want to say, even before writing a first draft. This procedure can be helpful in planning a tentative organization, but remember that in revising a draft you'll likely generate some new ideas and have to modify the outline accordingly. A preliminary outline is chiefly useful as a means of getting going, not as a guide to the final essay.

THE OUTLINE AS A WAY OF CHECKING A DRAFT   Whether or not you use a preliminary outline, we strongly suggest that after writing what you hope is your last draft, you make an outline of it; there is no better way of finding out whether the essay is well organized.

Go through the draft and write down the chief points in the order in which you make them. That is, prepare a table of contents — perhaps a phrase for each paragraph. Next, examine your notes to see what kind of sequence they reveal in your paper:

- Is the sequence reasonable? Can it be improved?
- Are any passages irrelevant?
- Does something important seem to be missing?

If no coherent structure or reasonable sequence clearly appears in the outline, the full prose version of your argument probably doesn't have any either. Therefore, produce another draft by moving things around, adding or subtracting paragraphs — cutting and pasting them into a new sequence, with transitions as needed — and then make another outline to see if the sequence now is satisfactory.

A CHECKLIST FOR ORGANIZING AN ARGUMENT

❏ Does the introduction let the readers know where the author is taking them?

    ❏ Does the introduction state the problem or issue?

    ❏ Does it state the claim (the thesis)?

    ❏ Does it suggest the organization of the essay, thereby helping the reader follow the argument?

❏ Do subsequent paragraphs support the claim?

    ❏ Do they offer evidence?

    ❏ Do they face objections to the claim and offer reasonable responses?

    ❏ Do they indicate why the author's claim is preferable?

    ❏ Do transitions (signposts such as *Furthermore, In contrast,* and *Consider as an example*) guide the reader through the argument?

❏ Does the essay end effectively, with a paragraph (at most, two paragraphs) bringing a note of closure?

TONE AND THE WRITER'S PERSONA

Although this book is chiefly about argument in the sense of rational discourse — the presentation of reasons in support of a thesis or conclusion — the appeal to reason (*logos*) is only one form of persuasion, as we have shown in earlier chapters. Another form is the appeal to emotion (*pathos*) — to pity, for example — and a third form of persuasion is the appeal to the speaker's character (*ethos*). What Aristotle called the **ethical appeal** is the idea that effective speakers convey the suggestion that they are

- informed,
- intelligent,
- fair minded (persons of goodwill), and
- honest

Because they are perceived as trustworthy, their words inspire confidence in their listeners. It is a fact that when reading an argument we're often aware of the *person* or *voice* behind the words, and our assent to the argument depends partly on the extent to which we share the speaker's assumptions and see the matter from his or her point of view — in short, the extent to which we can *identify* with the speaker.

How can a writer inspire the confidence that lets readers identify with him or her? First, the writer should possess the virtues Aristotle specified: intelligence or good sense, honesty, and benevolence or goodwill. As a Roman proverb puts it, "No one gives what he does not have." Still, possession of these qualities is not a guarantee that you will convey them in your writing. Like all other writers, you'll have to revise your drafts so that these qualities become apparent; stated more moderately, you'll have to revise so that nothing in the essay causes a reader to doubt your intelligence, honesty, and goodwill. A blunder in logic, a misleading quotation, a snide remark, even an error in spelling — all such slips can cause readers to withdraw their sympathy from the writer.

Of course, all good argumentative essays do not sound exactly alike; they do not all reveal the same speaker. Each writer develops his or her own voice, or (as literary critics and instructors call it) **persona**. (We discussed persona in more detail in Chapter 5, Examining the Author's Persona, pp. 178–79.) In fact, one writer may have several voices or personae, depending on the topic and the audience. The president of the United States delivering an address on the State of the Union has one persona; when chatting with a reporter at his summer home, he has another. This change is not a matter of hypocrisy. Different circumstances call for different language. As a French writer put it, there is a time to speak of "Paris" and a time to speak of "the capital of the nation." When Abraham Lincoln spoke at Gettysburg, he didn't say "Eighty-seven years ago"; instead, he intoned "Four score and seven years ago." We might say that just as some occasions required him to be the folksy Honest Abe during election campaigns, the occasion of the dedication of hallowed ground at Gettysburg, where so many Civil War soldiers lost their lives, required him to be formal and solemn — thus, as president of the United States he appropriately used biblical language.

When we talk about a writer's persona, we mean the way in which the writer presents his or her attitudes

- toward *the self,*
- toward *the audience,* and
- toward *the subject.*

Thus, if a writer says:

I have thought long and hard about this subject, and I can say with assurance that . . .

we may feel that he is a self-satisfied egotist who probably is mouthing other people's opinions. Certainly he's mouthing clichés: "long and hard," "say with assurance."

Let's look at a subtler example of an utterance that reveals certain attitudes:

President Nixon was hounded out of office by journalists.

The statement above conveys a respectful attitude toward Nixon ("President Nixon") and a hostile attitude toward the press (they are beasts, curs who "hounded" our elected leader). If the writer's attitudes were reversed, she might have said something like this:

The press turned the searchlight on Tricky Dick's criminal shenanigans.

"Tricky Dick" and "criminal" are obvious enough, but notice that "shenanigans" also implies the writer's contempt for Nixon, and "turned the searchlight" suggests that the press is a source of illumination, a source of truth. The original version and the opposite version both say that the press was responsible for Nixon's resignation, but the original version ("President Nixon was hounded") conveys indignation toward journalists, whereas the revision conveys contempt for Nixon.

These two versions suggest two speakers who differ not only in their view of Nixon but also in their manner, including the seriousness with which they take themselves. Although the passage is very short, it seems to us that the first speaker conveys righteous indignation ("hounded"), whereas the second conveys amused contempt ("shenanigans"). To our ears, the tone, as well as the point, differs in the two versions.

> **WRITING TIP**
> Present yourself so that readers see you as knowledgeable, honest, open-minded, and interested in helping them to think about the significance of an issue.

LOADED WORDS We are talking now about **loaded words**, which convey the writer's attitude and, through their connotations, seek to win the reader to the writer's side. Compare the words in the left-hand column with those in the right:

freedom fighter	terrorist
pro-choice	pro-abortion
pro-life	antichoice
economic refugee	illegal alien
terrorist surveillance	domestic spying

The words in the left-hand column sound like good things; speakers who use them seek to establish themselves as virtuous people supporting worthy causes. The **connotations** (associations, overtones) of these pairs of words differ, even though the **denotations** (explicit meanings, dictionary definitions) are the same — just as the connotations of *mother* and *female parent* differ, although the denotations are the same. Similarly, although Lincoln's "four score and seven" and "eighty-seven" both denote "thirteen less than one hundred," they differ in connotation.

Tone is not only a matter of connotation (*hounded out of office* versus, let's say, *compelled to resign*, or *pro-choice* versus *pro-abortion*); it is also a matter of such things as the selection and type of examples. A writer who offers many examples, especially ones drawn from ordinary life, conveys a persona different from that of a writer who offers no examples or only an occasional invented instance. The first writer seems friendlier, more honest, more down-to-earth.

USING TONE TO ADDRESS OPPOSITION On the whole, when writing an argument, it's advisable to be courteous and respectful of your topic, your audience, and people who hold views opposite to yours. It is rarely good for one's own intellectual development to regard as villains or fools persons who hold views different from one's own, especially if some of them are in the audience. Keep in mind the story of two strangers on a train who, striking up a conversation, found that both were clergymen, although of different faiths. Then one said to the other, "Well, why shouldn't we be friends? After all, we both serve God, you in your way and I in His."

Complacency is all right when telling a joke, but not when offering an argument:

- Recognize opposing views.
- Assume that they are held in good faith.
- State them fairly. If you don't, you do a disservice not only to the opposition but also to your own position because the perceptive reader won't take you seriously.
- Be temperate in arguing your own position: "If I understand their view correctly . . .";
  "It seems reasonable to conclude that . . ."; "Perhaps, then, we can agree that . . ."
- Write calmly. If you become overly emotional, readers may interpret you as biased or unreasonable, and they may lose their confidence in you.

WE, ONE, OR I?

The use of *we* in the last paragraph brings us to another point: Is it correct to use the first-person pronouns *I* and *we*? In this book, because three of us are writing, we often use *we* to mean the three authors. Sometimes we use *we* to mean the authors and the readers, or *we* the people in general. This shifting use of one word can be troublesome, but we hope (clearly, the *we* here refers only to the authors) that we have avoided ambiguity. But can, or should, or must an individual use *we* instead of *I*? The short answer is no.

If you're simply speaking for yourself, use *I*. Attempts to avoid the first-person singular by saying things like "This writer thinks . . ." and "It is thought that . . ." and "One thinks that . . ." are far more irritating (and wordy) than the use of *I*. The so-called editorial *we* sounds as odd in a student's argument as the royal *we* does. (Mark Twain said that the only ones who can appropriately say *we* are kings, editors, and people with a tapeworm.) It's advisable to use *we* only when you are sure you're writing or speaking directly to an audience who holds membership in the same group, as in "We *students of this university should . . .*" or "We *the* members of Theta Chi fraternity need to. . . ." If the *we* you refer to has a referent, simply refer to what it means: Say "Americans are" rather than "We are," or "College students should" rather than "We should," or "Republicans need to" rather than "We need to."

Many students assume that using *one* will solve the problem of pronouns. But because one *one* leads to another, the sentence may end up sounding, as James Thurber once said, "like a trombone solo." It's best to admit that you are the author and to use *I*. However, there is no need to preface every sentence with "I think." The reader knows that the essay is yours and that the opinions are yours; so use *I* when you must, but not needlessly. Do not write, "I think *X* movie is terrible"; simply say, "*X* movie is terrible." And do not add extra words that say more obvious things, like "*It is my idea that* the company needs a new mission statement." Just write, "*The company needs a new mission statement.*"

Often you'll see *I* in journalistic writing and autobiographical writing — and in some argumentative writing, too — but in most argumentative writing, it's best to state the facts and (when drawing reasonable conclusions from them) to keep yourself in the background. Why? The more you use *I* in an essay, the more your readers will attach *you* directly to the argument and may regard your position as personal rather than as relevant to themselves.

THINKING CRITICALLY *Eliminating* We, One, *and* I

Rewrite the following sentences to eliminate unnecessary uses of *we, one, I,* and other gratuitous statements of opinion. (The first row has been completed as an example.)

ORIGINAL SENTENCE	REWRITTEN SENTENCE
I think fracking is the best way to achieve energy independence and to create jobs.	Fracking is the best way to achieve energy independence and to create jobs.
In our country, we believe in equality and freedom.	
One should consider one's manners at formal dinner parties.	
In my opinion, the government should not regulate the sizes of sodas we can order.	
It is clearly the case that the new policy treats employees unfairly.	

AVOIDING SEXIST LANGUAGE

Courtesy — as well as common sense — requires that you respect your readers' feelings. Many people today find offensive the implicit gender bias in the use of male pronouns ("As the reader follows the argument, he will find . . .") to denote not only men but also women or people who use nonbinary gender pronouns such as *ze* or *they*. And sometimes the use of the male pronoun to denote all people is ridiculous ("An individual, no matter what his sex, . . .").

In most contexts, there is no need to use gender-specific nouns or pronouns. One way to avoid using *he* when you mean any person is to use *he or she* (or *she or he*), but the result is sometimes cumbersome — although superior to the overly conspicuous *he/she* and *s/he*. Some people will accept *they*, even when the syntax of a sentence calls for a singular pronoun, to avoid this issue ("When a person enters the exhibit, they will see . . ."), but not everyone accepts this usage in formal writing yet.

Here are two simple ways to solve the problem:

- *Use the plural* ("As readers follow the argument, they will find . . .").
- *Recast the sentence* so that no pronoun is required ("Readers following the argument will find . . .").

Because *man* and *mankind* strike many readers as sexist when used in such expressions as "Man is a rational animal" and "Mankind has not yet solved this problem," consider using such words as *human being, person, people, humanity,* and *we* (e.g., "Human beings are rational animals"; "We have not yet solved this problem").

Peer Review

Your instructor may suggest — or require — that you submit an early draft of your essay to a fellow student or small group of students for comment. Such a procedure benefits both author and readers: You get the responses of a reader, and the student-reader gets experience

A CHECKLIST FOR PEER REVIEW

Read through the draft quickly. Then read it again, with the following questions in mind. Remember: You are reading a draft, a work in progress. You're expected to offer suggestions, and you're expected to offer them courteously.

In a sentence, indicate the degree to which the draft shows promise of fulfilling the assignment.

- ☐ Is the writer's tone appropriate? Who is the audience?
- ☐ Looking at the essay as a whole, what thesis (main idea) is advanced?
- ☐ Are the needs of the audience kept in mind? For instance, do some words need to be defined?
- ☐ Is the evidence (e.g., the examples and the testimony of authorities) clear and effective?
- ☐ Can I accept the assumptions? If not, why not?
- ☐ Is any obvious evidence (or counterevidence) overlooked?
- ☐ Is the writer proposing a solution? If so,
    - ☐ Are other equally attractive solutions adequately examined?
    - ☐ Has the writer overlooked some unattractive effects of the proposed solution?

Look at each paragraph separately.

- ☐ What is the basic point?
- ☐ How does each paragraph relate to the essay's main idea or to the previous paragraph?
- ☐ Should some paragraphs be deleted? Be divided into two or more paragraphs? Be combined? Be moved elsewhere? (If you outline the essay by writing down the gist of each paragraph, you'll get help in answering these questions.)
- ☐ Is each sentence clearly related to the sentence that precedes and to the sentence that follows? If not, in a sentence or two indicate examples of good and bad transitions.
- ☐ Is each paragraph adequately developed? Are there sufficient details, perhaps brief supporting quotations from the text?
- ☐ Are the introductory and concluding paragraphs effective?

Look at the paper as a whole.

- ☐ What are the paper's chief strengths?
- ☐ Make at least two specific suggestions that you think will help the author improve the paper.

in thinking about the problems of developing an argument, especially such matters as the degree of detail that a writer needs to offer to a reader and the importance of keeping the organization evident to a reader.

Oral peer reviews allow for the give and take of discussion, but probably most students and most instructors find written peer reviews more helpful because reviewers think more carefully about their responses to the draft, and they help essayists to get beyond a knee-jerk response to criticism. Online reviews on a class website, through email, or via another platform such as a file-sharing service or internet-based document tool are especially helpful precisely because they are not face to face; the peer reviewer gets practice *writing*, and the essayist is not directly challenged.

A Student's Essay, from Rough Notes to Final Version

While we were revising this textbook, we asked the students in one of our classes to write a short essay (500–750 words) on some ethical problem that concerned them. Because this assignment was the first writing assignment in the course, we explained that a good way to generate ideas is to ask oneself some questions, write down responses, question those responses, and write freely for ten minutes or so, not worrying about contradictions. We invited our students to hand in their initial notes along with the finished essay so that we could get a sense of how they proceeded as writers. Not all of them chose to hand in their notes, but we were greatly encouraged by those who did. What encouraged us was the confirmation of an old belief — we call it a fact — that students will hand in a thoughtful essay if before preparing a final version they ask themselves *why* they think this or that, write down their responses, and are not afraid to change their minds as they proceed.

Here are the first notes of a student, Emily Andrews, who elected to write about whether to give money to street beggars. She simply put down ideas, one after the other.

Help the poor? Why do I (sometimes) do it?

I feel guilty, and think I should help them: poor, cold, hungry (but also some of them are thirsty for liquor, and will spend the money on liquor, not on food).

I also feel annoyed by them — most of them.

Where does the expression "the deserving poor" come from?

And "poor but honest"? Actually, that sounds odd. Wouldn't "rich but honest" make more sense?

Why don't they work? Fellow with red beard, always by bus stop in front of florist's shop, always wants a handout. He is a regular, there all day every day, so I guess he is in a way "reliable," so why doesn't he put the same time in on a job?

Or why don't they get help? Don't they know they need it? They *must* know they need it.

Maybe that guy with the beard is just a con artist. Maybe he makes more money by panhandling than he would by working, and it's a lot easier!

Kinds of poor — how to classify??

> drunks, druggies, etc.
> mentally ill (maybe drunks belong here, too)
> decent people who have had terrible luck

Why private charity?

Doesn't it make sense to say we (fortunate individuals) should give something — an occasional handout — to people who have had terrible luck? (I suppose some people might say there's no need for any of us to give anything — the government takes care of the truly needy — but I *do* believe in giving charity. A month ago a friend of the family passed away, and the woman's children suggested that people might want to make a donation in her name to a shelter for battered women. I know my parents made a donation.)

BUT how can I tell who is who, which are which? Which of these people asking for "spare change" really need (deserve???) help, and which are phonies? Impossible to tell.

Possibilities:

> Give to no one.
> Give to no one but make an annual donation, maybe to United Way.
> Give a dollar to each person who asks. This would probably not cost me even a dollar a day.
> Occasionally do without something — maybe a new album or a meal in a restaurant — and give the money I save to people who seem worthy.

WORTHY? What am I saying? How can I, or anyone, tell? The neat-looking guy who says he just lost his job may be a phony, and the dirty bum — probably a drunk — may desperately need food. (OK, so what if he spends the money on liquor instead of food? At least he'll get a little pleasure in life. No! It's not all right if he spends it on drink.)

Other possibilities:

> Do some volunteer work?
> To tell the truth, I don't want to put in the time. I don't feel *that* guilty.

So what's the problem?

Is it, How I can help the very poor (handouts, or through an organization)? or

How I can feel less guilty about being lucky enough to be able to go to college and to have a supportive family?

I can't quite bring myself to believe I should help every beggar who approaches, but I also can't bring myself to believe that I should do nothing, on the grounds that:

> a. it's probably their fault
> b. if they are deserving, they can get gov't help. No, I just can't believe that. Maybe some are too proud to look for government help, or don't know that they're entitled to it.

What to do?

On balance, it seems best to:

    a. give to United Way
    b. maybe also give to an occasional individual, if I happen to be moved, without worrying about whether he or she is "deserving" (since it's probably impossible to know)

A day after making these notes Emily reviewed them, added a few points, and then made a very brief selection from them to serve as an outline for her first draft:

Opening para.: "poor but honest"? Deserve "spare change"?

Charity: private or through organizations?

    pros and cons
    guy at bus
    it wouldn't cost me much, but . . . better to give through organizations

Concluding para.: still feel guilty?

    maybe mention guy at bus again?

After writing and revising a draft, Emily submitted her essay to a fellow student for review. She then revised her work in light of the peer's suggestions and her own further thinking.

Emily's final essay appears below. If after reading the final version you reread Emily's early notes, you'll notice that some of her notes never made it into the final version. But without the notes, the essay probably wouldn't have been as interesting as it is. When Emily made the notes, she wasn't so much putting down her ideas as *finding* ideas through the process of writing. (By the way, Emily told us that in her next-to-last draft, the title was "Is It Right to Spare 'Spare Change'?" This title, unlike the revision, introduces the topic but not the author's position.)

Emily Andrews

Professor Barnet

English 102

January 15, 2019

Why I Don't Spare "Spare Change"

"Poor but honest." "The deserving poor." I don't know the origin of these quotations, but they always come to mind when I walk through my city, Boston, and encounter "the poor" on the streets asking for money. When I do, I have to face an ethical dilemma—not as to whether or not I *can* spare my spare change, but whether or not I *should*. Panhandlers by definition are people who solicit money for their personal use without providing goods or services. This forces me to consider the behavior I am enabling by giving away money on the street. Many of these people, perhaps through alcohol or drugs, have ruined not only their own lives but also the lives of others in order to indulge in their own habits. Perhaps alcoholism and drug addiction really are "diseases," as many people say, but my own feeling—based, of course, not on any serious study—is that most alcoholics and drug addicts can be classified with the "undeserving poor." And that is largely why I don't distribute spare change to panhandlers.

Surely among street people there are also some who can rightly be called "deserving." Deserving of what? A fair shake in life, or government assistance? Perhaps. But my spare change? It happens that I have been brought up to believe that it is appropriate to make contributions to charity—let's say a shelter for battered women—but if I give some change to a panhandler, I may be helping someone, or, on the contrary, I could just as easily be encouraging someone to continue their alcohol or drug abuse, and not to get help. Maybe even worse: maybe I am supporting a criminal, or con artist, or someone who could use my money to get high and take advantage of someone else. The fact is, I don't know.

If one believes in the value of private charity, one can give either to needy individuals or to charitable organizations. Money given to panhandlers may indeed help a person badly in need, but it could just as easily be misused and cause greater harm. In giving to an organization

---

Title is informative, alerting the reader to the topic and the author's position.

Opening paragraph holds readers' interest by alluding to familiar phrases and an anecdote.

Defines a key term: *panhandler*.

Author presents general outline of argument and thesis.

Voices the reader's probably uneasy response to the opening, showing audience awareness.

Supports her argument with reason.

Clearly sets forth the alternatives. A reader may disagree with them, but they are stated fairly.

such as the United Way, in contrast, one can feel that one's money is likely to be used wisely. True, confronted by a panhandler one may feel that *this* particular unfortunate individual needs help at *this* moment—a cup of coffee or a sandwich—and the need will not be met unless I put my hand in my pocket right now. But I have come to think that the beggars whom I encounter can get along without my spare change. If they choose, they can go to shelters where charitable contributions can be collected and spent wisely. Indeed, panhandlers may actually be better off if people did not give them spare change which they can subsequently use on alcohol or drugs.

It happens that in my neighborhood I encounter a few panhandlers regularly. There is one fellow who is always by the bus stop where I catch the bus to the college, and I never give him anything precisely because he is always there. He is such a regular that, I think, he ought to be able to hold a regular job. Putting him aside, I routinely encounter about three or four beggars in an average week. (I'm not counting street musicians. These people seem quite able to work for a living. If they see their "work" as playing or singing, let persons who enjoy their performances pay them. I do not consider myself among their audience.) The truth of the matter is that since I meet so few beggars, I could give each one a dollar and hardly feel the loss. At most, I might go without seeing a movie some week. But I know nothing about these people, and it's my impression—based on what I see—that they simply prefer begging to working.

That's why I usually do not give "spare change," and I don't think I will in the future. These people will get along without me, and may get along better without me if their needs eventually lead them to a shelter or a food bank. Someone else will have to come up with money for their coffee or their liquor, or, at worst, they will just have to do without. I will continue to contribute occasionally to a charitable organization, not simply (I hope) to salve my conscience but because I believe that these organizations actually do good work. But I will not attempt to be a mini-charitable organization, distributing spare change likely to go to an unworthy cause.

Paragraphs 4 and 5 are more personal than the earlier paragraphs. The writer, more or less having stated what she takes to be the facts, now is entitled to offer a highly personal response to them.

The final paragraph nicely concludes with a reference to the title, giving the reader a sense of completeness.

Topics for Critical Thinking and Writing

1. Does the writer establish a good sense of *ethos* in this essay? Explain what works best and what works least in terms of establishing credibility or goodwill.

2. Do you think this essay has a strong thesis? A strong argument? Explain.

3. What assumptions are made about panhandlers in this essay? If you wanted to challenge these assumptions, what kinds of questions could you ask and what evidence could you seek?

4. What are some alternative solutions or counterarguments that the writer did not address?

5. Who is the writer's intended audience? Do you think the writer's language and tone are appropriate?

ASSIGNMENT FOR DEVELOPING AN ARGUMENT OF YOUR OWN

In a brief essay, state a claim and support it with evidence. Choose an issue in which you are genuinely interested and about which you already know something. You may want to interview a few experts and do some reading, but don't try to write a highly researched paper. Be sure to organize your argument thoughtfully, with consideration of your audience, the context of the argument, and alternative viewpoints. Sample topics:

1. Students in laboratory courses should not be required to participate in the dissection of animals.

2. Washington, DC, should be granted statehood.

3. In wartime, women should be subject to the military draft.

4. The annual Miss America contest was right to eliminate the swimsuit competition.

5. The government should not offer financial support to the arts.

6. The chief fault of the curriculum in high school was . . .

7. No specific courses should be required in colleges or universities.

7

Using Sources

Research is formalized curiosity. It is poking and prying with a purpose.
— ZORA NEALE HURSTON

There is no way of exchanging information that does not involve an act of judgment.
— JACOB BRONOWSKI

I have yet to see any problem, however complicated, which, when you looked at it in the right way, did not become still more complicated.
— POUL ANDERSON

A university is just a group of buildings gathered around a library.
— SHELBY FOOTE

Why Use Sources?

We have pointed out that one gets ideas by writing. While prewriting and drafting, ideas form and stimulate further ideas, especially when you question and *think critically* about what you are writing. Of course, when writing about complex, serious questions, nobody is expected to invent all the answers out of thin air. On the contrary, a writer is expected to be familiar with the chief answers already produced by others and to make use of them through selective incorporation and criticism. When you write about an issue, you are not expected to reinvent the wheel; sometimes, simply adding a spoke is enough.

You may be familiar with some directives about research from previous courses. Your instructors may have asked you to locate three sources, or four sources, or six sources, and to use those sources in support of an argument (perhaps with some added requirement that one or more of these be scholarly sources). However, your teachers generally do not want you simply to go out and find a fixed number of sources to plug in to your essay for the sake of it. The goal of research is more idealistic. The point is not that a minimum number of sources is right for every argument, nor is it to send you off on a scavenger hunt for types of sources. Instead, research is intended to encourage learning, thoughtful engagement with a topic, and the production of an informed view.

ENTERING A DISCOURSE

Kenneth Burke (1887–1993), one of America's most important theorists of rhetoric, wrote:

> Imagine that you enter a parlor. You come late. When you arrive, others have long preceded you, and they are engaged in a heated discussion, a discussion too heated for them to pause and tell you exactly what it is about. In fact, the discussion had already begun long before any of them got there, so that no one present is qualified to retrace for you all the steps that had gone before. You listen for a while, until you decide that you have caught the tenor of the argument; then you put in your oar. Someone answers; you answer him; another comes to your defense; another aligns himself against you, to either the embarrassment or gratification of your opponent, depending upon the quality of your ally's assistance. However, the discussion is interminable. The hour grows late, you must depart. And you do depart, with the discussion still vigorously in progress.[1]

When you are writing, imagine you are entering a discussion, but not a live one as in Burke's analogy. Imagine instead you are entering into a **discourse**. A discourse is a type of discussion, surely. But unlike a live conversation, a discourse takes place over a longer period of time among many participants in various types of writing and public venues. A discourse is a conversation writ large, one that has gone on before you enter the fray, and one that will likely continue after you leave.

So why are sources important in discourse?

- The first answer is practical: You use sources because they are where conversations about important topics occur.
- The second is more idealistic: It is your responsibility as an intelligent citizen to participate meaningfully in discourses.

From sources, you learn what the facts are, what issues are current, and what positions certain people or groups are taking on the issues. Through sources, you discover new ideas, questions, and answers. When you perform research on a topic, you are *finding, evaluating,* and *synthesizing* sources so as to position yourself to speak within that kind of conversation known as a discourse.

Two caveats are important. First, although we will discuss finding, evaluating, and synthesizing sources separately, once you begin researching you will see that these activities are not entirely separable. As you find sources, you will simultaneously be assessing their relevancy and value (evaluating) and placing sources into conversation with one another (synthesizing) while considering ways to integrate them into your own writing.

Second, the boundaries of discourse are not clear-cut. Obviously, many conversations about many different topics occur constantly in a variety of places. We may speak generally of political discourse, scientific discourse, or economic discourse, and we may speak more particularly of discourses on women's rights, environmentalism, or taxation. Any subject at all may be thought

---

[1] *The Philosophy of Literary Form* (Baton Rouge: Louisiana State University Press, 1941), 110–11.

Intersecting discourses

of in terms of the discourses (or conversations) that take place about it. Consider, for example, the conversation about security and freedom in the United States. This conversation — this *discourse* — has been ongoing since the nation was founded, and it continues today. In articles, essays, speeches, legal reviews, court opinions, congressional debates, and elsewhere, people continue to weigh the appropriate balance between security and freedom: The country needs to be kept safe, and so law enforcement agencies are granted many powers to investigate, detect, and prevent lawbreaking, yet American citizens are also protected by the US Constitution from unwarranted harassment, search and seizure, and other invasions of privacy. Today, terrorism, illegal immigration, stop-and-frisk practices, and cybersecurity are just a few areas of focus in this conversation-writ-large. Within each of those categories, even narrower conversations occur. Airport security, border security, cell phone searches, facial recognition technology — the list goes on and on. Many combined, overlapping conversations (some very general, some quite specific) may all be said to be part of this *discourse* about freedom and security. Even fictional novels, plays, films, and television shows contribute to the discourse. A television series like *House of Cards* (2013–2018) or a blockbuster superhero movie like *Captain America: Winter Soldier* (2014) can represent and spur discussion about topical issues related to freedom and security — and potentially be a rich source for research and analysis to support your own argument and entry into the conversation.

A **discourse community** is any group of people who share general interests, assumptions, and values and who communicate with one another in some form of media, usually adhering to a set of conventions for that communication. For example, imagine a professor of physics who is active in the scientific discourse on thermodynamics, publishing his theories in academic books and articles. In those, he is addressing one discourse community of scientists and experts in a particular type of writing style or genre. But maybe he is also an environmentalist in his hometown who publishes on the Sierra Club blog and posts videos about local ecology. And maybe he is also a fan of X-Men and writes passionately about the Marvel mutants on a listserv dedicated to that series. In those cases, he is addressing narrower discourse communities.

Now, this hypothetical professor would be likely to research and write differently depending on which discourse community he is engaging. Understanding discourse communities is important because it can help you

- focus your own research by determining which types of sources you need to seek,
- evaluate the sources you find,

- define your audience and purpose in writing, and
- write more persuasively.

UNDERSTANDING INFORMATION LITERACY

During your college courses — and in work and daily life — you will be reading and listening to ongoing conversations within and among discourse communities. Sometimes, you will want (or need) to participate yourself. You will have to interject, responding to issues by speaking and writing. Thus, when you set out to learn about and contribute to a discourse, how you discover, evaluate, and use your sources is crucial. Together, these are integrated skills known as **information literacy**. According to the Association of College and Research Libraries, these skills encompass

- the thoughtful and reflective discovery of information,
- the understanding of how information is produced and valued, and
- the ethical use of information in creating new ideas by participating in various academic or civic discourses.

Information literacy involves being able to survey what and how knowledge circulates about a topic, thinking critically while you learn. It allows you to see what kinds of questions have been raised and what answers have been provided. As you poke and pry into a topic, you can distinguish between strong and weak sources and separate the wheat from the chaff.

Information literacy skills are necessary to be able to navigate the vast fields of information to which we are exposed constantly in the digital media environment. Even when we are trying to be diligent in our efforts to find quality sources, we face obstacles. Search engines, for example, simply cannot index, curate, and return results from the billions of websites on the ever-expanding internet. This means we need to develop skills on *how* to search: how to use search operators and phrases to limit the results we get and how to search for only certain kinds of websites or file types. But even the best search strategies will not return full-length published books or password-protected content such as subscription-only magazines, newspapers, and journals, many of which are carefully edited and vetted for quality (and are often the best possible sources).

Further, we should also be aware that search engines are not neutral. They commonly return results that are most popular (or most highly paid for), not necessarily those that are most thorough, interesting, or reliable. Some search engines tailor the top results to your previous searches and online activity through "personalized" search results, leading to an information ecosystem susceptible to "filter bubble" and "echo chamber" effects in which people are led to information limited by a single perspective or ideology. If you are searching for a political topic and your search engine knows your political leanings, it will likely return in your top results webpages that reflect your political views. This practice seriously raises the potential for confirmation bias (discussed on p. 79).

Once you narrow in on a topic and adopt a central idea or position on an issue — a thesis — your ability to persuade an audience will depend on the sources you provide, evaluate, and cite. Even one citation of a fraudulent website or one uncritical reference to a highly partisan or narrowly ideological source can undermine your credibility. On the other hand, well-researched and thoughtfully discussed sources show that you are an educated participant in a discourse — or even one small area of it — who is equipped with foundational facts and evidence drawn from reputable sources; you have an argument worth listening to.

Choosing a Topic

Because of the complexity of discourses — the plurality of topics, issues, ideas, and opinions (in so many different forms and from so many different groups) — the research process isn't straightforward and neat. Research is a form of inquiry that can range from finding answers to simple questions to exploring complex topics, problems, or issues discussed within or among discourse communities. Part of conducting a successful, fruitful research effort is first selecting an area of focus and narrowing the scope of your research to suit the needs of your assignments or interests.

If a topic is not assigned, choose one that

- interests you, and
- can be researched with reasonable thoroughness in the allotted time.

Topics such as censorship, the environment, and sexual harassment obviously impinge on our lives, and it may well be that one such topic is of special interest to you. But the breadth of these topics (like with freedom vs. security, discussed earlier) makes researching them potentially overwhelming. Type the word *censorship* into an internet search engine, and you will be referred to millions of information sources.

This brings us to our second point: getting a manageable topic. Any of the previous topics would need to be refined substantially before you could begin researching in earnest. Similarly, even more specific topics such as "the effects of the Holocaust" can hardly be mastered in a few weeks or argued in a ten-page paper. They are simply too big. (The questions that immediately come to mind are, What kind of effects do you mean? Political effects? Psychological effects? For whom? Where? When? Where will you find the evidence?) Getting a manageable topic often means working on one area of a larger puzzle, pinpointing the places where you can add your piece. You can do that by

- seeking gaps or areas of conflict within or among discourses (places where you can weigh in) or
- breaking down complex topics, issues, or debates into simpler questions (perhaps focusing on one question informing the larger issue).

> **WRITING TIP**
> You may think you have little to contribute to conversations whose participants are illustrious authorities and experts. However, by dint of being a student, you have a unique perspective: You are on the edge of the future, able to apply new questions and issues in the present to those old primary and secondary resources. Or maybe you may have a purpose for writing that is fundamentally different from anyone else's.

By focusing your research on one area within a broader discourse, you can limit the range and types of resources you consult based on your circumstances and goals. As you research, you may find yourself drawn toward even more specific questions. If you were writing about the psychological effects of the Holocaust, for instance, you could focus on an affected ethnic group like Jewish people or focus further on German, French, Russian, or American Jews; you could define a time frame; or you could deal with a specific postwar generation, or consider a group within that generation, such as women, men, children, or second-generation survivors (those born after the war). If you chose to develop your analysis around specific traumatic events, places, or even practices, such as the use of gas chambers, you might seek evidence in psychological studies, memoirs, and testimony or in the arts.

One strategy for narrowing your topic is, first, to find your general topic and then apply some basic questions to discover how you might find an entry point into the conversations about it.

Find Relevance

- What are some of the ways people have been discussing this topic recently?
- To whom — that is, to what groups or audiences — is this topic especially important now?
- Is there any data, any evidence, or an example that arguments on this topic have not yet accounted for?

Develop a New Approach

- What is most important or interesting to *me* about this topic?
- Is there a perspective or an application that has been underreported in the discourses on this topic?
- Can I ask new questions by thinking politically, historically, religiously, scientifically, psychologically, philosophically, culturally — or in some combination of these?

Determine Your Research Goals and Writing Context

- Where do I stand?
- What type of audience do I want to reach most?
- How do I want to position myself in the discourse on this topic (i.e., in what genre, in what format will I make myself heard, including considerations of length and depth)?

Exercise: Exploring Your Topic

Once you've narrowed your focus, spend a little time exploring your topic to see if you can locate interesting conversations and manageable topics or issues by taking one or more of these approaches:

- *Do a web search on the topic.* You can quickly put your finger on the pulse of popular approaches to a topic by scanning the first page or two of results to see who is talking about it (individuals, groups, etc.) and in what forms (articles, news, blogs, etc.).

- *Plug the topic into one of the library's article databases.* Just by scanning the titles in a general database, you can get a sense of what questions have been and are currently being raised about your topic.

- *Browse the library shelves where books on the topic are kept.* A quick check of the tables of contents of recently published books may give you ideas of how to narrow your topic.

- *Ask a librarian to show you where specialized reference books on your topic are found.* Instead of general encyclopedias, try sources like *CQ Researcher* or *Encyclopedia of Science, Technology, and Ethics.*

- *Talk to an expert.* Members of the faculty who specialize in the area of your topic might be able to point you to key sources and discourses.

Finding Sources

Your sources' quality and integrity are crucial to your own credibility and to the strength of your argument. In Chapters 5 and 6, we discussed *ethos* as an appeal that establishes credibility with readers. When you do competent research, you let your audience see that you have done your homework, which thereby increases your *ethos*. Sources, we mean to say, provide evidence in support of your argument, but they also collectively serve as evidence that you are familiar with the discourses on your topic, that you know what you're talking about, and that your interpretation is sound.

To find good sources, you must have a strategy for searching. What strategy you use will depend on your topic. Researching a social problem or a new economic policy may involve reading recent newspaper articles, scanning information on government websites, and locating current statistics. On the other hand, researching the meaning of a pop culture trend, for example, may be best tackled by seeking out books and scholarly journal articles on the sociological nature of fashion and also some popular style magazines or videos to use as evidence. In all your research, you will be attempting to identify the places where conversations on your topic are taking place — in specific academic journals, magazines, websites, annual conferences, and so on. By noting what is common among your sources, what data and evidence are shared, you may find other authoritative sources and get leads on further research.

If your topic warrants it, you may also want to supplement your library or internet research with your own fieldwork. You could conduct surveys or interviews, design an experiment, or visit a museum. You could perform research in an archive or other repository to analyze original documents or artifacts. This kind of research is called **primary research** because you are the one gathering the basic evidence and data. **Secondary research** is the term given to the kind of inquiry that involves your study of research done by others.

Visual Guide: Finding Discourse on Your Topic

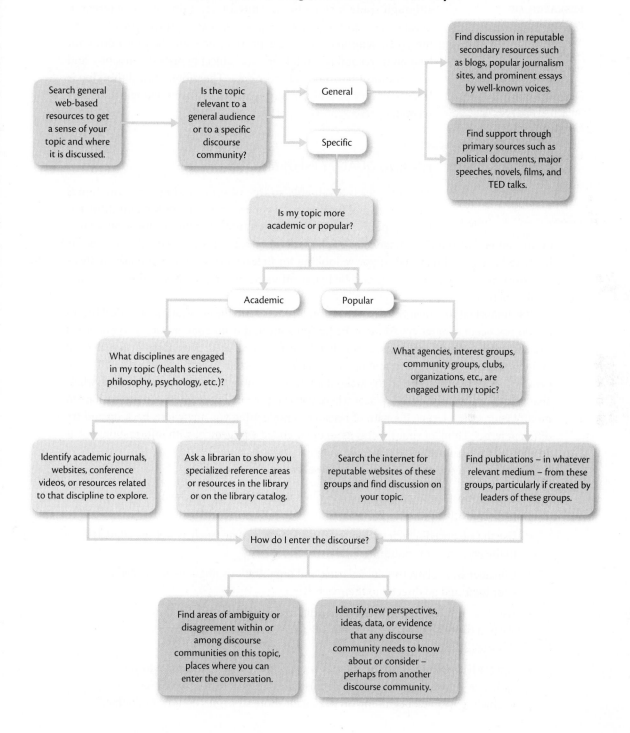

Search general web-based resources to get a sense of your topic and where it is discussed. → Is the topic relevant to a general audience or to a specific discourse community?

General → Find discussion in reputable secondary resources such as blogs, popular journalism sites, and prominent essays by well-known voices.

→ Find support through primary sources such as political documents, major speeches, novels, films, and TED talks.

Specific → Is my topic more academic or popular?

Academic → What disciplines are engaged in my topic (health sciences, philosophy, psychology, etc.)?
- Identify academic journals, websites, conference videos, or resources related to that discipline to explore.
- Ask a librarian to show you specialized reference areas or resources in the library or on the library catalog.

Popular → What agencies, interest groups, community groups, clubs, organizations, etc., are engaged with my topic?
- Search the internet for reputable websites of these groups and find discussion on your topic.
- Find publications – in whatever relevant medium – from these groups, particularly if created by leaders of these groups.

How do I enter the discourse?
- Find areas of ambiguity or disagreement within or among discourse communities on this topic, places where you can enter the conversation.
- Identify new perspectives, ideas, data, or evidence that any discourse community needs to know about or consider – perhaps from another discourse community.

One form of research is not necessarily better than the other, although some may be better suited to certain topics or research questions than others. Many types of research projects involve both methods. Whether research is primary or secondary also does not bear on its reliability. Both kinds are subject to biases, omissions, and assumptions that could color the data. Therefore, critical thinking is essential every step of the way, whether you are seeking primary or secondary research or are performing it.

FINDING QUALITY INFORMATION ONLINE

The internet is a valuable source of information for many topics and less helpful for others. In general, if you're looking for information on public policy, popular culture, current events, legal affairs, or any subject of interest to agencies of the federal or state government, the internet is likely to have useful material. If you're looking for literary criticism or scholarly analysis of historical or social issues, you may be better off using library databases, described later in this chapter.

It is important to remember that the research process and the application of critical thinking do not occur separately: You may be jumping around from contemporary to historical sources, databases, and webpages, evaluating them as you proceed. Seek more facts as needed and remain adaptable, flexible, and open-minded all the while. Be prepared to take different perspectives seriously and be on the lookout for areas of ambiguity, unsettled issues, and debatable questions. Again, these are places where you can potentially weigh in. Do not hesitate to modify your search terms. If a path of research is not getting you anywhere, back up and try different terms. Think of your process as an open-ended engagement with information, not as an effort to prove something you already think.

To make good use of the internet, try these strategies:

- Use the most specific terms possible when using a general search engine; put phrases in quotes.

- Use the advanced search option to limit a search by date (such as websites updated in the past week or month).

- Consider which government agencies and organizations might be interested in your topic and go directly to their websites.

- Use clues in URLs to see where sites originate. Delete everything after the first slash in the URL to go to the parent site to see if it provides information about the website's source, origin, or purpose.

- Always bear in mind that the sources you choose must be persuasive to your audience. Avoid sites that may be dismissed as unreliable or biased. (See Evaluating Sources, beginning on p. 255, for more strategies on how to do that.)

A WORD ABOUT *WIKIPEDIA* Links to *Wikipedia* often rise to the top of search results. This vast and decentralized site provides nearly six million articles on a wide variety of topics. However, anyone can contribute to the online encyclopedia, so the accuracy of articles varies, and in some cases, the coverage of a controversial issue is one-sided or disputed. In other cases, businesses, political campaigns, and public relations firms patrol *Wikipedia* and manage their own or their clients' "online reputation" by adding and subtracting information from the website. Nevertheless, many articles are accurate, particularly when they are noncontroversial; however, like any encyclopedia, they provide only basic information. *Wikipedia*'s founder, Jimmy Wales, cautions students against using it as a source, except for obtaining general background knowledge: "You're in college; don't cite the encyclopedia."[2] *Wikipedia* is most valuable when you use it for basic undisputed facts or to locate bibliographies that will help you conduct further independent research.

FINDING ARTICLES USING LIBRARY DATABASES

Your library has a wide range of general and specialized databases available through its website. When you search through a database, you are searching within an electronic index of citations from published sources, both popular and scholarly. Some databases provide references to articles (and perhaps abstracts or summaries), and some provide direct links to the full text of entire articles.

Through your school library, you may have access to general and interdisciplinary databases such as Academic Search Premier (produced by the EBSCOhost company) and Expanded Academic Index (from InfoTrac), which provide access to thousands of publications, including both scholarly and popular sources. LexisNexis or ProQuest Newsstand are particularly useful for newspaper articles that are not available for free online. More specialized databases include PsycINFO (for psychology research) and ERIC (focused on topics in education). Others, such as JSTOR, are full-text digital archives of scholarly journals. Some databases offer the archives of a single publication, like the *New York Times*, *Wall Street Journal*, or *JAMA* (the *Journal of the American Medical Association*). Others offer scientific, medical, or economic data exclusively (such as Web of Science, MEDLINE, EconLit), and still others are virtual archives (such as African American Newspapers of the Nineteenth Century or The Sixties, a searchable database of independent newspapers and ephemera of that age). Some databases offer art (ArtStor), video (Films on Demand), music (Database of Recorded American Music [DRAM]), or photography (Associated Press Images Collection). Others may offer excellent resources for highly specific material: The Burns Archive, for example, offers one million historic photographs and is recognized by

> **RESEARCH TIP**
> Beware of trying to find the "perfect source." Students often get frustrated with the research process because they have an excellent original idea but cannot find analysis, commentary, or opinion that directly supports it. Although it may not feel like it, not being able to find sources may actually be a *good* thing: It may indicate you have an original perspective or argument, a perfect place to add your voice.

---

[2]"Wikipedia Founder Discourages Academic Use of His Creation," *Chronicle of Higher Education Wired Campus*, June 12, 2006, http://www.chronicle.com/wiredcampus/article/1328/wikipedia-founder-discourages-academic-use-of-his-creation.

scholars as a primary resource for early medical photography. Look at your library's website and find out where you can browse the databases.

As you can see, databases abound. To navigate them and find the right one for your topic and project, look at your library's offerings and roll your cursor over database titles to get some information about the scope and holdings of each one. Never hesitate to ask a librarian at the reference desk for a quick tutorial on how to use your university databases — after all, you technically pay for these subscriptions through your tuition.

When using databases for research, first choose a topic, then narrow your topic using the strategies outlined earlier in this chapter. List synonyms for your key search terms. As you search, look at words used in titles and descriptors for alternative ideas and make use of the "advanced search" option so that you can easily combine multiple terms. Rarely will you find exactly what you're looking for right away. Try different search terms and different ways to narrow your topic. Consider limiting the date range of your search to find historical sources on your topic or narrowing results to show scholarly journal articles only.

Most databases have an advanced search option that offers fillable forms for combining multiple terms. In Figure 7.1, we show a search field using Boolean operators (AND, OR, and NOT) to seek targeted information on the use of anabolic steroids. Because a simple search of "anabolic steroids" retrieved far too many results, we used this advanced search to combine three concepts: anabolic steroids, legal aspects of their use, and use of them by athletes. Related terms are combined with the word "or": *law* or *legal*. The last letters of a word have been replaced with an asterisk so that any ending will be included in the search. *Athlet** will search for *athlete, athletes,* or *athletics.* Options on both sides of the list of articles retrieved offer opportunities to refine a search by date of publication or to restrict the results

Figure 7.1   A Database Search

to only academic journals, magazines, or newspapers. Notice in Figure 7.2 some further ways to limit your searches.

As with an internet search, when you search through databases, you'll need to make critical choices about which articles are worth pursuing. Some results may not be useful. A title might tell you right away that a source is not exactly about your topic, or you might notice that the publication date is not relevant to your questions. The subject lines may contain some keywords associated with your topic (or not), and if you open the source, you may find an abstract that tells you more about the contents and findings of the source. All these leads can let you know how much further to look into your source.

Don't forget that your sources need not have links to the full text for you to retrieve them easily. It is the role of a library to get you the information you need. If you cannot link to the full text of an article you want to read, find your library's Interlibrary Loan (ILL) system, which you can use to request books and copies of articles to be sent to your library for you. Often, ILL materials take less than a day for electronic delivery and anywhere from two days to two weeks for physical books.

As you choose and use sources, keep track of them. You can save them in a folder, or you can use your library's system for selecting and saving resources. You can save, email, or print the references you have selected. You may also have an option to export references to a citation management program such as RefWorks or EndNote. These programs allow you to create your own personal database of sources in which you can store your references and take notes. Later, when you're ready to create a bibliography, these programs will automatically format your references in MLA, APA, or another style. Ask a librarian if one of these programs is available to students on your campus.

RESEARCH TIP
Sources that at first appear to be unrelated to your topic may actually be *relatable* to your topic. If you are writing about poor labor conditions in US clothing companies' supply chains in Asia, and you find an article about the working conditions of agricultural laborers in South America, don't just cast that article aside. Rather, explore the possible overlaps. Determine whether or not you can apply one situation to the other.

Figure 7.2   Advanced Search Options

① Drop-down menus specify types of documents, types of publications, languages, and dates.

② Check boxes specify full text, references, cover stories, image types, and file types.

THINKING CRITICALLY *Using Search Terms*

Imagine that your research question is this: Should first-year college students be required to live on campus? Identify useful key issues, terms, and related terms that you can use to search. (The first row has been completed as an example.)

QUESTION	KEY TERMS	RELATED TERMS	SEARCH TERMS
Should first-year college students be required to live on campus?	first-year students required to live on campus	freshmen freshman year residency policies residence hall requirement dorm dormitory	freshman OR first-year student* Residency rules OR residence requirement dorm*
Which schools have a first-year residency requirement, and which do not?			
What are the benefits and drawbacks of living on campus?			
How do alternative on- or off-campus living situations compare?			

LOCATING BOOKS

The books that your library owns can be found through its online catalog. Typically, you can search by author or title or, if you don't have a specific book in mind, by keyword or subject. As with databases, think about different search terms to use, keeping an eye out for subject headings used for books that appear relevant. Take advantage of an "advanced search" option. You may, for example, be able to limit a search to books on a particular topic in English published within recent years. In addition to books, the catalog will also list DVDs, audio and video recordings, and other formats.

Unlike articles, books tend to cover broad topics, so be prepared to broaden your search terms. It may be that a book has a chapter or ten pages that are precisely what you need, but the catalog typically doesn't index the contents of books in detail. Think instead of what kind of book might contain the information you need.

Once you've found some promising books in the catalog, note down the call numbers, find them on the shelves, and then browse. Because books on the same topic are shelved together, you can quickly see what additional books are available by scanning the shelves. As you browse, be sure to look for books that have been published recently enough for your purposes. You do not have to read a book from cover to cover to use it in your research. Instead, skim the introduction to see if it will be useful and then use its table of contents and index to pinpoint the sections of the book that are the most relevant.

If you are searching for a very specific name or phrase, you might try typing it into Google Book Search (books.google.com), which searches the contents of more than twenty-five million scanned books. Although it tends to retrieve too many results for most topics and you may only be able to see a snippet of content, it can help you locate a particular quote or identify which books might include an unusual name or phrase. There is a "find in a library" link that will help you determine whether the books are available in your library.

Exercise: Practicing Research

Select one of the research questions below or use one you're currently working on. Using the Visual Guide: Finding Discourse on Your Topic as well as the instruction in this chapter, determine the best research strategy: General internet searching? Library databases? Books? Narrow it down: Which websites will you visit? Which databases will you use? What books can you peruse by searching your library's catalog?

Research Question 1: How do children's toys impact the development of gender?

Research Question 2: What are the dangers and benefits of nationalism?

Research Question 3: Should big college sports programs pay athletes?

Then, find your sources online, in the database, or in your library's catalog. Use words or phrases from the research question and combine them with your own words to search for related information to answer it. Practice maneuvers like limiting results by date range, looking for scholarly and popular sources, searching for images, or seeking only certain kinds of documents.

Evaluating Sources

Each step of the way in your research process, you will be making choices about your sources. As you proceed, from selecting promising items in a database search to browsing the book collection, you will want to use the techniques for previewing and skimming detailed on pages 33–36 in order to make your selections and develop your argument as you research. Begin by asking yourself some basic questions:

- Is this source relevant?
- Is it current enough?

- Does the title or abstract suggest it will address an important aspect of my topic?
- Am I choosing sources that represent a range of ideas, not simply ones that support my opinion?
- Do I have a reason to believe that these sources are trustworthy?

Once you have collected a number of likely sources, you will want to do further filtering. Examine each one with these questions in mind:

- *Is this source credible? Does it include information about the author and his or her credentials that can help me decide whether to rely on it?* In the case of books, you might check a database for book reviews for a second opinion. In the case of websites, find out where the site came from and why it has been posted online. Don't use a source if you can't determine its authorship or purpose.

- *Will my audience find this source credible and persuasive?* A story about US politics from the *Washington Post*, whose writers conduct firsthand reporting in the nation's capital, carries more clout than a story from a small-circulation newspaper that is drawing its information from a wire service.

- *Am I using the best evidence available?* Quoting directly from a government report may be more effective than quoting a news story that summarizes the report. Finding evidence that supports your claims in a president's speeches or letters is more persuasive than drawing your conclusions from a page or two of a history textbook.

RESEARCH TIP
During your research, write down observations and questions. This way, you won't find yourself with a pile of printouts and books and no idea what to say about them. What you have to say will flow naturally out of the prewriting you've already done — and that prewriting will help guide your further research.

- *Am I being fair to all sides?* Make sure you are prepared to address alternate perspectives, even if you ultimately take a position. Avoid sources that clearly promote an agenda in favor of ones that your audience will consider balanced and reliable.

- *Can I corroborate my key claims in more than one source?* Compare your sources to ensure that you aren't relying on facts that can't be confirmed. If you're having trouble confirming a source, check with a librarian.

- *Do I really need this source?* It's tempting to use all the books and articles you have found, but if two sources say essentially the same thing, choose the one that is likely to carry the most weight with your audience.

SCHOLARLY, POPULAR, AND TRADE SOURCES

An important part of finding and evaluating the reliability of your sources is determining whether they are **scholarly** or **popular** sources. In the table shown on p. 258, we cover some of the basic elements that distinguish these two types of publications. We also examine a third category called **trade** publications.

Scholarly publications are generally considered the gold standard of reliability in the production of knowledge and the circulation of discourse. This is primarily because scholarly publications are generally

- nonprofit;
- built on a mission to advance knowledge in a specific area;
- organized according to disciplinary methodologies, standards, and ethics; and
- peer-reviewed or refereed (meaning that before publication, the articles are reviewed and accepted by a group of experts in that field and in that specific area).

Popular publications — newspapers, magazines, newsletters, websites, blogs — may be more or less reliable sources, but they generally do not carry the academic weight of scholarly ones. Popular sources have relative value: Some have high journalistic and editorial standards — think of the *Los Angeles Times* or the *Economist* magazine — and may contain articles and essays by respected journalists and experts — even scholars. But even intellectual magazines like *Science* or the *New Yorker* are popular publications in the same sense that *Cosmopolitan, Game Informer, Better Homes and Gardens,* or *Car and Driver* are: They are written for a general audience, and they are driven by profit.

Consider the implications. Magazines and newspapers must publish articles that sell to broad audiences; indeed, the goal of any commercial media enterprise is to make money from sales, subscriptions, and sponsors. Therefore, they are not as likely as academic sources to offer the widest range of subjects or perspectives, the same level of complexity, or the deepest, most thorough, and thoughtful forms of analysis.

Trade publications, the third category of sources, are more related to publications in the popular category; however, trade sources are designed for people in particular industries and professional associations. They sometimes appear to be very complex because they assume that readers are familiar with an insider's vocabulary. However, they are not popular because they are not for a general audience, and they are not scholarly because they do not involve a peer review process. Nevertheless, trade publications often utilize the latest field-specific research and expert voices and may be considered reliable resources in many cases. That said, we must remember that industry groups are likely to interpret issues through the lens of their interests — so, for example, *Coal Age* magazine (published by Mining Media International) and *SNLEnergy* (published by the American Coal Council) are much more likely to view coal production and use favorably as compared to *Solar Today Magazine* (published by the American Solar Energy Society).

Remember that just because something is published in a scholarly journal doesn't mean it is peer reviewed. In some journals, a peer-reviewed article may sit side by side with a book review or an editorial. Popular magazines will almost never contain scholarly articles; a respected scholar might contribute an original essay to a popular magazine, but again that doesn't mean the article is "scholarly."

Types of Sources

	Scholarly	Popular	Trade
Publisher	Universities, government agencies, research foundations, and institutions	Media companies, for-profit groups, internet website owners, interest groups	Professional associations, trade groups, unions, business groups, consortiums
Purpose	To report on research, experiments, and theories to expand human knowledge	To inform, entertain, and engage; to expand influence or profit or both	To inform, entertain, and engage; to expand influence in a specific field or industry
Audience	Academics, intellectuals, specialists, researchers	General public	People who have interests in a specific trade or industry
Language	Complex, technical, authoritative	Accessible, conversational	Accessible but with insider-speak such as jargon and acronyms
Sources cited	Always	Sometimes, usually through in-text reference or hyperlinks	Sometimes, usually through in-text reference or hyperlinks
Features and characteristics	Plain style; lots of footnotes or endnotes, long articles; few advertisements (if any); often charts and graphs; longer paragraphs and titles; peer reviewed	Glossy, attractive style; shorter and easier-to-digest articles; many advertisements; simple charts and graphs; shorter paragraphs and titles (if any); not peer reviewed	Various styles ranging from newsprint to glossy styles; technical but easier-to-digest articles, titles indicating industry-specific issues, advertising related to field; not peer reviewed
Frequency	Usually quarterly, semiannually	Usually daily, weekly, biweekly, monthly	Sometimes quarterly or semiannually; most often daily, weekly, monthly, bimonthly
Examples	*American Journal of Sociology, Harvard Asia Pacific Review, Foreign Affairs,* government reports	*Time, New York Times, Vogue, Popular Mechanics, HuffPost, Business Insider*	*AdWeek, Publishers Weekly, Columbia Journalism Review, Chronicle of Higher Education, Comics and Games Retailer*

EVALUATING ONLINE SOURCES

Unlike the information found in a library or published and circulated widely in print, much information online does not go through an evaluative process, as when librarians curate their collections or an editor reviews and selects material for a publication. Thus, one of the first things you must do to determine the quality and reliability of information online is consider the pathway of its publication on the internet. Did the information pass through any review process? Who was doing the reviewing? If the comments section in the *New York Times* shows someone claiming to be a doctor giving advice on some health issue, should you believe it? After all, you too could claim to be a doctor and publish your comments somewhere. At the same time, it may be that the commentator *is* a doctor and *is* reliable — but how would you know? In this hypothetical case, we would recommend corroborating the alleged doctor's claim using a respectable, reviewed medical publication (even if it happens to be openly available online).

Today, most print publications offer their content online in a digital format. However, there are also reliable online resources that are not duplicated in print, from high-quality citizen journalism to TED talks to university lectures online. There may be thoughtful blogs or other publication formats (video, podcast, indexes) created or curated by people who have a high degree of credibility, but you must be cautious. The popularity of a website, blog, or podcast does not automatically confer expertise upon the creators or producers. Neither does the way a website *looks*. Given the ease of entry into the marketplace of ideas via the internet and the relative ease of designing a professional-looking webpage, the popularity and design of a website cannot be considered key criteria in evaluating reliability.

A further problem is caused by the surge in disreputable publication venues that offer open-access publishing in journals that appear to be peer reviewed but really have dramatically lower standards — or none at all. These venues are usually predatory: They project the veneer of a scholarly journal, often with academic-sounding titles to match. For a fee, or sometimes for free (if they are ad revenue–based), these "journals" will publish material with little or no quality control. They are primary locations for fraudulent and hoax papers. Be wary of online journals discovered on the open internet and review them very carefully. It is always safer to use your university databases for scholarly sources.

Nevertheless, it is likely most of us will seek sources on the internet. The best steps you can take to remain a skeptical but open-minded researcher is to apply critical thinking skills. The first thing to do is consider all the contexts that inform your online sources:

- How did they get onto the internet?
- What organizations or individuals are behind their publication?
- Were they originally published elsewhere?
- What are the limitations of this particular kind of online resource?

- Why is this type of source a legitimate form of evidence in the context of your analysis?
- What special authority does the individual or group cited have for speaking on an issue?

With so much information online, you don't always get the basic indicators of authority, such as author credentials or an indication of editorial review. Remember that anyone can publish online with no review process. All that is needed is access to the internet.

You need not discount information available online, though; the internet provides a stunning array of unique perspectives and analyses. It has made it possible for people everywhere to contribute their arguments, opinions, and comments to public discourses.

Many students have been told to examine the domains of websites to judge the reliability of a source; however, whether a website is a *.com*, *.org*, or *.edu* is a weak marker of a source's reliability. All domain types can host reliable or unreliable information. Similarly, tweets and comments, even when written by experts, may or may not carry much weight depending on the subject and occasion of their tweets or comments.

The information you will look for as you evaluate internet sources is often the same as what you need to record in any citation. Use clues in URLs to see where sites originate. For example, URLs containing *.k12* are hosted at elementary and secondary schools, so they may be intended for a young audience; those ending in *.gov* are government agencies, so they tend to provide official information, but if a *.gov* website is followed by a country code, you must also consider the context of place revealed by that origin. A website with a domain such as *.gov.ca* (Canada) may be more trustworthy than one from a country where freedoms of speech are curtailed, such as *.gov.kp* (North Korea). You can streamline the process of creating a list of works cited by identifying these elements as you find and begin to evaluate a source. (See Documentation later in this chapter for more on how to properly cite sources.)

In Figure 7.3, the URL includes the ending *.gov*, meaning it is a government website, an official document that has been vetted. There is an "about" link that will explain the government agency's mission. This appears to be a high-quality source of basic information on the issue. The information you need to cite this report is also on the page; make sure you keep track of where you found the source and when, since websites can change. One way to keep track is by creating an account at a social bookmarking site such as Diigo (diigo.com) where you can store and annotate websites.

Figure 7.3 A Page from a Government Website

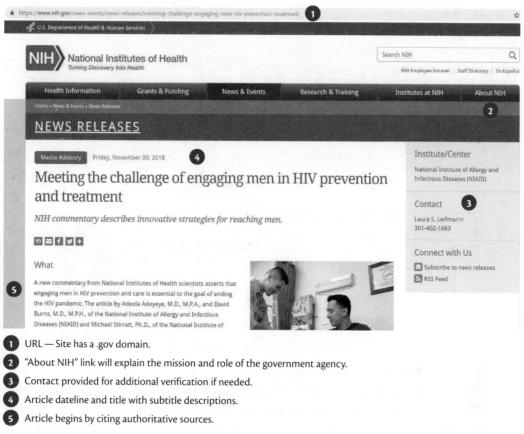

1. URL — Site has a .gov domain.
2. "About NIH" link will explain the mission and role of the government agency.
3. Contact provided for additional verification if needed.
4. Article dateline and title with subtitle descriptions.
5. Article begins by citing authoritative sources.

Figure 7.4 on page 262 shows how the information on a web page might lead you to reject it as a source. Clearly, although this site purports to provide educational information in a well-meaning way, its primary purpose is to sell services and products. The focus on marketing should send up a red flag.

Exercise: Finding Reliable Websites

Perform an internet search on a topic and find a more reliable and less reliable website, using the questions below (and continued on the next page) to help you determine the factors that indicate reliability. *Hint*: To get past the most popular results from major news organizations, go deeper in the search results.

- What kind of domain does the website have? Does it impact its reliability? How so?
- Can you follow an "about" link (or delete everything after the first slash in the URL to go to the parent site)? If so, who is behind the website?
- What is the purpose or mission of the individual or organization operating the website?

Figure 7.4   A Page from a Commercial Website

1. URL shows that the site is a .com (commercial) site.

2. Menu bar offers speaking services, recipes that use sponsored products, and shopping for sponsored products.

3. "About" link tells us that author's qualifications do not include formal education in health science.

4. Additional link to the "news" is actually an advertisement. (We suspect the "free newsletter" will also be ad-driven.)

5. Article on "proven" benefits of turmeric is list-based and anecdotal, and it supports the ad nearby.

- Are there advertisements visible on the page? If so, what kind of products are they? Is the content of the website related to the products being advertised? How?

- Is the information on the website reviewed by anyone before it is selected and posted? Who is selecting and reviewing? Is that person (or body) reputable and reliable? Why or why not?

WHY FINDING RELIABLE INTERNET SOURCES IS SO CHALLENGING

With our instant access to so much knowledge, and in the midst of an online cacophony of perspectives and voices, finding dependable, trustworthy sources of information can be difficult. Today, individuals can articulate their views publicly in a variety of online venues. With just a few clicks, individuals can expose poor customer service at a restaurant or abuses of power by police. They can report on news events as they happen, rally like-minded people to causes and activism, and share their opinions about almost anything in videos, blogs, tweets, and comments. This suggests an unprecedented democratic potential: The role of the internet in facilitating Arab Spring, a series of antigovernment protests across the Middle East in 2010–2011, or the #occupy, #blacklivesmatter, and #metoo movements in the United States, is inspiring. The internet's structure gives voice to the voiceless, allowing underrepresented and systematically marginalized people to share experiences and form discourse communities across the globe.

At the same time, this democratic potential is accompanied by serious perils. Hate groups and narrowly ideological activist organizations, for example, sometimes deliberately spread propaganda, promoting shallow conspiracy theories and outright lies. Consider a couple of claims popularized by such groups in recent years: that the Sandy Hook Elementary School shooting was staged by gun-control activists seeking to push through new firearms controls; that Barack Obama was not born in the United States; that the September 11, 2001, attacks on the World Trade Center were an "inside job"; that a secret society called the Illuminati controls the world. These false stories were created and perpetuated by highly partisan, conspiracy-driven, or fraudulent websites and were amplified by individual social media users vulnerable to such misinformation who shared the stories with networks of friends and followers.

Critical thinking can help mitigate the dangers of the media environment, which includes the possibility that lies, hysteria, and even violence can result from the unsafe, uncritical acceptance of information available on the internet. The proliferation of "fake news" stories and websites, viral misinformation campaigns, clickbait articles, and fraudulent websites all complicate our efforts to find quality information online. But not all fake news is created by political operatives, foreign agents, malicious bots, or entrepreneurs seeking to make money from advertising on bogus websites. Some fake news stories are created by everyday individuals. In 2016, Tim Tucker, a Twitter user who photographed a line of buses near a Donald Trump election rally in Austin, Texas, claimed that his photographs were evidence of Democratic Party busing in paid anti-Trump protesters. By his own admission, this claim was false, invented out of thin air, yet although he started with only 40 followers on Twitter, his post was shared 16,000 times on that site and 350,000 times on Facebook in a single day and subsequently was covered by a variety of conservative news outlets. Soon, it was referenced by Trump himself on his Twitter account. In just a few days, one user's incautious post created a national firestorm. ("Anytime

"Don't believe everything you read on the internet just because there's a quote next to it."

—Abraham Lincoln

Sometimes "authority" can be misleading.

you see me in the future," Tucker later said, "I can assure you I am going to try my best to be balanced with the facts and very clear about what is opinion and what is not.")

In sum, the internet gives us unprecedented access to information and to our own assertions of authority, but this empowerment also requires us to examine information carefully and proffer it responsibly. It is important to respect accuracy and reliability when sharing our ideas on the internet, to track the sources of viral stories, and to fact-check as much as possible the claims and details they offer.

A WORD ON "FAKE NEWS"

It has become somewhat fashionable to label as "fake news" any kind of information that does not accord with one's own worldview. For example, politicians often call into question the objectivity and reliability of news outlets that have been the standard-bearers of ethical journalism in the United States for decades — in some cases, more than a century (the *New York Times*, for example). Here we must be emphatic: The mainstream news media, such as the *New York Times*, CNN, FOX, MSNBC, and others, are *not* fake news outlets. These organizations may or may not exhibit political biases and may or may not privilege information likely to attract certain kinds of readers and viewers, but they also carefully demarcate what they consider to be news programs and opinion programs, and they follow the most rigorous standards of verifiable reporting. (Also remember that taking a thoughtful position is not the same as having a bias. In fact, taking a thoughtful position means *overcoming* biases, integrating a range of perspectives, meeting challenges to your own views, and adhering strictly to the goals of fairness and accuracy.)

Whether today's fake news stories are created by nefarious individuals or antagonistic intelligence agencies, their purpose is to sow confusion, doubt, and disorder by promoting falsehoods on the internet. Often these stories play upon base prejudices and superstitions. Their creators are not shy about telling wholesale lies, inventing quotations, and manipulating charts, graphs, and images, for example. They are indiscriminate in their attacks on truth: Liberals and conservatives, celebrities and everyday people have been targeted. Sometimes, fake news stories are built around issues: unscientific claims denying climate change, the efficacy of vaccinations, and the integrity of elections are just a few instances. Other types of fake news stories are created to further the agendas of activist organizations. Still others are designed merely to be eye-catching, their sole purpose to generate traffic to a website.

Unreliable or misleading news sources also include popular tabloids such as the *National Enquirer*, which blurs the lines between fiction and reality with salacious, screaming headlines like "Muslim Spies in Obama's CIA" and "Ted Cruz's Father Linked to JFK Assassination." Consider, too, satirical publications and programs like *The Onion*, *The Daily Show* (Comedy Central), or *Last Week Tonight* (HBO). Although such programs offer sometimes sharp commentary and analysis, their purpose is largely to entertain, not to inform. As such, they should not be considered quality sources of information.

ANATOMY OF A FAKE NEWS STORY   NewsPunch is a fake news website posing as a legitimate news outlet, which you can see in Figure 7.5. It has a respectable title and a "punchy" tagline ("Where Mainstream Fears to Tread"), as well as a clean design and layout characteristic of respectable news websites (a navigation menu of relevant topics and lists of recent and popular articles). There is even a headline ticker bar that scrolls between titles as if they were breaking news stories. When we visited the site, clickbait titles appeared such as "Under Obama, US Became World's #1 Hotspot for Pedophilia." Thus, although the site projects some signs of journalistic legitimacy, we knew we needed to look more closely to determine if it was actually reliable.

We looked at the first story on the page and searched for author Sean Adl-Tabatabai to verify his credentials as a writer. We discovered through a quick internet search that

Figure 7.5   A Fake News Website

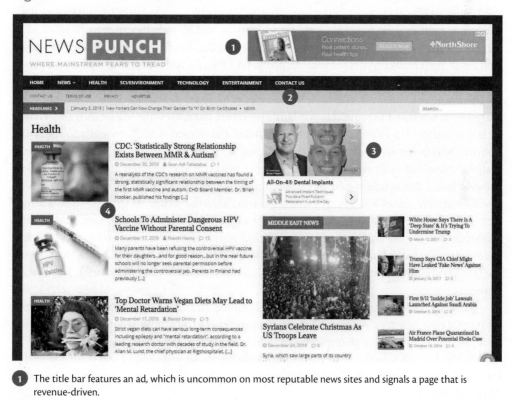

1. The title bar features an ad, which is uncommon on most reputable news sites and signals a page that is revenue-driven.

2. The navigation menu looks standard, but "Contact Us" is repeated on both lines, and there is an option for "Advertise," another warning sign.

3. Another ad, higher and more prominent on the page than most articles.

4. The stories mimic the layout of news sites: a photo with a category label ("Health") and a title, publication date, author, and first lines of the article.

the former television producer is the founder of this fake news site, and the site has been flagged by a European Union task force charged with investigating Russian efforts to destabilize Western democracies. We found no information about the second author listed, Niamh Harris.

The first headline, "CDC: 'Statistically Strong Relationship Exists Between MMR and Autism,'" suggests that the Centers for Disease Control and Prevention (CDC), the US government's national health protection agency, makes this claim. In fact, the CDC is *very* clear that MMR vaccines do NOT cause autism — the CDC uses huge letters on its website to emphasize its position — and it has devoted significant resources to debunking dangerous theories that they do. The quotation in the headline is actually attributed to Dr. Brian Hooker of the Children's Health Defense organization, an activist group widely discredited in the medical community for its antivaccine stance and not associated at all with the CDC.

Hooker's findings were first published (the NewsPunch article tells us) in the *Journal of American Physicians and Surgeons*. This publication sounds fairly impressive at first. However, further searching on Google and "source watch" websites such as Beall's List of Predatory Journals and Publications showed us that this journal is published by the Association of American Physicians and Surgeons (AAPS), an ultraconservative activist group advocating a range of scientifically discredited theories, including that HIV does not cause AIDS and that abortion leads to breast cancer. The *Journal of American Physicians and Surgeons* is not listed in reputable academic literature databases like MEDLINE and Web of Science, and the US Library of National Medicine has denied AAPS's requests to index the journal, which has also been listed by watchdog scholars as a predatory open-access journal. As a result of our evaluation of the website plus further research and cross-checking, we concluded this article is fake news and not to be trusted.

The article on MMR vaccines and autism, and the other examples cited earlier, are undoubtedly the strictest forms of fake news (spurious, mendacious, malicious). Websites like NewsPunch contain information mostly from other sources, recycled and reinterpreted through a sensationalistic or ideological lens. Other partisan websites may be less severe but nevertheless project the look of a news organization with none of its integrity.

What we cannot stress enough is that such information sources — and, in fact, *all* types of information sources — demand our most careful critical thinking and information literacy skills. Use the table that follows to help identify and evaluate resources that may be unreliable. Use the Checklist for Identifying Fake News on page 268 to ascertain a website's origins, legitimacy, and value and to dig further into the online sources you find to measure their validity.

NATIVE ADVERTISING AND BRANDED CONTENT

Some magazines, you probably have noticed, contain nearly as many (or even more) pages of advertisements than original content — a sign that the publication's content may be driven by the sponsors. In some publications, content itself can be part of an overall marketing scheme.

Types of "Fake News" and Unreliable Content

Type	Creator(s)	Purpose(s)	Features	Example(s)
Propaganda	Government agencies, activist groups, political organizations, corporations	To affect social and political beliefs, attitudes, and behaviors to further an agenda	Widespread, often misleading or biased; one-sided (not objective or neutral)	Advertising, issue-based political messages, public service announcements, recruitment or indoctrination materials
Clickbait	Companies and paid content creators	To entice viewers to navigate to websites designed to generate ad revenue based on traffic volume	Sensational "teaser" headlines with links	"Amazing" health news, discoveries, celebrity gossip, lists, inspirational or revolting personal stories
Sponsored content	Companies and marketing firms	To present advertisements as news or interest stories so as to drive revenue	Designed to look like news, will reference products or services in main text	Articles worked into major news sources and webpages directing users to third-party content; often labeled
Partisan news	Media companies and special-interest groups	To provide perspective-based information to like-minded viewers/readers	Ideological; not impartial (although may claim to be); facts may be present but selective; biased interpretations of facts	Self-identified liberal or conservative information outlets, news personalities; some mainstream networks
Conspiracy theory	Special-interest groups, individuals	To subvert, fool, or entertain (for political or other purposes)	Dismisses experts and authorities; provides simplistic or sensationalistic answers to complex questions; spreads beliefs rooted in paranoia, fear, uncertainty	Material claiming to provide the "real" truth contrary to accepted knowledge or beliefs; claims to expose "hoaxes" perpetuated by powerful persons or interests

In the magazine industry, this type of content is known as "ad-friendly copy" or "advertorial," with articles deliberately written to puff up a person, product, or service. On the internet, you have probably seen links to "sponsored content," which is like a digital version of advertorial (see Fig. 7.6, p. 268). Even reputable news agencies will include links to sponsored content (and will usually indicate as much). These are not good sources because they are not neutral: They are less interested in providing quality information and more interested in selling a product or service.

Figure 7.6   Sponsored Content

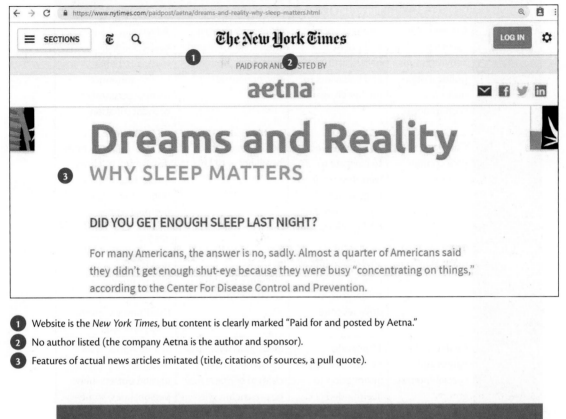

1. Website is the *New York Times*, but content is clearly marked "Paid for and posted by Aetna."
2. No author listed (the company Aetna is the author and sponsor).
3. Features of actual news articles imitated (title, citations of sources, a pull quote).

A CHECKLIST FOR IDENTIFYING FAKE NEWS

Website

☐ Does my source appear to be on a reputable website? Is it a .com, .edu, .org, or .net?

☐ Is there an "About" link (or a "Who We Are" or "Mission" link)? What individual or organization is behind the website?

☐ Is the content edited, or can users post anything?

☐ Does the website respect intellectual property? What website policies ensure (or compromise) source integrity?

☐ Do errors or misspellings on the website signal a lack of quality or reputability?

☐ How is the website supported (ads, donations, sponsorships)? What kinds of products and services are being sold, directly or indirectly, on the website? Are ads and sponsored content clearly marked as such?

(continues on next page)

❏ Are there a lot of pop-ups, surveys, or other distractions? Are visitors being asked for personal information or to sign up for something?

Authors

❏ Are authors or contributors named? Are they identifiable people with first and last names, or are they known just by "handles"?

❏ Are they real people? Can I find additional information about them?

❏ What authority do they have? What biases or other ideological predispositions might they have, if any?

Accuracy

❏ Does the information in my source check against other reputable sources?

❏ Are there links or citations in the articles (and do they point to other reputable, timely sources)? What kind of sources are being quoted and cited?

❏ Can I verify or cross-reference images to ensure that they have not been manipulated?

Comments

❏ What kind of audience seems to be involved in the debate?

❏ Do comments agreeing with the source tend to reflect reasonable ideas and common values? What about dissenting comments?

❏ If the site does not allow commenting, why?

CONSIDERING HOW CURRENT SOURCES ARE

Popular sources do have one major advantage in that they are very current. Newspapers and magazines publish frequently enough — daily, weekly, monthly — that they can respond to events as they occur. Although this schedule makes them prone to errors of fact and misreadings of developing situations, they have an indispensable immediacy. Academic journals, on the other hand, usually publish quarterly or semiannually because the peer-review process is so elaborate and the content so rich: Although it takes a longer time to write, review, and publish issues of an academic journal, the content tends not to age as fast. Because academic journals are so deeply researched, analyzed, and reviewed, their findings generally have staying power.

So far, we have been discussing the difference between scholarly, popular, and trade **periodicals** — that is, publications that appear on a regular basis. Whether they are scholarly, popular, or trade publications, or appear frequently or not, reputable publications have strong editorial review processes and abide by the codes of journalistic ethics. Full-length books, too, may be popular or scholarly, published by a university press or a respected organization. Although scholarly books are not always peer reviewed, many academic publishers are overseen by editorial boards who solicit feedback from expert reviewers. Academic books are also subject to a secondary review process in scholarly journals after they are published, so you can always examine how a source has been regarded by other experts if you wanted to verify its credibility. Like with popular and scholarly periodicals, full-length books may also have different levels of continuing relevance. Some books are published quickly and are intended to speak to current events; others take years to write, vet, and publish and may stick around as authoritative sources for a long time, even decades.

Remember, however, that academic books *do* age. Those you find on the library shelves may be much older than the relevant results from an internet or database search. Such books published long ago may be of historical interest, but they are rarely the strongest sources speaking directly to current issues, and they must be regarded in context. A book about juvenile delinquency published by a sociologist in 1955 cannot be used as evidence for a theory of adolescence nowadays, and even a landmark work, like Sigmund Freud's *The Interpretation of Dreams* (1899), may be an interesting book to study in and of itself or may prove to be an excellent background reference in your work, but it would not serve as evidence in an argument that the Oedipal complex — Freud's famous theory of psychosexual development — should inform how parents interact with their children today.

A CHECKLIST FOR EVALUATING SOURCES

☐ Can I identify the person or organization who produced the source?

☐ Can I identify the source's purpose?

☐ Are the authors real, reliable, and credentialed?

☐ Do sources cited represent a range of ideas, not simply ones that support one viewpoint?

☐ Are images verifiable from other sources?

☐ Is the source recent? If not, is the information I will be using from it likely or unlikely to change over time?

☐ Does the source treat the topic superficially or in depth?

☐ Does the article speak directly (or relevantly) to my topic and tentative thesis?

☐ If the article is from a scholarly journal, am I sure I understand it?

☐ Is the source titled and marketed as entertainment? If so, have I considered the author's commercial biases?

(continues on next page)

Performing Your Own Primary Research

Research isn't limited to the world of professors and scientists. In one way or another, everyone does research at some point. If you decided to open your own business, you would want to do market research to persuade the bank that you are likely to be profitable enough to repay a loan. If you wanted to find out how and why a campus monument was erected, you could visit the university library's institutional archives and seek out information on it. If you were reviewing a film or book, you would probably go to the cinema or read in a comfortable place. Doing any of these things is performing primary research. In college, you might find yourself working on primary research alongside faculty members or participating in a class project to collect data. In other circumstances, you may wish to supplement your arguments with primary sources. Here, we touch on several kinds of primary research commonly performed by students.

INTERVIEWING PEERS AND LOCAL AUTHORITIES

For many topics, consider that you are surrounded by experts at your college. You ought to try to consult them — for instance, members of the faculty or other authorities on art, business, law, university administration, and so forth. You can also consult interested laypersons. Remember that experts may have their biases and "ordinary" people may have knowledge that experts lack. When interviewing experts, keep in mind Pablo Picasso's comment: "You mustn't always believe what I say. Questions tempt you to tell lies, particularly when there is no answer."

If you are interviewing your peers, you will probably want to make an effort to get a representative sample. Of course, even within a group not all members share a single view — for example, many African Americans favor affirmative action, but not all do; some lawmakers support capital punishment, but again, many do not. Make an effort to talk to a range of people who might offer varied opinions. You may learn some unexpected things.

You may also collect **testimonial** evidence from professors, students, community members, or family members. If you are writing about the women's rights movement of the 1970s, you might interview a professor or family member who lived through the era or participated in civil rights activities. You may know veterans who can speak to issues surrounding US wars or the experience of military service. Or perhaps an expert on a particular subject is visiting your campus for a lecture or talk, and you can find a way to put some questions of interest to her.

Visual Guide: Conducting Interviews

1 Find subjects for interviews

If you are looking for expert opinions, you may want to start with a faculty member on your campus. Search department and college websites for information about the special interests of the faculty and also about lecturers who will be visiting the campus.

2 Request the interview

Request the interview, preferably in writing, a week in advance.

- Ask for ample time, but respect the interviewee's schedule.
- Indicate whether the material will be confidential and (if relevant) ask if you may record the interview.

If the person accepts the invitation:
- Ask if he or she recommends any reading.
- Establish a suitable time and place.

3 Prepare thoroughly

- Read any recommended or background material.
- Formulate some questions, keeping in mind that you want detailed answers. Questions beginning with *Why* and *How* will usually require the interviewee to go beyond yes and no answers.

4 Conduct the interview

- Begin by engaging in brief conversation, without taking notes.
- Come prepared with an opening question or two, but as the interview proceeds, don't hesitate to ask questions that you hadn't anticipated asking.
- Even if your subject has consented to let you record the interview, be prepared to take notes on points that strike you as especially significant.
- Near the end, ask the subject if he or she wishes to add anything, perhaps by way of clarifying some earlier comment.
- Conclude by thanking the interviewee and by offering to provide a copy of the final version of your paper.

5 Write up the interview

- As soon as possible, type up your notes and observations and clarify them, filling in any abbreviations or shorthand you used while you still remember.
- If you recorded the interview, transcribe it or use a transcription program such as Transcribe. (You can also upload the audio to YouTube and then click on the transcribe button as it plays.)
- Scan the transcription and mark the parts that now strike you as especially significant.
- Be especially careful to indicate which words are direct quotations from your interview and which are your own observations. If in doubt, check with the interviewee.

CONDUCTING OBSERVATIONS

Observational research is the process of collecting information by situating yourself in a real-life context and making observations of what is present or what occurs. It may be *structured*, which means that you spend time designing your observation in a systematic way so as to get consistent results. For example, perhaps you want to see if male and female children are more likely to select gender-specific toys from a toy chest if they are with peers of the same sex; to prepare, you might code each toy according to its gendered properties and then watch and record while same-sex and mixed-sex groups of children are at play in the toy chest. To aim for consistent results, you might conduct the observation in multiple sittings, but always at the same time with the same number of children in each group.

Observational research may also be *unstructured*, meaning that you simply immerse yourself in a situation and carefully note what you see or experience. If you visited a toy store to gather impressions about how children's toys are segregated according to gender, you would be performing unstructured observational research. The same goes for attending a political convention as an observer (as opposed to a participant) or riding along with a police officer.

However, when you conduct observations, you must be careful to abide by ethical standards; you should not record people without their consent, for example. You must also be aware of observer biases — the notion that people's behavior changes when they know they are being watched, for one thing, and also that you yourself as a researcher may get swept up in what you are observing to a degree that you are not able to be neutral or objective in your observations.

CONDUCTING SURVEYS

Surveys are excellent ways to ascertain the opinions and beliefs of a certain population. Whether you distribute your surveys via paper or set up an online survey through an online service like Doodle or SurveyMonkey, your college's in-house software such as Qualtrics, or even a Facebook poll, be sure to distribute your survey to the target population. Whether you are trying to collect opinions, values, behaviors, or facts, your survey questions should be constructed carefully to get the data that you want. Here are some other pitfalls of collecting surveys:

- *Not enough respondents/bad sample size:* If only five women responded to your survey on attitudes about fraternities on campus, you shouldn't use just five responses to say "80% of women on campus have a favorable view of fraternities."
- *Leading questions:* Leading questions use language likely to influence respondents' answers, such as "How fast should drivers be allowed to go on our serene campus roads?" As you can see, the language "leads" the respondent: For these questions, respondents are likely to answer lower speeds for "serene" roads. A more appropriate version of this question would be "What in your opinion is a safe driving speed for campus roads?"
- *Loaded questions:* Loaded questions push respondents to answer questions that don't fully or accurately represent their actual opinions. "On a scale of 1 to 5," a loaded question might ask, "how awful do you think it is that our

administration is raising tuition?" Such a question forces all respondents to answer in the "awful" range, even if they are somewhat satisfied with the tuition amount overall.

RESEARCH IN ARCHIVES AND SPECIAL COLLECTIONS

Archives are collections of material maintained and preserved by organizations such as college and university libraries, public libraries, corporations, governments, churches, museums, and historical societies. Archives generally contain records that are important to an institution's own history and that may be relevant to others. The National Archives in Washington, DC, for example, curates a vast number of resources, including America's founding documents and military service records. Coca-Cola's company archives and the Walt Disney archives are examples of corporate archives that hold a vast array of materials related to those companies' pasts. Your college or university probably keeps its own institutional archives in its library.

Special collections are bodies of original material — including photographs, films, letters, memos, manuscripts of unique interests, and often material artifacts — usually gathered around a specialized topic, theme, or individual. Special collections often include original, rare, and valuable artifacts that may require permission for access or examination. Many libraries and museums offer at least limited access to digital archives and special collections via their websites, and some databases offer access to primary research sources, too (letters, original newspapers, early manuscripts, and so on).

Some special collections are broad and deep: The Library of Congress, the Smithsonian, and other national museums, for example, hold special collections on a variety of subjects in American political, social, and natural history. Other special collections can be quite specific, ranging from collections of science fiction pulp novels of the 1950s; to letters from combat veterans of World War II; to photograph, film, art, and music collections, antique and contemporary. The Blues Archive at the University of Mississippi contains — among other treasures — the musician B.B. King's personal record collection. The popular culture collection at Bowling Green State University holds 10,000 comic books and graphic novels, among other curiosities like a complete Pokémon set and *Star Trek* memorabilia.

Exercises: Conducting Primary Research

1. *Observation*: Visit a location on campus or a local event and report on the subjects or interactions you find there. Try to formulate a question you want answered: Do people tend to eat lunch outside more often when the cafeteria is busy? Do more people dress in school colors on days when the football team or basketball team is competing?

2. *Survey*: Design three to five survey questions that will help you aggregate data about attitudes, beliefs, opinions, or behaviors of students on your campus. Your survey might be about a specific campus issue or political or social opinions, or you could imagine a demographic you are trying to reach, such as in-state or out-of-state or international students, African American or Latinx students, or students of a particular religion. Reflect on how you might distribute this survey — electronically or using paper — and why.

3. ***Archives***: Visit the website of your own school, or another local college or museum, and examine its special collections. Identify the special collections available and choose one that sounds especially interesting. Look further into it: What kinds of materials are in the collection? Is digital access available? If so, select an example of an original artifact (document, image, etc.) and save it or print it out for closer inspection. For what kind of research topics might it be an important or relevant item? If digital access is unavailable, identify an item you would like to get access to and outline the process of doing so.

Synthesizing Sources

When you are evaluating sources, consider the words of Francis Bacon, Shakespeare's contemporary:

> Some books are to be tasted, others to be swallowed, and some few to be chewed and digested.

Your instructor will expect you not just to find but to digest your sources. This doesn't mean you need to accept them but only that you need to read them thoughtfully. Your readers will expect you to tell them *what you make of your sources*, which means that you will go beyond writing a summary and will synthesize the material into your own contribution to the discourse. *Your* view is what is wanted, and readers expect this view to be thoughtful — not mere summary and not mere tweeting.

Let's pause for a moment and consider the word ***synthesis***. You probably are familiar with *photosynthesis*, the chemical process in green plants that produces carbohydrates from carbon dioxide and hydrogen. Synthesis combines preexisting elements and produces something new. In your writing, you will *synthesize* sources, combining existing material into something new, drawing nourishment from what has already been said (giving credit, of course), and converting it into something new — a view that you think is worth considering. In our use of the word *synthesis*, even a view that you utterly reject becomes a part of your new creation *because it helped stimulate you to formulate your view*; without the idea that you reject, you might not have developed the view that you now hold.

During the process of reading and evaluating sources, and afterward, you will want to listen, think, and say to yourself something like the following:

- "No, no, I see things very differently; it seems to me that . . ."
- "Yes, of course, but on one large issue I think I differ."
- "Yes, sure, I agree, but I would go further and add . . ."
- "Yes, I agree with the conclusion, but I hold this conclusion for reasons different from the ones offered."

> **WRITING TIP**
> In your final draft, *you must give credit to all your sources*. Let the reader know whether you are quoting (in this case, you will use quotation marks around all material directly quoted), whether you are summarizing (you will explicitly say so), or whether you are paraphrasing (again, you will explicitly say so).

Taking Notes

Whether you are performing primary or secondary research, using library special collections or online resources, you should be keeping notes along the way. When it comes to taking notes, all researchers have their own habits that they swear by: We still prefer to take notes on four-by-six-inch index cards; others use a notebook or a computer for note taking. If you use a citation management program such as RefWorks or EndNote, you can store your personal notes and commentary with the citations you have saved. By using the program's search function, you can easily pull together related notes and citations, or you can create project folders for your references so that you can easily review what you've collected.

Whatever method you use, the following techniques should help you maintain consistency and keep organized during the research process:

1. If you use a notebook or index cards, organize them carefully, write in ink (pencil gets smudgy), and write on only one side of the paper or card to avoid losing track of your material. If you keep notes electronically, consider an online tool such as Microsoft OneNote, a Google Doc, or another cloud-based service so that you will not lose your research in the event of a computer crash or a lost laptop.

2. Summarize, for the most part, rather than quote at length. Quote only passages in which the writing is especially effective or passages that are in some way crucial. Make sure that all quotations are exact.

3. Indicate the source. The author's last name is enough if you have consulted only one work by the author, but if you consult more than one work by an author, you need further identification, such as both the author's name and a short title.

4. Add your own comments about the substance of what you are recording. Such comments as "but contrast with Sherwin" or "seems illogical" or "evidence?" will ensure that you are thinking as well as reading and writing.

5. In a separate computer file, or on a separate card or page, write a bibliographic entry for each source. The information in each entry will vary, depending on whether the source is a book, a periodical, an electronic document, and so forth. The kind of information (e.g., author and title) needed for each type of source can be found in the sections MLA Format: The List of Works Cited (p. 287) and APA Format: The List of References (p. 297).

A Note on Plagiarizing

Plagiarism is the unacknowledged use of someone else's work. The word comes from a Latin word for "kidnapping," and plagiarism is indeed the stealing of something engendered by someone else. Your college or your class instructor probably has issued a statement concerning plagiarism. If there is such a statement, be sure to read it carefully.

We won't deliver a sermon on the dishonesty (and folly) of plagiarism; we intend only to help you understand exactly what plagiarism is. The first thing to say is that plagiarism is not limited to the unacknowledged quotation of words.

PARAPHRASING A *paraphrase* is a sort of word-by-word or phrase-by-phrase translation of the author's language into your own language. Unlike a summary, then, a paraphrase is approximately as long as the original.

Paraphrase thus has its uses, but writers often use it unnecessarily, and students who overuse it may find themselves crossing the border into plagiarism. True, if you paraphrase you are using your own words, but you are also using someone else's ideas, and, equally important, you are using this other person's sequence of thoughts.

Even if you change every third word in your source, you are plagiarizing. Here is an example of this sort of plagiarism, based on the previous sentence:

> Even if you alter every second or third word that your source gives, you still are plagiarizing.

Further, even if the writer of this paraphrase had cited a source after the paraphrase, he or she would still have been guilty of plagiarism. How, you may ask, can a writer who cites a source be guilty of plagiarism? Easy. Readers assume that only the gist of the idea is the source's and that the development of the idea — the way it is set forth — is the present writer's work. A paraphrase that runs to several sentences is in no significant way the writer's work: The writer is borrowing not only the idea but also the shape of the presentation, the sentence structure. What the writer needs to do is to write something like this:

> Changing an occasional word does not free the writer from the obligation to cite a source.

And, if the central idea were not a commonplace one, the source would still need to be cited.

Now consider this question: *Why* paraphrase? As we explained in Summarizing and Paraphrasing in Chapter 2 (pp. 46–49), the chief reason to paraphrase a passage is to clarify it — that is, to ensure that you and your readers understand a passage that — perhaps because it is badly written — is obscure. Often there is no good answer for why you should paraphrase. Since a paraphrase is as long as the original, you might as well quote the original, if you think that a passage of that length is worth quoting. Probably it is *not* worth quoting in full; probably you should *not* paraphrase but rather should drastically *summarize* most of it, and perhaps quote a particularly effective phrase or two.

Compiling an Annotated Bibliography

When several sources have been identified and gathered, many researchers prepare an annotated bibliography. That's a list providing all relevant bibliographic information (just as it will appear in your Works Cited list or References list), as well as a brief descriptive and evaluative summary of each source — perhaps one to three sentences. Your instructor may ask you to provide an annotated bibliography for your research project.

An annotated bibliography serves four main purposes:

1. It helps you master the material contained in any given source. To find the heart of the argument presented in an article or book, to phrase it briefly, and to comment on it, you must understand it fully.

2. It helps you think about how each portion of your research fits into the whole of your project, how you will use it, and how it relates to your topic and thesis.

3. It allows your readers to see quickly which items may be especially helpful in their own research.

4. It gives you hands-on practice at bibliographic format, thereby easing the job of creating your final bibliography (the Works Cited list or References list of your paper).

Following is an example entry for an annotated bibliography in MLA (Modern Language Association) format for a project on the effect of violence in the media. Notice that the entry does three things:

1. It begins with a bibliographic entry — author (last name first), title, and so forth.

2. Then it provides information about the content of the work under consideration.

3. Then it suggests how the source might work to support your argument in the final research paper you are writing.

Clover, Carol J. *Men, Women, and Chain Saws: Gender in the Modern Horror Film*. Princeton UP, 1992. The author focuses on Hollywood horror movies of the 1970s and 1980s. She studies representations of women and girls in these movies and the responses of male viewers to female characters, suggesting that this relationship is more complex and less exploitative than the common wisdom claims. Could use this source to establish a counterpoint to the idea that all women are represented stereotypically in horror films.

CITATION GENERATORS   There are many citation generators available online. These generators allow you to enter the information about your source, and, with a click, they will create Works Cited entries in APA or MLA format. But just as you cannot trust spell- and grammar-checkers in Microsoft Word, you cannot trust these generators completely. If you use them, be sure to double-check what they produce before submitting your essay. Always remember that responsible writers take care to cite their sources properly and that failure to do so puts you at risk for accusations of plagiarism.

Quoting from Sources

When is it necessary, or appropriate, to quote? Using your notes, consider where the reader would benefit by seeing the exact words of your source. If you are arguing that Z's definition of *rights* is too inclusive, your readers have to know exactly how Z defined *rights*, word for word. If your source material is so pithy and well worded that summarizing it would weaken its force, give your readers the pleasure of reading the original. Of course, readers won't give you credit for writing these words, but they will appreciate your taste and your effort to make their reading experience pleasant. In short, use (but don't overuse) quotations. Don't quote *too often* and don't quote *too much* of the original source (and never use quotations to achieve more length!). Speaking roughly,

- quotations should occupy no more than 10 to 15 percent of your paper;
- they may occupy much less; and
- most of your paper should set forth your ideas, not other people's ideas.

LONG AND SHORT QUOTATIONS   **Long quotations** (more than four lines of typed prose or three or more lines of poetry) are set off from the text. To set off material, start on a new line, indent one-half inch from the left margin, and type the quotation double-spaced. Do not enclose quotations within quotation marks if you are setting them off.

Short quotations are treated differently. They are embedded within the text; they are enclosed within quotation marks, but otherwise they do not stand out.

All quotations, whether set off or embedded, must be exact. If you omit any words, you must indicate the ellipsis by substituting three spaced periods for the omission; if you insert any words or punctuation, you must indicate the addition by enclosing it within square brackets, not to be confused with parentheses.

Original	The Montgomery bus boycott not only brought national attention to the discriminatory practices of the South, but elevated a twenty-six-year-old preacher to exalted status in the civil rights movement.
Quotation in student paper	"The Montgomery bus boycott . . . elevated [King] to exalted status in the civil rights movement."

LEADING INTO A QUOTATION   Now for a less mechanical matter: The way in which a quotation is introduced. To say that it is "introduced" implies that one leads into it, although on rare occasions a quotation appears without an introduction, perhaps immediately after the title. Normally one leads into a quotation by giving any one or more of the following (but be aware that using them all at once can get unwieldy and produce awkward sentences):

- the *name of the author* and (no less important) the author's expertise or authority
- an indication of *the source of the quotation*, by title and/or year
- *clues signaling the content of the quotation and the purpose* it serves in the present essay

For example:

William James provides a clear answer to Huxley when he says that ". . ."

In *The Will to Believe* (1897), psychologist William James provides a clear answer to Huxley when he says that ". . ."

Either of these lead-ins work, especially because William James is quite well known. When you're quoting from a lesser-known author, it becomes more important to identify his or her expertise and perhaps the source, as in

Biographer Theodora Bosanquet, author of *Henry James at Work* (1982), subtly criticized Huxley's vague ideas on religion by writing, " . . . ."

Notice that in all these samples, the writer uses the lead-in to signal to readers the general tone of the quotation to follow. The writer uses the phrase "a clear answer" to signal that what's coming is, in fact, clear, uses the terms "subtly criticized" and "vague" to indicate that the following words by Bosanquet will be critical and will point out a shortcoming in Huxley's ideas. In this way, the writer anticipates and controls the meaning of the quotation for the reader. If the writer believed otherwise, the lead-ins might have run thus:

> William James's weak response to Huxley does not really meet the difficulty Huxley calls attention to. James writes, ". . . ."

> Biographer Theodora Bosanquet, author of *Henry James at Work* (1982), unjustly criticized Huxley's complex notion of religion by writing ". . . ."

In these examples, clearly the words "weak" and "unjustly criticized" imply how the essayist wants the reader to interpret the quotation. In the second one, Huxley's idea is presented as "complex," not vague.

SIGNAL PHRASES Think of your writing as a conversation between you and your sources. As in conversation, you want to be able to move smoothly between different, sometimes contrary, points of view. You also want to be able to set your thoughts apart from those of your sources. Signal phrases make it easy for readers to know where your information came from and why it's trustworthy by pointing to key facts about the source:

> *According to* psychologist Stephen Ceci . . .

> A report published by the US Bureau of Justice Statistics *concludes* . . .

> Feminist philosopher Sandra Harding *argues* . . .

To avoid repetitiveness, vary your sentence structure:

> . . . *claims* Stephen Ceci.

> . . . *according to* a report published by the US Bureau of Statistics.

Some useful verbs to introduce sources include the following:

acknowledges	contends	points out
argues	denies	recommends
believes	disputes	reports
claims	observes	suggests

Note that papers written using MLA style refer to sources in the present tense (*acknowledge, argue, believe*). Papers written in APA style use the past tense (*acknowledged, argued, believed*).

LEADING OUT OF A QUOTATION   You might think of providing quotations as a three-stage process that includes the **lead-in**, the **quotation** itself, and the **lead-out**. The lead-out gives you a chance to interpret the quoted material, further controlling the intended meaning and telling the reader what is most important.

Visual Guide: Integrating Quotations

1 Lead-in
- Name of author(s)
- Author's (or authors') expertise or authority
- Title of source, publication title, publication year/date
- Signal phrases that indicate the content of the quotation and the purpose it serves for your argument

2 Quote
- "_____," concludes Smith.
- "_____." Smith boldly declares, "_____."
- "_____," Smith admits.

3 Lead-out
- Interpret the quotation.
- Reflect on its usefulness to your essay and argument.

In the lead-out, you have a chance to reflect on the quotation and to shift back toward your own ideas and analysis. Consider this three-stage process applied in the following two ways:

> In his first book, *A World Restored* (1954), future Secretary of Defense Henry Kissinger wrote the famous axiom "History is the memory of states." It is the collective story of an entire people, displayed in public museums and libraries, taught in schools, and passed on from generation to generation.

> In his first book, *A World Restored* (1954), Nixon's former Secretary of Defense Henry Kissinger wrote glibly, "History is the memory of states." By asserting that history is largely the product of self-interested propaganda, Kissinger's words suggest that the past is maintained and controlled by whatever groups happen to hold power.

Notice the three-step process, and notice especially how the two examples convey different meanings of Kissinger's famous phrase. In the lead-in to the first sample, Kissinger's "future" role suggests hope. It signals a figure whose influence is growing. By using "famous" and "axiom," the author presents the quotation as true or even timeless. In the lead-out, the role of the state in preserving history is optimistic and idealistic.

In the second sample, "former" is used in the lead-in, suggesting Kissinger's later association with the ousted president he served, Richard Nixon. Readers are told that Kissinger "wrote glibly" even before they are told what he wrote, so readers may tend to read the quoted words that way. In the lead-out, the state becomes a more nefarious source of history keeping, one not interested in accommodating marginal voices or alternative perspectives, or remembering events inconvenient to its authority or righteousness.

Again, we hope you can see in these examples how the three-step process facilitates a writer's control over the meanings of quotations. Returning to our earlier example, if after reading something by Huxley the writer

> **WRITING TIP**
> In introducing a quotation, it is usually advisable to signal the reader *why* you are using the quotation by means of a lead-in consisting of a verb or a verb and adverb, such as *admits* or *convincingly shows*.

had merely stated that "William James says . . . ," readers wouldn't know whether they were getting confirmation, refutation, or something else. The essayist would have put a needless burden on the readers. Generally speaking, the more difficult the quotation, the more important is the introductory or explanatory lead-in, but even the simplest quotation profits from some sort of brief lead-in, such as "James reaffirms this point when he says . . . "

Documentation

In the course of your essay, you will probably quote or summarize material derived from a source. You must give credit, and although there is no one form of documentation to which all scholarly fields subscribe, you will probably be asked to use one of two. One, established by the Modern Language Association (MLA), is used chiefly in the humanities; the other, established by the American Psychological Association (APA), is used chiefly in the social sciences.

We include two papers that use sources. "An Argument for Corporate Responsibility" (p. 303) uses the MLA format. "Does Ability Determine Expertise?" (p. 309) follows the APA format. (You may notice that various styles are illustrated in other selections we have included.)

In some online venues, you can link directly to your sources. If your assignment is to write a blog or some other online text, linking helps the reader look at a note or citation or the direct source quickly and easily. For example, in describing or referencing a scene in a movie, you can link to reviews of the movie, to a YouTube video of the trailer, or to the exact scene you're discussing. These kinds of links can help your audience get a clearer sense of your point. When formatting such a link in your text, make sure the link opens in a new window so that readers won't lose their place in your original text. In a blog, linking to sources usually is easy and helpful.

A NOTE ON FOOTNOTES (AND ENDNOTES)

Before we discuss these two formats, a few words about footnotes are in order. Before the MLA and the APA developed their rules of style, citations commonly appeared in footnotes. Although today footnotes are not so frequently used to give citations, they still may be useful for another purpose. (The MLA suggests endnotes rather than footnotes, but most readers seem to think that, in fact, footnotes are preferable to endnotes. After all, who wants to keep shifting from a page of text to a page of notes at the end?) If you want to include some material that may seem intrusive in the body of the paper, you may relegate it to a footnote. For example, you might translate a quotation given in a foreign language, or you might demote from text to footnote a paragraph explaining why you aren't taking account of such-and-such a point. By putting the matter in a footnote, you signal to the reader that it is dispensable — that it's relevant but not essential, something extra that you are, so to speak, tossing in. Don't make a habit of writing this sort of note, but there are times when it is appropriate to do so.

MLA Format: Citations within the Text

Brief citations within the body of the essay give credit, in a highly abbreviated way, to the sources for material you quote, summarize, or make use of in any other way. These *in-text citations* are made clear by a list of sources, titled Works Cited, appended to the essay. Thus, in your essay you may say something like this:

> Commenting on the relative costs of capital punishment and life imprisonment, Ernest van den Haag says that he doubts "that capital punishment really is more expensive" (33).

The **citation,** the number 33 in parentheses, means that the quoted words come from page 33 of a source (listed in the Works Cited) written by van den Haag. Without a Works Cited list, a reader would have no way of knowing that you are quoting from page 33 of an article that appeared in the February 8, 1985, issue of the *National Review.*

Usually, the parenthetic citation appears at the end of a sentence, as in the example just given, but it can appear elsewhere; its position will depend chiefly on your ear, your eye, and the context. You might, for example, write the sentence thus:

> Ernest van den Haag doubts "that capital punishment really is more expensive" than life imprisonment (33), but other writers have presented figures that contradict him.

Five points must be made about these examples:

1. *Quotation marks* The closing quotation mark appears after the last word of the quotation, not after the parenthetic citation. Because the citation is not part of the quotation, the citation is not included within the quotation marks.

2. *Omission of words (ellipsis)* If you are quoting a complete sentence or only a phrase, as in the examples given, you do not need to indicate (by three spaced periods) that you are omitting material before or after the quotation. But if for some reason you want to omit an interior part of the quotation, you must indicate the omission by inserting an ellipsis, the three spaced dots. To take a simple example, if you omit the word "really" from van den Haag's phrase, you must alert the reader to the omission:

> Ernest van den Haag doubts that "capital punishment . . . is more expensive" than life imprisonment (33).

3. *Punctuation with parenthetic citations* In the preceding examples, the punctuation (a period or a comma in the examples) follows the citation. If, however, the quotation ends with a question mark, include the question mark within the quotation, since it is part of the quotation, and put a period after the citation:

> Van den Haag asks, "Isn't it better — more just and more useful — that criminals, if they do not have the certainty of punishment, at least run the risk of suffering it?" (33).

But if the question mark is your own and not in the source, put it after the citation, thus:

> What answer can be given to van den Haag's doubt that "capital punishment really is more expensive" (33)?

4. *Two or more works by an author* If your list of Works Cited includes two or more works by an author, you cannot, in your essay, simply cite a page number — the reader will not know which of the works you are referring to. You must give additional information. You can give it in your lead-in; thus:

> In "New Arguments against Capital Punishment," van den Haag expresses doubt that "capital punishment really is more expensive" than life imprisonment (33).

Or you can give the title, in a shortened form, within the citation:

> Van den Haag expresses doubt that "capital punishment really is more expensive" than life imprisonment ("New Arguments" 33).

5. *Citing even when you do not quote* Even if you don't quote a source directly but instead use its point in a paraphrase or a summary, you will give a citation:

> Van den Haag thinks that life imprisonment costs more than capital punishment (33).

Notice that in all the previous examples, the author's name is given in the text (rather than within the parenthetic citation). But there are several other ways of giving the citation, and we shall look at them now.

AUTHOR AND PAGE NUMBER IN PARENTHESES

> It has been argued that life imprisonment is more costly than capital punishment (van den Haag 33).

AUTHOR, TITLE, AND PAGE NUMBER IN PARENTHESES

Doubt has been expressed that capital punishment is as costly as life imprisonment (van den Haag, "New Arguments" 33).

A GOVERNMENT DOCUMENT OR A WORK OF CORPORATE AUTHORSHIP

The Commission on Food Control, in *Food Resources Today*, concludes that there is no danger (37–38).

A WORK BY TWO AUTHORS

There is not a single example of the phenomenon (Christakis and Fowler 293).

Christakis and Fowler insist there is not a single example of the phenomenon (293).

A WORK BY MORE THAN TWO AUTHORS

If there are *more than two authors,* give the last name of the first author, followed by *et al.* (an abbreviation for *et alia,* Latin for "and others")

Gittleman et al. argue (43) that . . .

On average, the cost is even higher (Gittleman et al. 43).

PARENTHETICAL CITATION OF AN INDIRECT SOURCE (CITATION OF MATERIAL THAT ITSELF WAS QUOTED OR SUMMARIZED IN YOUR SOURCE)

Suppose you're reading a book by Jones in which she quotes Smith and you wish to use Smith's material. Your citation must refer the reader to Jones — the source you're using — but of course, you cannot attribute the words to Jones. You will have to make it clear that you are quoting Smith, so after a lead-in phrase like "Smith says," followed by the quotation, you will give a parenthetic citation along these lines:

(qtd. in Jones 324-25).

PARENTHETICAL CITATION OF TWO OR MORE WORKS

The costs are simply too high (Smith 301; Jones 28).

AN ANONYMOUS WORK

For an anonymous work, or for a work where the author is unknown, give the title in your lead-in or give it in a shortened form in your parenthetic citation:

A Prisoner's View of Killing includes a poll taken of the inmates on death row (32).

According to the website for the American Civil Liberties Union . . .

AN INTERVIEW

Vivian Berger, in an interview, said . . .

If you don't mention the source's name in the lead-in, you'll have to give it in the parentheses:

Contrary to popular belief, the death penalty is not reserved for serial killers and depraved murderers (Berger).

AN ONLINE SOURCE

Generally, you can use the same formatting of the entries we've discussed so far for an online source. If the source uses pages or breaks down further into paragraphs or screens, insert the appropriate identifier or abbreviation (*p.* or *pp.* for page or pages; *par.* or *pars.* for paragraph or paragraphs; *screen* or *screens*) before the relevant number:

The growth of day care has been called "a crime against posterity" by a spokesman for the Institute for the American Family (Terwilliger, screens 1-2).

MLA Format: The List of Works Cited

As the previous pages explain, parenthetic documentation consists of references that become clear when the reader consults the list titled Works Cited at the end of an essay. Here are some general guidelines.

FORM ON THE PAGE

The list of Works Cited begins on its own page.

- Continue the pagination of the essay: If the last page of text is 10, then the Works Cited begins on page 11.
- Type the heading Works Cited, centered, one inch from the top, and then double-space and type the first entry.
- Double-space the page; that is, double-space each entry, and double-space between entries.
- Begin each entry flush with the left margin, and indent a half inch for each succeeding line of the entry. This is known as a hanging indent, and you can set most word processing programs to achieve this formatting easily.
- Italicize titles of works published independently (which the MLA also calls *containers*; see page 288), such as books, pamphlets, and journals.
- Enclose within quotation marks a work not published independently — for instance, an article in a journal or a short story.

- Arrange the list of sources alphabetically by author, with the author's last name first. For anonymous works, use the title, and slot in your list alphabetically. For works with more than one author, and two or more works by one author, see sample entries that follow. If your list includes two or more works by one author, do not repeat the author's name for the second title; instead represent it by three hyphens followed by a period (---.).

- Anonymous works are listed under the first word of the title or the second word if the first is *A*, *An*, or *The* or a foreign equivalent. We discuss books by more than one author, government documents, and works of corporate authorship in the sample entries in this section.

CONTAINERS AND PUBLICATION INFORMATION

When a source being documented comes from a larger source, the larger source is considered a *container* because it contains the smaller source you are citing. For example, a container might be an anthology, a periodical, a website, a television program, a database, or an online archive. The context of a source will help you determine what counts as a container.

In Works Cited lists, the title of a container is listed after the period following the author's name. The container title is generally italicized and followed by a comma, since the information that follows describes the container. Here are some guidelines:

- Capitalize the first word and the last word of the title.

- Capitalize all nouns, pronouns, verbs, adjectives, adverbs, and subordinating conjunctions (e.g., *although, if, because*).

- Do not capitalize articles (e.g., *a, an, the*), prepositions (e.g., *in, on, toward, under*), coordinating conjunctions (e.g., *and, but, or, for*), or the *to* in infinitives, unless it's the first or last word of the title or the first word of the subtitle.

- Disregard any unusual typography, such as the use of all capital letters or the use of an ampersand (&) for *and*.

- Italicize the container title (and subtitle, if applicable; separate them by a colon), but do not italicize the period that concludes this part of the entry.

When citing a source within a container, the title of the source should be the first element following the author's name. The source title should be set within quotation marks with a period inside the closing quotation mark. The title of the container is then listed, followed by a comma, with additional information — including publication information, dates, and page ranges — about the container set off by commas.

The following example cites a story, "Achates McNeil," from an anthology — or container — called *After the Plague: Stories*. The anthology was published by Viking Penguin in 2001, and the story appears on pages 82 through 101.

Boyle, T. C. "Achates McNeil." *After the Plague: Stories*, Viking Penguin, 2001, pp. 82-101.

Notice that the full name of the publisher is listed. Always include the full names of publishers except for terms such as "Inc." and "Company"; retain terms such as "Books" and "Publisher." The only exception is university presses, which are abbreviated thus: *Yale UP, U of Chicago P, State U of New York P.*

On the following pages, you will find more specific information for listing different kinds of sources. Although we have covered many kinds of sources, it's entirely possible that you will come across a source that doesn't fit any of the categories that we have discussed. For greater explanations of these matters, covering the proper way to cite all sorts of troublesome and unbelievable (but real) sources, see the *MLA Handbook,* Eighth Edition (Modern Language Association of America, 2016).

BOOKS

A BOOK BY MORE THAN ONE AUTHOR

The book is alphabetized under the last name of the first author named on the title page. If there are *two authors*, the name of the second author is given in the normal order, *first name first, after the first author's name.*

> Gilbert, Sandra M., and Susan Gubar. *The Madwoman in the Attic: The Woman Writer and the Nineteenth-Century Literary Imagination.* Yale UP, 1979.

If there are *more than two authors*, give the name only of the first, followed by a comma, and then add *et al.* (Latin for "and others").

> Zumeta, William, et al. *Financing American Higher Education in the Era of Globalization.* Harvard Education Press, 2012.

WORKS OF CORPORATE AUTHORSHIP

Begin the citation with the corporate author, even if the same body is also the publisher.

> American Psychiatric Association. *Psychiatric Glossary.* American Psychiatric Association, 1984.

> Human Rights Watch. *World Report of 2018: Events of 2017.* Seven Stories Press, 2018.

A REPRINT

After the title, give the date of original publication (it can usually be found on the reverse of the title page of the reprint you are using), then a period, and then the publisher and date of the edition you are using.

> de Mille, Agnes. *Dance to the Piper.* 1951. Introduction by Joan Acocella, New York Review Books, 2015.

A BOOK WITH AN AUTHOR AND AN EDITOR

> Kant, Immanuel. *The Philosophy of Kant: Immanuel Kant's Moral and Political Writings.* Edited by Carl J. Friedrich, Modern Library, 1949.

A TRANSLATED BOOK

Ullmann, Regina. *The Country Road: Stories*. Translated by Kurt Beals, New Directions
    Publishing, 2015.

AN INTRODUCTION, FOREWORD, OR AFTERWORD

Usually, an introduction or comparable material is listed under the name of the
author of the book (here Karr) rather than under the name of the writer of the foreword
(here Dunham), but if you are referring to the apparatus rather than to the book itself,
use the form given.

Dunham, Lena. Foreword. *The Liars' Club*, by Mary Karr, Penguin Classics, 2015, pp. xi-xiii.

A BOOK WITH AN EDITOR BUT NO AUTHOR

Horner, Avril, and Anne Rowe, editors. *Living on Paper: Letters from Iris Murdoch*. Princeton UP,
    2016.

A WORK WITHIN A VOLUME OF WORKS BY ONE AUTHOR

The following entry indicates that a short work by Susan Sontag, an essay called "The
Aesthetics of Silence," appears in a book by Sontag titled *Styles of Radical Will*. Notice that
the inclusive page numbers of the short work are cited — not merely page numbers that you
may happen to refer to, but the page numbers of the entire piece.

Sontag, Susan. "The Aesthetics of Silence." *Styles of Radical Will*, Farrar, Straus, and Giroux,
    1969, pp. 3-34.

A BOOK REVIEW

Walton, James. "Noble, Embattled Souls." Review of *The Bone Clocks and Slade House*, by David
    Mitchell. *The New York Review of Books*, 3 Dec. 2015, pp. 55-58.

If a review is anonymous, list it under the first word of the title or under the second word if
the first is *A, An,* or *The*. If an anonymous review has no title, begin the entry with *Review of* and
then give the title of the work reviewed; alphabetize the entry under the title of the work reviewed.

AN ARTICLE OR ESSAY IN A COLLECTION

A book may consist of a collection (edited by one or more persons) of new essays by several
authors. Here, the essay by Sayrafiezadeh occupies pages 3 to 29 in a collection edited by Marcus.

Sayrafiezadeh, Saïd. "Paranoia." *New American Stories*, edited by Ben Marcus, Vintage Books,
    2015, pp. 3-29.

MULTIPLE WORKS FROM THE SAME COLLECTION

You may find that you need to cite multiple sources from within a single container, such
as several essays from the same edited anthology. In these cases, provide an entry for the

entire anthology (the entry for Marcus below) and a shortened entry for each selection. Alphabetize the entries by authors' or editors' last names.

Eisenberg, Deborah. "Some Other, Better Otto." Marcus, pp. 94-136.

Marcus, Ben, editor. *New American Stories*. Vintage Books, 2015.

Sayrafiezadeh, Saïd. "Paranoia." Marcus, pp. 3-29.

ARTICLES IN PERIODICALS

AN ARTICLE IN A REFERENCE WORK (INCLUDING A WIKI)

For a *signed* article, begin with the author's last name. Provide the name of the article, the publication title, edition number (if applicable), the publisher, and the copyright year. For an unsigned article, begin with the title of the article:

Robinson, Lisa Clayton. "Harlem Writers Guild." *Africana: The Encyclopedia of the African and African American Experience*. 2nd ed., Oxford UP, 2005.

"The Ball's in Your Court." *The American Heritage Dictionary of Idioms*. 2nd ed., Houghton Mifflin Harcourt, 2013.

For an online reference work, such as a wiki, include the author name and article name followed by the name of the website, the date of publication or the most recent update, and the URL (without *http://* before it).

Durante, Amy M. "Finn Mac Cumhail." *Encyclopedia Mythica*, 17 Apr. 2011, www.pantheon.org /articles/f/finn_mac_cumhail.html.

"House Music." *Wikipedia*, 16 Nov. 2015, en.wikipedia.org/wiki/House_music.

AN ARTICLE IN A SCHOLARLY JOURNAL

The title of the article is enclosed within quotation marks, and the title of the journal is italicized.

Matchie, Thomas. "Law versus Love in the Round House." *Midwest Quarterly*, vol. 56, no. 4, Summer 2015, pp. 353-64.

Matchie's article occupies pages 353 to 364 in volume 56, which was published in 2015. When available, give the issue number as well.

AN ARTICLE IN A MAGAZINE

Do not include volume or issue numbers, even if given.

Thompson, Mark. "Sending Women to War: The Pentagon Nears a Historic Decision on Equality at the Front Lines." *Time*, 14 Dec. 2015, pp. 53-55.

AN ARTICLE IN A NEWSPAPER

Because a newspaper usually consists of several sections, a section number or a capital letter may precede the page number. The example indicates that an article appears on page 1 of section C.

Bray, Hiawatha. "As Toys Get Smarter, Privacy Issues Emerge." *The Boston Globe*, 10 Dec. 2015, p. C1.

AN ARTICLE IN AN ONLINE PERIODICAL

Give the same information as you would for a print article, plus the URL. (See Fig. 7.7.)

Acocella, Joan. "In the Blood: Why Do Vampires Still Thrill?" *New Yorker*, 16 March 2009.
www.newyorker.com/magazine/2009/03/16/in-the-blood.

Figure 7.7   Citing an Online Magazine

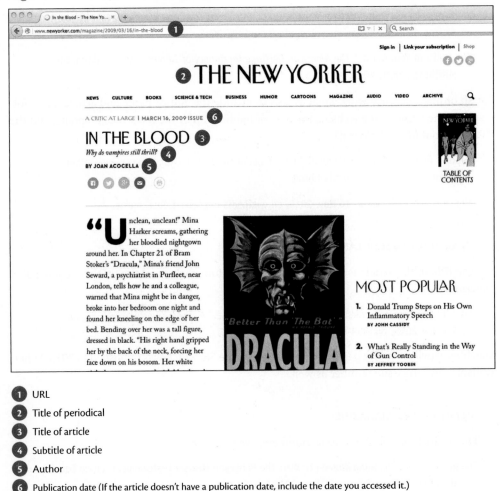

1 URL

2 Title of periodical

3 Title of article

4 Subtitle of article

5 Author

6 Publication date (If the article doesn't have a publication date, include the date you accessed it.)

AN UNSIGNED EDITORIAL OR LETTER TO THE EDITOR

Include the label "Editorial" or "Letter" at the end of the entry (and before any database information).

"The Religious Tyranny Amendment." *New York Times*, 15 Mar. 1998, p. 16. Editorial.

Adrouny, Salpi. "Our Shockingly Low Local Voter Turnout." *AJC.com*, 8 Nov. 2015, www.ajc.com /news/news/opinion/readers-write-nov-8/npHrS/. Letter.

A DATABASE SOURCE

Treat material obtained from a database like other printed material, but at the end of the entry add (if available) the title of the database (italicized) and a permalink or DOI (digital object identifier) if the source has one. If a source does not have that information, include a URL (without the protocol, such as *http://*).

Coles, Kimberly Anne. "The Matter of Belief in John Donne's Holy Sonnets." *Renaissance Quarterly*, vol. 68, no. 3, Fall 2015, pp. 899-931. JSTOR, doi:10.1086/683855.

Macari, Anne Marie. "Lyric Impulse in a Time of Extinction." *American Poetry Review*, vol. 44, no. 4, July/Aug. 2015, pp. 11-14. *General OneFile*, go.galegroup.com/.

GOVERNMENT DOCUMENTS

If the writer is not known, treat the government and the agency as the author.

United States, Department of Agriculture, Food and Nutrition Service, Child Nutrition Programs. *Eligibility Manual for School Meals: Determining and Verifying Eligibility*. July 2015, www.fns.usda.gov/sites/default/files/cn/SP40_CACFP18_SFSP20-2015a1.pdf.

INTERVIEWS

A PUBLISHED OR BROADCAST INTERVIEW

Give the name of the interview subject and the interviewer, followed by the relevant publication or broadcast information, in the following format:

Weddington, Sarah. "Sarah Weddington: Still Arguing for *Roe*." Interview by Michele Kort, *Ms.*, Winter 2013, pp. 32-35.

Tempkin, Ann, and Anne Umland. Interview by Charlie Rose. *Charlie Rose: The Week*, PBS, 9 Oct. 2015.

AN INTERVIEW YOU CONDUCT

Akufo, Dautey. Personal interview, 11 Apr. 2016.

ONLINE SOURCES

A WEBSITE AND PARTS OF WEBSITES

Include the following elements: the name of the person who created the site or authored the page (omit if not given, as in Figure 7.8); page title (in quotation marks), if applicable, and

Figure 7.8   Citing a Blog

1. URL
2. Sponsor of website
3. No author given; start citation with the title.
4. No date of publication given; include date of access in citation.

site title (italicized); any sponsoring institution or organization (if the title of the site and the sponsor are the same or similar, use the title of the site but omit the sponsor); date of electronic publication or of the latest update (if given; if not, provide the date you accessed the site at the end of the citation); and the URL (without *http://*).

Legal Guide for Bloggers. Electronic Frontier Foundation, www.eff.org/issues/bloggers/legal. Accessed 5 Apr. 2016.

Bae, Rebecca. Home page. Iowa State U, 2015, www.engl.iastate.edu/rebecca-bae-directory-page.

Enzinna, Wes. "Syria's Unknown Revolution." *Pulitzer Center on Crisis Reporting*, 24 Nov. 2015, pulitzercenter.org/projects/middle-east-syria-enzinna-war-rojava.

ENTIRE BLOG

Kiuchi, Tatsuro. Tatsuro Kiuchi: *News & Blog*. tatsurokiuchi.com. Accessed 3 Mar. 2016.

Ng, Amy. Pikaland. Pikaland Media, 2015, www.pikaland.com.

A SOCIAL MEDIA POST OR COMMENT

Include the name of the social media page (e.g., Facebook, Instagram) on which the post appeared, the name of the post (or the post on which the comment appears), the name of the site, the date, and the URL of the post or comment.

Bedford English. "Stacey Cochran Explores Reflective Writing in the Classroom and as a Writer: http://ow.ly/YkjVB." *Facebook*, 15 Feb. 2016, www.facebook.com/BedfordEnglish /posts/10153415001259607.

For Twitter, include the handle of the poster, the content of the tweet (enclosed in quotation marks), the name of the site, the date and time of the post, and the URL.

Curiosity Rover. "Can you see me waving? How to spot #Mars in the night sky: https://youtu .be/hv8hVvJlcJQ." *Twitter*, 5 Nov. 2015, 11:00 a.m., twitter.com/marscuriosity/status /672859022911889408.

@grammarphobia (Patricia T. O'Conner and Steward Kellerman). "When Dickens don't use 'doesn't' #English #grammar #usage." *Twitter*, 11 June 2018, 8:10 a.m., twitter.com /grammarphobia.

MULTIMEDIA SOURCES

WORK OF ART (INCLUDING PHOTOGRAPHS)

Bradford, Mark. *Let's Walk to the Middle of the Ocean*. 2015, Museum of Modern Art, New York.

Hura, Sohrab. *Old Man Lighting a Fire*. 2015. *Magnum Photos*, pro.magnumphotos.com /CS.aspx?VP3=SearchResult&VBID=2K1HZ04JVP42X8&SMLS=1&RW=1280&RH=692.

CARTOON OR COMIC

Zyglis, Adam. "City of Light." *Buffalo News*, 8 Nov. 2015, buffalonews.com/2015/11/08 /city-of-light/. Cartoon.

ADVERTISEMENT

AT&T. *National Geographic*, Dec. 2015, p. 14. Advertisement.

Toyota. *The Root*. Slate Group, 28 Nov. 2015, www.theroot.com. Advertisement.

VISUALS (TABLES, CHARTS, GRAPHICS, ETC.)

Add the type of visual at the end, if it's not obvious from the title or website. This is optional, but good for clarity.

"Number of Measles Cases by Year." *Centers for Disease Control and Prevention*, 6 June 2019, www.cdc.gov/measles/cases-outbreaks.html. Table.

Brown, Evan. "15 Golden Principles of Visual Hierarchy." *DesignMantic*, 15 Oct. 2014, www
.designmantic.com/blog/infographics/15-golden-principles-of-visual-hierarchy. Infographic.

A TELEVISION OR RADIO PROGRAM

Be sure to include the title of the episode or segment (in quotation marks), the title of the
show (italicized), the producer or director of the show, the network, and the date of the airing.
Other information, such as performers, narrator, and so forth, may be included if pertinent.

"Fast Times at West Philly High." *Frontline*, produced by Debbie Morton, PBS, 17 July 2012.

"Federal Role in Support of Autism." *Washington Journal*, narrated by Robb Harleston, C-SPAN,
1 Dec. 2012.

PODCAST

Include the podcast host(s) and the title of the episode. Then list the title of the podcast,
the network or service, the date, and the place where you access the episode. If you access the
podcast through an app or a platform such as Spotify, treat the app or platform as a separate
container, similar to a database.

McDougall, Christopher. "How Did Endurance Help Early Humans Survive?" *TED Radio Hour*, NPR, 20
Nov. 2015, www.npr.org/2015/11/20/455904655/how-did-endurance-help-early-humans
-survive.

FILM

Begin with whatever you are emphasizing in your work: entire film (first model), director
(second model), and so forth.

Birdman or (The Unexpected Virtue of Ignorance). Directed by Alejandro González Iñárritu,
performances by Michael Keaton, Emma Stone, Zach Galifianakis, Edward Norton, and
Naomi Watts, Fox Searchlight, 2014.

Scott, Ridley, director. *The Martian*. Performances by Matt Damon, Jessica Chastain, Kristen
Wiig, and Kate Mara, Twentieth Century Fox, 2015.

VIDEO FROM AN ONLINE SOURCE (SUCH AS YOUTUBE)

Nayar, Vineet. "Employees First, Customers Second." *YouTube*, 9 June 2015, www.youtube.com
/watch?v=cCdu67s_C5E.

APA Format: Citations within the Text

The APA style emphasizes the date of publication; the date appears not only in the list of references at the end of the paper but also in the paper itself, when you give a brief parenthetic citation
of a source that you have quoted or summarized or in any other way used. Here is an example:

Statistics are readily available (Smith, 1989, p. 20).

The title of Smith's book or article will be given at the end of your paper in the list titled References. We discuss the form of the material listed in the References after we look at some typical citations within the text of a student's essay.

A SUMMARY OF AN ENTIRE WORK

Smith (1988) holds the same view.

Similar views are held widely (Smith, 1988; Jones & Metz, 1990).

A REFERENCE TO A PAGE OR TO PAGES

Lanier (2018) argues that "to free yourself, to be more authentic . . . delete your accounts" (p. 24).

A REFERENCE TO AN AUTHOR WHO HAS MORE THAN ONE WORK IN THE LIST OF REFERENCES

If in the References you list two or more works that an author published in the same year, the works are listed in alphabetical order, by the first letter of the title. The first work is labeled *a*, the second *b*, and so on. Here is a reference to a second work that Smith published in 1989:

Florida presents "a fair example" of how the death penalty is administered (Smith, 1989b, p. 18).

APA Format: The List of References

Your paper will conclude with a separate page headed References, on which you list all your sources. If the last page of your essay is numbered 10, number the first page of the References 11. Here are some general guidelines.

FORM ON THE PAGE

- Begin each entry flush with the left margin, but if an entry runs to more than one line, indent five spaces for each succeeding line of the entry.
- Double-space each entry and double-space between entries.

ALPHABETICAL ORDER

- Arrange the list alphabetically by author.
- Give the author's last name first and then the initial of the first name and of the middle name (if any).
- If there is more than one author, name all of the authors up to seven, again inverting the name (last name first) and giving only initials for first and middle names. (But do not invert the editor's name when the entry begins with the name

of an author who has written an article in an edited book.) When there are two or more authors, use an ampersand (&) before the name of the last author. For example (here, of an article in the tenth volume of a journal called *Developmental Psychology*):

Drabman, R. S., & Thomas, M. H. (1974). Does media violence increase children's tolerance of real-life aggression? *Developmental Psychology, 10,* 418-421.

- For eight or more authors, list the first six followed by three ellipsis dots (. . .) and then the last author.

- If you list more than one work by an author, do so in the order of publication, the earliest first. If two works by an author were published in the same year, give them in alphabetical order by the first letter of the title, disregarding *A, An,* or *The,* and a foreign equivalent. Designate the first work as *a,* the second as *b,* and so forth. Repeat the author's name at the start of each entry.

Donnerstein, E. (1980a). Aggressive erotica and violence against women. *Journal of Personality and Social Psychology, 39,* 269-277.

Donnerstein, E. (1980b). Pornography and violence against women. *Annals of the New York Academy of Sciences, 347,* 227-288.

Donnerstein, E. (1983). Erotica and human aggression. In R. Green & E. Donnerstein (Eds.), *Aggression: Theoretical and empirical reviews* (pp. 87-103). New York, NY: Academic Press.

FORM OF TITLE

- In references to books, capitalize only the first letter of the first word of the title (and of the subtitle, if any) and capitalize proper nouns. Italicize the complete title (but not the period at the end).

- In references to articles in periodicals or in edited books, capitalize only the first letter of the first word of the article's title (and subtitle, if any) and all proper nouns. Do not put the title within quotation marks or italicize it. Type a period after the title of the article.

- In references to periodicals, give the volume number in arabic numerals, and italicize it. Do not use *vol.* before the number and do not use *p.* or *pg.* before the page numbers.

SAMPLE REFERENCES

For a full account of the APA method of dealing with all sorts of unusual citations, see the sixth edition (2010) of the APA manual, *Publication Manual of the American Psychological Association.*

BOOKS

A BOOK BY ONE AUTHOR

Pavlov, I. P. (1927). *Conditioned reflexes* (G. V. Anrep, Trans.). London, England: Oxford University Press.

A BOOK BY MORE THAN ONE AUTHOR

Belenky, M. F., Clinchy, B. M., Goldberger, N. R., & Torule, J. M. (1986). *Women's ways of knowing: The development of self, voice, and mind*. New York, NY: Basic Books.

A COLLECTION OF ESSAYS

Christ, C. P., & Plaskow, J. (Eds.). (1979). *Woman-spirit rising: A feminist reader in religion*. New York, NY: Harper & Row.

A WORK IN A COLLECTION OF ESSAYS

Fiorenza, E. (1979). Women in the early Christian movement. In C. P. Christ & J. Plaskow (Eds.), *Woman-spirit rising: A feminist reader in religion* (pp. 84-92). New York, NY: Harper & Row.

ARTICLES IN PERIODICALS

AN ARTICLE IN A JOURNAL

Tversky, A., & Kahneman, D. (1981). The framing of decisions and the psychology of choice. *Science, 211*, 453-458.

Foot, R. J. (1988-89). Nuclear coercion and the ending of the Korean conflict. *International Security, 13*(4), 92-112.

The reference informs us that the article appeared in issue number 4 of volume 13.

AN ARTICLE FROM A MAGAZINE

Bensman, D. (2015, December 4). Security for a precarious workforce. *The American Prospect*. Retrieved from http://prospect.org/

Greenwald, J. (1989, February 27). Gimme shelter. *Time, 133*, 50-51.

AN ARTICLE IN A NEWSPAPER

Connell, R. (1989, February 6). Career concerns at heart of 1980s campus protests. *Los Angeles Times*, pp. 1, 3.

Roberson, K. (2015, May 3). Innovation helps address nurse shortage. *Des Moines Register*. Retrieved from http://www.desmoinesregister.com/

(*Note:* If no author is given, simply begin with the title followed by the date in parentheses.)

AN ARTICLE FROM A DATABASE

Lyons, M. (2015). Writing upwards: How the weak wrote to the powerful. *Journal of Social History,* *49*(2), 317-330. https://doi.org/10.1093/jsh/shv038

A BOOK REVIEW

Daniels, N. (1984). Understanding physician power [Review of the book *The social transformation of American medicine*]. *Philosophy and Public Affairs, 13,* 347-356.

Daniels is the reviewer, not the author of the book. The book under review is called *The Social Transformation of American Medicine,* but the review, published in volume 13 of *Philosophy and Public Affairs,* had its own title, "Understanding Physician Power."

If the review does not have a title, retain the square brackets and use the material within as the title. Proceed as in the example just given.

GOVERNMENT PUBLICATIONS

If the writer is not known, treat the government and the agency as the author. If a document number has been assigned, insert that number in parentheses between the title and the following period.

U.S. Census Bureau, Bureau of Economic Analysis. (2015, December). *U.S. international trade in goods and services, October 2015* (Report No. CB15-197, BEA15-60, FT-900 [15-10]). Retrieved from http://www.census.gov/foreign-trade/Press-Release /current_press_release/ft900.pdf

ONLINE SOURCES

WEBSITES AND PARTS OF WEBSITES

Do not include an entire website in the reference list; instead, give the URL in parentheses within your paper.

Badrunnesha, M., & Kwauk, C. (2015, December). *Improving the quality of girls' education in madrasa in Bangladesh*. Retrieved from Brookings Institution website: http://www.brookings .edu/research/papers/2015/12/05-bangladesh-girls-education-madrasa-badrunnesha

BLOG POST

Costandi, M. (2015, April 9). Why brain scans aren't always what they seem [Blog post]. Retrieved from http://www.theguardian.com/science/neurophilosophy/2015/apr/09 /bold-assumptions-fmri

COMMENT ON AN ONLINE ARTICLE

MintDragon. (2015, December 9). Re: The very real pain of exclusion [Comment]. *The Atlantic*. Retrieved from http://www.theatlantic.com/

A SOCIAL MEDIA POST

National Science Foundation. (2015, December 8). Simulation shows key to building powerful magnetic fields 1.usa.gov/1TZUiJ6 #supernovas #supercomputers [Tweet]. Retrieved from https://twitter.com/NSF/status/674352440582545413

MULTIMEDIA SOURCES

WORK OF ART (INCLUDING PHOTOGRAPHS)

Sabogal, J. (2015). *Los hijos of the Revolution* [Outdoor mural]. San Francisco, CA.

Whitten, J. (2015). *Soul map* [Painting]. Retrieved from http://www.walkerart.org/

TELEVISION OR RADIO PROGRAM

Oliver, J. (Host), & Leddy, B. (Director). (2015, October 4). Mental health [Television series episode]. In *Last week tonight with John Oliver*. New York, NY: HBO.

PODCAST

Abumrad, J., & Krulwich, R. (2015, August 30). *Remembering Oliver Sacks* [Audio podcast]. Retrieved from https://www.wnycstudios.org/shows/radiolab/

DATA SET OR GRAPHIC REPRESENTATION OF DATA (GRAPH, CHART, TABLE)

Gallup. (2015). *Gallup worldwide research data collected from 2005-2018* [Data set]. Retrieved from http://www.gallup.com/services/177797/country-data-set-details.aspx

U.S. Department of Agriculture, Economic Research Service. (2015). *USDA expenditures for food and nutrition assistance, FY 1980-2014* [Chart]. Retrieved from http://www.ers.usda .gov/data-products/chart-gallery/detail.aspx?chartId=40105&ref=collection&embed=True

A VIDEO FROM AN ONLINE SOURCE (SUCH AS YOUTUBE)

Renaud, B., & Renaud, C. (2015, October 8). *Between borders: America's migrant crisis* [Video file]. Retrieved from https://www.youtube.com/watch?v=rxF0t-SMEXA

An Annotated Student Research Paper in MLA Format

The following argument makes good use of sources. Early in the semester, students were asked to choose one topic from a list of ten and to write a documented argument of 750 to 1,250 words (three to five pages of double-spaced typing) as a prelude to working on a research paper of 2,500 to 3,000 words. Citations are given in the MLA form.

Lesley Timmerman

Professor Jennifer Wilson

English 102

15 August 2016

An Argument for Corporate Responsibility

Opponents of corporate social responsibility (CSR) argue that a company's sole duty is to generate profits. According to them, by acting for the public good, corporations are neglecting their primary obligation to make money. However, as people are becoming more and more conscious of corporate impacts on society and the environment, separating profits from company practices and ethics does not make sense. Employees want to work for institutions that share their values, and consumers want to buy products from companies that are making an impact and improving people's lives. Furthermore, businesses exist in an interdependent world where the health of the environment and the well-being of society really do matter. For these reasons, corporations have to take responsibility for their actions, beyond making money for shareholders. For their own benefit as well as the public's, companies must strive to be socially responsible.

In his article "The Case against Corporate Social Responsibility," *Wall Street Journal* writer Aneel Karnani argues that CSR will never be able to solve the world's problems. Thinking it can, Karnani says, is a dangerous illusion. He recommends that instead of expecting corporate managers to act in the public interest, we should rely on philanthropy and government regulation. Karnani maintains that "Managers who sacrifice profit for the common good [. . .] are in effect imposing a tax on their shareholders and arbitrarily deciding how that money should be spent." In other words, according to Karnani, corporations should not be determining what constitutes socially responsible behavior; individual donors and the government should. Certainly, individuals should continue to make charitable gifts, and governments should maintain laws and regulations to protect the public interest. However, Karnani's reasoning for why corporations should be exempt from social responsibility is flawed. With very few exceptions, corporations' socially responsible actions are not arbitrary and do not sacrifice long-term profits.

Author concisely states her position.

In fact, corporations have already proven that they can contribute profitably and meaningfully to solving significant global problems by integrating CSR into their standard practices and long-term visions. Rather than focusing on shareholders' short-term profits, many companies have begun measuring their success by "profit, planet and people" — what is known as the "triple bottom line." Businesses operating under this principle consider their environmental and social impacts, as well as their financial impacts, and make responsible and compassionate decisions. For example, such businesses use resources efficiently, create healthy products, choose suppliers who share their ethics, and improve economic opportunities for people in the communities they serve. By doing so, companies often save money. They also contribute to the sustainability of life on earth and ensure the sustainability of their own businesses. In their book *The Triple Bottom Line: How Today's Best-Run Companies Are Achieving Economic, Social, and Environmental Success,* coauthors Savitz and Weber demonstrate that corporations need to become sustainable, in all ways. They argue that "the only way to succeed in today's interdependent world is to embrace sustainability" (xi). The authors go on to show that, for the vast majority of companies, a broad commitment to sustainability enhances profitability (Savitz and Weber 39).

Transitions ("For example," "also") alert readers to where the writer is taking them.

For example, PepsiCo has been able to meet the financial expectations of its shareholders while demonstrating its commitment to the triple bottom line. In addition to donating over $16 million to help victims of natural disasters, Pepsi has woven concerns for people and for the planet into its company practices and culture (Bejou 4). For instance, because of a recent water shortage in an area of India where Pepsi runs a plant, the company began a project to build community wells (Savitz and Weber 160). Though Pepsi did not cause the water shortage nor was its manufacturing threatened by it, "Pepsi realizes that the well-being of the community is part of the company's responsibility" (Savitz and Weber 161). Ultimately, Pepsi chose to look beyond the goal of maximizing short-term profits. By doing so, the company improved its relationship with this Indian community, improved people's daily lives and opportunities, and improved its own reputation. In other words, Pepsi embraced CSR and ensured a more sustainable future for everyone involved.

Another example of a wide-reaching company that is working toward greater sustainability on all fronts is Walmart. The corporation has issued a CSR policy that includes three ambitious goals: "to be fully supplied by renewable energy, to create zero waste and to sell products that sustain people and the environment" ("From Fringe to Mainstream"). As Dr. Doug Guthrie, dean of George Washington University's School of Business, noted in a recent lecture, if a company as powerful as Walmart were to succeed in these goals, the impact would be huge. To illustrate Walmart's potential influence, Dr. Guthrie pointed out that the corporation's exports from China to the United States are equal to Mexico's total exports to the United States. In committing to CSR, the company's leaders are acknowledging how much their power depends on the earth's natural resources, as well as the communities who produce, distribute, sell, and purchase Walmart's products. The company is also well aware that achieving its goals will "ultimately save the company a great deal of money" ("From Fringe to Mainstream"). For good reason, Walmart, like other companies around the world, is choosing to act in *everyone*'s best interest.

Recent research on employees' and consumers' social consciousness offers companies further reason to take corporate responsibility seriously. For example, studies show that workers care about making a difference (Meister). In many cases, workers would even take a pay cut to work for a more responsible, sustainable company. In fact, 45% of workers said they would take a 15% reduction in pay "for a job that makes a social or environmental impact" (Meister). Even more said they would take a 15% cut in pay to work for a company with values that match their own (Meister). The numbers are most significant among Millennials (those born between, approximately, 1980 and the early 2000s). Fully 80% of Millennials said they "wanted to work for a company that cares about how it impacts and contributes to society," and over half said they would not work for an "irresponsible company" (Meister). Given this more socially conscious generation, companies are going to find it harder and harder to ignore CSR.

> Author provides two examples of forward-thinking moves by major companies.

> Author now introduces statistical evidence that, if introduced earlier, might have turned the reader off.

To recruit and retain employees, employers will need to earn the admiration, respect, and loyalty of their workers by becoming "good corporate citizen[s]" (qtd. in "From Fringe to Mainstream").

Similarly, studies clearly show that CSR matters to today's consumers. According to an independent report, 80% of Americans say they would switch brands to support a social cause (Cone Communications 6). Fully 88% say they approve of companies' using social or environmental issues in their marketing (Cone Communications 5). And 83% say they "wish more of the products, services and retailers would support causes" (Cone Communications 5). Other independent surveys corroborate these results, confirming that today's customers, especially Millennials, care about more than just price ("From Fringe to Mainstream"). Furthermore, plenty of companies have seen what happens when they assume that consumers do not care about CSR. For example, in 1997, when Nike customers discovered that their shoes were manufactured by child laborers in Indonesia, the company took a huge financial hit (Guthrie). Today, Information Age customers are even more likely to educate themselves about companies' labor practices and environmental records. Smart corporations will listen to consumer preferences, provide transparency, and commit to integrating CSR into their long-term business plans.

> Author argues that it is in the *companies'* interest to be socially responsible.

In this increasingly interdependent world, the case against CSR is becoming more and more difficult to defend. Exempting corporations and relying on government to be the world's conscience does not make good social, environmental, or economic sense. Contributors to a recent article in the online journal *Knowledge@Wharton*, published by the Wharton School of Business, agree. Professor Eric Orts maintains that "it is an outmoded view to say that one must rely only on the government and regulation to police business responsibilities. What we need is re-conception of what the purpose of business is" (qtd. in "From Fringe to Mainstream"). The question is, what should the purpose of a business be in today's world? Professor of Business Administration David Bejou of Elizabeth City State University has a thoughtful and sensible answer to that question. He writes,

> Author's lead-in to the quotation guides the reader's response to the quotation.

> . . . it is clear that the sole purpose of a business is not merely that of generating profits for its owners. Instead, because compassion provides the necessary equilibrium between a company's purpose and the needs of its communities, it should be the new philosophy of business. (Bejou 1)

As Bejou implies, the days of allowing corporations to act in their own financial self-interest with little or no regard for their effects on others are over. None of us can afford such a narrow view of business. The world is far too interconnected. A seemingly small corporate decision — to buy coffee beans directly from local growers or to install solar panels — can affect the lives and livelihoods of many people and determine the environmental health of whole regions. A business, just like a government or an individual, therefore has an ethical responsibility to act with compassion for the public good.

Fortunately, corporations have many incentives to act responsibly. Customer loyalty, employee satisfaction, overall cost-saving, and long-term viability are just some of the advantages businesses can expect to gain by embracing comprehensive CSR policies. Meanwhile, companies have very little to lose by embracing a socially conscious view. These days, compassion is profitable. Corporations would be wise to recognize the enormous power, opportunity, and responsibility they have to effect positive change.

Author uses a block quotation for quotation longer than three lines in text.

Works Cited list begins on a new page.

Alphabetical by author's last name.

Hanging indent ½".

An article on a blog without a known author.

A clip from YouTube.

Timmerman 6

Works Cited

Bejou, David. "Compassion as the New Philosophy of Business." *Journal of Relationship Marketing,* vol. 10, no. 1, Apr. 2011, pp. 1-6. *Taylor and Francis,* doi:10.1080/15332667.2011.550098.

Cone Communications. 2010 *Cone Cause Evolution Study.* Cone, 2010, www.conecomm.com/research-blog/2010-cause-evolution-study.

"From Fringe to Mainstream: Companies Integrate CSR Initiatives into Everyday Business." *Knowledge@Wharton,* 23 May 2012, knowledge.wharton.upenn.edu/article/from-fringe-to-mainstream-companies-integrate-csr-initiatives-into-everyday-business/.

Guthrie, Doug. "Corporate Social Responsibility: A State Department Approach." *Promoting a Comprehensive Approach to Corporate Social Responsibility (CSR),* George P. Shultz National Foreign Affairs Training Center, 22 May 2012. *YouTube,* 23 Aug. 2013, www.youtube.com/watch?v=99cJMe6wERc.

Karnani, Aneel. "The Case against Corporate Social Responsibility." *Wall Street Journal,* 14 June 2012, www.wsj.com/articles/SB10001424052748703338004575230112664504890.

Meister, Jeanne. "Corporate Social Responsibility: A Lever for Employee Attraction & Engagement." *Forbes,* 7 June 2012, www.forbes.com/sites/jeannemeister/2012/06/07/corporate-social-responsibility-a-lever-for-employee-attraction-engagement/#6125425a7511.

Savitz, Andrew W., with Karl Weber. *The Triple Bottom Line: How Today's Best-Run Companies Are Achieving Economic, Social, and Environmental Success,* Jossey-Bass, 2006.

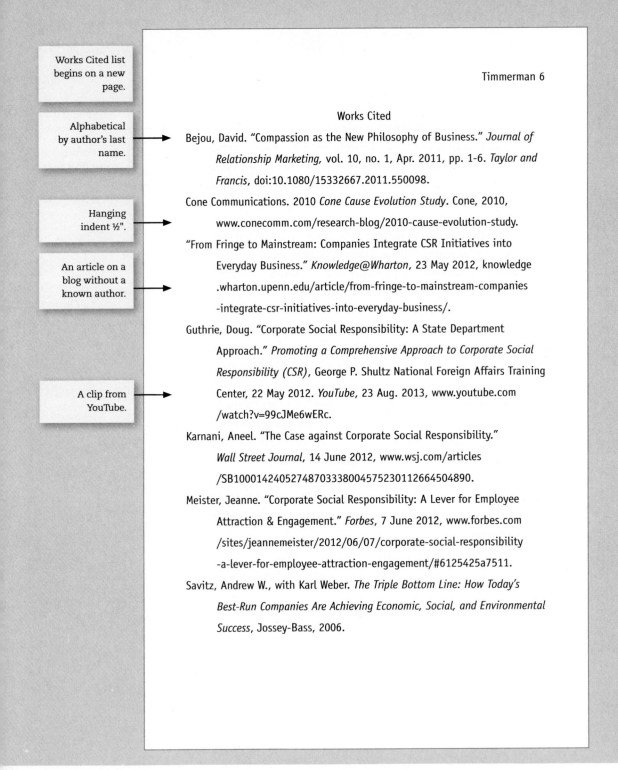

An Annotated Student Research Paper in APA Format

The following paper is an example of a student paper that uses APA format.

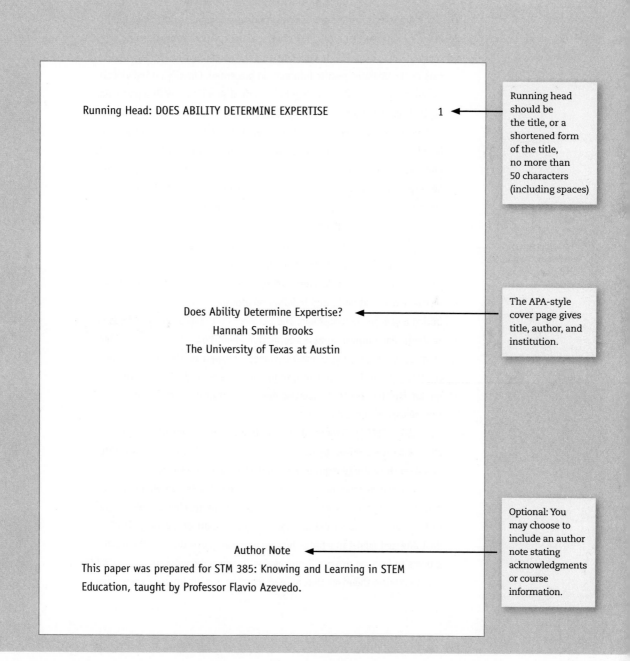

Running Head: DOES ABILITY DETERMINE EXPERTISE   1

Running head should be the title, or a shortened form of the title, no more than 50 characters (including spaces)

Does Ability Determine Expertise?

Hannah Smith Brooks

The University of Texas at Austin

The APA-style cover page gives title, author, and institution.

Author Note

This paper was prepared for STM 385: Knowing and Learning in STEM Education, taught by Professor Flavio Azevedo.

Optional: You may choose to include an author note stating acknowledgments or course information.

Short form of title
and page number
as running head.

Thesis explicitly
introduced.

Headings aligned
center and set in
boldface to help
readers navigate
the essay.

Does Ability Determine Expertise?

To become an expert requires long-term commitment to the field
of study, whether it be calculus or classroom instruction provided by a
teacher. Thus, expertise is dependent upon the context of the required
task or the domain specific information presented. Classifying individuals
as novices means only that they have limited experience with a particular
topic. If provided with an appropriate context, a novice may think deeply
and demonstrate effective problem-solving strategies. An individual may
be adept at managing student behavior, but he or she may have very little
understanding of the biological brain development of adolescents. His or
her expertise is defined by the required task of managing a classroom.
Importantly, domain experts have extensive experience interacting with the
content or skill throughout varied scenarios.

The Development of Expertise

Picture a classroom teacher who interacts with groups of students
each day. That teacher develops a deep understanding of student behavior,
instructional strategies, and building relationships with young people.
During a year in the classroom, the teacher is presented with hundreds of
students, each providing new information about how adolescence influences
learning. Over time, the teacher becomes an expert in understanding how
to effectively instruct student groups and manage student interactions,
reinforcing the idea that expertise develops out of many different
experiences within a domain.

Saxe (1992) suggests that cognitive development often follows
along a pathway driven by goal-directed activities. These goals can shift
based on the activity requirements and accumulation of new knowledge.
Our classroom teacher might use goals embedded in lesson plan design
and the building of diverse student groups. As the teacher completes each
goal, he or she builds more understanding of the art of teaching. This
goal-directed model illustrates how novices can move through the learning
process to become experts if provided with adequate supports and scaffolds.
Constructivism theorizes that all new learning is built on prior knowledge

and conceptions. Smith, diSessa, and Roschelle (1993/1994) discuss the role of student conceptions in the development of expertise. They argue that more complex cognitive structures must build on existing structures, illustrating how expertise can be developed exclusive of any innate ability. There must be a basic understanding of the foundational concepts in order for knowledge and information to build towards expertise, but these foundational concepts are learned, not inherent.

Many argue that an individual's natural interests may dictate success across domains. However, interest and expertise may not be directly related. Some would argue that all understanding occurs when new information is fully integrated into one's existing cognitive structure (Carey, 1985). ← Author and date cited for summary or paraphrase.
Using this definition, interest could be seen as driving an individual to understand and learn more about a particular topic or concept, but does not guarantee integration of information into the cognitive structure. Similarly, while an individual may move through the learning process at a unique speed, the rate of learning does not correlate to an underlying ability to become a "better expert." Individuals are not born with an inherent ability or pre-existing cognitive structure that allows immediate ← Author raises and refutes well-researched counterarguments.
and deep understanding of domain specific concepts, whether interested or not. In order to become recognized as an expert, the individual must actively build the domain-specific cognitive structure. Expertise is based on area specificity, where novices are only novices based on the contextual environment.

An important factor in the development of expertise is the learning environment in which the individual interacts. Cultural practices, social experiences, and the physical world influence how an individual sees and understands the world. The goal directed activities mentioned previously are determined by the specific cultural norms and expectations acting in the environment of the individual. In addition, the early interactions of childhood can greatly impact the belief system of a developing student. These influences can shape academic outcomes, but are not based on the inherent ability an individual may or may not be born with.

How Do Experts Differ From Novices?

There are some notable differences between experts and novices, and I would argue that each of the following skills or strategies is based on a repeated set of experiences and interactions with the domain specific content, not an inherent ability. Goldman and Petrosino (1999) conclude that experts are able to use acquired knowledge of their domain to improve the ability to notice subtle differences and characteristics of presented problems. They continue to suggest that expertise allows an individual to better develop problem-solving strategies and process information using complex creative mental representations. Each of these strategies is based on the continued experience and exposure to content-specific concepts and ideas, not an individual's inherent problem-solving ability. An expert is "not simply [a] 'general problem solver' who [has] learned a set of strategies that operate across all domains" (Bransford, Brown, & Cocking, 1999, p. 48). I consider myself a very creative problem solver inside the walls of a science classroom. If I was asked to solve for a derivative, I would be hopelessly lost and unable to draw upon my extensive problem-solving experience. As Goldman and Petrosino (1999) state, a deep domain-specific knowledge does not equate to an individual's general intelligence. Bransford, Brown and Cocking (1999) take this one step further and suggest that specialization within a specific domain actually reduces the amount of general knowledge an individual can hold at any given time.

Conclusion

If provided with the supports and scaffolds to learn the required mathematical processes and calculations, I could grow into an expert within that domain. Successful acquisition of skills or knowledge in either area is based on my desire to improve and learn, not an inherent ability. Expertise arises with extended and extensive study and exposure to a specific area of study or content. While a student may be more interested in science, they are not born with an inherent ability that precedes the learning process. Everyone must learn how to incorporate new ideas, strategies, and skills into a unique cognitive structure that promotes increased understanding of the world around us to become an expert.

When author's name appears in text, only the date is cited parenthetically.

Bracketed word not in quotation in the original source. Author, date, and page number are cited for a direct quotation.

Conclusion restates and strengthens thesis.

References

References begin on new page.

Bransford, J., Brown A. L., & Cocking, R. R. (1999). How experts differ from novices. In *How people learn: Brain, mind, experience, and school.* Retrieved from https://www.nap.edu/read/9853/chapter/1

Carey, S. (1985). *Conceptual change in childhood*. Cambridge, MA: MIT Press.

Goldman, S., & Petrosino, A. (1999). Design principles for instruction in content domains: Lessons from research on expertise and learning. In F. T. Durso & R. S. Nickerson (Eds.), *Handbook of applied cognition* (pp. 595-627). Chichester, NY: Wiley.

Saxe, G. B. (1992). Studying children's learning in context: Problems and prospects. *Journal of the Learning Sciences, 2*, 215-234.

Smith, J. P., diSessa, A., & Roschelle, J. (1993/1994). Misconceptions reconceived: A constructivist analysis of knowledge in transition. *Journal of the Learning Sciences, 3*, 115-163. Retrieved from http://www.jstor.org/stable/1466679

A book.

An article or a chapter in a book.

An article in a journal, retrieved from a database.

ASSIGNMENTS FOR USING SOURCES

1. Write an essay in which you enter a discourse (an ongoing conversation) on a topic and make an argument. To research effectively, you'll need to do the following:

   - Narrow your topic sufficiently to make the research manageable.

   - Research your topic thoroughly. Find appropriate sources through library or online research (see Finding Sources, pp. 248–55) or conduct your own primary research (see Performing Your Own Primary Research, pp. 271–75).

   - Evaluate your sources to determine if they are credible, relevant, and appropriate to your argument. (See Evaluating Sources, pp. 255–71.)

   - Take good, thorough notes that you can organize later to form the outline of your paper. Be sure to mark which ideas are your sources' and which are yours during this process. (See Taking Notes, p. 276.)

   When writing your essay, build your argument according to the strategies discussed in Chapter 6. In using sources, be sure to adequately introduce and describe the discourse you're entering: What are people saying about your topic? What "sides" or approaches are there, and who takes them? How will you contribute to the conversation? Support your argument with evidence from your research, making sure to summarize, paraphrase, and quote effectively and ethically, citing your source in the appropriate format (see Documentation, pp. 283–302). Address counterpositions and counterarguments you find in your sources to show you are aware of the various strains in the discourse, but be sure to return to and support your own argument and claims to persuade your audience of your thesis.

2. Find what you take to be a "fake news" article from a news source on the internet. Apply the evaluation methods outlined in this chapter to argue that the site or the story is "fake." Be sure to identify and analyze the three or four major factors that caused you to judge it as such. What visual features warned you the web page was suspicious? What other sources did you use to check, verify, or invalidate the source?

PART THREE

Further Views on Argument

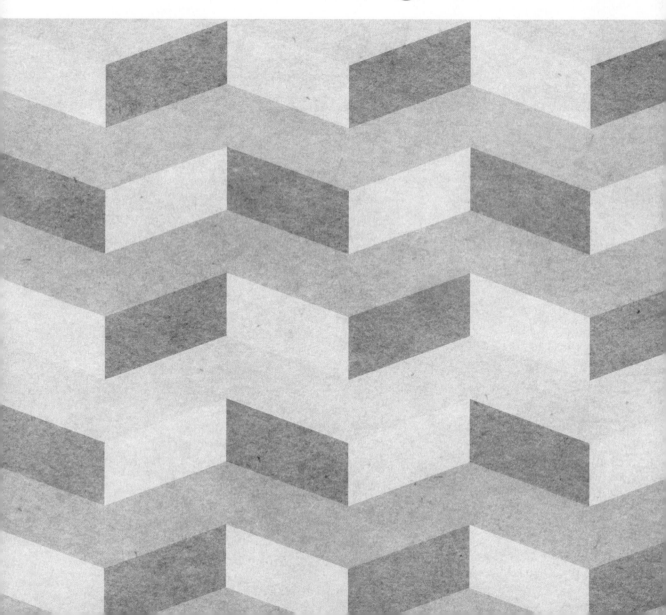

8

A Philosopher's View: The Toulmin Model

All my ideas hold together, but I cannot elaborate them all at once. — JEAN-JACQUES ROUSSEAU

[Philosophy is] a peculiarly stubborn effort to think clearly. — WILLIAM JAMES

Fight for the things you care about, but do it in a way that will lead others to join you. — RUTH BADER GINSBURG

In Chapter 3, we explained the contrast between making *deductive* and *inductive* arguments, the two main methods people use to reason. Either

- we make explicit something concealed in what we already accept (**deduction**), or
- we use what we have observed as a basis for asserting something new (**induction**).

These two types of reasoning share some structural features, as we also noticed. Both deductive and inductive reasoning seek to establish a thesis (or reach a conclusion) by offering *reasons*. Thus, every argument contains both a thesis and one or more supportive reasons.

After a little scrutiny, we can in fact point to several features shared by all arguments, whether deductive or inductive, good or bad. We use the vocabulary popularized by Stephen Toulmin, Richard Rieke, and Allan Janik in their book *An Introduction to Reasoning* (1979; second edition 1984) to explore the various elements of argument. Once these elements are understood, it is possible to analyze an argument using their approach and their vocabulary in what has come to be known as the Toulmin method.

The major components of arguments using this model are laid out in the Visual Guide to the Toulmin Method (p. 318), and we go into more detail about each of them throughout this chapter.

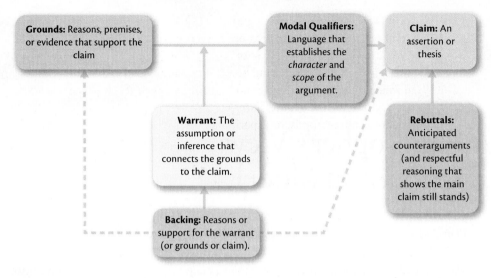

Components of the Toulmin Model

THE CLAIM

Every argument has a purpose, goal, or aim — namely, to establish a **claim** (*conclusion* or *thesis*). Claims may be general or specific. As we have noted in earlier chapters, arguments may attempt to persuade readers simply to change an opinion or adopt a belief, or they may advocate for some action or seek to convince people to take some action. In other words, the *claim* being made in an argument is the whole point of making the argument in the first place. Consequently, when you read or analyze an argument, the first questions you should ask are these:

1. What is the argument intending to prove or establish?
2. What claim is it making?

Different types of claims will lead to different types of grounds, warrants, and backing and to different types of qualifiers and rebuttals.

Suppose you are arguing in a very general sense that men and women should receive equal pay for equal work. You might state your thesis or claim as follows:

Men and women ought to be paid equally for the same kinds of jobs.

A more specific and precise claim might be the following:

The Equal Pay Act of 1963 should be strengthened in order to guarantee that men and women are paid equally for the same kinds of jobs.

Both formulations are arguments with strong claims. They make similar but still distinguishable arguments. One is general, and the other is solution-based. Thus, the components of each argument — their grounds, warrants, backing, and so on — will also be slightly different.

GROUNDS

If a claim is clearly formulated and unambiguously asserts what it advocates, it does not matter how general or specific it is. As long as the argument's chief purpose or point is present, we can look for the reasons — in short, the **grounds** — for that claim. You may think of the word *groundwork* to understand better the meaning of an argument's *grounds*. You may ask, On what *groundwork* — what *ground*, what firmament of fact — does the claim rest? In *deductive* arguments, the grounds are the premises; in *inductive* arguments, the grounds are the samples, observations, or experimental results that make the claim possible and plausible.

Consider the differences in the grounds for the two claims about equal pay.

Claim 1: Men and women ought to be paid equally for the same kinds of jobs.

Grounds: According to the US Census Bureau in 2018, women on average make 19.5 percent lower incomes than men for the same kinds of work.

Claim 2: The Equal Pay Act of 1963 should be strengthened in order to guarantee that men and women are paid equally for the same kinds of jobs.

Grounds: The Equal Pay Act was passed in 1963 to eliminate the gender pay gap. Because women still earn on average 19.5 percent lower incomes for the same kinds of work as men, the Equal Pay Act has not been effective.

But something is missing. We have provided the grounds and claim, but neither explains the reasoning or justifications that connects them. That women earn less money for similar work doesn't in and of itself justify the claim that pay should be equal among the sexes. One might simply counter that, no, women *should* make less money than men (and with only grounds and a claim you could not effectively argue back). Your opponent's argument might look like this:

Claim: Women and men get paid exactly what they deserve.

Grounds: According to the US Census Bureau in 2018, women on average currently make 19.5 percent lower incomes than men for the same kinds of work.

In this case, the grounds are the same as in the argument *against* pay inequity. Thus, good arguments exhibit — and require — another feature: the *warrant*.

WARRANTS

Once we have determined the claim of an argument and have isolated the grounds for its existence, the next question to ask is, What **warrants** it? That is, exactly what reasoning helps connect the claim and grounds, or why does the claim arise from the grounds?

The word *warrant* is related to the Old French word *gurant*, the root of our word *guarantee*. A warrant in this context is like the *warranty* you get when you buy something. It guarantees it. With an argument, you might ask what *guarantees* that a rational claim may arise given these grounds. What reasons could be proffered to justify the claim?

Warrants help establish the *connections* between the claim and the grounds. Imagine you establish your grounds (the existence of the pay gap). You claim women and men should be paid equally for similar work. Someone might ask you, What *warrants* your claim? *Why* should women and men get equivalent pay for the same kinds of jobs? You might offer something such as:

> Well, we live in a society where people are not to be discriminated against based on sex, and unequal pay based on sex is discriminatory.

In this case, your warrant is the legal (and perhaps moral) proposition about equality that connects the claim and grounds. (Part of your warrant, too, is that the US Census Bureau numbers are reliable.) Warrants are, in a sense, *interpretations* of how the data and the arguments stemming from them are inherently related.

In ordinary and straightforward *deductive* arguments, warrants may be quite simple. If John is six feet tall and Mary is five feet tall, you have the grounds to argue that John is taller than Mary. The warrant here is just a matter of language: "Taller than" means exceeding something in a measurement of height, so the warrant is "People are said to be taller than other people when they exceed them in measurements of height." The *warrant* here is the common understanding of what the phrase "taller than" means.

In ordinary *inductive* arguments, we are likely to point to the way in which observations or sets of data constitute a *representative sample*. When Anne McKee, a neuropathologist, examined the brains of 110 deceased professional football players and found that 99 percent of them showed signs of chronic traumatic encephalopathy (CTE), she claimed that playing professional football increases the likelihood of brain damage. Her warrant was the reasoning about such a high percentage of her sample showing signs of CTE — that one (football) caused the other (CTE); the warrant is the logic that connected her grounds and her claim.

Establishing the warrants for our reasoning can be a highly technical and exacting procedure when we are making more complex, ambiguous, or values-based claims — that is, when we are explaining why our grounds really do support our claims about why something is right or wrong, moral or immoral, just or unjust. Developing a "feel" for why grounds are or are not relevant to what they are alleged to support is important. "That's just my view" is *not* a convincing warrant for any argument.

Even without formal training, however, one can sense that something is wrong with many bad arguments. Here is one example. British professor C. E. M. Joad found himself standing on a station platform, annoyed because he had just missed his train. Then another train, making an unscheduled stop, pulled up to the platform in front of him. Joad decided to jump aboard, only to hear the conductor say, "I'm afraid you'll have to get off, Sir. This train doesn't stop here." "In that case," replied the professor, "don't worry. I'm not on it."

BACKING

Warrants, remember, explain why our *grounds* support our *claims*. The next task is to be able to show that we can back up what we have claimed by showing the reasons our warrants are good, reasonable, or rational. To establish that kind of further support for an argument is to provide **backing**.

What is appropriate backing for one kind of argument might be quite inappropriate for another kind of argument. For example, the kinds of reasons relevant to support the warrant that men and women should be paid equally may be completely different from the reason used to justify the claim that the Equal Pay Act should be amended. For the first argument, you might draw upon political documents, speeches, and other evidence showing that gender equality is a value and priority that necessitates action. In the second argument, you are claiming that the Equal Pay Act has been ineffective and needs strengthening, so your backing might consist of arguments about that piece of legislation specifically — theories and illustrations about what makes good, effective, and practical policy, for example. (Notice you are *not* arguing that women and men should be paid equally, per se; you are taking that for granted, making an assumption about shared beliefs.)

Another way of stating this point is to recognize that once you have given reasons for a claim, you are then likely to be challenged to explain why your reasons are good reasons — why, that is, anyone should believe your reasons rather than regard them skeptically. They have to be the right *kinds* of reasons given the field you are arguing about. A claim about the constitutionality of corporate personhood (in which corporations are regarded legally as sharing rights and responsibilities of natural persons) would have to be rationalized using backing quite different from the backing required to settle the question of what motivated Chinese people to immigrate to the United States in the nineteenth century. The *canons* (the established conventions, rules, laws, principles, and important texts) in two such dramatically different arguments have to do with the scholarly communities in law and history, respectively, that have developed over the years to justify, support, defend, challenge, and undermine ideas in those two areas of discourse.

Why (to give a simple example) should we accept the testimony of Dr. *X* when Dr. *Y*, equally renowned, supports the opposite side? What more do we need to know about "expert testimony" before it can be believably invoked? Consider a different kind of case: When and why is it safe to rest a prediction on a small — although admittedly carefully selected — sample? (McKee has been criticized for examining only the *donated* brains of professional football players, suggesting that those players or their families suspected CTE in the first place.) Why is it legitimate to argue that building a border wall, spanking children, or smoking cigarettes indoors is (or is not) appropriate? What evidence explains your thinking?

To answer questions of these sorts is to support one's reasons, to give them legitimate *backing*. No argument is any better than its backing.

MODAL QUALIFIERS

As we have seen, all arguments are made up of assertions or propositions that can be sorted into four categories:

- *claims* (theses to be established)
- *grounds* (explicit reasons advanced)
- *warrants* (guarantees, evidence, or principles that connect grounds and claims)
- *backing* (relevant support)

All the kinds of propositions that emerge when we assert something in an argument have what philosophers call a **modality**. In other words, propositions generally indicate — explicitly or tacitly — the *character* and *scope* of what is believed to be their likely truth.

CHARACTER   **Character** has to do with the nature of the claim being made, the extent of an argument's presumed reach. Both making and evaluating arguments require being clear about whether they are

- *necessary,*
- *probable,*
- *plausible,* or
- *possible.*

Consider, for example, a claim that it is to the advantage of a college to have a racially diverse student body. Is that *necessarily* true or only *probably* true? What about an argument that a runner who easily wins a 100-meter race should also be able to win a 200-meter race? Is that *plausible,* or is it only *possible*? Indicating the *character* with which an assertion is advanced is crucial to any argument for or against it. Furthermore, if there is more than one reason for making a claim and all those reasons are *good,* it is still possible that one of those good reasons may be *better* than the others. If so, the better reason should be stressed.

SCOPE   Indicating the **scope** of an assertion is equally crucial to how an argument plays out. *Scope* entails such considerations as whether the proposition is thought to be true *always* or just *sometimes.* Further, is the claim being made supposed to apply in *all* instances or just in *some*? Assertions are usually clearer, as well as more likely to be true, if they are explicitly *quantified* and *qualified*. Suppose, for example, you are arguing against smoking, and the ground for your claim is this:

Heavy smokers cut short their life span.

In this case, there are three obvious alternative quantifications to choose among: *All* smokers cut short their life span, *most* do, or only *some* do. Until the assertion is quantified in one of these ways, we really don't know what is being asserted, and so we don't know what degree and kind of evidence or counterevidence is relevant. Other quantifiers include *few, rarely, often, sometimes, perhaps, usually, more or less, regularly,* and *occasionally.*

Scope also reflects that empirical generalizations are typically **contingent** on various factors. Indicating such contingencies clearly is an important way to protect a generalization against obvious counterexamples. Thus, consider this empirical generalization:

Students do best on final examinations if they study hard for them.

Are we really to believe that students who cram ("study hard" in that concentrated sense) for an exam will do better than those who do the work diligently throughout the whole course ("study hard" in that broader sense) and therefore do not need to cram for the final? Probably not; what is really meant is that, *all other things being equal* (in Latin, *ceteris paribus*), concentrated study just before an exam will yield good results. Alluding in this way to the contingencies — the things that might derail the argument — shows that the writer is aware of possible exceptions and is conceding them from the start.

In sum, sensitivity to both character and (especially) scope — paying attention to the role played by quantifiers, qualifiers, and contingencies and making sure you use appropriate ones for each of your assertions — will strengthen your arguments enormously. Not least of the benefits is that you will reduce the peculiar vulnerabilities of an argument that is undermined by exaggeration and other misguided generalizations.

REBUTTALS

Very few arguments of any interest are beyond dispute, conclusively knockdown affairs. Only very rarely is the claim of an argument so rigidly tied to its grounds, warrants, and backing — and with its quantifiers and qualifiers argued in so precise a manner — that it proves its conclusion beyond any possibility of doubt. On the contrary, most arguments have many counterarguments, and sometimes one of these counterarguments is more convincing than the original argument. When writers raise counterarguments, they build their *ethos* and assure readers that other views are taken seriously; however, those counterarguments should not be raised simply to challenge your own position. If you indeed believe in your position, you can offer a **rebuttal** to the counterargument — telling your readers where it succeeds, perhaps, but also where it fails (thus implying or stating that *your* position is more convincing).

Suppose someone has taken a sample that appears to be random: An interviewer on your campus approaches the first ten students she encounters, and seven of them are fraternity or sorority members. She is now ready to argue that seven-tenths of enrolled students belong to Greek organizations.

You believe, however, that the Greeks are in the minority; you point out that she happens to have conducted her interview around the corner from the Panhellenic Society's office just off Sorority Row. Her random sample is anything but random. The ball is now back in her court as you await her response to your rebuttal.

As this example illustrates, it is safe to say that we do not understand our own arguments very well until we have tried to get a grip on the places in which they are vulnerable to criticism, counterattack, or refutation. As Edmund Burke astutely observed, "He that wrestles with us strengthens our nerves, and sharpens our skill. Our antagonist is our helper."

THINKING CRITICALLY *Constructing a Toulmin Argument*

Choose a topic or issue that interests you. In the spaces provided, supply a sentence or two for each step of a Toulmin argument about your topic.

STEP OF TOULMIN ARGUMENT	QUESTION THIS STEP ADDRESSES	YOUR SENTENCE(S)
Claim	*What is your argument?*	
Grounds	*What is your evidence?*	
Warrant	*What reasoning connects your evidence to your argument?*	
Backing	*What can you provide as support to convince the reader to agree with your grounds, claims, and warrants?*	
Qualifier	*What are the limits of your argument?*	
Rebuttal	*What are the objections to your argument—and can you reason that your argument still holds?*	

Putting the Toulmin Method to Work: Responding to an Argument

Let's take a look at another argument—on why buying directly from farmers near you won't save the planet—and see how the Toulmin method can be applied. The checklist on page 327 can help you focus your thoughts as you read.

JAMES E. McWILLIAMS

James E. McWilliams (b. 1968), the author of *Just Food: Where Locavores Get It Wrong and How We Can Truly Eat Responsibly* (2009), is a professor of history at Texas State University. This piece first appeared in *Forbes Magazine* on August 3, 2009.

The Locavore Myth: Why Buying from Nearby Farmers Won't Save the Planet

Buy local, shrink the distance food travels, save the planet. The locavore movement has captured a lot of fans. To their credit, they are highlighting the problems with industrialized food. But a lot of them are making a big mistake. By focusing on transportation, they overlook other energy-hogging factors in food production.

Take lamb. A 2006 academic study (funded by the New Zealand government) discovered that it made more environmental sense for a Londoner to buy lamb shipped from New Zealand than to buy lamb raised in the U.K. This finding is counterintuitive — if you're only counting food miles. But New Zealand lamb is raised on pastures with a small carbon footprint, whereas most English lamb is produced under intensive factory-like conditions with a big carbon footprint. This disparity overwhelms domestic lamb's advantage in transportation energy.

New Zealand lamb is not exceptional. Take a close look at water usage, fertilizer types, processing methods, and packaging techniques and you discover that factors other than shipping far outweigh the energy it takes to transport food. One analysis, by Rich Pirog of the Leopold Center for Sustainable Agriculture, showed that transportation accounts for only 11 percent of food's carbon footprint. A fourth of the energy required to produce food is expended in the consumer's kitchen. Still more energy is consumed per meal in a restaurant, since restaurants throw away most of their leftovers.

Locavores argue that buying local food supports an area's farmers and, in turn, strengthens the community. Fair enough. Left unacknowledged, however, is the fact that it also hurts farmers in other parts of the world. The U.K. buys most of its green beans from Kenya. While it's true that the beans almost always arrive in airplanes — the form of transportation that consumes the most energy — it's also true that a campaign to shame English consumers with small airplane stickers affixed to flown-in produce threatens the livelihood of 1.5 million sub-Saharan farmers.

Another chink in the locavores' armor 5 involves the way food miles are calculated. To choose a locally grown apple over an apple trucked in from across the country might seem easy. But this decision ignores economies of scale. To take an extreme example, a shipper sending a truck with 2,000 apples over 2,000 miles would consume the same amount of fuel per apple as a local farmer who takes a pickup 50 miles to sell 50 apples at his stall at the green market. The critical measure here is not food miles but apples per gallon.

The one big problem with thinking beyond food miles is that it's hard to get the information you need. Ethically concerned consumers know very little about processing practices, water availability, packaging waste, and fertilizer application. This is an opportunity for watchdog groups. They should make life-cycle carbon counts available to shoppers.

Until our food system becomes more transparent, there is one thing you can do to shrink the carbon footprint of your dinner: Take the meat off your plate. No matter how you slice it, it takes more energy to bring meat, as opposed to plants, to the table. It takes 6 pounds of grain to make a pound of chicken and 10 to 16 pounds to make a pound of beef. That difference translates into big differences in inputs. It requires 2,400 liters of water to make a burger and only 13 liters to grow a tomato. A majority of the water in the American West goes toward the production of pigs, chickens, and cattle.

The average American eats 273 pounds of meat a year. Give up red meat once a week and you'll save as much energy as if the only food miles in your diet were the distance to the nearest truck farmer.

If you want to make a statement, ride your bike to the farmer's market. If you want to reduce greenhouse gases, become a vegetarian.

Thinking with the Toulmin Method

Remember to make use of the Visual Guide on page 318 as you work to find the claim(s), grounds, and warrant(s) that McWilliams puts forward in this short essay.

1. What **claim** is the author making? Is it in the title? Is it in the opening sentence? Or is it buried in the first paragraph?

McWilliams really gives away his game in the title, even though he opens the essay itself in a way that might make the reader think he is about to launch into a defense of the locavore movement. He even goes out of his way to praise its members ("To their credit . . ."). The signal that his claim really appears already in the title and that he is *not* going to defend the locavore movement is the way he begins the fourth sentence. Notice that although you may have been told that starting a sentence with *But* isn't the best way to write, McWilliams here does so to good effect. Not only does he dramatically counter what he said just prior to that, but he also sets up the final sentence of the paragraph, which turns out to be crucial. In this way, he draws sharp attention to his *claim*. How would you state his claim?

2. What are the **grounds**, the evidence or reasons, that the author advances in support of his claim?

As it turns out, McWilliams spells out only one example as evidence for his claim. What is it? Is it convincing? Should he have provided more evidence or reasons at this point? It turns out that he does have other grounds to offer, but he mentions them only later. What are those other pieces of evidence?

3. What **warrants** does McWilliams offer to show why we should accept his grounds? What authority does he cite? How effective and convincing is this way of trying to get us to accept the grounds he offered in support of his claim?

The essence of the Toulmin method lies in these three elements: the claim(s), the grounds, and the warrant(s). If you have extracted these from McWilliams's essay, you are well on the way to being able to identify the argument he is putting forward. So far, so good. Further probing, however — looking for the other three elements of the Toulmin method (the backing, the modal qualifiers and quantifiers, and the rebuttal) — is essential before you are in a position to actually evaluate the argument. So let's go on.

4. What **backing** does McWilliams provide? What reasons does he give that might persuade us to accept his argument? Look for what he claimed came out of the analysis that was his basic warrant. He certainly seems to be using factual information — but what if you challenged him? Has he provided adequate reasons for us to believe him? What could he (or would he have to) be able to tell us if we challenged him with questions like "How do you know . . . ?" or "Why do you believe . . . ?" In other words, has he provided adequate backing? Or does he want us to just accept his statement of the facts?

5. Does McWilliams use **modal qualifiers**? Can you find phrases like "in most cases" or "generally it is true that . . ."? Or does he write so boldly — with little in the way of qualifiers or quantifiers — that readers are left uncertain about whether to accept his position? Where might he have effectively used qualifiers?

6. Does McWilliams prepare **rebuttals**, the reasons given in anticipation of someone rejecting the author's claim or conceding the claim but rejecting the grounds? Does he offer anything to forestall criticisms? If so, what is it that he does? If not, what could or should he have done?

Just how good an argument has McWilliams made? Is he convincing? If you identified weak points in his argument, what are they? Can you help strengthen the argument? If so, how?

> ## A CHECKLIST FOR USING THE TOULMIN METHOD
>
> ☐ What claim does the argument make?
>
> ☐ What grounds are offered for the claim?
>
> ☐ What warrants connect the grounds to the claim?
>
> ☐ What backing supports the claim?
>
> ☐ With what modalities are the claim and grounds asserted?
>
> ☐ To what rebuttals are the claim, grounds, and backing vulnerable?

9

A Logician's View: Deduction, Induction, and Fallacies

Logic is the anatomy of thought.

— JOHN LOCKE

Logic takes care of itself; all we have to do is to look and see how it does it.

— LUDWIG WITTGENSTEIN

In Chapter 3, we introduced the terms *deduction*, *induction*, and *fallacy*. In this chapter, we discuss them in more detail and present some principles of *formal logic* to help you develop your ability to understand arguments.

Using Formal Logic for Critical Thinking

Formal logic is a discipline of philosophy that studies the *nature* and *structure* of arguments abstracted from their content. Formal logic emerged in the ancient world and was developed further during the Enlightenment (ca. 1685–1815), a time of great scientific ferment, as an attempt to understand truth according to *a priori* rules — that is, rules that exist before, or *prior* to, any specific content. Formal logic is closely related to mathematics. Each expresses reality using symbols and variables. In math, the phrase *two plus two equals four* is true no matter if apples or oranges are being counted. Consider the structure of an equation:

If $A + B = C$, then $C + D = (A + B) + D$.

This formula expresses logical truth no matter what numbers you plug into the letters. The variables can change, but not the truth of the matter: If the first proposition is true, the second must be, too.

Perhaps for obvious reasons, formal logic is quite important in computer science, which is based on binaries of 0 and 1. But even in our everyday lives, we still use methods of formal logic to demonstrate truth ("If I take a lower-paying job, there will be less household income overall; if there is lower household income, there will be less money to pay for X, Y, and Z; therefore, some cuts to one or more of X, Y, or Z are inevitable if I take the lower-paying job").

But as soon as we enter the world of values, language, principles, and morals — where we encounter questions of what words mean and what we *should* or *ought* to do, or have a *right* to do — we must recognize the limits of formal logic's ability to demonstrate absolute truth. For arguments to work, the components must have meaning. Therefore, arguments that make assertions of human value involve applied reasoning, empirical observation, speculation, and other ways of thinking. Nevertheless, formal logic can assist us in seeing the ways even these types of arguments are structured and ultimately help us judge such arguments and think more carefully about our own.

Visual Guide: Deduction and Induction

DEDUCTION	Conclusion
Theory/Hypothesis	
Evidence	
Observation	
Conclusion	**INDUCTION**

Deduction

The basic aim of deductive reasoning is to start with some given premise and extract from it a conclusion — a logical consequence — that is concealed but implicit in it. When we introduced the idea of deduction in Chapter 3, we gave as our primary example the *syllogism*, and we provided a classical syllogism to represent how one aspect of formal logic, deduction, can lead to true conclusions:

Premise: All human beings are mortal.

Premise: Socrates is a human being.

Conclusion: Socrates is mortal.

If the premises are absolutely true, and the conclusion necessarily follows from them, the syllogism is *valid* and the argument is *sound*.

Here is another example:

Texas is larger than California.

California is larger than Arizona.

Therefore, Texas is larger than Arizona.

The conclusion in this syllogism can be derived from the two premises; that is, anyone who asserts the two premises is committed to accepting the conclusion as well, whatever one thinks of it. It is not a matter of perspective, opinion, or dispute.

Using formal logic, we can derive an equation of sorts to represent the argument graphically using nested circles:

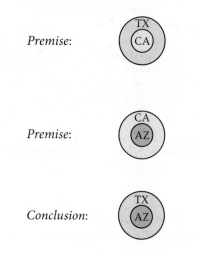

Premise:

Premise:

Conclusion:

We can see that this conclusion follows from the premises because it amounts to nothing more than what one gets by superimposing the two premises on each other. Thus, the whole argument can be represented like this:

The so-called middle term in the argument — California — disappears from the conclusion; its role is confined to be the link between the other two terms, Texas and Arizona, in the premises. In a graphic depiction, as with an equation, one can literally *see* that the conclusion follows from the premises. (This technique is an adaptation of one used in elementary formal logic known as Venn diagrams.)

In formal logic, the validity of a deductive inference depends on being able to show how the concepts in the premises are related to the concepts in the conclusion. In this case, the validity of the inference depends on the meaning of a key concept, *being larger than*. This concept has the property of *transitivity*, a property that many concepts share (e.g., *is equal to, is to the right of, is smarter than*). Transitive concepts can be represented symbolically in equations. Consequently, regardless of what is represented by A, B, and C, we can say:

If $A > B$, and $B > C$, then $A > C$.

This is all intended to show that the validity of deductive inference is a purely *formal* property of argument. You can substitute any state for Texas, California, and Arizona — or anything at all for the variables *A*, *B*, and *C* — as long as they adhere to the meaning of the transitive concept *larger than*.

Understanding this technique can help you see how some arguments can appear to be valid, but may also be challenged. For example:

If *A* is to the right of *B* and *B* is to the right of *C*, then *A* is to the right of *C*.

or

If *A* is smarter than *B* and *B* is smarter than *C*, then *A* is smarter than *C*.

Let's dig into these examples. First, on the earth, if *A* is to the right of *B* and *B* is to the right of *C*, it is purely logical that *A* is to the right of *C*, too — until we circle the globe and place *A* directly to the left of *C*, in which case the syllogism may be refuted on the grounds that it assumes an infinite plane surface. The very meaning of the phrase *to the right of* has been challenged. In the second example, *smarter than* is a category that needs definition. To challenge this argument, you can contest the comparative meaning of the term *smarter than*: Does "smart" refer to IQ level, grades earned in school, street smarts, or something else? Here you have two examples of valid syllogism, neither of which is necessarily true.

Now let's look at an example of another syllogism that is **valid** but not true.

Rhode Island is larger than Texas.

Texas is larger than Canada.

Therefore, Rhode Island is larger than Canada.

How, you might ask, can this syllogism be valid? Again, remember this about the formal properties of arguments: If you grant that the premises are true and the conclusion is inherently related to the premises, it is valid *even if it not true*.

Why is all this important to your learning about arguments? Well, if all one can say about an argument is that it is valid — that is, its conclusion follows from the premises — one has not given a sufficient reason for accepting the argument's conclusion. It has been said that the devil can quote scripture; similarly, an argument can be deductively valid and of no value whatsoever because valid (but false) conclusions can be drawn from false, misleading, or meaningless premises.

In short, a valid deductive argument doesn't prove anything unless the premises and the conclusion are *true*, but they can't be true unless they *mean* something in the first place. Consider this nonsense syllogism:

If the slithy toves, then the gyres gimble. The slithy toves. Therefore, the gyres gimble.

This argument has the following form:

If *A*, then *B*; *A*; therefore *B*.

As a piece of deductive inference, it is every bit as good (valid) as the other arguments above. Unlike them, however, it is of no interest at all because its assertions make no sense (unless you're a reader of Lewis Carroll's "Jabberwocky," and even then it is doubtful).

This example shows that the form of an argument can be good but the argument itself bad. We work through these problems because understanding the structures of arguments helps us better think about, analyze, and construct arguments ourselves. Think about this one:

> If President Truman knew the Japanese were about to surrender, then it was immoral of him to order that atom bombs be dropped on Hiroshima and Nagasaki. Truman knew the Japanese were going to surrender. Therefore, it was immoral of him to order dropping those bombs.

Once again, anyone who assents to the *if . . . then* proposition in the premise and accepts that Truman knew the Japanese were about to surrender must assent to the conclusion. But do the premises *prove* the conclusion? That depends on whether both premises are true. Well, are they? The answer turns on a number of considerations, and it is worth pausing to examine how we might think critically about this argument.

Let's begin by examining the second premise, which proposes a fact: Did Truman really know the Japanese were about to surrender? This question is controversial even today. Autobiography, memoranda, other documentary evidence — all are needed to assemble the evidence to back up the grounds for the thesis or claim made in the conclusion of this argument. Evaluating this material effectively may involve further deductions (and perhaps inductive reasoning as well).

As to the first premise, its truth doesn't depend on facts about the past but, rather, on moral principles. The first premise contains a hypothetical ("if") and asserts a connection between two very different kinds of things (prior knowledge and morality). This premise as a whole can thus be seen as expressing *a principle of moral responsibility*. The principle is this: If we have knowledge that makes violence unnecessary, it is immoral to act violently anyway. Someone could compare Truman's decision to an argument that shares its form: If someone is surrendering, it is immoral to do violence to him. Such principles can, of course, be supported or contested.

EXAMPLES OF DEDUCTION

When we engage with and construct arguments, it is useful to keep in mind some of the basic structures (including but not limited to *syllogism*) because they help us see what is going on under the surface of an argument.

DISJUNCTION One common form of argument occurs through **disjunctive syllogism**, so called because its major premise is a **disjunction**, or a relationship between distinct alternatives. For example:

> Either censorship of fake news is overdue or our society is indifferent to hostile forces meddling in elections.
>
> Our society is not indifferent to propaganda on social media affecting our elections.
>
> Therefore, censorship of fake news is overdue.

Notice, by the way, that the validity of an argument, as in this case, does not turn on pedantic repetition of every word or phrase: Nonessential elements can be dropped or equivalent expressions substituted without adverse effect on the reasoning as long as those relationships are established. Thus, in conversation or in writing, this argument might actually be presented like this:

> Either censorship of fake news is overdue or our society is indifferent to the role fake news propaganda has in our elections. Of course, our political elections are susceptible to the effects of fake news, which is why some kind of censorship is overdue.

The key feature of disjunctive syllogism is that the conclusion is whichever of the alternatives remains after the others have been negated. We could easily have a very complex disjunctive syllogism with a dozen alternatives in the first premise and seven of them denied in the second, leaving a conclusion of the remaining five. Usually, however, a disjunctive argument is formulated in this manner: Assert a disjunction with two or more alternatives in the major premise, *deny all but one* in the minor premise, and then infer validly the remaining alternative(s) as the conclusion.

DILEMMA   Another type of argument, especially favored by orators and rhetoricians, is the **dilemma**. Ordinarily, we use the term *dilemma* in the sense of an awkward predicament, as when we say, "His dilemma was that he didn't have enough money to pay the waiter." But when logicians refer to a dilemma, they mean a forced choice between two or more equally unattractive alternatives. For example, the predicament faced by the US government in fighting the Islamic State (ISIS) in Syria can be posed as a dilemma. The United States could ally itself with the Syrian government, a dictatorship under Bashar al-Assad, who is also trying to destroy ISIS influence in Syria. But al-Assad's government is hostile to the United States, has attempted to crush political reform movements in Syria, and actively supports groups the United States deems terrorist organizations. On the other hand, the United States could extend support to the Syrian Democratic Forces (SDF), a large militia inside Syria comprised mostly of Kurdish majority people who are fighting against ISIS and opposing al-Assad; however, in doing so, the United States risks expanding conflict in Syria, a Russian ally, and alienates its own ally, Turkey, which sees the SDF as a force of instability in its own country. The dilemma might be phrased as such:

> If the United States supports the Syrian government's fight against ISIS, it would be supporting a dictatorship linked to terrorism and crimes against humanity. If the United States supports the SDF, it risks further conflict with the Bashar al-Assad regime (and perhaps Russia) and also compromises its own relationship with Turkey. Thus, in fighting the Islamic State in Syria, either the United States supports a dictatorship or it supports a resistance group opposed to our own ally. In either case, unattractive consequences follow.

Notice first the structure of the argument: two conditional propositions asserted as premises followed by another premise that states a **necessary truth**. The premise, "Either we support the dictatorship or we support the SDF," is a disjunction; because the two alternatives are presented as exhaustive (the only options), one of the two alternatives must be true.

(Such a statement is often called analytically true, or a *tautology*.) No doubt the conclusion of this dilemma ("unattractive consequences") follows from its premises.

But does the argument *prove*, as it purports to do, that whatever the US government does, it will suffer "unattractive consequences"? It is customary to speak of "the horns of the dilemma," as though the challenge posed by the dilemma were like a bull ready to gore us no matter which direction we turn. But if the two conditional premises failed to exhaust the possibilities, we can escape from the dilemma by going "between the horns" — by finding a third alternative (or a fourth or fifth).

If alternatives are not possible, we can still ask whether both of the main premises are true. Neither of the main premises spells out all or even most of the consequences that could be foreseen, and perhaps backing the SDF would not result in compromising our relationship with Turkey. In cases where both of the conditional premises are true, then, it may be that the consequences of one alternative are not as bad as those of the other. If that is true, but our reasoning stops before evaluating that fact, we may be guilty of failing to distinguish between the greater and the lesser of two evils. The logic of the dilemma itself cannot decide this choice for us. Instead, we must bring to bear empirical inquiry and imagination to the evaluation of the grounds of the dilemma.

REDUCTIO AD ABSURDUM Finally, one of the most powerful and dramatic forms of argument is **reductio ad absurdum** (from the Latin, meaning "reduction to absurdity"). The idea of a reductio argument is to disprove a proposition by showing the absurdity of its inevitable conclusion. It is used, of course, to refute your opponent's position and prove your own. For example, in Plato's *Republic*, Socrates asks an old gentleman, Cephalus, to define *right conduct*. Cephalus says it consists of paying your debts and keeping your word. Socrates rejects this answer by showing that it leads to a contradiction. He argues that Cephalus cannot have given the correct answer because if we believe that he did, we will quickly encounter contradictions; in some cases, when you keep your word, you will nonetheless be doing the wrong thing. Suppose, says Socrates, you borrowed a weapon from a man, promising to return it when

Socrates Looking in a Mirror by Bernard Vaillant, c. 17th century.

he asks for it. One day he comes to your door, demanding his weapon and swearing angrily that he intends to murder a neighbor. Keeping your word under those circumstances would be absurd, Socrates implies, and the reader of the dialogue is left to infer that Cephalus's definition, which led to this result, has been refuted.

Let's look at another example. Suppose you are opposed to any form of gun control, whereas we are in favor of gun control. We might try to refute your position by attacking it with a reductio argument. We start out by assuming the very opposite of what we believe or favor and try to establish a contradiction that results from following out the consequences of your initial assumption:

Your position is that there ought to be no legal restrictions of any kind on the sale and ownership of guns. That means that you'd permit having every neighborhood hardware store sell pistols and rifles to whoever walks in the door. But that's not all. You apparently also would permit selling machine guns to children, antitank weapons to lunatics, and small-bore cannons to the nearsighted, as well as guns and ammunition to anyone with a criminal record. But that is utterly preposterous; no one could favor such a dangerous policy. So the only question worth debating is what kind of gun control is necessary.

Now in this example, our reductio of your position on gun control is not based on claiming to show that you have strictly contradicted yourself, for there is no purely logical contradiction in opposing all forms of gun control. Instead, what we have tried to do is to show that there is a contradiction between what you profess — no gun controls at all — and what you probably really believe, if only you'll stop to think about it — which is that no lunatic should be allowed to buy a loaded machine gun. Our refutation of your position rests on whether we succeed in establishing an inconsistency among your own beliefs. If it turns out that you really believe lunatics should be free to purchase guns and ammunition, our attempted refutation fails.

CONTRADICTION, CONSISTENCY, AND CONJUNCTION   In explaining reductio ad absurdum, we have had to rely on another idea fundamental to logic, that of **contradiction**, or inconsistency. The opposite of contradiction is **consistency**, a notion important to good reasoning. These concepts deserve a few words of further explanation and illustration. Consider this pair of assertions:

A. Abortion is homicide.

B. Racism is unfair.

No one would plausibly claim that we can infer or deduce B from A or, for that matter, A from B. There is no evident connection between these two assertions. They are unrelated assertions; logically speaking, they are *independent* of each other. The two assertions are potentially *consistent*; that is, both could be true — or both could be false. But now consider another proposition:

C. Euthanasia is not murder.

Could a person assert A (*Abortion is homicide*) and also assert C (*Euthanasia is not murder*) and be consistent? Could you assert these two propositions as a **conjunction**? Now consider:

D. Abortion is homicide, and euthanasia is not murder.

It's not so easy to say whether these are consistent or inconsistent. One person could assert one of these propositions and reject the other, leading to a conclusion of general inconsistency. Another could be convinced that there is no inconsistency in asserting that *Abortion is homicide* and that *Euthanasia is not murder*. (For instance, suppose you believe both that the unborn are persons who deserve a chance to live and that putting terminally ill persons to death in a painless manner and with their consent confers a benefit on them.)

Let us generalize: We can say of any set of propositions that they are consistent *if and only if* all could be true together. Remember that, once again, the truth of the assertions in question doesn't matter. Two propositions can be consistent or not, quite apart from whether they are true. That's not so with falsehood: It follows from our definition of consistency that an *inconsistent* proposition must be *false*. (We have relied on this idea in explaining how a reductio ad absurdum argument works.)

Assertions or claims that are not consistent can take either of two forms. Suppose you assert that abortion is homicide, early in an essay you are writing, but later you assert that abortion is harmless. You have now asserted a position on abortion that is strictly contrary to the one with which you began—both cannot be true. It is simply not true that if an abortion involves killing a human being (which is what *homicide* strictly means), it causes no one any harm (killing a person always causes harm—even if it is excusable, justifiable, not wrong, the best thing to do in the circumstances, and so on). Notice that while both cannot be true, they *can* both be false. In fact, many people who are perplexed about the morality of abortion believe precisely this. They concede that abortion does harm the fetus, but they also believe that abortion doesn't kill a person.

Let's consider another, simpler case. If you describe the glass as half empty and I describe it as half full, both of us can be right; the two assertions are consistent, even though they sound vaguely incompatible. (This is the reason that disputing over whether the glass is half full or half empty has become the popular paradigm of a futile, purely *verbal disagreement*.) But if I describe the glass as half empty whereas you insist that it is two-thirds empty, we have a real disagreement; your description and mine are strictly contrary, in that both cannot be true—although both *can* be false. (Both are false if the glass is only one-fourth full.)

This, by the way, enables us to define the difference between a pair of **contradictory** propositions and a pair of **contrary** propositions. Two propositions are contrary if and only if both cannot be true (though both can be false); two propositions are contradictory if and only if they are such that if one is true the other must be false, and vice versa. Thus, if Jack says that Alice Walker's *The Color Purple* is a better novel than Mark Twain's *Huckleberry Finn*, and Jill says, "No, *Huckleberry Finn* is better than *The Color Purple*," she is contradicting Jack. If what either one of them says is true, then what the other says must be false.

A more subtle case of contradiction arises when two or more of one's own beliefs implicitly contradict each other. We may find ourselves saying "Travel is broadening" and saying an hour later "People don't really change." Just beneath the surface of these two beliefs lies a self-contradiction: How can travel broaden us unless it influences—and changes—our beliefs, values, and outlook? But if we can't really change ourselves, traveling to new places won't change us, either. (Indeed, there is a Roman saying to the effect that travelers change the skies above them, not their hearts.) "Travel is broadening" and "People don't change" collide with each other; something has to give.

Our point, of course, is not that you must never say today something that contradicts something you said yesterday. Far from it; if you think you were mistaken yesterday, of course you will take a different position today. But what you want to avoid is what George Orwell called *doublethink* in his novel *1984*: "*Doublethink* means the power of holding two contradictory beliefs in one's mind simultaneously, and accepting them both."

PARADOX   While we're speaking of inconsistency, let's spend a moment on **paradox**. The word refers to two different things:

- an assertion that is essentially self-contradictory and therefore cannot be true
- a seemingly contradictory assertion that nevertheless may be true

An example of the first might be "Evaluations concerning quality in literature are all a matter of personal judgment, but Shakespeare is the world's greatest writer." It is hard to make any sense out of this assertion. Contrast it with a paradox of the second sort, a *seeming* contradiction that may make sense, such as "The longest way around is the shortest way home," or "Work is more fun than fun," or "The best way to find happiness is not to look for it." Here we have assertions that are striking because as soon as we hear them we realize that although they seem inconsistent and self-defeating, they contain (or may contain) profound truths. If you use the word *paradox* in your own writing—for instance, to characterize an argument you're reading—be sure the reader will understand in which sense you're using the word. (And, of course, you won't want to write paradoxes of the first, self-contradictory sort.)

Induction

Deduction involves logical thinking that applies to absolutely any assertion or claim — because every possible statement, true or false, has deductive logical consequences. Induction, remember, is the type of thinking that begins with specific **empirical** or *factual* observations and leads to general conclusions. Induction is relevant to one kind of assertion only. Other kinds of assertions (such as definitions, mathematical equations, and moral or legal norms) simply are not the product of inductive reasoning and cannot serve as a basis for further inductive thinking.

So, in studying the methods of induction, we are exploring tactics and strategies useful in gathering and then using **evidence** — empirical, observational, experimental — in support of a belief as its ground. Modern scientific knowledge is the product of these methods, and they differ somewhat from one science to another because they depend on the theories and technology appropriate to each of the sciences. Here all we can do is discuss generally the more abstract features common to inductive inquiry. For fuller details, you must eventually consult a physicist, chemist, geologist, or their colleagues and counterparts in other scientific fields.

OBSERVATION AND INFERENCE

Let's begin with a simple example. Suppose we have evidence (actually we don't, but that won't matter for our purposes) in support of this claim:

In a sample of 500 smokers, 230 persons observed have cardiovascular disease.

The basis — the evidence or grounds — for asserting this claim would be, presumably, straightforward physical examination of the 500 persons in the sample, one by one.

With this claim in hand, we can think of the purpose and methods of induction as pointing in two opposite directions: toward establishing the basis or ground of the very empirical proposition with which we start (in this example, the observation stated above) or toward understanding what that observation indicates or suggests as a more general, inclusive, or fundamental fact of nature.

In each case, we start from something we *do* know (or take for granted and treat as a sound starting point) — some fact of nature, perhaps a striking or commonplace event that we have observed and recorded — and then go on to something we do *not* fully know and perhaps cannot directly observe. In the smoking example above, only the second of these two orientations (the 230 persons with cardiovascular disease) is of any interest, so let's concentrate exclusively on it.

GENERALIZATION   Anyone truly interested in the observed fact that *230 of 500 smokers have cardiovascular disease* is likely to start speculating about, and thus be interested in finding out, whether any or all of several other propositions are also true. For example, one might wonder whether the following claim is true:

> *All* smokers have cardiovascular disease or will develop it during their lifetimes.

This claim is a straightforward generalization of the original observation as reported in the first claim. When we think inductively, we are reasoning from an observed sample (some smokers — i.e., 230 of the 500 *observed*) to the entire membership of a more inclusive class (*all* smokers, whether observed or not). The fundamental question raised by reasoning from the narrower claim to the broader claim is whether we have any ground for believing that what is true of *some* members of a class is true of them *all*. So the difference between these claims is that of *quantity* or scope.

RELATION   We can also think inductively about the *relation* between the factors mentioned in the original claim, *In a sample of 500 smokers, 230 persons observed have cardiovascular disease*. Having observed data, we may be tempted to assert a different and more profound kind of claim:

> Smoking *causes* cardiovascular disease.

Here our interest is not merely in generalizing from a sample to a whole class; it is the far more important one of *explaining* the observation with which we began. Certainly, the preferred, even if not the only, mode of explanation for a natural phenomenon is a *causal* explanation. In this claim, we propose to explain the presence of one phenomenon (cardiovascular disease) by the prior occurrence of an independent phenomenon (smoking). The original observation about the number of diseased smokers is now serving as evidence or support for this new conjecture.

But there is a third way to think inductively beyond our original claim. Instead of a straightforward generalization or a pronouncement on the cause of a phenomenon, we might have a more complex and cautious further claim in mind, such as this:

> Smoking is a factor in the causation of cardiovascular disease in some persons.

This proposition also advances a claim about causation, although it is obviously weaker than the claim *Smoking causes cardiovascular disease*. That is, other observations, theories, or evidence that would support the "factor" claim could easily fail to be enough to support the claim that smoking is the sole or main cause. Claiming that smoking is only one factor allows for other (unmentioned) factors in the causation of cardiovascular disease (e.g., genetic or dietary factors) that may not be found in all smokers.

INDUCTIVE INFERENCE (OR HYPOTHESIS) We began by assuming that our first proposition states an empirical fact based on direct observation but that the propositions that follow do not. Instead, they state empirical *hypotheses* or conjectures — tentative generalizations not fully confirmed — each of which goes beyond the observed facts. As such, they can be regarded as an *inductive inference* from the first proposition or observation.

PROBABILITY

Another way of thinking about inferences and hypotheses is to say that whereas a statement of observed fact (*230 out of 500 smokers have cardiovascular disease*) has a **probability** of 1.0 — that is, it is absolutely certain — the probability of each of the hypotheses that followed, *relative* to 1.0, is smaller than 1.0. (We need not worry here about how much smaller than 1.0 the probabilities are, nor about how to calculate these probabilities precisely.) But it takes only a moment's reflection to realize that no matter what the probability actually is, those probabilities in each case will be quite different relative to different information, such as this:

Ten persons observed in a sample of 500 smokers have cardiovascular disease.

The idea that *a given proposition can have different probabilities* relative to different bases is fundamental to all inductive reasoning. The following example makes a convincing illustration. Suppose we want to consider the probability of this proposition being true:

Susanne Smith will live to be eighty.

Taken as an abstract question of fact, we cannot even guess what the probability is with any assurance. But we can do better than guess; we can, in fact, even calculate the answer — if we get some further information. Thus, suppose we are told that Susanne Smith is seventy-nine. Our original question then becomes one of determining the probability that the proposition is true given this fact — that is, relative to the evidence. There's no doubt that if Susanne Smith really is seventy-nine, the probability that she will live to be eighty is greater than if we know only that Suzanne Smith is more than nine years old. Obviously, a lot can happen to Susanne in the seventy years between nine and seventy-nine that isn't very likely to happen in the one year between seventy-nine and eighty. So our proposition is more probable relative to the evidence of Susanne's age of seventy-nine than of "more than nine years old."

Let's suppose for the sake of the argument that the following is true:

Ninety percent of women alive at age seventy-nine live to be eighty.

Given this additional information and the information that Susanne is seventy-nine, we now have a basis for answering our original question about our proposition about Susanne's longevity with some precision. But suppose, in addition, we are also told that

Susanne Smith is suffering from inoperable cancer.

and also that

The survival rate for women suffering from inoperable cancer is 0.6 years (i.e., the average life span for women after a diagnosis of inoperable cancer is about seven months).

With this new information, the probability that Susanne will live to eighty drops significantly, all because we can now estimate the probability in relation to a new body of evidence.

The probability of an event, thus, is not a fixed number but one that varies because it is always relative to some evidence—and given different evidence, one and the same event can have different probabilities. In other words, the probability of any event is always relative to how much is known (assumed, believed), and because different persons may know different things about a given event or the same person may know different things at different times, one and the same event can have two or more probabilities. This conclusion is not a paradox but, rather, a logical consequence of the concept of what it is for an event to have (i.e., to be assigned) a probability.

S. Harris/Cartoonstock

MILL'S METHODS

Now let's return to our earlier discussion of smoking and cardiovascular disease and consider in greater detail the question of a causal connection between the two phenomena. We began thus:

In a sample of 500 smokers, 230 persons observed have cardiovascular disease.

We regarded this claim as an observed fact, although in truth, of course, it is mere supposition. Our question now is how we might augment this information so as to strengthen our confidence of our causal hypotheses that

Smoking *causes* cardiovascular disease.

or at least that

Smoking is a factor in the causation of cardiovascular disease in some persons.

Suppose further examination showed that

In the sample of 230 smokers with cardiovascular disease, no other suspected factor (such as genetic predisposition, lack of physical exercise, age over fifty) was also observed.

Such an observation would encourage us to believe that our hypotheses are true. Why? Because we're inclined to believe also that no matter what the cause of a phenomenon is, it must *always* be present when its effect is present. Thus, the inference from observed fact to our hypotheses is supported by this new evidence, using **Mill's Method of Agreement**, named after the British philosopher John Stuart Mill (1806–1873), who first formulated it. It's called a method of agreement because of the way in which the inference relies on *agreement* among the observed phenomena where a presumed cause is thought to be *present*.

Let's now suppose that in our search for evidence to support our hypotheses we conduct additional research and discover that

In a sample of 500 nonsmokers, selected to be representative of both sexes, different ages, dietary habits, exercise patterns, and so on, none is observed to have cardiovascular disease.

This observation would further encourage us to believe that we had obtained significant additional confirmation of our hypotheses. Why? Because we now know that factors present (such as male sex, lack of exercise, family history of cardiovascular disease) in cases where the effect is absent (no cardiovascular disease observed) cannot be the cause. This is an example of **Mill's Method of Difference**, so called because the cause or causal factor of an effect must be *different* from whatever factors are present when the effect is *absent*.

Suppose now that, increasingly confident we've found the cause of cardiovascular disease, we study our first sample of 230 smokers ill with the disease, and we discover this:

Those who smoke two or more packs of cigarettes daily for ten or more years have cardiovascular disease either much younger or much more severely than those who smoke less.

This is an application of **Mill's Method of Concomitant Variation**, perhaps the most convincing of the three methods. Here we deal not merely with the presence of the conjectured cause (smoking) or the absence of the effect we are studying (cardiovascular disease), as we were previously, but with the more interesting and subtler matter of the *degree and* *regularity of the correlation* of the supposed cause and effect. According to the observations reported here, it strongly appears that the more we have of the "cause" (smoking), the sooner or the more intense the onset of the "effect" (cardiovascular disease).

Notice, however, what happens to our confirmation if, instead, we had discovered this:

> In a representative sample of 500 nonsmokers, cardiovascular disease was observed in 34 cases.

(We won't pause here to explain what makes a sample more or less representative of a population, although the representativeness of samples is vital to all statistical reasoning.) Such an observation would lead us almost immediately to suspect some other or additional causal factor: Smoking might indeed be *a* factor in causing cardiovascular disease, but it can hardly be *the* cause because (using Mill's Method of Difference) we cannot have the effect, as we do in the observed sample of 34 cases reported above, unless we also have the cause.

An observation such as this is likely to lead us to think our hypothesis that *smoking causes cardiovascular disease* has been disconfirmed. But we have a fallback position ready — we can still defend our weaker hypothesis: *Smoking is a factor in the causation of cardiovascular disease in some persons.* It is still quite possible that smoking is a factor in causing this disease, even if it isn't the *only* factor.

Fallacies

The straight road on which sound reasoning proceeds gives little latitude for cruising about. Irrationality, carelessness, passionate attachment to one's unexamined beliefs, and the sheer complexity of some issues occasionally spoil the reasoning of even the best of us. An inventory of some common fallacies proves an instructive and potentially amusing exercise — instructive because the diagnosis and repair of error help us understand more principles of sound reasoning and amusing because we are so constituted that our perception of the nonsense of others can stimulate our minds, warm our hearts, and give us comforting feelings of superiority.

The discussion that follows, then, is a quick tour through the twisting paths, mudflats, and quicksands one sometimes encounters in reading arguments that stray from the way of clear thinking.

FALLACIES OF AMBIGUITY

AMBIGUITY Near the center of the town of Concord, Massachusetts, is an empty field with a sign reading "Old Calf Pasture." Hmm. A pasture in which calves grazed in former times? Or a pasture now in use for elderly calves? Or something that used to be a calf pasture but is now something else? These alternative readings arise because of **ambiguity**; brevity in the sign has produced a group of words that give rise to more than one possible interpretation, confusing the reader and (presumably) frustrating the sign writer's intentions.

Common Fallacies

	Fallacy	Definition	Example
Fallacies of Ambiguity	Ambiguity (p. 342)	Using a word, phrase, or claim that gives rise to more than one possible interpretation.	People have equal rights, and so everyone has a right to property.
	Division (p. 345)	Assuming all members of a set share characteristics of the set as a whole.	PETA is a radical organization; therefore, anyone who is a member of PETA is radical.
	Composition (p. 345)	Assuming that a set shares characteristics with a given member of a set (the reverse of division fallacy).	Kimberly is a freelance writer and makes a lot of money; freelance writers must make a lot of money.
	Equivocation (p. 345)	Making two words or phrases equivalent in meaning while ignoring contextual differences.	Evolution is a natural process, so this company's growth is natural and good.
	Non sequitur (p. 346)	Literally, "it does not follow." Drawing conclusions that are unrelated or do not follow logically from the premises.	Because Sammy is good at math, we should let him draw up our annual budget.
Fallacies of Presumption	Distorting the Facts (p. 346)	Misrepresenting information, data, or facts in an argument.	Video games have been shown to cause violence in one out of five kids; 20 percent of the next generation will be violent citizens.
	Post Hoc, Ergo Propter Hoc (p. 346)	Literally, "after this, therefore because of this." Assuming that sequence equals consequence.	After the invention of the birth control pill, the divorce rate increased; therefore, the "pill" contributed to the rising divorce rate.
	Many Questions (p. 347)	Presupposing facts that are assumed in the question itself.	Can selfish and self-interested politicians be trusted to do anything to bring about banking reform?
	Hasty Generalization (p. 347)	Jumping to conclusions based on insufficient evidence or biases.	I'm not moving to that neighborhood. When I visited it, there were two people fighting in the street.
	Slippery Slope (p. 347)	Arguing that an idea or action will lead inevitably to unrealistically steeper and steeper consequences.	If we allow legal recreational marijuana, other drugs will soon follow, and soon there will be addicts everywhere.
	False Analogy (p. 348)	Comparing two things that may be similar in some ways but remain different in other ways.	Building a border wall is just like fencing in our backyards; it is simply a safe and reasonable precaution.
	Straw Man (p. 348)	Misrepresenting an argument so that you can attack the misrepresentation rather than the actual argument.	If you want prison reform, you are basically saying you want to treat criminals like they're at a resort. We should not be rewarding criminals!
	Special Pleading (p. 348)	Making an unwarranted claim by misapplying or misusing rules and standards.	I should get an A because I worked really hard.
	Begging the Question (p. 348)	Making an argument in which the premises are based on the truth of the conclusion.	We have a free press because the Constitution guarantees it.

(Continued)

Common Fallacies (Continued)

	Fallacy	Definition	Example
Fallacies of Presumption	False Dichotomy (p. 349)	Establishing only two opposing positions or points when more might be available or when the opposing positions are not mutually exclusive.	Either we drill for natural gas, or we keep using carbon fuel.
	Oversimplification (p. 349)	Reducing a complex thing to a simple cause or consequence.	With all the bullying on the internet, it is no wonder school shootings are happening.
	Red Herring (p. 349)	Presenting a question or issue intended to divert and distract from the central or most relevant question or issue.	I recognize that the issue of race and police violence needs to be addressed, but the real question is whether or not athletes should kneel during the national anthem.
Fallacies of Irrelevance	Tu Quoque (p. 350)	Literally, "you also." Discrediting an argument by attacking the speaker's failure to adhere to his or her conclusion.	How can my professor say that electric vehicles are the future when he still drives a fuel-cell car?
	Genetic Fallacy (p. 350)	Arguing a position based on the real or imagined origin, history, or source of the idea.	In ancient times, men were hunters and women were gatherers — that's why women tend to be more domestic than men.
	Appeal to Ignorance (p. 350)	Saying that something is true because there is no evidence against it.	No one has complained about our new chili recipe, so it must be good.
	Poisoning the Well (p. 351)	Creating negative associations preemptively to discredit another person or position.	Now that I have highlighted the importance of keeping the controversial monument on campus, watch out because all the liberal snowflakes are going to argue that it "injures" them.
	Ad Hominem (p. 351)	Literally, "against the man [person]." Attacking the character of a person by providing irrelevant negative information.	How can this woman be the mayor when she can't even hold her own family together?
	Appeal to Authority (p. 351)	Asserting that a claim is true by citing someone thought to be an authority, regardless of the merits of the position or the relevance of the authority's expertise.	If the coach says throwing balls at the players makes them tougher, it must be true.
	Appeal to Fear (p. 352)	Supporting a position by instilling irrational fear of the alternatives.	If we don't strengthen our drug laws, drug dealers will see our community as a place to buy and sell openly on the streets.
Other	Death by a Thousand Qualifications (p. 352)	Justifying a weak idea or position by changing (or qualifying) it each time it is challenged.	Television is so bad for kids. (Well, not all television, and not all kids, and not in moderation, etc.)
	Protecting the Hypothesis (p. 352)	Distorting evidence to support a preexisting belief or idea.	According to the prophecy, the world was supposed to end. It didn't end. Therefore, the prophecy was not wrong, but we must have misinterpreted it.

Consider a more complex example. Suppose someone asserts *People have equal rights* and also *Everyone has a right to property.* Many people believe both these claims, but their combination involves an ambiguity. According to one interpretation, the two claims entail that everyone has an *equal right* to property. (That is, you and I each have an equal right to whatever property we have.) But the two claims can also be interpreted to mean that everyone has a *right to equal property.* (That is, whatever property you have a right to, I have a right to the same, or at least equivalent, property.) The latter interpretation is revolutionary, whereas the former is not. Arguments over equal rights often involve this ambiguity.

DIVISION   In the Bible, we read that the apostles of Jesus were twelve and that Matthew was an apostle. Does it follow that Matthew was twelve years old? No. To argue in this way from a property of a group to a property of a member of that group is to commit the **fallacy of division**. The example of the apostles may not be a very tempting instance of this error. A classic version may be a bit more interesting: If it is true that the average American family has 1.8 children, does it follow that your brother and sister-in-law are likely to have 1.8 children? If you think it does, you have committed the fallacy of division.

COMPOSITION   Could an all-star team of professional basketball players beat the Boston Celtics in their heyday — say, the team of 1985–1986? Perhaps it could in one game or two, but probably not in seven out of a dozen games in a row. As students of the game know, teamwork is an indispensable part of outstanding performance, and the 1985–1986 Celtics were famous for their self-sacrificing style of play.

The **fallacy of composition** can therefore be convincingly illustrated in this argument: *A team of five NBA all-stars is the best team in basketball if each of the five players is the best at his position.* The fallacy is called composition because the reasoning commits the error of arguing from the true premise that each member of a group has a certain property to the not necessarily true conclusion that the group (the composition) itself has the property (i.e., because *A* is the best player at forward, *B* is the best center, and so on; therefore, the team of *A*, *B*, . . . is the best team).

EQUIVOCATION   In a delightful passage in Lewis Carroll's *Through the Looking-Glass*, the king asks his messenger, "Who did you pass on the road?" and the messenger replies, "Nobody." This prompts the king to observe, "Of course, Nobody walks slower than you," provoking the messenger's sullen response: "I do my best. I'm sure nobody walks much faster than I do." At this the king remarks with surprise, "He can't do that or else he'd have been here first!" (This, by the way, is the classic predecessor of the famous comic dialogue "Who's on First?" between the comedians Bud Abbott and Lou Costello.) The king and the messenger are equivocating on the term *nobody*. The messenger uses it in the normal way as an indefinite pronoun equivalent to "not anyone." But the king uses the word as though it were a proper noun, *Nobody*, the rather odd name of some person. It's no wonder the king and the messenger talk right past each other.

Equivocation (from the Latin for "equal voice" — i.e., giving utterance to two meanings at the same time in one word or phrase) can ruin otherwise good reasoning, as in this example: *Euthanasia is a good death; one dies a good death when one dies peacefully in old age; therefore, euthanasia is dying peacefully in old age.* The etymology of *euthanasia* is literally "a good death," so the first premise is true. And the second premise is certainly plausible. But the conclusion of this syllogism is false. Euthanasia cannot be defined as a peaceful death in one's old age for two reasons. First, euthanasia requires the intervention of another person who kills someone (or lets the person die); second, even a very young person can be euthanized. The problem arises because "a good death" works in the second premise in a manner that does not apply to euthanasia. Both meanings of "a good death" are legitimate, but when used together, they constitute an equivocation that spoils the argument.

NON SEQUITUR   The fallacy of equivocation takes us from the discussion of confusions in individual claims or grounds to the more troublesome fallacies that infect the linkages between the claims we make and the grounds (or reasons) for them. These fallacies occur in statements that, following the vocabulary of the Toulmin method, are called the *warrant* of reasoning. Each fallacy is an example of reasoning that involves a **non sequitur** (Latin for "it does not follow"). That is, the *claim* (the conclusion) does not follow from the *grounds* (the premises).

For a start, here is an obvious non sequitur: "He went to the movies on three consecutive nights, so he must love movies." Why doesn't the claim ("He must love movies") follow from the grounds ("He went to the movies on three consecutive nights")? Perhaps the person was just fulfilling an assignment in a film course (maybe he even hated movies so much that he had postponed three assignments to see films and now had to see them all in quick succession), or maybe he went with a girlfriend who was a movie buff, or maybe . . . — there are any number of other possible reasons.

FALLACIES OF PRESUMPTION

DISTORTING THE FACTS   Facts can be distorted either intentionally (to deceive or mislead) or unintentionally, and in either case usually (but not invariably) to the benefit of whoever is doing the distortion. Consider this case. In 1964, the US surgeon general reported that smoking cigarettes increased the likelihood that smokers would eventually suffer from lung cancer. The cigarette manufacturers vigorously protested that the surgeon general relied on inconclusive research and was badly misleading the public about the health risks of smoking. It later turned out that the tobacco companies knew that smoking increased the risk of lung cancer — a fact established by the company's own laboratories but concealed from the public. Today, thanks to public access to all the facts, it is commonplace knowledge that inhaled smoke — including secondhand smoke — is a risk factor for many illnesses.

POST HOC, ERGO PROPTER HOC   One of the most tempting errors in reasoning is to ground a claim about causation on an observed temporal sequence — that is, to argue "after this, therefore because of this" (which is what **post hoc, ergo propter hoc** means in Latin). When the medical community first announced that smoking tobacco caused lung cancer, advocates for the tobacco industry replied that doctors were guilty of this fallacy.

These industry advocates argued that medical researchers had merely noticed that in some people, lung cancer developed *after* considerable smoking — indeed, years after — but (they insisted) that this correlation was not at all the same as a causal relation between smoking and lung cancer. True enough. The claim that *A causes B* is not the same as the claim that *B comes after A*. After all, it was possible that smokers as a group had some other common trait and that this factor was the true cause of their cancer.

As the long controversy over the truth about the causation of lung cancer shows, to avoid the appearance of fallacious post hoc reasoning one needs to find some way to link the observed phenomena (the correlation between smoking and the onset of lung cancer). This step requires some further theory and preferably some experimental evidence for the exact sequence or physical mechanism, in full detail, of how ingestion of tobacco smoke is a crucial factor — and is not merely an accidental or happenstance prior event — in the subsequent development of the cancer.

MANY QUESTIONS   Some questions contain presuppositions that are presented as true and are built into the question itself. Loaded questions, leading questions, and trick questions are all part of the many questions fallacy. The old saw, "When did you stop beating your wife?" is sometimes used to illustrate the **fallacy of many questions**. This question, as one can readily see, is unanswerable unless all three of its implicit presuppositions are true. The questioner presupposes that (1) the addressee has or had a wife, (2) he or she has beaten her, and (3) he or she has stopped beating her. If any of these presuppositions is false, the question is pointless; it cannot be answered strictly and simply with a date or time.

HASTY GENERALIZATION   From a logical point of view, **hasty generalization** is the precipitous move from true assertions about *one* or a *few* instances to dubious or even false assertions about *all*. For example, although it may be true that the only native Hungarians you personally know do not speak English very well, that is no basis for asserting that all Hungarians do not speak English very well. Likewise, if the clothes you recently ordered online turn out not to fit very well, it doesn't follow that *all* online clothes turn out to be too large or too small. A hasty generalization usually lies behind a **stereotype** — that is, a person or event treated as typical of a whole class.

SLIPPERY SLOPE   One of the most familiar arguments against any type of government regulation is that if it is allowed, it will be just the first step down the path that leads to ruinous interference, overregulation, and totalitarian control. Fairly often we encounter this mode of argument in the public debates over handgun control, the censorship of pornography, and physician-assisted suicide. The argument is called the **slippery slope** (or the wedge argument, from the way people use the thin end of a wedge to split solid things apart; it is also called, rather colorfully, "letting the camel's nose under the tent"). The fallacy here is in implying that the first step necessarily leads to the second and so on down the slope to disaster, when in fact there is no necessary slide from the first step to the second. (Would handgun registration lead to a police state? Well, it hasn't in Switzerland.)

Closely related to the slippery slope is what lawyers call a **parade of horrors**, an array of examples of terrible consequences that will or might follow if we travel down a certain path.

A good example appears in Justice William Brennan's opinion for the US Supreme Court in *Texas v. Johnson* (1989) regarding a Texas law against burning the American flag in political protest. If this law is allowed to stand, Brennan suggests, we may next find laws against burning the presidential seal, state flags, and the Constitution.

FALSE ANALOGY   Argument by analogy, as we point out in Chapter 3 and as many of the selections in this book show, is a familiar and even indispensable mode of argument. But it can be treacherous because it runs the risk of the **fallacy of false analogy**. Unfortunately, we have no simple or foolproof way of distinguishing between the useful, legitimate analogies and the others. The key question to ask yourself is, Do the two things put into analogy differ in any essential and relevant respect, or are they different only in unimportant and irrelevant aspects?

In a famous example from his discussion in support of suicide, philosopher David Hume rhetorically asked: "It would be no crime in me to divert the Nile or Danube from its course, were I able to effect such purposes. Where then is the crime of turning a few ounces of blood from their natural channel?" This is a striking analogy — except that it rests on a false assumption. No one has the right to divert the Nile or the Danube or any other major international watercourse; it would be a catastrophic crime to do so without the full consent of people living in the region, their government, and so forth. Therefore, arguing by analogy, one might well say that no one has the right to take his or her own life either. Thus, Hume's own analogy can be used to argue against his thesis that suicide is no crime. But let's ignore the way in which his example can be turned against him. The analogy is a terrible one in any case. Isn't it obvious that the Nile, regardless of its exact course, would continue to nourish Egypt and the Sudan, whereas the blood flowing out of someone's veins will soon leave that person dead? The fact that the blood is the same blood, whether in a person's body or in a pool on the floor (just as the water of the Nile is the same body of water no matter what path it follows to the sea) is, of course, irrelevant to the question of whether one has the right to commit suicide.

STRAW MAN   It is often tempting to reframe or report your opponent's thesis to make it easier to attack and perhaps refute it. If you do so in the course of an argument, you are creating a straw man, a thing of no substance that's easily blown away. The straw man you've constructed is usually a radically conservative or extremely liberal thesis, which few if any would want to defend. That is why it is easier to refute the straw man than refute the view your opponent actually holds: "So you defend the death penalty — and all the horrible things done in its name." It's highly unlikely that your opponent supports *everything* that has been done in the name of capital punishment — crucifixion and beheading, for example, or execution of the children of the guilty offender.

SPECIAL PLEADING   We all have our favorites — relatives, friends, and neighbors — and we're all too likely to show that favoritism in unacceptable ways. Here is an example: "I know my son punched another boy but he is not a bully, so there must have been a good reason."

BEGGING THE QUESTION   The fallacy called "begging the question," *petitio principii* in Latin, is so named because the conclusion of the argument is hidden among its assumptions — and so the conclusion, not surprisingly, follows from the premises. The argument over whether the death penalty is a deterrent to crime illustrates this fallacy. From the facts that you live in a death-penalty state and were not murdered yesterday, we cannot infer that the death penalty was a deterrent. Yet it is tempting to make this inference, perhaps because — all unaware — we are relying on the **fallacy of begging the question**. If someone tacitly assumes from the start that the death penalty is an effective deterrent, the fact that you weren't murdered yesterday certainly looks like evidence for the truth of that assumption. But it isn't, as long as there are competing but unexamined alternative explanations, as in this case.

Of course, that you weren't murdered is *consistent* with the claim that the death penalty is an effective deterrent, just as someone else being murdered is also consistent with that claim (because an effective deterrent need not be a *perfect* deterrent). In general, from the fact that two propositions are consistent with each other, we cannot infer that either is evidence for the other.

Note: "Begging the question" is often wrongly used to mean "raises the question," as in "His action of burning the flag begs the question, What drove him to do such a thing?"

FALSE DICHOTOMY Sometimes, oversimplification takes a more complex form in which contrary possibilities are wrongly presented as though they were exhaustive and exclusive. "Either we get tough with drug users, or we must surrender and legalize all drugs." Really? What about doing neither and instead offering education and counseling, detoxification programs, and incentives to "Say no"? A favorite of debaters, **either/or reasoning** always runs the risk of ignoring a third (or fourth) possibility. Some disjunctions are indeed exhaustive: "Either we get tough with drug users, or we do not." This proposition, although vague (what does "get tough" really mean?), is a tautology; it cannot be false, and there is no third alternative. But most disjunctions do not express a pair of *contradictory* alternatives: They offer only a pair of *contrary* alternatives, and mere contraries do not exhaust the possibilities (recall our discussion of contraries versus contradictories on pp. 335–36).

OVERSIMPLIFICATION "Poverty causes crime," "Taxation is unfair," "Truth is stranger than fiction" — these are examples of generalizations that exaggerate and therefore oversimplify the truth. Poverty as such can't be the sole cause of crime because many poor people do not break the law. Some taxes may be unfairly high, others unfairly low — but there is no reason to believe that *every* tax is unfair to all those who have to pay it. Some true stories do amaze us as much or more than some fictional stories, but the reverse is true, too. (In the language of the Toulmin method, **oversimplification** is the result of a failure to use suitable modal qualifiers in formulating one's claims or grounds or backing.)

RED HERRING The fallacy of **red herring**, less colorfully named "irrelevant thesis," occurs when one tries to distract one's audience by invoking a consideration that is irrelevant to the topic under discussion. (This fallacy probably gets its name from the fact that a rotten herring, or a cured herring, which is reddish, will throw pursuing hounds off the right track.) Consider this case: Some critics, seeking to defend the US government's refusal to sign the Kyoto accords to reduce climate change, argue that signing is supported mainly by left-leaning scientists. This argument supposedly shows that climate change is not a serious, urgent issue. But claiming that the supporters of these accords are left-inclined is a red herring, an irrelevant thesis. By raising doubts about the political views of the advocates of signing, critics distract attention from the scientific question (Is there climate change?) and also from the separate political question (Ought the US government to sign the accords?). The refusal of a government to sign the accords doesn't show there is no such thing as climate change. And even if all the advocates of signing were left-leaning (they aren't), this fact (if it were a fact, but it isn't) would not show that worries about climate change are exaggerated.

FALLACIES OF IRRELEVANCE

TU QUOQUE   The Romans called one particular type of fallacy *tu quoque*, for "you also." Consider this: "You're a fine one, trying to persuade me to give up smoking when you indulge yourself with a pipe and a cigar from time to time. Maybe I should quit, but then so should you. It's hypocritical of you to complain about my smoking when you persist in the same habit." The fallacy is this: The merit of a person's argument has nothing to do with the person's character or behavior. Here the assertion that smoking is bad for one's health is *not* weakened by the fact that a smoker offers the argument.

GENETIC FALLACY   A member of the family of fallacies that includes poisoning the well and ad hominem (see below) is the **genetic fallacy**. Here the error takes the form of arguing against a claim by pointing out that its origin (genesis) is tainted or that it was invented by someone deserving our contempt. For example, an opponent of the death penalty might argue this:

> Capital punishment arose in barbarous times, but we claim to be civilized; therefore, we should discard this relic of the past.

Such reasoning shouldn't be persuasive because the question of the death penalty for our society must be decided by the degree to which it serves our purposes — justice and defense against crime, presumably — to which its historic origins are irrelevant. The practices of beer- and wine-making are as old as human civilization, but their origin in antiquity is no reason to outlaw them in our time. The curious circumstances in which something originates usually play no role in its validity. Anyone who would argue that nothing good could possibly come from molds and fungi is refuted by Sir Alexander Fleming's discovery of penicillin in 1928.

APPEAL TO IGNORANCE   In the controversy over the death penalty, the issues of deterrence and executing the innocent are bound to be raised. Because no one knows how many innocent persons have been convicted for murder and wrongfully executed, it is tempting for abolitionists to argue that the death penalty is too risky. It is equally tempting for proponents of the death penalty to argue that since no one knows how many people have been deterred from murder by the threat of execution, we abolish it at society's peril.

Each of these arguments suffers from the same flaw: the **fallacy of appeal to ignorance**. Each argument invites the audience to draw an inference from a premise that is unquestionably true, but what is that premise? It asserts that there is something "we don't know." But what we *don't* know cannot be *evidence* for (or against) anything. Our ignorance is no reason for believing anything, except perhaps that we ought to undertake an appropriate investigation so as to replace our ignorance with reliable information.

POISONING THE WELL   During the 1970s, some critics of the Equal Rights Amendment (ERA) argued against it by pointing out that Marx and Engels, in their *Communist Manifesto*, favored equality of women and men — and therefore the ERA was immoral, undesirable, and perhaps even a Communist plot. This kind of reasoning is an attempt to **poison the well**; that is, it is an attempt to shift attention from the merits of the argument — the validity of the reasoning, the truth of the claims — to the source or origin of the argument. Such criticism deflects attention from the real issue — namely, whether the view in question is true and what the quality of evidence is in its support. The mere fact that Marx (or Hitler, for that matter) believed something does not show that the belief is false or immoral; just because some scoundrel believes the world is round is no reason for you to believe it is flat.

AD HOMINEM   Closely allied to poisoning the well is another fallacy, **ad hominem** argument (from the Latin for "against the person"). A critic can easily yield to the temptation to attack an argument or theory by trying to impeach or undercut the credentials of its advocates.

Consider this example: Jones is arguing that prayer should not be permitted in public schools, and Smith responds by pointing out that Jones has twice been convicted of assaulting members of the clergy. Jones's behavior doubtless is reprehensible, but the issue is not Jones, it is prayer in school, and what must be scrutinized is Jones's argument, not his police record or his character.

APPEAL TO AUTHORITY   One might easily imagine someone from the South in 1860 defending the slave-owning society of that day by appealing to the fact that no less a person than Thomas Jefferson — a brilliant public figure, thinker, and leader by any measure — owned slaves. Or today one might defend capital punishment on the ground that Abraham Lincoln, surely one of the nation's greatest presidents, signed many death warrants during the Civil War, authorizing the execution of Union soldiers. No doubt the esteem in which such figures as Jefferson and Lincoln are deservedly held amounts to impressive endorsement for whatever acts and practices, policies, and institutions, they supported. But the **authority** of these figures in itself is not evidence for the truth of their views, so their authority cannot be a reason for anyone to agree with them.

Sometimes, the appeal to authority is fallacious because the authoritative person is not an expert on the issue in dispute. The fact that a high-energy physicist has won the Nobel Prize is no reason for attaching any special weight to her views on the causes of cancer, the reduction of traffic accidents, or the legalization of marijuana. We all depend heavily on the knowledge of various experts and authorities, so we tend to respect their views. Conversely, we should resist the temptation to accord their views on diverse subjects the same respect that we grant them in the area of their expertise.

APPEAL TO FEAR The Romans called the **appeal to fear** fallacy *ad baculum*, for "resorting to violence" (*baculum* means "stick" or "club"). Trying to persuade people to agree with you by threatening them with painful consequences is obviously an appeal that no rational person would contemplate. The violence need not be physical; if you threaten someone with the loss of a job, for instance, you are still using a stick. Violence or the threat of harmful consequences in the course of an argument is beyond reason and always shows the haste or impatience of those who appeal to it. It is also an indication that the argument on its merits would be unpersuasive, inconclusive, or worse. President Theodore Roosevelt's epigrammatic doctrine for the kind of foreign policy he favored — "Speak softly but carry a big stick" — illustrates an attempt to have it both ways; an appeal to reason for starters, but a recourse to coercion, or the threat of coercion, as a backup if needed.

ADDITIONAL FALLACIES

Finally, we add two fallacies, not easily embraced by Engels's three categories that have served us well thus far (ambiguity, erroneous presumption, and irrelevance): death by a thousand qualifications and protecting the hypothesis.

DEATH BY A THOUSAND QUALIFICATIONS **Death by a thousand qualifications** gets its name from the ancient torture of death by a thousand small cuts. Thus, a bold assertion can be virtually killed and its true content reduced to nothing, bit by bit, as all the appropriate or necessary qualifications are added to it. Consider an example. Suppose you hear a politician describing another country (let's call it Ruritania so as not to offend anyone) as a "democracy" — except it turns out that Ruritania doesn't have regular elections, lacks a written constitution, has no independent judiciary, prohibits religious worship except of the state-designated deity, and so forth. So what remains of the original claim that Ruritania is a democracy is little or nothing. The qualifications have taken all the content out of the original description.

PROTECTING THE HYPOTHESIS In Chapter 3, we contrasted *reasoning* and *rationalization* (or the finding of bad reasons for what one intends to believe anyway). Rationalization can take subtle forms, as the following example indicates. Suppose you're standing with a friend on the shore or on a pier and you watch as a ship heads out to sea. As it reaches the horizon, it slowly disappears — first the hull, then the upper decks, and finally the tip of the mast. Because the ship (you both assume) isn't sinking, it occurs to you that this sequence of observations provides evidence that the earth's surface is curved. Nonsense, says your companion. Light waves sag, or bend down, over distances of a few miles, and so a flat surface (such as the ocean) can intercept them. Therefore, the ship, which appears to be going "over" the horizon, really isn't: It's just moving steadily farther and farther away in a straight line. Your friend, you discover to your amazement, is a card-carrying member of the Flat Earth Society, a group who insists the earth is a plane surface. Now most of us would regard the idea that light rays bend down in the manner required by the Flat Earther's argument as a rationalization whose sole purpose is to protect the flat-earth doctrine against counterevidence. We would be convinced it was a rationalization, and not a very good one at that, if the Flat Earther held to it despite a patient and thorough explanation from a physicist that showed modern optical theory to be quite incompatible with the view that light waves sag.

This example illustrates two important points about the *backing* of arguments. First, it is always possible to **protect a hypothesis** by abandoning adjacent or connected hypotheses; this is the tactic our Flat Earth friend has used. This maneuver is possible, however, only because — and this is the second point — whenever we test a hypothesis, we do so by taking for granted (usually, quite unconsciously) many other hypotheses as well. So the evidence for the hypothesis we think we are confirming is impossible to separate entirely from the adequacy of the connected hypotheses. As long as we have no reason to doubt that light rays travel in straight lines (at least over distances of a few miles), our Flat Earth friend's argument is unconvincing. But once that hypothesis is itself put in doubt, the idea that seemed at first to be a pathetic rationalization takes on an even more troublesome character.

There are, then, not one but two fallacies exposed by this example. The first and perhaps graver one is in rigging your hypothesis so that *no matter what* observations are brought against it, you will count nothing as falsifying it. The second and subtler one is in thinking that as you test one hypothesis, all your other background beliefs are left safely to one side, immaculate and uninvolved. On the contrary, our beliefs form a corporate structure, intertwined and connected to one another with great complexity, and no one of them can ever be singled out for unique and isolated application, confirmation, or disconfirmation to the world around us.

> ## A CHECKLIST FOR EVALUATING AN ARGUMENT WITH LOGIC
>
> ☐ Can I identify the premises and the conclusion of the argument?
>
> ☐ Given the premises, is the argument valid?
>
> ☐ If it is valid, are all its premises true?
>
> ☐ If all the premises are true, does the conclusion necessarily follow from them?
>
> ☐ Are there any claims that are inconsistent in the argument?
>
> ☐ Does the argument contain one or more fallacies?
>
> ☐ If the argument is inductive, on what observations is it based?
>
> ☐ Do the observations or data make the conclusion probable?
>
> ☐ Is there enough evidence to disconfirm the conclusion?

THINKING CRITICALLY *Identifying Fallacies*

Here are some fallacies in action. Using the explanations in this section, identify what type of fallacy the argument example commits and then explain your reasoning.

EXAMPLE	TYPE OF FALLACY	EXPLANATION
Senator Case was friends with a disgraced racketeer; he shouldn't be your selection in the upcoming election.		
These activists say they want justice, but is it really justice to clog up the streets with the protests?		
East Coast urban liberals are going to say that hunting is inhumane. They do not realize how narrow-minded they are.		
There have been few terrorist attacks since September 11, 2001; therefore, our national security efforts must be working.		
If you start out with a bottle of beer a day and then go on to a glass or two of wine on the weekends, you're well on your way to becoming a hopeless drunk.		
My marriage was a failure, which just proves my point: Don't ever get married in the first place.		
Not until astronauts sailed through space around the moon did we have adequate reason to believe that the moon even had a back side.		
Going to church on a regular basis is bad for your health. Instead of sitting in a pew for an hour each Sunday, you'd be better off taking an hour's brisk walk.		

EXAMPLE	TYPE OF FALLACY	EXPLANATION
A professional baseball player has a good-luck charm. When he wears it, the team wins.		
How come herbivores don't eat herbs?		

MAX SHULMAN

Max Shulman (1919–1988) began his career as a writer when he was a journalism student at the University of Minnesota. Later he wrote humorous novels, stories, and plays. One of his novels, *Barefoot Boy with Cheek* (1943), was made into a musical, and another, *Rally Round the Flag, Boys!* (1957), was made into a film starring Paul Newman and Joanne Woodward. *The Tender Trap* (1954), a play he wrote with Robert Paul Smith, still retains its popularity with theater groups.

"Love Is a Fallacy" was first published in 1951, when demeaning stereotypes about women and minorities were widely accepted in the marketplace, as well as the home. Thus, jokes about domineering mothers-in-law or about dumb blondes routinely met with no objection.

Love Is a Fallacy

Cool was I and logical. Keen, calculating, perspicacious, acute, and astute — I was all of these. My brain was as powerful as a dynamo, as precise as a chemist's scales, as penetrating as a scalpel. And — think of it! — I was only eighteen.

It is not often that one so young has such a giant intellect. Take, for example, Petey Bellows, my roommate at the university. Same age, same background, but dumb as an ox. A nice enough fellow, you understand, but nothing upstairs. Emotional type. Unstable. Impressionable. Worst of all, a faddist. Fads, I submit, are the very negation of reason. To be swept up in every new craze that comes along, to surrender yourself to idiocy just because

everybody else is doing it — this, to me, is the acme of mindlessness. Not, however, to Petey.

One afternoon I found Petey lying on his bed with an expression of such distress on his face that I immediately diagnosed appendicitis. "Don't move," I said. "Don't take a laxative. I'll call a doctor."

"Raccoon," he mumbled thickly.

"Raccoon?" I said, pausing in my flight. 5

"I want a raccoon coat," he wailed.

I perceived that his trouble was not physical, but mental. "Why do you want a raccoon coat?"

"I should have known it," he cried, pounding his temples. "I should have known they'd come back when the Charleston came back.

Like a fool I spent all my money for textbooks, and now I can't get a raccoon coat."

"Can you mean," I said incredulously, "that people are actually wearing raccoon coats again?"

"All the Big Men on Campus are wearing 10 them. Where've you been?"

"In the library," I said, naming a place not frequented by Big Men on Campus.

He leaped from the bed and paced the room. "I've got to have a raccoon coat," he said passionately. "I've got to!"

"Petey, why? Look at it rationally. Raccoon coats are unsanitary. They shed. They smell bad. They weigh too much. They're unsightly. They ——"

"You don't understand," he interrupted impatiently. "It's the thing to do. Don't you want to be in the swim?"

"No," I said truthfully. 15

"Well, I do," he declared. "I'd give anything for a raccoon coat. Anything!"

My brain, that precision instrument, slipped into high gear. "Anything?" I asked, looking at him narrowly.

"Anything," he affirmed in ringing tones.

I stroked my chin thoughtfully. It so happened that I knew where to get my hands on a raccoon coat. My father had had one in his undergraduate days; it lay now in a trunk in the attic back home. It also happened that Petey had something I wanted. He didn't *have* it exactly, but at least he had first rights on it. I refer to his girl, Polly Espy.

I had long coveted Polly Espy. Let me 20 emphasize that my desire for this young woman was not emotional in nature. She was, to be sure, a girl who excited the emotions, but I was not one to let my heart rule my head. I wanted Polly for a shrewdly calculated, entirely cerebral reason.

I was a freshman in law school. In a few years I would be out in practice. I was well aware of the importance of the right kind of wife in furthering a lawyer's career. The successful lawyers I had observed were, almost without exception, married to beautiful, gracious, intelligent women. With one omission, Polly fitted these specifications perfectly.

Beautiful she was. She was not yet of pin-up proportions, but I felt sure that time would supply the lack. She already had the makings.

Gracious she was. By gracious I mean full of graces. She had an erectness of carriage, an ease of bearing, a poise that clearly indicated the best of breeding. At table her manners were exquisite. I had seen her at the Kozy Kampus Korner eating the specialty of the house — a sandwich that contained scraps of pot roast, gravy, chopped nuts, and a dipper of sauerkraut — without even getting her fingers moist.

Intelligent she was not. In fact, she veered in the opposite direction. But I believed that under my guidance she would smarten up. At any rate, it was worth a try. It is, after all, easier to make a beautiful dumb girl smart than to make an ugly smart girl beautiful.

"Petey," I said, "are you in love with Polly 25 Espy?"

"I think she's a keen kid," he replied, "but I don't know if you'd call it love. Why?"

"Do you," I asked, "have any kind of formal arrangement with her? I mean are you going steady or anything like that?"

"No. We see each other quite a bit, but we both have other dates. Why?"

"Is there," I asked, "any other man for whom she has a particular fondness?"

"Not that I know of. Why?" 30

I nodded with satisfaction. "In other words, if you were out of the picture, the field would be open. Is that right?"

"I guess so. What are you getting at?"

"Nothing, nothing," I said innocently, and took my suitcase out of the closet.

"Where you going?" asked Petey.

"Home for the weekend." I threw a few 35 things into the bag.

"Listen," he said, clutching my arm eagerly, "while you're home, you couldn't get some money from your old man, could you, and lend it to me so I can buy a raccoon coat?"

"I may do better than that," I said with a mysterious wink and closed my bag and left.

"Look," I said to Petey when I got back Monday morning. I threw open the suitcase and revealed the huge, hairy, gamy object that my father had worn in his Stutz Bearcat in 1925.

"Holy Toledo!" said Petey reverently. He plunged his hands into the raccoon coat and then his face. "Holy Toledo!" he repeated fifteen or twenty times.

"Would you like it?" I asked. 40

"Oh yes!" he cried, clutching the greasy pelt to him. Then a canny look came into his eyes. "What do you want for it?"

"Your girl," I said, mincing no words.

"Polly?" he said in a horrified whisper. "You want Polly?"

"That's right."

He flung the coat from him. "Never," he 45 said stoutly.

I shrugged. "Okay. If you don't want to be in the swim, I guess it's your business."

I sat down in a chair and pretended to read a book, but out of the corner of my eye I kept watching Petey. He was a torn man. First he looked at the coat with the expression of a waif at a bakery window. Then he turned away and set his jaw resolutely. Then he looked back at the coat, with even more longing in his face. Then he turned away, but with not so much resolution this time. Back and forth his head swiveled, desire waxing, resolution waning. Finally he didn't turn away at all; he just stood and stared with mad lust at the coat.

"It isn't as though I was in love with Polly," he said thickly. "Or going steady or anything like that."

"That's right," I murmured.

"What's Polly to me, or me to Polly?" 50

"Not a thing," said I.

"It's just been a casual kick — just a few laughs, that's all."

"Try on the coat," said I.

He complied. The coat bunched high over his ears and dropped all the way down to his shoe tops. He looked like a mound of dead raccoons. "Fits fine," he said happily.

I rose from my chair. "Is it a deal?" I asked, 55 extending my hand.

He swallowed. "It's a deal," he said and shook my hand.

I had my first date with Polly the following evening. This was in the nature of a survey; I wanted to find out just how much work I had to do to get her mind up to the standard I required. I took her first to dinner. "Gee, that was a delish dinner," she said as we left the restaurant. Then I took her to a movie. "Gee, that was a marvy movie," she said as we left the theater. And then I took her home. "Gee, I had a sensaysh time," she said as she bade me good night.

I went back to my room with a heavy heart. I had gravely underestimated the size of my task. This girl's lack of information was terrifying. Nor would it be enough merely to supply her with information. First she had to be taught to *think*. This loomed as a project of no small dimensions, and at first I was tempted to give her back to Petey. But then I got to thinking about her abundant physical charms and about the way she entered a room and the way she handled a knife and fork, and I decided to make an effort.

I went about it, as in all things, systematically. I gave her a course in logic. It happened that I, as a law student, was taking a course in logic myself, so I had all the facts at my fingertips. "Polly," I said to her when I picked her up on our next date, "tonight we are going over to the Knoll and talk."

"Oo, terrif," she replied. One thing I will say for this girl: You would go far to find another so agreeable.

We went to the Knoll, the campus trysting place, and we sat down under an old oak, and she looked at me expectantly: "What are we going to talk about?" she asked.

"Logic."

She thought this over for a minute and decided she liked it. "Magnif," she said.

"Logic," I said, clearing my throat, "is the science of thinking. Before we can think correctly, we must first learn to recognize the common fallacies of logic. These we will take up tonight."

"Wow-dow!" she cried, clapping her hands delightedly.

I winced, but went bravely on. "First let us examine the fallacy called Dicto Simpliciter."

"By all means," she urged, batting her lashes eagerly.

"Dicto Simpliciter means an argument based on an unqualified generalization. For example: Exercise is good. Therefore everybody should exercise."

"I agree," said Polly earnestly. "I mean exercise is wonderful. I mean it builds the body and everything."

"Polly," I said gently, "the argument is a fallacy. *Exercise is good* is an unqualified generalization. For instance, if you have heart disease, exercise is bad, not good. Many people are ordered by their doctors *not* to exercise. You must *qualify* the generalization. You must say exercise is *usually* good, or exercise is good *for most people*. Otherwise you have committed a Dicto Simpliciter. Do you see?"

"No," she confessed. "But this is marvy. Do more! Do more!"

"It will be better if you stop tugging at my sleeve," I told her, and when she desisted, I continued. "Next we take up a fallacy called Hasty Generalization. Listen carefully: You can't speak French. I can't speak French. Petey Bellows can't speak French. I must therefore conclude that nobody at the University of Minnesota can speak French."

"Really?" said Polly, amazed. "*Nobody?*"

I hid my exasperation. "Polly, it's a fallacy. The generalization is reached too hastily. There are too few instances to support such a conclusion."

"Know any more fallacies?" she asked breathlessly. "This is more fun than dancing even."

I fought off a wave of despair. I was getting nowhere with this girl, absolutely nowhere. Still, I am nothing if not persistent. I continued. "Next comes Post Hoc. Listen to this: Let's not take Bill on our picnic. Every time we take him out with us, it rains."

"I know somebody just like that," she exclaimed. "A girl back home — Eula Becker, her name is. It never fails. Every single time we take her on a picnic ——"

"Polly," I said sharply, "it's a fallacy. Eula Becker doesn't *cause* the rain. She has no connection with the rain. You are guilty of Post Hoc if you blame Eula Becker."

"I'll never do it again," she promised contritely. "Are you mad at me?"

I sighed. "No, Polly, I'm not mad."

"Then tell me some more fallacies."

"All right. Let's try Contradictory Premises."

"Yes, let's," she chirped, blinking her eyes happily.

I frowned, but plunged ahead. "Here's an example of Contradictory Premises: If God can do anything, can He make a stone so heavy that He won't be able to lift it?"

"Of course," she replied promptly.

"But if He can do anything, He can lift the stone," I pointed out.

"Yeah," she said thoughtfully. "Well, then I guess He can't make the stone."

"But He can do anything," I reminded her.

She scratched her pretty, empty head. "I'm all confused," she admitted.

"Of course you are. Because when the premises of an argument contradict each other, there can be no argument. If there is an irresistible force, there can be no immovable object. If there is an immovable object, there can be no irresistible force. Get it?"

"Tell me some more of this keen stuff," she said eagerly.

I consulted my watch. "I think we'd better call it a night. I'll take you home now, and you go over all the things you've learned. We'll have another session tomorrow night."

I deposited her at the girls' dormitory, where she assured me that she had had a perfectly terrif evening, and I went glumly home to my room. Petey lay snoring in his bed, the raccoon coat huddled like a great hairy beast at his feet. For a moment I considered waking him and telling him that he could have his girl back. It seemed clear that my project was doomed to failure. The girl simply had a logic-proof head.

But then I reconsidered. I had wasted one evening; I might as well waste another. Who knew? Maybe somewhere in the extinct crater of her mind a few embers still smoldered. Maybe somehow I could fan them into flame. Admittedly it was not a prospect fraught with hope, but I decided to give it one more try.

Seated under the oak the next evening I said, "Our first fallacy tonight is called Ad Misericordiam."

She quivered with delight.

"Listen closely," I said. "A man applies for a job. When the boss asks him what his qualifications are, he replies that he has a wife and six children at home, the wife is a helpless cripple, the children have nothing to eat, no clothes to wear, no shoes on their feet, there are no beds in the house, no coal in the cellar, and winter is coming."

A tear rolled down each of Polly's pink cheeks. "Oh, this is awful, awful," she sobbed.

"Yes, it's awful," I agreed, "but it's no argument. The man never answered the boss's question about his qualifications. Instead he appealed to the boss's sympathy. He committed the fallacy of Ad Misericordiam. Do you understand?"

"Have you got a handkerchief?" she blubbered.

I handed her a handkerchief and tried to keep from screaming while she wiped her eyes. "Next," I said in a carefully controlled tone, "we will discuss False Analogy. Here is an example: Students should be allowed to look at their textbooks during examinations. After all, surgeons have X rays to guide them during an operation, lawyers have briefs to guide them during a trial, carpenters have blueprints to guide them when they are building a house. Why, then, shouldn't students be allowed to look at their textbooks during an examination?"

"There now," she said enthusiastically, "is the most marvy idea I've heard in years."

"Polly," I said testily, "the argument is all wrong. Doctors, lawyers, and carpenters aren't taking a test to see how much they have learned, but students are. The situations are altogether different, and you can't make an analogy between them."

"I still think it's a good idea," said Polly.

"Nuts," I muttered. Doggedly I pressed on. "Next we'll try Hypothesis Contrary to Fact."

"Sounds yummy," was Polly's reaction.

"Listen: If Madame Curie had not happened to leave a photographic plate in a drawer with a chunk of pitchblende, the world today would not know about radium."

"True, true," said Polly, nodding her head. "Did you see the movie? Oh, it just knocked me out. That Walter Pidgeon is so dreamy. I mean he fractures me."

"If you can forget Mr. Pidgeon for a moment," I said coldly, "I would like to point out that the statement is a fallacy. Maybe Madame Curie would have discovered radium at some later date. Maybe somebody else would have discovered it. Maybe any number of things would have happened. You can't start with a hypothesis that is not true and then draw any supportable conclusions from it."

"They ought to put Walter Pidgeon in more pictures," said Polly. "I hardly ever see him anymore." 110

One more chance, I decided. But just one more. There is a limit to what flesh and blood can bear. "The next fallacy is called Poisoning the Well."

"How cute!" she gurgled.

"Two men are having a debate. The first one gets up and says, 'My opponent is a notorious liar. You can't believe a word that he is going to say.' . . . Now, Polly, think. Think hard. What's wrong?"

I watched her closely as she knit her creamy brow in concentration. Suddenly a glimmer of intelligence — the first I had seen — came into her eyes. "It's not fair," she said with indignation. "It's not a bit fair. What chance has the second man got if the first man calls him a liar before he even begins talking?"

"Right!" I cried exultantly. "One hundred percent right. It's not fair. The first man has *poisoned the well* before anybody could drink from it. He has hamstrung his opponent before he could even start. . . . Polly, I'm proud of you." 115

"Pshaw," she murmured, blushing with pleasure.

"You see, my dear, these things aren't so hard. All you have to do is concentrate. Think — examine — evaluate. Come now, let's review everything we have learned."

"Fire away," she said with an airy wave of her hand.

Heartened by the knowledge that Polly was not altogether a cretin, I began a long, patient review of all I had told her. Over and over and over again I cited instances, pointed out flaws, kept hammering away without letup. It was like digging a tunnel. At first everything was work, sweat, and darkness. I had no idea when I would reach the light, or even *if* I would. But I persisted. I pounded and clawed and scraped, and finally I was rewarded. I saw a chink of light. And then the chink got bigger and the sun came pouring in and all was bright.

Five grueling nights this took, but it was worth it. I had made a logician out of Polly; I had taught her to think. My job was done. She was worthy of me at last. She was a fit wife for me, a proper hostess for my many mansions, a suitable mother for my well-heeled children. 120

It must not be thought that I was without love for this girl. Quite the contrary. Just as Pygmalion loved the perfect woman he had fashioned, so I loved mine. I decided to acquaint her with my feelings at our very next meeting. The time had come to change our relationship from academic to romantic.

"Polly," I said when next we sat beneath our oak, "tonight we will not discuss fallacies."

"Aw, gee," she said, disappointed.

"My dear," I said, favoring her with a smile, "we have now spent five evenings together. We have gotten along splendidly. It is clear that we are well matched."

"Hasty Generalization," said Polly brightly. 125

"I beg your pardon," said I.

"Hasty Generalization," she repeated. "How can you say that we are well matched on the basis of only five dates?"

I chuckled with amusement. The dear child had learned her lessons well. "My dear," I said, patting her hand in a tolerant manner, "five dates is plenty. After all, you don't have to eat a whole cake to know that it's good."

"False Analogy," said Polly promptly. "I'm not a cake. I'm a girl."

I chuckled with somewhat less amuse- 130 ment. The dear child had learned her lesson perhaps too well. I decided to change tactics. Obviously the best approach was a simple, strong, direct declaration of love. I paused for a moment while my massive brain chose the proper words. Then I began:

"Polly, I love you. You are the whole world to me, and the moon and the stars and the constellations of outer space. Please, my darling, say that you will go steady with me, for if you will not, life will be meaningless. I will languish. I will refuse my meals. I will wander the face of the earth, a shambling, hollow-eyed hulk."

There, I thought, folding my arms, that ought to do it.

"Ad Misericordiam," said Polly.

I ground my teeth. I was not Pygmalion; I was Frankenstein, and my monster had me by the throat. Frantically I fought back the tide of panic surging through me. At all costs I had to keep cool.

"Well, Polly," I said, forcing a smile, "you 135 certainly have learned your fallacies."

"You're darn right," she said with a vigorous nod.

"And who taught them to you, Polly?"

"You did."

"That's right. So you do owe me something, don't you, my dear? If I hadn't come along you never would have learned about fallacies."

"Hypothesis Contrary to Fact," she said 140 instantly.

I dashed perspiration from my brow. "Polly," I croaked, "you mustn't take all these things so literally. I mean this is just classroom stuff. You know that the things you learn in school don't have anything to do with life."

"Dicto Simpliciter," she said, wagging her finger at me playfully.

That did it. I leaped to my feet, bellowing like a bull. "Will you or will you not go steady with me?"

"I will not," she replied.

"Why not?" I demanded. 145

"Because this afternoon I promised Petey Bellows that I would go steady with him."

I reeled back, overcome with the infamy of it. After he promised, after he made a deal, after he shook my hand! "That rat!" I shrieked, kicking up great chunks of turf. "You can't go with him, Polly. He's a liar. He's a cheat. He's a rat."

"Poisoning the Well," said Polly, "and stop shouting. I think shouting must be a fallacy too."

With an immense effort of will, I modulated my voice. "All right," I said. "You're a logician. Let's look at this thing logically. How could you choose Petey Bellows over me? Look at me — a brilliant student, a tremendous intellectual, a man with an assured future. Look at Petey — a knothead, a jitterbug, a guy who'll never know where his next meal is coming from. Can you give me one logical reason why you should go steady with Petey Bellows?"

"I certainly can," declared Polly. "He's got a 150 raccoon coat."

Topic for Critical Thinking and Writing

After you have finished reading "Love Is a Fallacy," consider the following hypothetical conversation and then join the conversation: Write your own, final response that points out to these three peers how their arguments succeed or fail, using the elements of logic from this chapter (premises, conclusions, assumptions, fallacies, etc.). Finally, make your own argument about the nature of this story and how it bears on the question of sexism and publication.

CAITLYN: The story is condescending and even insulting to women. You could even call it sexist. Sexist stories should not be in college textbooks, and therefore this story should not have been published in this college textbook.

JOSHUA: This story may be sexist, but that is acceptable in the context of learning. Now if any story were racist, you would have a point about not including it in a textbook. But this story was written in 1951, and it wasn't considered sexist in its own time.

SAM: Max Shulman was a great humorist who worked in old-time television and invented the iconic character Dobie Gillis. The story is intended to be funny; therefore, it is not sexist. If anything, it should not be included in this textbook because it is not funny.

10

A Psychologist's View:
Rogerian Argument

Real communication occurs . . . when we listen with understanding. — CARL ROGERS

The first duty of a wise advocate is to convince his opponents that he understands their arguments, and sympathizes with their just feelings. — SAMUEL TAYLOR COLERIDGE

Rogerian Argument: An Introduction

Carl R. Rogers (1902–1987), perhaps best known for his book entitled *On Becoming a Person* (1961), was a psychotherapist, not a teacher of writing. Nonetheless, Rogers's approach to argument (put forth in the short essay by Rogers beginning on p. 366) has exerted much influence on instructors who teach argument.

On the surface, many arguments seem to show *A* arguing with *B*, presumably seeking to change *B*'s mind, but *A*'s argument is really directed not to *B* but to *C*. This attempt to persuade a nonparticipant is evident in the courtroom, where neither the prosecutor (*A*) nor the defense lawyer (*B*) is really trying to convince the opponent. Rather, both are trying to convince a third party, the jury (*C*). Prosecutors don't care whether they convince defense lawyers; they don't even mind infuriating defense lawyers because their only real goal is to convince the jury. Similarly, the writer of a letter to a newspaper, taking issue with an editorial, doesn't expect to change the paper's policy. Rather, the writer hopes to convince a third party, the reader of the newspaper.

Carl R. Rogers (second from the right) leading a panel discussion in 1966.

But suppose *A* really does want to bring *B* around to *A*'s point of view and suppose *B* is also arguing with *A*, too, trying to persuade *A* that his or her way is best. Politicians often argue with one another in just such ways. In such instances, both parties may be reluctant to listen to the other. Rogers points out that when we engage in an argument, if we feel our integrity or our identity is threatened, we will stiffen our position. The sense of threat may be so great that we are unable to consider the alternative views being offered, and we therefore remain unpersuaded. Threatened, we may defend ourselves rather than our argument, and little communication will take place. Of course, a third party might say that we or our opponent presented the more convincing case, but we, and perhaps the opponent, have scarcely listened to each other, and so the two of us remain apart.

Rogers therefore suggests that a writer who wishes to communicate with someone (as opposed to convincing a third party) needs to reduce the threat. In a sense, the participants in the argument need to become partners rather than adversaries. Rogers, a therapist, was keen to highlight **empathy**, the understanding of someone else's perspective or experiences, as a fundamental part of effective communication. But writers, like therapists, also must work toward understanding their partners in communication. That is achieved partially through an honest attempt to inhabit the psyche of the other, to see and feel the issues through the other's perspectives, in light of their perceptions and feelings. Instead of point–counterpoint argument, the goal is to foster emotional and intellectual reciprocity. Listeners are more willing to be persuaded when they see their partner in communication as an honest collaborator instead of an opponent. Rogers wrote, "Mutual communication tends to be pointed toward solving a problem rather than toward attacking a person or group."

Thus, in an essay on standardized testing, for instance, the writer need not — and probably should not — see the issue as black or white, as *either/or*. Such an essay might indicate that testing is undesirable because it has negative effects on students or teaching, *but in some circumstances* it may be seen as reasonable and acceptable. This qualification does not mean that one must compromise. Thus, the essayist might argue that high-stakes testing increases student

Visual Guide: Rogerian Argument

1 State the problem.

2 Give the opponent's position.

3 Grant whatever validity the writer finds in that position.

4 (If possible) Attempt to show how the opposing position will be improved if the writer's own position is accepted.

anxiety, constrains teachers, and devalues the arts, but may also recognize the value of the tests in ensuring educational consistency across public school systems.

A writer who wishes to reduce the psychological threat to the opposition and thus facilitate partnership in the study of some issue can do several things:

- show sympathetic understanding of the opposing argument
- recognize what is valid in it
- recognize and demonstrate that those who take the other side are nonetheless persons of goodwill

Advocates of Rogerian argument are likely to contrast it with Aristotelian argument, saying that the style of argument associated with Aristotle (384–322 BCE, Greek philosopher and rhetorician) has these two characteristics:

- It is adversarial, seeking to refute other views.
- It sees the listener as wrong, as someone who now must be overwhelmed by evidence.

> ## A CHECKLIST FOR ANALYZING ROGERIAN ARGUMENT
>
> ❏ Have I stated the problem and indicated that a dialogue is possible?
>
> ❏ Have I stated at least one other point of view in a way that would satisfy its proponents?
>
> ❏ Have I been courteous to those who hold views other than mine?
>
> ❏ Have I enlarged my own understanding to the extent that I can grant validity, at least in some circumstances, to at least some aspects of other positions?
>
> ❏ Have I stated my position and indicated the contexts in which I believe it is valid?
>
> ❏ Have I pointed out the ground that we share?
>
> ❏ Have I shown how other positions will be strengthened by accepting some aspects of my position?

In contrast to the confrontational Aristotelian style, which allegedly seeks to present an airtight case that compels belief, Rogerian argument (it is said) has the following characteristics:

- It is nonconfrontational, collegial, and friendly.
- It respects other views and allows for multiple truths.
- It seeks to achieve some degree of assent and empathy rather than convince utterly.

Sometimes, of course, the differing positions may be so far apart that no reconciliation can be proposed, in which case the writer will probably seek to show how the problem can best be solved by adopting the writer's own position. These matters are discussed in Chapter 6, but not from the point of view of a psychotherapist, and so we reprint Rogers's essay here.

CARL R. ROGERS

Carl R. Rogers (1902–1987), perhaps best known for his book *On Becoming a Person* (1961), was a psychotherapist. The following essay was originally presented on October 11, 1951, at Northwestern University's Centennial Conference on Communications. In it, Rogers reflects the political climate of the cold war between the United States and the Soviet Union, which dominated headlines for more than forty years (1947–1989). Several of Rogers's examples of bias and frustrated communication allude to the tensions of that era.

Communication: Its Blocking and Its Facilitation

It may seem curious that a person whose whole professional effort is devoted to psychotherapy should be interested in problems of communication. What relationship is there between providing therapeutic help to individuals with emotional maladjustments and the concern of this conference with obstacles to communication? Actually the relationship is very close indeed. The whole task of psychotherapy is the task of dealing with a failure in communication. The emotionally maladjusted person, the "neurotic," is in difficulty first because communication within himself has broken down, and second because as a result of this his communication with others has been damaged. If this sounds somewhat strange, then let me put it in other terms. In the "neurotic" individual, parts of himself which have been termed unconscious, or repressed, or denied to awareness, become blocked off so that they no longer communicate themselves to the conscious or managing part of himself. As long as this is true, there are distortions in the way he communicates himself to others, and so he suffers both within himself, and in his interpersonal relations. The task of psychotherapy is to help the person achieve, through a special relationship with a therapist, good communication within himself. Once this is achieved he can communicate more freely and more effectively with others. We may say then that

psychotherapy is good communication, within and between men. We may also turn that statement around and it will still be true. Good communication, free communication, within or between men, is always therapeutic.

It is, then, from a background of experience with communication in counseling and psychotherapy that I want to present here two ideas. I wish to state what I believe is one of the major factors in blocking or impeding communication, and then I wish to present what in our experience has proven to be a very important way to improving or facilitating communication.

I would like to propose, as an hypothesis for consideration, that the major barrier to mutual interpersonal communication is our very natural tendency to judge, to evaluate, to approve or disapprove, the statement of the person, or the other group. Let me illustrate my meaning with some very simple examples. As you leave the meeting tonight, one of the statements you are likely to hear is, "I didn't like that man's talk." Now what do you respond? Almost invariably your reply will be either approval or disapproval of the attitude expressed. Either you respond, "I didn't either. I thought it was terrible," or else you tend to reply, "Oh, I thought it was really good." In other words, your primary reaction is to evaluate what has just been said to you, to evaluate it from *your* point of view, your own frame of reference.

Or take another example. Suppose I say with some feeling, "I think the Republicans are behaving in ways that show a lot of good sound sense these days," what is the response that arises in your mind as you listen? The overwhelming likelihood is that it will be evaluative. You will find yourself agreeing, or disagreeing, or making some judgment about me such as "He must be a conservative," or "He seems solid in his thinking." Or let us take an illustration from the international scene. Russia says vehemently, "The treaty with Japan is a war plot on the part of the United States." We rise as one person to say "That's a lie!"

This last illustration brings in another element connected with my hypothesis. Although the tendency to make evaluations is common in almost all interchange of language, it is very much heightened in those situations where feelings and emotions are deeply involved. So the stronger our feelings, the more likely it is that there will be no mutual element in the communication. There will be just two ideas, two feelings, two judgments, missing each other in psychological space. I'm sure you recognize this from your own experience. When you have not been emotionally involved yourself, and have listened to a heated discussion, you often go away thinking, "Well, they actually weren't talking about the same thing." And they were not. Each was making a judgment, an evaluation, from his own frame of reference. There was really nothing which could be called communication in any genuine sense. This tendency to react to any emotionally meaningful statement by forming an evaluation of it from our own point of view, is, I repeat, the major barrier to interpersonal communication.

But is there any way of solving this problem, of avoiding this barrier? I feel that we are making exciting progress toward this goal and I would like to present it as simply as I can. Real communication occurs, and this evaluative tendency is avoided, when we listen with understanding. What does that mean? It means *to see the expressed idea and attitude from the other person's point of view, to sense how it feels to him, to achieve his frame of reference in regard to the thing he is talking about.*

Stated so briefly, this may sound absurdly simple, but it is not. It is an approach which we have found extremely potent in the field of psychotherapy. It is the most effective agent we know for altering the basic personality structure of an individual, and improving his relationships and his communications with others. If I can listen to what he can tell me, if I can understand how it seems to him, if I can see its personal meaning for him, if I can sense the emotional flavor which it has for him, then I will be releasing potent forces of change in him. If I can really understand how he hates his father, or hates the university, or hates communists — if I can catch the flavor of his fear of insanity, or his fear of atom bombs, or of Russia — it will be of the greatest help to him in altering those very hatreds and fears, and in establishing realistic and harmonious relationships with the very people and situations toward which he has felt hatred and fear. We know from our research that such empathic understanding — understanding *with* a person, not *about* him — is such an effective approach that it can bring about major changes in personality.

Some of you may be feeling that you listen well to people, and that you have never seen such results. The chances are very great indeed that your listening has not been of the type I have described. Fortunately I can suggest a little laboratory experiment which you can try to test the quality of your understanding. The next time you get into an argument with your wife, or your friend, or with a small group of friends, just stop the discussion for a moment and for an experiment, institute this rule. "Each person can speak up for himself only *after* he has first restated the ideas and feelings of the previous speaker accurately, and to that speaker's satisfaction." You see what this would mean. It would simply mean that before presenting your own point of view, it would be necessary for you to really achieve the other speaker's frame of reference — to understand his thoughts and feelings so well that you could summarize them for him. Sounds simple, doesn't it? But if you try it you will discover it one of the most difficult things you have ever tried to do. However, once you have been able to see the other's point of view, your own comments will have to be drastically revised. You will also find the emotion going out of the discussion, the differences being reduced, and those differences which remain being of a rational and understandable sort.

Can you imagine what this kind of an approach would mean if it were projected into larger areas? What would happen to a labor-management dispute if it was conducted in such a way that labor, without necessarily agreeing, could accurately state management's point of view in a way that management could accept; and management, without approving labor's stand, could state labor's case in a way that labor agreed was accurate? It would mean that real communication was established, and one could practically guarantee that some reasonable solution would be reached.

If then this way of approach is an effec- 10 tive avenue to good communication and good relationships, as I am quite sure you will agree if you try the experiment I have mentioned, why is it not more widely tried and used? I will try to list the difficulties which keep it from being utilized.

In the first place it takes courage, a quality which is not too widespread. I am indebted to Dr. S. I. Hayakawa, the semanticist, for pointing out that to carry on psychotherapy in this fashion is to take a very real risk, and that courage is required. If you really understand another person in this way, if you are willing to enter his private world and see the way life appears to him, without any attempt to make evaluative judgments, you run the risk of being changed yourself. You might see it his way, you might find yourself influenced in your attitudes or your personality. This risk of being changed is one of the most frightening prospects most of us can face. If I enter, as fully as I am able, into the private world of a neurotic or psychotic individual, isn't there a risk that I might become lost in that world? Most of us are afraid to take that risk. Or if we had a Russian communist speaker here tonight, or Senator Joe McCarthy, how many of us would dare to try to see the world from each of these points of view? The great majority of us could not *listen*; we would find ourselves compelled to *evaluate*, because listening would seem too dangerous. So the first requirement is courage, and we do not always have it.

But there is a second obstacle. It is just when emotions are strongest that it is most difficult to achieve the frame of reference of the other person or group. Yet it is the time the attitude is most needed, if communication is to be established. We have not found this to be an insuperable obstacle in our experience in psychotherapy. A third party, who is able to lay aside his own feelings and evaluations, can assist greatly by listening with understanding to each person or group and clarifying the views and attitudes each holds. We have found this very effective in small groups in which contradictory or antagonistic attitudes exist. When the parties to a dispute realize that they are being understood, that someone sees how the situation seems to them, the statements grow less exaggerated and less defensive, and it is no longer necessary to maintain the attitude, "I am 100 percent right and you are 100 percent wrong." The influence of such an understanding catalyst in the group permits the members to come closer and closer to the objective truth involved in the relationship. In this way mutual communication is established and some type of agreement becomes much more possible. So we may say that though heightened emotions make it much more difficult to understand *with* an opponent, our experience makes it clear that a neutral, understanding, catalyst type of leader or therapist can overcome this obstacle in a small group.

This last phrase, however, suggests another obstacle to utilizing the approach I have described. Thus far all our experience has been with small face-to-face groups — groups exhibiting industrial tensions, religious tensions, racial tensions, and therapy groups in which many personal tensions are present. In these small groups our experience, confirmed by a limited amount of research, shows that this basic approach leads to improved communication, to greater acceptance of others and by others, and to attitudes which are more positive and more problem-solving in nature. There is a decrease in defensiveness, in exaggerated statements, in evaluative and critical behavior. But these findings are from small groups. What about trying to achieve understanding between larger groups that are geographically remote? Or between face-to-face groups who are not speaking for themselves, but simply as representatives of others, like the delegates at Kaesong?[1] Frankly we do not know the answers to these questions. I believe the situation might be put this way. As social scientists we have a tentative test-tube solution of the problem of breakdown in communication. But to confirm the validity of this test-tube solution, and to adapt it to the enormous problems of communication breakdown between classes, groups, and nations, would involve additional funds, much more research, and creative thinking of a high order.

Even with our present limited knowledge we can see some steps which might be taken, even in large groups, to increase the amount of listening *with*, and to decrease the amount of evaluation *about*. To be imaginative for a moment, let us suppose that a therapeutically oriented international group went to the Russian leaders and said, "We want to achieve a genuine understanding of your views and even more important, of your attitudes and feelings, toward the United States. We will summarize and resummarize the views and feelings if necessary, until you agree that our description represents the situation as it seems to you." Then suppose they did the same thing with the leaders in our own country. If they then gave the widest possible distribution to these two views, with the feelings clearly described but not expressed in name-calling, might not the effect be very great? It would not guarantee the type of understanding I have been describing, but it would make it much more possible. We can understand the feelings of a person who hates us much more readily when his attitudes are accurately described to us by a neutral third party, than we can when he is shaking his fist at us.

But even to describe such a first step is to suggest another obstacle to this approach of understanding. Our civilization does not yet have enough faith in the social sciences to utilize their findings. The opposite is true of the physical sciences. During the war[2] when a test-tube solution was found to the problem of synthetic rubber, millions of dollars and an army of talent was turned loose on the problem of using that finding. If synthetic rubber could be made in milligrams, it could and would be made in the thousands of tons. And it was. But in the social science realm, if a way is found of facilitating communication and mutual understanding in small groups, there is no guarantee that the

15

---

[1] **the delegates at Kaesong** Representatives of North Korea and South Korea met at the border town of Kaesong to arrange terms for an armistice to hostilities during the Korean War (1950–1953). [Editors' note]

---

[2] **the war** World War II. [Editors' note]

finding will be utilized. It may be a generation or more before the money and the brains will be turned loose to exploit that finding.

In closing, I would like to summarize this small-scale solution to the problem of barriers in communication, and to point out certain of its characteristics.

I have said that our research and experience to date would make it appear that breakdowns in communication, and the evaluative tendency which is the major barrier to communication, can be avoided. The solution is provided by creating a situation in which each of the different parties come to understand the other from the *other's* point of view. This has been achieved, in practice, even when feelings run high, by the influence of a person who is willing to understand each point of view empathically, and who thus acts as a catalyst to precipitate further understanding.

This procedure has important characteristics. It can be initiated by one party, without waiting for the other to be ready. It can even be initiated by a neutral third person, providing he can gain a minimum of cooperation from one of the parties.

This procedure can deal with the insincerities, the defensive exaggerations, the lies, the "false fronts" which characterize almost every failure in communication. These defensive distortions drop away with astonishing speed as people find that the only intent is to understand, not judge.

This approach leads steadily and rapidly [20] toward the discovery of the truth, toward a realistic appraisal of the objective barriers to communication. The dropping of some defensiveness by one party leads to further dropping of defensiveness by the other party, and truth is thus approached.

This procedure gradually achieves mutual communication. Mutual communication tends to be pointed toward solving a problem rather than toward attacking a person or group. It leads to a situation in which I see how the problem appears to you, as well as to me, and you see how it appears to me, as well as to you. Thus accurately and realistically defined, the problem is almost certain to yield to intelligent attack, or if it is in part insoluble, it will be comfortably accepted as such.

This then appears to be a test-tube solution to the breakdown of communication as it occurs in small groups. Can we take this small-scale answer, investigate it further, refine it; develop it and apply it to the tragic and well-nigh fatal failures of communication which threaten the very existence of our modern world? It seems to me that this is a possibility and a challenge which we should explore.

Topics for Critical Thinking and Writing

1. What obstacles to effective argument does Carl R. Rogers outline in his essay? Consider that it was written in the 1950s. Are there any additional obstacles we face today? How might they be overcome through critical thinking and effective argument?

2. Rogers writes in paragraph 12 that it is "when emotions are strongest that it is most difficult to achieve the frame of reference of the other person or group." Select a current debate in the news and explain how strong emotions — about issues or in relation to particular factors — inhibit effective communication in that debate. Is each side equally emotional, or do emotions inhibit one side more than the other? How can one or the other side argue more effectively not by discounting the emotions of the other but expressing understanding?

3. List three additional debate topics with two generally opposing positions. Then identify potentially shared goals or outcomes among the two positions. (Use the Visual Guide on p. 364 as a model.) Reflect on the exercise: What challenges did you face following the Rogerian framework for argument? What do you think may help and hinder empathy between the two positions?

EDWARD O. WILSON

Edward O. Wilson, born in Birmingham, Alabama, in 1929, is an emeritus professor of evolutionary biology at Harvard University. A distinguished writer as well as a researcher and teacher, Wilson has twice won the Pulitzer Prize for General Non-Fiction. We reprint a piece first published in 2006 in Wilson's book *The Creation: An Appeal to Save Life on Earth*.

Letter to a Southern Baptist Minister

Dear Pastor:

We have not met, yet I feel I know you well enough to call you friend. First of all, we grew up in the same faith. As a boy I too answered the altar call; I went under the water. Although I no longer belong to that faith, I am confident that if we met and spoke privately of our deepest beliefs, it would be in a spirit of mutual respect and good will. I know we share many precepts of moral behavior. Perhaps it also matters that we are both Americans and, insofar as it might still affect civility and good manners, we are both Southerners.

I write to you now for your counsel and help. Of course, in doing so, I see no way to avoid the fundamental differences in our respective worldviews. You are a literalist interpreter of Christian Holy Scripture. You reject the conclusion of science that mankind evolved from lower forms. You believe that each person's soul is immortal, making this planet a way station to a second, eternal life. Salvation is assured those who are redeemed in Christ.

I am a secular humanist. I think existence is what we make of it as individuals. There is no guarantee of life after death, and heaven and hell are what we create for ourselves, on this planet. There is no other home. Humanity originated here by evolution from lower forms over millions of years. And yes, I will speak plain, our ancestors were apelike animals. The human species has adapted physically and mentally to life on Earth and no place else. Ethics is the code of behavior we share on the basis of reason, law, honor, and an inborn sense of decency, even as some ascribe it to God's will.

For you, the glory of an unseen divinity; for me, the glory of the universe revealed at last. For you, the belief in God made flesh to save mankind; for me, the belief in Promethean[1] fire seized to set men free. You have found your final truth; I am still searching. I may be wrong, you may be wrong. We may both be partly right.

Does this difference in worldview separate us in all things? It does not. You and I and every other human being strive for the same

---
[1] **Promethean** In Greek mythology, Prometheus was a Titan who looked after mankind, going so far as to steal fire from Mount Olympus to give it to humans. [Editors' note]

imperatives of security, freedom of choice, personal dignity, and a cause to believe in that is larger than ourselves.

Let us see, then, if we can, and you are willing, to meet on the near side of metaphysics in order to deal with the real world we share. I put it this way because you have the power to help solve a great problem about which I care deeply. I hope you have the same concern. I suggest that we set aside our differences in order to save the Creation. The defense of living Nature is a universal value. It doesn't rise from, nor does it promote, any religious or ideological dogma. Rather, it serves without discrimination the interests of all humanity.

Pastor, we need your help. The Creation — living Nature — is in deep trouble. Scientists estimate that if habitat conversion and other destructive human activities continue at their present rates, half the species of plants and animals on Earth could be either gone or at least fated for early extinction by the end of the century. A full quarter will drop to this level during the next half century as a result of climate change alone. The ongoing extinction rate is calculated in the most conservative estimates to be about a hundred times above that prevailing before humans appeared on Earth, and it is expected to rise to at least a thousand times greater or more in the next few decades. If this rise continues unabated, the cost to humanity, in wealth, environmental security, and quality of life, will be catastrophic.

Surely we can agree that each species, however inconspicuous and humble it may seem to us at this moment, is a masterpiece of biology, and well worth saving. Each species possesses a unique combination of genetic traits that fits it more or less precisely to a particular part of the environment. Prudence alone dictates that we act quickly to prevent the extinction of species and, with it, the pauperization of Earth's ecosystems — hence of the Creation.

You may well ask at this point, Why me? Because religion and science are the two most powerful forces in the world today, including especially the United States. If religion and science could be united on the common ground of biological conservation, the problem would soon be solved. If there is any moral precept shared by people of all beliefs, it is that we owe ourselves and future generations a beautiful, rich, and healthful environment.

I am puzzled that so many religious [10] leaders, who spiritually represent a large majority of people around the world, have hesitated to make protection of the Creation an important part of their magisterium.[2] Do they believe that human-centered ethics and preparation for the afterlife are the only things that matter? Even more perplexing is the widespread conviction among Christians that the Second Coming is imminent, and that therefore the condition of the planet is of little consequence. Sixty percent of Americans, according to a 2004 poll, believe that the prophecies of the book of Revelation are accurate. Many of these, numbering in the millions, think the End of Time will occur within the life span of those now living. Jesus will return to Earth, and those redeemed by Christian faith will be transported bodily to heaven, while those left behind will struggle through severe hard times and, when they die, suffer eternal damnation. The condemned will remain in hell, like those already consigned in the generations before them, for a trillion trillion years, enough for the universe to expand to its own, entropic

---

[2]**magisterium** The official teaching of the Roman Catholic Church. [Editors' note]

death, time enough for countless universes like it afterward to be born, expand, and likewise die away. And that is just the beginning of how long condemned souls will suffer in hell — all for a mistake they made in choice of religion during the infinitesimally small time they inhabited Earth.

For those who believe this form of Christianity, the fate of 10 million other life forms indeed does not matter. This and other similar doctrines are not gospels of hope and compassion. They are gospels of cruelty and despair. They were not born of the heart of Christianity. Pastor, tell me I am wrong!

However you will respond, let me here venture an alternative ethic. The great challenge of the twenty-first century is to raise people everywhere to a decent standard of living while preserving as much of the rest of life as possible. Science has provided this part of the argument for the ethic: the more we learn about the biosphere, the more complex and beautiful it turns out to be. Knowledge of it is a magic well: the more you draw from it, the more there is to draw. Earth, and especially the razor-thin film of life enveloping it, is our home, our wellspring, our physical and much of our spiritual sustenance.

I know that science and environmentalism are linked in the minds of many with evolution, Darwin, and secularism. Let me postpone disentangling all this (I will come back to it later) and stress again: to protect the beauty of Earth and of its prodigious variety of life forms should be a common goal, regardless of differences in our metaphysical beliefs.

To make the point in good Gospel manner, let me tell the story of a young man, newly trained for the ministry, and so fixed in his Christian faith that he referred all questions of morality to readings from the Bible. When he visited the cathedral-like Atlantic rainforest of Brazil, he saw the manifest hand of God and in his notebook wrote, "It is not possible to give an adequate idea of the higher feelings of wonder, admiration, and devotion which fill and elevate the mind."

That was Charles Darwin in 1832, early into the voyage of HMS *Beagle*, before he had given any thought to evolution.

And here is Darwin, concluding *On the Origin of Species* in 1859, having first abandoned Christian dogma and then, with his newfound intellectual freedom, formulated the theory of evolution by natural selection: "There is grandeur in this view of life, with its several powers, having been originally breathed into a few forms or into one; and that, whilst this planet has gone cycling on according to the fixed law of gravity, from so simple a beginning endless forms most beautiful and most wonderful have been, and are being, evolved."

Darwin's reverence for life remained the same as he crossed the seismic divide that divided his spiritual life. And so it can be for the divide that today separates scientific humanism from mainstream religion. And separates you and me.

You are well prepared to present the theological and moral arguments for saving the Creation. I am heartened by the movement growing within Christian denominations to support global conservation. The stream of thought has arisen from many sources, from evangelical to unitarian. Today it is but a rivulet. Tomorrow it will be a flood.

I already know much of the religious argument on behalf of the Creation, and would like to learn more. I will now lay before you and others who may wish to hear it the scientific argument. You will not agree with all that I say about the origins of life — science and religion do not easily mix in such matters — but I like to think that in this one life-and-death issue we have a common purpose.

Topics for Critical Thinking and Writing

1. Edward O. Wilson claims to be a "secular humanist" (para. 3). How would you define that term? Are you a secular humanist? Why, or why not?

2. What does Wilson mean by "metaphysics" (para. 6)? Which if any of his views qualify as metaphysical?

3. Wilson obviously seeks to present his views in a fashion that makes them as palatable as possible to his reader. Do you think he succeeds in this endeavor? Write an essay of about 500 words arguing for or against his achievement in this regard, pointing to instances in the text where he succeeds or fails.

11

A Literary Critic's View: Arguing about Literature

Literary criticism [is] a reasoned account of the feeling produced upon the critic by the book he is reading.
— D. H. LAWRENCE

A true classic ... is an author who has enriched the human mind, increased its treasure, and caused it to advance a step; who has discovered some moral and not equivocal truth, or revealed some eternal passion in that heart where all seemed known and discovered; who has expressed his thought, observation, or invention, in no matter what form, only provided it be broad and great, refined and sensible, sane and beautiful in itself; who has spoken to all in his own peculiar style, a style which is found to be also that of the whole world, a style new without neologism, new and old, easily contemporary with all time.
— CHARLES AUGUSTIN SAINTE-BEAUVE

Stories have been used to dispossess and to malign. But stories can also be used to empower, and to humanize. Stories can break the dignity of a people. But stories can also repair that broken dignity.
— CHIMAMANDA NGOZI ADICHIE

You might think that literature — fiction, poetry (including songs), drama — is meant only to be enjoyed, not to be argued about. Yet literature is constantly the subject of argumentative writing — not all of it by teachers of English. For instance, if you glance at the current issue of a local city newspaper or the *New Yorker*, you probably will find a review of a play suggesting that the play is worth seeing or is not worth seeing. In the same publication, you may find an article reporting that a senator or member of Congress argued that the National Endowment for the Arts insulted taxpayers by making an award to a writer who defamed the American family.

Probably most writing about literature, whether done by college students, professors, journalists, politicians, or whomever, is devoted to one or more of these goals: interpreting, judging (evaluating), or theorizing. Let's look at each of these, drawing our examples chiefly from comments about Shakespeare's *Macbeth*.

Interpreting

Interpreting literature in an argument is centrally a matter of setting forth the *meaning* (or meanings) of a work. However, the meaning of a work of literature is a complex question.

Take Shakespeare's tragedy *Macbeth* as an example of a work that has yielded many interpretations over time. Let's take two fairly simple and clearly opposed views:

> Macbeth is a villain who, by murdering his lawful king, offends God's rule, so he is overthrown by God's earthly instruments, Malcolm and Macduff. Macbeth is justly punished; the reader or spectator rejoices in his defeat.

> Macbeth is a hero-villain, a man who commits terrible crimes but who never completely loses the reader's sympathy; although he is justly punished, the reader believes that with the death of Macbeth the world has become a smaller place.

A writer *must* offer evidence in an essay that presents one of these theses or indeed presents any interpretation. For instance, to support the latter thesis, a writer might argue that although Macbeth's villainy is undeniable, his conscience never deserts him — here one would point to specific passages and would offer some brief quotations.

For many readers, a work of literature might appear to have meanings clearly intended by the writer. For others, the meanings might be latent in the text itself (whether or not intended by the author). So, we have two basic kinds of interpretation, one *author-centered* and one *text-centered*. Further, because individual readers experience texts in unique ways, we may add a third general category of interpretation, a *reader-centered* one.

Author-centered interpretation deals chiefly with the meanings intended by the author. Let's again take up our example of *Macbeth*, sometimes called "The Scottish Play." It is about a Scottish king, written by Shakespeare soon after a Scot — James VI of Scotland — had been installed as James I, King of England. One thing James did was announce that he would be the new sponsor of Shakespeare's Theater Company. If someone asked,

> Was Shakespeare paying homage to James I, his king and patron, in *Macbeth*?

he or she might seek evidence by exploring Shakespeare's relationship to James I and tracing allusions to the king apparent in *Macbeth*. For example, *Macbeth* is overflowing with biblical imagery, and King James was an avid reader and eventually the first translator of the Bible into English. Add to that the "two-fold balls and treble scepters" of James's double coronation, another allusion to the foiled Gunpowder Plot of 1607 to kill James, and the fact that the play was presented at James's court, and a convincing argument emerges that Shakespeare was indeed paying homage to James I in the play.

Author-centered arguments need not be strictly about the author's intentions. They may also be rooted in efforts to show the meaning of the work in the author's *milieu* — how it was read or how it impacted people (or a specific group of people) at the particular time of publication (or performance) regardless of the author's intentions. In such arguments, one might explore how specific themes of *Macbeth* — heredity, ambition, blood, power, and the supernatural — would have been interpreted by ordinary English audiences sharing with

Shakespeare the general worldview of the early seventeenth century and the particularities of life in England at the time. Or someone might ask,

> How would the portrayal of Banquo have been understood by members of James's court, where we know it was presented?

Author-centered arguments, in other words, may consider the author's intentions, or they may consider the time and place in which the author, text, and audience coexisted.

Text-centered interpretation usually focuses on "the text itself" as the primary source of meaning. For some critics, it is futile to attempt to discern an author's intentions and only marginally interesting to argue about what a text might have meant in its own time. What is more immediately important is how literature's formal elements — plot, characterization, language, symbols, setting, tension, ironies — combine to make its meanings. By performing **close reading**, one can discern and describe *how* literary texts produce powerful meanings. A text-centered interpretation of *Macbeth* might examine a certain set of metaphors to discover a theme in the play, asking questions such as:

> How do images of clothing (and nakedness) recur in the play to demonstrate the artificiality of social positions?
>
> How does blood appear in the play as a symbol of guilt?
>
> How are Macbeth, MacDuff, and Banquo similarly and differently characterized?

Arguments in this vein may be supported by prior interpretations, but in text-centered arguments, the text itself is often the primary source of evidence.

Reader-centered interpretations of literature concern the experience of reading itself, especially the ways in which a work becomes meaningful to an individual reader. From this perspective, the point of reading is not to discover biographical or historical meanings (author-centered) or to construct meanings thought to be inherent within the text itself (text-centered). Instead, the point is to pay attention to the reading experience as a means to discover the self — to understand oneself and one's own relationship to the world at large. In this view, literature can help people articulate their views on the world, clarify their own personal values, and connect to others. A reader-centered critic might ask,

> How does Macbeth relate to ambition in my own life and times?

Reader-centered interpretation does not always mean purely subjective interpretation; it may also concentrate on meanings that are relevant to particular groups of people. Thus, political interpretations, feminist readings, psychological approaches, and a range of cultural studies methodologies may be considered reader-focused. Such readings might focus on marginalized or oppressed groups evident (or absent) from texts or examine how ideologies are extended or suppressed through works of literature. One reader-centered argument might claim that Lady Macbeth — the devious schemer who convinces her husband to murder King Duncan and usurp the throne — presents a vision not of evil but of rebellion against gender norms. (At one point in the play, she asks the spirits to "unsex" her so she may gain the will to power.) Sometimes undermining or challenging previous interpretations with one's own idiosyncratic interpretation can be an empowering act. Reader-centered interpretation recognizes that meaning itself is not permanent or universal but changes according to reader, time, and place.

For most critics today, a work of literature has many meanings — the meaning it had for the writer and the audience, the meanings it has accumulated over time, and the meanings it has for today's diverse readers. In the end, the meaning of a work of literature involves readers, texts, and authors, all of which are important. Arguments about literature in this sense may be thought of as **intersectional**. Consider the reader-centered interpretation of Lady Macbeth above. To fully articulate the argument, it may be important to analyze the symbolic power of blood, motherhood, and heredity in the play (a text-centered approach) and also to attempt to understand Elizabethan values about the proper roles of women (an author-centered approach).

Judging (or Evaluating)

Evaluative arguments about literature are primarily concerned with the value of a work: Is *Macbeth* a great tragedy? Is *Macbeth* a greater tragedy than *Romeo and Juliet*? What is the importance of *Macbeth*? Does *Macbeth* contribute positively to our understanding of the nature and limits of ambition? As with any thesis statement, if a writer judges the worth of a play, the claim must be supported by an argument and expressed in sentences that offer supporting evidence.

Let's pause for a moment to think about evaluation in general. When we say "This is a great play," are we in effect saying only "I like this play"? That is, are we merely *expressing* our taste rather than *asserting* something independent of our tastes and feelings? On the other hand, a statement such as "I like the New York Yankees" is not an argument that requires justification — it is merely an opinion. However, statements such as "The New York Yankees are the best team in the league" or "The Yankees are the most important franchise in Major League Baseball" would require an argument and evidence.

Now consider another statement, "This is a really good book." It is entirely reasonable for someone to ask you *why* you say that. You might answer with any one of the following:

- "Well, the author really captured the tensions of a rapidly transforming society." (author-centered)
- "The characters are realistically portrayed, and the plot is dramatic with a gripping climax." (text-centered)
- "I really gained insights into the question of betrayal, which is important to me because I was once betrayed and now I can see how forgiveness is the only path." (reader-centered)

Even when we are *evaluating*, we are also often *interpreting* in various modes at the same time. The key in judging or evaluating the worth of a work of literature, then, is to state as clearly as possible what kind of **criteria** you are using, such as

- the skill or motivation of the author
- the innovation, uniqueness, or originality of the work
- the faithfulness of the work in its depiction of *X*
- the importance, status, or durability of the work
- the degree to which the work helps people understand themselves or another group better
- the artistic quality in terms of the work's structure, balance, coherence, unity, or use of other literary devices (characterizations, settings, dialogue, etc.)

At the very least, we should show *why* we evaluate the work as we do and suggest that if readers try to see it from our point of view, they may then accept our evaluation.

Evaluations are always based on assumptions, although these assumptions may be unstated; in fact, the writer may even be unaware of them. For instance, what does it mean to be a "skillful" author? Is "originality" a good thing in and of itself? Is the "faithfulness" of a literary depiction dependent upon a realistic description of a time and place, or can abstraction or impressionism also do the job? Can a work of literature be awful but important or be excellent but insignificant? As usual with arguments, the more you define your criteria (and the reasons you use those criteria), the more convincing you may be.

Some common ideas about art often play the role of criteria in literary judgments.

1. A good work of art, even when fictional, says something about real life. If you believe that art is a means by which people connect themselves to enduring human ideas and values, or to society at large, you bring to your evaluation of art an assumption that a good work of art reflects reality (or even impacts it) in some meaningful way. If you hold the view that human beings encounter fairly common experiences and behave in fairly consistent ways — that is, that each of us has an enduring "character" — you probably will judge as inferior a work in which the plot is implausible or one in which characters are inconsistent or inadequately motivated. The novelist Henry James said, "You will not write a good novel unless you possess the sense of reality."

However, there are plenty of arguments to be made for the worth of artworks that do not reflect reality in the usual or expected ways. Some kinds of literary expression are not intended to *say* anything at all (in and of themselves, at least). Consider the poetic form haiku or this imagistic piece by the Japanese poet Matsuo Bashō (1644–1694):

An old pond
Leap, splash
A frog.

This poem, like a haiku, presents an image only and tells us little to nothing about how to interpret it. Experimental fiction and poetry, absurdist drama, and other forms often challenge us to reconceive our ideas about the role and goal of literature. Can a story be successful or good if it offers two or more different endings? Should supernatural events occur in otherwise true-to-life plots? We do not have the answers, but we think the questions are worth pondering.

    2. *A good work of art is complex yet unified.* One of the staples of literary criticism is the idea that a successful work of art exhibits a unified, complex whole constructed out of carefully arranged elements. In many ways, today's audiences continue to value those works in which structure, character, setting, irony, paradox, language, symbol, plot — indeed any of the imaginable literary devices — all work together in meaningful, interconnected ways. *Macbeth* is a good work of art, one might argue, partly because it shows us so many aspects of

A seventeenth-century artist's interpretation of Macbeth's murder of King Duncan.

life (courage, fear, loyalty, treachery, for a start) through richly varied language (the diction ranges from a grand passage in which Macbeth says that his bloody hands will "incarnadine," or make red, "the multitudinous seas" to colloquial passages such as the drunken porter's "Knock, knock"). The play shows the heroic Macbeth tragically destroying his own life through villainy, and it shows the comic porter making coarse jokes about deceit and damnation, jokes that (although the porter doesn't know it) connect with Macbeth's crimes. A work may be considered complex yet unified when it contains a rich and multivalent symbolic structure in which all the parts contribute to the complexity of the whole.

    Of course, wholeness itself is also an aspect of successful art explicitly challenged by some artists and critics. In the twentieth century, "fragmented" texts were deliberately constructed by some authors to defy the principle of wholeness: James Joyce's *Finnegan's Wake*, for example, contains this indicative passage:

> The great fall of the offwall entailed at such short notice the pftjschute of Finnegan, erse solid man, that the humptyhillhead of humself prumptly sends an unquiring one well to the west in quest of his tumptytumtoes: and their upturapikepointandplace is at the knock out in the park where oranges have been laid to rust upon the green since dev-linsfirst loved livvy.

Joyce's language reflects the basically random, nonlinear, and episodic nature of experience — all mixed in with inner monologues, daydreams, puns, and breakdowns of language that defy any

Print Collector/Getty Images

sense of coherence in the mind or art. Today, authors readily combine genres, mix historical fiction and nonfiction, create plots that go nowhere, or include other unaccustomed elements such as stream of consciousness, shifting narrators, or multiple endings that disrupt the ideal of unity in literature.

3. *A good work of art sets forth a wholesome view of life.* The general public widely believes that a work should be judged partly or largely on the moral view that it sets forth. (Esteemed philosophers, notably Plato, have felt the same way.) Thus, a story that demeans women — perhaps one that takes a casual view of sexual assault — would be held in low estimation, as would a play that treats a mass murderer as a hero.

Implicit in this approach is what is called an *instrumentalist* view — the idea that a work of art is an instrument, a means, to some higher value. Thus, many people hold that reading great works of literature makes us better — or at least does not make us worse. In this view, a work that is pornographic or in some other way considered immoral will be devalued.

Moral judgments, of course, must be considered very carefully in arguments about the quality of art or literature. Historically, platitudes about what is decent and good have led in some instances to censorship. Changing values have also transformed the ways artists have been regarded and how artworks have been interpreted. Edgar Allan Poe, a pioneer of the horror genre and now a celebrated American author, was castigated in his own time for moral shortcomings in his life and stories. Walt Whitman's landmark poem *Leaves of Grass* (1855), one of the most influential works of American literature, was accused by one critic in *Criterion* magazine as exhibiting "a degrading, beastly sensuality that is fast rotting the health core of all social virtues." Finally, Kate Chopin, a southern realist — whose short story "The Story of an Hour" appears in this chapter — had her career ruined by critics who deemed her 1899 novel *The Awakening* "immoral" for its depiction of a married woman's sexuality and her transgression of gender norms. Even today, arguments about the ways in which art may instruct or corrupt audiences remain at the heart of cultural debates. For instance, current law requires the National Endowment for the Arts to take into account standards of decency when making awards.

4. *A good work of art is original.* The assumption that a good work of art is original puts special value on new techniques and new subject matter in art. If a writer employs a new or innovative way to structure a novel, for instance, he or she might get a kind of critical extra credit. Nicholson Baker's novel *The Mezzanine* (1988), for example, takes place over the course of a character's single trip up an escalator — a digressive exploration of the spectacular array of thoughts that occur in the mind of a person in just a few short moments. New kinds of characters and story lines tend to be valued, as do new ways of representing reality in literature, such as techniques that help represent email, text messaging, and tweeting. Sometimes, the *first* text to introduce a new subject (say, AIDS) gets that critical extra credit, so to speak, for opening a needed conversation or debate. Or returning to Shakespeare, consider that one sign of his genius, it is held, is that he was so highly varied — none of his tragedies seems merely to duplicate another;

each is a world of its own, a new kind of achievement. (Compare, for instance, *Romeo and Juliet*, with its two youthful and innocent heroes, with *Macbeth*, with its deeply guilty hero.)

Of course, just because a work is new or innovative may not reflect qualitatively on it. A full-length novel written entirely through tweets might be a neat idea or a somewhat interesting concept, but it need not signal genius. Newness or originality, that is, is not necessarily synonymous with excellence.

5. *A good work of art is important.* When we consider if a piece of art deals with an important subject, we are often concerned with themes: Great works, in this view, must deal with great themes. Love, death, patriotism, and God, say, are great themes; a work that deals with these subjects may achieve a height, an excellence, that, say, a work describing a dog scratching for fleas may not achieve. (Of course, if the reader believes that the dog is a symbol of humanity plagued by invisible enemies, the poem about the dog may reach the heights; but then, too, it is *not* a poem about a dog and fleas: It is really a poem about humanity and the invisible.)

Another way to construe the importance of a work of literature is to regard it as a social or political object. Works of literature commonly derive their importance by being relevant to public beliefs and attitudes. Some may be important to specific communities. Some may help mark in public memory the meaning of historical events. In this sense, a work's importance is found in its ability to reflect (and reproduce) culture.

The point is that in writing an evaluation, you must let the reader know *why* you value the work as you do. Obviously, it is not enough just to keep saying that *this* work is great whereas *that* work is not so great; the reader wants to know *why* you offer the judgments you do, which means that you must

- set forth your criteria and then
- offer evidence that is in accord with them.

Theorizing

Another kind of argument about literature is more theoretical; as such, it is more of a metacognitive discourse, one that attempts to understand and define the very nature of literary expression and interpretation. Some literary criticism is concerned with such theoretical questions as these:

- What is tragedy? Can the hero be a villain? How does tragedy differ from melodrama?
- Why do tragedies — works showing good or at least interesting people destroyed — give us pleasure?
- How did the detective genre develop over time, and how is it different in different places and times?

Other kinds of criticism might explore theories about the value of literature and ask questions such as these:

- Are classic works of Western literature great because they contain great wisdom or beauty, or are they great because they have been privileged over time?
- Can a work of art really be said to offer anything that can be called "truth"?
- Does a work of art have meaning in itself, or is the meaning simply whatever anyone wishes to say it is?

Yet again, one hopes that anyone asserting a thesis concerned with any of these topics will offer evidence — will, indeed, *argue* rather than merely assert.

A CHECKLIST FOR ARGUING ABOUT LITERATURE

❏ Can I identify if my argument is primarily author-centered, text-centered, or reader-centered?

❏ Can I determine whether my thesis is based on interpreting, judging, or theorizing about the work of literature at hand (or whether it is some combination of the three)?

❏ Do I have a good reason to make my reader interested in hearing my point of view about a work?

❏ Is my essay supported with evidence from the text itself?

❏ If I am using sources such as interpretations written by others or other contextual material, am I integrating them well to support my argument?

Examples: Two Students Interpret Robert Frost's "Mending Wall"

Let's consider two competing interpretations of a poem, Robert Frost's "Mending Wall." We say "competing" because these interpretations clash head-on. Differing interpretations need not be incompatible, of course. For instance, a historical interpretation of *Macbeth*, arguing that an understanding of the context of English–Scottish politics around 1605 helps us appreciate the play, need not be incompatible with a psychoanalytic interpretation that tells us that Macbeth's murder of King Duncan is rooted in an Oedipus complex, the king being a father figure. Different approaches thus can illuminate different aspects of the work, just as they can emphasize or subordinate different elements in the plot or characters portrayed. But, again, in the next few pages we will deal with mutually incompatible interpretations of the meaning of Frost's poem.

After reading the poem and the two interpretations written by students, spend a few minutes thinking about the questions that we raise after the second interpretation.

ROBERT FROST

Robert Frost (1874–1963) studied for part of one term at Dartmouth College in New Hampshire, then did odd jobs (including teaching), and from 1897 to 1899 was enrolled as a special student at Harvard. He then farmed in New Hampshire, published a few poems in newspapers, did some more teaching, and in 1912 left for England, where he hoped to achieve success as a writer. By 1915, he was known in England, and he returned to the United States. By the time of his death, he was the nation's unofficial poet laureate. "Mending Wall" was first published in 1914.

Mending Wall

Something there is that doesn't love a wall,
That sends the frozen-ground-swell under it,
And spills the upper boulders in the sun;
And makes gaps even two can pass abreast.
The work of hunters is another thing: 5
I have come after them and made repair
Where they have left not one stone on a stone,
But they would have the rabbit out of hiding,
To please the yelping dogs. The gaps I mean,
No one has seen them made or heard them   10
    made,
But at spring mending-time we find them there.
I let my neighbor know beyond the hill;
And on a day we meet to walk the line
And set the wall between us once again.
We keep the wall between us as we go.   15
To each the boulders that have fallen to each.
And some are loaves and some so nearly balls
We have to use a spell to make them balance:
"Stay where you are until our backs are turned!"
We wear our fingers rough with handling them.   20
Oh, just another kind of outdoor game,
One on a side. It comes to little more:
There where it is we do not need the wall:
He is all pine and I am apple orchard.

My apple trees will never get across   25
And eat the cones under his pines, I tell him.
He only says, "Good fences make good
    neighbors."
Spring is the mischief in me, and I wonder
If I could put a notion in his head:
"*Why* do they make good neighbors? Isn't it   30
Where there are cows? But here there are
    no cows.
Before I built a wall I'd ask to know
What I was walling in or walling out,
And to whom I was like to give offense.
Something there is that doesn't love a wall,   35
That wants it down." I could say "Elves" to him,
But it's not elves exactly, and I'd rather
He said it for himself. I see him there
Bringing a stone grasped firmly by the top
In each hand, like an old-stone savage armed.   40
He moves in darkness as it seems to me,
Not of woods only and the shade of trees.
He will not go behind his father's saying,
And he likes having thought of it so well
He says again, "Good fences make good   45
    neighbors."

Jonathan Deutsch
Professor Walton
English 102
5 March 2016

The Deluded Speaker in Frost's "Mending Wall"

Our discussions of "Mending Wall" in high school showed that most people think Frost is saying that walls between people are a bad thing and that we should not try to separate ourselves from each other unnecessarily. Perhaps the wall, in this view, is a symbol for race prejudice or religious differences, and Frost is suggesting that these differences are minor and that they should not keep us apart. In this common view, the neighbor's words, "Good fences make good neighbors" (lines 27 and 45), show that the neighbor is shortsighted. I disagree with this view, but first I want to present the evidence that might be offered for it, so that we can then see whether it really is substantial.

First of all, someone might claim that in lines 23 to 26 Frost offers a good argument against walls:

> There where it is we do not need the wall:
> He is all pine and I am apple orchard.
> My apple trees will never get across
> And eat the cones under his pines, I tell him.

The neighbor does not offer a valid reply to this argument; in fact, he doesn't offer any argument at all but simply says, "Good fences make good neighbors."

Another piece of evidence supposedly showing that the neighbor is wrong, it is said, is found in Frost's description of him as "an old-stone savage" and someone who "moves in darkness" (40, 41). And a third piece of evidence is said to be that the neighbor "will not go behind his father's saying" (43), but he merely repeats the saying.

There is, however, another way of looking at the poem. As I see it, the speaker is a very snide and condescending person. He is confident that he

Indication of an author-centered approach.

Thesis and preliminary map of essay.

Textual evidence presented as opposition to the writer's view.

Writer examines language closely to criticize the speaker of the poem.

knows it all and that his neighbor is an ignorant savage; he is even willing to tease his supposedly ignorant neighbor. For instance, the speaker admits to "the mischief in me" (28), and he is confident that he could tell the truth to the neighbor but arrogantly thinks that it would be a more effective form of teaching if the neighbor "said it for himself" (38).

The speaker is not only unpleasantly mischievous and condescending toward his neighbor, but he is also shallow, for he does not see the great wisdom that there is in proverbs. The *American Heritage Dictionary of the English Language*, Third Edition, defines a proverb as "A short, pithy saying in frequent and widespread use that expresses a basic truth." Frost, or at least the man who speaks this poem, does not seem to realize that proverbs express truths. He just dismisses them, and he thinks the neighbor is wrong not to "go behind his father's saying" (43). But there is a great deal of wisdom in the sayings of our fathers. For instance, in the Bible (in the Old Testament) there is a whole book of proverbs, filled with wise sayings such as "Reprove not a scorner, lest he hate thee: rebuke a wise man, and he will love thee" (9:8); "He that trusteth in his riches shall fall" (11:28); "The way of a fool is right in his own eyes" (12:15; this might be said of the speaker of "Mending Wall"); "A soft answer turneth away wrath" (15:1); and (to cut short what could be a list many pages long), "Whoso diggeth a pit shall fall therein" (26:27).

The speaker is confident that walls are unnecessary and probably bad, but he doesn't realize that even where there are no cattle, walls serve the valuable purpose of clearly marking out our territory. They help us to preserve our independence and our individuality. Walls — manmade structures — are a sign of civilization. A wall more or less says, "*This* is mine, but I respect *that* as yours." Frost's speaker is so confident of his shallow view that he makes fun of his neighbor for repeating that "Good fences make good neighbors" (27, 45). But he himself repeats his own saying, "Something there is that doesn't love a wall" (1, 35). And at least the neighbor has age-old tradition on his side, since the proverb is the

Writer treads the line between author-centered and text-centered interpretation. It is not clear that the writer thinks Frost intended to characterize the speaker of the poem in this way.

Author reinterprets the phrases of the neighbor not as simple or archaic but as time-tested and the speaker's ideas as vague.

saying of his father. In contrast, the speaker has only his own opinion, and he can't even say what the "something" is.

It may be that Frost meant for us to laugh at the neighbor and to take the side of the speaker, but I think it is much more likely that he meant for us to see that the speaker is mean-spirited (or at least given to unpleasant teasing), too self-confident, foolishly dismissing the wisdom of the old times, and entirely unaware that he has these unpleasant characteristics.

Felicia Alonso

Professor Walton

English 102

5 March 2016

The Debate in Robert Frost's "Mending Wall"

I think the first thing to say about Frost's "Mending Wall" is this: The poem is not about a debate over whether good fences do or do not make good neighbors. It is about two debaters: one of the debaters is on the side of vitality, and the other is on the side of an unchanging, fixed—dead, we might say—tradition.

How can we characterize the speaker? For one thing, he is neighborly. Interestingly, it is *he*, and not the neighbor, who initiates the repairing of the wall: "I let my neighbor know beyond the hill" (line 12). This seems strange, since the speaker doesn't see any point in this wall, whereas the neighbor is all in favor of walls. Can we explain this apparent contradiction? Yes; the speaker is a good neighbor, willing to do his share of the work and willing (perhaps in order not to upset his neighbor) to maintain an old tradition even though he doesn't see its importance. It may not be important, he thinks, but it is really rather pleasant, "another kind of outdoor game" (21). In fact, sometimes he even repairs fences on his own, after hunters have destroyed them.

Second, we can say that the speaker is on the side of nature. "Something there is that doesn't love a wall," he says (1, 35), and of course, the "something" is nature itself. Nature "sends the frozen-ground-swell" under the wall and "spills the upper boulders in the sun; / And makes gaps even two can pass abreast" (2–4). Notice that nature itself makes the gaps and that "two can pass abreast"—that is, people can walk together in a companionable way. It is hard to imagine the neighbor walking side by side with anyone.

Third, we can say that the speaker has a sense of humor. When he thinks of trying to get his neighbor interested in the issue, he admits that "the mischief" is in him (28), and he amusingly attributes his

---

Text-based approach.

Writer uses textual evidence to show irony: despite being against walls, the speaker is willing to play this outdoor game.

Writer continues to offer a positive reading of the speaker by associating him with nature.

playfulness to a natural force, the spring. He playfully toys with the obviously preposterous idea of suggesting to his neighbor that elves caused the stones to fall, but he stops short of making this amusing suggestion to his very serious neighbor. Still, the mere thought assures us that he has a playful, genial nature, and the idea also again implies that not only the speaker but also some sort of mysterious natural force dislikes walls.

Finally, though, of course, he thinks he is right and that his neighbor is mistaken, he at least is cautious in his view. He does not call his neighbor "an old-stone savage" (40); rather, he uses a simile ("like") and then adds that this is only his opinion, so the opinion is softened quite a bit. Here is the description of the neighbor, with italics added to clarify my point. The neighbor is . . .

> *like* an old-stone savage armed.
> He moves in darkness *as it seems to me* . . . (40–41)

Of course, the only things we know about the neighbor are those things that the speaker chooses to tell us, so it is not surprising that the speaker comes out ahead. He comes out ahead not because he is right about walls (real or symbolic) and his neighbor is wrong — that's an issue that is not settled in the poem. He comes out ahead because he is a more interesting figure, someone who is neighborly, thoughtful, playful. Yes, maybe he seems to us to feel superior to his neighbor, but we can be certain that he doesn't cause his neighbor any embarrassment. Take the very end of the poem. The speaker tells us that the neighbor

> . . . will not go behind his father's saying,
> And he likes having thought of it so well
> He says again, "Good fences make good neighbors."

The speaker is telling *us* that the neighbor is utterly unoriginal and that the neighbor confuses *remembering* something with *thinking*. But the speaker doesn't get into an argument; he doesn't rudely challenge his

Writer examines language very closely to derive the meaning of what might first be taken as insulting.

neighbor and demand reasons, which might force the neighbor to see that he can't think for himself. And in fact we probably like the neighbor just as he is, and we don't want him to change his mind. The words that ring in our ears are not the speaker's but the neighbor's: "Good fences make good neighbors." The speaker of the poem is a good neighbor. After all, one can hardly be more neighborly than to let the neighbor have the last word.

Reading a Poem and a Story

RICHARD BLANCO

Richard Blanco (b. 1968) is a native-born Cuban who emigrated to the United States with his family as an infant. A 1991 graduate of Florida International University, Blanco worked as an engineer in Miami before returning to that university to pursue poetry, earning his MFA in 1997. His first collection of poems, *City of a Hundred Fires* (1998), won the Agnes Lynch Starret Poetry Prize from the University of Pittsburgh, and his later efforts, *Directions to the Beach of the Dead* (2005) and *Looking for the Gulf Motel* (2012), earned him international recognition. Blanco's recent work includes a critically acclaimed memoir, *The Prince of Los Cocuyos: A Miami Childhood* (2014), and his latest collection of poems, *How to Love a Country* (2019). In 2012, President Barack Obama invited Blanco to become the fifth presidential inaugural poet, the first Latino, immigrant, and openly gay person in that role. On January 21, 2013, Blanco read "One Today," a poem written for that inauguration and reprinted here.

One Today

One sun rose on us today, kindled over our
    shores,
peeking over the Smokies, greeting the faces
of the Great Lakes, spreading a simple truth
across the Great Plains, then charging across
    the Rockies.
One light, waking up rooftops, under each   5
    one, a story
told by our silent gestures moving behind
    windows.

My face, your face, millions of faces in morn-
    ing's mirrors,
each one yawning to life, crescendoing into
    our day:
pencil-yellow school buses, the rhythm of traf-
    fic lights,
fruit stands: apples, limes, and oranges arrayed   10
    like rainbows
begging our praise. Silver trucks heavy with
    oil or paper — bricks or milk, teeming over
    highways alongside us,

on our way to clean tables, read ledgers, or save
    lives —
to teach geometry, or ring up groceries, as my
    mother did
for 20 years, so I could write this poem.   15

All of us as vital as the one light we move through,
the same light on blackboards with lessons for
    the day:
equations to solve, history to question, or
    atoms imagined,
the "I have a dream" we keep dreaming,
or the impossible vocabulary of sorrow that   20
    won't explain
the empty desks of 20 children marked absent°
today, and forever. Many prayers, but one light
breathing color into stained glass windows,
life into the faces of bronze statues, warmth

---

[21]**empty desks of 20 children** Reference to the December 14, 2012, Sandy Hook Elementary School massacre in Newtown, Connecticut.

onto the steps of our museums and park 25
    benches
as mothers watch children slide into the day.

One ground. Our ground, rooting us to
    every stalk
of corn, every head of wheat sown by sweat
and hands, hands gleaning coal or planting
    windmills
in deserts and hilltops that keep us warm, 30
    hands
digging trenches, routing pipes and cables,
    hands
as worn as my father's cutting sugarcane
so my brother and I could have books and
    shoes.

The dust of farms and deserts, cities and
    plains
mingled by one wind — our breath. Breathe. 35
    Hear it
through the day's gorgeous din of honking cabs,
buses launching down avenues, the symphony
of footsteps, guitars, and screeching subways,
the unexpected song bird on your clothes line.

Hear: squeaky playground swings, trains 40
    whistling,
or whispers across cafe tables, Hear: the
    doors we open
for each other all day, saying: hello, shalom,
buon giorno, howdy, namaste, or buenos días
in the language my mother taught me — in
    every language
spoken into one wind carrying our lives   45
without prejudice, as these words break
    from my lips.

One sky: since the Appalachians and Sierras
    claimed

their majesty, and the Mississippi and Colorado
    worked
their way to the sea. Thank the work of our
    hands:
weaving steel into bridges, finishing one more 50
    report
for the boss on time, stitching another wound
or uniform, the first brush stroke on a
    portrait,
or the last floor on the Freedom Tower°
jutting into a sky that yields to our resilience.

One sky, toward which we sometimes lift our 55
    eyes
tired from work: some days guessing at the
    weather
of our lives, some days giving thanks for
    a love
that loves you back, sometimes praising a
    mother
who knew how to give, or forgiving a father
who couldn't give what you wanted.   60

We head home: through the gloss of rain or
    weight
of snow, or the plum blush of dusk, but
    always — home,
always under one sky, our sky. And always
    one moon
like a silent drum tapping on every rooftop
and every window, of one country — all 65
    of us —
facing the stars
hope — a new constellation
waiting for us to map it,
waiting for us to name it — together

---

[53]**Freedom Tower** The main building of the rebuilt World
Trade Center in New York City, completed in 2013.

Topics for Critical Thinking and Writing

1. The word *one* appears in the title and throughout the poem. What do you think Richard Blanco was trying to accomplish with repetition of this word? Explain your answer.

2. This poem was written on the occasion of Barack Obama's second inauguration; it was read aloud by Blanco and broadcast nationally during the ceremony. (Find the clip on YouTube and watch it if you can.) How do you think these facts affect the meaning of the poem? What do you think Blanco intended to convey?

3. How do colors and sounds work in the poem to support its meanings?

4. What does time signify, and how is it captured in the poem?

5. What twenty-first-century events are important to understanding this poem? Are there events outside the text (i.e., not mentioned directly) that inform the ways audiences would understand it at the time of its recitation and publication?

6. In your opinion, is the poem overly optimistic? Explain your answer in about 500 words.

7. Blanco identifies as a gay male Latino immigrant. Do you think these biographical facts assist in deciphering the meaning of the poem, or are they irrelevant?

KATE CHOPIN

Kate Chopin (1851–1904) was born in St. Louis and named Katherine O'Flaherty. At the age of nineteen she married a cotton broker in New Orleans, Oscar Chopin (the name is pronounced something like "show pan"), who was descended from the early French settlers in Louisiana. After her husband's death in 1883, Kate Chopin turned to writing fiction. The following story was first published in 1894.

The Story of an Hour

Knowing that Mrs. Mallard was afflicted with a heart trouble, great care was taken to break to her as gently as possible the news of her husband's death.

It was her sister Josephine who told her, in broken sentences, veiled hints that revealed in half concealing. Her husband's friend Richards was there, too, near her. It was he who had been in the newspaper office when intelligence of the railroad disaster was received, with Brently Mallard's name leading the list of "killed." He had only taken the time to assure himself of its truth by a second telegram, and had hastened to forestall any less careful, less tender friend in bearing the sad message.

She did not hear the story as many women have heard the same, with a paralyzed inability to accept its significance. She wept at once, with sudden, wild abandonment, in her sister's arms. When the storm of grief had spent itself she went away to her room alone. She would have no one follow her.

There stood, facing the open window, a comfortable, roomy armchair. Into this she sank, pressed down by a physical exhaustion that haunted her body and seemed to reach into her soul.

She could see in the open square before 5 her house the tops of trees that were all aquiver with the new spring life. The delicious breath of rain was in the air. In the street below a peddler was crying his wares. The notes of a distant song which some one was singing reached her faintly, and countless sparrows were twittering in the eaves.

There were patches of blue sky showing here and there through the clouds that had met and piled one above the other in the west facing her window.

She sat with her head thrown back upon the cushion of the chair, quite motionless, except when a sob came up into her throat and shook her, as a child who has cried itself to sleep continues to sob in its dreams.

She was young, with a fair, calm face, whose lines bespoke repression and even a certain strength. But now there was a dull stare in her eyes, whose gaze was fixed away off yonder on one of those patches of blue sky. It was not a glance of reflection, but rather indicated a suspension of intelligent thought.

There was something coming to her and she was waiting for it, fearfully. What was it? She did not know; it was too subtle and elusive to name. But she felt it, creeping out of the sky, reaching toward her through the sounds, the scents, the color that filled the air.

Now her bosom rose and fell tumultu- 10 ously. She was beginning to recognize this thing that was approaching to possess her, and she was striving to beat it back with her will — as powerless as her two white slender hands would have been.

When she abandoned herself a little whispered word escaped her slightly parted lips. She said it over and over under her breath: "Free, free, free!" The vacant stare and the look of terror that had followed it went from her eyes. They stayed keen and bright. Her pulses beat fast, and the coursing blood warmed and relaxed every inch of her body.

She did not stop to ask if it were not a monstrous joy that held her. A clear and exalted perception enabled her to dismiss the suggestion as trivial.

She knew that she would weep again when she saw the kind, tender hands folded in death; the face that had never looked save with love upon her, fixed and gray and dead. But she saw beyond that bitter moment a long procession of years to come that would belong to her absolutely. And she opened and spread her arms out to them in welcome.

There would be no one to live for her during those coming years; she would live for herself. There would be no powerful will bending her in that blind persistence with which men and women believe they have a right to impose a private will upon a fellow creature. A kind intention or a cruel intention made the act seem no less a crime as she looked upon it in that brief moment of illumination.

And yet she had loved him — sometimes. 15 Often she had not. What did it matter! What could love, the unsolved mystery, count for in face of this possession of self-assertion which she suddenly recognized as the strongest impulse of her being.

"Free! Body and soul free!" she kept whispering.

Josephine was kneeling before the closed door with her lips to the keyhole, imploring for admission. "Louise, open the door! I beg; open the door — you will make yourself ill. What are you doing, Louise? For heaven's sake open the door."

"Go away. I am not making myself ill." No; she was drinking in a very elixir of life through that open window.

Her fancy was running riot along those days ahead of her. Spring days, and summer days, and all sorts of days that would be her own. She breathed a quick prayer that life might be long. It was only yesterday she had thought with a shudder that life might be long.

She arose at length and opened the door 20 to her sister's importunities. There was a feverish triumph in her eyes, and she carried herself unwittingly like a goddess of Victory. She clasped her sister's waist, and together they descended the stairs. Richards stood waiting for them at the bottom.

Some one was opening the front door with a latchkey. It was Brently Mallard who entered, a little travel-stained, composedly carrying his gripsack and umbrella. He had been far from the scene of accident, and did not even know there had been one. He stood amazed at Josephine's piercing cry; at Richards' quick motion to screen him from the view of his wife.

But Richards was too late.

When the doctors came they said she had died of heart disease — of joy that kills.

Topics for Critical Thinking and Writing

Read the following assertions and consider whether you agree or disagree, and why. For each assertion, draft a paragraph with your arguments.

1. The railroad accident is a symbol of the destructiveness of the Industrial Revolution.
2. The story accurately captures how trapped many women felt by marriage in the nineteenth century.
3. This story's setting is unclear, which makes the story less effective than if the setting had been specified.
4. Mrs. Mallard's death at the end is a just punishment for the joy she takes in her husband's death.
5. The story is rich in irony. Some examples: (1) The other characters think Mrs. Mallard is grieving, but she is rejoicing; (2) she prays for a long life, but she dies almost immediately; (3) the doctors say she died of the "joy that kills," but they think her joy was seeing her husband alive.
6. The story is excellent because it has a surprise ending.

Thinking about the Effects of Literature

What about the *consequences* of literature? Does literature shape our character and therefore influence our behavior? It is generally believed that it does have an effect. One hears, for example, that literature (like travel) is broadening, that it makes us aware of, and tolerant of, kinds of behavior that differ from our own and from what we see around us. One of the chief arguments against pornography, for instance, is that it desensitizes us, makes us too tolerant of abusive relationships, relationships in which people (usually men) use other people (usually women) as mere things or instruments for pleasure.

(A contrary view: Some people argue that pornography provides a relatively harmless outlet for fantasies that otherwise might be given release in the real world. In this view, pornography acts as a sort of safety valve.)

Other topics are also the subjects of controversy. For instance, in recent decades, parents and educators have been much concerned with fairy tales. Does the violence in some fairy tales ("Little Red Riding Hood," "The Three Little Pigs") have a negative effect on children? Do some of the stories teach the wrong lessons, implying that women should be passive and men active ("Sleeping Beauty," for instance, in which the sleeping woman is brought to life by the action of the handsome prince)? The Greek philosopher Plato (427–347 BC) strongly believed that the literature we hear or read shapes our later behavior, and since most of the ancient Greek traditional stories (notably Homer's *Odyssey* and *Iliad*) celebrate acts of love and war rather than of justice, he prohibited the reading of such material in his ideal society. (We reprint a relevant passage from Plato on p. 397.)

Exercise: Thinking about the Effects of Literature

1. If you have responded strongly (favorably or unfavorably) to some aspect of the social content of a literary work — for instance, its depiction of women, a particular minority group, or a political perspective —analyze the response in a 250- to 500-word essay and try to determine whether you are talking chiefly about yourself or the work. Can we really see literary value — *really* see it — in a work that deeply offends us?

2. Read the following brief claims about literature; then choose one and write a 250-word essay offering support or taking issue with it.

   The pen is mightier than the sword.   — EDWARD BULWER-LYTTON

   [The arts] supply our best data for deciding which experiences are more valuable than others.   — I. A. RICHARDS

   I believe as the Victorian novelists did that a novel isn't simply a vehicle for private expression, but that it also exists for social examination.   — MARGARET ATWOOD

   Poetry makes nothing happen.   — W. H. AUDEN

   Literature is *without proofs*. By which it must be understood that it cannot prove, not only *what* it says, but even that it is worth the trouble of saying it.

   — ROLAND BARTHES

   Of course the illusion of art is to make one believe that great literature is very close to life, but exactly the opposite is true. Life is amorphous, literature is formal.

   — FRANÇOISE SAGAN

   Of course I'm a black writer. . . . I'm not just a black writer, but categories like black writer, woman writer and Latin American writer aren't marginal anymore. We have to acknowledge that the thing we call "literature" is more pluralistic now, just as society ought to be.   — TONI MORRISON

3. Do you think authors control the meaning of their poems and stories? Is the author's intention the correct meaning of a work of literature? Explain your answer in approximately 500 words.

4. What possible public benefit can come from supporting the arts? Can one argue that we should support the arts for the same reasons that we support public schools — that is, to have a civilized society? Explain your response.

PLATO

Plato (427–347 BC), an Athenian aristocrat by birth, was the student of one great philosopher (Socrates) and the teacher of another (Aristotle). His legacy of more than two dozen dialogues — imaginary discussions between Socrates and one or more other speakers, usually young Athenians — has been of such influence that the whole of Western philosophy can be characterized, A. N. Whitehead wrote, as "a series of footnotes to Plato." Plato's interests encompassed the full range of topics in philosophy: ethics, politics, logic, metaphysics, epistemology, aesthetics, psychology, and education.

This selection from Plato's *Republic*, one of his best-known and longest dialogues, is about the education suitable for the rulers of an ideal society. *The Republic* begins, typically, with an investigation into the nature of justice. Socrates (who speaks for Plato) convincingly explains to Glaucon that we cannot reasonably expect to achieve a just society unless we devote careful attention to the moral education of the young men who are scheduled in later life to become the rulers. (Here as elsewhere, Plato's elitism and aristocratic bias shows itself; as readers of *The Republic* soon learn, Plato is no admirer of democracy or of a classless society.) Plato cares as much about what the educational curriculum should exclude as what it should include. His special target was the common practice in his day of using for pedagogy the Homeric tales and other stories about the gods. He readily embraces the principle of censorship, as the excerpt explains, because he thinks it is a necessary means to achieve the ideal society.

The Greater Part of the Stories Current Today We Shall Have to Reject

"What kind of education shall we give them then? We shall find it difficult to improve on the time-honored distinction between the physical training we give to the body and the education we give to the mind and character."

"True."

"And we shall begin by educating mind and character, shall we not?"

"Of course."

"In this education you would include stories, 5 would you not?"

"Yes."

"These are of two kinds, true stories and fiction.[1] Our education must use both, and start with fiction."

"I don't know what you mean."

"But you know that we begin by telling children stories. These are, in general, fiction,

---

[1] The Greek word *pseudos* and its corresponding verb meant not only "fiction" — stories, tales — but also "what is not true" and so, in suitable contexts, "lies": and this ambiguity should be borne in mind. [Editors' note: All footnotes are by the translator, but some have been omitted.]

though they contain some truth. And we tell children stories before we start them on physical training."

"That is so."

"That is what I meant by saying that we must start to educate the mind before training the body."

"You are right," he said.

"And the first step, as you know, is always what matters most, particularly when we are dealing with those who are young and tender. That is the time when they are easily molded and when any impression we choose to make leaves a permanent mark."

"That is certainly true."

"Shall we therefore readily allow our children to listen to any stories made up by anyone, and to form opinions that are for the most part the opposite of those we think they should have when they grow up?"

"We certainly shall not."

"Then it seems that our first business is to supervise the production of stories, and choose only those we think suitable, and reject the rest. We shall persuade mothers and nurses to tell our chosen stories to their children, and by means of them to mold their minds and characters which are more important than their bodies. The greater part of the stories current today we shall have to reject."

"Which are you thinking of?"

"We can take some of the major legends as typical. For all, whether major or minor, should be cast in the same mold and have the same effect. Do you agree?"

"Yes: but I'm not sure which you refer to as major."

"The stories in Homer and Hesiod and the poets. For it is the poets who have always made up fictions and stories to tell to men."

"What sort of stories do you mean and what fault do you find in them?"

"The worst fault possible," I replied, "especially if the fiction is an ugly one."

"And what is that?"

"Misrepresenting the nature of gods and heroes, like a portrait painter whose portraits bear no resemblance to their originals."

"That is a fault which certainly deserves censure. But give me more details."

"Well, on the most important of subjects, there is first and foremost the foul story about Ouranos[2] and the things Hesiod says he did, and the revenge Cronos took on him. While the story of what Cronos did, and what he suffered at the hands of his son, is not fit as it is to be lightly repeated to the young and foolish, even if it were true; it would be best to say nothing about it, or if it must be told, tell it to a select few under oath of secrecy, at a rite which required, to restrict it still further, the sacrifice not of a mere pig but of something large and difficult to get."

"These certainly are awkward stories."

"And they shall not be repeated in our state, Adeimantus," I said. "Nor shall any young audience be told that anyone who commits horrible crimes, or punishes his father unmercifully, is doing nothing out of the ordinary but merely what the first and greatest of the gods have done before."

"I entirely agree," said Adeimantus, "that these stories are unsuitable."

"Nor can we permit stories of wars and plots and battles among the gods; they are quite untrue, and if we want our prospective guardians to believe that quarrelsomeness is one of the worst of evils, we must certainly not let them be told the story of the Battle of the Giants or embroider it on robes, or tell them other tales about many and various

---

[2]**Ouranos** The sky, the original supreme god. Ouranos was castrated by his son Cronos to separate him from Gaia (mother earth). Cronos was in turn deposed by Zeus in a struggle in which Zeus was helped by the Titans.

quarrels between gods and heroes and their friends and relations. On the contrary, if we are to persuade them that no citizen has ever quarreled with any other, because it is sinful, our old men and women must tell children stories with this end in view from the first, and we must compel our poets to tell them similar stories when they grow up. But we can admit to our state no stories about Hera being tied up by her son, or Hephaestus being flung out of Heaven by his father for trying to help his mother when she was getting a beating, nor any of Homer's Battles of the Gods, whether their intention is allegorical or not. Children cannot distinguish between what is allegory and what isn't, and opinions formed at that age are usually difficult to eradicate or change; we should therefore surely regard it as of the utmost importance that the first stories they hear shall aim at encouraging the highest excellence of character."

"Your case is a good one," he agreed, "but if someone wanted details, and asked what stories we were thinking of, what should we say?"

To which I replied, "My dear Adeimantus, you and I are not engaged on writing stories but on founding a state. And the founders of a state, though they must know the type of story the poet must produce, and reject any that do not conform to that type, need not write them themselves."

"True: but what are the lines on which our poets must work when they deal with the gods?"

"Roughly as follows," I said. "God must 35 surely always be represented as he really is, whether the poet is writing epic, lyric, or tragedy."

"He must."

"And in reality of course god is good, and he must be so described."

"Certainly."

"But nothing good is harmful, is it?"[3]

"I think not." 40

"Then can anything that is not harmful do harm?"

"No."

"And can what does no harm do evil?"

"No again."

"And can what does no evil be the cause of 45 any evil?"

"How could it?"

"Well then; is the good beneficial?"

"Yes."

"So it must be the cause of well-being."

"Yes." 50

"So the good is not the cause of everything, but only of states of well-being and not of evil."

"Most certainly," he agreed.

"Then god, being good, cannot be responsible for everything, as is commonly said, but only for a small part of human life, for the greater part of which he has no responsibility. For we have a far smaller share of good than of evil, and while god must be held to be the sole cause of good, we must look for some factors other than god as cause of the evil."

"I think that's very true," he said.

"So we cannot allow Homer or any other 55 poet to make such a stupid mistake about the gods, as when he says that

Zeus has two jars standing on the floor
of his palace, full of fates, good in one and
evil in the other

_____

[3]The reader of the following passage should bear the following ambiguities in mind: (1) the Greek word for good (*agathos*) can mean (a) morally good, (b) beneficial or advantageous; (2) the Greek word for evil (*kakos*) can also mean harm or injury; (3) the adverb of *agathos* (*eu* — the well) can imply either morally right or prosperous. The word translated "cause of" could equally well be rendered "responsible for."

and that the man to whom Zeus allots a mixture of both has "varying fortunes sometimes good and sometimes bad," while the man to whom he allots unmixed evil is "hased by ravening despair over the face of the earth."[4] Nor can we allow references to Zeus as "dispenser of good and evil." And we cannot approve if it is said that Athene and Zeus prompted the breach of solemn treaty and oath by Pandarus, or that the strife and contentions of the gods were due to Themis and Zeus. Nor again can we let our children hear from Aeschylus that

> God implants a fault in man, when he
> wishes to destroy a house utterly.

No: We must forbid anyone who writes a play about the sufferings of Niobe (the subject of the play from which these last lines are quoted), or the house of Pelops, or the Trojan war, or any similar topic, to say they

---

[4]Quotations from Homer are generally taken from the translations by Dr. Rieu in the Penguin series. At times (as here) the version quoted by Plato differs slightly from the accepted text.

are acts of god; or if he does he must produce the sort of interpretation we are now demanding, and say that god's acts were good and just, and that the sufferers were benefited by being punished. What the poet must not be allowed to say is that those who were punished were made wretched through god's action. He may refer to the wicked as wretched because they needed punishment, provided he makes it clear that in punishing them god did them good. But if a state is to be run on the right lines, every possible step must be taken to prevent anyone, young or old, either saying or being told, whether in poetry or prose, that god, being good, can cause harm or evil to any man. To say so would be sinful, inexpedient, and inconsistent."

"I should approve of a law for this purpose and you have my vote for it," he said.

"Then of our laws laying down the principles which those who write or speak about the gods must follow, one would be this: *God is the cause, not of all things, but only of good.*"

"I am quite content with that," he said.

Topics for Critical Thinking and Writing

1. In the beginning of the dialogue, Plato says that adults recite fictions to very young children and that these fictions help mold character. Think of some story that you heard or read when young, such as "Snow White and the Seven Dwarfs" or "Ali Baba and the Forty Thieves." Try to think of a story that, in the final analysis, is not in accord with what you consider to be proper morality, such as a story in which a person triumphs through trickery or a story in which evil actions — perhaps murders — are set forth without unfavorable comment. (Was it naughty of Jack to kill the giant?) On reflection, do you think children should not be told such stories? Why, or why not? Or think of the early film westerns in which, on the whole, the Indians (except for an occasional Uncle Tonto) are depicted as bad guys and the white cowboys (except for an occasional coward or rustler) are depicted as good guys. Many people who now have gray hair enjoyed such films in their childhood. Are you prepared to say that such films are not damaging? Or, in contrast, are you prepared to say they are damaging and should be prohibited?

2. It is often objected that censorship of reading matter and of television programs available to children underrates children's ability to think for themselves and to discount the dangerous, obscene, and tawdry. Do you agree with this objection? Does Plato? Explain your response.

3. Plato says that allowing poets to say what they please about the gods in his ideal state would be "inconsistent." Explain what he means by this criticism and then explain why you agree or disagree with it.

4. Do you believe that parents should censor the "fiction" their children encounter (literature, films, pictures, music) but that the community should not censor the "fiction" of adults? Write an essay of about 500 words on one of these topics: "Censorship and Hip-Hop Lyrics," "X-Rated Films," or "Ethnic Jokes." (These topics are broadly worded; you can narrow one and offer any thesis you wish.)

5. Were you taught that any of the founders of the United States ever acted disreputably or that any American hero had any serious moral flaw? Or that the United States ever acted immorally in its dealings with other nations? Do you think it appropriate for children to hear such things? Explain your responses.

12

A Debater's View: Oral Presentations and Debate

He who knows only his own side of the case knows little of that. — JOHN STUART MILL

A philosopher who is not taking part in discussions is like a boxer who never goes into the ring. — LUDWIG WITTGENSTEIN

Freedom is hammered out on the anvil of dissension, dissent, and debate. — HUBERT HUMPHREY

Oral Presentations

Forensic comes from the Latin word *foris*, meaning "out of doors," which also produced the word *forum*, an open space in front of a public building. In the language of rhetoricians, the place where one delivers a speech to an audience is the forum — whether it is a classroom, a court of law, or the steps of the Lincoln Memorial. In fact, the earliest meaning of *forensics* in English was related to public discussion and debate.

Your instructor may ask you to make an oral presentation (in which case, the forum would be the classroom), and if he or she doesn't make such a demand, later life almost certainly will. For example, you'll find that at a job interview, you will be expected to talk persuasively (perhaps to a group) about what good qualities or experience you can bring to the place of employment. Similarly, when you have a job, you'll sometimes have to summarize a report orally or argue your case out loud, perhaps so that your colleagues might do something they are hesitant to do.

The goal of your classroom talk is to persuade the audience to share your view or, if you can't get them to agree completely, to get them to see that at least there is something to be said for this view — that it is a position a reasonable person can hold.

Elsewhere in this book we have said that the subjects of persuasive writing are usually

- matters of fact (e.g., statistics show that the death penalty does — or does not — deter crime),

- matters of value (e.g., separating families is — or is not — immoral), or

- matters of policy (e.g., government should — or should not — make college "free").

Similarly, many kinds of public speaking involve just such matters, and the habits of critical thinking, argument, and persuasion we have discussed to this point now need to be personified and articulated.

No matter what your subject is, when you draft and revise your talk, make certain that a thesis statement underlies the whole (e.g., "Proposition 2 is a bad idea because . . .").

The text of an oral presentation ought not to be identical with the text of a written presentation. Both must have a clear organization, but oral presentations usually require making the organization a bit more obvious, with abundant **signposts**. Signposts help audiences listen to your key points. For example, audiences benefit from knowing how long they are expected to listen. (Think about it: Who hasn't checked the time remaining in a movie or television show to help anticipate where they are in the plot?) It sometimes helps to inform your audience: "In *the next ten minutes*, I will be speaking to you about *X*"; "Before I talk about *X*, I am going *to spend a minute or two* on background"; or "Now, *with just few minutes remaining*, I would like to make my key point." Skilled speakers know how to raise their audience's perceptions at key moments. Following are some more signpost words and phrases that can help an audience hear what you them to hear most.

> **SPEAKING TIPS**
> - *In preparing your oral presentation, keep your thesis in mind.* You may be giving counterarguments, examples, definitions, and so forth, but make sure that your thesis is evident to the audience and return to it occasionally as a reminder.
> - *Keep your audience in mind.* Inevitably, you will have to make assumptions about what the audience does and does not know about your topic. Do not overestimate their knowledge and do not underestimate their intelligence.

Transitioning to a new topic or another point

Up to this point we have been discussing *X*. *Turning now to Y*, we can see something different.

Now *let me pause for a second* before moving on. My first point was *X*. This supports my argument. But so does *Y*, a different kind of case.

Exploring something further

Now, *for just a minute*, let's look at this more deeply.

X is worth *elaborating on for a couple minutes* before I continue.

Digressing

Let's *take a detour* for a second.

I am going *to stop for a minute and tell a brief story* to show a perfect example.

Summarizing or returning to the beginning

To recap everything I have said here, *let me walk through the key points* . . .

Going back to my previous points, A, B, and C, we can safely conclude . . .

In general, when speaking, you will have to repeat a bit more than you would in a written presentation. An old rule of thumb suggests that to make your audience remember something, you may need only to write it only once but say it three times. After all, a reader can turn back to check a sentence or a statistic, but a listener cannot. Thus, you may find yourself saying things out loud that you would scarcely or ever write, such as "The authorities were wrong. So that's my first conclusion. The authorities were wrong," or "The reason Jones was arrested was unjust. *I repeat*: The reasons were unjust."

You will want to think carefully about the **organization** of your talk. We've already stressed the need to develop essays with clear thesis statements and logical supporting points. Oral presentations are no different, but remember that when you are speaking in public, a clear organization will always help alleviate anxiety and reassure you. Thus, you can deliver a powerful message without getting tripped up yourself. We suggest you try the following:

- Outline your draft in advance to ensure it has clear organization.
- Inform the audience at the start about the organization of your presentation. Early in the talk, you probably should say something along these lines, although not in as abbreviated a form:

  In talking about *A*, I'll have to define a few terms, *B* and *C*, and I will also have to talk about two positions that differ from mine, *D* and *E*. I'll then try to show why *A* is the best policy to pursue, clearly better than *D* and *E*.

- So that the listeners can easily follow your train of thought, be sure to use transitions such as "Furthermore," "Therefore," "Although it is often said," and "Some may object that." Sometimes, you may even remind the listeners what the previous stages were, with a comment such as "We have now seen three approaches to the problem of . . ."

METHODS OF DELIVERY

After thinking about helping the audience follow your speech, consider how much help you'll need delivering it. Depending on your comfort level with the topic and your argument, you might decide to

- deliver a memorized talk without notes,
- read the talk from a written text, or

- speak from an outline, perhaps with quotations and statistics written down.

Each of these methods has strengths and weaknesses. A memorized talk allows for plenty of eye contact with the audience, but unless you are a superb actor, it is almost surely going to seem a bit mechanical. A talk that you read from a text will indeed let you say to an audience exactly what you intend (with the best possible wording), but reading a text inevitably establishes some distance between you and the audience, even if you occasionally glance up from your pages. If you talk from a mere outline, almost surely some of your sentences will turn out to be a bit awkward — although a little awkwardness may help convey sincerity and therefore be a plus.

No matter what form of delivery you choose, try to convey the impression that you're conversing with the audience, not talking down to them (even though if you're standing on a platform you will be literally talking down).

You may want to use **multimedia aids** in your presentation. These can range from such low-tech materials as handouts, blackboards, and whiteboards to high-tech PowerPoint presentations, Prezis, or videos and recordings. Each has advantages and disadvantages. For instance, if you distribute handouts when the talk begins, the audience may start thumbing through them during your opening comments. And although software like PowerPoint can provide highly useful aids, some speakers make too much use of it simply because it's available. Any software you use, or any supplementary materials you introduce, should be essential to communicating your message effectively, not superfluous or merely decorative. And these materials should be legible: If you do use visuals, make certain that your words and images are large enough to be seen by all given the size of the room and the expectation that not everyone can see equally clearly. A graph with tiny words won't impress your audience, nor will words that cannot be read by everyone. Also, to accommodate as many people as possible, it helps to describe your slides even when you have created them to be extremely clear.

AUDIENCE

It is not merely because topics are complicated that we cannot agree that one side is reasonable and correct and the other side irrational and wrong. The truth is that we are swayed not only by reason (*logos*) but also by appeals to the emotions (*pathos*) and by the speaker's character (*ethos*). (For more on these appeals, see Persuasion, Argument, and Rhetorical Appeals on pp. 75–79 in Chapter 3.) We can combine these last two factors and put it this way: Sometimes we are inclined to agree with X rather than with Y because X strikes us as a more appealing person (perhaps more open-minded, more intelligent, better informed, more humane, and less cold). X is the sort of person we want to have as a friend. We disagree with Y — or at least we're unwilling to associate ourselves with Y — because Y is, well, Y just isn't the sort of person we want to agree with. Y's statistics don't sound right, or Y seems like a bully;

for some reason, we just don't have confidence in *Y*. Confidence is easily lost: Alas, even a mispronunciation will diminish the audience's confidence in *Y*. As Peter de Vries said, "You can't be happy with someone who pronounces both *d*'s in Wednesday."

Earlier in the book, we talked about the importance of **tone** and of the writer's **persona**. We have also made the point that the writer's tone will depend partly on the audience. A person writing for a conservative journal whose readership is almost entirely conservatives can adopt a highly satiric manner in talking about liberals and will win much approval. But if this conservative writer is writing in a liberal journal and hopes to get a sympathetic hearing, he or she will have to avoid satire and wisecracks and, instead, present himself or herself as a person of goodwill who is open-minded and eager to address the issue seriously.

The **language** you use — the degree to which it is formal as opposed to colloquial and the degree to which it is technical as opposed to general — will also depend on the audience. Speaking broadly, in oral argument you should speak politely but not formally. You do not want to be one of those people who "talk like a book." But you also don't want to be overly colloquial. Choose a middle course, probably a notch below the style you would use in a written paper. For instance, in an oral presentation you might say, "We'll consider this point in a minute or two," whereas in a written paper you probably would write, "We will consider this point shortly."

Technical language is entirely appropriate if your audience is familiar with it. If you are arguing before members of Amnesty International about the use of torture, you can assume certain kinds of specialized knowledge. You can, for instance, breezily speak of the DRC and of KPCS, and your listeners will know what you're talking about because Amnesty International has been active with issues concerning the Democratic Republic of Congo and the Kimberley Process Certification Scheme. In contrast, if you are arguing the same case before a general public, you'll have to explain these abbreviations, and you may even have to explain what Amnesty International is. If you are arguing before an audience of classmates, you probably have a good idea of what they know and don't know.

DELIVERY

Your audience will in some measure determine not only your tone but also the way you appear when giving the speech. Part of the delivery is the speaker's appearance. The medium is part of the message. The president can appear in golf clothes when he chats about his reelection plans, but he wears a suit and a tie when he delivers the State of the Union address. Just as we wear one kind of clothing when playing tennis, another when attending classes, and yet another when going for a job interview, an effective speaker dresses appropriately. A lawyer arguing before the Supreme Court wears a dark suit or dress. The same lawyer, arguing at a local meeting, speaking as a community resident, may well dress informally — maybe in jeans — to show that he or she is not stuffy or overly formal but, rather, a regular member of the community.

Your appearance when you speak is not merely a matter of clothing; it includes your **facial expressions**, your **posture**, your **gestures**, and your general demeanor. In general, you should avoid bodily motions — swaying, thumping the table, craning your neck, smirking — that are so distracting that they cause the audience to concentrate on the distraction rather than on the argument. ("That's the third time he straightened his necktie. I wonder how many more times he will — oops, that's the fourth!") Most of us are unaware of our annoying habits; if you're lucky, a friend, when urged, will tell you about them. In preparation, you may also film yourself speaking to observe your physical gestures from a third-person perspective.

You probably can't do much about your **voice** and its unique character — it may be high-pitched, or it may be gravelly — but you can make sure to speak loudly enough for the audience members to hear you and slowly and clearly enough for them to understand you.

We have some advice about quotations, too. First, if possible, use an effective quotation or two, partly because — we'll be frank here — the quotations may be more impressively worded than anything you come up with on your own. A quotation may be the chief thing your audience comes away with: "Hey, yes, I liked that: 'War is too important to be left to the generals'"; "When it comes down to it, I agree with that Frenchman who said 'If we are to abolish the death penalty, I should like to see the first step taken by the murderers'"; or "You know, I think it was all summed up in that line by Margaret Mead, something like, 'No one would remember the Good Samaritan if he'd had only good intentions. He had money as well.' Yes, that's pretty convincing. Morality isn't enough. You need money." You didn't invent the words that you quote, but you did bring them to your listeners' attention, and they will be grateful to you.

Our second piece of advice concerning quotations is this: If the quotation is only a phrase or a brief sentence, you can memorize it and be confident that you'll remember it, but if it's longer than a sentence, write it on a sheet in your notes or on a four-by-six-inch card in print large enough for you to read easily. You have chosen these words because they are effectively put, so you don't want to misquote them or hesitate in delivering them.

CONTENT

As for the talk itself, well, we have been touching on it in our discussion of such matters as the speaker's relation to the audience, the need to provide signposts, and the use of quotations. All our comments in earlier chapters about developing a written argument are also relevant to oral arguments, but here we should merely emphasize that because the talk is oral and the audience cannot look back to an earlier page to remind itself of some point, the speaker may have to repeat and summarize a bit more than is usual in a written essay.

Remember, too, that a reader can see when the essay ends — there is blank space at the end of the page — but a listener depends on aural cues. Nothing is more embarrassing — and less effective as argument — than a speaker who seems (to the audience) to suddenly stop and sit down. In short, give your hearers ample clues that you are ending (post such signs as "Finally," "Last," or "Let me end by saying"), and be sure to end with a strong sentence. It may not be as good as the end of the Gettysburg Address ("government of the people, by the people, for the people, shall not perish from the earth"), nor will it be as good as the end of Martin Luther King Jr.'s "I Have a Dream" speech ("Free at last! Free at last! Thank God Almighty, we are free at last!"), but those are the models to emulate.

Formal Debates

It would be nice if all arguments ended with everyone, participants and spectators, agreeing that the facts are clear, that one presentation is more reasonable than the other, and therefore that one side is right and the other side is wrong. But in life, most issues are complicated. High school students may earnestly debate — this is a real topic in a national debate —

> Resolved: That education has failed its mission in the United States but it takes only a moment of reflection to see that neither the affirmative nor the negative can be true. Yes, education has failed its mission in many ways, but, no, it has succeeded in many ways. Its job now is (in the words of Samuel Beckett) to try again: "Fail. Fail again. Fail better."

Debates of this sort, conducted before a judge and guided by strict rules concerning "Constructive Speeches," "Rebuttal Speeches," and "Cross-Examinations," are not attempts to get at the truth; like lawsuits, they are attempts to win a case. Each speaker seeks not to persuade the opponent but only to convince the judge. Although most of this section is devoted not to forensics in the strictest sense but more generally to the presentation of oral arguments, we begin with the standard format.

STANDARD DEBATE FORMAT

Formal debates occur within a structure that governs the number of speeches, their order, and the maximum time for each one. The format may vary from place to place, but there is always a structure. In most debates, a formal resolution states the reason for the debate ("Resolved: That capital punishment be abolished in juvenile cases"). The affirmative team supports the resolution; the negative team denies its legitimacy. The basic structure has three parts:

- *The constructive phase*, in which the debaters construct their cases and develop their arguments (usually for ten minutes).

- *The rebuttal*, in which debaters present their responses and also present their final summary (usually for five minutes).

- *The preparation*, in which the debater prepares for presenting the next speech. (During the preparation — a sort of time-out — the debater is not addressing the opponent or audience. The total time allotted to a team is usually six or eight minutes, which the individual debaters divide as they wish.)

We give, very briefly, the usual structure of each part, although we should mention that another common format calls for a cross-examination of the First Affirmative Constructive by the Second Negative, a cross-examination of the First Negative Constructive by the First Affirmative, a cross-examination of the Second Affirmative by the First Negative, and a cross-examination of the Second Negative by the Second Affirmative:

First Affirmative Constructive Speech: Serves as introduction, giving summary overview, definitions, criteria for resolution, major claims and evidence, statement, and intention to support the resolution.

First Negative Constructive Speech: Responds by introducing the basic position, challenges the definitions and criteria, suggests the line of attack, emphasizes that the burden of proof lies with the affirmative, rejects the resolution as unnecessary or dangerous, and supports the status quo.

US Democratic presidential candidates Hillary Clinton and Bernie Sanders during a debate at the University of New Hampshire in Durham on February 4, 2016. A successful debate can help change the tide of a candidate's campaign.

- ☐ Have I done adequate preparation in my research?

- ☐ Are my notes legible, with accurate quotations and credible sources?

- ☐ Am I prepared to take good notes during the debate?

- ☐ Is my proposition clearly stated?

- ☐ Do I have adequate evidence to support the thesis (main point)?

- ☐ Do I have backup points in mind?

- ☐ Have I given thought to issues my opponents might raise?

- ☐ Does the opening properly address the instructor, the audience, the opponents? (Remember, you are addressing an audience, not merely the opponents.)

- ☐ Are my visual aids focused on major points?

- ☐ Is my demeanor professional and is my dress appropriate?

Second Affirmative Constructive: Rebuilds the affirmative case; refutes chief attacks, especially concerning definitions, criteria, and rationale (philosophic framework); and further develops the affirmative case.

Second Negative Constructive: Completes the negative case, if possible advances it by rebuilding portions of the first negative construction, and contrasts the entire negative case with the entire affirmative case.

First Negative Rebuttal: Attacks the opponents' arguments and defends the negative constructive arguments (but a rebuttal may not introduce new constructive arguments).

First Affirmative Rebuttal: Usually responds first to the second negative construction and then to the first negative rebuttal.

Second Negative Rebuttal: Constitutes final speech for the negative, summarizing the case and explaining to the judge why the negative should be declared the winner.

Second Affirmative Rebuttal: Summarizes the debate, responds to issues pressed by the second negative rebuttal, and suggests to the judge that the affirmative team should win.

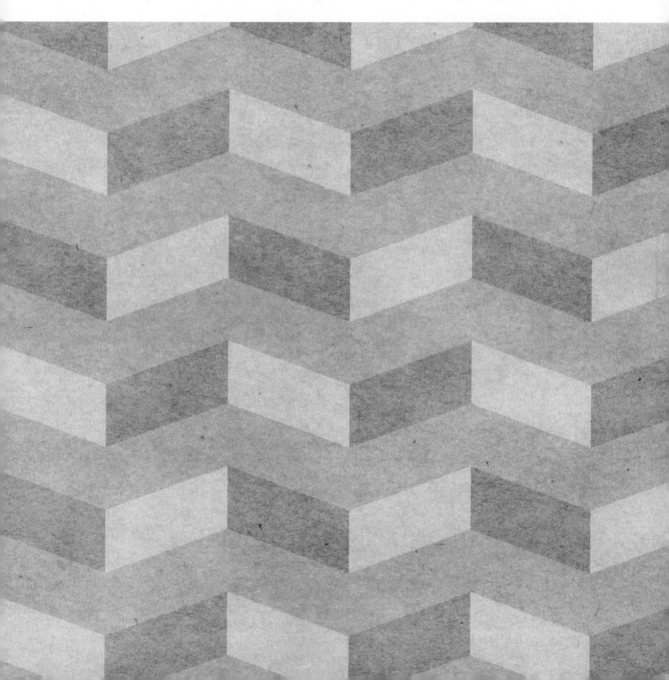

PART FOUR

Casebooks

13

A College Education: What Is Its Purpose?

ANDREW DELBANCO

Andrew Delbanco (b. 1952) is a widely published author who teaches at Columbia University, where he is the Alexander Hamilton Professor of American Studies. The following essay first appeared in *Parade*, a magazine-like supplement that is part of the Sunday edition of many newspapers, and was later included in Delbanco's book *College: What It Was, Is, and Should Be* (2012). In 2012, Delbanco was awarded the National Humanities Medal by President Barack Obama.

3 Reasons College Still Matters

The American college is going through a period of wrenching change, buffeted by forces — globalization, economic instability, the information technology revolution, the increasingly evident inadequacy of K–12 education, and, perhaps most important, the collapse of consensus about what students should know — that make its task more difficult and contentious than ever before.

For a relatively few students, college remains the sort of place that Anthony Kronman, former dean of Yale Law School, recalls from his days at Williams, where his favorite class took place at the home of a philosophy professor whose two golden retrievers slept on either side of the fireplace "like bookends beside the hearth" while the sunset lit the Berkshire Hills "in scarlet and gold." For many more students, college means the anxious pursuit of marketable skills in overcrowded, underresourced institutions. For still others, it means traveling by night to a fluorescent office building or to a "virtual classroom" that only exists in cyberspace.

It is a pipe dream to imagine that every student can have the sort of experience that our richest colleges, at their best, provide. But it is a nightmare society that affords the chance to learn and grow only to the wealthy, brilliant, or lucky few. Many remarkable teachers in America's community colleges, unsung private colleges, and underfunded public colleges live this truth every day, working to keep the ideal of democratic education alive. And so it is my unabashed aim to articulate in my forthcoming book, *College: What It Was, Is, and Should Be*, what a college — any college — should seek to do for its students.

What, then, are today's prevailing answers to the question, what is college for? The most common answer is an economic one. It's clear that a college degree long ago supplanted the high school diploma as the minimum qualification for entry into the skilled labor market, and there is abundant evidence that people with a college degree earn more money over the course of their lives than people without one. Some estimates put the worth of a bachelor of arts degree at about a million dollars in incremental lifetime earnings.

For such economic reasons alone, it is 5 alarming that for the first time in history, we face the prospect that the coming generation of Americans will be less educated than its elders.

Within this gloomy general picture are some especially disturbing particulars. For one thing, flat or declining college attainment rates (relative to other nations) apply disproportionately to minorities, who are a growing portion of the American population. And financial means have a shockingly large bearing on educational opportunity, which, according to one authority, looks like this in today's America: If you are the child of a family making more than $90,000 per year, your odds of getting a BA by age twenty-four are roughly one in two; if your parents make less than $35,000, your odds are one in seventy.

Moreover, among those who do get to college, high-achieving students from affluent families are four times more likely to attend a selective college than students from poor families with comparable grades and test scores. Since prestigious colleges serve as funnels into leadership positions in business, law, and government, this means that our "best" colleges are doing more to foster than to retard the growth of inequality in our society. Yet colleges are still looked to as engines of social mobility in American life, and it would be shameful if they became, even more than they already are, a system for replicating inherited wealth.

Not surprisingly, as in any discussion of economic matters, one finds dissenters from the predominant view. Some on the right say that pouring more public investment into higher education, in the form of enhanced subsidies for individuals or institutions, is a bad idea. They argue against the goal of universal college education as a fond fantasy and, instead, for a sorting system such as one finds in European countries: vocational training for the low scorers, who will be the semiskilled laborers and functionaries; advanced education for the high scorers, who will be the diplomats and doctors.

Other thinkers, on the left, question whether the aspiration to go to college really makes sense for "low-income students who can least afford to spend money and years" on such a risky venture, given their low graduation rates and high debt. From this point of view, the "education gospel" seems a cruel distraction from "what really provides security to families and children: good jobs at fair wages, robust unions, affordable access to health care and transportation."

One can be on either side of these ques- 10 tions, or somewhere in the middle, and still believe in the goal of achieving universal college education. Consider an analogy from another sphere of public debate: health care. One sometimes hears that eliminating smoking would save untold billions because of the immense cost of caring for patients who develop lung cancer, emphysema, heart disease, or diabetes. It turns out, however, that reducing the incidence of disease by curtailing smoking may actually end up costing us more, since people who don't smoke live longer and eventually require expensive therapies for chronic diseases and the inevitable infirmities of old age.

In other words, measuring the benefit as a social cost or gain does not quite get the point — or at least not the whole point. The best reason to end smoking is that people who don't smoke have a better chance to lead better lives. The best reason to care about college — who goes, and what happens to them when they get there — is not what it does for society in economic terms but what it can do for individuals, in both calculable and incalculable ways.

The second argument for the importance of college is a political one, though one rarely hears it from politicians. This is the argument on behalf of democracy. "The basis of our government," as Thomas Jefferson put the matter near the end of the eighteenth century, is "the opinion of the people." If the new republic was to flourish and endure, it required, above all, an educated citizenry.

This is more true than ever. All of us are bombarded every day with pleadings and persuasions — advertisements, political appeals, punditry of all sorts — designed to capture our loyalty, money, or, more narrowly, our vote. Some say health care reform will bankrupt the country, others that it is an overdue act of justice; some believe that abortion is the work of Satan, others think that to deny a woman the right to terminate an unwanted pregnancy is a form of abuse. The best chance we have to maintain a functioning democracy is a citizenry that can tell the difference between demagoguery and responsible arguments.

Education for democracy also implies something about what kind of education democratic citizens need. A very good case for college in this sense has been made recently by Kronman, the former Yale dean who now teaches in a Great Books program for Yale undergraduates. In his book *Education's End*, Kronman argues for a course of study that introduces students to the constitutive ideas of Western culture, including, among many others, "the ideals of individual freedom and toleration," "a reliance on markets as a mechanism for the organization of economic life," and "an acceptance of the truths of modern science."

Anyone who earns a BA from a reputable 15 college ought to understand something about the genealogy of these ideas and practices, about the historical processes from which they have emerged, the tragic cost when societies fail to defend them, and about alternative ideas both within the Western tradition and outside it. That's a tall order for anyone to satisfy on his or her own — and one of the marks of an educated person is the recognition that it can never be adequately done and is therefore all the more worth doing.

There is a third case for college, seldom heard, perhaps because it is harder to articulate without sounding platitudinous and vague. I first heard it stated in a plain and passionate way after I had spoken to an alumni group from Columbia, where I teach. The emphasis in my talk was on the Jeffersonian argument — education for citizenship. When I had finished, an elderly alumnus stood up and said more or less the following: "That's all very nice, professor, but you've missed the main point." With some trepidation, I asked him what that point might be. "Columbia," he said, "taught me how to enjoy life."

What he meant was that college had opened his senses as well as his mind to experiences that would otherwise be foreclosed to him. Not only had it enriched his capacity to read demanding works of literature and to grasp fundamental political ideas, it had also heightened and deepened his alertness to color and form, melody and harmony. And now, in the late years of his life, he was grateful. Such an education is a hedge against utilitarian values. It slakes the human craving for contact with works of art that somehow register one's own longings and yet exceed what one has been able to articulate by and for oneself.

If all that seems too pious, I think of a comparably personal comment I once heard my colleague Judith Shapiro, former provost of Bryn Mawr and then president of Barnard, make to a group of young people about what they should expect from college: "You want the inside of your head to be an interesting place to spend the rest of your life."

What both Shapiro and the Columbia alum were talking about is sometimes called "liberal education" — a hazardous term today, since it has nothing necessarily to do with liberal politics in the modern sense of the word. The phrase "liberal education" derives from the classical tradition of *artes liberales*, which was reserved in Greece and Rome — where women were considered inferior and slavery was an accepted feature of civilized society — for "those free men or gentlemen possessed of the requisite leisure for study." The tradition of liberal learning survived and thrived throughout European history but remained largely the possession of ruling elites. The distinctive American contribution has been the attempt to democratize it, to deploy it on behalf of the cardinal American principle that all persons, regardless of origin, have the right to pursue happiness — and that "getting to know," in poet and critic Matthew Arnold's much-quoted phrase, "the best which has been thought and said in the world" is helpful to that pursuit.

This view of what it means to be educated [20] is often caricatured as snobbish and narrow, beholden to the old and wary of the new; but in fact it is neither, as Arnold makes clear by the (seldom quoted) phrase with which he completes his point: "and through this knowledge, turning a stream of fresh and free thought upon our stock notions and habits."

In today's America, at every kind of institution — from underfunded community colleges to the wealthiest Ivies — this kind of education is at risk. Students are pressured and programmed, trained to live from task to task, relentlessly rehearsed and tested until winners are culled from the rest. Too many colleges do too little to save them from the debilitating frenzy that makes liberal education marginal — if it is offered at all.

In this respect, notwithstanding the bigotries and prejudices of earlier generations, we might not be so quick to say that today's colleges mark an advance over those of the past.

Consider a once-popular college novel written a hundred years ago, *Stover at Yale*, in which a young Yalie declares, "I'm going to do the best thing a fellow can do at our age, I'm going to loaf." The character speaks from the immemorial past, and what he says is likely to sound to us today like a sneering boast from the idle rich. But there is a more dignified sense in which "loaf" is the colloquial equivalent of contemplation and has always been part of the promise of American life. "I loaf and invite my soul," says Walt Whitman in that great democratic poem "Song of Myself."

Surely, every American college ought to defend this waning possibility, whatever we call it. And an American college is only true to itself when it opens its doors to all — the rich, the middle, and the poor — who have the capacity to embrace the precious chance to think and reflect before life engulfs them. If we are serious about democracy, that means everyone.

Topics for Critical Thinking and Writing

1. In two or three sentences, describe what Andrew Delbanco is arguing for. Then, in another two or three sentences, describe what he is he arguing against.

2. What do you think Delbanco considers to be the most important outcomes of a college education? What outcomes are less important to him?

3. In 300 to 500 words, explain whether you think the higher education system perpetuates inequalities or whether it helps resolve inequalities in the United States. Or is it a little of both? Explain.

4. Why is higher education good for freedom and democracy? What evidence can you cite from Delbanco as support for your answer? What evidence can you cite on your own?

5. In paragraph 10, Delbanco introduces, as an analogy, the cost of lung cancer and other life-threatening diseases (although he goes on to reject this comparison). Do you think his use of this analogy is effective? Why, or why not?

6. Using Delbanco's own formulation of a "liberal education" in paragraph 19, assess your own university's liberal education requirements and explain whether you think it is a valuable part of your education. Would you prefer an education that trained you only in your chosen career field or one that spreads learning across disciplines and experiences? If possible, talk to a humanities professor at your institution about the importance of a liberal education and include his or her thoughts, agreeing or countering them as you see fit, in your assessment.

CARLO ROTELLA

Carlo Rotella (b. 1964) is a professor in the English Department at Boston College and a writer for the *New York Times Magazine*. A former columnist for the *Boston Globe*, his work has also appeared in magazines such as the *New Yorker*, *Harper's*, and *Slate* and in academic journals such as *Critical Inquiry*, *American Quarterly*, and the *American Scholar*. This piece appeared in the *Boston Globe* on December 24, 2011.

No, It Doesn't Matter What You Majored In

I woke up on Wednesday morning with two routine but pressing jobs to accomplish: I had a column to write, and I had a stack of twenty-page papers to grade. The two duties wouldn't seem to have anything to do with each other. But they do, and what they have in common says something about the value of higher education.

Almost everybody agrees that college costs too much. If a relative handful of relatively rich people want to pay a lot to go to the most exclusive schools, that's up to them; it's a victimless crime. But if a good college education costs too much across the board, that's a major social problem, especially because a college degree has increasingly become a minimum qualification for the kind of job that puts you in the middle class — which is where most Americans, wishfully or not, still imagine themselves to belong. And this all looks worse because the economic crisis has hit many public institutions especially hard.

Some have called this situation a higher-education bubble. Some have begun to investigate what students are really getting out of college for their money. They're asking necessary questions about curriculum and teaching, and about institutions' and students' commitment to academic excellence.

But this vitally important discussion is often hamstrung by a tendency to reduce college to vocational education in the crudest, most unrealistic ways. This kind of reduction often zeroes in on the humanities and parts of the social sciences — together often mislabeled as "the liberal arts" (when, in fact, math and science are also part of the liberal arts) — as the most overvalued, least practical aspect of higher education. If you study engineering you can become an engineer, if you study biology or physics you can be a scientist, and if you're pre-med or pre-law then you can go on to be a doctor or a lawyer. But what kind of job can you get if you study Renaissance art, or Indonesian history, or any kind of literature at all?

It's a fair question, even when asked ₅ unfairly. If Deval Patrick,[1] an English major, was available, I'd let him answer. But he's busy being governor, so I'll take a shot at it.

Let's first defenestrate a mistaken assumption that many students and their parents cling to. Prospective employers frequently don't really care what you majored in. They might look at where you went to school and how you did, and they will definitely consider whether you wrote a decent cover letter, but they don't sit there and think, "Anthropology?! We don't need an anthropologist."

They do care that you're a college graduate. What that means, if you worked hard and did your job properly and your teachers did theirs, is that you have spent four years developing a set of skills that will serve you in good stead in the postindustrial job market. You can assimilate and organize large, complex bodies of information; you can analyze that information to create outcomes that have value to others; and you can express your ideas in clear, purposeful language. Whether you honed these skills in the study of foreign policy or Russian novels is secondary, even trivial. What matters is that you pursued training in the craft of mastering complexity, which you can apply in fields from advertising to zoo management.

The papers on my desk are from a course on the city in literature and film. They're about, among other things, 9/11 stories, inner-city documentaries, and the literary tradition of Washington, D.C. Instead of worrying about whether you can get paid to know about these topics, consider this: You can't fake a twenty-page paper. Either you've done the work this semester and know what you're talking about, or you don't. Either you can deliver a sustained reasoned argument, or you can't. It's a craft, like cabinet making.

I make my living building such figurative cabinets — like this column, a miniature one I assembled using skills I learned first in school and then honed doing various jobs in the private and public sectors: policy analyst, teacher, reporter, writer, very small businessman. Whatever else happens at college, higher education is about learning to drive the postindustrial nails straight.

---

[1] **Deval Patrick** Governor of Massachusetts when Rotella's article was published. [Editors' note]

Topics for Critical Thinking and Writing

1. Carlo Rotella's thesis appears in his title. Do you think he presents a convincing argument in the essay? Why, or why not?

2. Rotella references a course he teaches about the role of the city in literature and film. Do you think such a course would be a valuable addition to your own higher education?

3. Do you think students deciding what major to select would benefit from reading Rotella's essay? Explain your reasoning.

4. On what points do you think Delbanco would agree with Rotella's argument? On what points might Delbanco differ? Explain.

EDWARD CONARD

Edward Conard (b. 1956), who has an MBA from Harvard, is best known for his controversial book on the US economy, *Unintended Consequences: Why Everything You've Been Told about the Economy Is Wrong* (2012). He has made more than one hundred television appearances, debating luminaries such as Paul Krugman and Jon Stewart. This article appeared as part of a Pro/Con debate in the *Washington Post* on July 30, 2013.

We Don't Need More Humanities Majors

It's no secret that innovation grows America's economy. But that growth is constrained in two ways. It is constrained by the amount of properly trained talent, which is needed to produce innovation. And it is constrained by this talent's willingness to take the entrepreneurial risks critical to commercializing innovation. Given those constraints, it is hard to believe humanities degree programs are the best way to train America's most talented students.

According to the Bureau of Labor Statistics (BLS), U.S. employment has grown roughly 45 percent since the early 1980s. Over the same period, Germany's employment grew roughly 20 percent, while France's employment grew less than 20 percent and Japan's only 13 percent. U.S. employment growth put roughly 10 million immigrants to work since the BLS started keeping track in 1996 and it has employed tens of millions of people offshore.

The share of people in the world living on less than $1.25-a-day has fallen from over 50 percent to nearly 20 percent today, according to The World Bank. Name another high-wage economy that has done more than the United States for the employment of the world's poor and middle class during this time period.

Contrary to popular belief, U.S. employment growth isn't outpacing other high-wage economies because of growing employment in small businesses. Europe has plenty of small family-owned businesses. U.S. growth is predominately driven by successful high-tech startups, such as Google, Microsoft, and Apple, which have spawned large industries around them.

A Kauffman Institute survey of over 500 engineering and tech companies established between 1995 and 2005 reveals that 55 percent of the U.S.-born founders held degrees in the science, engineering, technology or mathematics, so called STEM-related fields, and over 90 percent held terminal degrees in STEM, business, economics, law and health care. Only 7 percent held terminal degrees in other areas — only 3 percent in the arts, humanities or social sciences. It's true some advanced degree holders may have earned undergraduate degrees in humanities, but they quickly learned humanities degrees alone offered inadequate training, and they returned to school for more technical degrees.

Other studies reach similar conclusions. 5 A seminal study by Stanford economics professor Charles Jones estimates that 50 percent of the growth since the 1950s comes from increasing the number of scientific researchers relative to the population.

Another recent study from UC–Davis economics professor Giovanni Peri and Colgate economics associate professor Chad Sparber finds the small number of "foreign scientists and engineers brought into this country under the H-1B visa program have contributed to 10%–20% of the yearly productivity growth in the U.S. during the period 1990–2010." Despite the outsized importance of business and technology to America's economic growth, nearly half of all recent bachelor's degrees in the 2010–2011 academic year were awarded in fields outside these areas of study. Critical thinking is valuable in all forms, but it is more valuable when applied directly to the most pressing demands of society.

At the same time, U.S. universities expect to graduate a third of the computer scientists our society demands, according to a study released by Microsoft. The talent gap in the information technology sector has been bridged by non-computer science majors, according to a report by Daniel Costa, the Economic Policy Institute's director of immigration law and policy research. Costa finds

that the sector has recruited two-thirds of its talent from other disciplines — predominately workers with other technical degrees. But with the share of U.S. students with top quintile SAT/ACT scores and GPAs earning STEM-related degrees declining sharply over the last two decades, the industry has turned to foreign-born workers and increasingly offshore workers to fill its talent needs. While American consumers will benefit from discoveries made in other countries, discoveries made and commercialized here have driven and will continue to drive demand for U.S. employment — both skilled and unskilled.

UC–Berkeley economics professor Enrico Moretti estimates each additional high-tech job creates nearly five jobs in the local economy, more than any other industry. Unlike a restaurant, for example, high-tech employment tends to increase demand overall rather than merely shifting employment from one competing establishment to another. If talented workers opt out of valuable training and end up underemployed, not only have they failed to create employment for other less talented workers, they have taken jobs those workers likely could have filled.

Thirty years ago, America could afford to misallocate a large share of its talent and still grow faster than the rest of the world. Not anymore; much of the world has caught up. My analysis of data collected by economics professors Robert Barro of Harvard University and Jong-Wha Lee of Korea University reveals that over the last decade America only supplied 10 percent of the increase in the world's college graduates, much less than the roughly 30 percent it supplied thirty years ago. Fully harnessing America's talent and putting it to work addressing the needs of mankind directly would have a greater impact on raising standards of living in both the United States and the rest of the world than other alternatives available today.

Topics for Critical Thinking and Writing

1. In paragraph 1, Edward Conard makes clear his thesis: "It is hard to believe humanities degree programs are the best way to train America's most talented students." What assumption is Conard making about college degrees and the economy? Do you agree? Why, or why not?

2. Conard argues in paragraph 2 that the rate of employment in the United States has outpaced that of other advanced nations. To what does he attribute this growth? How does the US economy in turn provide worldwide prosperity?

3. Conard argues that economic growth is not generated by small businesses, as many people believe, but by start-up companies that become huge, such as Google, Microsoft, and Apple (para. 3). What other companies, if any, have started up in recent decades outside of the technological fields that have had a major impact on the economy, including job growth?

4. In paragraph 7, Conard points out that the United States is graduating only about one-third of the number of graduates needed in the fields of science, technology, engineering, and mathematics (STEM). Why is that? Do some research to support your answer.

5. Conard's arguments are driven almost entirely by economic concerns, not issues of personal happiness or career satisfaction. In your opinion, to what extent should those factors, as opposed to economic concerns, play a role in one's choice of a major? Explain your answer.

CHRISTIAN MADSBJERG AND MIKKEL B. RASMUSSEN

Christian Madsbjerg and Mikkel B. Rasmussen are senior partners at ReD Associates, a consulting firm that, in the words of its website, uses "social science tools to understand how people experience their reality" so that businesses can better reach customers. Together, Madsbjerg and Rasmussen wrote *The Moment of Clarity: Using Human Sciences to Solve Your Toughest Business Problems* (2014). This article appeared as part of a Pro/Con debate in the *Washington Post* on July 30, 2013.

We Need More Humanities Majors

It has become oddly fashionable to look down on the humanities over the last few decades. Today's students are being told that studying the classics of English literature, the history of the twentieth century, or the ethics of privacy are a fun but useless luxury. To best prioritize our scarce education resources, we ought instead to focus on technical subjects such as math and engineering.

This short-term market logic doesn't work across the thirty-or-so-year horizon of a full career. A generation ago, lawyers made more money than investment bankers. Today, we have too many law graduates (though there appears to be data to support it's still worth the money) and the investment banks complain about a lack of talent. It is basically impossible to project that sort of thing into the far future.

We are also told that a degree in the humanities is unlikely to make you successful. Take North Carolina Governor Pat McCrory (R), who, while making the case for subsidizing state community colleges and universities based on how well they do in terms of placing students in the workforce, said this in January:

> " . . . frankly, if you want to take gender studies, that's fine. Go to a private school and take it, but I don't want to subsidize that if that's not going to get someone a job. . . . It's the tech jobs that we need right now."

But quite a few people with humanities degrees have had successful careers and, in the process, created numerous jobs. According to a report from *Business Insider*, the list includes A.G. Lafley of Procter & Gamble (French and History), former Massachusetts Governor and Republican presidential nominee Mitt Romney (English), George Soros (Philosophy), Michael Eisner of Disney (English and Theater), Peter Thiel of Paypal (Philosophy), Ken Chenault of American Express (History), Carl Icahn (Philosophy), former Secretary of the Treasury Hank Paulson (English), Supreme Court Justice Clarence Thomas (English), Ted Turner of CNN (History), and former IBM CEO Sam Palmisano (History). *Business Insider* has a list of 30 business heavyweights in total.

One might think that most people starting 5 out or running tech companies in the heart of Silicon Valley would be from the science, technology, engineering and mathematics (STEM) fields. Not so. Vivek Wadhwa, a columnist for *The Washington Post*'s Innovations section and a fellow at the Rock Center for Corporate Governance at Stanford University, found that 47 percent of the 652 technology and engineering company founders surveyed held terminal degrees in the STEM fields, with 37 percent of those degrees being in either engineering or computer technology and 2 percent in mathematics. The rest graduated with a healthy combination of liberal arts, healthcare and business degrees.

This leads us to a very important question: What good is a degree in the humanities in the real world of products and customers? Here's the answer: Far more than most people think. It all comes down to this: Is it helpful to know your customers? Deeply understanding their world, seeing what they see and understanding why they do the things they do, is not an easy task. Some people have otherworldly intuitions. But for most of us, getting under the skin of the people we are trying to serve takes hard analytical work.

By analytical work we mean getting and analyzing data that can help us understand the bigger picture of people's lives. The real issue with understanding people, as opposed to bacteria, or numbers, is that we change when we are studied. Birds or geological sediments do not suddenly turn self-conscious, and change their behavior just because someone is looking. Studying a moving target like this requires a completely different approach than the one needed to study nature. If you want to understand the kinds of beings we are, you need to use your own humanity and your own experience.

Such an approach can be found in the humanities. When you study the writings of, say, David Foster Wallace, you learn how to step into and feel empathy for a different world than your own. His world of intricate, neurotic detail and societal critique says more about living as a young man in the 1990s than most market research graphs. But more importantly: The same skills involved in being a subtle reader of a text are involved in deeply understanding Chinese or Argentinian consumers of cars, soap or computers. They are

CHAPTER 13 | A COLLEGE EDUCATION: WHAT IS ITS PURPOSE?

hard skills of understanding other people, their practices and context.

The market is naturally on to this: In a recent study, Debra Humphreys from the Association of American College & Universities concludes that 95 percent of employers say that "a candidate's demonstrated capacity to think critically, communicate clearly, and solve complex problems is more important than their undergraduate major." These all are skills taught at the highest level in the humanities.

Companies — with the most sophisticated ones such as Intel, Microsoft and Johnson & Johnson leading the charge — are starting to launch major initiatives with names such as "customer-centric marketing" and "deep customer understanding." The goal of these programs is to help companies better understand the people they're selling to.

The issue is that engineers and most designers, by and large, create products for people whose tastes resemble their own. They simply don't have the skill set of a humanities major — one that allows a researcher or executive to deeply understand what it is like to be an Indonesian teenager living in Jakarta and getting a new phone, or what kind of infused beverages a Brazilian 25-year-old likes and needs.

The humanities are not in crisis. We need humanities majors more now than before to strengthen competitiveness and improve products and services. We have a veritable goldmine on our hands. But, in order for that to happen, we need the two cultures of business and the humanities to meet. The best place to start is collaboration between companies and universities on a research level — something that ought to be at the top of the minds of both research institutions and R&D departments in the coming decade.

Topics for Critical Thinking and Writing

1. Christian Madsbjerg and Mikkel B. Rasmussen note at the beginning of their article that there has been a significant trend of pushing students to major in the fields of science, technology, engineering, and mathematics (STEM). Why has that trend occurred? What do they say is the problem with doing so? Why?

2. In paragraph 4, the authors list several big-name businesspeople, politicians, and others who have degrees in the humanities. Are they merely cherry-picking examples (i.e., finding the few examples that support your position while ignoring the vast majority that do not), or do those examples accurately reflect the broader whole? Do research to support your answer.

3. What argument do the authors make about the abilities of humanities majors being superior to the abilities of those who major in technical fields? Do you find the authors' argument credible? Why, or why not?

4. In paragraph 9, the authors use the example of studying literature as a way to better understand human nature. Is that a fair claim? Why, or why not?

5. The authors point out that employers want to see employment candidates who can "think critically, communicate clearly, and solve complex problems" (para. 9). The authors argue that humanities graduates best fit that description. In your opinion, is that true or not? Be specific in your response.

6. In paragraph 11, the authors state, "The issue is that engineers and most designers, by and large, create products for people whose tastes resemble their own." Consider a specific recent product or invention and argue whether its design is reflective of what a customer wants or what an engineer or designer wants. Why?

7. In their conclusion, the authors argue that the "two cultures of business and the humanities" need to come together (para. 12). What does that statement assume about the purpose of higher education? What objections to it can you think of? Why?

CAROLINE HARPER

Caroline Harper holds a PhD in political science with concentrations in black politics and international relations from Howard University, where she is a lecturer. Located in Washington, DC, Howard is the most prominent historically black university in the United States. This essay was first published in May 14, 2018, on the blog *Higher Education Today*, operated by the American Council on Education.

HBCUs, Black Women, and STEM Success

The demand for professionals in science, technology, engineering, and math, or STEM, has been on the rise since 2000 — and projections indicate that the need for qualified candidates will not slow down any time soon. As new technology has driven market growth around the world, the United States has struggled to develop a workforce capable of maintaining a competitive edge in the global market. The ability to compete in the global market is contingent upon our ability to maximize resources that educate and prepare a diverse pipeline of students who understand the necessity of global citizenship.

During the White House College Opportunity Summit in 2014, President Obama reiterated the need to develop long-term strategies that expose students to STEM disciplines in elementary and middle school, increase college access, and maintain postsecondary affordability. These goals become increasingly important as projections indicate that more students from low-income and underrepresented minorities will pursue college degrees by 2025. According to the Bureau of Labor Statistics, women will make up 47.2 percent of the total labor force by 2024. It has become clear that postsecondary education is the gateway to obtaining professional opportunities in STEM occupations. In 2015, the Bureau of Labor Statistics confirmed that more than 99 percent of jobs in STEM required postsecondary education, compared to 36 percent of occupations overall.

The ability to create a pathway from degree attainment to gainful employment ensures that the STEM workforce reflects the diversity of our country. In recognizing this, the White House Council on Women and Girls and the Office of Science and Technology Policy have worked to encourage more women and girls to earn college degrees and pursue careers in STEM fields. But do existing strategies ensure a diverse STEM pipeline? Do these strategies reduce disparities between degree attainment and labor force outcomes among women and minorities?

CONDITIONS OF THE STEM PIPELINE

Although policy efforts to encourage STEM degree attainment are laudable, the STEM pipeline is leaky when it comes to underrepresented minorities. At the high school level, it is difficult to maintain a campus culture that encourages equity in the pursuit of STEM degrees when calculus and physics courses are available in only 33 percent and 48 percent of high schools with high black and Latino student enrollment, respectively.

Beyond access to courses that serve as the 5 foundation to STEM careers, many black and Latino students have limited access to college and career readiness counselors. According to a national survey of school counselors, in high schools in which the student body is primarily low-income and/or underrepresented minority, the average caseload is at least 1,000 students per counselor — at least twice the national average. As a consequence of factors beyond their control, it is especially difficult for these students to successfully navigate a career trajectory that incorporates course selection, experiential learning opportunities, extracurricular activities, and college admission requirements.

Although many of the students aspire to attend college, black students are struggling to meet mathematics (13 percent), science (11 percent) and general STEM (4 percent) ACT test benchmarks, which are often seen as a measure of college readiness. What is the alternative for students who are interested in pursuing STEM careers but need additional resources to overcome limitations in their K–12 education?

CAMPUS CULTURE AND COLLEGE SUCCESS

Despite limited access to resources during high school, students who choose to pursue their undergraduate degrees at Historically Black Colleges and Universities (HBCUs) are welcomed by a nurturing environment that provides critical resources to overcome academic, social, and financial hurdles. For more than 150 years, HBCUs have continued to serve first-generation, low-income, and underprepared students.

According to the U.S. Census Bureau, the number of traditional college-aged Americans is projected to grow to 13.3 million by 2025. The largest growth is expected to occur among students who identify as black, Hispanic, or Asian/Pacific Islander. In an analysis of black student graduation rates, about half of all four-year HBCUs enrolled freshmen classes where 75 percent of students were from low-income backgrounds, compared to 1 percent of the 676 non-HBCUs in the study. Among the institutions where 40–75 percent of the freshman class was low-income, the graduation rate for black students who attended HBCUs was 37.8 percent — five percentage points higher than their counterparts at non-HBCUs.

HBCUs produced 46 percent of black women who earned degrees in STEM disciplines between 1995 and 2004. HBCUs produced 25 percent of all bachelor's degrees in STEM fields earned by African Americans in 2012. In 2014, black women represented the highest percentage of minority women who earned bachelor's degrees in computer sciences. HBCUs such as North Carolina A&T State University, Howard University, Florida A&M University, and Xavier University of Louisiana continue producing undergraduate STEM degree earners who pursue graduate degrees in their field.

Beyond producing bachelor's degrees, 10 research confirms that HBCUs are the institution of origin among almost 30 percent of blacks who earned doctorates in science and engineering. According to the National Science Foundation, within STEM fields such as mathematics, biological sciences, physical sciences, agricultural sciences, and earth, atmospheric, and ocean sciences, a large percentage of doctorate degree holders earned their bachelor's degrees at HBCUs.

CAREER OUTCOMES

While the campus culture at HBCUs provides black students with a sense of community, self-confidence, and efficacy, the workforce provides a stark contrast. Relative to their share of degree attainment, blacks are underrepresented in the overall context of the workforce and earnings.

Research has shown that compared to their Hispanic and Asian counterparts, blacks have the highest rate of unemployment. Among minorities currently employed in a STEM occupation, 41.4 percent are Asian, 18.4 percent are Hispanic or Latino, and only 17.4 percent are black. Moreover, blacks who work full time, year-round in STEM occupations are paid less than their Asian and Hispanic counterparts.

Despite disparities in employment rates and income, there are still important achievements that should be considered as the STEM workforce continues to grow. Within mathematical occupations, there were more black operations research analysts than any other minority group in 2011. In engineering occupations, black engineers outnumbered other minorities in the petroleum engineering field and rivaled Asians in roles related to environmental engineering, surveyors, cartographers, and photogrammetrists. Black scientists outnumbered other minorities in chemical technician and nuclear scientist roles. Compared to their Hispanic counterparts, there was a higher percentage of black professionals in conservation sciences and forestry occupations and geological and petroleum technician roles.

NEXT STEPS

While HBCUs do their share of producing black graduates with STEM degrees, there is a greater need for equity throughout the education pipeline and in workforce hiring practices. Suggestions to fill gaps in the STEM pipeline and ensure a diverse workforce that increases our ability to compete internationally include:

- Ensure that high schools serving low-income and minority students are provided with adequate resources to hire additional school counselors proportional to the student body and with the capacity to help students develop strategies to achieve college and career readiness.

- Provide funding to support collaborations with organizations that encourage academic rigor in STEM disciplines, including calculus and physics, in addition to advanced placement and honors courses. Specifically, funds should be designated to increase access to STEM foundation courses, advanced placement, and honors courses.

- Encourage private corporations to actively engage in the process of creating a diverse workforce by developing partnerships that encourage diversity in recruitment, hiring, and development of African American college students pursuing degrees in STEM disciplines.

- Develop internship opportunities in collaboration with HBCU campuses to provide students with opportunities to put their coursework into practice while developing skills that can be transferred into the workforce.

HBCUs have maintained their legacies of [15] producing African American professionals in critical professions. Staying true to their mission, HBCUs continue to provide a nurturing environment where students gain academic and professional training to drive innovation in STEM fields and make valuable contributions in communities around the world.

Topics for Critical Thinking and Writing

1. What is Caroline Harper's argument? Describe how she lays out the problem and solution over the course of the essay. Use details and examples from her essay in your description.

2. What does Harper mean by the STEM pipeline? In 250 words or so, define the STEM pipeline in your own words, using your own examples.

3. In approximately 250 words, explain why Harper thinks HBCUs are the ideal places for correcting the inequities between different economic, racial, and gender groups.

4. Does Harper's argument imply that the kind of humanities-based, liberal arts education advocated by Delbanco and by Madsbjerg and Rasmussen is not as important for underrepresented minorities as advancement in STEM skills and fields? In 300 to 500 words, supplement Harper's argument with your own ideas on why it might be important for underrepresented minorities to take courses in history, art, or other humanities fields.

14

What Is the Ideal Society?

THOMAS MORE

The son of a prominent London lawyer, Thomas More (1478–1535) served as a page in the household of the Archbishop of Canterbury, went to Oxford University, and then studied law in London. More's charm, brilliance, and gentle manner caused Erasmus, the great Dutch humanist who became his friend during a visit to London, to write to a friend: "Did nature ever create anything kinder, sweeter, or more harmonious than the character of Thomas More?"

More served in Parliament, became a diplomat, and after holding several important positions in the government of Henry VIII, rose to become lord chancellor. But when Henry married Anne Boleyn, broke from the Church of Rome, and established himself as head of the Church of England, More refused to subscribe to the Act of Succession and Supremacy. Condemned to death as a traitor, he was executed in 1535, nominally for treason but really because he would not recognize the king rather than the pope as the head of his church. A moment before the ax fell, More displayed a bit of the whimsy for which he was known: When he put his head on the block, he brushed his beard aside, commenting that his beard had done no offense to the king. In 1886, the Roman Catholic Church beatified More, and in 1935, the four-hundredth anniversary of his death, it canonized him as St. Thomas More.

More wrote *Utopia* (1514–1515) in Latin, the international language of the day. The book's name, however, is Greek for "no place" (*ou topos*), with a pun on "good place" (*eu topos*). *Utopia* owes something to Plato's *Republic* and something to then-popular accounts of voyagers such as Amerigo Vespucci. *Utopia* purports to record an account given by a traveler named Hytholodaeus (Greek for "learned in nonsense"), who allegedly visited Utopia. The work is playful, but it is also serious. In truth, it is hard to know exactly where it is serious and how serious it is. One inevitably wonders, for example, if More the devoted Roman Catholic could really have advocated euthanasia. And could More the persecutor of heretics really have approved of the religious tolerance practiced in Utopia? Is he perhaps in effect saying, "Let's see what reason, unaided by Christian revelation, can tell us about an ideal society"? But if so, is he nevertheless also saying, very strongly, that Christian countries, although blessed with the revelation of Christ's teachings, are far behind these unenlightened pagans? Utopia has been widely praised by all sorts of readers — from Roman Catholics to communists — and for all sorts of reasons. The selection presented here is about one-twelfth of the book (in a translation by Paul Turner).

From *Utopia*

[A DAY IN UTOPIA]

And now for their working conditions. Well, there's one job they all do, irrespective of sex, and that's farming. It's part of every child's education. They learn the principles of agriculture at school, and they're taken for regular outings into the fields near the town, where they not only watch farm work being done, but also do some themselves, as a form of exercise.

Besides farming which, as I say, is everybody's job, each person is taught a special trade of his own. He may be trained to process wool or flax, or he may become a stonemason, a blacksmith, or a carpenter. Those are the only trades that employ any considerable quantity of labor. They have no tailors or dressmakers, since everyone on the island wears the same sort of clothes — except that they vary slightly according to sex and marital status — and the fashion never changes. These clothes are quite pleasant to look at, they allow free movement of the limbs, they're equally suitable for hot and cold weather — and the great thing is, they're all home-made. So everybody learns one of the other trades I mentioned, and by everybody I mean the women as well as the men — though the weaker sex are given the lighter jobs, like spinning and weaving, while the men do the heavier ones.

Most children are brought up to do the same work as their parents, since they tend to have a natural feeling for it. But if a child fancies some other trade, he's adopted into a family that practices it. Of course, great care is taken, not only by the father, but also by the local authorities, to see that the foster father is a decent, respectable type. When you've learned one trade properly, you can, if you like, get permission to learn another — and when you're an expert in both, you can practice whichever you prefer, unless the other one is more essential to the public.

The chief business of the Stywards[1] — in fact, practically their only business — is to see that nobody sits around doing nothing, but that everyone gets on with his job. They don't wear people out, though, by keeping them hard at work from early morning till late at night, like cart horses. That's just slavery — and yet that's what life is like for the working classes nearly everywhere else in the world. In Utopia they have a six-hour working day — three hours in the morning, then lunch — then a two-hour break — then three more hours in the afternoon, followed by supper. They go to bed at 8 p.m., and sleep for eight hours. All the rest of the twenty-four they're free to do what they like — not to waste their time in idleness or self-indulgence, but to make good use of it in some congenial activity. Most people spend these free periods on further education, for there are public lectures first thing every morning. Attendance is quite voluntary, except for those picked out for academic training, but men and women of all classes go crowding in to hear them — I mean, different people go to different lectures, just as the spirit moves them. However, there's nothing to stop you from spending this extra time on your trade, if you want to. Lots of people do, if they haven't the capacity for intellectual work, and are much admired for such public-spirited behavior.

---

[1]**Stywards** In Utopia, each group of thirty households elects a steward; each town has two hundred stywards, who elect the mayor. [Editors' note]

After supper they have an hour's recreation, 5 either in the gardens or in the communal dining-halls, according to the time of year. Some people practice music, others just talk. They've never heard of anything so silly and demoralizing as dice, but they have two games rather like chess. The first is a sort of arithmetical contest, in which certain numbers "take" others. The second is a pitched battle between virtues and vices, which illustrates most ingeniously how vices tend to conflict with one another, but to combine against virtues. It also shows which vices are opposed to which virtues, how much strength vices can muster for a direct assault, what indirect tactics they employ, what help virtues need to overcome vices, what are the best methods of evading their attacks, and what ultimately determines the victory of one side or the other.

But here's a point that requires special attention, or you're liable to get the wrong idea. Since they only work a six-hour day, you may think there must be a shortage of essential goods. On the contrary, those six hours are enough, and more than enough to produce plenty of everything that's needed for a comfortable life. And you'll understand why it is, if you reckon up how large a proportion of the population in other countries is totally unemployed. First you have practically all the women — that gives you nearly 50 percent for a start. And in countries where the women *do* work, the men tend to lounge about instead. Then there are all the priests, and members of so-called religious orders — how much work do they do? Add all the rich, especially the landowners, popularly known as nobles and gentlemen. Include their domestic staffs — I mean those gangs of armed ruffians that I mentioned before. Finally, throw in all the beggars who are perfectly hale and hearty, but pretend to be ill as an excuse for being lazy. When you've counted them up, you'll be surprised to find how few people actually produce what the human race consumes.

And now just think how few of these few people are doing essential work — for where money is the only standard of value, there are bound to be dozens of unnecessary trades carried on, which merely supply luxury goods or entertainment. Why, even if the existing labor force were distributed among the few trades really needed to make life reasonably comfortable, there'd be so much overproduction that prices would fall too low for the workers to earn a living. Whereas, if you took all those engaged in nonessential trades, and all who are too lazy to work — each of whom consumes twice as much of the products of other people's labor as any of the producers themselves — if you put the whole lot of them on to something useful, you'd soon see how few hours' work a day would be amply sufficient to supply all the necessities and comforts of life — to which you might add all real and natural forms of pleasure.

[THE HOUSEHOLD]

But let's get back to their social organization. Each household, as I said, comes under the authority of the oldest male. Wives are subordinate to their husbands, children to their parents, and younger people generally to their elders. Every town is divided into four districts of equal size, each with its own shopping center in the middle of it. There the products of every household are collected in warehouses, and then distributed according to type among various shops. When the head of a household needs anything for himself or his family, he just goes to one of these shops and asks for it. And whatever he asks for, he's allowed to take away without any sort of payment, either in money or in kind. After all, why shouldn't he? There's more than enough of everything to go round, so there's no risk of his asking for more than he needs — for why should anyone want to start hoarding, when he knows he'll never have to go short of anything? No living creature is naturally greedy, except from fear of want — or in the case of human beings, from vanity, the notion that you're better than people if you can display more superfluous property than they can. But there's no scope for that sort of thing in Utopia.

[UTOPIAN BELIEFS]

The Utopians fail to understand why anyone should be so fascinated by the dull gleam of a tiny bit of stone, when he has all the stars in the sky to look at — or how anyone can be silly enough to think himself better than other people, because his clothes are made of finer woollen thread than theirs. After all, those fine clothes were once worn by a sheep, and they never turned it into anything better than a sheep.

Nor can they understand why a totally 10 useless substance like gold should now, all over the world, be considered far more important than human beings, who gave it such value as it has, purely for their own convenience. The result is that a man with about as much mental agility as a lump of lead or a block of wood, a man whose utter stupidity is paralleled only by his immorality, can have lots of good, intelligent people at his beck and call, just because he happens to possess a large pile of gold coins. And if by some freak of fortune or trick of the law — two equally effective methods of turning things upside down — the said coins were suddenly transferred to the most worthless member of his domestic staff, you'd soon see the present owner trotting after his money, like an extra piece of currency, and becoming his own servant's servant. But what puzzles and disgusts the Utopians even more is the idiotic way some people have of practically worshipping a rich man, not because they owe him money or are otherwise in his power, but simply because he's rich — although they know perfectly well that he's far too mean to let a single penny come their way, so long as he's alive to stop it.

They get these ideas partly from being brought up under a social system which is directly opposed to that type of nonsense, and partly from their reading and education. Admittedly, no one's allowed to become a full-time student, except for the very few in each town who appear as children to possess unusual gifts, outstanding intelligence, and a special aptitude for academic research. But every child receives a primary education, and most men and women go on educating themselves all their lives during those free periods that I told you about. . . .

In ethics they discuss the same problems as we do. Having distinguished between three types of "good," psychological, physiological, and environmental, they proceed to ask whether the term is strictly applicable to all of them, or only to the first. They also argue about such things as virtue and pleasure. But their chief subject of dispute is the nature of human happiness — on what factor or factors does it depend? Here they seem rather too much inclined to take a hedonistic view, for according to them human happiness consists largely or wholly in pleasure. Surprisingly enough, they defend this self-indulgent doctrine by arguments drawn from religion — a thing normally associated with a more serious view of life, if not with gloomy asceticism. You see, in all their discussions of happiness they invoke certain religious principles to supplement the operations of reason, which they think otherwise ill-equipped to identify true happiness.

The first principle is that every soul is immortal, and was created by a kind God, Who meant it to be happy. The second is that we shall be rewarded or punished in the next world for our good or bad behavior in this one. Although these are religious principles, the Utopians find rational grounds for accepting them. For suppose you didn't accept them? In that case, they say, any fool could tell you what you ought to do. You should go all out for your own pleasure, irrespective of right and wrong. You'd merely have to make sure that minor pleasures didn't interfere with major ones, and avoid the type of pleasure that has painful aftereffects. For what's the sense of struggling to be virtuous, denying yourself the pleasant things of life, and deliberately making yourself uncomfortable, if there's nothing you hope to gain by it? And what *can* you hope to gain by it, if you receive no compensation after death for a thoroughly unpleasant, that is, a thoroughly miserable life?

Not that they identify happiness with every type of pleasure — only with the higher ones. Nor do they identify it with virtue — unless they belong to a quite different school of thought. According to the normal view, happiness is the *summum bonum*[2] toward which we're naturally impelled by virtue — which in their definition means following one's natural impulses, as God meant us to do. But this includes obeying the instinct to be reasonable in our likes and dislikes. And reason also teaches us, first to love and reverence Almighty God, to Whom we owe our existence and our potentiality for happiness, and secondly to get through life as comfortably and cheerfully as we can, and help all other members of our species to do so too.

The fact is, even the sternest ascetic tends 15 to be slightly inconsistent in his condemnation of pleasure. He may sentence *you* to a life of hard labor, inadequate sleep, and general discomfort, but he'll also tell you to do your best to ease the pains and privations of others. He'll regard all such attempts to improve the human situation as laudable acts of humanity — for obviously nothing could be more humane, or more natural for a human being, than to relieve other people's sufferings, put an end to their miseries, and restore their *joie de vivre*, that is, their capacity for pleasure. So why shouldn't it be equally natural to do the same thing for oneself?

Either it's a bad thing to enjoy life, in other words, to experience pleasure — in which case you shouldn't help anyone to do it, but should try to save the whole human race from such a frightful fate — or else, if it's good for other people, and you're not only allowed, but positively obliged to make it possible for them, why shouldn't charity begin at home? After all, you've a duty to yourself as well as to your neighbor, and, if Nature says you must be kind to others, she can't turn round the next moment and say you must be cruel to yourself. The Utopians therefore regard the enjoyment of life — that is, pleasure — as the natural object of all human efforts, and natural, as they define it, is synonymous with virtuous. However, Nature also wants us to help one another to enjoy life, for the very good reason that no human being has a monopoly of her affections. She's equally anxious for the welfare of every member of the species. So of course she tells us to make quite sure that we don't pursue our own interests at the expense of other people's.

---

[2]*summum bonum* Latin for "the highest good." [Editors' note]

On this principle they think it right to keep one's promises in private life, and also to obey public laws for regulating the distribution of "goods" — by which I mean the raw materials of pleasure — provided such laws have been properly made by a wise ruler, or passed by common consent of a whole population, which has not been subjected to any form of violence or deception. Within these limits they say it's sensible to consult one's own interests, and a moral duty to consult those of the community as well. It's wrong to deprive someone else of a pleasure so that you can enjoy one yourself, but to deprive yourself of a pleasure so that you can add to someone else's enjoyment is an act of humanity by which you always gain more than you lose. For one thing, such benefits are usually repaid in kind. For another, the mere sense of having done somebody a kindness, and so earned his affection and goodwill, produces a spiritual satisfaction which far outweighs the loss of a physical one. And lastly — a belief that comes easily to a religious mind — God will reward us for such small sacrifices of momentary pleasure, by giving us an eternity of perfect joy. Thus they argue that, in the final analysis, pleasure is the ultimate happiness which all human beings have in view, even when they're acting most virtuously.

Pleasure they define as any state or activity, physical or mental, which is naturally enjoyable. The operative word is *naturally*. According to them, we're impelled by reason as well as an instinct to enjoy ourselves in any natural way which doesn't hurt other people, interfere with greater pleasures, or cause unpleasant after-effects. But human beings have entered into an idiotic conspiracy to call some things enjoyable which are naturally nothing of the kind — as though facts were as easily changed as definitions. Now the Utopians believe that, so far from contributing to happiness, this type of thing makes happiness impossible — because, once you get used to it, you lose all capacity for real pleasure, and are merely obsessed by illusory forms of it. Very often these have nothing pleasant about them at all — in fact, most of them are thoroughly disagreeable. But they appeal so strongly to perverted tastes that they come to be reckoned not only among the major pleasures of life, but even among the chief reasons for living.

In the category of illusory pleasure addicts they include the kind of person I mentioned before, who thinks himself better than other people because he's better dressed than they are. Actually he's just as wrong about his clothes as he is about himself. From a practical point of view, why is it better to be dressed in fine woollen thread than in coarse? But he's got it into his head that fine thread is naturally superior, and that wearing it somehow increases his own value. So he feels entitled to far more respect than he'd ever dare to hope for, if he were less expensively dressed, and is most indignant if he fails to get it.

Talking of respect, isn't it equally idiotic to [20] attach such importance to a lot of empty gestures which do nobody any good? For what real pleasure can you get out of the sight of a bared head or a bent knee? Will it cure the rheumatism in your own knee, or make you any less weak in the head? Of course, the great believers in this type of artificial pleasure are those who pride themselves on their "nobility." Nowadays that merely means that they happen to belong to a family which has been rich for several generations, preferably in landed property. And yet they feel every bit as "noble" even if they've failed to inherit any of the said property, or if they have inherited it and then frittered it all away.

Then there's another type of person I mentioned before, who has a passion for jewels, and feels practically superhuman if he manages to get hold of a rare one, especially if it's a kind that's considered particularly precious in his country and period—for the value of such things varies according to where and when you live. But he's so terrified of being taken in by appearances that he refuses to buy any jewel until he's stripped off all the gold and inspected it in the nude. And even then he won't buy it without a solemn assurance and a written guarantee from the jeweler that the stone is genuine. But my dear sir, why shouldn't a fake give you just as much pleasure, if you can't, with your own eyes, distinguish it from a real one? It makes no difference to you whether it's genuine or not—any more than it would to a blind man!

And now, what about those people who accumulate superfluous wealth, for no better purpose than to enjoy looking at it? Is their pleasure a real one, or merely a form of delusion? The opposite type of psychopath buries his gold, so that he'll never be able to use it, and may never even see it again. In fact, he deliberately loses it in his anxiety not to lose it—for what can you call it but lost, when it's put back into the earth, where it's no good to him, or probably to anyone else? And yet he's tremendously happy when he's got it stowed away. Now, apparently, he can stop worrying. But suppose the money is stolen, and ten years later he dies without ever knowing it has gone. Then for a whole ten years he has managed to survive his loss, and during that period what difference has it made to him whether the money was there or not? It was just as little use to him either way.

Among stupid pleasures they include not only gambling—a form of idiocy that they've heard about but never practiced—but also hunting and hawking. What on earth is the fun, they ask, of throwing dice onto a table?

Besides, you've done it so often that, even if there was some fun in it at first, you must surely be sick of it by now. How can you possibly enjoy listening to anything so disagreeable as the barking and howling of dogs? And why is it more amusing to watch a dog chasing a hare than to watch one dog chasing another? In each case the essential activity is running—if running is what amuses you. But if it's really the thought of being in at the death, and seeing an animal torn to pieces before your eyes, wouldn't pity be a more appropriate reaction to the sight of a weak, timid, harmless little creature like a hare being devoured by something so much stronger and fiercer?

So the Utopians consider hunting below the dignity of free men, and leave it entirely to butchers, who are, as I told you, slaves. In their view hunting is the vilest department of butchery, compared with which all the others are relatively useful and honorable. An ordinary butcher slaughters livestock far more sparingly, and only because he has to, whereas a hunter kills and mutilates poor little creatures purely for his own amusement. They say you won't find that type of blood lust even among animals, unless they're particularly savage by nature, or have become so by constantly being used for this cruel sport.

There are hundreds of things like that, [25] which are generally regarded as pleasures, but everyone in Utopia is quite convinced that they've got nothing to do with real pleasure, because there's nothing naturally enjoyable about them. Nor is this conviction at all shaken by the argument that most people do actually enjoy them, which would seem to indicate an appreciable pleasure content. They say this is a purely subjective reaction caused by bad habits, which can make a person prefer unpleasant things to pleasant ones, just as pregnant women sometimes lose their sense of taste, and find suet or turpentine more delicious than honey. But however much one's judgment may be impaired by habit or ill health, the nature of pleasure, as of everything else, remains unchanged.

Real pleasures they divide into two categories, mental and physical. Mental pleasures include the satisfaction that one gets from understanding something, or from contemplating truth. They also include the memory of a well-spent life, and the confident expectation of good things to come. Physical pleasures are subdivided into two types. First there are those which fill the whole organism with a conscious sense of enjoyment. This may be the result of replacing physical substances which have been burnt up by the natural heat of the body, as when we eat or drink. Or else it may be caused by the discharge of some excess, as in excretion, sexual intercourse, or any relief of irritation by rubbing or scratching. However, there are also pleasures which satisfy no organic need, and relieve no previous discomfort. They merely act, in a mysterious but quite unmistakable way, directly on our senses, and monopolize their reactions. Such is the pleasure of music.

Their second type of physical pleasure arises from the calm and regular functioning of the body — that is, from a state of health undisturbed by any minor ailments. In the absence of mental discomfort, this gives one a good feeling, even without the help of external pleasures. Of course, it's less ostentatious, and forces itself less violently on one's attention than the cruder delights of eating and drinking, but even so it's often considered the greatest pleasure in life. Practically everyone in Utopia would agree that it's a very important one, because it's the basis of all the others.

It's enough by itself to make you enjoy life, and unless you have it, no other pleasure is possible. However, mere freedom from pain, without positive health, they would call not pleasure but anesthesia.

Some thinkers used to maintain that a uniformly tranquil state of health couldn't properly be termed a pleasure since its presence could only be detected by contrast with its opposite — oh yes, they went very thoroughly into the whole question. But that theory was exploded long ago, and nowadays nearly everybody subscribes to the view that health is most definitely a pleasure. The argument goes like this — illness involves pain, which is the direct opposite of pleasure, and illness is the direct opposite of health, therefore health involves pleasure. They don't think it matters whether you say that illness *is* or merely *involves* pain. Either way it comes to the same thing. Similarly, whether health *is* a pleasure, or merely *produces* pleasure as inevitably as fire produces heat, it's equally logical to assume that where you have an uninterrupted state of health you cannot fail to have pleasure.

Besides, they say, when we eat something, what really happens is this. Our failing health starts fighting off the attacks of hunger, using the food as an ally. Gradually it begins to prevail, and, in this very process of winning back its normal strength, experiences the sense of enjoyment which we find so refreshing. Now, if health enjoys the actual battle, why shouldn't it also enjoy the victory? Or are we to suppose that when it has finally managed to regain its former vigor — the one thing that it has been fighting for all this time — it promptly falls into a coma, and fails to notice or take advantage of its success? As for the idea that one isn't conscious of health except through its opposite, they say that's quite untrue. Everyone's perfectly aware of feeling well, unless he's asleep or actually feeling ill. Even the most insensitive and apathetic sort of person will admit that it's delightful to be healthy — and what is delight, but a synonym for pleasure?

They're particularly fond of mental pleasures, which they consider of primary importance, and attribute mostly to good behavior and a clear conscience. Their favorite physical pleasure is health. Of course, they believe in enjoying food, drink, and so forth, but purely in the interests of health, for they don't regard such things as very pleasant in themselves — only as methods of resisting the stealthy onset of disease. A sensible person, they say, prefers keeping well to taking medicine, and would rather feel cheerful than have people trying to comfort him. On the same principle it's better not to need this type of pleasure than to become addicted to it. For, if you think that sort of thing will make you happy, you'll have to admit that your idea of perfect felicity would be a life consisting entirely of hunger, thirst, itching, eating, drinking, rubbing, and scratching — which would obviously be most unpleasant as well as quite disgusting. Undoubtedly these pleasures should come right at the bottom of the list, because they're so impure. For instance, the pleasure of eating is invariably diluted with the pain of hunger, and not in equal proportions either — for the pain is both more intense and more prolonged. It starts before the pleasure, and doesn't stop until the pleasure has stopped too.

So they don't think much of pleasures like that, except insofar as they're necessary. But they enjoy them all the same, and feel most grateful to Mother Nature for encouraging her children to do things that have to be done so often, by making them so attractive. For just think how dreary life would be, if those chronic ailments, hunger and thirst, could only be cured by foul-tasting medicines, like the rarer types of disease!

They attach great value to special natural gifts such as beauty, strength, and agility. They're also keen on the pleasures of sight, hearing, and smell, which are peculiar to human beings — for no other species admires the beauty of the world, enjoys any sort of scent, except as a method of locating food, or can tell the difference between a harmony and a discord. They say these things give a sort of relish to life.

However, in all such matters they observe the rule that minor pleasures mustn't interfere with major ones, and that pleasure mustn't cause pain — which they think is bound to happen, if the pleasure is immoral. But they'd never dream of despising their own beauty, overtaxing their strength, converting their agility into inertia, ruining their physique by going without food, damaging their health, or spurning any other of Nature's gifts, unless they were doing it for the benefit of other people or of society, in the hope of receiving some greater pleasure from God in return. For they think it's quite absurd to torment oneself in the name of an unreal virtue, which does nobody any good, or in order to steel oneself against disasters which may never occur. They say such behavior is merely self-destructive, and shows a most ungrateful attitude toward Nature — as if one refused all her favors, because one couldn't bear the thought of being indebted to her for anything.

Well, that's their ethical theory, and short of some divine revelation, they doubt if the human mind is capable of devising a better one. We've no time to discuss whether it's right or wrong — nor is it really necessary, for all I undertook was to describe their way of life, not to defend it.

[TREATMENT OF THE DYING]

As I told you, when people are ill, they're 35 looked after most sympathetically, and given everything in the way of medicine or special food that could possibly assist their recovery. In the case of permanent invalids, the nurses try to make them feel better by sitting and talking to them, and do all they can to relieve their symptoms. But if, besides being incurable, the disease also causes constant excruciating pain, some priests and government officials visit the person concerned, and say something like this:

"Let's face it, you'll never be able to live a normal life. You're just a nuisance to other people and a burden to yourself — in fact you're really leading a sort of posthumous existence. So why go on feeding germs? Since your life's a misery to you, why hesitate to die? You're imprisoned in a torture chamber — why don't you break out and escape to a better world? Or say the word, and we'll arrange for your release. It's only common sense to cut your losses. It's also an act of piety to take the advice of a priest, because he speaks for God."

If the patient finds these arguments convincing, he either starves himself to death, or is given a soporific and put painlessly out of his misery. But this is strictly voluntary, and, if he prefers to stay alive, everyone will go on treating him as kindly as ever.

[THE SUMMING UP]

Well, that's the most accurate account I can give you of the Utopian Republic. To my mind, it's not only the best country in the world, but the only one that has any right to call itself a republic. Elsewhere, people are always talking about the public interest, but all they really care about is private property. In Utopia, where's there's no private property, people take their duty to the public seriously. And both attitudes are perfectly reasonable. In other "republics" practically everyone knows that, if he doesn't look out for himself, he'll starve to death, however prosperous his country may be. He's therefore compelled to give his own interests priority over those of the public; that is, of other people. But in Utopia, where everything's under public ownership, no one has any fear of going short, as long as the public storehouses are full. Everyone gets a fair share, so there are never any poor men or beggars. Nobody owns anything, but everyone is rich — for what greater wealth can there be than cheerfulness, peace of mind, and freedom from anxiety? Instead of being worried about his food supply, upset by the plaintive demands of his wife, afraid of poverty for his son, and baffled by the problem of finding a dowry for his daughter, the Utopian can feel absolutely sure that he, his wife, his children, his grandchildren, his great-grandchildren, his great-great-grandchildren, and as long a line of descendants as the proudest peer could wish to look forward to, will always have enough to eat and enough to make them happy. There's also the further point that those who are too old to work are just as well provided for as those who are still working.

Now, will anyone venture to compare these fair arrangements in Utopia with the so-called justice of other countries? — in which I'm damned if I can see the slightest trace of justice or fairness. For what sort of justice do you call this? People like aristocrats, goldsmiths, or moneylenders, who either do no work at all, or do work that's really not essential, are rewarded for their laziness or their unnecessary activities by a splendid life of luxury. But laborers, coachmen, carpenters, and farmhands, who never stop working like cart horses, at jobs so essential that, if they *did* stop working, they'd bring any country to a standstill within twelve months — what happens to them? They get so little to eat, and have such a wretched time, that they'd be almost better off if they *were* cart horses. Then at least, they wouldn't work quite such long hours, their food wouldn't be very much worse, they'd enjoy it more, and they'd have no fears for the future. As it is, they're not only ground down by unrewarding toil in the present, but also worried to death by the prospect of a poverty-stricken old age — since their daily wages aren't enough to support them for one day, let alone leave anything over to be saved up when they're old.

Can you see any fairness or gratitude in 40 a social system which lavishes such great rewards on so-called noblemen, goldsmiths, and people like that, who are either totally unproductive or merely employed in producing luxury goods or entertainment, but makes no such kind provision for farmhands, coal heavers, laborers, carters, or carpenters, without whom society couldn't exist at all? And the climax of ingratitude comes when they're old and ill and completely destitute. Having taken advantage of them throughout the best years of their lives, society now forgets all the sleepless hours they've spent in its service, and repays them for all the vital work they've done, by letting them die in misery. What's more, the wretched earnings of the poor are daily whittled away by the rich, not only through private dishonesty, but through public legislation. As if it weren't unjust enough already that the man who contributes most to society should get

the least in return, they make it even worse, and then arrange for injustice to be legally described as justice.

In fact, when I consider any social system that prevails in the modern world, I can't, so help me God, see it as anything but a conspiracy of the rich to advance their own interests under the pretext of organizing society. They think up all sorts of tricks and dodges, first for keeping safe their ill-gotten gains, and then for exploiting the poor by buying their labor as cheaply as possible. Once the rich have decided that these tricks and dodges shall be officially recognized by society — which includes the poor as well as the rich — they acquire the force of law. Thus an unscrupulous minority is led by its insatiable greed to monopolize what would have been enough to supply the needs of the whole population. And yet how much happier even these people would be in Utopia! There, with the simultaneous abolition of money and the passion for money, how many other social problems have been solved, how many crimes eradicated! For obviously the end of money means the end of all those types of criminal behavior which daily punishments are powerless to check: fraud, theft, burglary, brawls, riots, disputes, rebellion, murder, treason, and black magic. And the moment money goes, you can also say goodbye to fear, tension, anxiety, overwork, and sleepless nights. Why, even poverty itself, the one problem that has always seemed to need money for its solution, would promptly disappear if money ceased to exist.

Let me try to make this point clearer. Just think back to one of the years when the harvest was bad, and thousands of people died of starvation. Well, I bet if you'd inspected every rich man's barn at the end of that lean period you'd have found enough corn to have saved all the lives that were lost through malnutrition and disease, and prevented anyone from suffering any ill effects whatever from the meanness of the weather and the soil. Everyone could so easily get enough to eat, if it weren't for that blessed nuisance, money. There you have a brilliant invention which was designed to make food more readily available. Actually it's the only thing that makes it unobtainable.

I'm sure that even the rich are well aware of all this, and realize how much better it would be to have everything one needed, than lots of things one didn't need — to be evacuated altogether from the danger area, than to dig oneself in behind a barricade of enormous wealth. And I've no doubt that either self-interest, or the authority of our Savior Christ — Who was far too wise not to know what was best for us, and far too kind to recommend anything else — would have led the whole world to adopt the Utopian system long ago, if it weren't for that beastly root of all evils, pride. For pride's criterion of prosperity is not what you've got yourself, but what other people haven't got. Pride would refuse to set foot in paradise, if she thought there'd be no underprivileged classes there to gloat over and order about — nobody whose misery could serve as a foil to her own happiness, or whose poverty she could make harder to bear, by flaunting her own riches. Pride, like a hellish serpent gliding through human hearts — or shall we say, like a sucking-fish that clings to the ship of state? — is always dragging us back, and obstructing our progress toward a better way of life.

But as this fault is too deeply ingrained in human nature to be easily eradicated, I'm glad that at least one country has managed to develop a system which I'd like to see universally adopted. The Utopian way of life provides not only the happiest basis for a civilized community, but also one which, in all human probability, will last forever. They've eliminated the root causes of ambition, political conflict, and everything like that. There's therefore no danger of internal dissension, the one thing that has destroyed so many impregnable towns. And as long as there's unity and sound administration at home, no matter how envious neighboring kings may feel, they'll never be able to shake, let alone to shatter, the power of Utopia. They've tried to do so often enough in the past, but have always been beaten back.

Topics for Critical Thinking and Writing

1. Thomas More, writing early in the sixteenth century, was living in a primarily agricultural society. Laborers were needed on farms, but might More have had any other reason for insisting (para. 1) that all people should do some farming and that farming should be "part of every child's education"? Do you think everyone should put in some time as a farmer? Why, or why not?

2. More indicates that in the England of his day, many people loafed or engaged in unnecessary work (producing luxury goods, for one thing), putting an enormous burden on those who engaged in useful work. Is this condition, or any part of it, true of our society? Explain.

3. The Utopians cannot understand why the people of other nations value gems, gold, and fine clothes. If you value any of these items, can you offer an explanation as to why such things are valued?

4. What arguments can you offer against the Utopians' treatment of persons who are incurably ill and in pain?

5. What aspects of More's Utopia do not sound particularly "utopian" to you? Why?

6. In three or four paragraphs, summarize More's report of the Utopians' idea of pleasure.

7. More's Utopians cannot understand why anyone takes pleasure in gambling or in hunting. If either activity gives you pleasure, explain why in an essay of 500 words, offering an argument on behalf of your view. If neither activity gives you pleasure, tell whether it accords with the Utopians' views.

8. As More makes clear in the part called "The Summing Up," in Utopia there is no private property. In a sentence or two, summarize the reasons he gives for this principle and then, in a paragraph, evaluate them.

NICCOLÒ MACHIAVELLI

Niccolò Machiavelli (1469–1527) was born in Florence at a time when Italy was divided into five major states: Venice, Milan, Florence, the Papal States, and Naples. Although these states often had belligerent relations with one another as well as with lesser Italian states, under the Medici family in Florence they achieved a precarious balance of power. In 1494, however, Lorenzo de' Medici, who had ruled from 1469 to 1492, died, and two years later Lorenzo's successor was exiled when the French army arrived in Florence. Italy became a field where Spain, France, and Germany competed for power. From 1498 to 1512, Machiavelli held a high post in the diplomatic service of the Florentine Republic, but when the French army reappeared and the Florentines in desperation recalled the Medici, Machiavelli lost his post and was imprisoned, tortured, and then exiled. Banished from Florence, he nevertheless lived in comfort on a small estate nearby, writing his major works and hoping to obtain an office from the Medici. In later years, he was employed in a few minor diplomatic missions, but even after the collapse and expulsion of the Medici in 1527 and the restoration of the republic, he did not regain his old position of importance. He died shortly after the restoration.

This selection comes from *The Prince*, which Machiavelli wrote in 1513 during his banishment, hoping that it would interest the Medici and thus restore him to favor; but the book was not published until 1532, five years after his death. In this book of twenty-six short chapters, Machiavelli begins by examining different kinds of states, but the work's enduring power resides in the discussions (in Chapters 15–18, reprinted here) of qualities necessary to a prince — that is, a head of state. Any such examination obviously is based in part on assumptions about the nature of the citizens of the realm.

This selection was taken from a translation by W. K. Marriott.

From *The Prince*

CONCERNING THINGS FOR WHICH MEN, AND ESPECIALLY PRINCES, ARE PRAISED OR BLAMED

It remains now to see what ought to be the rules of conduct for a prince towards subject and friends. And as I know that many have written on this point, I expect I shall be considered presumptuous in mentioning it again, especially as in discussing it I shall depart from the methods of other people. But, it being my intention to write a thing which shall be useful to him who apprehends it, it appears to me more appropriate to follow up the real truth of the matter than the imagination of it; for many have pictured republics and principalities which in fact have never been known or seen, because how one lives is so far distant from how one ought to live, that he who neglects what is done for what ought to be done, sooner effects his ruin than his preservation; for a man who wishes to act entirely up to his professions of virtue soon meets with what destroys him among so much that is evil.

Hence it is necessary for a prince wishing to hold his own to know how to do wrong, and to make use of it or not according to necessity. Therefore, putting on one side imaginary things concerning a prince, and discussing those which are real, I say that all men when they are spoken of, and chiefly princes for being more highly placed, are remarkable for some of those qualities which bring them either blame or praise; and thus it is that one is reputed liberal, another miserly, using a Tuscan term (because an avaricious person in our language is still he who desires to possess by robbery, whilst we call one miserly who deprives himself too much of the use of his own); one is reputed generous, one rapacious; one cruel, one compassionate; one faithless, another faithful; one effeminate and cowardly, another bold and brave; one affable, another haughty; one lascivious, another chaste; one sincere, another cunning; one hard, another easy; one grave, another frivolous; one religious, another unbelieving, and the like. And I know that everyone will confess that it would be most praiseworthy in a prince to exhibit all the above qualities that are considered good; but because they can neither be entirely possessed nor observed, for human conditions do not permit it, it is necessary for him to be sufficiently prudent that he may know how to avoid the reproach of those vices which would lose him his state; and also to keep himself, if it be possible, from those which would not lose him it; but this not being possible, he may with less hesitation abandon himself to them. And again, he need not make himself uneasy at incurring a reproach for those vices without which the state can only be saved with difficulty, for if everything is considered carefully, it will be found that something which looks like virtue, if followed, would be his ruin; whilst something else, which looks like vice, yet followed brings him security and prosperity.

CONCERNING LIBERALITY AND MEANNESS

Commencing then with the first of the above-named characteristics, I say that it would be well to be reputed liberal. Nevertheless, liberality exercised in a way that does not bring you the reputation for it, injures you; for if one exercises it honestly and as it should be exercised, it may not become known, and you will not avoid the reproach of its opposite. Therefore, anyone wishing to maintain among men the name of liberal is obliged to avoid no attribute of magnificence; so that a prince thus inclined will consume in such acts all his property, and will be compelled in the end, if he wish to maintain the name of liberal, to unduly weigh down his people, and tax them, and do everything he can to get money. This will soon make him odious to his subjects, and becoming poor he will be little valued by anyone; thus, with his liberality, having offended many and rewarded few, he is affected by the very first trouble and imperiled by whatever may be the first danger; recognizing this himself, and wishing to draw back from it, he runs at once into the reproach of being miserly.

Therefore, a prince, not being able to exercise this virtue of liberality in such a way that it is recognized, except to his cost, if he is wise he ought not to fear the reputation of being mean, for in time he will come to be more considered than if liberal, seeing that with his economy his revenues are enough, that he can defend himself against all attacks, and is able to engage in enterprises without burdening his people; thus it comes to pass that he exercises liberality towards all from whom he does not take, who are numberless, and meanness towards those to whom he does not give, who are few.

We have not seen great things done in our 5 time except by those who have been considered mean; the rest have failed. Pope Julius the Second was assisted in reaching the papacy by a reputation for liberality, yet he did not strive afterwards to keep it up, when he made war on the King of France; and he made many wars without imposing any extraordinary tax on his subjects, for he supplied his additional expenses out of his long thriftiness. The present King of Spain would not have undertaken or conquered in so many enterprises if he had been reputed liberal. A prince, therefore, provided that he has not to rob his subjects, that he can defend himself, that he does not become poor and abject, that he is not forced to become rapacious, ought to hold of little account a reputation for being mean, for it is one of those vices which will enable him to govern.

And if anyone should say: Caesar obtained empire by liberality, and many others have reached the highest positions by having been liberal, and by being considered so, I answer: Either you are a prince in fact, or in a way to become one. In the first case this liberality is dangerous, in the second it is very necessary to be considered liberal; and Caesar was one of those who wished to become pre-eminent in Rome; but if he had survived after becoming so, and had not moderated his expenses, he would have destroyed his government. And if anyone should reply: Many have been princes, and have done great things with armies, who have been considered very liberal, I reply: Either a prince spends that which is his own or his subjects' or else that of others. In the first case he ought to be sparing, in the second he ought not to neglect any opportunity for liberality. And to the prince who goes forth with his army, supporting it by pillage, sack, and extortion, handling that which belongs to others, this liberality is necessary, otherwise he would not be followed by soldiers. And of that which is neither yours nor your subjects' you can be a ready giver, as were Cyrus, Caesar, and Alexander; because it does not take away your reputation if you squander that of others, but adds to it; it is only squandering your own that injures you.

And there is nothing wastes so rapidly as liberality, for even whilst you exercise it you lose the power to do so, and so become either poor or despised, or else, in avoiding poverty, rapacious and hated. And a prince should guard himself, above all things, against being despised and hated; and liberality leads you to both. Therefore it is wiser to have a reputation for meanness which brings reproach without hatred, than to be compelled through seeking a reputation for liberality to incur a name for rapacity which begets reproach with hatred.

CONCERNING CRUELTY AND CLEMENCY, AND WHETHER IT IS BETTER TO BE LOVED THAN FEARED

Coming now to the other qualities mentioned above, I say that every prince ought to desire to be considered clement and not cruel. Nevertheless he ought to take care not to misuse this clemency. Cesare Borgia[1] was considered cruel; notwithstanding, his cruelty reconciled the Romagna, unified it, and restored it to peace and loyalty. And if this be rightly considered, he will be seen to have been much more merciful than the Florentine people, who, to avoid a reputation for cruelty, permitted Pistoia[2] to be destroyed. Therefore a prince, so long as he keeps his subjects united and loyal, ought not to mind the reproach of cruelty; because with a few examples he will be more merciful than those who, through too much mercy, allow disorders to arise, from which follow murders or robberies; for these are wont to injure the whole people, whilst those executions which originate with a prince offend the individual only.

And of all princes, it is impossible for the new prince to avoid the imputation of cruelty, owing to new states being full of dangers. Hence Virgil, through the mouth of Dido, excuses the inhumanity of her reign owing to its being new, saying, "against my will, my fate / A throne unsettled, and an infant state, / Bid me defend my realms with all my pow'rs, / And guard with these severities my shores."[3] Nevertheless, he ought to be slow to believe and to act, nor should he himself show fear, but proceed in a temperate manner with prudence and humanity, so that too much confidence may not make him incautious and too much distrust render him intolerable.

Upon this a question arises: whether it 10 be better to be loved than feared or feared than loved? It may be answered that one should wish to be both, but, because it is difficult to unite them in one person, it is much safer to be feared than loved, when, of the two, either must be dispensed with. Because this is to be asserted in general of men, that they are ungrateful, fickle, false, cowardly, covetous, and as long as you succeed they are yours entirely; they will offer you their blood, property, life, and children, as is said above, when the need is far distant; but when it approaches they turn against you. And that prince who, relying entirely on their promises, has neglected other precautions, is ruined; because friendships that are obtained by payments, and not by greatness or nobility of mind, may indeed be earned, but they are not secured, and in time of need cannot be relied upon; and men have less scruple in offending one who is beloved than one who is feared, for love is preserved by the link of obligation which, owing to the baseness of men, is broken at every opportunity for their advantage;

---

[1]**Cesare Borgia** The son of Pope Alexander VI, Cesare Borgia (1476–1507) was ruthlessly opportunistic. Encouraged by his father, in 1499 and 1500 he subdued the cities of Romagna, the region including Ferrara and Ravenna. [All notes are the editors']
[2]**Pistoia** A town near Florence; Machiavelli suggests that the Florentines failed to treat dissenting leaders with sufficient severity.

[3]In *Aeneid* I, 563–64, **Virgil** (70–19 BC) puts this line into the mouth of **Dido**, the queen of Carthage.

but fear preserves you by a dread of punishment which never fails.

Nevertheless, a prince ought to inspire fear in such a way that, if he does not win love, he avoids hatred; because he can endure very well being feared whilst he is not hated, which will always be as long as he abstains from the property of his citizens and subjects and from their women. But when it is necessary for him to proceed against the life of someone, he must do it on proper justification and for manifest cause, but above all things he must keep his hands off the property of others, because men more quickly forget the death of their father than the loss of their patrimony. Besides, pretexts for taking away the property are never wanting; for he who has once begun to live by robbery will always find pretexts for seizing what belongs to others; but reasons for taking life, on the contrary, are more difficult to find and sooner lapse. But when a prince is with his army, and has under control a multitude of soldiers, then it is quite necessary for him to disregard the reputation of cruelty, for without it he would never hold his army united or disposed to its duties.

Among the wonderful deeds of Hannibal[4] this one is enumerated: that having led an enormous army, composed of many various races of men, to fight in foreign lands, no dissensions arose either among them or against the prince, whether in his bad or in his good fortune. This arose from nothing else than his inhuman cruelty, which, with his boundless valor, made him revered and terrible in the sight of his soldiers, but without that cruelty, his other virtues were not sufficient to produce this effect. And short-sighted writers admire his deeds from one point of view and from another condemn the principal cause of them.

That it is true his other virtues would not have been sufficient for him may be proved by the case of Scipio,[5] that most excellent man, not only of his own times but within the memory of man, against whom, nevertheless, his army rebelled in Spain; this arose from nothing but his too great forbearance, which gave his soldiers more license than is consistent with military discipline. For this he was upbraided in the Senate by Fabius Maximus, and called the corrupter of the Roman soldiery. The Locrians were laid waste by a legate of Scipio, yet they were not avenged by him, nor was the insolence of the legate punished, owing entirely to his easy nature. Insomuch that someone in the Senate, wishing to excuse him, said there were many men who knew much better how not to err than to correct the errors of others. This disposition, if he had been continued in the command, would have destroyed in time the fame and glory of Scipio; but, he being under the control of the Senate, this injurious characteristic not only concealed itself, but contributed to his glory.

Returning to the question of being feared or loved, I come to the conclusion that, men loving according to their own will and fearing according to that of the prince, a wise prince should establish himself on that which is in his own control and not in that of others; he must endeavor only to avoid hatred, as is noted.

CONCERNING THE WAY IN WHICH PRINCES SHOULD KEEP FAITH

Everyone admits how praiseworthy it is in a prince to keep faith, and to live with integrity and not with craft. Nevertheless our

---

[4]**Hannibal** The Carthaginian general (247–183 BC) whose crossing of the Alps with elephants and full baggage train is one of the great feats of military history.

[5]**Scipio** Publius Cornelius Scipio Africanus the Elder (235–183 BC), the conqueror of Hannibal in the Punic Wars. The mutiny of which Machiavelli speaks took place in 206 BC.

experience has been that those princes who have done great things have held good faith of little account, and have known how to circumvent the intellect of men by craft, and in the end have overcome those who have relied on their word. You must know there are two ways of contesting, the one by the law, the other by force; the first method is proper to men, the second to beasts; but because the first is frequently not sufficient, it is necessary to have recourse to the second. Therefore it is necessary for a prince to understand how to avail himself of the beast and the man. This has been figuratively taught to princes by ancient writers, who describe how Achilles and many other princes of old were given to the Centaur Chiron[6] to nurse, who brought them up in his discipline; which means solely that, as they had for a teacher one who was half beast and half man, so it is necessary for a prince to know how to make use of both natures, and that one without the other is not durable. A prince, therefore, being compelled knowingly to adopt the beast, ought to choose the fox and the lion; because the lion cannot defend himself against snares and the fox cannot defend himself against wolves. Therefore, it is necessary to be a fox to discover the snares and a lion to terrify the wolves. Those who rely simply on the lion do not understand what they are about. Therefore a wise lord cannot, nor ought he to, keep faith when such observance may be turned against him, and when the reasons that caused him to pledge it exist no longer. If men were entirely good this precept would not hold, but because they are bad, and will not keep faith with you, you too are not bound to observe it with them. Nor will there ever be wanting to a prince legitimate reasons to excuse this non-observance. Of

this endless modern examples could be given, showing how many treaties and engagements have been made void and of no effect through the faithlessness of princes; and he who has known best how to employ the fox has succeeded best.

But it is necessary to know well how to disguise this characteristic, and to be a great pretender and dissembler; and men are so simple, and so subject to present necessities, that he who seeks to deceive will always find someone who will allow himself to be deceived. One recent example I cannot pass over in silence. Alexander the Sixth[7] did nothing else but deceive men, nor ever thought of doing otherwise, and he always found victims; for there never was a man who had greater power in asserting, or who with greater oaths would affirm a thing, yet would observe it less; nevertheless his deceits always succeeded according to his wishes, because he well understood this side of mankind.

Therefore it is unnecessary for a prince to have all the good qualities I have enumerated, but it is very necessary to appear to have them. And I shall dare to say this also, that to have them and always to observe them is injurious, and that to appear to have them is useful; to appear merciful, faithful, humane, religious, upright, and to be so, but with a mind so framed that should you require not to be so, you may be able and know how to change to the opposite. And you have to understand this, that a prince, especially a new one, cannot observe all those things for which men are esteemed, being often forced, in order to maintain the state, to act contrary to fidelity, friendship, humanity, and religion. Therefore it is necessary for him to have a mind ready to turn itself accordingly as the winds and

15

---

[6]**Chiron** (Kīʹron) A centaur (half man, half horse) who was said in classical mythology to have been the teacher not only of Achilles but also of Theseus, Jason, Hercules, and other heroes.

[7]**Alexander the Sixth** Pope from 1492 to 1503; father of Cesare Borgia.

variations of fortune force it, yet, as I have said above, not to diverge from the good if he can avoid doing so, but, if compelled, then to know how to set about it.

For this reason a prince ought to take care that he never lets anything slip from his lips that is not replete with the above-named five qualities, that he may appear to him who sees and hears him altogether merciful, faithful, humane, upright, and religious. There is nothing more necessary to appear to have than this last quality, inasmuch as men judge generally more by the eye than by the hand, because it belongs to everybody to see you, to few to come in touch with you. Everyone sees what you appear to be, few really know what you are, and those few dare not oppose themselves to the opinion of the many, who have the majesty of the state to defend them; and in the actions of all men, and especially of princes, which it is not prudent to challenge, one judges by the result.[8]

For that reason, let a prince have the credit of conquering and holding his state, the means will always be considered honest, and he will be praised by everybody; because the vulgar are always taken by what a thing seems to be and by what comes of it; and in the world there are only the vulgar, for the few find a place there only when the many have no ground to rest on. One prince of the present time, whom it is not well to name, never preaches anything else but peace and good faith, and to both he is most hostile, and either, if he had kept it, would have deprived him of reputation and kingdom many a time.

_____

[8]**one judges by the result** The original Italian, *si guarda al fine*, has often been translated erroneously as "the ends justify the means." Although this saying is often attributed to Machiavelli, he never actually wrote it.

Topics for Critical Thinking and Writing

1. In the opening paragraph, Niccolò Machiavelli claims that a ruler who wishes to keep in power must "know how to do wrong" — that is, must know where and when to ignore the demands of conventional morality. In the rest of the excerpt, does he give any convincing evidence to support this claim? Can you think of any recent political event in which a political leader violated the requirements of morality, as Machiavelli advises? Explain your response.

2. In paragraph 2, Machiavelli claims that it is impossible for a ruler to exhibit *all* the conventional virtues (trustworthiness, liberality, and so on). Why does he make this claim? Do you agree with it? Why, or why not?

3. Machiavelli says that Cesare Borgia's cruelty brought peace to Romagna and that, in contrast, the Florentines who sought to avoid being cruel in fact brought pain to Pistoia. Can you think of recent episodes supporting the view that cruelty can be beneficial to society? If so, restate Machiavelli's position, using these examples from recent history. Then go on to write two paragraphs, arguing on behalf of your two examples. Or if you believe that Machiavelli's point here is fundamentally wrong, explain why, again using current examples.

4. In *The Prince*, Machiavelli is writing about how to be a successful ruler. He explicitly says that he is dealing with things as they are, not as they should be. Do you think that one can, in fact, write usefully about governing without considering ethics? Explain.

5. In the next-to-last paragraph, Machiavelli declares that "in the actions of all men, . . . one judges by the result." Taking account of the context, do you think the meaning is (a) that

any end, goal, or purpose of anyone justifies using any means to reach it or (b) that the end of governing the state, nation, or country justifies using any means to achieve it? Or do you think Machiavelli means both? Or something else entirely?

6. In about 500 words, argue that an important contemporary political figure does or does not act according to Machiavelli's principles.

7. Read the selection from Thomas More's *Utopia*, and write an essay of 500 words on one of these two topics: (a) why More's book is or is not wiser than Machiavelli's or (b) why one of the books is more interesting than the other.

8. More and Machiavelli wrote their books at almost exactly the same time. In 500 to 750 words, compare and contrast the two authors' arguments about the nature of the state, examining their assumptions about human beings and the role of government.

THOMAS JEFFERSON

Thomas Jefferson (1743–1826) was a congressman, the governor of Virginia, the first secretary of state, and the president of the United States, but he said he wished to be remembered for only three things: drafting the Declaration of Independence, writing the Virginia Statute for Religious Freedom, and founding the University of Virginia. All three were efforts to promote freedom.

Jefferson was born in Virginia and educated at William and Mary College in Williamsburg, Virginia. After graduating, he studied law, was admitted to the bar, and in 1769 was elected to the Virginia House of Burgesses, his first political office. In 1776, he went to Philadelphia as a delegate to the second Continental Congress, where he was elected to a committee of five to write the Declaration of Independence. Jefferson drafted the document, which was then subjected to some changes by the other members of the committee and by the Congress. Although he was unhappy with the changes (especially with the deletion of a passage against slavery), his claim to have written the Declaration is just.

The Declaration of Independence

When in the course of human events, it becomes necessary for one people to dissolve the political bands which have connected them with another, and to assume among the Powers of the earth, the separate and equal station to which the Laws of Nature and of Nature's God entitle them, a decent respect to the opinions of mankind requires that they should declare the causes which impel them to the separation.

We hold these truths to be self-evident, that all men are created equal, that they are endowed by their Creator with certain unalienable Rights, that among these are Life, Liberty and the pursuit of Happiness.

That to secure these rights, Governments are instituted among Men, deriving their just powers from the consent of the governed.

That whenever any Form of Government becomes destructive of these ends, it is the Right of the People to alter or to abolish it, and to institute a new Government, laying its foundation on such principles and organizing its powers in such form, as to them shall seem most likely to effect their Safety and Happiness. Prudence, indeed, will dictate that Governments long established should not be changed for light and transient causes; and accordingly all experience hath shown that mankind are more disposed to suffer, while evils are sufferable, than to right themselves by abolishing the forms to which they are accustomed. But when a long train of abuses and usurpations pursuing invariably the same Object evinces a design to reduce them under absolute Despotism, it is their right, it is their duty, to throw off such government, and to provide new Guards for their future security.

Such has been the patient sufferance of 5 these Colonies; and such is now the necessity which constrains them to alter their former Systems of Government. The history of the present King of Great Britain is a history of repeated injuries and usurpations, all having in direct object the establishment of an absolute Tyranny over these States. To prove this, let Facts be submitted to a candid world.

He has refused his Assent to Laws, the most wholesome and necessary for the public good.

He has forbidden his Governors to pass Laws of immediate and pressing importance, unless suspended in their operation till his Assent should be obtained; and when so suspended, he has utterly neglected to attend to them.

He has refused to pass over Laws for the accommodation of large districts of people, unless those people would relinquish the right of Representation in the Legislature, a right inestimable to them and formidable to tyrants only.

He has called together legislative bodies at places unusual, uncomfortable, and distant from the depository of their Public Records, for the sole purpose of fatiguing them into compliance with his measures.

He has dissolved Representative Houses 10 repeatedly, for opposing with manly firmness his invasions on the rights of the people.

He has refused for a long time, after such dissolutions, to cause others to be elected; whereby the Legislative Powers, incapable of Annihilation, have returned to the People at large for their exercise; the State remaining in the mean time exposed to all the dangers of invasion from without, and convulsions within.

He has endeavored to prevent the population of these States, for that purpose obstructing the Laws of Naturalization of Foreigners; refusing to pass others to encourage their migration hither, and raising the conditions of new Appropriations of Lands.

He has obstructed the Administration of Justice, by refusing his Assent to Laws for establishing Judiciary Powers.

He has made Judges dependent on his Will alone, for the tenure of their offices, and the amount and payment of their salaries.

He has erected a multitude of New Offices, 15 and sent hither swarms of Officers to harass our People, and eat out their substance.

He has kept among us, in time of peace, Standing Armies without the consent of our Legislature.

He has affected to render the Military independent of and superior to the Civil Power.

He has combined with others to subject us to jurisdictions foreign to our constitution, and unacknowledged by our laws; giving his Assent to their acts of pretended Legislation:

For quartering large bodies of armed troops among us:

For protecting them, by a mock Trial, 20 from Punishment for any Murders which they should commit on the Inhabitants of these States:

For cutting off our Trade with all parts of the world:

For imposing Taxes on us without our Consent:

For depriving us in many cases, of the benefits of Trial by Jury:

For transporting us beyond Seas to be tried for pretended offenses:

For abolishing the free System of English Laws in a Neighbouring Province, establishing therein an Arbitrary government, and enlarging its boundaries so as to render it at once an example and fit instrument for introducing the same absolute rule into these Colonies:

For taking away our Charters, abolishing our most valuable Laws, and altering fundamentally the Forms of our Governments.

For suspending our own Legislatures, and declaring themselves invested with Power to legislate for us in all cases whatsoever.

He has abdicated Government here, by declaring us out of his Protection and waging War against us.

He has plundered our seas, ravaged our Coasts, burnt our towns and destroyed the Lives of our people.

He is at this time transporting large Armies of foreign Mercenaries to compleat the works of death, desolation and tyranny, already begun with circumstances of Cruelty & perfidy scarcely paralleled in the most barbarous ages, and totally unworthy the Head of a civilized nation.

He has constrained our fellow Citizens taken Captive on the high Seas to bear Arms against their Country, to become the executioners of their friends and Brethren, or to fall themselves by their Hands.

He has excited domestic insurrections amongst us, and has endeavored to bring on the inhabitants of our frontiers, the merciless Indian Savages, whose known rule of warfare is an undistinguished destruction of all ages, sexes and conditions.

In every stage of these Oppressions We Have Petitioned for Redress in the most humble terms: Our repeated petitions have been answered only by repeated injury. A Prince, whose character is thus marked by every act which may define a Tyrant, is unfit to be the ruler of a free People.

Nor have We been wanting in attention to our British brethren. We have warned them from time to time of attempts by their legislature to extend an unwarrantable jurisdiction over us. We have reminded them of the circumstances of our emigration and settlement here. We have appealed to their native justice and magnanimity and we have conjured them by the ties of our common kindred to disavow these usurpations, which would inevitably interrupt our connections and correspondence. They too have been deaf to the voice of justice and of consanguinity. We must, therefore, acquiesce in the necessity, which denounces our Separation, and hold them, as we hold the rest of mankind, Enemies in War, in Peace Friends.

We, therefore, the Representatives of the United States of America, in General Congress, Assembled, appealing to the Supreme Judge of the world of the rectitude of our intentions, do, in the Name, and by Authority of the good People of these Colonies, solemnly publish and declare, That these United Colonies are, and of Right ought to be, Free and Independent States; that they are Absolved from all Allegiance to the British Crown, and that all political connection between them and the State of Great Britain, is and ought to be totally dissolved; and that as Free and Independent States, they have full power to levy War, conclude Peace, contract Alliances, establish Commerce, and to do all other Acts and Things which Independent States may of right do. And for the support of this Declaration, with a firm reliance on the protection of Divine Providence, we mutually pledge to each other our lives, our Fortunes and our sacred Honor.

Topics for Critical Thinking and Writing

1. According to the first paragraph, for what audience was the Declaration of Independence written? To what other audiences do you think the document was (in one way or another) addressed?

2. In the Declaration of Independence, it is argued that the colonists are entitled to certain things and that under certain conditions they may behave in a certain way. Make explicit the syllogism that Thomas Jefferson is arguing.

3. What evidence does Jefferson offer to support his major premise? His minor premise?

4. In paragraph 2, the Declaration cites "certain unalienable Rights" and mentions three: "life, liberty and the pursuit of happiness." What is an unalienable right? If someone has an unalienable (or inalienable) right, does that imply that he or she also has certain duties? If so, what are these duties? John Locke, a century earlier (1690), asserted that all men have a natural right to "life, liberty, and property." Do you think the decision to drop "property" and substitute "pursuit of happiness" improved Locke's claim? Explain how or why you think Jefferson changed the phrase.

5. The Declaration states that it is intended to "prove" that the acts of the government of George III had as their "direct object the establishment of an absolute Tyranny" in the American colonies (para. 5). Write an essay of 500 to 750 words showing whether the evidence offered in the Declaration "proves" this claim to your satisfaction. (You will want to define *absolute tyranny*.) If you think further evidence is needed to "prove" the colonists' point, indicate what this evidence might be.

6. King George III has asked you to reply, on his behalf, to the colonists. Write this reply in 500 to 750 words. (Caution: A good reply will probably require you to do some reading about the period.)

7. Write a declaration of your own, setting forth in 500 to 750 words why some group is entitled to independence. You may want to argue that adolescents should not be compelled to attend school, that animals should not be confined in zoos, or that persons who use drugs should be able to buy them legally. Begin with a premise, then set forth facts illustrating the unfairness of the present condition, and conclude by stating what the new condition will mean to society.

ELIZABETH CADY STANTON

Elizabeth Cady Stanton (1815–1902), a lawyer's daughter and journalist's wife, proposed in 1848 a convention to address the "social, civil, and religious condition and rights of women." Responding to Stanton's call, women and men from all over the Northeast traveled to the Woman's Rights Convention held in the village of Seneca Falls, New York. Her declaration, adopted by the convention — but only after vigorous debate and some amendments by others — became the platform for the women's rights movement in the United States.

Declaration of Sentiments and Resolutions

When, in the course of human events, it becomes necessary for one portion of the family of man to assume among the people of the earth a position different from that which they have hitherto occupied, but one to which the laws of nature and of nature's God entitle them, a decent respect to the opinions of mankind requires that they should declare the causes that impel them to such a course.

We hold these truths to be self-evident: that all men and women are created equal; that they are endowed by their Creator with certain inalienable rights; that among these are life, liberty and the pursuit of happiness; that to secure these rights governments are instituted, deriving their just powers from the consent of the governed. Whenever any form of government becomes destructive of these ends, it is the right of those who suffer from it to refuse allegiance to it, and to insist upon the institution of a new government, laying its foundation on such principles, and organizing its powers in such form, as to them shall seem most likely to effect their safety and happiness. Prudence, indeed, will dictate that governments long established should not be changed for light and transient causes; and accordingly all experience hath shown that mankind are more disposed to suffer, while evils are sufferable, than to right themselves by abolishing the forms to which they were accustomed. But when a long train of abuses and usurpations, pursuing invariably the same object, evinces a design to reduce them under absolute despotism, it is their duty to throw off such government, and to provide new guards for their future security. Such has been the patient sufferance of the women under this government, and such is now the necessity which constrains them to demand the equal station to which they are entitled.

The history of mankind is a history of repeated injuries and usurpations on the part of man toward woman, having in direct object the establishment of an absolute tyranny over her. To prove this, let facts be submitted to a candid world.

He has never permitted her to exercise her inalienable right to the elective franchise.

He has compelled her to submit to laws, in 5 the formation of which she had no voice.

He has withheld from her rights which are given to the most ignorant and degraded men — both natives and foreigners.

Having deprived her of this first right of a citizen, the elective franchise, thereby leaving her without representation in the halls of legislation, he has oppressed her on all sides.

He has made her, if married, in the eye of the law, civilly dead.

He has taken from her all right in property, even to the wages she earns.

He has made her, morally, an irresponsible 10 being, as she can commit many crimes with impunity, provided they be done in the presence of her husband. In the covenant of marriage, she is compelled to promise obedience to her husband, he becoming to all intents and purposes, her master — the law giving him power to deprive her of her liberty, and to administer chastisement.

He has so framed the laws of divorce, as to what shall be the proper causes, and in case of separation, to whom the guardianship of the children shall be given, as to be wholly regardless of the happiness of women — the law, in all cases, going upon a false supposition of the supremacy of man, and giving all power into his hands.

After depriving her of all rights as a married woman, if single, and the owner of property, he has taxed her to support a government which recognizes her only when her property can be made profitable to it.

He has monopolized nearly all the profitable employments, and from those she is permitted to follow, she receives but a scanty remuneration. He closes against her all the avenues to wealth and distinction which he considers most honorable to himself. As a teacher of theology, medicine, or law, she is not known.

He has denied her the facilities for obtaining a thorough education, all colleges being closed against her.

He allows her in Church, as well as State, but a subordinate position, claiming Apostolic authority for her exclusion from the ministry, and, with some exceptions, from any public participation in the affairs of the Church.

He has created a false public sentiment by giving to the world a different code of morals for men and women, by which moral delinquencies which exclude women from society, are not only tolerated, but deemed of little account in man.

He has usurped the prerogative of Jehovah himself, claiming it as his right to assign for her a sphere of action, when that belongs to her conscience and to her God.

He has endeavored, in every way that he could, to destroy her confidence in her own powers, to lessen her self-respect, and to make her willing to lead a dependent and abject life.

Now, in view of this entire disfranchisement of one-half the people of this country, their social and religious degradation — in view of the unjust laws above mentioned, and because women do feel themselves aggrieved, oppressed, and fraudulently deprived of their most sacred rights, we insist that they have immediate admission to all the rights and privileges which belong to them as citizens of the United States.

In entering upon the great work before us, we anticipate no small amount of misconception, misrepresentation, and ridicule; but we shall use every instrumentality within our power to effect our object. We shall employ agents, circulate tracts, petition the State and National legislatures, and endeavor to enlist the pulpit and the press in our behalf. We hope this Convention will be followed by a series of Conventions embracing every part of the country.

[The following resolutions were discussed by Lucretia Mott, Thomas and Mary Ann McClintock, Amy Post, Catharine A. F. Stebbins, and others, and were adopted:]

Whereas, The great precept of nature is conceded to be, that "man shall pursue his own true and substantial happiness." Blackstone in his Commentaries remarks, that this law of Nature being coeval with mankind, and dictated by God himself, is of course superior in obligation to any other. It is binding over all the globe, in all countries, and at all times; no human laws are of any validity if contrary to this, and such of them as are valid, derive all their force, and all their validity, and all their authority, mediately and immediately, from this original; therefore,

Resolved, That such laws as conflict, in any way, with the true and substantial happiness of woman, are contrary to the great precept of nature and of no validity, for this is "superior in obligation to any other."

Resolved, That all laws which prevent woman from occupying such a station in society as her conscience shall dictate, or which place her in a position inferior to that of man, are contrary to the great precept of nature, and therefore of no force or authority.

Resolved, That woman is man's equal — was intended to be so by the Creator, and the highest good of the race demands that she should be recognized as such.

Resolved, That the women of this country 25 ought to be enlightened in regard to the laws under which they live, that they may no longer publish their degradation by declaring themselves satisfied with their present position, nor their ignorance, by asserting that they have all the rights they want.

Resolved, That inasmuch as man, while claiming for himself intellectual superiority, does accord to woman moral superiority, it is preeminently his duty to encourage her to speak and teach, as she has an opportunity, in all religious assemblies.

Resolved, That the same amount of virtue, delicacy, and refinement of behavior that is required of woman in the social state, should also be required of man, and the same transgressions should be visited with equal severity on both man and woman.

Resolved, That the objection of indelicacy and impropriety, which is so often brought against woman when she addresses a public audience, comes with a very ill-grace from those who encourage, by their attendance, her appearance on the stage, in the concert, or in feats of the circus.

Resolved, That woman has too long rested satisfied in the circumscribed limits which corrupt customs and a perverted application of the Scriptures have marked out for her, and that it is time she should move in the enlarged sphere which her great Creator has assigned her.

Resolved, That it is the duty of the women 30 of this country to secure to themselves their sacred right to the elective franchise.

Resolved, That the equality of human rights results necessarily from the fact of the identity of the race in capabilities and responsibilities.

Resolved, therefore, That, being invested by the Creator with the same capabilities, and the same consciousness of responsibility for their exercise, it is demonstrably the right and duty of woman, equally with man, to promote every righteous cause by every righteous means; and especially in regard to the great subjects of morals and religion, it is self-evidently her right to participate with her brother in teaching them, both in private and in public, by writing and by speaking, by any instrumentalities proper to be used, and in any assemblies proper to be held; and this being a self-evident truth growing out of the divinely implanted principles of human nature, any custom or authority adverse to it, whether modern or wearing the hoary sanction of antiquity, is to be regarded as a self-evident falsehood, and at war with mankind.

[At the last session Lucretia Mott offered and spoke to the following resolution:]

Resolved, That the speedy success of our cause depends upon the zealous and untiring efforts of both men and women, for the overthrow of the monopoly of the pulpit, and for the securing to woman an equal participation with men in the various trades, professions, and commerce.

Topics for Critical Thinking and Writing

1. Elizabeth Cady Stanton echoes the Declaration of Independence because she wishes to associate her ideas and the movement she supports with a document and a movement that her readers esteem. She must have believed that if readers esteem the Declaration of Independence, they must grant the justice of her goals. Does her strategy work, or does it backfire by making her essay seem strained? Explain your response.

2. When Stanton insists that women have an "inalienable right to the elective franchise" (para. 4), what does she mean by "inalienable"?

3. Stanton complains that men have made married women, "in the eye of the law, civilly dead" (para. 8). What does she mean by "civilly dead"? How is it possible for a person to be biologically alive and yet civilly dead?

4. Stanton objects that women are "not known" as teachers of "theology, medicine, or law" (para. 13). Is that still true today? Do some research in your library and then write three 100-word biographical sketches, one each on well-known female professors of theology, medicine, and law.

5. The Declaration of Sentiments and Resolutions claims that women have "the same capabilities" as men (para. 32). Yet in 1848 Stanton and the others at Seneca Falls knew, or should have known, that history recorded no example of a woman philosopher comparable to Plato or Kant, a composer comparable to Beethoven or Chopin, a scientist comparable to Galileo or Newton, or a mathematician comparable to Euclid or Descartes. Do these facts contradict the Declaration's claim? If not, why not? How else but by different intellectual capabilities do you think such facts can be explained?

6. Stanton's declaration is more than 165 years old. Have all the issues she raised been satisfactorily resolved? If not, which ones remain?

7. In our society, children have very few rights. For instance, a child cannot decide to drop out of elementary school or high school, and a child cannot decide to leave his or her parents to reside with some other family that he or she finds more compatible. Whatever your view of children's rights, compose the best Declaration of the Rights of Children that you can.

MARTIN LUTHER KING JR.

Martin Luther King Jr. (1929–1968) was born in Atlanta and educated at Morehouse College, Crozer Theological Seminary, and Boston University. In 1954, he was called to serve as a Baptist minister in Montgomery, Alabama. During the next two years, he achieved national fame when, using a policy of nonviolent resistance, he successfully led the boycott against segregated bus lines in Montgomery. He then helped organize the Southern Christian Leadership Conference, which furthered civil rights, first in the South and then nationwide. In 1964, he was awarded the Nobel Peace Prize. Four years later, he was assassinated in Memphis, Tennessee, while supporting striking garbage workers.

The speech presented here was delivered from the steps of the Lincoln Memorial, in Washington, DC, in 1963, the hundredth anniversary of the Emancipation Proclamation. King's immediate audience consisted of more than two hundred thousand people who had come to demonstrate for civil rights.

I Have a Dream

I am happy to join with you today in what will go down in history as the greatest demonstration for freedom in the history of our nation.

Five score years ago, a great American, in whose symbolic shadow we stand today, signed the Emancipation Proclamation. This momentous decree came as a great beacon light of hope to millions of Negro slaves who had been seared in the flames of withering injustice. It came as a joyous daybreak to end the long night of their captivity. But one hundred years later, the Negro still is not free. One hundred years later, the life of the Negro is still sadly crippled by the manacles of segregation and the chains of discrimination. One hundred years later, the Negro lives on a lonely island of poverty in the midst of a vast ocean of material prosperity. One hundred years later, the Negro is still anguished in the corners of American society and finds himself in exile in his own land. And so we have come here today to dramatize a shameful condition.

In a sense we have come to our nation's capital to cash a check. When the architects of our republic wrote the magnificent words of the Constitution and the Declaration of Independence, they were signing a promissory note to which every American was to fall heir. This note was the promise that all men — yes, black men as well as white men — would be guaranteed the inalienable rights of life, liberty, and the pursuit of happiness.

It is obvious today that America has defaulted on this promissory note insofar as her citizens of color are concerned. Instead of honoring this sacred obligation, America has given the Negro people a bad check, a check which has come back marked "insufficient funds." But we refuse to believe that the bank of justice is bankrupt. We refuse to believe that there are insufficient funds in the great vaults of opportunity of this nation; and so we have come to cash this check, a check that will give us upon demand the riches of freedom and the security of justice.

We have also come to this hallowed spot 5 to remind America of the fierce urgency of *now*. This is no time to engage in the luxury of cooling off or to take the tranquilizing drug of gradualism. *Now* is the time to make real promises of democracy. *Now* is the time to rise from the dark and desolate valley of segregation to the sunlit path of racial justice. *Now* is the time to lift our nation from the quicksands of racial injustice to the solid rock of brotherhood. *Now* is the time to make justice a reality for all of God's children.

It would be fatal for the nation to overlook the urgency of the moment. This sweltering summer of the Negro's legitimate discontent will not pass until there is an invigorating autumn of freedom and equality. Nineteen sixty-three is not an end, but a beginning. And those who hope that the Negro needed to blow off steam and will now be content will have a rude awakening if the nation returns to business as usual. There will be neither rest nor tranquility in America until the Negro is granted his citizenship rights. The whirlwinds of revolt will continue to shake the foundations of our nation until the bright day of justice emerges.

But there is something that I must say to my people who stand on the warm threshold which leads into the palace of justice. In the process of gaining our rightful place, we must not be guilty of wrongful deeds. Let us not seek to satisfy our thirst for freedom by drinking from the cup of bitterness and hatred. We must forever conduct our struggle on the high plane of dignity and discipline. We must not allow our creative protest to degenerate into physical violence. Again and again we must rise to the majestic heights of meeting physical force with soul force. And the marvelous new militancy which has engulfed the Negro community must not lead us to a distrust of all white people; for many of our white brothers, as evidenced by their presence here today, have come to realize that their destiny is tied up with our destiny, and they have come to realize that their freedom is inextricably bound to our freedom.

We cannot walk alone. And as we walk we must make the pledge that we shall always march ahead. We cannot turn back. There are those who are asking the devotees of civil rights, "When will you be satisfied?" We can never be satisfied as long as the Negro is the victim of the unspeakable horrors of police brutality. We can never be satisfied as long as our bodies, heavy with the fatigue of travel, cannot gain lodging in the motels of the highways and the hotels of the cities. We cannot be satisfied as long as the Negro's basic mobility is from a smaller ghetto to a larger one. We can never be satisfied as long as our children are stripped of their selfhood and robbed of their dignity by signs stating "For Whites Only." We cannot be satisfied as long as the Negro in Mississippi cannot vote and a Negro in New York believes he has nothing for which to vote. No, no, we are not satisfied, and we will not be satisfied until justice rolls down like waters and righteousness like a mighty stream.[1]

I am not unmindful that some of you have come here out of great trials and tribulations. Some of you have come fresh from narrow jail cells. Some of you have come from areas where your quest for freedom left you battered by the storms of persecution and staggered by the winds of police brutality. You have been the veterans of creative suffering. Continue to work with the faith that unearned suffering is redemptive.

Go back to Mississippi, and go back to Alabama. Go back to South Carolina. Go back to Georgia. Go back to Louisiana. Go back to the slums and ghettos of our Northern cities, knowing that somehow this situation can and will be changed. Let us not wallow in the valley of despair.

I say to you today, my friends, even though we face the difficulties of today and tomorrow,

I still have a dream. It is a dream deeply rooted in the American dream. I have a dream that one day this nation will rise up and live out the true meaning of its creed: "We hold these truths to be self-evident, that all men are created equal." I have a dream that one day, on the red hills of Georgia, sons of former slaves and the sons of former slave owners will be able to sit down together at the table of brotherhood. I have a dream that one day even the state of Mississippi, a state sweltering with the heat of injustice, sweltering with the heat of oppression, will be transformed into an oasis of freedom and justice. I have a dream that my four little children will one day live in a nation where they will not be judged by the color of their skin, but by the content of their character.

I have a dream today. I have a dream that one day down in Alabama — with its vicious racists, with its governor's lips dripping with the words of interposition and nullification — one day right there in Alabama, little black boys and black girls will be able to join hands with little white boys and white girls as sisters and brothers.

I have a dream today. I have a dream that one day every valley shall be exalted and every hill and mountain shall be made low, the rough places will be made plain and the crooked places will be made straight, and the glory of the Lord shall be revealed, and all flesh shall see it together.[2]

This is our hope. This is the faith that I go back to the South with. And with this faith we will be able to hew out of the mountain of despair a stone of hope. With this faith we will be able to transform the jangling discords of our nation into a beautiful symphony of brotherhood. With this faith we will be able

---

[1]**justice ... stream** A quotation from the Hebrew Bible: Amos 5:24. [Editors' note]

[2]**every valley ... see it together** Another quotation from the Hebrew Bible: Isaiah 40:4–5. [Editors' note]

to work together, to play together, to struggle together, to go to jail together, to stand up for freedom together, knowing that we will be free one day.

And this will be the day — this will be the day when all of God's children will be able to sing with new meaning:

My country, 'tis of thee,
Sweet land of liberty,
    Of thee I sing;
Land where my fathers died,
Land of the Pilgrim's pride,
From every mountainside
    Let freedom ring.

And if America is to be a great nation, this must become true.

And so let freedom ring from the prodigious hilltops of New Hampshire. Let freedom ring from the mighty mountains of New York. Let freedom ring from the heightening Alleghenies of Pennsylvania. Let freedom ring from the snow-capped Rockies of Colorado. Let freedom ring from the curvaceous slopes of California.

But not only that. Let freedom ring from Stone Mountain of Georgia. Let freedom ring from Lookout Mountain of Tennessee. Let freedom ring from every hill and molehill of Mississippi. "From every mountainside let freedom ring."

And when this happens — when we allow freedom to ring, when we let it ring from every village and every hamlet, from every state and every city — we will be able to speed up that day when all of God's children, Black men and white men, Jews and Gentiles, Protestants and Catholics, will be able to join hands and sing in the words of the old Negro spiritual: "Free at last! Free at last! Thank God Almighty. We are free at last!"

Topics for Critical Thinking and Writing

1. Analyze the rhetoric — the oratorical art — of the second paragraph. What, for instance, is gained by saying "five score years ago" instead of "a hundred years ago"? By metaphorically calling the Emancipation Proclamation "a great beacon light of hope"? By saying that "Negro slaves . . . had been seared in the flames of withering injustice"? And what of the metaphors "daybreak" and "the long night of . . . captivity"?

2. Do the first two paragraphs make an effective opening? Why?

3. In paragraphs 3 and 4, Martin Luther King Jr. uses the metaphor of a bad check. Rewrite paragraph 3 *without* using any of King's metaphors and then in a paragraph evaluate the differences between King's version and yours.

4. King's highly metaphoric speech appeals to emotions, but it also offers *reasons*. What reasons, for instance, does King give to support his belief that African Americans should not resort to physical violence in their struggle against segregation and discrimination?

5. When King delivered the speech, his audience at the Lincoln Memorial was primarily African American. Do you think the speech is also addressed to other Americans? Explain.

6. The speech can be divided into three parts: paragraphs 1 through 6; paragraphs 7 ("But there is") through 10; and paragraph 11 ("I say to you today, my friends") to the end. Summarize each of these three parts in a sentence or two so that the basic organization of the speech is evident.

7. King says (para. 11) that his dream is "deeply rooted in the American dream." First, what is the American dream, as King seems to understand it? Second, how does King establish his point — that is, what evidence does he use to convince us — that his dream is the American dream?

8. King delivered his speech in 1963, more than half a century ago. In an essay of 500 words, argue that the speech still is — or is not — relevant. Or write an essay of 500 words in which you state what you take to be the "American dream" and argue that it now is or is not readily available to African Americans.

W. H. AUDEN

Wystan Hugh Auden (1907–1973) was born in York, England, and educated at Oxford University. In the 1930s his witty left-wing poetry earned him wide acclaim as the leading poet of his generation. In 1939 he came to the United States, becoming a citizen in 1946 but returning to England for his last years. Much of Auden's poetry is characterized by a combination of colloquial diction and technical dexterity. The poem reprinted here was originally published in 1940.

The Unknown Citizen

(To JS/07/M/378
This Marble Monument
Is Erected by the State)

He was found by the Bureau of Statistics to be
One against whom there was no official
    complaint,
And all the reports on his conduct agree
That, in the modern sense of an old-fashioned
    word, he was a saint,
For in everything he did he served the Greater 5
    Community.
Except for the War till the day he retired
He worked in a factory and never got fired,
But satisfied his employers, Fudge Motors Inc.
Yet he wasn't a scab or odd in his views,
For his Union reports that he paid his dues, 10
(Our report on his Union shows it was sound)
And our Social Psychology workers found
That he was popular with his mates and liked
    a drink.
The Press are convinced that he bought a
    paper every day
And that his reactions to advertisements were 15
    normal in every way.
Policies taken out in his name prove that he
    was fully insured,
And his Health-card shows he was once in
    hospital but left it cured.
Both Producers Research and High-Grade
    Living declare
He was fully sensible to the advantages of the
    Installment Plan
And had everything necessary to the Modern 20
    Man,
A phonograph, radio, a car and a frigidaire.
Our researches into Public Opinion are content
That he held the proper opinions for the time
    of year;
When there was peace, he was for peace;
    when there was war, he went.

He was married and added five children to   25
   the population,
Which our Eugenist says was the right number for a parent of his generation,
And our teachers report that he never inter-
   fered with their education.

Was he free? Was he happy? The question is
   absurd:
Had anything been wrong, we should certainly have heard.

Topics for Critical Thinking and Writing

1. Who is the narrator in W. H. Auden's poem, and on what sort of occasion is the narrator speaking? How do you know?

2. France, Great Britain, and the United States all have monuments to "The Unknown" (formerly "The Unknown Soldier"). How is Auden's proposed monument like and unlike these war memorials?

3. The poem ends by asking "Was he free? Was he happy?" and the questions are dismissed summarily. Is that because the answers are so obvious? What answers (obvious or subtle) do you think the poem offers to these questions?

4. What does it mean in line 23 that the unknown citizen "held the proper opinions for the time of year"? Explain and tell why this attribute is presented as something lamentable.

5. Read the selection from Thomas More's *Utopia*, and write an essay of 500 to 750 words setting forth More's likely response to Auden's poem.

6. Reread the section on author-based, text-based, and reader-based approaches to literature (pp. 376–78). Select one type of approach, and evaluate Auden's poem using that approach.

EMMA LAZARUS

Emma Lazarus (1849–1887) was born in New York City as the fourth of seven children in a well-established family. Her parents provided her with a private education, and her father supported her writing: When Lazarus was just seventeen, her father had a collection of Lazarus's poetry, called *Poems and Translations: Written between the Ages of Fourteen and Sixteen*, printed for private circulation. In addition to poetry, Lazarus wrote essays, plays, several highly respected translations, and a novel, going on to become part of the literary elite in late nineteenth-century New York. Lazarus is probably known best for the poem that follows, "The New Colossus." She wrote this sonnet in 1883 as a donation to an auction held to raise money to build the pedestal for the Statue of Liberty. The poem was installed on the base of the statue in 1903, nearly two decades after Lazarus's death in 1887.

The New Colossus

Not like the brazen giant of Greek fame,
With conquering limbs astride from land to land;
Here at our sea-washed, sunset gates shall stand
A mighty woman with a torch, whose flame
Is the imprisoned lightning, and her name   5
Mother of Exiles. From her beacon-hand
Glows world-wide welcome; her mild eyes command

The air-bridged harbor that twin cities frame.
"Keep, ancient lands, your storied pomp!"
   cries she
With silent lips. "Give me your tired, your poor,   10
Your huddled masses yearning to breathe free,
The wretched refuse of your teeming shore.
Send these, the homeless, tempest-tost to me,
I lift my lamp beside the golden door!"

Topics for Critical Thinking and Writing

1. In the opening line of the poem, Emma Lazarus alludes to the Colossus of Rhodes — a statue of the Greek titan-god of the sun Helios that was erected in the city of Rhodes in 280 BC. The Colossus was 98 feet tall, making it one of the tallest statues of the ancient world. Compare the language Lazarus uses to describe this "brazen giant of Greek fame" (l. 1) to the language she uses to describe the Statue of Liberty, the "Mother of Exiles" (l. 6). If both statues are symbols for nations, what kind of argument does Lazarus make by describing the two statues as she does?

2. Lazarus refers to the Statue of Liberty as the "Mother of Exiles." Do you think this description still holds up today in light of current debates about immigration laws? Write a brief essay of about 500 words using both historical evidence and current events to support your argument.

3. Notice the description of the Statue of Liberty's eyes as "mild" in line 7. Do you think it is an accurate depiction of how "the homeless, tempest-tost" are generally seen in the United States today? Why, or why not?

4. Do some research into immigration in the United States today and then write an essay in which you judge whether or not the current immigration debate lives up to the ideals of "The New Colossus."

WALT WHITMAN

Walt Whitman (1819–1892) is one of the most renowned poets in the American canon. He was born in Huntington, New York, as the second of nine children to Walter and Louisa Van Velsor Whitman. He attended public school until age eleven, at which time he concluded his formal schooling and took a job as a printer's assistant. He quickly learned the printing trade, and at age seventeen, he became a teacher. He continued to teach until 1841, when he became a full-time journalist. Whitman founded and served as editor of the *Long-Islander*, a weekly Huntington newspaper, and went on to edit several other newspapers in the New York area before leaving the newspaper business in 1848. He moved back in with his parents at that point, working as a part-time carpenter and beginning work on *Leaves of Grass*, his most enduring and famous collection of poems. He first published *Leaves* at his own expense in 1855, although he continued to revise it several times throughout the rest of his life. "One Song, America, Before I Go" first appeared in the 1900 edition of *Leaves of Grass*.

One Song, America, Before I Go

One song, America, before I go,
I'd sing, o'er all the rest, with trumpet sound,
For thee — the Future.

I'd sow a seed for thee of endless Nationality;
I'd fashion thy Ensemble, including Body and 5
    Soul;
I'd show, away ahead, thy real Union, and how
    it may be accomplish'd.

(The paths to the House I seek to make,
But leave to those to come, the House itself.)

Belief I sing — and Preparation;
As Life and Nature are not great with 10
    reference to the Present only,
But greater still from what is yet to come,
Out of that formula for Thee I sing.

Topics for Critical Thinking and Writing

1. Walt Whitman identifies his poem as a song for America. What kinds of songs do you usually think of when you think about America? How does Whitman's tone compare to other songs about the country?

2. Why is the future important in this poem? What argument is Whitman making about the present and past of the country?

3. "One Song, America, Before I Go" was originally published in 1900. If Whitman were alive today, how do you think he would assess the state of the country? Do you think he would think that the "Belief" and "Preparation" (l. 9) he advised had been heeded? Why, or why not?

URSULA K. LE GUIN

Ursula K. Le Guin (1929–2018) was born in Berkeley, California, the daughter of a distinguished mother (Theodora Kroeber, a folklorist) and father (Alfred L. Kroeber, an anthropologist). After graduating from Radcliffe College, she earned a master's degree at Columbia University; in 1952, she held a Fulbright Fellowship for study in Paris, where she met and married Charles Le Guin, a historian. She began writing in earnest while bringing up three children. Although her work is most widely known to buffs of science fiction, it interests many other readers who normally do not care for sci-fi because it usually has large moral or political dimensions.

Le Guin said that she was prompted to write the following story by a remark she encountered in William James's "The Moral Philosopher and the Moral Life." James suggests there that if millions of people could be "kept permanently happy on the one simple condition that a certain lost soul on the far-off edge of things should lead a life of lonely torment," our moral sense "would make us immediately feel" that it would be "hideous" to accept such a bargain. This story first appeared in *New Dimensions* 3 (1973).

The Ones Who Walk Away from Omelas

With a clamor of bells that set the swallows soaring, the Festival of Summer came to the city Omelas, bright-towered by the sea. The rigging of the boats in harbor sparkled with flags. In the streets between houses with red roofs and painted walls, between old moss-grown gardens and under avenues of trees, past great parks and public buildings, processions moved. Some were decorous: old people in long stiff robes of mauve and gray, grave master workmen, quiet, merry women carrying their babies and chatting as they walked. In other streets the music beat faster, a shimmering of gong and tambourine, and the people went dancing, the procession was a dance. Children dodged in and out, their high calls rising like the swallows' crossing flights over the music and the singing. All the processions wound towards the north side of the city, where on the great water-meadow called the Green Fields boys and girls, naked in the bright air, with mudstained feet and ankles and long, lithe arms, exercised their restive horses before the race. The horses wore no gear at all but a halter without bit. Their manes were braided with streamers of silver, gold, and green. They flared their nostrils and pranced and boasted to one another; they were vastly excited, the horse being the only animal who has adopted our ceremonies as his own. Far off to the north and west the mountains stood up half encircling Omelas on her bay. The air of morning was so clear that the snow still crowning the Eighteen Peaks burned with white-gold fire across the miles of sunlit air, under the dark blue of the sky. There was just enough wind to make the banners that marked the racecourse snap and flutter now and then. In the silence of the broad green meadows one could hear the music winding through the city streets, farther and nearer and ever approaching, a cheerful faint sweetness of the air that from time to time trembled and gathered together and broke out into the great joyous clanging of the bells.

Joyous! How is one to tell about joy? How describe the citizens of Omelas?

They were not simple folk, you see, though they were happy. But we do not say the words of cheer much any more. All smiles have become archaic. Given a description such as this one tends to make certain assumptions. Given a description such as this one tends to look next for the King, mounted on a splendid stallion and surrounded by his noble knights, or perhaps in a golden litter borne by great-muscled slaves. But there was no king. They did not use swords, or keep slaves. They were not barbarians. I do not know the rules and laws of their society, but I suspect that they were singularly few. As they did without monarchy and slavery, so they also got on without the stock exchange, the advertisement, the secret police, and the bomb. Yet I repeat that these were not simple folk, not dulcet shepherds, noble savages, bland utopians. They were not less complex than us. The trouble is that we have a bad habit, encouraged by pedants and sophisticates, of considering happiness as something rather stupid. Only pain is intellectual, only evil interesting. This is the treason of the artist: a refusal to admit the banality of evil and the terrible boredom of pain. If you can't lick 'em, join 'em. If it hurts, repeat it. But to praise despair is to condemn delight, to embrace violence is to lose hold of everything else. We have almost lost hold, we can no longer describe a happy man, nor make any celebration of joy. How can I tell you about the people of Omelas? They were not naïve and happy children — though their children were, in fact, happy. They were mature, intelligent, passionate adults whose lives were not wretched. O miracle! But I wish I could describe it better. I wish I could convince you. Omelas sounds in my words like a city in a fairy tale, long ago and far away, once upon a time. Perhaps it would be best if you imagined it as your own fancy bids, assuming it will rise to the occasion, for certainly I cannot suit you all. For instance, how about technology? I think that there would be no cars or helicopters in and above the streets; this follows from the fact that the people of Omelas are happy people. Happiness is based on a just discrimination of what is necessary, what is neither necessary nor destructive, and what is destructive. In the middle category, however — that of the unnecessary but undestructive, that of comfort, luxury, exuberance, etc. — they could perfectly well have central heating, subway trains, washing machines, and all kinds of marvelous devices not yet invented here, floating light-sources, fuelless power, a cure for the common cold. Or they could have none of that: it doesn't matter. As you like it. I incline to think that people from towns up and down the coast have been coming in to Omelas during the last days before the Festival on very fast little trains and double-decked trams, and that the train station of Omelas is actually the handsomest building in town, though plainer than the magnificent Farmers' Market. But even granted trains, I fear that Omelas so far strikes some of you as goody-goody. Smiles, bells, parades, horses, bleh. If so, please add an orgy. If an orgy would help, don't hesitate. Let us not, however, have temples from which issue beautiful nude priests and priestesses already half in ecstasy and ready to copulate with any man or woman, lover or stranger, who desires union with the deep godhead of the blood,

although that was my first idea. But really it would be better not to have any temples in Omelas — at least, not manned temples. Religion yes, clergy no. Surely the beautiful nudes can just wander about, offering themselves like divine soufflés to the hunger of the needy and the rapture of the flesh. Let them join the processions. Let tambourines be struck above the copulations, and the glory of desire be proclaimed upon the gongs, and (a not unimportant point) let the offspring of these delightful rituals be beloved and looked after by all. One thing I know there is none of in Omelas is guilt. But what else should there be? I thought that first there were no drugs, but that is puritanical. For those who like it, the faint insistent sweetness of *drooz* may perfume the ways of the city, *drooz* which first brings a great lightness and brilliance to the mind and limbs, and then after some hours a dreamy languor, and wonderful visions at last of the very arcana and inmost secrets of the Universe, as well as exciting the pleasure of sex beyond all belief; and it is not habit-forming. For more modest tastes I think there ought to be beer. What else, what else belongs in the joyous city? The sense of victory, surely, the celebration of courage. But as we did without clergy, let us do without soldiers. The joy built upon successful slaughter is not the right kind of joy; it will not do; it is fearful and it is trivial. A boundless and generous contentment, a magnanimous triumph felt not against some outer enemy but in communion with the finest and fairest in the souls of all men everywhere and the splendor of the world's summer: this is what swells the hearts of the people of Omelas, and the victory they celebrate is that of life. I really don't think many of them need to take *drooz*.

Most of the processions have reached the Green Fields by now. A marvelous smell of cooking goes forth from the red and blue tents of the provisioners. The faces of small children are amiably sticky; in the benign grey beard of a man a couple of crumbs of rich pastry are entangled. The youths and girls have mounted their horses and are beginning to group around the starting line of the course. An old woman, small, fat, and laughing, is passing out flowers from a basket, and tall young men wear her flowers in their shining hair. A child of nine or ten sits at the edge of the crowd, alone, playing on a wooden flute. People pause to listen, and they smile, but they do not speak to him, for he never ceases playing and never sees them, his dark eyes wholly rapt in the sweet, thin magic of the tune.

He finishes, and slowly lowers his hands 5 holding the wooden flute.

As if that little private silence were the signal, all at once a trumpet sounds from the pavilion near the starting line: imperious, melancholy, piercing. The horses rear on their slender legs, and some of them neigh in answer. Sober-faced, the young riders stroke the horses' necks and soothe them, whispering, "Quiet, quiet, there my beauty, my hope. . . ." They begin to form in rank along the starting line. The crowds along the racecourse are like a field of grass and flowers in the wind. The Festival of Summer has begun.

Do you believe? Do you accept the festival, the city, the joy? No? Then let me describe one more thing.

In a basement under one of the beautiful public buildings of Omelas, or perhaps in the cellar of one of its spacious private homes, there is a room. It has one locked door, and no window. A little light seeps in dustily between cracks in the boards, secondhand from a cobwebbed window somewhere across the cellar. In one corner of the little room a couple of mops, with stiff, clotted, foul-smelling heads, stand near a rusty bucket. The floor is dirt, a little damp to the touch, as cellar dirt usually is. The room is about three paces long and two wide: a mere broom closet or disused tool room. In the room a child is sitting. It could be a boy or a girl. It looks about six, but actually is nearly ten. It is feeble-minded. Perhaps it was born defective, or perhaps it has become imbecile through fear, malnutrition, and neglect. It picks its nose and occasionally fumbles vaguely with its toes or genitals, as it sits hunched in the corner farthest from the bucket and the two mops. It is afraid of the mops. It finds them horrible. It shuts its eyes, but it knows the mops are still standing there; and the door is locked; and nobody will come. The door is always locked; and nobody ever comes, except that sometimes — the child has no understanding of time or interval — sometimes the door rattles terribly and opens, and a person, or several people, are there. One of them may come in and kick the child to make it stand up. The others never come close, but peer in at it with frightened, disgusted eyes. The food bowl and the water jug are hastily filled, the door is locked, the eyes disappear. The people at the door never say anything, but the child, who has not always lived in the tool room, and can remember sunlight and its mother's voice, sometimes speaks. "I will be good," it says. "Please let me out. I will be good!" They never answer. The child used to scream for help at night, and cry a good deal, but now it only makes a kind of whining, "eh-haa, eh-haa," and it speaks less and less often. It is so thin there are no calves to its legs; its belly protrudes; it lives on a half-bowl of corn meal and grease a day. It is naked. Its buttocks and thighs are a mass of festered sores, as it sits in its own excrement continually.

They all know it is there, all the people of Omelas. Some of them have come to see it, others are content merely to know it is there. They all know that it has to be there. Some of them understand why, and some do not, but they all understand that their happiness, the beauty of their city, the tenderness of their friendships, the health of their children, the wisdom of their scholars, the skill of their makers, even the abundance of their harvest and the kindly weathers of their skies, depend wholly on this child's abominable misery.

This is usually explained to children when they are between eight and twelve, whenever they seem capable of understanding; and most of those who come to see the child are young people, though often enough an adult comes, or comes back, to see the child. No matter how well the matter has been explained to them, these young spectators are always shocked and sickened at the sight. They feel disgust, which they had thought themselves superior to. They feel anger, outrage, impotence, despite all the explanations. They would like to do something for the child. But there is nothing they can do. If the child were brought up into the sunlight out of that vile place, if it were cleaned and fed and comforted, that would be a good thing, indeed; but if it were done, in that day and hour all the prosperity and beauty and delight of Omelas would wither and be destroyed. Those are the terms. To exchange all the goodness and grace of every life in Omelas for that single, small improvement: to throw away the happiness of thousands for the chance of the happiness of one: that would be to let guilt within the walls indeed.

The terms are strict and absolute; there may not even be a kind word spoken to the child.

Often the young people go home in tears, or in a tearless rage, when they have seen the child and faced this terrible paradox. They may brood over it for weeks or years. But as time goes on they begin to realize that even if the child could be released, it would not get much good of its freedom: a little vague pleasure of warmth and food, no doubt, but little more. It is too degraded and imbecile to know

any real joy. It has been afraid too long ever to be free of fear. Its habits are too uncouth for it to respond to humane treatment. Indeed, after so long it would probably be wretched without walls about it to protect it, and darkness for its eyes, and its own excrement to sit in. Their tears at the bitter injustice dry when they begin to perceive the terrible justice of reality, and to accept it. Yet it is their tears and anger, the trying of their generosity and the acceptance of their helplessness, which are perhaps the true source of the splendor of their lives. Theirs is no vapid, irresponsible happiness. They know that they, like the child, are not free. They know compassion. It is the existence of the child, and their knowledge of its existence, that makes possible the nobility of their architecture, the poignancy of their music, the profundity of their science. It is because of the child that they are so gentle with children. They know that if the wretched one were not there snivelling in the dark, the other one, the flute-player, could make no joyful music as the young riders line up in their beauty for the race in the sunlight of the first morning of summer.

Now do you believe in them? Are they not more credible? But there is one more thing to tell, and this is quite incredible.

At times one of the adolescent girls or boys who go to see the child does not go home to weep or rage, does not, in fact, go home at all. Sometimes also a man or woman much older falls silent for a day or two, and then leaves home. These people go out into the street, and walk down the street alone. They keep walking, and walk straight out of the city of Omelas, through the beautiful gates. They keep walking across the farmlands of Omelas. Each one goes alone, youth or girl, man or woman. Night falls; the traveler must pass down village streets, between the houses with yellow-lit windows, and on out into the darkness of the fields. Each alone, they go west or north, towards the mountains. They go on. They leave Omelas, they walk ahead into the darkness, and they do not come back. The place they go towards is a place even less imaginable to most of us than the city of happiness. I cannot describe it at all. It is possible that it does not exist. But they seem to know where they are going, the ones who walk away from Omelas.

Topics for Critical Thinking and Writing

1. The narrator suggests, "Perhaps it would be best if you imagined it [Omelas] as your own fancy bids . . . for certainly I cannot suit you all" (para. 3). Do you think leaving the description of Omelas to the reader is an effective strategy for storytelling? Why, or why not?

2. Consider the narrator's assertion in paragraph 3 that happiness "is based on a just discrimination of what is necessary." Do you agree? Why, or why not?

3. Summarize the point of the story — not the plot, but what the story adds up to, what the author is getting at. What do you think is the intended meaning of the story?

4. Why do you think the citizens of Omelas hold a child captive, and why do you think they refer to the child as "it"?

5. Do you think the story implies a criticism of contemporary American society? Explain.

TEXT CREDITS

Index of Authors, Titles, and Terms

Argument (*continued*)
evidence in, 92–102
images as, 131–170
induction, 80, 337–342
as instrument of inquiry, 206
logical, 80–85
nonrational appeals in, 103–107
peer review of, 234–236
vs. persuasion, 75–79
planning, 205–220
prevalence of, 107–108
rhetorical appeals and, 75–79
Rogerian, 363–373
sound, 81–83
stasis theory, 210–213
Toulmin method, 317–327
true, 81–83
valid, 81–83
weak and invalid, 84–85
Argument ad misericordiam, 104
Argument ad populam, 104
"An Argument for Corporate Responsibility"
(Timmerman), 303–308
Aristotelian argument, 365
Aristotle, 78, 211, 230
Articles in periodicals
APA style, citing in, 299–300
MLA style, citing in, 291–293
Assignments
argument, development of, 241
arguments, analysis of, 204
argument using sources, 314
for critical reading, 72–74, 130
critical summary, 74
for critical thinking, 31–32
definition, 73, 130
letter to the editor, 73
rhetorical analysis, 130
visual rhetoric, 171–172
Assumptions
arguments and, 90–92, 107–108
checklist for, 26–27
evaluations based on, 379
examination of, 25–30
explicit, 25–26
implicit, 25–26

Attitude
of author, 231
skeptical, 6
Auden, W. H., "The Unknown Citizen,"
458–459
Audience
analysis of, 179–180, 186–187
beliefs of, 216–217
checklist for imagining, 220
common ground with, 218–220
imagining, 216–218
intended, checklist for analyzing, 180
in oral presentation, 403–406
visuals and, 163
Audiovisual aids, 405
Aural cues, in oral presentations, 408
Author
attitude of, 231
citation of. *see* Citations
methods of, 177, 186–187
noting in research, 276
persona of, 178–181, 186–187, 230–232, 234, 406
in previewing, 33, 34, 37
purpose of, 176–177
in quotation lead-in, 280–281
thesis of, 175–176, 186
Author-centered interpretation, 376–377, 378
Authoritative testimony, 97–99, 187
Authority, 78
appeal to, 344, 351–352

Backing, 318, 320–321, 327
Bandwagon appeals, 136
Bar graphs, 159, 160, 162
Begging the question, fallacy of, 343, 348–349
Beliefs, 6, 90, 145, 216–217, 335
Benedict, Helen, "The Military Has a Man
Problem," 27–30
Bias
confirmation, 79–80, 245
gender, 234
observer, 272
in testimony, 97
Bibliography
annotated, 278–279
source information, 276

Deductive reasoning, 80
Definition
    in argument, 85–90
    assignments for, 73
    as classical topic, 16
    concepts, 44–45
    example, 87–88
    in stasis theory, 211
    statistics and, 102
    stipulation, 86–87
    sufficient and necessary conditions, 88–89
    synonym, 87
    terms, 44–45
Delbanco, Andrew, "3 Reasons College Still Matters," 413–416
Delivery, oral presentations, 404–405
Denotations, 232
Denotative meaning, 139
Detail, attention to, 78
Diagramming, 208–209
Dialogue, between reader and text, 206
Difference, Mill's Method of, 341
Dilemma, 333–334
Discourse, 243–245, 249
Discourse community, 244, 263
Disjunction, 332–333
Disjunctive syllogism, 332–333
Distorting the facts, fallacy of, 343, 346
Division, fallacy of, 343, 345
Documentation, 283–284. *see also* Citations
"Does Ability Determine Expertise?" (Brooks), 309–313
Domains of websites, 260–261
Drafts
    of an argument, 220–234
    student essay, 236–240

Editorial *we*, 232–233
Either/or reasoning, 349
Electronic sources. *see* Web, research on
Ellipsis, 285
Emotional appeals. *see also Pathos*
    definition of, 75
    fallacy of, 105–107
    images and, 131–136
    overview of, 76–77

    in Shakespeare, 104–105
    types of, 133–136
Empathy, 364, 365
Empirical claims, 337
Encyclopedia, online, 251
Endnotes, 284
Enthymeme, 83–84
Ephron, Nora, "The Boston Photographs," 166–170
Equivocation, fallacy of, 343, 345–346
Ethical appeal, 133, 230
Ethical standards, in research, 272
Ethos
    appeals to, 230
    establishing, 132, 176, 178
    identifying, 78–79
    images, using to establish, 132
    in oral presentations, 405
    ridicule and, 104
    sources and, 248
Evaluation
    of issues, 6–7
    in literary criticism, 378–382
    from multiple perspectives, 4–6
Evaluative approach, 20
Evidence, 92–102, 337
    authoritative testimony, 97–99
    author's use of, 178
    example, 94–97
    experimentation, 93–94
    forms of, 145
    numerical data, 99–102
    probability and, 340
Example, 87–88
    as evidence, 94–97, 187
"Executions Should Be Televised" (Shemtob and Lat), 64–65
Exercises
    assumptions, 92
    audience, imagining, 218
    brainstorming, 210
    definitions, 89–90
    emotional appeals in visual arguments, 136
    "First and Last" rule, 41
    images, accommodating, resisting, and negotiating, 148

A COMPACT AND COMPLETE GUIDE TO CRITICAL THINKING AND ACADEMIC ARGUMENT

Critical Thinking, Reading, and Writing is a brief yet versatile resource that makes complex argument concepts approachable and helps students move from critical thinking to argumentative and researched writing.

"*Critical Thinking, Reading, and Writing* reveals the mechanics of thought behind the very active processes of reading and writing. This guide is an excellent foundation for argument—from inception to final presentation."

— Meghan Tutolo, *University of Pittsburgh at Greensburg*

Cover art: Torben Giehler, German, born in 1973, *BOOGIE WOOGIE*, 1999, Acrylic on canvas, 205.7 x 195.6 cm (81 x 77 in.), Museum of Fine Arts, Boston, The Living New England Artist Purchase Fund, created by The Stephen and Sybil Stone Foundation 1999.499. Photo ©2020 Museum of Fine Arts, Boston.

AUTHENTIC

macmillanlearning.com

bedford/st.martin's
Macmillan Learning

ISBN 978-1-319-19451-2

90000

9 781319 194512